MW00817939

# Treating Addiction
# as a Human Process

# Treating Addiction as a Human Process

*Edward J. Khantzian, M.D.*

A JASON ARONSON BOOK

ROWMAN & LITTLEFIELD PUBLISHERS, INC.
*Lanham • Boulder • New York • Toronto • Oxford*

A JASON ARONSON BOOK

ROWMAN & LITTLEFIELD PUBLISHERS, INC.

Published in the United States of America
by Rowman & Littlefield Publishers, Inc.
A wholly owned subsidary of The Rowman & Littlefield Publishing Group, Inc.
4501 Forbes Boulevard, Suite 200, Lanham, Maryland 20706
www.rowmanlittlefield.com

PO Box 317
Oxford
OX2 9RU, UK

Copyright © 1999 by Jason Aronson Inc.
First Rowman & Littlefield edition 2004

British Library Cataloguing in Publication Information Available

**Library of Congress Cataloging-in-Publication Data**

Khantzian, Edward J.
    Treating addiction as a human process / Edward J. Khantzian.
        p.  cm.
    Includes bibliographical references and index.
    ISBN 0-7657-0186-3
    1. Substance abuse—Etiology. 2. Substance abuse—Psychological aspects. 3.
Narcotic addicts—Mental health. 4. Alcoholics—Mental health. 5. Substance abuse—
Treatment. I. Title.
RC564.K535  1999
616.86—dc21                                                    98-36955

Printed in the United States of America

⊖™ The paper used in this publication meets the minimum requirements of American
National Standard for Information Sciences—Permanence of Paper for Printed Library
Materials, ANSI/NISO Z39.48-1992.

To my grandchildren

*How should we be able to forget those ancient myths about dragons that at the last minute turn into princesses who are only waiting to see us once beautiful and brave . . . perhaps everything terrible is in its deepest being something helpless that wants help from us.*

Rainer Maria Rilke

# Contents

## PART III:
## THE SELF-MEDICATION HYPOTHESIS
## OF SUBSTANCE USE DISORDERS

## PART IV:
## UNDERSTANDING ADDICTIVE
## VULNERABILITY—PSYCHODYNAMICS

## PART V:
## TREATMENT OF THE ADDICTIONS

## PART VI:
## EPILOGUE: FUTURE PROSPECTS
## FOR UNDERSTANDING AND TREATING
## THE ADDICTED PERSON

# Foreword

*Jerome D. Levin*

When Professor Khantzian agreed to bring together a substantial portion of his work in one volume for the Library of Substance Abuse and Addiction Treatment (LSAAT), I felt elated. As the series editor I felt certain that I had pulled of something of a coup and that I was about to publish a major work. Why, you may ask, is a publication of Khantzian's most important papers so significant? The answer is that Edward J. Khantzian has changed the ways we think of and understand addiction and addicts to a degree matched by few, if any, others. And this change in perception and perspective is not only an intellectual or scientific one but also a moral one. Khantzian's insight into the dynamics, the inner world, of addicts offers understanding, an understanding with direct clinical implications that significantly raise the likelihood of successful treatment; it de-demonizes a demonized population, altering the addiction specialist's countertransference so that feelings of contempt and condemnation, conscious and unconscious, do not contaminate and disable the therapy but, perhaps even more important, alter both the public's and self-conception of the addict. The scorn of others is all too readily internalized by the addict or substance abuser, setting up a vicious cycle of shame, drugging to obliterate that shame, and then using yet more of the drug to obliterate the shame induced by previous drug use. Khantzian's insights undercut all of this whether "this"—hatred, fear, devaluation, distancing, and opprobrium—resides in the society, the therapist, or the patient's own self.

How does Khantzian accomplish this? First and foremost, this transformation is attitudinal. Like Harry Stack Sullivan, Khantzian believes deep in his core self that "We are all more human than anything else." It isn't we and them; it is us—human beings struggling with our limitations and pain and aspirations and trying to get through as best we can. The addicted have fewer resources than most, and try in different and often tragic ways to get by and to live as fully as possible, in face of their relatively limited emotional and coping capacities. Over and above and no less vital to Khantzian's view than its attitudinal component, is his brilliant intellectual contribution that throws much illumination on the nature of those limitations and the strategies employed by the addicted to deal with them. This hard-to-come-by combination of moral and scientific strength is only possible because Khantzian is a truly humble and open man—although no less tenacious in defense of what he believes to be true, nor unaware of the importance of his contribution for that humility and openness. Yes, tenacious in defense of the truth as he sees it, yet never dogmatic and never losing sight of the complexion of reality and of life including the complexity of the addicted life and its treatment. He knows that his perspective, highly valuable as it may be, isn't the whole truth nor the whole picture, and that kind of sanity is hard to find in the field in which science all too easily becomes religion at its dogmatic worst instead of an open-ended search for truth. Unfortunately, this can be said with equal validity of the study of psychodynamics and of addiction theory. If his contribution was only his sanity and the saliency of his theoretical and clinical contribution was far less than it is, he would still be a giant in the field not distinguished by sanity, openness, or more than ritualistic acknowledgment of complexity. Khantzian is different because both the work and the man are characterized by passion without dogmatism and compassion without sentimentality.

Khantzian's work is important—very important—because he, along with Leon Wurmser and Henry Krystal, are the major psychodynamic theorists of addiction of the second half of the twentieth century. These men, as well as a handful of neuropsychological researchers and theorists like C. Robert Cloninger and Ralph Tarter, have taught us things we did not know, so that now standing on the shoulders of giants we see further. Khantzian and his few peers in the psychodynamic tradition also know that addiction is indeed a human process and that in unraveling the enigma of addiction—in discovering why some and not others become addicted, and the forces: neurochemical, societal, cultural, and psychodynamic that drive the addiction—we will discover not only something about "them," but something about "us." In short, there is no way to expand our knowledge of the nature of addiction without expanding our knowledge of human nature. The specialist is ineluctably the generalist, and Khantzian knows this. So what started out as his moral strength became inevitably his intellectual and scientific strength. What Khantzian has discovered about addiction is *mutatis mutandis* true of psychopathology in general and, in its own way, of all human emotional life.

A word about Khantzian's writing style. The great American literary critic Edmund Wilson taught that good writing is characterized by "lucidity, clarity and force." By that standard, Khantzian is a good writer indeed, so that his work not only enlightens but gives pleasure.

What about the content? What is it that Edward Khantzian has to teach us? I am about to tell you, but first let me place Khantzian in two traditions of which he is very much a part. One is the tradition of psychodynamic understanding of addiction, and the other is the Western tradition of rationalism which goes back to classical antiquity. The psychodynamic tradition could be said to start with Benjamin Rush, Surgeon General of the American Revolutionary Army, who described dynamic denial in his pioneering conceptualization of alcoholism as a disease, and with the British naval physician Thomas Trotter, who possessed prescient 1820 insight into the etiology of alcoholism as the result of heredity and premature weaning—that is, environmental trauma. Dynamic thinking about addiction resurfaced with Freud's work in the early twentieth century when he postulated that every addiction was a displacement and re-enactment of the primal addiction—addiction to masturbation. Later Freud cited addiction as evidence for the existence of a repetition compulsion. Drive theorists, early and late, who are essentially id psychologists, elaborated on Freud's thinking and these analysts emphasized the use of elatants or intoxicants, as they called them, to enable expression of forbidden sexual and aggressive wishes. Almost a century later, ego, self, and object relations theorists have all taken a crack at elucidating the dynamics of addition. And among the ego psychologists, Khantzian has been preeminent.

His contribution has been complex and multifaceted, but perhaps his most lasting contribution will turn out to be the self-medication hypothesis. Elaborated and refined over three decades with ever increasing subtlety, Khantzian's hypothesis has given us a new way to look at and to understand why human beings do such a strange thing to themselves as to self-poison. Khantzian's answer to why people do such a manifestly crazy thing has been to show that they can do no other because they suffer not only unconsciously self-diagnosed psychiatric illnesses such as Attention Deficit Disorder, which they by serendipity or intuition have learned to self-medicate with uppers, but all sorts of subclinical deficits and deficiencies that they also self-medicate with varying degrees of specificity (in terms of preferred drug). The subclinical part of Khantzian's self-medication hypothesis is currently accruing more and more empirical evidence both from clinical research and from studies of high-risk children of alcoholics. The self-medication hypothesis has been truly revolutionary. It is not pleasure-seeking or release of forbidden impulses that eventuates in addiction—it is the attempt, however misguided, to remediate deficit. That changes not only the way the therapist, and ultimately the society and the addict him- or herself, understands the addictive behavior, it changes how the therapist, the society, and the addict treat the addiction. And that makes a huge difference, which is why Edward Khantzian is one of the preeminent psychodynamic addictions theorists of his generation. Like all truly revolutionary ideas, it seems, in spite of the continuing controversy around it, almost self-evident. But that is only because we stand on the shoulders of a giant.

The self-medication hypothesis is only one of Khantzian's contributions. The second lies in his elaboration of the nature of the addict's deficits which he sees as a paucity in the capacities for self-care and self-governance. To be sane, it is necessary to know how to be sane. And these deficits in the capacities for self-care and self-governance can be seen as ignorance—as not knowing how. This conceptualization shifts the locus of the addict's difficulties from expression of impulses to ego and superego malformation and the optimal treatment to remediation of these abnormalities. It also throws entirely new light on the "self-destructiveness" of addicts, now not seen as unconsciously motivated and indeed the "payoff" of the addiction but rather as the ineluctable consequences of not knowing how to adequately care for oneself or to regulate oneself either behaviorally or affectively. Khantzian has taught us that addiction (whatever else it may be) is a futile attempt to remediate affect dysregulation. Finally, Khantzian has taught us that all substance abuse including that eventuating in addiction is primarily driven not by pleasure-seeking, but by an attempt to relieve *suffering*. It is pain, not pleasure, that drives the addictive process.

Having located Khantzian in the psychodynamic tradition, I would like to also place him in the great tradition of Western rationalism. When Plato's Socrates says, "To know the good is to do the good," with its corollary that evil (pathology) is ignorance, he was anticipating by implication—2,500 years early—Edward Khantzian's self-medication hypothesis as well as his notion of deficit in self-care and self-governance. Western rationalism holds that the irrational is at some ultimate level rational in the sense that the irrational can be explained. And that is precisely what Khantzian has done: made the irrationality of addiction with its self-destructiveness understandable. According to the rationalist tradition, to become more rational, more sane, to move toward what the Greeks called the "good," is to move from ignorance to knowledge. Here, too, Khantzian is a rationalist, one who is insistent on the efficacy of insight as against behavioral manipulation alone in the treatment of addiction. For Plato to move from ignorance to knowledge was to move from slavery to freedom. So, too, for Khantzian's patients who become free even as they become more enlightened.

Finally, I would like to comment on Edward Khantzian's courage. For many years he has fought a three-front war against more traditional psychoanalysts who have attacked him as betraying Freud's legacy of unconscious motivation by the seething drives of the id pressing for discharge; against the more dogmatic members of the recovering community who see his as insufficiently committed to the disease model; and against the more radical behavioral and neurochemical theorists and practitioners who have attacked him for incarnating a redundant and illusionary emphasis on the inner life. A man with such enemies can't be all wrong. Who else is attacked by the recovery lobby for prescribing medications for psychiatric distress, including anxiety, as a part of treating target symptoms, even as he is attacked by some in the analytic community for disbelieving in the centrality of unconsciously motivated self-destruction in the addictive dynamic? Further, he has held his own with quiet grace, disparaging no one, recognizing what he sees as valid in the positions of others, while steadily accumulating evidence for his own unique and powerful take on the addictive process, even as he continues to fine tune his theoretical concepts and to make more efficacious his clinical technique.

# Acknowledgments

Acknowledgments are about people and institutions that have made it feasible for a person to do his work. I have been most fortunate in both respects. Many special people and several important organizations have made it possible for me to develop a body of work and pursue a point of view that I hope has contributed to a more humane clinical understanding of individuals who suffer with substance use disorders (SUDs).

First of all, I want to express my appreciation to my most recent collaborators, Jason Aronson, my publisher, and Jerome Levin, my editor, for so generously and magnanimously responding to my proposal to publish my collected works. I truly consider it an honor and an opportunity beyond my wildest dreams to have my most important and interesting works published in one place. In doing so, Drs. Aronson and Levin have provided a stamp of affirmation that has encouraged me to take on the work of pulling together these selected papers and the considerable additional commentary and new (previously unpublished) writing to make this volume complete. I am also indebted to Elaine Lindenblatt, my production editor, for her support, patience, and wisdom in guiding me to make the manuscript tighter and more readable.

John Mack was of singular importance in getting me started and supporting me in pursuing my ideas. He was an important collaborator in several publications, which are included in this volume. Beyond his support in the realm of ideas, he was a superb leader and administrator, permitting the development of programs that effectively treated patients with substance use disorders at the same time we learned from them. Over the next three decades I was blessed to be associated with a number of collaborators with whom there was a generous exchange of clinical experiences and sharing of our growing understanding of our patients. I can list only some of them here. Alan Corman, Bert Johnson, William Kates, and Jancis Long were there at the beginning when we started our methadone maintenance program in 1970. Gerald McKenna and Steve Leff then joined with me in our first major research project evaluating and treating polysubstance abusers. Alan Schatzberg and Catherine Treece, in the 1970s, and, subsequently in the 1980s, Lance Dodes, William McAuliffe, Kurt Halliday, Sarah Golden, Nancy Brehm, and Carolyn Bell came aboard in our Department of Psychiatry at The Cambridge Hospital, which was enjoying a growing reputation as an institution that cared about and treated the substance abusing patient respectfully and well. All of these colleagues were extremely important and a major impetus for me to more systematically consolidate my ideas and publish them. More recently this impetus is sustained by Mark Albanese at Tewksbury Hospital, who has embraced a humanistic appreciation of addictive suffering, especially among the severely mentally ill. I suspect and hope he will be an important part of assuring that such a legacy will continue in the next generation of clinicians who devote themselves to such problems.

There are numerous friends and colleagues outside my affiliated institutions who have influenced the development of my perspective. To acknowledge them all would make for an unwieldy list. Most of them will recognize who they are in the pages of this book, but I should make special mention of Leon Wurmser and Henry Krystal, two very gifted and kind scholars, who were singularly important in influencing and validating the development of my ideas.

I was twice rewarded in being associated with special hospitals that not only did not turn their institutional backs on these problems, but in fact were committed to assuring services to this population of patients for whom so many other hospital were unresponsive. For the first two decades of my career it was The Cambridge Hospital, and for the past decade it has been Tewksbury Hospital. I am indebted to John O'Brien at The Cambridge Hospital, and Raymond Sanzone and Katherine Domoto at Tewksbury Hospital for their support and their readiness to assure provision of excellent services to patients who suffer with SUDs. I am also grateful to Robert Dorwart, the Psychiatrist-in-Chief at The Cambridge Hospital for his continued support and encouragement for maintaining the ongoing programmatic support and respect for the psychodynamic perspective represented in this book. I owe a debt of gratitude as well to Jan Kaufman and Howard Shaffer for continuing excellent treatment and training programs in Cambridge and at Harvard Medical School, ongoing contexts that have generously contributed to make my work possible. A special note of gratitude for Jeffrey Simmons, Chief of Service at Tewksbury Hospital and my esteemed colleague and friend, is in order. He has been an inestimable source of wise counsel and support in this late stage of my career by "hanging in" with this work, and validating and guiding me through the administrative and intellectual minefields that are invariably present in working with addictive disorders.

Finally, in the preparation of a work such as this, there are a number of special helpers without whom such a publication would not be possible. Steven Dilts was invaluable in providing important input to assure clarity of presentation of previously unpublished material in this book, and special help with carefully articulating the importance of the biopsychosocial paradigm and the inseparability of the psychological (or psychodynamic) dimension from the biological and social ones. It was also a special privilege to have my daughter Nancy Jo as a collaborator on several projects. As a fair-minded parent it would be improper to not mention my other children, Susan, Jane, and John, who have been special fans that have helped to maintain my commitment to this work. Again, going back to the beginning, a special note of gratitude to Helen Modica, who over the years labored in her own way, as much I did, over multiple versions of these chapters. Her transcriptions, feedback, and astute editing have been invaluable. More recent important special helpers have been Dennis Wolbach with his effective editorial assistance, and Tracy Roach and Linda Bishop in their generous help in the preparation of manuscripts. CarolAnn Khantzian has been a constant partner, directly and indirectly, in making all of my work possible. She has been a major source of help as a most competent administrative assistant, but mostly as a life partner and assistant who was always been there with her support, wise advice, and appreciation for my life work.

# Collaborators

**Sarah J. Golden**, Ph.D. Associate Director of Psychology, Department of Psychiatry, Beth Israel Deaconess Medical Center; Instructor in Psychology, Harvard Medical School.

**Kurt Halliday**, Ph.D. Private practice, Denver, CO.

**William W. Kates**, M.D. Assistant Clinical Professor of Psychiatry, Harvard Medical School; Staff Psychiatrist, Beth Israel Deaconess Medical Center.

**Nancy Jo Khantzian Modlish**, MSW, LICSW. Groveland, MA.

**Jerome David Levin**, Ph.D. Editor, Library of Substance Abuse and Addiction Treatment; Director, Alcoholism and Substance Abuse Counselor Training Program, New School for Social Research, New York

**John E. Mack**, M.D. Professor of Psychiatry, Harvard Medical School; Staff Psychiatrist, The Cambridge Hospital.

**William E. McAuliffe**, Ph.D. Associate Professor of Psychiatry, Harvard Medical School; Director, National Technical Center for Substance Abuse Needs Assessment; Cambridge, MA.

**Gerald J. McKenna**, M.D. Associate Clinical Professor of Psychiatry, University of Hawaii School of Medicine; Medical Director, Ke Ala Pono Recovery Center.

**Alan F. Schatzberg**, M.D. Professor and Chairman, Department of Psychiatry and Behavioral Sciences, Stanford University School of Medicine.

**Catherine Treece**, Ph.D. Assistant Professor of Psychology, Department of Psychiatry, University of Wisconsin Medical School; private practice.

# PART I

# Overview: Potentials and Limitations for Understanding and Treating Addictive Vulnerability

Individuals with addictive disorders suffer in the extreme with two basic aspects of human nature. They cannot control their emotions and they cannot control their behaviors. They either feel too much or they feel too little; they are over controlled or they are out of control. These two extremes are crucial if not essential aspects of addictive disorders. Such generalizations are a risky way to start a book. In doing so I run the risk of seeming to know the truth or of being dogmatic. What I intend in this book is not so much to find or speak the truth but to present a particular perspective.

There are, obviously, other perspectives than mine, and very important ones at that. Some of these perspectives, ones that are particularly popular now, focus on the brain, genes, and heredity. They employ highly sophisticated macroscopic and microscopic methods and technology to reveal new and exciting findings about the biological substrate of addictive disorders. They have important implication for probing and altering our brains, our chemistry, and even our genes, which could and do affect how we understand and treat substance use disorders (SUDs).

My perspective is a different one. It focuses more on the mind and human processes. It is a perspective that has evolved out of psychoanalytic methods, first developed by Sigmund Freud, for understanding and treating the workings of the human mind and its aberrations. For many clinicians, including myself, the perspective adopted here grew out of the psychoanalytic tradition and I refer to it as the *psychodynamic perspective.*

The psychodynamic perspective takes into account that the mind and the person form a complex system in which there are psychological structures and functions that organize or regulate our internal life (e.g., drives, affects, cognition, perception) and our adaptation to external reality (e.g., behavior, action, relationship to others). This perspective, when applied to understanding and treating people in individual psychotherapy and in groups, provides a powerful method in its own right to fathom the causes and consequences of human psychological suffering, including those involved in addictive suffering.

The treatment relationship is a rich source of data. A psychodynamic perspective permits the gathering of these data by providing a more or less structured and supportive relationship, avoiding extremes of activity or passivity, which allows for a natural unfolding of the characteristic ways a person feels, thinks, and behaves. These characteristic ways of being reveal a person's strengths and vulnerabilities, including those vulnerabilities that predispose a person to addiction. These observations evolve out of the clinician's empathic attention to patients' stories and experiences that they bring into their therapy (individual or group therapy), and how these stories and experiences play out in therapy and what they evoke in the therapist (or in the case of group therapy, the group leader and the other patients). This approach is an extraordinary way for a patient and a therapist to learn about and know self, and to explore ways to modify aspects of self that need correction or repair. In this volume, almost all of what I have to say about the human problem of addictive vulnerability is based on this perspective.

In the neurobehavioral sciences we are accustomed to paying homage to the biopsychosocial perspective. We remind ourselves and each other of the importance of acknowledging this tripartite aspect of understanding and managing our human nature. Yet too often it seems that we only pay lip service to it and then go on to elaborate one particular aspect of the biopsychosocial formula without acknowledging how or if one's perspective or data fits with the rest of the formula. In my opinion, the biopsychosocial model should be viewed holistically. All three areas interact and cannot exist separately. In the case of the psychodynamic perspective, it is the model that I am best versed in and most comfortable with. Nevertheless, the psychodynamic perspective derives from what is perceived through our eyes and ears, mediated by biological processes within a social context. Thus my perspective is the human view of what the biological and social psychiatrists are seeing. The psychodynamic perspective is an integral and unavoidable (but too often overlooked) part of psychiatry. It is a perspective that does not or should not compete with these other perspectives.

My perspective has evolved over a period of three decades. As is evident in my early writings, I employ and apply psychoanalytic terms and formulations that are more complicated and (at times) more dense to explain some of the psychodynamics and mechanisms involved in addictive disorders. Notwithstanding this early trend, I have always tried to use as little as possible convoluted psychoanalytic jargon or concepts to explain my ideas or point of view. I have tried to write or speak in such a way that I never presume that the terms or concepts I employ are self-evident to my audience. I, like many of my colleagues, have lived through two eras in which investigators of very different persuasions (or perspectives) have made such presumptions and have used highly technical methods, language, and concepts that obscure more than clarify aspects of our human nature. Early in my career, when psychoanalytic concepts of the mind predominated, this obscuring was more often done with "psychobabble"; more recently, when scientific concepts and methods about the brain predominate, it is frequently done with "technobabble."

Accordingly, over the years that I have tried to explain how I understand and treat addictive disorders, I have attempted to adopt a parsimonious psychodynamic model, one in which, for the most part, the language and concepts are basic and as clear as possible. I try always to have a focus. At first it was an adaptational one, namely that every human trouble or psychological symptom has its reasons and represents an attempt to solve a problem; I then focused on what was disordered or broken in one's ego or psychological structure that needed understanding and repair. This shift allowed me to focus on deficits in affects, self-esteem, relationships, and self-care, deficits that seemed repeatedly to be part of the addictive equation. Out of this focus I evolved and articulated a self-medication perspective. The focus on self-medication factors in addictive disorders raised questions and inconsistencies that required clarification. As a result, I adopted a more overarching perspective in which I increasingly focused on addictive behaviors as a disorder in self-regulation. This focus has required me more and more to consider what is disordered in the person(ality) (i.e., the way the person is) that causes the person to suffer the way he or she does, which in turn heightens his or her disordered personality. This repetition and the insidious interaction of both the disordered person and the person who suffers are key factors in explaining why individuals revert to and become dependent on substances as a means to cope.

This volume of my collected works amplifies and makes more evident the modes and methods of a psychodynamic perspective. It should reveal the rich potential of this method for fathoming the nature of addictive disorders and their treatment.

The book is organized into four parts, as follows:

- The Internal World of the Addicted Person
- The Self-Medication Hypothesis of Substance Use Disorders
- Understanding Addictive Vulnerability—Psychodynamics
- Treatment of the Addictions

This book is a compilation of my collected works. All the chapters except Chapters 27, 39, and 40 have been previously published as journal articles or book chapters. The new chapters discuss in more detail my perspective on the relationship between posttraumatic stress disorder (PTSD) and SUDs (Chapter 27) and my approach to individual and group psychotherapy (Chapters 39 and 40). Although the majority of the chapters in this volume are reproduced in their entirety, as originally published, in certain segments we have deleted or condensed portions of the text to avoid repetition or redundancy. In these instances, the reader is referred to other chapters where the same material has been covered.

The chapters in each section are organized in chronological sequence, earlier papers proceeding to more recent ones. I have written an introduction for each part to guide the reader, so to speak, as to what was on my mind, then and now, when I wrote or published these articles. I did this to provide an historical view that places my work in the context of the developments and the controversies that have occurred in the field of addictive studies over the last third of this century—a period in which the devastating and widespread use and the consequences of legal and illegal addictive substances have become all too evident. We have also witnessed during this same period significant advances in our understanding and treatment of these disorders. I have also used the introductory sections to ensure that the reader appreciates the human processes and the psychodynamic underpinnings of SUDs.

I have admittedly tried to make a case in this book for the special advantages of a psychodynamic perspective. I have done so because it is the one with which I am most comfortable—by temperament, preference, and training. I am drawn more to process and narrative data than to data of an empirical nature. It is likely these pages will reveal that I am not dispassionate about my subject matter—namely, the lot of my patients who have suffered and are recovering from addictive disorders. I hope what follows will make self-evident (or more apparent) the potentials of this perspective for appreciating their vulnerabilities, resiliency, and strengths. In the final chapter of this book I make a plea for more integrative thinking and how we all need to more humbly remain in the "margins" of the biological, social, and psychological domains in considering the nature of addictive vulnerability. Although there is a consistent emphasis in this book on a particular conceptualization and approach, it should be considered in parallel with other approaches and not in competition with them.

This book is intended for the students, clinicians, and patients and their families who are interested in the psychology and treatment of addictive disorders. It should provide understanding and hope as well as meaningful insights and answers. I do not assume to have all the answers here, only some special ones, answers that are often not enough considered in an era of biological psychiatry and empiricism. As in any approach, there are potentials and limitations. To the extent that there are limitations in this volume, I trust they can be offset by other perspectives and approaches. I believe it is the obligation

of all of us, however, to try and appreciate the potentials and limitations of the various approaches we adopt, to find complementarity
when we can, and, when we cannot, to explore the advantages of other
perspectives. I hope that whoever reads this book will be more guided
that limited by it. Most of all, what I hope this book can avoid, in its
contents and in what it evokes, is rigid and polarized reactions that
too often have obscured or stood in the way of understanding and feeling compassion for our patients and their needs.

# PART II

# The Internal World
# of the Addicted Person

## INTRODUCTION

Viewed from a psychodynamic perspective, the addicted person has made a short-term discovery that addictive substances make it more easy to adjust to one's inner emotional world and one's external reality. Addictive drugs are seductive because their action (or effects) can powerfully alter a person's feelings and how the person experiences his or her surroundings. All of us as humans are susceptible to these drugs, but some are more susceptible than others because they cannot adequately cope without them. Their temperament, parenting, or life experience has affected them in such a way that they more often experience their emotions in the extreme, and cannot adequately control or regulate their self-other relations or their behaviors. For some, intense emotions such as rage and anger unhinge them because of fragile or inadequate defenses, and opiates or obliterating doses of alcohol may calm or contain them. For the more timid or shy, restrictive character shields are dissolved by more moderate (but frequent) doses of alcohol and other depressants. Stimulants have a wider range of appeal because both high- and low-energy individuals exploit the powerful energizing and/or activating properties of these drugs. Overtly and covertly depressed individuals overcome states of depletion and anergia and temporarily "enjoy" a boost in their self-esteem, and more expansive, high-energy types augment this "best" sense of themselves with the stimulants. Moreover, attention deficit and hyperactive individuals welcome what for them is the paradoxical calming and focusing effects of cocaine and speed.

The chapters in this section explore how the internal world of addicts causes them major difficulty in coping with a range of life challenges. With one exception (Chapter 7) the chapters in this section span the first decade of my work with substance use disorders (SUDs) and herald most of the important themes I have tried to further clarify and develop over the subsequent two decades of my career. The themes are the use of addictive substances as coping agents; addictions as disorders in self-regulation; the self-medication hypothesis of SUDs; implications for self-help, individual and group (modified or dynamic) psychotherapy, and pharmacotherapy; and a psychodynamic appreciation of the causes and consequences of addictive suffering. This section should guide the reader in appreciating how the internal world of the addicted person is regulated (or not regulated) in such ways that makes the use and dependence on addictive substances more likely if not compelling. It also gives some early and preliminary account of what the treatment implications are for individuals with SUDs.

Chapter 1, which discusses heroin use as an attempt to cope, was written at a time when I had been working with addicts for approximately five years and was beginning to appreciate better some of the general and specific psychological factors that govern individuals' tendencies to become and remain dependent on narcotic drugs. I had just completed my psychoanalytic training at the Boston Psychoanalytic Institute, and my perspective was significantly influenced by an ego psychological perspective in which the emphasis was always to try to understand what was evident from the "ego side," namely, the observable psychological characteristics and defenses that determined the ways individuals managed their internal emotional life and their adjustment to external reality. As a consequence of these influences, most of the chapters in this section spell out in more detail and more precisely what I thought were some of the particular disturbances in the ego structures and related sense of self that made life so unbearable for the patients I was seeing, and how, at least for a while, drugs, and especially opiates, could relieve their suffering and make life more bearable.

Chapter 1 examines how individuals use opiates to adapt to a range of human psychological challenges. The case vignettes reveal that the challenges for the patients derive from overwhelming internal and external realities that produce distress and suffering that, in the short term, become more bearable or manageable with the use of drugs. In this chapter I hint at or touch on two major themes that I repeatedly return to and elaborate upon throughout this volume: (1) that addictive drugs relieve suffering, and (2) that individuals who risk this option do so because they are underdeveloped in a capacity for self-care. Chapter 2 provides the first and probably best description of self-care functions in addicted individuals, their component mechanisms, and the compensatory defenses that are apparent when self-care functions are underdeveloped.

In short, these early papers herald the core vulnerabilities of patients with substance use disorders, namely, their major difficulties in regulating their feelings and self-care. In Chapter 2 and the subsequent ones in this section, the clinical work, and the practice theory that derives from it, provides ample basis to appreciate how emotional and behavioral dysregulation is at the heart of addictive disorders. Contemporary investigators have popularized and emphasized the hereditary, cultural, and biophysiologic underpinnings of addictive disorders (DuPont 1997, Gold and Miller 1994, Schuckit and Smith 1996, Vaillant 1983). Recent empirical longitudinal and cross-sectional studies, however, from a psychosocial perspective (Brook et al. 1992, Kellam et al. 1991, Moss et al. 1995, Shedler and Block 1990), provide robust evidence that addictive vulnerability (including heavy use of "gateway" drugs such as marijuana and nicotine in early and late adolescence) just as much has its origins in troubled, disrupted intra-familial life. What I have repeatedly tried to focus on in my work is to understand from my patients' life experiences and my clinical observations of them, how they are constructed (or broken) in their psychological (ego) structures and how these differences cause them to suffer and behave in such ways that makes dependence on addictive drugs more likely and compelling. As the title of this book suggests, we need to appreciate much better the psychological dimension of SUDs in order to understand the human processes involved and how we can access and modify them. We can best do this by adopting a biopsychosocial perspective that empathically and clinically attunes to and ameliorates the psychological pain that governs addictive behavior.

Chapter 3 has its origins in a necessity I felt at that time to articulate what I was discovering about impulse problems and aggression associated with substances of abuse. In part, I felt compelled to write this chapter to overcome the rampant simplistic stereotype of addicted individuals as "drug crazed," who would do anything, including hurt, maim, or kill, either to get their drugs or while they were under their influence. It is noteworthy that at the time I wrote the paper (1973–1974) amphetamines were the most prevalent stimulant and cocaine abuse was not yet widespread. Accordingly, in describing the appeal and the consequences of stimulant use/abuse, most of the case examples involve those where amphetamine was the main stimulant of choice, and each patient has a story to tell. Drugs work to contain temporarily or relieve intense emotions for some, or can under less opportune circumstances inadvertently backfire and compound difficulties with aggression and impulsivity.

Chapter 4 was written at the invitation of the National Institute of Drug Abuse, which wanted to publish a monograph on the main prevalent theories of drug abuse at that time. Essentially, it codifies and summarizes germinal ideas I had explored over the previous ten years. It is probably important to single out my emphasis on "severe and significant psychopathology." This is in contrast to later publications in which my emphasis is more on "sectors of vulnerability in personality organization" and self-regulation disturbances (Khantzian 1990, 1995, 1997).

Chapter 5 provides empirical data documenting the emotional distress and behavioral dysregulation in narcotic and polydrug users. This chapter is an exception to most of the remaining chapters in this book, which are primarily based on clinical observations and case studies.

Chapter 6 was originally published in a book (Bean and Zinberg 1981) in which all of the authors (all from my own Department of Psychiatry at The Cambridge Hospital), were, with the exception of John

Mack, at variance with my views. In my chapter I elaborated on structural (ego and self) deficits in self-care and affect regulation and explored the treatment implications of these deficits, psychotherapeutically and psychopharmacologically. Of note, in this chapter I elaborated on a rationale for combining pharmacotherapy and psychotherapy in the treatment of alcoholics, an approach not widely embraced at that time by addiction specialists. In particular, I explored the potential and actual benefits of targeting and treating symptoms of depression and anxiety that I judged to be important in contributing to patients' dependence on alcohol. Three of the other authors in the book (George E. Vaillant, Norman Zinberg, and Margaret Bean) were explicitly critical of considering either the diagnosis or treatment of co-occurring depression and anxiety in alcoholics. Arguments against such considerations included contentions that alcoholism caused depression, not the other way around (Vaillant); that psychotherapy and the substitution of drug therapy for alcoholism plays into patients' denial of alcoholism as a primary disease; that psychotherapy could foster unhealthy or toxic dependency; and that drug therapy runs the risks of the addictive or toxic effects of these drugs. Both Zinberg and Vaillant at that time were considered premier investigators and critical thinkers in the alcoholism-addictions field and leading spokespersons for these widely held positions. (Bean would soon come into her own as a leading authority.) I was junior to both of them and I was in a distinct minority both in my own department and in the country in holding to a clinical position that psychological vulnerabilities and psychiatric symptoms were at the root of addictive vulnerability.

Over the subsequent two decades, clinical studies and empirical reports have proven that the bias against a psychiatric-psychodynamic perspective of patients with SUDs is unfounded and have provided evidence for the utility and efficacy of targeting an individual's suffering and psychiatric symptoms and the safety and effectiveness of treating patients with substance abuse disorders. The University of Pennsylvania/VA Medical Center group (Woody et al. 1983, 1986, 1995) have provided the most convincing studies demonstrating the benefits of psychotherapy in addicts. Ciraulo and associates (1988) and Adinoff (1992) provide reassurance that when coexisting anxiety is carefully diagnosed and treated with certain benzodiazepines (i.e., those that have a low abuse potential, for example, oxazepam or clonazepam) treatment can be efficacious and safe in reducing anxiety and the related dependence on alcohol. More recently, a series of reports has demonstrated that the utilization of antidepressants positively affects treatment outcome, reducing both the co-occurring depression and alcohol consumption. McGrath and colleagues (1996) showed that imipramine reduced depressive symptoms in alcoholics, and Mason and colleagues (1996) showed desipramine to be effective in reducing depression and relapses to alcohol. In a double-blind, placebo-controlled trial, Cornelius and associates (1997) demonstrated the Selective Serotonin Reuptake Inhibitor (SSRI) fluoxetine to be effective in alleviating depressive symptoms and reducing alcohol consumption in patients suffering with major depression and comorbid alcohol dependence. Their findings were consistent with two previous reports by this same group (1993, 1995) showing the efficacy of fluoxetine in depressed alcoholics. Most recently, Greenfield and colleagues (1998) came to similar conclusions on the relationship between depression and drinking behavior. Their study followed over a one-year period, a sample of forty women and sixty-one men who were diagnosed as depressed at the time of admission and showed that a diagnosis of major depression at admission predicted a significantly shorter period to first drink and relapse, regardless of gender. Furthermore, depressed patients who received antidepressants at hospital discharge returned more slowly to drinking than patients who received no medications.

Although I argue elsewhere in this volume (see Chapter 15) that patients do not necessarily self-medicate their psychiatric disorders, but more likely self-medicate subjective states of distress and suffering (that might or might not be associated with *DSM-IV* psychiatric diagnoses), I believe these more recent studies uphold my convictions, dating back to my early works, and especially my impressions spelled out in Chapter 6, that we need to target the psychological and psychiatric suffering that is so often associated with SUDs. The *DSM-IV* psychiatric diagnoses associated with SUDs, in my opinion, are the more extreme cases in the spectrum of psychological pain and suffering entailed in alcohol and drug dependency.

Chapter 6 is also noteworthy for a more detailed elaboration of the developmental origins of the pathological ego and self formations. In the latter case I focus on faulty or pathological ego-ideal structures to account for alcoholics' self-esteem problems and their inability to comfort or soothe themselves. Of significance here is my portrayal of alcoholics as uniformly suffering from more severe pathology. This is in contrast to subsequent works where I place greater emphasis on degrees of addictive vulnerability and viewing drug-alcohol dependence as disorders in self-regulation (Khantzian 1990, 1995, 1997). This shift in emphasis evolved out of my increasing experience with patients in long-term psychotherapy, and seeing patients coming from twelve-step programs for therapy, who exhibited much more resiliency, characterological strength, and psychological flexibility, than I witnessed earlier in my career. I believe this tendency to perceive more severe and pervasive psychopathology was in part influenced by my exposure, when I first started working in the addictions, to patients who primarily were either opiate or polysubstance dependent, a population that I still believe is more severely impaired. Finally, in this chapter I describe how I help patients achieve abstinence as a process, a process that can be alliance-building versus one that can be adversarial. As for the goal of obtaining abstinence, patients' accounts of their drinking behavior in Chapter 3 and 6 (its "rewards" and its consequences, and its meaning and role in their lives) graphically if not poignantly convey the preeminently human basis of addictive vulnerability, and how achieving abstinence and sobriety more often is a process rather than an event.

Chapter 7 was my first attempt to explain from a psychodynamic perspective how it was that addicts seem to "intentionally" perpetuate psychological suffering as much as they seek to relieve it. I pick up on and explore this theme in more detail in a series of papers in the 1990s (Khantzian 1993, 1995, 1997, Khantzian and Wilson 1993). Two of these reports that I published on the nature of addictive suffering (1995, 1997) are included in this volume (see Chapters 14 and 15).

## REFERENCES

Adinoff, B. (1992). Long term therapy with benzodiazepine despite alcohol dependence: seven case reports. *American Journal on Addictions* 1:288–293.

Bean, M. H., and Zinberg, N. E., eds. (1981). *Dynamic Approaches to the Understanding and Treatment of Alcoholism.* New York: Free Press.

Brook, J. S., Whiteman, M., Cohen, P., and Tanaka, J. S. (1992). Childhood precursors of adolescent drug use: a longitudinal analysis. *Genetics, Society and General Psychology Monograph* 118:195–213.

Ciraulo, D. A., Sands, B. F., and Shader, R. I. (1988). Critical review of liability for benzodiazepine abuse among alcoholics. *American Journal of Psychiatry* 145:1501–1506.

Cornelius, J. R., Salloum, I. M., Cornelius, M. D., et. al. (1993). Fluoxetine trial in suicidal depressed alcoholics. *Psychopharmacology Bulletin* 29:195–199.

——— (1995). Preliminary report: double blind, placebo-controlled study of fluoxetine in depressed alcoholics. *Psychopharmacology Bulletin* 31:297–303.

Cornelius, J. R., Salloum, I. M., Eliler, J. G., et al. (1997). Fluoxetine in depressed alcoholics: a double blind, placebo controlled trial. *Archives of General Psychiatry* 54:700–705.

DuPont, R. L. (1997). *The Selfish Brain: Learning from the Addictions.* Washington, DC: American Psychiatric Press.

Gold, M. S., and Miller, M. S. (1994). The biology of addictive and psychiatric disorders. In *Treating Co-existing Psychiatric and Addictive Disorders: A Practical Guide*, ed. N. S. Miller, pp. 35–49. Center City, MN: Hazelden.

Greenfield, S. J., Weiss, R. D., Muenz, L. R., et al. (1998). The effect of depression on return to drinking: a prospective study. *Archives of General Psychiatry* 55:259–265.

Kellam, S. G., Wethamer-Larson, L., Dollan, L. J., et al. (1991). Developmental epidemiologically based preventive trials: baseline modeling of early target behaviors and depressive symptoms. *American Journal of Community Psychology* 19:563–584.

Khantzian, E. J. (1990). Self-regulation and self-medication factors in alcoholism and the addiction: similarities and differences. In *Recent Developments in Alcoholism*, Vol. 8, ed. M. Galanter, pp. 225–271. New York: Plenum.

——— (1993). Affects and addictive suffering: a clinical perspective. In *Human Feelings: Explorations in Affect Development and Meaning*, ed. S. Ablon, D. Brown, E. J. Khantzian, and J. E. Mack, pp. 259–279. Hillsdale, NJ: Analytic Press.

——— (1995). Self-regulation vulnerabilities in substance abusers: treatment implications. In *The Psychology and Treatment of Addictive Behavior*, ed. S. Dowling, pp. 17–41. New York: International Universities Press.

——— (1997). The self-medication hypothesis of substance use disorders: a reconsideration and recent applications. *Harvard Review of Psychiatry* 4:231–244.

Khantzian, E. J., and Wilson, A. (1993). Substance abuse, repetition and the nature of addictive suffering. In *Hierarchical Conceptions in Psychoanalysis*, ed. A. Wilson and J. E. Gedo, pp. 263–283. New York: Guilford.

Mason, B. J., Kocsis, J. H., Ritvo, C. E., and Cutler, R. B. (1996). A double-blind, placebo-controlled trial of desipramine for primary alcohol dependence stratified on the presence or absence of major depression. *Journal of the American Medical Association* 275:761–767.

McGrath, P. J., Nunes, E. V., Stewart, J. W., et al. (1996). Imipramine treatment of alcoholics with major depression: a placebo controlled clinical trial. *Archives of General Psychiatry* 53:232–240.

Moss, N. B., Mezzich, A., Yao, J. K., et al. (1995). Aggressivity among sons of substance abusing fathers: association with psychiatric disorder in the father and son, paternal personality, pubertal development and socioeconomic status. *American Journal of Drug and Alcohol Abuse* 21:195–208.

Schuckit, M. A., and Smith, T. L. (1996). An 8-year follow-up of 450 sons of alcoholic and control subjects. *Archives of General Psychiatry* 53:202–210.

Shedler, J., and Block, J. (1990). Adolescent drug use and psychological health. *American Psychology* 45:612–630.

Vaillant, G. E. (1983). *The Natural History of Alcoholism*. Cambridge: Harvard University Press.

Woody, G. E., Luborsky, L., McLellan, A. T., et al. (1983). Psychotherapy for opiate addicts: Does it help? *Archives of General Psychiatry* 40:639–645.

Woody, G. E., McLellan, A. T., Luborsky, L., and O'Brien, C. P. (1986). Psychotherapy for substance abuse. *Psychiatric Clinics of North America* 9:547–562.

———— (1995). Psychotherapy in community methadone programs. *American Journal of Psychiatry* 152:1302–1308.

# 1

# Heroin Use As an Attempt to Cope

*with John E. Mack and*
*Alan F. Schatzberg*

There are numerous studies and reports that describe the psychological and personality characteristics of narcotic addicts as documented by psychological tests and personality inventories (Gerard and Kornetsky 1955, Haertzen and Hooks 1969, Hill et al. 1960, Zimmering et al. 1952). But surprisingly few clinical reports of addicted patients are based on psychiatric interviews and observations in long-term psychotherapy. Chein and associates (1964) were the first to attempt a systematic exploration of addicts' ego pathology, their problems with narcissism, and the manner in which they use narcotics to deal with their environment. Many of these observations were based on clinical work with addicts previously reported by Gerard and Kornetsky (1954). Clinical reports by Fort (1954), Guttman (1965), and Wurmser (1972) document strikingly the immense difficulties that addicts have with their narcissism and aggression. These reports offer ample evidence that narcotics addiction is symptomatic of underlying personality problems. However, the reports fail to indicate how the personality organization of these individuals distinguishes them from other groups of patients with significant character pathology or ego disturbances.

Our aim here is to demonstrate that addicts' use of opiates represents a unique and characteristic way of dealing with a range of human problems involving emotional pain, stress, and dysphoria. We show how addicts take advantage of the powerful action of the drug to mute and extinguish their emotions and to solve, at least in the short run, problems associated with interpersonal relationships. In addition, we describe how the transactions and practices of the pseudoculture in which the addict immerses himself also play a part in filling his social vacuum and providing an alternative to the establishment of meaningful attachments to other people.

Five brief case histories are reported. Emphasis is placed on the circumstances surrounding and leading up to the use of heroin, patients' subjective reactions to the drug, and the specific ways in which the patients employed the drug to manage their daily lives. The clinical material was collected by psychiatric interview and individual psychotherapy.

## CASE REPORTS

### Case 1

Mark, a 21-year-old single white man of Mediterranean descent, was the youngest of six children born to parents from a working-class background. He had been addicted to heroin for three years when he sought treatment.

At that time he claimed that he was using twelve bags of heroin per day and indicated that he had used up to a "bundle" (twenty-four bags) daily. He supported his habit by dealing in heroin and boasted that he could earn $800 in one hour on his own "turf." The verve and pride with which he described his success as a freewheeling, independent drug entrepreneur were in sharp contrast to his own admitted "depression and feeling bummed out and not caring" after being jilted by an older girlfriend when he was 16. Immediately after this he had turned to a group of older boys who were using drugs heavily and was introduced to amphetamines and proprietary opiates. By the time he was 18 he was using heroin regularly and exclusively.

Amphetamines had helped him to be more active, but they also had made him feel "tense, shaky, and aggressive." He contrasted this with the tranquilizing effects of heroin, saying, "That's why I like heroin—it calms me down. I love it almost as much as girlfriends." In reviewing his sexual history, it was learned that he had considerable self-consciousness about his sexual prowess, including concerns about the size of his penis and premature ejaculation. He suggested that amphetamines helped him to copulate more frequently and that he had no problems with premature emission while on heroin.

Although he enjoyed the euphoriant "nod" of heroin, he stressed that he felt "relaxed, mellow, and didn't think about bad things on dope—but you can get up and do what you like, for example, play football." He also stressed that heroin seemed to keep him going, that he had worked steadily as an electrician for two years while addicted to heroin.

## Case 2

Bob, a black technician, is married and the father of two children. He first sought treatment at a drug dependency clinic at age 25. He began to smoke marijuana regularly at age 19 and was experimenting with heroin by age 20. Despite a moderately heavy habit he always held responsible jobs and supported his family.

Bob was the eldest of five children. His parents were divorced when he was 6, and until recently he rarely saw his father. Three of his four siblings had also been addicted to heroin. His mother always worked at maintaining the household despite insufficient food and clothing for the children and her own significant illness, physical disability, and pain, which included vertebral disk problems dating back to her adolescence, long-standing hypertension, headaches, and chronic heart disease. She was hospitalized on several different occasions, including once for a psychiatric disorder when Bob was in high school. The poverty in his background led to considerable shame and self-consciousness, as well as resentment and anger, which he focused and vented on his mother. In later years he felt considerable guilt for the blame that he had placed on her.

Bob made no connection between his background of poverty, and its associated feelings, and his drug addiction. In general, he denied using drugs consciously for the purposes of dealing with personal distress. When giving his drug history, however, he claimed that heroin helped him to feel better when he was angry, nervous, or depressed. Bob said that he enjoyed the "high" he attained with heroin. Although he described heroin as a "monster," he said that it helped him to relax and gave him a "mellow feeling."

At about age 6 or 7 he had developed biweekly headaches (later diagnosed as migraines) that persisted into adolescence with increasing frequency. He discovered that he did not have headaches when using heroin or when maintained on methadone, but they returned during detoxification.

### Case 3

John, a 24-year-old white graduate student, sought psychotherapy for his drug problem. He had been mainlining heroin intermittently for five years, during which time he had had two treatment courses of methadone maintenance and several periods of abstinence. These periods were marked by a craving for heroin.

John was raised by well-educated, devoted, but rather doting parents. Although he readily acknowledged his mother's devotion to him, his chief complaint was that her love for him seemed contingent upon performances and achievement, an expectation that he was frequently determined to thwart. In the course of treatment, a picture emerged of an indulgent mother–child relationship, in which the mother seemed to have been constantly ready and eager to meet her son's dependency needs and spare him unnecessary frustrations. The description that the patient provided of his total dependence on the drug, which seemed to gratify his every need, corresponded precisely to the perception of his attachment to his mother. According to the patient, the mother insisted throughout his childhood and youth on seeing him as a brilliant and gifted Adonis without limitations, qualities that he knew realistically he did not possess and would not be able to acquire. He felt that he had been denied the experience of facing and accepting the pain of his own limitations. Instead he had grown up always fearing that he might disappoint his mother and lose her love if she discovered his actual shortcomings.

As the patient entered adolescence he became increasingly uneasy about himself, especially in regard to his capacities as a student, his ability to make friends, and his success with girls. He constantly felt a nameless dread, a vague fear of rejection, and a kind of emotional void. His use of heroin, which began as a shared experience with a high school acquaintance, seemed to help greatly. In his words, it was "mind-filling" and "all-solving." The substance itself was seen as tremendously powerful and the experience of shooting drugs so intensely pleasurable that nothing, not even sex, seemed to be its equal. The drug also helped to solve his recurrent problem of premature ejaculation. On heroin he could sustain an erection and perform the sexual act more effectively.

With the drug in his system he felt instantly and dramatically transformed; all reality problems would disappear and his fear of rejection would be replaced by a feeling of solidarity with other drug takers. Pain, distress, and depression were replaced by a feeling of being part of a special subculture, with its peculiar rituals and drug-taking paraphernalia, a group privileged to have tasted "the apple in the Garden of Eden." With his addict friends he would imagine a romantic vagabond existence, where a financial windfall would make hard work unnecessary. The solidarity that he felt with other drug-taking contemporaries was highly important to him and contrasted sharply with his bitter memories of the lack of self-confidence and anxiety that he had felt with his peers in high school. These relationships, although important, were less vital than the drug itself, for he readily acknowledged that members of the group would not hesitate to steal from each other when necessary to maintain their habits.

## Case 4

Paul, a 28-year-old white college graduate from an upper-class family background, is a divorced father of two children. When Paul sought psychiatric help he had been addicted to heroin for a little more than two years and was using up to twenty bags of heroin per day. The patient was the oldest of three boys. His father, a successful executive, was characterized as remote and authoritarian. Paul felt that he was close to his mother, whom he claimed indulged him in all his wants and needs. In comparison, his brothers were more self-reliant and like their father. He felt that his parents, who were both college graduates, were extremely conscious of status and exerted great pressure on him to perform in prep school and to gain entrance into a prestigious college. His ultimate failure in both of these expectations was accompanied by much apprehension and depression.

When he was first seen, he had been using heroin exclusively. However, he had become heavily involved with other drugs in high school, where he used significant amounts of amphetamines, hallucinogens, hashish, marijuana, cough syrup with codeine, and combinations such as amyl nitrate with alcohol. He explained his indiscriminate use of every drug he could obtain as a way of gaining acceptance from "hippie-intellectual types" after he had gotten into trouble with the law and had become disillusioned with society.

In the course of treatment it became clear that "society" represented the patient's father, whom he felt he could never be like. He described him as "awesome, self-disciplined, predictable, and successful." Despite his admitted mistrust of his fellow junkies, he felt that he could gain acceptance and success more easily and on his own terms with a group of drug-taking friends.

In giving his drug history the patient focused particularly on how irritable and mean he was, particularly when on amphetamines, and he described many violent situations in which he was sadistically "beating on" someone or was similarly being beaten. He explained that a good part of his violent behavior was calculated and deliberate to impress his buddies and girlfriend with his "manliness," but there was also an impulsive side to this, over which he felt he had no control. He listed many situations of unprovoked assaults on people at parties and also while roaming the street with friends, for which he had been arrested a number of times. According to the patient his impulsive behavior was prominent when he used alcohol and stimulant drugs but was more controlled and contained when he used opiates.

Immediately prior to the patient's initiation to heroin, there was a protracted period of several months during which he used large amounts of "methcrystal" ("speed") during the day and barbiturates at night. He recalled that the first time he went looking for heroin he was "hassling" with his wife. He described his first experience with heroin as follows: "It was the epitome of everything I had tried. It made me feel good, and it made me relax." The first time he used heroin someone else gave him the injection, and he said, "I really dug the rush—it made my whole body relax instantly." In his interviews he stressed that he became subdued after taking narcotics but that he was a "madman" when he was coming off them. He asserted that once he had satisfied his craving for narcotics he was able to "get going and do things." For example, he went to a job interview at a prestigious company after injecting the contents of eight bags of heroin. After ascertaining that the interviewer was as status-minded as his father, he assumed an aristocratic attitude and sufficiently impressed the man to get the job. He was still holding the job one year later when he entered treatment.

## Case 5

Tony, a 21-year-old single white man, was the second youngest of four children in a middle-class family of Greek descent. His father, an executive in a food supply company, worked his way up from the position of laborer in the same company. At the time of his discharge from the military Tony was not using drugs, but he volunteered to be a subject in a prospective study following veterans who had become involved with narcotics while stationed in Vietnam. The following is a summary of his first interview.

Tony said that before going to Vietnam he frequently smoked "grass" after duty hours during the week, and on the weekends he used a fair amount of alcohol with his buddies back home. Upon arriving in Vietnam he immediately looked for marijuana and was surprised to find that it was scarce and that "everyone" was smoking heroin. He said that this was the first time he had been away from home and claimed he was lonesome. He noticed that heroin smoking was most widespread and obvious in the barracks during "sleeping hours." He decided to try it and discovered that it made him feel "secure and better about being away from home." (Then, and subsequently, he only smoked it.) In addition to relating how heroin helped him with his feelings of loneliness, he graphically described what else it did for him and for other men: "Things don't penetrate when you're on heroin, like if you were straight." He gave a number of examples: "Guys get letters [i.e., Dear John letters] from their girls and if they are stoned on heroin, they say 'Fuck it' and throw the letter away—you get very relaxed and into a state of mind of not caring. You have no sexual feelings but physically, you feel OK. Let's say you have to go to the bathroom. You can overlook it. You nod, relax. You can read a book for hours and days. It can make you tired, but you can stay awake and relax."

Tony emphasized that heroin was inexpensive in Vietnam and that it was not necessary to steal in order to support a habit. He said that he had looked forward to going to Vietnam, but once there he felt himself surrounded with danger (although he was never in combat) and trusted no one, including native troops, regular troops, blacks, and officers. He said, "Everybody is doing something [i.e., drugs, alcohol, etc.], and you can't trust anybody. If someone argues with somebody, they could just set a satchel charge [a homemade time bomb]. I would rather spend a year in jail than a month in Vietnam." In this context he again stated, "But with heroin I didn't care." Significantly, he said that he drank only twice in the six months he was in Vietnam, but that he thought he might have drunk more had his buddies imbibed. He stressed that it was the E6s and E7s, "the career soldiers who were for the war, that did all the drinking." In this same context he compared the effects of heroin to those of alcohol and barbiturates. He said that alcohol and barbiturates affected the head, whereas heroin affected the whole body.

## DISCUSSION

What appears to be unique about patients addicted to heroin—and an aspect of the disorder that has not been adequately described or explored—is the special role that the drug comes to play in the personality organization of these patients. They have not successfully established familiar defensive, neurotic, characterological, or other common adaptive mechanisms as a way of dealing with their distress. Instead, they have resorted to the use of opiates as a way of coping with a range of problems involving ordinary human pain, disappointment, anxiety, loss, anguish, sexual frustration, and other suffering. Failing to discover or adopt more common adaptive mechanisms to resolve their suffering, they have resorted to an extraordinary solution through the powerful action of the drug. In other words, the more familiar pathways to stability and predictability in personality organization, whether healthy or pathological, have been supplanted by the stability of the moment that can be provided by the drug and all of the attendant rituals, practices, and pseudoculture that are involved with its use.

An impreciseness in the diagnosis of individuals addicted to opiates is reflected in discussions by Chein and associates (1964), who refer to subgroups of pseudo "psychopaths" and to "latent schizophrenia" and by Vaillant (1966), who refers to addicts' schizoid and borderline qualities and underlying depression, which, however, is "highly defended against." These patients probably defy a more precise characterological or symptomatic diagnosis because the psychophysiological action of the drug attenuates and subdues feelings and emotions that would ordinarily be resolved in a more familiar way through symptom formation or other adaptive mechanisms.

In the clinical material presented, we noted an absence of the more usual mechanisms of defense and of attempts at conflict resolution. Instead, the opiates have been used by addicts as a costly form of adaptation, a kind of total solution to a variety of conflicts within the individual and in his interpersonal and work areas. All of the patients gave clear indications that the pharmacological properties of opiates strongly influenced a range of feelings and emotions. The loss of a girlfriend, a sense of failure in social relations, painful self-consciousness among peers in adolescence, worries about success and achievement, anticipated inability to live up to parental expectations, loneliness, psychosomatic pain, feelings of rage, violent impulses, and many other forms of emotional distress and bodily tension are relieved and made more manageable through the use of narcotic drugs. Indeed, our patients also offered evidence that the drugs did not necessarily interfere with gainful employment. In some instances the opiates seemed to facilitate their obtaining and holding a job by quieting a range of fears and tensions. Three of the patients (Mark, John, and Tony) indicated that opiates helped them to overcome difficulties with sexual performance and/or to eliminate and subdue distressing feelings associated with sexual tensions, heterosexual intimacy, and concerns about sexual adequacy.

The special practices, transactions, rituals, and pseudoculture that surround the opiate addict are not unrelated to the use of opiates as an adaptive and coping mechanism. As indicated earlier, opiates provide a chemical buffer for dealing with various human interactions; however, the various activities and involvements that surround addiction are often significant. For some, it is the great investment made in achieving success as a heroin "wheeler and dealer." For others, the drug culture represents the first place where they achieved a sense of belonging and acceptance. In many cases a social vacuum is filled, and problems of emotional emptiness and of forming and sustaining friendships and relationships are overcome, albeit in a tenuous and often shallow fashion. The powerful action of the drug may obviate the need for more lasting object relations and personal involvement.

The cases of the black addict and the Vietnam veteran who became addicted warrant special mention. In the case of the black addict, factors of poverty, family disorganization, and deprivation may loom particularly large. However, a serious question remains as to whether economic and emotional deprivations cause heroin addiction and whether heroin becomes a way of dealing with this kind of painful reality. In a brief discussion such as this the question can only be touched upon.

It is not uncommon to hear many addicts and others insist that the reason they repeatedly and avidly return to using opiates is that they have not escaped from those same societal influences that originally caused their problem. What tends to be overlooked in such a broad, oversimplified generalization is how these societal influences and intra-familial factors can produce early ego impairments that leave a person less equipped to deal with later developmental challenges and adult stresses. The reversion to drugs may then be viewed more as an indication that an individual needs the adaptive value offered by the psychophysiological action of the drug because he lacks or has failed to discover alternative coping devices or mechanisms.

In the case of the Vietnam veteran, one may feel compelled to justify and explain the use of opiates on the basis of environmental factors, although in this case the influences appeared later in the individual's life. However, most soldiers found alternative ways to deal with the disillusionment of an unpopular war and the loneliness, mistrust, fear, and danger associated with their experience. Tony made a compelling case for using drugs to combat all the painful feelings he described, but it is probably safe to say that his addiction was as adaptive or maladaptive as other reactions in this and previous wars (e.g., shell shock in World War I, traumatic or combat neurosis in World War II, and, more recently, combat exhaustion [Bloch 1969]).

However, Lifton (1972) has observed special problems in survival emotion involving guilt, violence, and rage associated with the Vietnam war that might encourage the use of the readily available heroin as a "symptom choice." That is, the Vietnam veterans had participated in a war that had no victory parades and no enemy that was commonly recognized, by either the soldiers or the citizens back home, to justify the feelings of violence and hatred engendered by war. One of us has described elsewhere (Khantzian 1972) how narcotics are particularly effective in muting and attenuating feelings of violence and rage, which probably accounts in part for some of the appeal of heroin in Vietnam.

It is from the Vietnam addict or the addict from a low-income minority background that one most often hears how external factors such as peer-group pressures, increased availability of drugs, or the "ills of society" caused his addiction. However much these factors may contribute to the problem, many of these arguments are used by individuals who remain addicted as justifications and rationalizations to psychologically support the continued use of the drug because they lack the capacity or fear the inability to find other ways to solve their problems. As with deprivation, certain forms of overindulgence in the mother–child relationship can also result in early ego impairments that may later lead to addiction problems. In the case of John, his mother's lifelong indulgence of his dependency needs and her need to minimize his frustrations apparently denied him the opportunity for learning to tolerate the experience of limitations in himself and in the outside world and for developing adequate defensive and adaptive mechanisms for dealing with the inevitable disappointments he was to encounter once he left home. Instead, he resorted to opiate use and its attendant subculture and rituals as a way of eliminating all fears of rejection, emotional pain, and anxiety.

We have been impressed with a rather specific ego impairment having to do with self-care and self-regulation that characterizes many addicted individuals. Ordinarily such functions protect individuals from hurting themselves, serve to avoid danger, and in general ensure that an individual can take care of himself. We believe that the adequate establishment of this function has to do with optimal nurturing and caring in the early mother–child relationship. Failure to establish these self-preservation functions may result from extremes of deprivation or indulgence.

Approaching this problem from another viewpoint, Lewis and associates (1966) have described how lapses and failures in adequate mother–child caring cause the child to be prone to accidental ingestion of poison. We believe that part of the apparent self-disregard evident in a number of our addicted patients is an adult derivative of similar failures of the mother–child relationship as described by these authors. Our own observations and those of Lewis and associates suggest that we need to learn more about how deprivation and indulgence can impair the development, internalization, and maintenance of self-care functions and about how impairments in such ego functions can result in an individual's susceptibility to addiction.

Rather than stretching the boundaries of our existing diagnostic categories to find a place for addicts, either symptomatically or characterologically, we would do better to consider the centrality of the addict's dependence on his drug in trying to describe and understand the addicted individual. The central problem for most people who have become addicted to opiates is that they have failed to develop effective symptomatic, characterological, or other adaptive solutions in response to developmental crises, stress, deprivation, and other forms of emotional pain, which may not in themselves be extraordinary. Their response has been to revert repeatedly to the use of opiates as an all-powerful device, thereby precluding other solutions that would normally develop and that might better sustain them. It is on this basis that addicts are probably so desperately dependent on their drugs and have so little confidence that they can endure without them. That is, the use of the drug is their characteristic or characterological way of adapting and dealing with their inner world of feelings and emotions and the real world around them.

The implications for treatment can be considered only briefly here. In appreciating the central role that opiates play for the addict in adapting to a range of problems and conflicts, it is less difficult to understand the initially high dropout rates from most forms of treatment. Regardless of which treatment approach is considered, we feel that it is most important that one understand the role that the drug plays in the addict's adaptation to his inner and outer world. Considered in this context, it does not seem as germane to engage in polemics about abstinence or maintenance. Rather, the main consideration becomes one of controlling the addiction through a variety of ways until such time as the original areas of avoidance and failures in mastery have been sufficiently influenced to allow for alternative ways of life and other adaptive solutions.

Specifically, we believe that psychotherapy must be of an educational variety in which the therapist actively pursues with the patient the ways in which he has used drugs to avoid life's inevitable pain and vicissitudes. To do this, the therapist must be willing to make significant aspects of his own personality available to the patient and to share with him some alternative ways to bear disappointment and endure distress. In such a process the therapist provides opportunities for the patient to identify with the healthier qualities of the therapist, who more successfully adapts to and masters his or her own conflicts and life experiences through other means.

## REFERENCES

Bloch, S. (1969). Army clinical psychiatry in the combat zone: 1967–1968. *American Journal of Psychiatry* 126:289–298.

Chein, I., Gerard, D. L., Lee R. S., and Rosenfeld, S. (1964). *The Road to H.* New York: Basic Books.

Fort, J. P. (1954). Heroin addiction among young men. *Psychiatry* 17:251–259.

Gerard, D. L., and Kornetsky, C. (1954). Adolescent opiate addiction: a case study. *Psychiatric Quarterly* 28:367–380.

———— (1955). Adolescent opiate addiction: a study of control and addict subjects. *Psychiatric Quarterly* 29:457–486.

Guttman, O. (1965). The psychodynamics of a drug addict. *American Journal of Psychotherapy* 19:653–665.

Haertzen, C. A., and Hooks, N. T. (1969). Changes in personality and subjective experience associated with the chronic administration and withdrawal of opiates. *Journal of Nervous and Mental Disease* 148:606–614.

Hill, H. E., Haertzen, C. A., and Glasser, R. (1960). Personality characteristics of narcotic addicts as indicated by the MMPI. *Journal of General Psychology* 62:127–139.

Khantzian, E. J. (1972). A preliminary dynamic formulation of the psychopharmacologic action of methadone. In *Proceedings of the Fourth National Conference on Methadone Treatment,* San Francisco, pp. 371–374. New York: National Association for the Prevention of Addictions to Narcotics.

Lewis, M., Solnit, A. J., Stark, M. H., et al. (1966). An exploration study of accidental ingestion of poison in young children. *Journal of the American Academy of Child Psychiatry* 5:255–271.

Lifton, R. J. (1972). Home from the war: the psychology of survival. *Atlantic Monthly,* November, pp. 56–72.

Vaillant, G. E. (1966). A 12-year follow-up of New York narcotic addicts, II: some social and psychiatric characteristics. *Archives of General Psychiatry* 15:599–609.

Wurmser, L. (1972). Methadone and the craving for narcotics: observations of patients on methadone maintenance in psychotherapy. In *Proceedings of the Fourth National Conference on Methadone Treatment*, San Francisco, pp. 525–528. New York: National Association for the Prevention of Addictions to Narcotics.

Zimmering, P., Toolan, J., Safrin, N. S., et al. (1952). Drug addiction in relation to problems of adolescence. *American Journal of Psychiatry* 109:272–279.

# 2

# The Ego, the Self, and Opiate Addiction

Until recently, the psychoanalytic literature on addiction stressed the pleasurable aspects of drug use to explain the compelling nature of addiction (Abraham 1908, Freud 1905, Rado 1933, 1957). Although Rado and others (Fenichel 1945, Savitt 1963, Wikler and Rasor 1953) appreciated underlying factors of depression, tension, and anxiety, many of these same workers continued to place particular emphasis on the euphoric-pleasurable aspects of drug use. Most of this literature on addiction focuses on the regressive gratification of libidinal instincts achieved through the use of addictive substances. Glover's (1932) work stands in striking contrast to the other theoretical explanations of addiction. He stressed that addicts used their substance progressively (as opposed to regressively) to defend against primitive, sadistic impulses and to avoid psychosis. He seemed to appreciate better the enormous difficulties addicts have with their aggression and viewed the sexual and pleasurable aspects of drug use as defensive responses to the underlying problems with aggression.

Later works (Chein et al. 1964, Khantzian 1974, 1975, Khantzian et al. 1974, Krystal and Raskin 1970, Milkman and Frosch 1973, Wieder and Kaplan 1969, Wurmser 1974) have stressed the adaptive use of drugs and have tried to incorporate a better appreciation of how the psychopharmacological action of the different drugs interact with the personality organization of addicted individuals. These reports have focused on ego function and ego impairments, and in particular on problems with affect tolerance (Krystal and Raskin 1970, Wurmser 1974) and drive defense (Khantzian 1974). Zinberg (1975) has stressed the importance of setting and how it interacts with ego function and drug effect. Some of these reports have also tried to take into account narcissistic problems that contribute to the individual's general predisposition to addiction, and to some of the related specific ego impairments and psychopathology that are evident in addicted individuals.

This chapter selectively reviews and expands on theoretical and clinical investigative work that has focused on the ego impairments of narcotic addicts, particularly in relation to problems with affect and drive defense, and explores how certain problems with self-care and self-regulation are related to failures in internalization, and how these failures in development leave such individuals vulnerable to a range of hazardous behavior and involvements, but in particular to addictions. Finally, the chapter examines certain unique and characteristic traits that are related to narcissistic processes and defenses so common among addicts. These characteristics serve to compensate for their developmental impairments, but at the same time impede such individuals in establishing and obtaining sufficient satisfactions in their involvement with people, work, and play. On the basis of these theoretical considerations, some implications for treatment interventions are explored.

## AFFECT AND DRIVE DEFENSE

In working with narcotic addicts one often hears the claim that they are psychologically "healthier" than other types of addicts or psychiatric patients. Such claims are bolstered by arguments that one would have to be healthier and "better put together" to survive the challenges and dangers involved in obtaining the money and drugs to support an addiction to heroin. Such claims are based on observations of how successful such individuals seem to be in acting upon and extracting from their surroundings what they want for themselves. This apparent "success" detracts both the observer and the addict from indications of failure in functioning that are often equally as apparent, namely the addict's inability to cope with his emotions and his relations with other people. The so-called successful functioning of the heroin addict says less about his mental health, but more about how the ego of such individuals is shaped and developed along certain lines to serve their addiction and related requirements. However, I also suspect that these special qualities of addicts represent attempts to make up for and to offset major deficits, impairments, and failures in defense against their affects and drives.

I believe that these failures and deficits in defense are developmental and are intimately related to problems with internalization. Internalization is a process by which the developing infant and child acquires qualities and functions from parental figures in the process of maturation. Ideally, the person eventually can care for himself as a result of this internalization. This process is probably related to the ways in which the developing person is exposed to the "good enough (caring) environment" and how "the good enough mothering" in infancy and childhood affects the person as a function of adequate nurturing (Winnicott 1953). If successful, this process of internalization establishes within the person a coherent sense of the self, an appreciation of the separate existence of others, as well as the establishment of adequate ego functions that serve purposes of defense and adaptation. In this section I shall focus on those aspects of internalization related to ego mechanisms of defense, especially against affects and drives, and I shall stress particularly ego impairments and problems associated with drive and affect defense in narcotic addicts.

Based on direct child observation and clinical practice with adults, there is rather convincing evidence that normal development requires certain amounts of frustration (Kohut 1971, Mahler 1968, Meissner et al. 1975, Winnicott 1953). Optimally, extremes of deprivation or indulgence are avoided and the child is confronted with enough tolerable disappointment that a capacity to tolerate emotional distress and pain is gradually built up. To summarize how this capacity evolves, the individual gradually incorporates into a sense of the self and into the ego the parents' protective role and their function as a stimulus barrier. Used in this sense, *stimulus barrier* refers to those aspects of ego functions that operate either to maintain a minimal level of unpleasant affects or tension, or to defend against such feelings through appropriate action and mechanisms of defense when they reach high or intolerable levels.

Krystal and Raskin (1970) have traced how affects also develop along certain lines and serve the ego to defend against internal emotional states and drives. They have delineated in a most helpful way how anxiety and depression develop out of a common undifferentiated matrix, and evolve through differentiation, de-somatization, and verbalization. Ideally, this process of development ultimately allows the person to use feelings as a guide and signal to mobilize the ego in response to the constant barrage of internal and external stimuli involved in human living. Krystal and Raskin further review how trauma in the course of development (or as a result of catastrophic events later in life) may lead to both affective disturbances and drug dependence. They stress how traumatization produces a reversal and regression resulting in dedifferentiation of affects. In addition to trauma, they also stress how the failure of parents to act as adequate models in managing affects leads to an arrest in development, which precludes successful differentiation. In the case of addicts, a major consequence of such developmental arrest is that they are unable to make use of anxiety and feelings as signals or guides because their feelings are undifferentiated and overwhelming.

Krystal and Raskin are fully aware of the specific anesthetic action of heroin on painful affects and explain most cogently why individuals involved with heroin are subject to and are unable to manage overwhelming affect states. However, in my estimation, they do not sufficiently distinguish the action of opiates from other sedatives, including alcohol. In addition to its antiaggression action, I believe that the capacity of heroin to relieve specifically overwhelming, distressful affect states is what makes it such a compelling substance for narcotic addicts. This observation might seem to state the obvious, but to specify and more precisely define what affect states are relieved by heroin and other drugs has most important implications for management and treatment, especially with psychotropic drugs.

Kohut (1971) has traced how problems with internalization are linked to narcissistic disturbances and, in particular, how such disturbances lie at the root of addictive disorders. Traumatic disappointments with the mother because of her lack of empathy with the child, and her failure to act as an adequate stimulus barrier or to provide adequate stimuli and gratification of tension, lead to a failure in development of the child's psychic apparatus. Later in life many of these individuals discover that drugs substitute for defects in their ability to cope with inevitable life distresses and disappointments. Kohut makes this provocative statement: "The drug serves not as a substitute for loved or loving objects, or for a relationship with them, but as a replacement for a defect in the psychological structure" (p. 46). Wieder and Kaplan (1969) similarly appreciate this aspect of drug use referring to drugs as a "corrective—and prosthetic." Wurmser (1974) comes to the same conclusion referring to the addict's "defect of affect defense." He emphasizes the addict's enormous difficulties in handling painful affects, and how opiates in particular act to relieve feelings of narcissistic rage, shame, hurt, and loneliness. In lieu of adequate defense, Wurmser speculates that narcotics act by dampening such feelings directly and/or raising the threshold against reactions of narcissistic disappointment.

A recent case example highlights nicely some of the problems with internalization and defects in affect defense that have been reviewed thus far:

A 29-year-old man was struggling with much rage and anxiety. Despite all good intentions, he found himself reverting to previous addictive behavior. His reversion had occurred in the context of a visit from his mother, whom he had not seen in over a year. She had reprimanded him about some recent financial indiscretions that concerned her, but had totally failed to appreciate how anxious, fragmented, and overwhelmed he was feeling at the time. The painful consequences of the defects in his ego structure and the quality of the overwhelming feelings in the absence of such structure was poignantly conveyed in the account of his reactions to his mother's visit. He also gave some hints about how such deficits originate in parental attitudes and disappointment. He complained: "My mother is utterly disregarding. She doesn't know me at all— what I feel or think or what I'm like. When I feel anxious, I feel it all over, not just butterflies in my stomach or sweaty hands. I feel it all over. When I get anxious, I get anxiouser, and anxiouser, and anxiouser. When I get afraid, the only thing that makes it go away [at this point he struggled to explain and finally offered:] is a stronger person." In this context he pleaded that the therapist prescribe a medication for his anxiety.

In my own work with narcotic addicts, I have been impressed with the lifelong difficulties such individuals have had with aggression and derivative problems with rage and depression. After obtaining repeated histories from addicts about how dysphoric feelings associated with restlessness, anger, and rage were relieved by heroin and other opiates, and after observing narcotic addicts stabilize on methadone, I began to suspect that narcotics might have a direct anti-aggression action. In a previous report (Khantzian 1974) I summarized these findings and concluded that problems with aggression predisposed certain individuals to dependence on opiates and played a central role in the development of addiction. I stressed the addict's use of the antiaggression action of opiates in the service of drive defense, and formulated how the longer but similar action of methadone was the basis for the "success" of methadone maintenance. In the report cited and elsewhere (Khantzian 1972) I stressed the disorganizing influence of aggression on ego function in individuals whose ego stability was already subject to dysfunction and impairment either as a result of developmental arrest or regression.

Zinberg (1975) has questioned seriously the role of preexisting psychopathology as a major determinant of addiction. He has perceptively and persuasively proposed that regression in addicts is less a function of personality disturbance and drug effect, but more the result of being labeled as deviant, the loss of varied contact with social and family relationships, and the necessity to "cop" (i.e., obtain drugs). Although his work is at variance with the emphasis on developmental impairments in this chapter, his point of view is not incompatible with what we have proposed. His study reminds us of the importance of "stimulus nutriment" from the environment in maintaining autonomous ego functions.

Although my own work with narcotic addicts has stressed problems with drive defense, particularly in relation to aggressive drives, it is important to note and emphasize that all the more recently cited reports of clinical investigative work with narcotic addicts are remarkably consistent with each other. They stress problems with drive and affect defense and focus on developmental impairments in the ego. More remarkable, much of this consensus has been arrived at almost simultaneously and independently. I believe that further work on the ego side of the problem, with cross-fertilization of thinking among various investigators, promises to yield further understanding of the relationship between drive and affect states, and various ego defenses and modes of adaptation. Milkman and Frosch (1973), for example, have reported on a promising line of inquiry in applying to addicts a systematic study of ego functions developed by Bellak and Hurvich. Their preliminary findings show a relationship between an abuser's characteristic mode of adaptation and his preference for either amphetamines or heroin.

I have said little up to this point specifically about character pathology, and yet we know that our patients most often are referred to as psychopaths, sociopaths, and antisocial characters. I believe these labels, so often used pejoratively, describe little that is meaningful or accurate about addicts. Perhaps such descriptions mostly indicate how little we understand character pathology. I suspect that as we study such problems, we shall gain a better appreciation of the relationship between various drive and affect states and the ways in which such states contribute to or drive so-called character pathology and related behavioral disorders such as narcotic addiction. In my work with character problems, I am in agreement with the proposition offered by Vaillant (1975) and Wishnie (1974) that, as control is gained over the behavior problems, underlying psychopathology that was previously masked by the destructive behavior emerges. Vaillant and Wishnie stress in particular the underlying depression. My own experience not only emphasizes the underlying depression, but the presence as well of a range and variety of mood disorders, phobic-anxious states, and other neurotic, characterological, and psychotic symptoms. As we more precisely identify such target symptoms and affect states, we shall be in a better position to decide on suitable forms and types of psychological and psychopharmacological interventions.

## SELF-CARE AND SELF-REGULATION[1]

There is an aspect of addiction that seems to have received little systematic attention in the literature. It is related to a particular type of gap or vulnerability in ego function of drug-dependent individuals. Namely, I have been impressed with an apparent disregard that drug-

---

1. The author is indebted to Dr. John E. Mack for his assistance in the development of the germinal idea and concept of self-care as an ego function.

dependent individuals show to a range of real or possible dangers to their well-being, including their substance involvement. I believe this type of self-disregard is associated with impairments of a generic or global ego function that I have chosen to designate as *self-care and self-regulation.* I say "generic or global" because I suspect such functions and their impairments are related to component ego functions such as signal anxiety, reality testing, judgment, control and synthesis, and, when impaired, to such defenses as denial, justification, and projection. As used here, the concept of self-care combines elements of all of these component functions, and in this respect it is a complex function. But in other respects the functions of self-care and -regulation are so basic and elementary for survival that they are sufficiently developed and present to be evident in normal young children.

Before proceeding to elaborate on problems with self-care as an ego function, I would like to stress what I am *not* referring to or emphasizing in this discussion. The literature refers to the obvious self-destructive nature of addictions. In some cases reference is made to unconscious "death wishes." In other cases, as referred to in the previous section, the apparent disregard and not caring is related to desperate attempts to ward off painful feelings. In still other instances, dangerous and violent behavior serves to counteract feelings of helplessness and dependency and, as Wieder and Kaplan (1969) have correctly indicated, it is a mode that is adopted against one's sense of terror and vulnerability. In these cases the actual and potential problems and danger for the person are driven, overdetermined, and defensive. These self-destructive aspects of addiction have received considerable attention and will not be the main focus of this discussion.

The addict's self-disregard is not so consciously or unconsciously motivated, but more a reflection of defects in self-care functions as a result of failures to adopt and internalize these functions from the caring parents in early and subsequent phases of development. The overdetermined and defensive forms of self-destructive behavior among addicts do not adequately account for all the terribly dangerous and destructive activity, to the point of death, that such people get into. In such cases danger is not so much consciously or unconsciously welcomed, or counterphobically denied, but rather is never anticipated, perceived, or appreciated. These are problems that I consider to be related to self-care (ego) functions that are impaired, deficient, or absent in so many of the addicts we see. The problems with self-care and -regulation are apparent in their past histories (predating their addiction) by a high incidence of preventable medical and dental problems, accidents, fights and violent behavior, and delinquent behavioral problems. Their impaired self-care function is also evident in relation to their drug problems, where despite obvious deterioration and imminent danger as a result of their drug use, there is little evidence of fear, anxiety, or realistic assessment about their substance involvement. One might correctly argue that in this latter instance the lack of self-care is secondary to regression as a result of prolonged drug use. Although this is probably quite true, we have been impressed with the presence and persistence of these described tendencies in such individuals both prior to becoming addicted, and subsequent to becoming drug-free and stabilized. In fact much of our therapeutic work beyond detoxification involves helping our patients to identify these impairments around self-care, and to help them learn to incorporate these functions for the first time in their daily living and behavior.

In contrast to the compulsive aspects of drug use where drugs serve purposes of defense and adaptation, some of the more malignant aspects of drug addiction that we are stressing here are related to the impulsive, maladaptive side of the problem. That is, the addiction to drugs and the associated involvements and activities, which are often equally as dangerous, represent a failure in the person's ego to properly assess, warn, and protect the individual against the dangers in a whole variety of settings and situations, not the least of which is the setting associated with addictions. Some examples taken from a women's correctional institution where most of the individuals have been drug-free and relatively stable for some time are presented for purposes of illustration.[2] Some of the most telling examples are evident in relation to health issues. For example, failure to clean needles that are shared is common. Gross dietary indiscretions, such as the diabetic failing to adhere to a proper diet, or the inmate who buys the most spicy foods despite a chronic ulcer, and failures in the sexual sphere to take precautions against pregnancy, or to worry about the possibility of venereal disease, or to obtain regular gynecologic examinations are but a few examples.

---

2. The author is indebted to Ms. Catherine Treece for these vignettes and case examples.

Then there are the people who just happen to be in the wrong place at the wrong time; for example, the inmate who went shopping with her boyfriend and was arrested for shoplifting after the boyfriend asked her to hold a bag containing a suit he had shoplifted, or the woman who landed in jail because she believed her male friend who told her that she was just "live parking" the car while he went to the bank, when in fact she was driving the getaway car.

Another inmate went for a walk with a girlfriend who she knew was planning to shoplift. She was caught and arrested for shoplifting and protested that she was only going along for the fresh air and "can't figure out" why she was charged.

In our own drug program we have been impressed with the many eleventh-hour lapses, oversights, mistakes, and crises in which patients find themselves, which undermine employment opportunities and treatment and education plans that the patient and the program staff have worked so hard to realize.

In all of the above examples it is not uncommon to hear such people reply, "I didn't think about it," when questioned as to how they could leave themselves so vulnerable. Usually our dynamic formulations about such behavior stress such considerations as regression, unconscious wishes, conflict, denial, and repetition compulsion. I believe that these formulations do a disservice to understanding the problems of these individuals. These explanations fail to consider at face value that the apparent oblivion in their "not thinking" statements accurately reflects the locus of the problem. Khantzian and Kates (1978) summarized the problem as follows:

> Although much of this behavior is dynamically motivated and defensive in nature, as well as symptomatic of regression, in other respects these individuals' apparent self-disregard ("thoughtlessness"), delinquency, failure to comply with assigned treatment plans, missed appointments, tardiness, etc., reflect a particular kind of absence and impairment in ego function, that predisposes people to mishaps and mistakes. These are functions which when better established, either automatically guide most of us away from trouble, or once in trouble, these and similar ego functions are mobilized, again fairly automatically, to direct us out of trouble. [p. 93]

In my opinion, it is specifically around this kind of impairment that we need to structure treatment programs. We must provide measures that actively and directly both respond to the overdetermined need to fend off help, and deal with the tendency of these individuals to be insufficiently anxious, concerned, and responsive about so many aspects of their life, but especially about self-care measures.

As indicated previously, my description of self-care and -regulation as an ego function probably consists of elements, components, and processes related to other ego functions. In my estimation, the adoption of a construct such as self-care as a possible unique ego function has particular utility and explanatory value in trying to understand behavioral problems in general, and the maladaptive aspects of addiction in particular. This function is related to signal anxiety and, along lines developed by Krystal and Raskin (1970), serves to guide us in relation to external dangers, threats, and involvements. Krystal and Raskin stress the role of signal anxiety in relation to internal states and how in its absence the individual tends to be overcome by overwhelming affects. With self-care functions, our emphasis is on the person's external world and his surrounding; when self-care functions are inadequate, the individual fails to perceive or judge realistically various dangers and threats. This function and its impairments are also related to ego functions involving synthesis and bear many similarities to this function as explained and applied by Chein and colleagues (1964) to the ego impairment of narcotic addicts. However, I believe this emphasis on self-care as an ego function, with the emphasis on external dangers and threats, is warranted because both the concepts of signal anxiety and synthetic functions stress intrapsychic processes and mechanisms, and fail to stress and take into account sufficiently the individual's adaptation to reality and the world around him.

## THE SELF AND NARCISSISTIC DEFENSE

There are some distinctive character features and traits common among addicts. In the previous two sections of this paper I have stressed ego mechanisms that serve a function in personality organization and adaptation. In this section, attitudes about the self and others, and the ways in which such attitudes are incorporated into character traits/styles, are stressed. Kohut (1971) and Kernberg (1975) have elaborated on how disturbances in early child-rearing, especially about nurturance and dependency needs, lead to narcissistic disturbances in adult life. Although both Kohut and Kernberg have indicated that narcissistic pathology predisposes certain individuals to addiction, neither has systematically explored the relationship between narcissistic disturbances and addiction. Wurmser has made a major contribution by expanding on this work and carefully reviewing the narcissistic basis for defects in affect defense, faulty ego ideal formation, pathological dependency, and the enormous problems that addicts have with rage, shame, hurt, and loneliness.

Wurmser's (1974) work has placed emphasis on narcissistic decompensation and the part that drugs play in allaying and countering painful affect states and narcissistic disturbances that result from an overwhelming crisis in the individual's life. In my own work, I am interested in trying to identify and understand some of the unique and characteristic traits of compensated addicts that are related to narcissistic processes and disturbances. More specifically, in psychotherapeutic work with stabilized addicts (i.e., postdetoxified or on drug maintenance) I am interested in exploring some of the special qualities and problems addicts display in obtaining satisfaction of their needs. Despite their totally or relatively drug-free state, extreme and often alternating patterns of reactions in relation to their need-satisfactions persist. In the therapeutic relationship, the most commonly observed feature is the extent to which such patients go to be compliant and cooperative, and, most of all, what little demand the patient places on the therapist for very long periods of time. Most often this takes such forms as passivity, indifference, solicitousness, disavowal, and self-sufficiency.

Occasionally such patients lapse and display another side of themselves, for example a most inappropriate intrusiveness into the life and activities of the therapist, and an assumption that their curiosity will or ought to be satisfied; on other occasions a request will be made that superficially sounds innocent and undemanding, but actually reveals an enormous sense of entitlement and total lack of appreciation of the magnitude and sensitivity of their request. One such patient in the course of his employment discovered he needed some confidential information on a person who was affiliated with an institution in which the therapist worked. In a matter-of-fact way he asked the therapist to obtain this information for him. He seemed totally surprised and hurt when he was tactfully informed that his request was unreasonable. Most of these same patterns carry over to their everyday life. In reviewing these patterns with such patients, one discovers that many of their complaints of boredom, depression, and dissatisfaction are related to these same rigidly maintained patterns of self-denial observable in therapy. At other times one hears accounts of massive explosions of anger and frustration as a result of chancing some wish or want and then experiencing massive disappointment.

Kernberg (1975) has stressed mechanisms of splitting and primitive dissociation in narcissistic disturbances where, for example, seemingly opposite ego attitudes of shyness and arrogance may coexist. Kohut has emphasized massive repression and disavowal of needs to describe how narcissistic personalities attempt to defend against their passive wishes and wants.

These are not at all uncommon characteristics and modes of defense in narcotic addicts with whom I have worked, and I believe these characteristics account for much of the unevenness in function and the unpredictability and contradiction in attitudes in such patients. In one patient, Arnold,[3] the following characteristics have been persistently and simultaneously evident:

*Solicitousness*: When Arnold first came for treatment he went out of his way to be extremely chatty and friendly with all the secretaries in a nearby administrative area. He has always gone out of his way to light people's cigarettes, including his therapist's. When the therapist has been late, he has never complained, and more often goes out of his way to dismiss any resulting inconvenience to himself. In his job he has the reputation of being most kind and supportive.

*Ruthlessness*: In business negotiations he is not adverse to subterfuge and intimidation to exact an outcome to his liking.

*Violent, sadistic, and explosive behavior*: While addicted to heroin, Arnold was involved in a number of brawls and fights and broke his hand on one occasion, and sustained a number of other injuries and lacerations in other fights. On more than one occasion he brutally beat a pet cat to death because the cat scratched, disobeyed, or frustrated him. At work his executive director avoided him because of menacing, explosive confrontations.

---

3. We elaborate on Arnold's case, especially his development, in Chapter 10.

*Passivity*: Whatever dates or social contacts he had were usually at the initiative of friends and family. Despite his passivity, and probably because he is likable, women at work ask him for dates and do favors for him. He spends many weekends alone watching television.

*Active behavior/restlessness*: Arnold went out of his way at work to assume risky security responsibilities and functions. He has always been attracted to leisure activities and sports that are the most active, exciting, and dangerous. His hobbies barely sublimate his aggression. Although his drug involvement has often placed him on the other side of the law, he has always been intrigued with law enforcement activities and enjoyed his contact with law enforcement personnel. He recently took up martial arts.

*Disavowal*: He insists that he must be tough in his work or he will be considered "a patsy and soft." He has insisted that he can handle his loneliness and does not need companionship. Despite this, he will often cruise in his car seeking a pickup. Recently, after much therapeutic work, he now admits that he is worried less about rejection in asking for dates, but feels awkward and embarrassed to reveal his need and interest in companionship.

The need for satisfaction, such as in the patient described, is countered by a need to maintain psychological equilibrium and homeostasis. Such patients are in constant fear that their precarious equilibrium will be disrupted. Defenses that are commonly employed to maintain such an equilibrium include denial and disavowal. Passive longings and wishes are frequently defended against by activity and the defensive assumption of aggressive attitudes. To indulge wishes and wants is felt to be hazardous because one runs the risk of disappointment, frustration, rage, and narcissistic decompensation. Defenses are employed in the service of containing a range of longings and aspirations, but particularly those related to dependency and nurturance needs. It is because of massive repression of these needs that such individuals feel cut off, hollow, and empty.

I suspect that addicts' inability to acknowledge and pursue actively their needs to be admired, and to love and be loved, leave them vulnerable to reversion to narcotic addiction on at least two counts. First, in failing to find suitable outlets for their needs, they fail to build up gradually a network of relationships, activities, and involvements that act as buffers against boredom, depression, and narcissistic withdrawal; this triumvirate of affects acts powerfully to compel such individuals to use opiates. Second, in failing to practice at expressing and chancing their wants and needs, they are then subject to sporadic, uneven breakthroughs of their impulses and wishes in unpredictable and inappropriate ways that are often doomed to frustration and failure. The resulting rage and anger that grow out of such disappointment also compel a reversion to opiates.

## TREATMENT IMPLICATIONS

I believe that effective treatment of narcotic addicts rests on identifying more precisely the underlying psychopathology and character disturbance. To do this requires the establishment of control over the addiction and the destructive activity and behavior often associated with it. However, this is understandably no easy task. The addict trusts his solutions more than ours. We also know that the use of drugs has played a most important part in regulating and controlling the addict's otherwise overwhelming anxiety, depression, and rage. The challenge of initial treatment interventions is to provide acceptable provisions and substitutes for the drugs in order to create the structure and time that makes understanding and management of the addict's problems possible. Briefly, our main allies for intervention and treatment remain the traditional institutions (courts, prisons, and hospitals), drug substitution (e.g., methadone maintenance, other psychoactive drugs), and human relationships.

There are specific ways in which we employ these interventions. In many instances, institutional treatment will continue to be imposed and, in certain cases, required. Such options continue to be distasteful to most of us, but are often necessary. As time goes on we may devise institutions that will avoid the extremes of prisons where there is too little understanding and hospitals where there is perhaps too much understanding but insufficient controls. The balance of controls and understanding is essential for the management and treatment of behavioral problems.

Although we, and others, have advanced specific hypotheses that propose a psychological and physiological basis for the clinical effectiveness of methadone maintenance, I suspect that one of the main benefits of methadone maintenance is the general control and internal chemical support the individual derives, which then makes other human interventions possible. Methadone and other psychotropic drugs similarly have a generally "prosthetic" value and act as a benign chemical substitute for those used by addicts.

As the available interventions help to establish control over the malignant aspects of drug use, in subsequent phases of treatment we are in a better position to identify and grapple with the specific impairments, vulnerabilities, and characteristics of narcotics addicts. As I have already indicated, drug use and its attendant activities have substituted for defenses, relationships, and other satisfactions. As this process is reversed with increasing control, the usual result is the emergence of underlying psychopathology and characterological problems. Some psychotherapeutic implications for these problems have already been hinted at. The necessity for consistency, empathy, activity, and availability is apparent. Readiness to put into words the addict's feelings that he can hardly recognize or identify for himself, or others, is essential. Firm, but nonpunitive, confrontation of violent and unacceptable behavior is also often required. The therapist must also be as active in pointing out the patient's inability or disinclination to perceive danger and risk in his daily living.

The fragile to nonexistent self-esteem in addicts must be appreciated continually. Massive confrontations about their problems with violence and rage should be avoided. Similarly, passive longings and dependency problems should not be overexposed; defenses that serve to disguise such problems should be dealt with gingerly and respectfully. However, one should not ignore the destructive consequences and/or withdrawal when such defenses are extreme and exaggerated. I have found it useful to approach these problems gradually by identifying the difficulties around the inability of such patients to gain sufficient satisfaction out of life. This is done by repeatedly but tactfully identifying, whenever it comes up, the patient's tendencies to pursue extremes of indulgence or self-denial in relation to his wishes, relationships, and activities. In the therapeutic relationship, extremes of aloofness or exaggerated friendliness are avoided by the therapist. Questions are answered; sharing of personal experience and requests for practical assistance around daily living problems are dealt with by again avoiding extremes of withholding or giving. Generally, attempts are made to gradually help our patients overcome their exaggerated self-sufficiency and to see that they can overcome their fears and mistrust about involving themselves, and that the world can provide reasonable degrees of satisfaction.

Finally, some brief considerations about the use of psychoactive drugs seem pertinent. Clearly, addicts to some extent know what is good for them. Had they not medicated themselves, many would not have survived or lived as well or as long as they did. It is surprising, then, to see how often psychotropic drugs are withheld or not considered in many treatment programs. I believe that it is heroic and unrealistic to believe that we can reverse or resolve the enormous psychological damage and impairment in addicts through our psychotherapeutic interventions alone. We should be ready to consider flexibly the use of psychotropic drugs as an adjunct to psychotherapy, or as the primary therapy, depending on the assessment of the degree and nature of the addict's impairment, and a precise identification of target symptoms and affect states. Klein (1975) has reviewed psychopharmacological approaches to borderline states and strongly urges that we work to identify target symptoms better, with a particular emphasis on affect states. He also stresses the efficacy of matching specific types of antidepressants, for example, monoamine oxidase (MAO) inhibitors versus tricyclics, and phenothiazines to target symptoms and affect states, and the use of lithium for stabilizing affect swings and behavior. These are promising findings that are applicable to the understanding and treatment of narcotics addiction and warrant further study.

## REFERENCES

Abraham, K. (1908). The psychological relation between sexuality and alcoholism. In *Selected Papers of Karl Abraham*, pp. 80–89. New York: Basic Books, 1960.

Chein, I., Gerard, D. L., Lee, R. S., and Rosenfeld, E. (1964). *The Road to H.* New York: Basic Books.

Fenichel, O. (1945). *The Psychoanalytic Theory of Neurosis.* New York: Norton.

Freud, S. (1905). Three essays on the theory of sexuality. *Standard Edition* 7:125–245.

Glover, E. (1932). On the etiology of drug addiction. In *On the Early Development of Mind*, pp. 187–215. New York: International Universities Press, 1956.

Kernberg, O. F. (1975). *Borderline Conditions and Pathological Narcissism.* New York: Jason Aronson.

Khantzian, E. J. (1972). A preliminary dynamic formulation of the psychopharmacologic action of methadone. In *Proceedings of the Fourth National Conference on Methadone Treatment,* pp. 371–374. New York: National Association for the Prevention of Addictions to Narcotics.

―― (1974). Opiate addiction: a critique of theory and some implications for treatment. *American Journal of Psychotherapy* 28:59–70.

―― (1975). Self selection and progression in drug dependence. *Psychiatry Digest* 36:19–22.

Khantzian, E. J., and Kates, W. (1978). Group treatment of unwilling addicted patients: programmatic and clinical aspects. *International Journal of Group Psychotherapy* 28:81–94.

Khantzian, E. J., Mack, J. E., and Schatzberg, A. F. (1974). Heroin use as an attempt to cope: clinical observations. *American Journal of Psychiatry* 131:160–164.

Klein, D. F. (1975). Psychopharmacology and the borderline patient. In *Borderline States in Psychiatry,* ed. J. E. Mack, pp. 75–91. New York: Grune & Stratton.

Kohut, H. (1971). *The Analysis of the Self.* New York: International Universities Press.

Krystal, H., and Raskin, H. A. (1970). *Drug Dependence: Aspects of Ego Functions.* Detroit: Wayne State University Press.

Mahler, M. S. (1968). *On Human Symbiosis and Vicissitudes of Individuation.* New York: International Universities Press.

Meissner, W. W., Mack, J. E., and Semrad, E. (1975). Classical psychoanalysis. In *Comprehensive Textbook of Psychiatry,* ed. A. Freedman et al., pp. 482–566. Baltimore: Williams & Wilkins.

Milkman, H., and Frosch, W. A. (1973). On the preferential abuse of heroin and amphetamine. *Journal of Nervous and Mental Disease* 156:242–248.

Rado, S. (1933). The psychoanalysis of pharmacothymia. *Psychoanalytic Quarterly* 2:1–23.

―― (1957). Narcotic bondage. A general theory of the dependence on narcotic drugs. *American Journal of Psychiatry* 114:165–171.

Savitt, R. A. (1963). Psychoanalytic studies on addiction: ego structure in narcotic addiction. *Psychoanalytic Quarterly* 32:43–57.

Vaillant, G. E. (1975). Sociopathy as a human process. *Archives of General Psychiatry* 32:178–183.

Wieder, H., and Kaplan, E. H. (1969). Drug use in adolescence: psychodynamic meaning and pharmacogenic effect. *Psychoanalytic*

*Study of the Child* 24:399–431. New York: International Universities Press.

Wikler, A. A., and Rasor, R. W. (1953). Psychiatric aspects of drug addiction. *American Journal of Medicine* 14:566–570.

Winnicott, D. W. (1953). Transitional objects and transitional phenomena. *International Journal of Psycho-Analysis* 34:89–97.

Wishnie, H. (1974). Opioid addiction: a masked depression. In *Masked Depression*, ed. S. Lesse, pp. 350–363. New York: Jason Aronson.

Wurmser, L. (1974). Psychoanalytic considerations of the etiology of compulsive drug use. *Journal of the American Psychoanalytic Association* 22:820–843.

Zinberg, N. E. (1975). Addiction and ego function. *Psychoanalytic Study of the Child* 30:567–588. New Haven, CT: Yale University Press.

# 3

# Impulse Problems in Addiction

This chapter explores some of the important interrelationships of drug use/dependency and impulse problems. Over the past several decades mental health professionals and citizens alike have been inundated by accounts in the mass media and in the scientific literature that link drug use/dependency with criminality, violence, brutality, and other forms of antisocial behavior. Not infrequently, the characterizations and accounts of such cases blur the links between the drugs and the disturbed behavior, and the consequent suggested or implied relationship between the two is overdrawn, stereotyped, or unspecified. The chapter specifies some of the relationships between impulse problems and drugs, placing a particular emphasis on problems with aggression, and gives clinical examples to show how the specific psychopharmacological actions of the three main classes of drugs on which individuals become dependent—stimulants, sedatives/hypnotics, and opiates—interact with personality and other emotional factors, and how this interaction may affect behavior.

## BACKGROUND AND OVERVIEW

The early psychiatric and psychoanalytic literature on addiction emphasizes the pleasurable and regressive aspects of drug use in accounting for why people become dependent on drugs (Khantzian 1974). Rado (1933), an American psychoanalyst who pioneered in exploring the psychodynamics of drug use, strongly influenced this trend in his early writings on drug dependence. Although he seemed to appreciate underlying factors of depression, he unduly emphasized the "hedonic" interests of the addict and the seeking of a "super-pleasure" to explain the compelling nature of addiction. Over the subsequent quarter century, other investigators and social commentators repeatedly cited and concurred with Rado's findings, and popular street terms reflect this emphasis in describing the drug experience—"high," "getting off," "cheap thrills," and so forth. It is little wonder then that we are quick to associate drug dependency with "pleasure seekers," irresponsibility, and impulsivity.

In contrast to early emphasis on gratification of instinctual impulses, subsequent investigators (Chein et al. 1964, Khantzian 1974, Krystal and Raskin 1970, Wieder and Kaplan 1969, Wurmser 1974) placed greater emphasis on problems of impulse control and regulation, affect tolerance, and management of drives in drug-dependent people. These reports stress an adaptive use of drugs wherein individuals, in lieu of adequate defenses and impaired ego capacities, adopt the use of drugs in the service of drive and affect defense (Khantzian 1974, Wurmser 1974) or to augment or facilitate certain desired ego states (Wieder and Kaplan 1969). In simpler and less technical terms, these latter formulations suggest that drug dependency has less to do with pleasure seeking than with an individual's boundaries and defenses regarding both internal feelings and the external world.

The addict suffers immensely with his feelings, drives, and relationships with other people. His boundaries and ego defense mechanisms are either rigidly overdrawn and painfully limiting (Wurmser 1977), or alarmingly brittle or absent (Kohut 1971). In other cases they are only poorly developed and barely adequate for negotiating any challenge or satisfaction. At other times the addict's boundaries and defenses play even crueler tricks on him, resulting in rapid, unpredictable, and seemingly unmanageable shifts: he either feels too much or not enough. It is in response to this state of affairs within different drug-dependent individuals, or at different points in time within the same individual, that various drugs take on such a compelling quality. Most addicts take drugs to compensate for developmental impairments in the ego. They augment shaky or absent defenses with a particular drug, or take advantage of a drug effect to produce certain feelings, actions, or activities for which they otherwise feel incapable.

It is also from this state of affairs that some of the cause-and-effect relationships between drugs and impulsive behavior develop. Some individuals become addicted to drugs because of an inability to cope with particular feelings; without the drug they are subject to overwhelming affects and impulses that seem intolerable. In other instances, drugs permit individuals to overcome sufficient inhibitions and barriers against interpersonal involvement, often related to fear of impulses, to allow them to seek out (possibly for the first time) some semblance of human contact and involvement with work and play. This defensive or facilitating use of drugs to deal with powerful affects that might lead to impulsive acts, or to liberate individuals from fears of impulsivity, illustrates the "cause" aspect of drug-dependency problems. In other instances, drug-dependent people, as a result of drug use, display massive rage and anger, bizarre and totally inappropriate behavior, or significant pathological withdrawal and regression. These latter examples of extreme behavior reflect the "effect" aspect of drug abuse.

Fortunately, and in most instances, the examples of drug dependency that follow are not as apparent, extreme, or problematic; rather, they range along a continuum. In the majority of cases, the desired effect produces an altered state of consciousness in order to enhance control, facilitate performance, or relieve distress. Only rarely is behavior affected to an extreme. But it is in these extreme instances that drug dependence leads to alarming, dramatic impulses and behavior, and becomes the focus of grave concern.

I will delineate the continuum of drug effects and reactions in relation to stimulants, sedatives/hypnotics, and opiates, and spell out some of the adaptive and maladaptive results of using such drugs. With a focus on impulsivity, I emphasize issues of aggression and control, that is, how in certain instances these drugs support and enhance control of impulses and aggression, while in others they undermine or abolish controls, leading to impulsive and destructive behavior.

## INTERRELATION OF IMPULSIVITY AND DRUG GROUPS

Previous reports, (Khantzian 1975, Milkman and Frosch 1973, Wieder and Kaplan 1969) have stressed the fact that despite experimentation with a variety of drugs, individuals tend to self-select and have particular preferences. This predilection for particular drugs is in many cases based on the "fit" of an individual's personality structure, including his reactive patterns, with the distinctive psychopharmacological action of the drug of choice. In most instances, the appeal of drugs rests on this specific interrelation, wherein the drug helps to relieve internal dysphoric and distressful states or leads to improved function. The following descriptions and clinical examples illustrate some of the interrelations of impulse problems and the three main categories of drugs that are misused.

### Stimulants

Amphetamines and cocaine are the two main drugs in the stimulant category and share an energizing or drive-augmenting action. For many, these drugs are appealing because they assist in overcoming fatigue and depletion states associated with depression. Wurmser (1974) states that they help to overcome depression by inducing a sense of "aggressive mastery, control, invincibility and grandeur" (p. 834). In my own clinical experience, I have been repeatedly impressed by how the use of these drugs became compelling for certain people as they discovered they were able to accomplish chores and overcome various tasks for which they previously felt incapable. The following case excerpt illustrates this nicely:

> A 25-year-old separated mother of two young children described an impoverished, lonely existence in which she cared for her children in a two-room flat in a congested, low-income neighborhood. Residence in this particular neighborhood had in part been chosen because of her husband's ethnic background. When he abandoned her,

her distressful feelings of estrangement and loneliness were compounded by the isolation she experienced in a community whose
cultural and ethnic traditions were alien to her. A friend introduced
her to methamphetamine (which she initially took orally). She
experienced a surge of energy that resulted in a frenetic, welcome
burst of enthusiasm to clean up her flat. The disheveled state of
the apartment resulted from and further compounded a depression
she only vaguely perceived. As she repeatedly tried to recapture
feelings of newfound energy and the elation of being able to complete some tasks, she required larger doses, including intravenous
use. This soon led to a two-year binge of protracted "amphetamine
runs" that resulted in the personal and physical deterioration ac-
companying major physiological dependence.

Many drug-dependent individuals have enormous difficulty in identifying and tolerating painful emotional states, particularly depression
(Krystal and Raskin 1970). The foregoing clinical excerpt is not atypical
of a person who only dimly perceives his or her depression, despite
overwhelming subjective and external reality factors that would dis-
pose one to this state. Physiologically, the drug presumably mobilizes
and energizes the patient by acting on catecholamine metabolism and
release of norepinephrine in certain central nervous system receptor
sites (Schildkraut 1965). In my opinion, we too often misidentify the
nature of the drug effect, namely that the chemical transformation of
depressive anergia and dysphoria to elation and hyperactivity is perceived as the "high" or euphoria obtained with stimulants.

Wieder and Kaplan (1969) posit a somewhat different basis on
which individuals use and become dependent on stimulants. They have
observed that amphetamines enhance feelings of mastery and activity, resulting in greater assertiveness, self-esteem, and frustration tolerance. This is congruent with my own clinical observations of how
certain individuals depend on the effect of stimulants to augment a
hyperactive, restless lifestyle and an exaggerated need for self-sufficiency. The following case illustrates how stimulants may be used in
this way.

A 22-year-old white, single man sought treatment because of an
inability to stop his drug use despite complications in his physical
health and much upheaval in his family life resulting from his drug

dependency. His history established that he was an individual who had always been extremely active, restless, and competitive. It was later learned that athletic prowess, which he insisted he always had, was highly valued in his family. His father and his two younger siblings, both boys, were accomplished athletes, and competition among them manifested itself in flagrant challenges and recurrent, thinly disguised contests. The patient also described the reputation he earned in early adolescence by doing the wildest, most outlandish, and dangerous things. Before discovering cocaine, he used marijuana heavily, emphasizing how it helped him to slow down and mellow, especially if he wished to stay in one place to enjoy music, an evening of conversation, or a motion picture. Subsequently he became heavily dependent on cocaine, and he stressed, with exhilaration and enthusiasm, how cocaine complemented his personality and helped him to remain active, effective, and mobile, particularly in his athletic, business, and social involvements. He said, "It was the only drug that relaxed me and gave me a good feeling." Opiate dependence followed when he began using increasing amounts of heroin to counteract the crashing letdown and feelings of inadequacy and impotence subsequent to cocaine withdrawal.

The above case exemplifies the appeal that stimulants hold for some individuals but says little about problems with impulsivity associated with these drugs. Stimulants augment both libidinal and aggressive drives. For individuals who are depressed and/or those whose self-esteem depends on maintaining high performance and activity levels, the presumed relation between these drugs and improved subjective states and behavior results from the increased mobilization of energy and aggressive drives. Unfortunately, in many instances the mobilized aggression exceeds the individual's capacity to harness and use it adaptively, and it is in these circumstances that impulse problems are precipitated by use of stimulants. In some cases problems with aggression and impulsivity are directly related to mobilized rage and violent feelings.

A 26-year-old man described how amphetamines originally appealed to him in his late teenage years because they helped him overcome feelings of vulnerability and weakness in social situations and in contact sports (despite his hefty muscular physique). With continued use, however, he found himself repeatedly involved in brutally damaging fights, both for himself and his victims. In some instances the fights were provoked and premeditated, but in other instances they erupted unpredictably and precipitously with little or no provocation. Initially he rationalized and glorified these episodes in a manner consistent with his need to maintain a sense of omnipotence and invulnerability. Later, upon more sober reflection, he admitted to acute terror and dysphoria as a result of his uncontrollable impulses while under the influence of stimulants.

Much of the bizarre, explosive, and dangerous behavior associated with amphetamine use is the result of acting upon drug-induced psychotic and delusional thinking. At these times feelings of violence and aggression are projected on and subsequently perceived in others and in the surroundings as hostile and threatening. Paranoid thinking focused on menacing and terrifying ideas and content is not uncommon and is often the basis on which individuals attack and retaliate. Unfortunately, as the following case excerpt illustrates, imagined attackers and enemies are often innocent bystanders:

> After almost continuous use of amphetamines over a two-year period that had increased to very heavy daily doses, a 24-year-old white man began imagining that passersby in automobiles suspected that he possessed large amounts of drugs. His preoccupation escalated to terror to a point that he descended into the nearby subway station and ran through the tunnel to the next station in the vicinity of his father's home, for which he headed. In his mad dash he fantasized a scenario in which menacing police with messages coming from their radios were pursuing him. Upon arriving at his father's home, which was empty at the time, he imagined that all the windows of the surrounding houses were focused on him. Losing more and more contact he sought out and gathered up his father's guns to protect himself. Upon returning home, the father was almost shot as the patient blasted away with the guns down the corridor of the house, thinking his father was the police.

From these last two examples it should be abundantly clear that stimulant drugs can profoundly influence and produce impulsive, dangerous behavior. An extensive literature has documented the devastating destructive consequences of amphetamine use and dependence

(Ellinwood 1971, Griffith 1966, Grinspoon and Hedblom 1975, Kramer 1969, Lemere 1966, Shader 1972). I am convinced that in the majority of instances, amphetamines are used in an adaptive, relatively benign or self-limited way. However, when used heavily over a prolonged period of time, they cause extremely violent, dangerous, and impulsive behavior, and represent one of the most dangerous types of misused drugs.

## Sedatives/Hypnotics

Fenichel's (1945) observation that "the super-ego is that part of the mind that is soluble in alcohol" (p. 379) captures the basis of appeal for sedatives and hypnotics. Smith and Wesson (1974) designated this effect of the drugs as "disinhibition euphoria." As previously cited (Khantzian 1974), sedatives/hypnotics help to overcome distressful feeling states associated with anxiety and conflict, which may be viewed in two ways. These distressing feelings can be seen as neurotic reactions related to inhibitions and defenses against unacceptable sexual impulses. Or, in my view, anxiety and conflict leading to heavy dependency on these drugs are more often associated with personality structures characterized by rigid and unstable defenses against more primitive narcissistic longings and aggressive impulses.

Krystal and Raskin (1970) stress the special and exaggerated defenses of denial and splitting employed by individuals dependent on short-acting sedatives/hypnotics and alcohol. These defenses are used in the service of "walling-off" and suppressing aggressive and loving feelings in relation to the self and others. These authors emphasize the great difficulty these individuals have with feelings of ambivalence, and how they prefer to use short-acting drugs to experience and give vent to such feelings briefly and therefore safely.

Although Kohut (1971) and Kernberg (1975) do not specify particular drug actions, they too refer to the prominence of massive repression, the splitting mechanism, and other rigid defenses in addicts. Kohut refers to developmental trauma and narcissistic disturbances in addicts that result in failures to internalize caring and protective functions for the self in the ego. Drugs consequently compensate for "a defect in the psychological structure" (p. 46). Hypnotics can overcome rigid and overdrawn defenses and can facilitate and regulate the expression of affectionate or aggressive feelings in the absence of ego structures that help to modulate such affects and drives. For these reasons they are welcomed by individuals with rigid and exaggerated defenses, as well as those who experience the absence of controls and modulation of impulses. However, the balance between adaptive release or regulation of feelings and a potentially destructive disinhibition of impulses is a precarious one with these drugs, often resulting in impulsive and threatening behavior.

A 22-year-old divorcée described both the adaptive and maladaptive effects of barbiturates for her. She said she started using barbiturates in her late teens to adopt an "I-don't-care" attitude after her husband left her, and that the barbiturates helped her "deal with" her feelings of sadness and resentment. She preferred barbiturates to alcohol because she could readily obtain just the desired subjective effect by limiting herself to two 100-mg capsules, whereas she could not regulate alcohol as well and became "sloppy." More important, she stressed that barbiturates helped her to overcome her "uptightness" so that she could begin to date and enjoy herself in the company of other men. In contrast to alcohol, she emphasized that she could "loosen up" just enough with the barbiturates to overcome her inhibitions about socializing in barrooms and seeking male companionship. Subsequently she began to experience increasing irritability and uncontrollable anger in various relationships when using the drug. The reactions of anger began to escalate with continued and increasing use to the point where she felt like actually killing people in the middle of an argument. At about this same time she became involved with a man who was a heroin addict and she too became thoroughly addicted. She made sharp contrasts between the effects of heroin and barbiturates, reporting that heroin helped her to feel "peaceful and in control" and that she found companionship to be more easy and comfortable with the use of heroin.

With this patient, an obvious shift occurred over time in the way she used and experienced drugs. At the outset, her troubled feelings and inhibitions caused her repeatedly to seek out a drug effect to overcome her depression, isolation, and loneliness. However, with protracted use, she found herself increasingly unable to regulate her feelings, and the same drug produced mounting and uncontrollable outbursts of aggression and killer rage. In other cases, however, the use of these drugs is associated with a long-standing history of impulsivity predating drug use and dependency, as exemplified by the following excerpt:

> A 23-year-old convicted felon with a history of acute school adjustment problems and delinquent, impulsive behavior going back to his early teen years was admitted to a polydrug treatment unit as part of a prison prerelease rehabilitation program. He was dishonorably discharged from the Army because of charges involving larceny and stolen goods. His fourteen-month imprisonment in the maximum security jail from which he had just been released was the result of a drug/alcohol incident. After an evening of moderately heavy drinking with friends and after ingesting several barbiturate capsules, he agreed to accompany one of these friends to the home of another acquaintance whom they abducted with the intention of committing robbery. When their intended victim resisted, the patient reacted by violently and uncontrollably beating and pummeling the man, as well as threatening him with a knife. He and his companion were ultimately apprehended, convicted, and incarcerated.
>
> In reviewing his drug history the patient reported that during his mid-teens, he and his contemporaries did not use drugs but did drink alcohol (mostly beer). He said that he generally avoided drugs, except for five or six instances of combining alcohol with barbiturates, including the instance that resulted in imprisonment. He stated that when he was a teenager, alcohol made him jovial and relaxed, but that this could shift quickly to irritability and angry outbursts. In looking back to his teenage reactions with alcohol and in reviewing the drug/alcohol episode of assault that led to confinement, he indicated that he had discovered in himself terrifying and violent feelings that he "never wanted to come out again." He said he tended to become particularly irritable and violent when someone had done a favor for him for which he believed the other person expected something in return. In the course of the interview he repeatedly resorted to such justification and projections. (The therapist subsequently learned that such reaction was related to long-standing bitterness and resentment toward his mother, who had abandoned him to the care of his maternal grandmother when he was 2 years old.)

This man apparently realized the potential devastating danger of his impulsivity as a result of shaky impulse controls, especially when under the influence of alcohol or sedative-hypnotic drugs. That he was not entirely without controls was evident in his own deliberate attempts to limit his drug use, his horror and fear of the magnitude and intensity of his rage, and his convincing desire for help and treatment. However, it was equally evident from his past and recent history that he had been only barely, if at all, able to manage his feelings and impulses, with tenuous to nonexistent controls in many instances and rigid denial and projection in others. Similarly, his past delinquent behavior and misconduct suggested a poorly developed ego and means of impulse control, evidenced by the unreflective and insufficiently anxious quality with which he anticipated trouble and danger.

## Opiates

More than any other drug, opiates, and heroin in particular, have been associated with violence and crime. This link has been condensed, distorted, and translated into terms such as *crimes of violence, drug-crazed junkies*, and *killer heroin*, and reflects public concern and alarm about heroin addicts as impulsive, intimidating people. The criminal behavior associated with heroin addiction is not primarily one of crimes associated with violence or attack on other individuals (Patch et al. 1973a,b). Rather, criminality is associated more with property theft (breaking and entering and robbery) and is the result of stringent arrest laws against opiate possession and the requirement of large amounts of cash to maintain the expensive heroin habit. Rather than producing violent behavior, opiates are, in my opinion, more sought after to produce the opposite effect.

Previous formulations have stressed either the euphorogenic-pleasurable effect of narcotics or their ability to relieve a range of distressful or unpleasant affects in explanation of their powerful tendency to induce and sustain addiction. Although these formulations have merit, I have been more impressed with the specific muting and stabilizing action of narcotics on the individual's rage and aggressive drives.

After evaluation and treatment of over 200 addicts, developmental impairments and deficiencies in the egos of the narcotic addicts seemed paramount (Khantzian 1974). These deficiencies were reflected in outbursts of rage, poor impulse control, and a general sense of dysphoria resulting from the felt threat to themselves and others because of their violent feelings and impulses. I was repeatedly impressed with the addicts' subjective reports of their initial experience with opiates in which they discovered the immediate calming and stabilizing action of the drug. More specifically, in the course of responding to a carefully taken drug history, patients gave ample descriptions of dysphoric states of bodily tensions and restlessness, anger, rage, violent feelings, and depression that were relieved by heroin and other opiates. With almost monotonous regularity, patients said they felt "relaxed," "mellow," and "calm," and emphasized a total body response to describe the effects of opiates when they first began to use such drugs.

On the basis of these findings, we hypothesized that individuals were predisposed and became addicted to opiates because they discovered the stabilizing action of these drugs on their egos. The short-term effect of the drugs acted specifically to reverse regressive states by attenuating and making more bearable painful drives and affects involving aggression, rage, and related depression. In Chapter 2 and 10 we use as an example the case of Arnold, a man who was overwhelmed with rageful affect and violent impulses, to show how opiates acted powerfully to contain his troubling feelings and behavior.

Although heroin addicts describe the calming and stabilizing effects of heroin, the muting effect on rage and aggression is not as apparent, and the short-acting nature of the drug, together with repeated cycles of withdrawal, tend to produce physical and psychological instability and regressed behavior. Because methadone is long-acting, addicts are able to use its muting and antiaggression action more adaptively, and thereby reverse their regressed states—an action of the drug accounting for the dramatic improvement in behavior often seen in methadone program participants. Conversely, as Wurmser (1977) has observed and as I have witnessed, there is an almost predictable reemergence of impulsive behavior, aggression, and rage as narcotic addicts withdraw from methadone or other opiates. Because opiates counteract disorganizing rage, aggression, and associated dysphoria, we have hypothesized that narcotic addicts are predisposed to become dependent on opiates. That is, rather than opiate dependence causing impulsive behavior, we believe that impulse problems may predispose to and cause opiate dependence.

## SUMMARY AND CONCLUSIONS

This chapter has reviewed how the specific psychopharmacological effects of each class of drugs interact with different personality structures of drug-dependent individuals to influence behavior. I have stressed drug effects in relation to impulses, particularly aggressive impulses, and have clarified how drug use/dependency can be viewed in some instances as attempts of individuals to solve problems of impulsivity. Too often the mode of solution causes the very problems the individuals sought to avoid.

In my opinion, undue emphasis has been placed on pleasure, sociopathy, and absence of adequate superego to account for drug use. Such emphases detract from a more careful examination of the ego impairments in this patient population. These patients do not necessarily suffer because they lack an adequate superego or conscience. They suffer because developmental ego impairments have rendered them ill-equipped to manage their feelings, drives, and behavior in relation to themselves and others. For most, drug use at the outset represents attempts to solve problems in day-to-day living. For those that become drug dependent, the struggle is more extreme and desperate and, in my experience, represents attempts to compensate for major ego gaps and impairments.

## REFERENCES

Chein, I., Gerard, D. L., Lee, R. S., and Rosenfeld, E. (1964). *The Road to H.* New York: Basic Books.

Ellinwood, E. (1971). Assault and homicide associated with amphetamine use. *American Journal of Psychiatry* 127:1170–1175.

Fenichel, O. (1945). *The Psychoanalytic Theory of Neurosis.* New York: Norton.

Griffith, J. (1966). A study of illicit amphetamine drug traffic in Oklahoma city. *American Journal of Psychiatry* 123:560–569.

Grinspoon, L., and Hedblom, P. (1975). *The Speed Culture: Amphetamine Use and Abuse in America.* Cambridge, MA: Harvard University Press.

Kernberg, O. F. (1975). *Borderline Conditions and Pathological Narcissism.* New York: Jason Aronson.

Khantzian, E. J. (1974). Opiate addiction: a critique of theory and some implications for treatment. *American Journal of Psychotherapy* 28:59–70.

—— (1975). Self-selection and progression in drug dependence. *Psychiatry Digest* 36:19–22.

Kohut, H. (1971). *The Analysis of the Self.* New York: International Universities Press.

Kramer, J. C. (1969). Introduction to amphetamine abuse. *Journal of Psychedelic Drugs* 2:8–13.

Krystal, H., and Raskin, H. A. (1970). *Drug Dependence: Aspects of Ego Functions.* Detroit: Wayne State University Press.

Lemere, F. (1966). The danger of amphetamine dependency. *American Journal of Psychiatry* 123:569–571.

Milkman, H., and Frosch, W. A. (1973). On the preferential abuse of heroin and amphetamine. *Journal of Nervous and Mental Disease* 156:242–248.

Patch, V. D., Fisch, A., Levine, M. E., et al. (1973a). Heroin addicts and violent crime. In *Proceedings of the Fifth National Conference on Methadone Treatment*, pp. 386–392. New York: National Association for the Prevention of Addictions to Narcotics.

—— (1973b). Urban versus suburban addict crime. In *Proceedings of the Fifth National Conference on Methadone Treatment*, pp. 393–400. New York: National Association for the Prevention of Addictions to Narcotics.

Rado, S. (1933). The psychoanalysis of pharmacothymia. *Psychoanalytic Quarterly* 2:1–23.

Schildkraut, J. J. (1965). The catecholamine hypothesis of affective disorders: a review of supporting evidence. *American Journal of Psychiatry* 122:509–522.

Shader, R., ed. (1972). *Psychiatric Complications of Medical Drugs.* New York: Raven Press.

Smith, D. E., and Wesson, D. R. (1974). *Diagnosis and Treatment of Adverse Reactions to Sedatives-Hypnotics.* Washington, DC: National Institute on Drug Abuse.

Wieder, H., and Kaplan, E. (1969). Drug use in adolescents. *Psychoanalytic Study of the Child* 24:399–431. New York: International Universities Press.

Wurmser, L. (1974). Psychoanalytic considerations of the etiology of compulsive drug use. *Journal of the American Psychoanalytic Association* 22:820–843.

—— (1977). Mr. Pecksniff's horse? (Psychodynamics in compulsive drug use.) In *Psychodynamic Aspects of Opiate Dependence*, research monograph 12, pp. 36–72. Rockville, MD: National Institute on Drug Abuse.

# 4

# An Ego/Self Theory of Substance Dependence

Drug dependence is tied intimately to an individual's attempt to cope with his or her internal emotional and external social and physical environment. Viewed from a contemporary psychoanalytic perspective, drug dependency can best be understood by examining how such a person's ego organization and sense of self serve or fail the individual's attempts to cope, and how the specific effects of various substances facilitate or impede such attempts.

Although early psychoanalytic investigators appreciated the presence of underlying depression, tension, and distress in addicts, most of the early psychoanalytic formulations of substance dependence emphasized the instinctive, pleasurable aspects of drug use to explain the compelling nature of addiction (Khantzian 1974, Khantzian and Treece 1977, Yorke 1970). Other psychoanalytic formulations have placed greater emphasis on problems in adaptation, ego and self disturbances, and related psychopathology as etiological factors in drug dependence (Khantzian 1978, Krystal and Raskin 1970, Wurmser 1974).

A variety of drug-use patterns and degrees of dependence in which everyday problems of living are involved may be identified (Khantzian et al. 1974). Nevertheless, I have become convinced, as has Wurmser (1974), that becoming and remaining addicted to drugs is in most instances associated with severe and significant psychopathology. Necessarily, some of the observed pathology evident in addicts is the result of drug use and its attendant interpersonal involvements (Khantzian and Treece 1979, Meyer and Mirin 1979, Zinberg 1975). However, it is my opinion that drug-dependent individuals are predisposed to use and to become dependent on their substances mainly as a result of severe ego impairments and disturbances in the sense of self, involving difficulties with drive and affect defense, self-care, dependency, and need satisfaction. Hence, my theoretical work has focused on these impairments and disturbances in the ego and the sense of self.

## ADAPTATION AND DRUG USE

In one of our first papers on substance dependence (Khantzian et al. 1974), we explored the relationship of heroin use to a range of human problems, including pain, stress, and dysphoria. In attempting to adapt to one's emotions and environment, the powerful action of heroin and immersion in the attendant rituals and subculture could be used to mute, extinguish, and avoid a range of feelings and emotions. That is, rather than settling for more ordinary defensive, neurotic, characterological, or other adaptive mechanisms as a way of dealing with distress, heroin addicts had adopted a more extraordinary solution by using a powerful drug and immersing themselves in the associated rituals, practices, and pseudoculture. In this early report, we stressed the costly consequences of the heroin involvement and why the addict was so desperately dependent on the drug:

> The central problem for most people who have become addicted to opiates is that they have failed to develop effective symptomatic, characterologic, or other adaptive solutions in response to developmental crises, stress, deprivation, and other forms of emotional pain which

may not in themselves be extraordinary. Their response has been to revert repeatedly to the use of opiates as an all powerful device, thereby precluding other solutions that would normally develop and that might better sustain them. [p. 164]

## AGGRESSION AND HEROIN DEPENDENCE

In contrast to a general sense that heroin could be used to deal with a range of human emotions and troubles, I also quickly became impressed with a rather specific reason why opiates could be so appealing to many heroin addicts. From the outset of my clinical-investigative work with drug dependency, I was immediately impressed with the enormous, lifelong difficulties heroin addicts had with feelings and impulses associated with aggression. In repeated life histories obtained from addicts, I was impressed with how dysphoric feelings associated with anger, rage, and restlessness were relieved in the short term by heroin and other opiates. This was even more apparent when observing addicts in treatment as they became stabilized on methadone and their aggression and restlessness subsided. I began to suspect that heroin addicts might be using opiates specifically as an antiaggression drug.

As a result of these initial impressions, I published a preliminary report (Khantzian 1972) and subsequently expanded and formulated a hypothesis (Khantzian 1974) that proposed that problems with aggression predisposed certain individuals to opiate dependence and was central in the development and maintenance of an addiction. I emphasized how addicts took advantage of the antiaggression action of opiates in the service of drive defense. I stressed the disorganizing influence of aggression on ego functions in individuals whose ego stability was already subject to dysfunction and impairment as a result of developmental arrest or regression. I also proposed that the same but sustained, longer antiaggression action of methadone was the basis for the "success" of methadone maintenance.

## SELF (NARCISSISTIC) PATHOLOGY

In contrast to ego pathology, in which the emphasis is on disturbance in structure and function in coping with drives and emotions, self pathology relates more to troubled attitudes and experiences about the self and others. Kohut (1971) and Kernberg (1975) have explored how disruptions and disturbances in a person's early development, particularly around nurturance and dependency needs, lead to self pathology in adult life. Both investigators consider substance dependencies as manifestations of such disorders, although neither Kohut nor Kernberg has systematically explored this relationship. A number of investigators have attempted to relate this recent better understanding of narcissistic processes and disturbances to substance dependence. Reports by Wieder and Kaplan (1969), Wurmser (1974), and Krystal and Raskin (1970) have stressed narcissistic vulnerabilities and decompensation as predisposing factors. Wurmser, in particular, has emphasized how drugs are used to counteract the distress and dysphoria associated with decompensated, narcissistic states.

In my own psychotherapeutic work with addicts, I became interested in some of the unique and characteristic traits of compensated addicts (i.e., addicts who were either drug free or on drug maintenance) that are related to underlying narcissistic processes and disturbances, and how such traits might predispose an individual to drug dependence. I repeatedly observed the addict's special problems in accepting dependency and actively acknowledging and pursuing goals and satisfactions related to needs and wants. Extreme and alternating patterns in pursuing need satisfaction were evident: cooperation and compliance might suddenly alternate with outbursts of rage, refusal, or resistance; passivity and indifference could shift rapidly or coexist with active, intense, and restless involvements that often led to danger, violence, and death; disavowal of needs and solicitousness of others might suddenly convert to angry demands and an entitlement that was totally oblivious of other people.

To explain such patterns, I proposed that the rigid character traits and alternating defenses employed by addicts were adopted against underlying needs and dependency in order to maintain a costly psychological equilibrium. Prominent defenses and traits included extreme repression, disavowal, self-sufficiency, activity, and assumption of aggressive attitudes. I concluded,

> Defenses (and the associated character traits) are employed in the service of containing a whole range of longings and aspirations, but particularly those related to dependency and nurturance needs. It is because of massive repression of these needs that such individuals feel

cut off, hollow and empty . . . [and that the] addicts' inability to acknowledge and pursue actively their needs to be admired, and to love
and be loved, leave them vulnerable to reversion to narcotics.
[Khantzian 1978, p. 196]

## SELF-SELECTION AND
## THE SPECIFIC APPEAL OF HEROIN

Most substance-dependent individuals prefer and self-select a particular drug. This preference and selection is the result of the drug of
choice and its distinctive psychopharmacological effects interacting
with the unique personality organization and reactive patterns of an
individual. It is this interaction between drug effect and personality
organization that predisposes a person to dependency on a particular
drug. The specific appeal of opiates, stimulants, sedative-hypnotic
drugs (including alcohol), and other drugs has been explored from a
psychodynamic perspective (Khantzian 1975, Milkman and Frosch
1973, Wieder and Kaplan 1969, Wurmser 1974). Wieder and Kaplan,
and others, continue to stress the regressive and pleasurable ego states
produced by these drugs (including opiates) to explain their appeal,
while Wurmser and I have placed greater emphasis on the progressive and adaptive use of drugs. In this respect, I have been particularly interested in the narcotics addict's preference for opiates. As already indicated, my early work with heroin addicts led me to conclude
that the compelling nature of opiates for many narcotics addicts resides in a specific antiaggression action of narcotics, namely, to relieve
and counteract regressed, disorganized, and dysphoric ego states related to overwhelming feelings of rage, anger, and related depression.
Whereas the use of drugs such as the amphetamines and hypnotics
(including alcohol) results in the mobilization and expression of aggressive and sexual impulses, opiates have the opposite effect. This
effect is particularly needed and welcomed in certain individuals whose
ego mechanisms of defense, particularly against aggressive drives, are
shaky or absent. On close examination, we have been impressed repeatedly that the so-called high or euphoria produced by opiates is
more correctly a relief of dysphoria associated with unmitigated aggression. The short-term effect of the drug is to reverse regressed
dysphoric ego states by muting and containing otherwise uncontrollable rage and aggression (Khantzian 1972, 1974, 1978).

## SELF-CARE DISTURBANCES

The previous sections have focused on how drug addicts attempt to use drugs adaptively to overcome and cope with ego and self problems. This section focuses on a more obvious maladaptive aspect of drug use.

The influences of early psychoanalysis are evident in id formulations of addictions that invoke and presuppose the existence of unconscious death wishes and self-destructive trends (death instincts) to account for the destructiveness and dangers associated with drug dependence. Clearly, certain individuals are driven or are compelled to be self-destructive, with suicide the most extreme manifestation of such a compulsion. Indeed, it has been suggested rather cynically by some that drug dependence and abuse is a form of suicide on the installment plan. Menninger (1938) is representative in presenting such a point of view, referring to such behavior as "chronic suicide." The psychology of conscious and unconscious human destructiveness is complex and may well be a component in the destructive aspects of substance dependence. However, in my experience, many of the self-destructive aspects of drug dependence represent failures in ego functions involving self-care and self-protection.

Self-care functions originate and are established in early phases of human development. They become internalized as a result of and through the ministrations of the caring and protective role of the parents, particularly the mother. If optimal, children gradually incorporate a capacity to care for themselves and to protect against and anticipate harm and danger. Extremes of indulgence and deprivation may do injury to individuals' developing ego and sense of self around vital functions of self-preservation and care, and may leave them vulnerable to a whole range of hazards and dangers, not the least of which is the use of dangerous drugs (Khantzian 1978).

Self-care as an ego function is complex. It is probably the result of a number of component functions and defenses such as signal anxiety, reality testing, judgment, control, and synthesis, and, when impaired, such defenses as denial, justification, and projection. We are all subject to our instincts, drives, and impulses, and if they are expressed indiscriminately, we are subject to hazard and danger. Most of us check ourselves more or less and automatically exercise caution, or we are appropriately worried and fearful of the prospects of danger or hazardous involvements. Such checking or cautionary responses are an integral part of our ego mechanisms of defense. However, it is exactly in this regard that addicts are deficient in their ego. We elaborate in more detail on these deficiencies and their telltales in Chapter 2.

## REFERENCES

Kernberg, O. F. (1975). *Borderline Conditions and Pathological Narcissism*. New York: Jason Aronson.

Khantzian, E. J. (1972). A preliminary dynamic formulation of the psychopharmacologic action of methadone. In *Proceedings of the Fourth National Conference on Methadone Treatment*, pp. 371–374. New York: National Association for the Prevention of Addictions to Narcotics.

———— (1974). Opiate addiction: a critique of theory and some implications for treatment. *American Journal of Psychotherapy* 28:59–70.

———— (1975). Self-selection and progression in drug dependence. *Psychiatry Digest* 10:19–22.

———— (1978). The ego, the self and opiate addiction: theoretical and treatment considerations. *International Review of Psychoanalysis* 5:189–198.

Khantzian, E. J., Mack, J. E., and Schatzberg, A. F. (1974). Heroin use as an attempt to cope: clinical observations. *American Journal of Psychiatry* 131:160–164.

Khantzian, E. J., and Treece, C. J. (1977). Psychodynamics of drug dependence: an overview. In *Psychodynamics of Drug Dependence*, ed. J. D. Blaine and D. A. Julius. Research Monograph 12, pp. 11–25. Rockville, MD: National Institute on Drug Abuse.

———— (1979). Heroin addiction—the diagnostic dilemma for psychiatry. In *Psychiatric Factors in Drug Abuse*, ed. R. W. Pickens and L. L. Heston, pp. 21–45. New York: Grune & Stratton.

Kohut, H. (1971). *The Analysis of the Self*. New York: International Universities Press.

Krystal, H., and Raskin, H. A. (1970). *Drug Dependence. Aspects of Ego Functions*. Detroit: Wayne State University Press.

Menninger, K. (1938). *Man Against Himself*. New York: Free Press.

Meyer, R. E., and Mirin, S. M. (1979). *The Heroin Stimulus: Implications for a Theory of Addiction*. New York: Plenum.

Milkman, H., and Frosch, W. A. (1973). On the preferential abuse of heroin and amphetamine. *Journal of Nervous and Mental Disease* 156:242–248.

Wieder, H., and Kaplan, E. H. (1969). Drug use in adolescence: psychodynamic meaning and pharmacogenic effect. *Psychoanalytic Study of the Child* 24:399–431. New York: International Universities Press.

Wurmser, L. (1974). Psychoanalytic considerations of the etiology of compulsive drug use. *Journal of the American Psychoanalytic Association* 22:820–843.

Yorke, C. (1970). A critical review of some psychoanalytic literature on drug addiction. *British Journal of Medical Psychotherapy* 43:141–159.

Zinberg, N. E. (1975). Addiction and ego function. *Psychoanalytic Study of the Child* 30:567–588. New Haven, CT: Yale University Press.

# 5

# Ego Functions and Psychopathology in Narcotics and Polydrug Users

## *with Gerald J. McKenna*[1]

This chapter compares ego functions and psychopathology in narcotics and polydrug users, based on preliminary findings using the Psychiatric Status Schedule (PSS) of Spitzer and Endicott. The tendency to view all drug-dependent individuals as deviants has detracted from a more careful assessment of their psychological vulnerabilities and the part that drugs play in the personality organization of these individuals and their attempts to adapt to their environment. Thus there is a need to study and clarify further the nature and degree of psychopathology in both opiate- and polydrug-dependent individuals.

---

1. Dr. McKenna was first author on this paper.

## REVIEW OF THE LITERATURE

Over the past fifty years, attempts by psychologists and psychiatrists to characterize drug-dependent individuals, particularly with regard to the presence of psychopathology, has produced confusing and contradictory findings. Early work by Kolb (1927) suggested that there were different types of addicted individuals and that personality characteristics determined the pattern of drug use and different subjective effects. Rado (1933) appreciated the presence of an underlying "tense depression" in addicts, but stressed more the "hedonic" interests and the pursuit of a "super-pleasure" to account for the compelling nature of drug dependence. In contrast to this, Glover (1932) stressed the use of drugs in the service of defense against paranoid tendencies and psychosis.

With the exception of these early reports, over the next twenty years there were few reports from the psychiatric, psychoanalytic, or psychological literature characterizing drug-dependent people. A major impetus for a more systematic study and understanding of drug-dependent individuals evolved out of the federal prison for narcotics addicts at Lexington, Kentucky. Initial efforts were predominantly focused on studies of the physiological basis of drug dependence. However, by the late 1940s and early 1950s, reports began to appear that delineated some of the psychological characteristics of individuals who were predominantly narcotics dependent. Early reports by Wikler (1952, Wikler and Rasor 1953) reflected an appreciation of drug-dependent persons' anxieties related to aggression and sexuality, and how neurotic individuals took these drugs to relieve such anxieties ("negative euphoria"). Vaillant (1966) and Wishnie (1974) subsequently observed that the opiate-dependent individual's involvement with drugs defended against and "masked" underlying depression.

With the development of the Minnesota Multiphasic Personality Inventory (MMPI), a number of reports began to appear in the early 1960s presenting "psychological profiles" of opiate-dependent individuals (see review by Treece 1977). An early report by Hill and colleagues (1960) stressed the "psychopathic" deviance of the group they tested. Subsequent reports suggested the MMPI profiles to be influenced by setting (for example, inpatient versus outpatient status) (Sutker and Allain 1973, Sutker et al. 1974), length of institutionalization (Fraccia et al. 1973), and treatment status. In a study by Berzins and colleagues (1974), there was a higher frequency than in earlier studies of elevation in the depression and schizophrenia scales, suggesting more distress, confusion, and schizoid features.

Works by Fenichel (1945), Savit (1954, 1963), and Wieder and Kaplan (1969) emphasized the presence of tension and psychic distress, including depression in those who were drug dependent, but tended still to place emphasis on a regressive pleasurable use of drugs. Wieder and Kaplan, however, made a notable contribution by stressing that certain psychological and developmental factors predisposed a person to use a particular type of drug.

The work of Chein and colleagues (1964) and the previous related work by Gerard and Kornetsky (1954) marked a significant departure in the psychiatric and psychoanalytic literature. They attempted to study adolescent opiate dependence in the ghetto rather than adult drug dependence in an institutional setting or a private practice. They better appreciated the specific effects of the drugs, and they attempted to explore how the drugs interacted with the addict's ego and superego pathology, problems with narcissism, and other psychopathology. They placed major emphasis on the individual's attempts to use drugs adaptively to cope with overwhelming adolescent anxiety associated with anticipated adult roles in the absence of adequate preparation, models, and prospects.

Other work on drug-dependent individuals has focused more precisely on ego functions and ego impairments. Krystal and Raskin (1970) stressed problems with recognizing and tolerating painful affects with a tendency to somatize emotional distress. Wurmser (1974) proposed that this group suffers major narcissistic injury, and along with Khantzian (1974) proposed that they are inadequately defended against their rage and aggression.

Most of the previously cited reports were based on studies of opiate dependence. Only later was there any attempt to study more carefully the characteristics of non–opiate- or "polydrug"-dependent individuals. Initial (Benvenuto and Bourne 1975, Wesson et al. 1975) and subsequent reports (McKenna 1977) have uniformly shown the presence of severe and significant underlying psychopathology in the polydrug-dependent population, including depression, severe anxiety, and psychosis. Straus and colleagues (1977) compared MMPI profiles of this group with psychiatric inpatients and found them to be similar.

## METHOD

A group of ninety-seven patients admitted to the inpatient detoxification/treatment unit of our polydrug treatment program was administered the Psychiatric Status Schedule of Spitzer and Endicott shortly after admission. There were three fairly distinct groups according to drug use pattern:

1. Narcotics alone (primarily heroin users who only occasionally used another drug)
2. Polydrug (whose multiple drug use excluded narcotics)
3. Combination of 1 and 2 (multiple substance users who used narcotics and sedative hypnotics with about equal frequency)

It is difficult to find drug users whose use is limited to a single substance. The older alcoholic may be the last vestige of the single substance abuser (Carroll 1977). One can, however, identify predominant drug patterns and look more closely for similarities and/or differences among individuals who choose one drug use pattern over another. We compared the PSS profiles for these three groups.

## DATA

Figure 5–1 presents the narcotics users' PSS Scores, based on PSS summaries of seventeen narcotics users. Figure 5–2 presents the scores of the forty-eight polydrug users. Figure 5–3 presents the PSS scores of the thirty-two combination polydrug/narcotics users. Figure 5–4 compares the PSS scores of the three groups. On Figures 5–1 through 5–3 the standardized PSS scores of an inpatient psychiatric population ($N = 470$), an outpatient psychiatric population ($N = 55$), and a community sample ($N = 130$) are shown so that they can be easily compared with the various drug populations.

The most striking result in this data is that there is no significant difference among the three drug groups in their PSS scores, while all three groups show evidence of considerable psychopathology as measured by most of the categories.

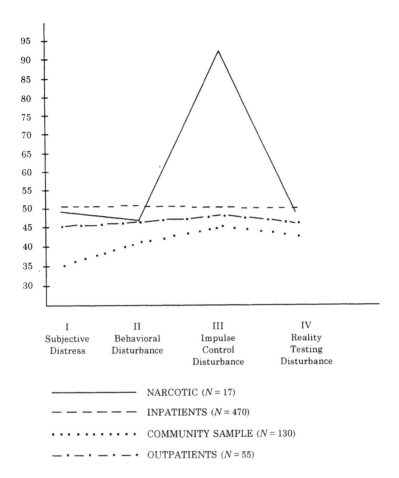

**Figure 5-1. Narcotic users' PSS scores**

On Figures 5–1 through 5–3, which compare the three drug groups with the psychiatric inpatient, outpatient, and community samples, it is clear that subjective distress is close to or above the levels of psychiatric inpatients. This would indicate that all three groups experience considerable symptoms of anxiety, depression, and somatic concerns, and are troubled by frequent thoughts of suicide. In addition, they experience feelings of social isolation and impairment of the ego functions involved in maintaining a daily routine.

Behavioral disturbance was elevated above the psychiatric inpatient level for the polydrug and combination polydrug/narcotics groups. The score for the narcotics-only group was at the level of psychiatric outpatients, but, nonetheless, elevated.

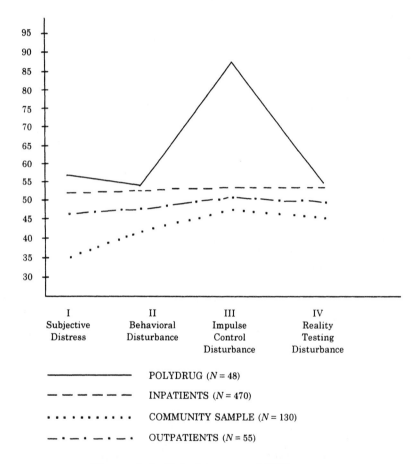

**Figure 5–2. Polydrug users' PSS scores**

Impulse control disturbance is very high for all of the drug-using groups. This finding is to be expected in part because the PSS uses items in this section that involve illegal acts or impulses to commit illegal acts along with behaviors frequently seen in drug intoxication and withdrawal, such as reported overt anger. The high score for all three groups is thus skewed.

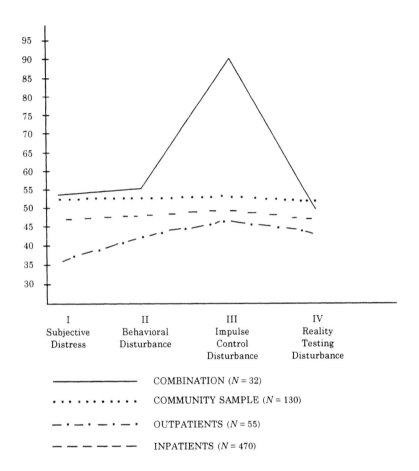

Figure 5–3. Combination polydrug/narcotics users' PSS scores

Reality testing disturbance is similarly elevated for the three groups to a level approaching or above the inpatient psychiatric group.

## DISCUSSION

While it is obviously not possible to generalize these data to any group of drug users other than those entering our detoxification unit, the data nonetheless lead us to question the clinical assumption that there are major differences among various groups of drug-dependent individuals. It may well be that those dependent on narcotics mask their

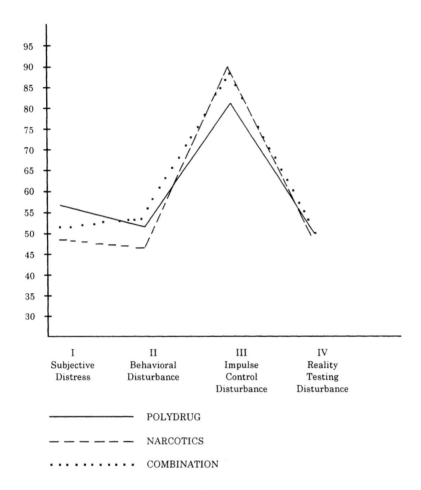

**Figure 5-4. Combination polydrug/narcotics/polydrug–narcotics
users' PSS scores**

internal psychological distress by their seeming ability to function in
the highly complex narcotics world. While our sample in this study was
restricted to individuals entering an inpatient unit for detoxification,
recent reports support the notion of psychopathology in outpatient
drug treatment groups. Weissman and colleagues (1976) reported
moderate depression in one-third of 106 patients in a methadone
maintenance clinic in New Haven using standard tests for depression.
These results were consistent with those found by Senay and col-

leagues (1977) in Chicago. A pilot study by Woody and colleagues (1975) in Philadelphia again showed depression in a number of narcotics addicts on methadone maintenance. An earlier report by McKenna and colleagues (1973) discussed various types of psychotic illness occurring among methadone maintenance patients. A report by Mirin and colleagues (1976) demonstrated an increase in psychopathology with chronic self-administration of heroin in a controlled setting. These reports, and the findings in this report, should encourage us to apply more individual diagnostic and treatment criteria in assessing an individual who is narcotics or polydrug dependent.

## REFERENCES

Benvenuto, J., and Bourne, P. G. (1975). The federal polydrug abuse project. Initial report. *Journal of Psychedelic Drugs* 7:115–120.

Berzins, J. I., Ross, W. F., English, G. E., and Haley, J. V. (1974). Subgroups among opiate addicts: a typological investigation. *Journal of Abnormal Psychology* 83:65–73.

Carroll, J. (1977). *The National Drug/Alcohol Collaborative Project Final Report*. Rockville, MD: National Institute on Drug Abuse.

Chein, I., Gerard, D. L., Lee, R. S., and Rosenfeld, E. (1964). *The Road to H*. New York: Basic Books.

Fenichel, O. (1945). The *Psychoanalytic Theory of Neurosis*. New York: Norton.

Fraccia, J., Sheppard, C., and Merlis, S. (1973). Some comments about the personality comparison of incarcerated and street heroin addicts. *Psychology Report* 33:413–414.

Gerard, D. L., and Kornetsky, C. (1954). Adolescent opiate addiction: a case study. *Psychiatric Quarterly* 28:367–380.

Glover, E. (1932). On the etiology of drug addiction. In *On the Early Development of Mind*, pp. 187–215. New York: International Universities Press, 1956.

Hill, H. E., Haertzen, C. A., and Glasser, R. (1960). Personality characteristics of narcotic addicts as indicated by the MMPI. *Journal of General Psychology* 62:127–139.

Khantzian, E. J. (1974). Opiate addiction: a critique of theory and some implications for treatment. *American Journal Psychotherapy* 28:59–70.

Kolb, L. (1927). Clinical contributions to drug addiction: the struggle for cures and the conscious reasons for relapse. *Journal of Nervous and Mental Disease* 66:22–43.

Krystal, H., and Raskin, H. A. (1970). *Drug Dependence: Aspects of Ego Functions.* Detroit: Wayne State University Press.

McKenna, G. J. (1977). *The drug/alcohol/psychiatry interface.* Presented at the Third National Drug Abuse Conference.

McKenna, G. J., Fisch, A., Levine, M., et al. (1973). The use of methadone as a psychotropic agent. In *Proceedings of the Fifth National Conference on Methadone Treatment,* Washington, DC. New York: National Association for the Prevention of Addictions to Narcotics.

Mirin, S. M., Meyer, R. E., and McNamee, H. B. (1976). Psychopathology, craving, and mood during heroin acquisition: an experimental study. *International Journal of Addictions* 11:525–544.

Rado, S. (1933). The psychoanalysis of pharmacothymia. *Psychoanalytic Quarterly* 2:1–23.

———— (1954). Extramural psychoanalytic treatment of a case of narcotic addiction. *Journal of the American Psychoanalytic Association* 2:494.

Savit, R. A. (1963). Psychoanalytic studies on addiction: ego structure in narcotic addiction. *Psychoanalytic Quarterly* 32:43–57.

Senay, E. C., Dorus, W., and Yufit, R. (1977). *Depression in drug abusers.* Paper presented at the American Psychiatric Convention, Toronto, May.

Straus, F., Ousley, N., and Carlin, A. (1977). Psychopathology and drug abuse: an MMPI comparison of polydrug abuse patients with psychiatric inpatients and outpatients. *Addictive Behavior* 2:75–78.

Sutker, P. B., and Allain, A. N. (1973). Incarcerated and street heroin addicts: a personality comparison. *Journal of Abnormal Psychology* 83(4).

Sutker, P. B., Allain, A., and Cohen, G. H. (1974). MMPI indices of personality change following short- and long-term hospitalization of heroin addicts. *Psychology Reports* 34(2).

Treece, C. J. (1977). *Narcotic use in relation to selected ego functions among incarcerated women.* Unpublished Doctoral Dissertation, Boston University.

Vaillant, G. E. (1966). A 12-year follow-up of New York narcotic addicts, III: some social and psychiatric characteristics. *Archives of General Psychiatry* 15:599–609.

Weissman, M., Slobetz, F., Prusoff, B., et al. (1976). Clinical depression among narcotics addicts maintained on methadone in the community. *American Journal of Psychiatry* 133:1434–1438.

Wesson, D. R., Smith, E. E., and Lerner, S. (1975). Streetwise and nonstreetwise polydrug typology. *Journal of Psychedelic Drugs* 7:121–134.

Wieder, H., and Kaplan, E. H. (1969). Drug use in adolescence: psychodynamic meaning and pharmacogenic effect. *Psychoanalytic Study of the Child* 24:399–431. New York: International Universities Press.

Wikler, A. A. (1952). A psychodynamic study of a patient during experimental self-regulated re-addiction to morphine. *Psychiatric Quarterly* 26:270.

Wikler, A. A., and Rasor, R. W. (1953). Psychiatric aspects of drug addiction. *American Journal of Medicine* 14:566–570.

Wishnie, H. (1974). Opioid addiction: a masked depression. In *Masked Depression*, ed. S. Lesse, pp. 350–367. New York: Jason Aronson.

Woody, G. E., O'Brien, C. P., and Rickels, K. (1975). Depression and anxiety in heroin addicts: a placebo-controlled study of doxepin in combination with methadone. *American Journal of Psychiatry* 132:447–450.

Wurmser, L. (1974). Psychoanalytic considerations of the etiology of compulsive drug use. *Journal of the American Psychoanalytic Association* 22:820–843.

# 6

# Treatment Implications of Ego and Self Disturbances in Alcoholism

Effective treatment of alcoholism must address the core problems of the alcoholic, namely, the enormous difficulties that such people have had in controlling and regulating their behavior, feelings, and self-esteem. Although psychoanalysis is rarely the treatment of choice for alcoholics, it does offer a special understanding of many of the alcoholic's problems and a rationale for the treatment choices and decisions that must be made to help the alcoholic.

Although in its early application to alcoholism psychoanalysis stressed the instinctual and regressive-pleasurable aspects of alcohol use (Abraham 1908, Freud 1905, Knight 1937, Rado 1933, Simmel 1948), many of these investigators also appreciated other contributing factors such as mood disturbance, particularly depression, diminished self-esteem, faulty ego ideal formation, and other forms of narcissistic disturbance. Blum (1966), Blum and Blum (1967), Rosenfeld (1965), and Yorke (1970) have published excellent reviews and critiques of these trends in the literature. This chapter elaborates on more recent psychoanalytic explanations that have attempted to identify more precisely impairments and disturbances in the ego and self, especially involving problems in self-care, affect management, and self-other relationships and related problems in coping, and reviews through case examples some important implications for treatment of these ego and self disturbances in alcoholics.

Some of the distinctions made in this presentation between *ego* and *self* are arbitrary and artificial. Although structure and function are stressed in relation to the ego, and subjective attitudes and states in relation to the self, clearly the ego has subjective elements associated with it, and the self has structural and functional aspects. The distinctions are made for heuristic purposes and to delineate more precisely the nature and qualities of the alcoholic's psychological disturbances.

## EGO FUNCTIONS AND THE ALCOHOLIC

As already indicated, early formulations of alcoholism were heavily influenced by an instinct psychology that stressed the oral dependency and fixation of the alcoholic. More recent attempts to explain alcoholism from a psychoanalytic point of view have understandably focused on the ego to delineate better the nature of the structural impairments that cause alcohol to become such a compelling and devastating influence in an individual's life. The nature of the ego disturbances and impairments in the alcoholic are varied and manifold. I shall selectively focus on and explore some of those that seem to me most germane in understanding a person's problems with alcohol.

In the broadest terms, it seems to me that the alcoholic has been most vulnerable and impaired in two areas of ego functioning. One area involves functions of self-care; whether sober or drunk, the alcoholic demonstrates a repeated tendency to revert to or persist in drinking behavior despite all the apparent indications that such behavior is self-damaging and dangerous. The second area of obvious difficulty has been in the alcoholic's inability to regulate his/her feelings. When sober, he/she often denies or is unable to identify or verbalize feelings. At other times he/she experiences nameless fears and suffers with depression that might be vaguely perceived or experienced as over-whelming and unbearable, even leading to suicide.

## The Ego and Self-Care

The defense mechanism of denial is frequently invoked to explain why or how alcoholics persist in their self-defeating behavior. In such in-stances the presence of conscious and unconscious destructive im-pulses, intentions, and behavior is assumed; presumably there is awareness of real or potential danger, but the individual resorts to an active process or defense against such awareness. Although there is probably a reasonable basis for these assumptions, such explana-tions are excessively influenced by early instinct theory that stressed pleasure seeking and life-death instincts to the exclusion of other con-siderations. In contradistinction to such a formulation, I believe that the self-damaging aspects of alcoholism can be better accounted for by considering a deficiency or impairment in development of an ego function I have designated as "self-care."

The self-destructiveness apparent in alcoholism is not willed or un-consciously motivated by suicidal wishes (i.e., the model of the neuro-ses) as often as it is the result of impairments and deficiencies in ego functions whereby an individual fails to be aware, cautious, worried, or frightened enough to avoid or desist in behavior that has damag-ing consequences. This function originates in the early mother–child relationship when the caring and protective functions of the mother are gradually internalized so that the individual can eventually take care of and adequately protect himself/herself from harm and danger-ous situations (Khantzian 1978, Khantzian et al. 1974). Extremes of parental deprivation or indulgence may have devastating subsequent effects, and it is not surprising that both patterns are frequently iden-tified in the background of alcoholics (Blum 1966, Knight 1937, Simmel 1948).

Self-care is a generic or global function and is related to ego func-tions such as signal anxiety, reality testing, judgment, and synthesis. When self-care is impaired, certain other ego mechanisms of defense are prominent or exaggerated. In fact I suspect such mechanisms might be related to and perhaps even secondary to impairments in self-care. That is, in working with individuals who have self-care prob-lems, I have been impressed by how they are vaguely aware of their susceptibility to mishaps and danger, and they sense in themselves the lack of a self-protective or self-caring ability and thus need and depend on others to protect them and to help in making judgments about dangerous situations. The ill-defined fears of vulnerability and feelings of helplessness associated with such states also compel those who are so affected to counteract these feelings and to externalize their problem by resorting to such mechanisms as justification, projection, phobic avoidance, and/or counterphobic attitudes. In the absence of self-care, such defenses are prominent in alcoholics.

I believe that self-care is deficient, impaired, or absent in many if not most alcoholics and that this accounts for much of the disastrous and destructive behavior in their lives, in addition to the malignant involvement with alcohol. In studying over fifty alcoholics, I have observed the problem of self-care in their histories of poor attention to preventable medical and dental problems, patterns of delinquent, accident-prone and violent behavior, and other forms of impulsivity that predate their alcoholism. It is most obvious in their apparent disregard for the consequences of drinking; there is little evidence of fear, anxiety, or realistic evaluation of the deterioration and danger when they revert to or persist in drinking. Although much of this is secondary to the regression and deterioration in judgment as a function of continued drinking, I have been impressed by the presence and persistence of these tendencies in such individuals both prior to their becoming alcoholic and subsequent to detoxification and stabilization (Khantzian 1978, 1979b).

## The Ego and Regulation of Feelings

Whereas self-care serves to warn and protect against external dangers and the consequences of careless behavior, the ego functions involved in regulation of feelings serve as signals and guides in managing and protecting against instability and chaos in our internal emotional life. Many of the same processes that establish self-care functions and originate from the nurturing and protective role of the mother in infancy are involved in the development of ego functions that serve to regulate feelings. It is not surprising, then, that alcoholics also suffer from a range of ego impairments that affect their capacity to regulate their feeling life. These impairments take such forms as an inability to identify and verbalize feelings, an incapacity to tolerate painful feelings such as anxiety and depression, an inability to modulate feelings, problems in activation and initiative, and a tendency to exhibit extreme manifestations of feelings including hypomania, phobic-anxious states, panic attacks, and labile emotional outbursts.

As has been suggested for other mental processes and functions, affects develop along certain lines and are subject to fixation, distortions, and regression. Krystal and Raskin (1970) have helpfully traced and formulated how the affects of anxiety and depression develop out of a common undifferentiated matrix. At the outset feelings are undifferentiated, somatized, and not verbalized. Normally, the tendency is for feelings to become differentiated, de-somatized, and verbalized. If this process proceeds optimally, it contributes significantly to the development of an effective *stimulus barrier*, that is, aspects of ego function that maintain minimal levels of unpleasant feelings through appropriate action and mechanisms of defense when they reach high or intolerable levels (Khantzian 1978, Krystal and Raskin 1970). In such instances, feelings act as a guide or signal to mobilize ego mechanisms of defense in response to internal emotions and external stimuli. Either as a result of developmental arrest or because of regression caused by traumatic events later in life, alcoholics fail to differentiate successfully, with the consequence that they are unable to use feelings as signals or guides because they are unable to identify affects or their feelings are unbearable or overwhelming. Because of defects in the stimulus barrier, alcoholics use denial or the effects of alcohol to ward off overwhelming affects (e.g., undifferentiated anxiety-depression). That is, in lieu of an affective stimulus barrier "drugs or alcohol are used to avoid impending psychic trauma in circumstances which would not be potentially traumatic to other people" (Krystal and Raskin 1970, p. 31).

Borderline and narcissistic pathology has been implicated in alcoholism (Kernberg 1975, Klein 1975, Kohut 1971), but there has been little systematic attempt to understand the relationship between the structural impairments of such pathology and alcoholism. Kernberg has emphasized ego weakness in borderline conditions and has singled out lack of anxiety tolerance and impulse control, primitive defensive operations including rigid walling off of good and bad introjects, and splitting and denial in the service of preventing anxiety related to aggression. Kernberg fails to make it clear whether he believes that such borderline symptomatology is at the root of alcohol problems or that borderline conditions and alcoholism have similar processes operating that affect both conditions. Presumably, the borderline processes delineated by Kernberg are consistent with those identified by Krystal and Raskin, who have detailed more precisely how such problems in coping with feelings affect alcoholics.

Taking a somewhat more descriptive approach, Klein (1975) has similarly focused on unpleasant dysphoric affect states associated with borderline conditions and alcoholism. He discounts the role of "ego defects" in borderline conditions and instead emphasizes the importance of a descriptive approach for purposes of diagnosis and classification. Klein stresses the ubiquity of labile, anxious, and depressive states associated with so-called borderline pathology. He believes the "border" in such conditions is more with affective disorders than with neurosis, character pathology, or schizophrenia, and that it is on such a basis that certain individuals welcome the effects of alcohol. He has singled out several syndromes in which alcohol and antianxiety agents are sought for relief, namely hysteroid ("rejection sensitive") dysphoria, chronic anxiety-tension states, and phobic neurosis with panic attacks. Despite his disclaimer about ego defects in such conditions, I believe his own description of these problems as an "affective or activation disorder, or a stereotyped affective overresponse" (Klein 1975, p. 369) speaks for an impairment in the ego's capacity to regulate feelings in such individuals. This is further supported by his observation that psychoactive drugs are effective with such patients because "they modify states of dysregulation of affect and activation." Along these lines, Quitkin and associates (1972) have impressively demonstrated that a small but significant proportion of alcoholics suffer from a phobic-anxious syndrome and respond to imipramine with marked symptomatic improvement and elimination of their dependence on alcohol.

In brief, then, I believe there is convincing evidence from several convergent lines of inquiry to support the point of view that significant impairments in ego structure predispose to alcoholism. Impairments in self-care leave individuals ill equipped to properly weigh, anticipate, and assess the consequences of risky and self-damaging behavior, but particularly in relation to the consequences of their alcohol involvement. The other area of ego impairment in alcoholics involves problems in recognizing, regulating, and harnessing feeling states to the point that conditions of immobilization or being overwhelmed with affects result, and alcohol is sought to overcome or relieve such dilemmas.

## THE SELF AND THE ALCOHOLIC

Alcoholics suffer not only because of impairments in their ego. They also suffer because of impairments and injury in their sense of self. As in ego disturbances, developmental problems loom large in the self disturbances of alcoholics. Both the development of the ego and the sense of self are results of internalization processes. Optimally, the developing child acquires qualities and functions from the caring parents such that the individual can eventually take care of himself. When successful, the process of internalization establishes within the person a coherent sense of the self, an appreciation of the separate existence of others, and adequate ego functions that serve purposes of defense and adaptation (Khantzian 1978).

In the previous sections we focused on how alcohol problems were related to impairments in ego function that resulted in a deficiency and/or inability to appreciate consequences of dangerous behavior and to regulate emotion. In this section I emphasize and explore how alcohol problems are also the result of impairments in the sense of self whereby the individual is unable or ill equipped to value, comfort, soothe, care for, and express himself/herself. Although I have designated the impairments around self-care and affect regulation as ego disturbances, such problems are not entirely distinguishable from self disturbances. As indicated at the outset of this chapter, some of these distinctions are arbitrary. It is likely that the nature of the self disturbances I will delineate in this section significantly impact upon and interact with ego disturbances involving self-care and (affect) regulation.

### Dependency and the Self

Alcoholics are desperately dependent people. Formulations about the nature of this dependency have, however, been overly simplistic and reductionistic, placing undue emphasis on the symbolic, oral, regressive aspects of the alcoholic's dependency on the substance itself. Similarly, the personal relationships of the alcoholic are characterized as infantile and clinging (Khantzian 1979b). The dependency of alcoholics is not primarily the result of oral fixations and oral cravings. The dependency has more to do with deficits and defects in psychological structure and sense of self whereby the alcoholic depends on the effects of alcohol and attaches himself to others to compensate for deficiencies in self-care, affect regulation, self-esteem, and subjective sense of well-being.

Balint (1968) has characterized the alcoholic's dependency as a "basic fault." He emphasizes that it does not have the form of an instinct or of conflict, but is "something wrong in the mind, a kind of deficiency which must be put right" (p. 56). According to Balint, the alcoholic seeks the effects of alcohol to establish a feeling of "harmony—a feeling that everything is now well between them and their environment—and . . . the yearning for this feeling of harmony is the most important cause of alcoholism or, for that matter, any form of addiction" (p. 56). Along these same lines, Kohut (1971) has observed that dependency of such people on substances (Kohut does not distinguish between alcohol and other substances) says less about the person's attachment to substances and/or people as loved or loving objects than about the search for "a replacement for a defect in psychological structure" (p. 46).

The "fault" or "defect" that alcoholics experience in their psychological self structure is the result of developmental failures in ego-ideal formation. The developing child and adolescent insufficiently experience admired and admiring feelings in response to parents and other adult figures. Because of this deficiency in the relationship with parents and others, such individuals fail to internalize and identify with the encouraging, valued, and idealized qualities of important adults.

Although alcoholics indeed suffer as a result of conscience or superego and seek to drown their guilt and self-condemnation in alcohol, I am impressed that they suffer more from the lack of an adequate ego ideal that would otherwise help them to evaluate themselves as worthwhile and good enough in a whole range of human involvements and activities. Because of faulty ego ideal formation, self-esteem suffers and there is an inability or failure to judge one's relationships, work, or play as sufficient or satisfactory. As a result, individuals so afflicted constantly seek external sources of reassurance, recognition, solace, and approval. Such individuals feel especially wanting from within for an approved self by an approving ego ideal, and it is in this respect that they are so desperately dependent. They seek out alcohol, people, and activities not primarily for gratification of oral, infantile drives and wishes, but more in an attempt to feel better or good about themselves, as they are almost totally unable to achieve this feeling for themselves from within.

Corollary to the disturbance in ego-ideal formation are disturbances related to the capacity to comfort, soothe, and care for oneself. Alcoholics seem to adopt modes of polar extremes with regard to such needs and functions. Alcoholics' search for external supplies, their dependence on alcohol, and leaning on others are the result of a failure to internalize adequately and to develop capacities for nurturance within the self, which causes them to turn primarily outside themselves for comfort, soothing, and caring, or defensively to deny such needs or wants.

## Pathological Self-Formations

One of the main consequences of the ego and self disturbances in alcoholics is that such individuals have developed and display troublesome and self-defeating compensatory defenses and pathological self structures in response to underlying conflicts around need satisfaction and dependency. In some instances the defenses that are employed serve to compensate for and counteract the sense of incompleteness such people feel as a result of deficits in affect defense and self-esteem; in other instances the more rigid and primitive defenses that are employed seem to be the result of pathological internalizations, identifications, and self structures. The alcoholic seeks the releasing effect of alcohol to overcome rigid and overdrawn defenses and to facilitate and regulate the experiencing and expression of affectionate or aggressive feelings in the absence of ego and self structure that helps to modulate such affects and drives (Khantzian 1979a).

Some elaborations on self pathology are probably pertinent with regard to the facilitating and regulating influences of alcohol and help to explain why alcoholics need to depend on such effects. Kernberg (1975) has emphasized the importance of pathological self structures in borderline conditions and has also implicated them in alcoholism. He believes that rigid and primitive defenses of splitting, denial, and projection serve to cause the repression, splitting off, and dissociation of parts of the self, and that the effect of alcohol acts to "refuel" the grandiose self, to activate the "all good" self and object images, and to deny the "all bad" internalized objects (p. 222). Despite the emphasis on a deficit psychology, Kohut places equal if not greater emphasis on compensatory and defensive reactions such as massive repression, self-disavowal, and denial of needs. According to Kohut, substance users resort to the effects of substances to lift these defenses in order to feel the soothing and resurgence of self-esteem they are otherwise unable to experience (Kohut 1977). Although Kohut does not specify any particular drugs or substance, in my experience it is precisely this effect that the alcoholic seeks to achieve with the use of alcohol.

On a similar basis, Krystal and Raskin (1970) and Krystal (1977) stress the special and exaggerated defenses of denial and splitting that are adopted by individuals dependent on alcohol. These defenses serve to wall off and suppress aggressive and loving feelings in relation to the self and others. Krystal emphasizes the great difficulty alcoholics have with ambivalence, and how they prefer to use the short-acting effect of alcohol to experience and give vent to such feelings briefly, and therefore safely.

Finally, on a somewhat different basis, Silber (1970, 1974) has focused on the developmental impairments of alcoholics that have been the result of pathological and destructive identifications with psychotic and/or very disturbed parents. The self-damaging and destructive aspects of alcohol involvement parallel and represent identifications with self-neglecting, self-destructive aspects of the parents.

## TREATMENT IMPLICATIONS

As I have indicated, alcoholics suffer tremendously in their attempts to regulate their behavior, feelings, and relationships with other people. Effective treatment of these problems must be based on a more precise identification of the disturbances in the ego and self structures of alcoholics, and our psychotherapeutic and psychopharmacological interventions should be based on such an appreciation. This section, using case material, explores some treatment implications of the alcoholic's ego and self disturbances.

### Implications for Initial Care

At the outset, the most urgent and often life-threatening aspect of alcoholism must be faced, namely, the impulsive unbridled use of alcohol. Alcoholics Anonymous (AA) has been most effective in helping alcoholics gain control over their drinking: "They have become experts in sobriety" (John Mack, personal communication). It is little wonder that AA's success rests upon an emphasis on abstinence as the single most important goal to be achieved by the alcoholic. AA has often worked because it skillfully manages and compensates for the impairments in self-care. AA also works because it contains and partly satisfies some of the other determinants of alcoholism, namely, problems in regulating emotions and maintaining self-esteem and related dependency problems. Unfortunately, AA is unacceptable for many if not a majority of alcoholics. For many alcoholics, psychiatric and psychological approaches become a logical, or necessary, alternative. If such becomes the case, it remains critical that the clinician appreciate, as much as AA has, the urgency and dangers of the uncontrolled drinking, as the equally important determinants and causes of the alcoholism are explored and understood. Clearly, until control over the drinking is established, exploration of predisposing causes is of little value.

I have evolved an approach that has proved to be surprisingly useful and effective in dealing with uncontrolled drinking when contact is first made with the alcoholic. As indicated, it is in regard to the uncontrolled drinking that impairments in self-care are most alarmingly and dangerously apparent, and this must become the first focus of any treatment intervention. Rather than stress abstinence or sobriety, I immediately attempt to ascertain the amount and pattern of drinking and I ask patients, respectfully and empathically, to share with me their own reasons for drinking, especially what the drinking does for them. I also ask patients as tactfully as I can to reflect on how much danger and harm they have caused themselves as a result of their drinking. Such an approach helps patients to ease into a treatment relationship where their enormous shame about and desperate dependence on alcohol are not immediately challenged or threatened, but which at the same time begins to focus early on some of the important determinants of the uncontrolled drinking.

Once satisfied that the drinking is out of control, I emphatically point this out with undisguised concern and stress that it is the single most immediate problem to be faced. Unrecognized impairments and evident rationalizations are identified as well as the unacknowledged physical and behavioral consequences of the drinking. I openly discuss how difficult it will be to stop drinking, but share with the patient my conviction about the urgency for control and an intention to keep this the main focus for both of us until it is achieved. Keeping the focus on control allows a strategy to develop that avoids premature insistence on permanent abstinence, or an equally untenable permissive acceptance of uncontrolled drinking. Alternative models and methods of control are described explicitly, such as gradual curtailment or abrupt cessation with short-term drug substitution if physiological dependence is evident. If the latter is the case, or if deterioration is evident and/or there is need for external support and control, hospitalization is recommended. In some cases I insist upon it if it seems necessary. Surprisingly, this is rarely the case, and often there is a margin of opportunity in such an approach for the therapist to share with the patient information, experiences, and knowledge about how others have gained control over their drinking. In most instances, then, the emphasis in this approach is on establishing control and giving the patient a chance to make a choice.

In one case the discovery that a choice about one's drinking can be made in collaboration with the therapist evolved over several months.

### Case 1

This patient, a 51-year-old tradesman who had worked successfully at his job, had consumed large amounts of distilled alcohol daily dating back to his late teenage years. He was considered a leader among his peers and until four years prior to seeking treatment had functioned effectively as the elected shop steward for his union. His drinking usually began at midday, and he continued drinking from the end of the workday at 4:00 P.M. until supper. He drank with his co-workers in a local pub, which was also a gathering place for people of his own nationality. He insisted and his wife confirmed that he never was drunk or reacted adversely to alcohol until four years before, when his shoe shop went out of business and he was unable to find employment because most of the other shoe shops in the area were also going out of business.

At the time of evaluation he indicated that over the past year and a half his drinking had been totally out of control, stating, "I wouldn't dare count how much I was drinking a day this past year or so—all I know is I needed it to start the day and finish the day." He stated that during this period he was experiencing "shakes" every morning. I immediately shared with him my sense that his drinking was out of control and agreed with him that it probably dated back to the loss of his job. I indicated that it would be extremely important to gain control, but I avoided explaining then what this would entail. During the initial sessions he alternated between being garrulous, expansive, and bantering and being irritable and defensive, especially about his drinking. According to the patient, again confirmed by his wife, who was reliable, he made significant but only moderately successful efforts to curtail his drinking over the first two months of weekly contacts with me. After his ninth session I felt he was more at ease with me as he was sharing both pleasant and troubling reminiscences from his childhood years, as well as his challenges and experiences as a union steward. In this context of a more relaxed treatment relationship with me, I expressed my concern that he was not sufficiently controlling his drinking. I told him that I was not sure he could take one or two drinks and then leave it alone. I told him that curtailment could be one form of control but I suspected it was not working for him. I shared with him my own discovery that I could not control my use of cigarettes and that smoking one cigarette inevitably led to my resuming smoking a pack a day, and how after much experimentation I had learned that abstinence from cigarettes (and the occasional substitution of a cigar) worked best for me. I reviewed with him my knowledge of AA and my experience with other patients for whom abstinence from alcohol seemed to work best as a form of control, but I said it remained to be seen what would work for him.

In an interview one month later he reported being discouraged in his efforts to modify his drinking and appeared dejected and depressed. In this context I told him that he seemed to be least able to control his drinking when he felt "lousy." Shortly after this session he stopped drinking. In an interview another month later in which he was evidently feeling much better, he indicated he was not craving alcohol at all. After a thoughtful review on his part of how he planned to approach finding a new job, I puzzled out loud with him how he had managed to gain control over his drinking. He told me that he had thought about my comment two months previously about whether he could have one or two drinks and then stop. He said he decided to try it out and he discovered he couldn't. Again he stressed that once he had stopped drinking, he didn't crave alcohol at all. Reflecting out loud, he reminded me again how much alcohol he needed to get a "little high," an amount that would make others "go staggering." Not without significance and characteristic of this man, he made a playful reference to my example of substituting cigars for cigarettes and revealed some successful substitutions of his own—he said he was "drinking lots of Moxie [a bittersweet, pungent carbonated beverage] and milk." He also added that he was eating well. Over two years of follow-up this man has remained totally sober and abstinent, and he has resumed working in a supervisory capacity. He has also considerably improved his relationship with his wife.

## Discussion

Taking an approach such as the one I have presented here, I have now had the experience of seeing several patients significantly modify and ultimately gain control over their drinking behavior. However, in the majority of the cases I have treated, the patients have chosen abstinence as the most reliable means of control. For some, this occurs at the outset; for others, after some tentative experimentation and attempts at continued drinking, such as those I described in this case. What has been most impressive has been the salutary discovery by the patient and myself that some choice can be exercised in achieving the goal of control over drinking behavior. In taking such an approach, struggles tend to be avoided, the patient feels a gradual sense of mastery over his/her own problems, and the joint effort to solve a problem fosters a healthy alliance rather than an adversary role between patient and therapist (Khantzian 1980).

As the urgency and danger of the destructive drinking behavior recede and the patient begins to develop an alliance with the therapist, examination and treatment of the predisposing disturbances can and should be considered. Although psychotherapeutic and psychopharmacological treatment of alcoholics has often been dismissed as ineffective and possibly even dangerous, I believe growing clinical understanding and experience with alcoholics suggest that alcoholics are eminently suitable for such treatment. In the preliminary phases of treatment it is most important that decisions about treatment alternatives (psychotherapy and/or drug therapy) be based on identifying more precisely the particular qualities and extent of the ego and self disturbances and other target symptoms that are ascertained. Although I have stressed certain ego and self disturbances in this chapter, it should be apparent that a whole range of psychiatric problems may contribute to or be a part of an alcohol problem, and specific treatment modalities should be tailored to the particular psychopathology or symptoms that may be identified. Of course allowances should also be made in the early phases of treatment, especially with psychotherapy, for cognitive impairments due to toxic aftereffects of prolonged drinking (usually reversible) that make integration of information and interpretations more difficult for the patient (Krystal 1962, Moore 1962, Rosett, unpublished).

## Implications for Psychotherapy

Critics of psychotherapy for alcoholism have focused on the impulsive, dependent, and demanding characteristics and lack of introspection of alcoholics, which make them ill suited for therapy, and others have stressed the destructive and unworkable regressive transferences that develop in psychotherapeutic relationships with alcoholics (Canter 1969, Hill and Blane 1967, Pattison 1972). These accounts give an unnecessarily pessimistic view of the alcoholic and do not consider how such reactions surface as a result of passivity on the part of the therapist and an outmoded model of therapy that emphasizes uncovering techniques alone. These approaches reflect once again the influences of an early instinct psychology that is based on the assumption that recovery and cure take place by making the unconscious conscious, reconstructing the past, and uncovering feelings. Other approaches have better taken into account the alcoholic's impairments and disturbances in identifying and tolerating painful feelings, and have a clearer appreciation of the nature of alcoholics' dependency needs and major problems around self-esteem. In contrast to early psychotherapeutic models, later approaches have appreciated the importance of structure, continuity, activity, and empathy in engaging and retaining alcoholics in treatment (Chafetz et al. 1962, Khantzian 1980, Krystal and Raskin 1970, Silber 1970, 1974).

For some, the initial work of therapy becomes that of gradually discovering and identifying states of anxiety and/or depression that have been relieved by drinking. For others, a gradual identification of the forms their dependency has taken, such as a denial of their needs or counterdependent attitudes, becomes important. In early phases of treatment there is a need for the therapist to be active, and to share openly his understanding of the alcoholic's problems, particularly how his use of alcohol has interacted with the particular ego and self disturbances that have been identified.

Some of the alcoholic's disturbances in identifying and experiencing his feelings and rigidly defending against affects have particular psychotherapeutic implications. Krystal (personal communication) has suggested that a "pre-therapy" phase of psychotherapy may be necessary with such patients to teach them about their feelings by helping them to identify and label them, particularly feelings of anxiety, fear, and depression. Krystal (1977) has also focused on alcoholics' use of splitting and other rigid defenses to wall off their ambivalent feelings. He has emphasized that effective therapy with such individuals hinges on helping them to master their fear of closeness with the therapist (related to reactivated childhood longings and feelings of aggression), to learn to grieve effectively, to take responsibility for their destructive feelings, and, perhaps most important, to overcome the barriers (i.e., rigid defenses) that prevent effective comforting of themselves. In my own work with alcoholics I have been impressed with how the affect disturbances significantly contribute to the self-care impairments of alcoholics and how necessary and useful it is to help such patients realize how feelings can be used as a guide for one's behavior and actions.

### Case 2

Psychotherapeutic interaction with a 51-year-old man who had a combined alcohol and drug problem nicely demonstrated elements of such affect disturbance, and how such disturbances may be psychotherapeutically managed and brought into the patient's awareness. This patient also gave dramatic evidence of impairments in self-care and some of the more extreme and primitive defenses that are adopted in the absence of self-care, namely, denial, counterphobia, and massive repression.

This man had achieved a significant amount of success in his life and his work despite an early childhood in which he suffered much traumatic neglect as a result of his mother's alcoholism and father's chronic depression and absorption with his wife's alcoholism.

Subsequent to the patient's 11-year-old son's contracting a severe illness, the patient had recently become more withdrawn, depending increasingly on alcohol and drugs himself, and he had been mandated for treatment as a result of indiscriminate behavior at work because of his drug-alcohol use. The two most outstanding features of this man, not unrelated to each other, were (1) the direction his interests took starting in early adolescence, and (2) his almost total inability to talk about his feelings. Starting at around age 10 he precociously and actively became sexually involved with the opposite sex. Early in his teenage years he turned to and became involved with hobbies that he has continued up until the present, which have definite danger and/or violence associated with them. Except for his quick wit (sometimes biting) he displays very little emotion, usually appearing indifferent or apathetic in his facial expressions. Attempts to elicit or draw out feelings are met with either frank denial or, at best, tentative acknowledgment that he might be feeling something.

During one group therapy session the patient reviewed some of his recent indiscretions in his work situation that resulted in possibly jeopardizing his job. He went into great detail about the events, which could have resulted in harm to himself and others. He appeared to be strikingly devoid of feelings as he elaborated on his behavior. A group member immediately exclaimed, "Didn't you realize how vulnerable you were leaving yourself?" The patient insisted that he never gave the situation a thought and denied being fearful about dangerous consequences for himself or others. Other members of the group persisted in inferring an unconscious self-destructive motive. I chose to comment on the patient's insistence that he had neither thought about the danger nor experienced any fear in relation to his behavior. I shared with him and the group my sense of his reluctance and inability to "fuss" over himself or to admit to any worry or fear. I suggested that this difficulty was perhaps a reflection of insufficient "fussing" over him earlier in his life when his parents were too tied up with themselves and their own problems.

As the group meeting continued, a curious and revealing exchange developed between myself and the patient in which he gave further evidence of his deficiencies in signal affects (i.e., feelings in the service of mobilizing mechanisms of defense and/or restraint over impulses). This exchange also demonstrated the necessity for the therapist to be ready to use his/her own feelings and reactions with such patients as an object lesson in helping them to use feelings to better serve and care for themselves. The patient commented on and inquired about my seemingly gruff response in a recent individual psycho-

therapy hour when he had corrected me on some technicality. I hesitantly acknowledged that he might have been correct in his impression, and I indicated that I knew this was a trait of mine when I am
worried and I believed it reflected my worrying about his problem. I
subsequently offered that I was worrying for him when he was not
sufficiently worrying about himself.

He next disclosed to the group and myself how at times in our individual sessions he often deliberately "eyeballed" me and stared me
down and that he was surprised that I repeatedly looked away, and
again he asked why I reacted in that way. I was surprised again and
somewhat caught off guard (perhaps I should not have been) that a
man who was so unaware of his own reactions could be so finely tuned
to my reactions. Pausing for a moment to get over my surprise, I answered him by acknowledging once again that he was most likely correct in his observation and that my reaction was probably a function
of some self-consciousness as a result of his staring at me. I told him
that I thought his puzzlement and surprise were some indication that
he was unable to admit to any such part of himself, but that if he could
continue to watch for other people's self-consciousness, especially in
group therapy, he might better develop this in himself to his own
benefit. I emphasized how my self-consciousness and others' can actually act as a guide and that being insufficiently self-conscious caused
him to get into trouble. Toward the end of the group meeting he began mildly to taunt one of the patients on the number of cups of coffee he drank during the group meeting. Piecing this together with his
uncharacteristic confrontations about my behavior, I interpreted his
provocativeness to be a function of having overexposed himself and
his behavioral difficulties early in the meeting. I pointed out that it
was to his credit that he was courageous enough to share his problems with the group, but that I was also equally concerned that he
might have overexposed himself; I told him that someone else might
not have been as open and as explicit, leading to so much exposure,
but that in his case he was not sufficiently self-conscious to protect
himself from overexposure.

## Duration and Goals of Psychotherapy

Decisions about the duration and goals of psychotherapy with alcoholics should remain flexible and should be based on a consideration

of the patient's wishes and a judgment by the therapist, weighing the indications and necessity for continued treatment against the hazards and risks. Many patients feel great relief and appreciation when they are able to control their drinking and know that someone who understands and accepts their problems is available. Such patients often decide for themselves that this is enough of a goal. If the patient is out of immediate danger, I often agree to stop, albeit my decision at times might be based as much on my clinical judgments about the patient as simply on what the patient wants to do, or even based more on my judgment. The following case illustrates how clinical judgments to stop treatment and what the patient wants are not mutually exclusive.

## Case 3

This patient, a 42-year-old, very intense and conscientious man, gave me good reasons pragmatically and clinically to take him seriously when he proposed that it was best to settle for the initial gains we had made and to discontinue his individual psychotherapy with me after a brief intervention that lasted about three months.

His initial meeting with me was prompted by a crisis that had been precipitated in his second marriage as a result of continued recurrent, alcoholic binges. He had recently remarried, entered into a new small business venture, and relocated to the East Coast—all in an attempt to build a new life. He was originally from an extremely wealthy Midwestern family. After attending an exclusive college and doing a tour of duty as a jet pilot in the military, he joined his family's large corporate business. From his late college years and through the military he was a heavy social drinker. Upon joining the family business and over the subsequent ten years, his drinking became increasingly heavy, which ultimately led to a decline and deterioration in his social standing, his marriage, and his job.

By the time he came for his first interview he had rejoined Alcoholics Anonymous (he belonged once before) and was having some success in abstaining from alcohol. In the first visit with me he reviewed how success, ambition, and achievement had always been tremendously important. He went back and forth from examining my professional certificates on the wall, to discussing his father's great business success (despite being an extremely heavy drinker himself), to his own lack of achievement and his alcoholic decline. He then went on to express in a most poignant way how there had been a lifelong strained relationship of aloofness and distance between his father and himself and how he had always longed for a better relationship. In this and subsequent interviews it was quickly evident that his longings for a closer relationship with his father coexisted with feelings of just as much bitterness and hatred. Strikingly, and in contrast, during the same initial interview he reviewed with me some of his work in Alcoholics Anonymous and how it was helping him. He said the people there were "real—and seeking alternatives to destructiveness." He stressed how they were able to get into the issues of alcohol, and that the feelings of "warmness, camaraderie, and family" were very important to him. At the end of the first hour we agreed that there was a "cauldron of issues bubbling inside" with which he struggled, but that for a while we would focus on his marital problems and he would continue to work on his sobriety through Alcoholics Anonymous. He agreed to join a couples group in which a common denominator was that the wife of one of the spouses in each couple had been affected by drug or alcohol dependence. He also agreed to see me for individual psychotherapy.

Over the next several months his ambivalence toward me became evident. On the one hand he admired my achievements and how I seemed to be able to understand him. On the other hand he regularly made it clear that psychiatrists understood little about alcoholism or alcoholics. In his first interview with me he said, "My [previous] psychiatrist never even asked about the alcohol—he gave me medicine saying it might help to deal with some of the underlying feelings so that I wouldn't have to use alcohol—and that when we got to the root of the problem, then maybe I wouldn't need to drink. I liked him, but I don't think he understood anything about alcohol." In subsequent visits he either would totally accept my clarifications and interpretations or just as arbitrarily would argue a point based on "strict principles" and a conviction that AA could serve him better, adding, furthermore, that it didn't cost anything.

After two months of individual and couples group meetings he became more clear and explicit about the reasons for his reluctance to continue in individual and group psychotherapy. He worried that his dependency on me and my ideas might be too consuming emotionally and financially (despite relatively unlimited financial backing from his family). References to competitive situations and stories where someone or an animal was killed or hurt only thinly masked concerns about his relationship with me. In one group meeting someone asked him about his tendency to avoid people with whom he identified. He responded that he tended to become anxious and then resort to "impulsive and compulsive behavior." About six weeks into the treatment (in association with a drinking setback) he sent a letter to me stating he would not see me anymore, indicating he did "not want to go back into the 'cauldron of issues' anymore." With one phone call from me he agreed to return, but he persisted in his ambivalence about continuing in individual psychotherapy. I told him I respected his wishes, and we met a few more times. In one of his final regularly scheduled meetings he once again spoke with concern about his tendency to adopt and depend on others wholesale, but said that he wanted and intended to continue group because he could "sample" other people's ideas and thoughts with "a little more protection." In this hour he made a reference to "symbiotic relationships" and commented on some stories about the Pharaoh and the "tooth scraper," and a crocodile who had a bird picking his teeth.

Considering that his drinking was under control, that he had by then joined several AA groups in which he felt comfortable, and the help obtained from the couples group, I decided that he had gained enough personal support and control over his drinking to stop his individual meetings. He also asked if he might periodically see me should he feel the need (which he has since done). I felt that the limited goals and involvement of obtaining support, clarification, and sobriety for this man were sufficient and outweighed the risks that were possible, given the intensity of his ambivalence toward me.

## Discussion

As this case demonstrates, the risks of ongoing psychotherapy with certain alcoholics outweigh the advantages that might be achieved, and limited goals of clarification and support are preferable. However, in many other cases disabilities and problems surface for which psychoanalytic psychotherapy should be considered, and in fact might be the treatment of choice. Many patients continue to evidence considerable impairment and vulnerability, and the constant threat of reversion to alcohol and other forms of impulsivity remains apparent. In still other instances, despite considerable stability and improvement, the patient and the therapist begin to sense and identify the persistence of subtle indications that things are not right: dissatisfactions in relationships or feelings of loneliness, isolation, and unhappiness emerge; or vague feelings of tension, anxiety, and depression continue; or self-defeating personality characteristics continue to plague a person, and related complaints and conflicts previously masked by the alcohol and associated acting out become more apparent. Qualities and characteristics often emerge in the treatment relationship that are symptomatic of ego and self impairments and become the basis for judgments about continued, long-term treatment.

In some cases more definitive long-term analysis/treatment of the determinants of the ego and self disturbances is not only possible but indicated. In my experience there is no basis to conclude categorically that a person with an alcohol problem lacks the requisite ego strength and capacity for an alliance to do such psychotherapeutic work. In such cases it is important for the therapist to combine elements of empathy and ego analysis to help patients gain an understanding of their dilemmas, as the following case illustrates.

### Case 4

Taking such an approach with a 29-year-old resident internist was particularly useful. Worried that he might be prone to alcoholism, he described a drinking pattern that involved regular, daily consumption of moderate to heavy amounts of beer interspersed with periodic episodes of extremely heavy drinking at various social get-togethers in which he might become amnesic for part of or all the episode.

The developments over the course of a particular treatment hour demonstrated how empathy with the patient's embarrassment and shame over his need to be appreciated, reassured, and understood led to a better elucidation and understanding of certain ego traits (cynicism and suspiciousness) and the uneven and self-defeating ways in which he satisfied his dependency including his use of alcohol. At the beginning of the hour he mentioned that he had to present a problem case to a senior attending physician at grand rounds. With a certain degree of detachment he observed that it would be interesting to see what the attending physician had to say on the case. He quickly became aware of and commented on his own "cynicism" and then conceded that the attending physician might also feel under pressure to do a good job. He wondered out loud some more as to the meaning of his cynicism. He speculated that it had to do with feeling "on the outside" and trying to get "in" himself. In an aside he complained of feeling "hung over" from the previous evening, when he had drunk a considerable amount of beer. He then joked about a new symptom of bruxism and lightly reviewed in the same vein how he frequently washed his hands, drank a lot, and "twiddled" his fingers. At this point I observed that he began to be self-conscious and wonder about his own cynicism and then to make light of his symptoms at the point where he indicated his more sympathetic appreciation that both the attending physician and myself might feel pressure to do a good job. He quickly agreed, and volunteered that he was quick to disbelieve the intentions of people. He gave the example of people in medicine professing a motive of wanting to help when he suspected the motive of wanting money and prestige. He went on to say that he became defensive when a consultant such as the attending physician "delivers on what I implicitly ask for—want." He also indicated he felt the same with me when I delivered on what he wanted. Among the forms his "defensiveness" might take he listed cynicism, humor, and a "carping anger." He reflected that he might be self-defeating, for example with the attending physician at grand rounds, and he might become obsequious, and he then questioned whether there might be a parallel pattern with me. I gently confirmed that such alternating patterns had occurred with me.

After a slight pause he began quietly to review how he thought a lot went into his reactions. He said, "Part of me wants to make repair of the things that are bad; part of me wants to exaggerate and make too much or the most of things. Somewhere in here there is a part of me that emerges that I don't know very well—it reminds me of how I recently told you I didn't know what my father thought of me. I still wonder how people see me."

He then began to address himself more directly to me. "Although you don't see me in action, I think you know me pretty well and have a pretty fair idea of how I interact with people. But I don't know how you see me—so I wonder what I am." His mood shifted abruptly and with a hint of embarrassment and some more evident impatience with himself he protested, "This is getting too complicated for this hour of the morning." I told him that I thought he was talking about something important but that he became uncomfortable when he approached a part of himself that he wanted me to know and understand better; he had become embarrassed as he did so, as was evident when he tried to dismiss his thoughts by commenting on the hour of the morning. He then associated to wanting to have children but returned to his embarrassment reaction and the wishes behind such reactions that I had been "able to pick up." He said, "You will think, how self-centered of me." I responded that he not only was embarrassed, but even more, he was ashamed of his wishes toward me. I suggested that he was experiencing in a small way with me the ways he got stuck in his life with his defensiveness, wherein he went from one extreme to the other, not allowing himself anything he wanted or indulging himself too much. He quickly interjected that drinking was his main "self-indulgence" and then chastised himself, saying twice, "God, I wish I didn't drink!" He promptly qualified this, reassuring me and himself he had been doing better. He then just as promptly castigated himself for reassuring himself. I ended the hour by pointing out that he berated and put himself down for reassuring himself. I said that reassuring himself was important and that if he could not allow that kind of indulgence for himself, it was understandable how he could continue to resort to more extreme, self-defeating indulgences.

## Discussion

This case demonstrates how certain patients adopt exaggerated postures of indifference and self-sufficiency to defend against their dependent longings and needs. Empathically focusing on the patient's discomfort, shame, and embarrassment reactions allowed the therapist to analyze with the patient how he repeatedly and characteristically denied and avoided his wish for recognition and approbation. Taking such an approach also makes extreme and alternating patterns of self-indulgence and denial more understandable, and thus more controllable—patterns that are otherwise driven, repetitious, and self-defeating. Such reactions suggest the operation of narcissistic resistances analogous to neurotic transference resistances, and represent opportunities for the patient and therapist to understand together, in the treatment relationship, the nature and origins of core conflicts around need satisfaction and dependency problems.

Many of the defenses and reactive patterns of alcoholics, including those of the patient just reviewed, resemble aspects and features of borderline and narcissistic conditions described by Kohut and Kernberg. Although they differ in their theoretical understanding and clinical application of these problems, they have both implicated such processes in drug and alcohol problems, and certain of their observations and approaches to such patients seem worth considering. In my opinion it is not clear whether borderline and narcissistic conditions share in common with alcoholics processes that are similar though not necessarily the same, or whether borderline and narcissistic pathology is at the root of alcoholism. However, the emphasis on treatment of the deficits and pathology in ego and self structures is a promising and hopeful development for alcoholism treatment. I also believe we are still in a discovery phase of understanding narcissistic pathology in general, and how such pathology and its treatment applies in cases of alcoholism.

## Implications for Psychopharmacological Treatment

The use of psychotropic drugs has a legitimate place among the treatment alternatives for alcohol problems and alcoholism. However, the literature on the efficacy of psychotropic agents in the treatment of alcoholism is for the most part confusing and discouraging. Part of the problem in drawing conclusions from these reports is that few if any of the studies are comparable. First, standard criteria for diagnosis of the alcoholism or the presumed underlying condition that is being treated are lacking. Another problem is that, depending on the study, different facets of the problem are studied to judge the usefulness of various psychopharmacological agents. In some reports relief of target symptoms such as sleeplessness, anorexia, and anergia is studied, in others whether abstinence is achieved, and in still others overall improvement of depression. Reviews by Mottin (1973), Viamontes (1972), and Greenblatt and Shader (1973) are generally pessimistic about all classes of psychopharmacological agents in the treatment of alcoholism. Mottin is most negative with regard to drug therapy. Viamontes' review reveals that the majority of uncontrolled clinical trials using antidepressants, phenothiazines, and benzodiazepines are effective in the treatment of alcoholism. Mottin, Viamontes, and Greenblatt and Shader uniformly emphasize the methodological problems of clinical trials with these drugs and cite the lack of double-blind controlled studies that might better establish the efficacy of these drugs.

Notwithstanding these methodological inconsistencies and short-comings, a number of carefully controlled and executed studies have proved to be promising and hopeful with regard to the use of drug therapy in alcoholism. Bliding (1973) demonstrated the benzodiazepine oxazepam to be more effective than chlorprothixene or placebo in the treatment of chronic alcoholism. Kissin and Gross (1968) showed chlordiazepoxide combined with imipramine to be effective in controlling drinking behavior and furthering overall improvement. In studies by Butterworth (1971) and Overall and colleagues (1973), the use of tricyclic antidepressants and to a lesser extent phenothiazines has proved effective in relieving symptoms of underlying depression (also anxiety in the Overall study). In another important study conducted by Quitkin and associates (1972), target symptoms of phobia and anxiety in a subsegment of alcoholics were dramatically relieved by imipramine with significant improvement of drinking behavior. Reports by Wren and associates (1974), Kline and colleagues (1974), and Merry and his collaborators (1976) suggest that lithium is effective in cases of alcoholism associated with depression. But more recent evidence (Dorus et al. 1989) fails to support the utility of lithium in depressed alcoholics.

What is to be made of these often confusing and contradictory findings? What should guide the practitioner in the decision to treat or not treat the alcoholic with these pharmacological agents? Do the findings of a dynamic approach that identifies structural impairments have any relevance to a descriptive approach that suggests such individuals might have pharmacologically treatable problems? Most if not all of the drug studies with alcoholics have been based on descriptive approaches in which target symptoms and psychopathology are identified. Nevertheless, I believe there is a basis for speculation that such target symptoms and psychopathology are the result of failures and deficits in ego and self structures, particularly those involving regulation of affects. I expect that these drugs work with alcoholics because they serve, support, and augment otherwise impaired ego capacities and disturbances in self-regulation.

The findings of descriptive psychiatry complement an approach aimed at identifying the ego and self disturbances in alcoholics. This is particularly so given recent trends in both descriptive psychiatry and psychoanalysis to state more explicitly the criteria for diagnosis and identify more precisely the nature of the psychopathology. Such approaches are consistently demonstrating the ubiquity of depression, phobia, anxiety, and panic states in association with alcoholism (Behar and Winokur 1979, Klein 1975, Quitkin et al. 1972, Weisman and Meyers 1980, Weisman et al. 1980, Winokur et al. 1970). There is evidence that these conditions are as treatable in alcoholics as they are in other patients and that they are contributory to the alcoholism (Behar and Winokur 1979, Klein 1975, Quitkin et al. 1972). Although the incidence of depression in alcoholism has ranged from 3 to 98 percent in different studies (Keeler et al. 1979), the application of precise diagnostic criteria for depression and phobic anxious states has produced more uniform results when attempts have been made to identify these conditions in alcoholics (Weisman et al. 1980). Moreover, when considered from a point of view taken by Klein (1975), where a more generic view of affective disturbance is considered, symptoms of dysphoria, anergia, anxiety, and depression become interacting, overlapping, and on a continuum, and seem more to be evidence of the "dysregulation of affects" and "disorders of activation" to which Klein refers.

In the first part of this chapter I explored how self-care disturbances and disturbances in affect regulation predisposed individuals to alcoholism. I speculated that in the absence of adequate self-care functions, the individuals' vague sense of vulnerability might contribute to phobias in alcoholics. I also suggested that because of developmental failures alcoholics either overregulated or underregulated their affects and depended on the effects of alcohol to release or submerge their "good and bad" feelings. In my estimation, many of the symptomatic features of alcoholics, including, for example, anxiety, depression, dysphoria, and sleeplessness, are indicators and the result of more fundamental and serious disturbances in the ego and self structures that are responsible for affect regulation and the achievement of subjective states of well-being, including the maintenance of self-esteem. These disturbances seriously incapacitate the alcoholic and are not easily or readily influenced by psychotherapeutic interventions alone, especially early in treatment. It is exactly in this respect that many alcoholics need assistance with the intolerable and overwhelming feeling states with which they suffer and why psychopharmacological agents might be considered useful if not necessary.

The common and prevalent distrust of alcoholics' suitability for drug therapy is unwarranted, in my opinion. Much of the controversy over drug use in alcoholism stems from a misunderstanding of the alcoholic's dependency problems. When considering psychopharmacological treatment of the alcoholic, it is understandable that we remain apprehensive about the "regressive-oral" needs and inclinations of the alcoholic. However, when we consider the structural impairments with which alcoholics suffer, the use of psychoactive drugs becomes a logical alternative that should be seriously considered. In my own experience, using predominantly tricyclic antidepressants and/or benzodiazepines (particularly oxazepam), I have very rarely had patients abuse or misuse these drugs. On the other hand, I have seen several alcoholic patients in consultation who had overused prescribed benzodiazepines, and it has been my clinical impression that this was more likely to occur when they were prescribed in lieu of a treatment relationship that considered and tried to understand all aspects of the physiological and psychological disturbances associated with alcohol problems.

For some the duration of need for these psychopharmacological agents is short, and for others the need continues for longer periods. For many others there is no need for medication at all. The timing, duration, and choice of these agents should be based on clinical observations and judgments about each patient as he or she gains or attempts to gain control over drinking. I believe the cases requiring no medication or only short-term use of medication are those in which the disturbances are less severe and/or the regression is more readily reversible. The more usual case in my experience involves situations where as control is gained over the drinking, depressive anxious syndromes, including phobias, surface, which are evident and are most often quite disabling. For some, the severity of these symptoms seems to be secondary and related to regressive states associated with protracted drinking, but the symptoms nevertheless respond to antidepressants and/or benzodiazepines. In my experience the decision as to which of the two drugs to use or whether to combine them should be based on clinical judgment as to the predominant symptomatology.

Perhaps Klein has properly elaborated on what one rationale might be for using these drugs in combination, namely that the phobic and panic states often involved with alcohol problems respond to imipramine, but the anticipatory anxiety associated with the phobic states is unresponsive to this drug. The anticipatory anxiety does, however, respond to antianxiety drugs, and therefore these drugs might be indicated in alcohol problems associated with phobic states. In many instances the disturbances I have outlined are severe, ubiquitous, and persistent. The buffering, supporting action of these drugs in helping to manage affects is needed, and the need for a longer and more indefinite period of drug therapy is indicated. In those instances where the patient was slow to abstain or curtail his/her drinking, where all other efforts on the part of myself, AA, the family, and others had failed, and where continued drinking threatened to be disastrous, I deliberately chose to initiate the use of antianxiety agents or antidepressants to help the patient contain and cope with painful affects of anxiety and/or depression. This is admittedly risky, and I have in such cases involved family members for supervision and dispensed only small amounts of the medication. Fortunately these instances are rare.

In summary, I would suggest that it is often the combination of psychotherapeutic and psychopharmacologic interventions, especially early in treatment, that is critical in helping alcoholics overcome their dependence on alcohol and assisting them with their enormous problems with self-care and affect regulation. In some instances the psychopharmacologic intervention may be time-limited and an adjunct to psychotherapy and other approaches, but in other instances it may be a definitive treatment for identified target symptoms and psychopathology.

## REFERENCES

Abraham, K. (1908). The psychological relation between sexuality and alcoholism. In *Selected Papers of Karl Abraham*, pp. 80–89. New York: Basic Books, 1960.

Balint, M. (1968). *The Basic Fault*. London: Tavistock.

Behar, D., and Winokur, G. (1979). Research in alcoholism and depression: a two way street under construction. In *Psychiatric Factors in Drug Abuse*, ed. R. W. Pickens and L. L. Heston, pp. 125–152. New York: Grune & Stratton.

Bliding, A. (1973). Efficacy of anti-anxiety drug therapy in alcoholic post intoxication symptoms: a double-blind study of chlorpromazine, oxazepam and placebo. *British Journal of Psychiatry* 122:465–468.

Blum, E. M. (1966). Psychoanalytic views on alcoholism. *Quarterly Journal of Studies on Alcohol* 27:259–299.

Blum, E. M., and Blum, R. H. (1967). *Alcoholism*. San Francisco: Jossey-Bass.

Butterworth, A. T. (1971). Depression associated with alcohol withdrawal in imipramine therapy compared with placebo. *Quarterly Journal of Studies on Alcohol* 32:343–348.

Canter, F. M. (1969). The future of psychotherapy with alcoholics. In *The Future of Psychotherapy*. Boston: Little, Brown.

Chafetz, P., Blane, H. T., Abram, H. S., et al. (1962). Establishing treatment relations with alcoholics. *Journal of Nervous and Mental Disease* 134:395–409.

Dorus, W., Ostrow, D. G., Anton, R., et al. (1989). Lithium treatment of depressed and nondepressed alcoholics. *Journal of the American Medical Association* 262:1646–1652.

Freud, S. (1905). Three essays on the theory of sexuality. *Standard Edition* 7:125–243.

Greenblatt, D. J., and Shader, R. I. (1973). *Benzodiazepines in Clinical Practice*. New York: Raven.

Hill, M., and Blane, H. T. (1967). Evaluation of psychotherapy with alcoholics: a critical review. *Journal of Studies on Alcoholism* 28:76–104.

Keeler, M. H., Taylor, I. C., and Miller, W. C. (1979). Are all recently detoxified alcoholics depressed? *American Journal of Psychiatry* 136:586–588.

Kernberg, O. F. (1975). *Borderline Conditions and Pathological Narcissism*. New York: Jason Aronson.

Khantzian, E. J. (1978). The ego, the self and opiate addiction: theoretical and treatment considerations. *International Review of Psycho-Analysis* 5:189–199.

——— (1979a). On the nature of the dependency and denial problems of alcoholics. *Journal of Geriatric Psychiatry* 11:191–202.

——— (1979b). Impulse problems in addiction: cause and effect relationships. In *Clinical Approaches to Impulsive Patients*, ed. H. Wishnie and J. N. Olesen, pp. 97–112. New York: Plenum.

——— (1980). The alcoholic patient: an overview and perspective. *American Journal of Psychotherapy* 34:4–19.

Khantzian, E. J., Mack, J. E., and Schatzberg, A. F. (1974). Heroin use as an attempt to cope: clinical observations. *American Journal of Psychiatry* 131:160–164.

Kissin, B., and Gross, M. M. (1968). Drug therapy in alcoholism. *American Journal of Psychiatry* 125:31–41.

Klein, D. F. (1975). Psychopharmacology and the borderline patient. In *Borderline States in Psychiatry*, ed. J. E. Mack, pp. 75–91. New York: Grune & Stratton.

Kline, N. S., Wren, J. C., Cooper, T. B., et al. (1974). Evaluation of lithium therapy in chronic and periodic alcoholism. *American Journal of Medical Science* 268:15–22.

Knight, R. P. (1937). The dynamics and treatment of chronic alcohol addiction. *Bulletin of the Menninger Clinic* 1:233–250.

Kohut, H. (1971). *The Analysis of the Self.* New York: International Universities Press.

——— (1977). Preface. In *Psychodynamics of Drug Dependence*, ed. J. D. Blaine and D. A. Julius. Research monograph 12, pp. vii–ix. Rockville, MD: National Institute on Drug Abuse.

Krystal, H. (1962). The problem of abstinence by the patient as a requisite for the psychotherapy of alcoholism. *Quarterly Journal on the Study of Alcohol* 23:112–122.

——— (1977). Self- and object-representation in alcoholism and other drug dependence: implications for therapy. In *Psychodynamics of Drug Dependence*, research monograph 12, pp. 88–100. Rockville, MD: National Institute on Drug Abuse.

Krystal, H., and Raskin, H. A. (1970). Drug Dependence. *Aspects of Ego Functions.* Detroit: Wayne State University Press.

Merry, J., Reynolds, C. M., Bailey, J., and Coppen, A. (1976). Prophylactic treatment of alcoholism by lithium carbonate. *Lancet* 2:481–482.

Moore, R. A. (1962). The problem of abstinence by the patient as a requisite for the psychotherapy of alcoholism. *Quarterly Journal of Studies on Alcohol* 23:105–111.

Mottin, J. L. (1973). Drug induced attenuation of alcohol consumption. *Quarterly Journal of Studies on Alcohol* 34:444–463.

Overall, J. E., Brown, D., Williams, J. D., et al. (1973). Drug treatment of anxiety and depression in detoxified alcoholic patients. *Archives of General Psychiatry* 29:218–221.

Pattison, E. M. (1972). Rehabilitation of the chronic alcoholic. In *The Biology of Alcoholism*, vol. 3, ed. B. Kissin and H. Begleiter, pp. 587–658. New York: Plenum.

Quitkin, F. M., Rifkin, A., Kaplan, J., and Klein, D. F. (1972). Phobic anxiety syndrome complicated by drug dependence and addiction. *Archives of General Psychiatry* 27:159–162.

Rado, S. (1933). The psychoanalysis of pharmacothymia. *Psychoanalytic Quarterly* 2:1–23.

Rosenfeld, H. A. (1965). The psychopathology of drug addiction and alcoholism: a critical review of the psychoanalytic literature. In *Psychotic States*, pp. 217–252. London: Hogarth.

Rosett, H. L. *Alcohol, brain physiology and ego function: implications for psychotherapy.* Unpublished.

Silber, A. (1970). An addendum to the technique of psychotherapy with alcoholics. *Journal of Nervous and Mental Disease* 150:423–437.

——— (1974). Rationale for the technique of psychotherapy with alcoholics. *International Journal of Psychoanalytic Psychotherapy* 28:47.

Simmel, E. (1948). Alcoholism and addiction. *Psychoanalytic Quarterly* 17:6–31.

Viamontes, J. A. (1972). Review of drug effectiveness in the treatment of alcoholism. *American Journal of Psychiatry* 128:1570–1571.

Weisman, M. M., and Meyers, J. K. (1980). Clinical depression in alcoholism. *American Journal of Psychiatry* 137:372–373.

Weisman, M. M., Meyers, J. K., and Harding, P. S. (1980). The prevalence rates and psychiatric heterogeneity of alcoholism in a United States urban community. *Quarterly Journal of Studies of Alcohol* 41:672–681.

Winokur, G., Reich, T. J., and Pitts, F. N. (1970). Alcoholism: III. diagnosis and familial psychiatric illness in 259 alcoholic probands. *Archives of General Psychiatry* 23:104–111.

Wren, J., Kline, N., and Cooper, T. (1974). Evaluation of lithium therapy in chronic alcoholism. *Clinical Medicine* 81:33–36.

Yorke, C. (1970). A critical review of some psychoanalytic literature on drug addiction. *British Journal of Medical Psychology* 43:141.

# 7

# Addiction: Self-Destruction or Self-Repair?[1]

The *JSAT* paper by Schiffer (1988) is a noteworthy contribution in a number of respects. First, it is a carefully thought out paper attempting to link treatment to theory. It is also unique in that it is grounded in psychodynamic theory, and the focus of the recommended psychotherapy is based on an understanding of that theory. Dr. Schiffer also benefits us with follow-up data, documenting significant improvement in status regarding drug use, mood, and overall adjustment. The pa-

---

1. This chapter was written in response to an article published in the *Journal of Substance Abuse Treatment (JSAT)* by F. Schiffer (1988) about the treatment of nine cocaine addicts in psychotherapy. It was a notable article in several respects, upon which I elaborate in the chapter.

per builds on existing theory and then moves beyond it to explain better some of the more maladaptive and self-destructive aspects of addictive involvements.

The author appreciates how addicts attempt to adaptively "self-medicate" painful affect states as a major motivation for drug dependence. However, he has also perceptively identified a "less obvious . . . self-destructive" (p. 135) mechanism in the addictive process. In his formulations he reinvokes pleasure and destructive motives, deriving from early instinct theory in psychoanalysis, in order to explain the maladaptive and self-defeating aspects of the cocaine dependence. I believe this emphasis is unwarranted and not as germane as his more novel application of the "repetition compulsion" to the addictions. I agree that there are many similarities between the dysphoria associated with the unwanted side effects of addictive drugs and their withdrawal or aftereffects and dysphoric states dating back to childhood in these patients. These patients attempt to achieve a sense of "safety and control," albeit misguided, through their repetitious use of drugs. However, rather than stressing, alone, the negative, self-destructive mechanism and motives such as denial, reaction formation, and turning against the self, I would also look to how addicts try to master dysphoria from the present and the past as a prime motivator of their repetitious drug-related behaviors.

As the author indicates, in my own formulation I have emphasized self-medication motives as a major factor to explain compulsive drug use. However, I, too, have found that this perspective alone does not adequately explain or deal with the just as obvious reality that our patients perpetuate their suffering as much as or more than they relieve it. It is heartening to see once again that the psychodynamic paradigm is heuristic and valid, given that, independent of each other, Dr. Schiffer and I have recently reached similar conclusions regarding the "repetition compulsion" and the suffering that addicts endure. In two publications (Khantzian 1987, Treece and Khantzian 1986) I introduced these themes as a modification of the self-medication hypothesis and then presented an expansion of these ideas in a paper entitled, "Substance Dependence, Repetition and the Nature of Addictive Suffering" at the May 1987 American Psychoanalytic Association meetings (Khantzian and Wilson 1993). In my own formulation, I have stressed less the self-punishing and destructive intrapsychic mechanisms proposed by Dr. Schiffer and, instead, have linked the sense of dysphoria to affect deficits and dysfunction related to very early life experiences for which unfortunately there are no symbols or memories (Gedo 1986). The unbearable features of affects for substance abusers are related to their specificity and intensity, but affects are unbearable because they are also vague, confusing, and undifferentiated. In either case, affects are threatening for addicts because they feel so out of control. The suffering of addicts is linked to attempts, then, to change the passive, nameless dysphoria, which they do not control, to an active dysphoria associated with drug effects, which they do control. The core dynamic then seems to be governed less by pleasurable or self-destructive motives than by the motive of turning passive suffering into active suffering, as much to master and overcome it as to punish oneself with it. Although these dynamics are preoedipal and indeed preverbal in origin, as Dr. Schiffer suggests, they may subsequently be elaborated on and attach themselves to oedipal dynamics and conflicts.

## REFERENCES

Gedo, J. (1986). *Conceptual Issues in Psychoanalysis: Essays in History and Method.* Hillsdale, NJ: Analytic Press.

Khantzian, E. J. (1987). A clinical perspective of the cause-consequence controversy in alcoholic and addictive suffering. *Journal of the American Academy of Psychoanalysis* 15:521–537.

Khantzian, E. J., and Wilson, A. (1993). Substance abuse, repetition and the nature of addictive suffering. In *Hierarchical Conceptions in Psychoanalysis*, ed. A. Wilson and J. E. Gedo, pp. 263–283. New York: Guilford.

Schiffer, F. (1988). Psychotherapy of nine successfully treated cocaine abusers: techniques and dynamics. *Journal of Substance Abuse Treatment* 5:131–137.

Treece, C., and Khantzian, E. J. (1986). Psychodynamic factors in the development of drug dependence. *Psychiatric Clinics of North America* 9:399–412.

# PART III

# The Self-Medication Hypothesis of Substance Use Disorders

## INTRODUCTION

This section contains a series of papers that highlights a core theme in my work, namely, that suffering or psychological pain is at the root of addictive vulnerability, and that individuals discover the pain-relieving properties of addictive substances. Spanning a quarter of a century, I have tried to articulate and expand on this theme, progressively refining my observations that each class of drugs of abuse has a predominant effect (i.e., pharmacological specificity), and that individuals discover what drug suits them best. Based on individuals' psychological organization or characterological makeup, they suffer with particular painful affect states, and they are drawn by the specific action of a drug that best ameliorates or relieves their suffering. This process has come to be referred to as the "self-medication hypothesis," and I suppose it has most commonly come to be associated with my name. As this section traces and reveals, however, a number of distinguished psychoanalysts, dating back to the late 1960s, have provided clinical observations and theoretical underpinnings that have contributed to this perspective. Although reductionistic in its own right, I have tried to clarify for nearly three decades that this point of view best gets at the human psychological vulnerabilities and roots of addictive suffering. As Chapter 8 indicates, it is only in the last third of the twentieth century that we have moved beyond other reductionistic theories such as "pleasure" motives, whether they originate from early psychoanalytic theory or from more contemporary cognitive-behavioral or conditioning theory, to account for the compelling appeal of addictive substances.

I wrote Chapter 8 in 1973, when I was completing my psychoanalytic training. It was intended as a critical review of the then existent theories of and treatments for opiate dependence. My main focus was on the specific appeal of opiates. In addition to the adaptive perspective influenced by my psychoanalytic training, I believe I was equally influenced by the exciting developments emerging in the field of psychopharmacology. Not the least of these developments was the then emerging new psychopharmacological agents and the change in terminology used to designate the psychoactive drugs we were employing in the practice of psychiatry. When I first started my residency in psychiatry in 1964, we still referred to medications for psychosis as "major tranquilizers," and medications for anxiety as "minor tranquilizers." Within a year of commencing my residency, we were instructed that this terminology would be abandoned, and we would designate the psychotropic medications by their specific action, thus the terminology "antipsychotic, antianxiety, and antidepressant medications."

It was this shift to thinking about the specific action of legitimate psychotropic medications, combined with an adaptational view of psychopathology, that stimulated my thinking about what the general and specific appeal might be of addictive drugs. This line of thinking was not activated (or could not be) until I realized and overcame my own initial subjective prejudices and doubts (i.e., countertransference) about opiate addicts as people to be feared and not trusted. In adopting a conventional clinical approach that focused on presenting symptoms and a developmental history/background, I was quickly able to appreciate the preeminently human basis of addictive vulnerability. Patients, with rare exceptions, responded to a nonjudgmental, understanding approach to their drug histories and life issues, and helped me to understand the meaning of their need for these powerful drugs. My detailed clinical observations of narcotics addicts' distress, appearance, and behaviors are presented in Chapter 8. The specific appeal of opiates is described, namely their powerful muting effect on feelings of rage and aggression. I touch on the developmental origins of their problems with rage and aggression as originating in family and social backgrounds that were violent, abusive, and harsh. Although I repeatedly come back to the theme of trauma and physical abuse in this book, I did not specifically elaborate on this important theme until the most recent articulation of the self-medication hypothesis (SMH) when I applied it to patients with co-occurring posttraumatic stress disorder (PTSD) and substance use disorders (SUDs). (See Chapter 15 and Chapter 26; I wrote the latter specifically for this volume.)

It is worth mentioning that, more so than I do in subsequent explanations of the SMH, in this early paper on opiate dependence I make more mention of "instinctual life," "sadomasochistic tendencies," and "aggressive drives," in part because during my psychoanalytic training and personal analysis, instinct and drive theory were still in vogue. It is fair to say that I was as impressionable as most young investigators, and I was quick to adopt as we often do the most popular and accepted conceptual tools. This is not too dissimilar to the current trend to adopt a narrow biological perspective to explain psychopathology in general and addictive disorders in particular. As is evident in subsequent chapters, the concepts and language of an ego-psychological (or structural) approach, and a focus on affects (and their interaction with ego structures) became much more central and persuasive for me in my trying to understand and explain my patients' struggles with drug dependency.

Starting with Chapter 9 on the self-selection of drugs, I began to move beyond the more narrow focus on opioid dependence and the aggressive drives that govern such a dependence. I became interested in the way a person is built (i.e., "psychological set" and "structural" factors), and how such factors predilect individuals for a particular drug. In a sense, it heralds my first definitive paper on the SMH (Khantzian 1985) that I would publish ten years later. In this 1975 version I felt the necessity to address not only the specific appeal of opiates, but the specific appeal of depressants and stimulants. In part, this was the result of a growing appreciation by myself and other practitioners that by the mid-1970s (beyond the so-called heroin epidemic), there was growing and widespread dependence on other addictive drugs. In this early version of the SMH, which was a concept not yet articulated in such terms, I categorize the appeal of stimulants, depressants (or sedative-hypnotics), and analgesic-opiates as "energizing," "releasing," and "controlling-stabilizing" drugs, respectively. In retrospect, this was as good a description of how each class of drugs has its special appeal as I could devise. Not without significance, the cocaine epidemic of the late 1970s and 1980s had not yet struck. Amphetamines were the most prevalent stimulant of abuse during this period and thus the representative stimulant that I refer to in these early papers; similarly, benzodiazepines had not yet surfaced as widely abused drugs and the representative depressants of abuse, aside from alcohol, were the barbiturate or barbiturate-like drugs (e.g., quaaludes).

Chapter 10, on the structural vulnerabilities of narcotics addicts and the specific appeal of opiates, represents for me a watershed publication. It grew out of an invitation to speak at and chair a session of a three-day conference convened by the distinguished neuroscientist Karl Vereby and the New York Academy of Sciences. The conference (and the publication that followed [Vereby 1982]) was entitled "Opioids in Mental Illness: Theories, Clinical Observations and Treatment Possibilities." In the course of eleven sections and nearly fifty presentations, there was an exhaustive review of the role and influence of external and internal (i.e., endorphins) opioids on mental life and psychiatric illness. Psychological, clinical-psychopharmacological, and neurochemical aspects of opioids were exhaustively reviewed. I was surprised and honored when I was asked to chair and speak in the main leadoff section (after a brief section on historical perspectives), the title of which was "Addiction and Psychological Disorders: The Self-Medication Hypothesis." As is evident in the beginning of Chapter 10, somewhat defensively I express trepidation about my audience's receptivity to a psychological-psychoanalytic perspective. I was not unaware that the foremost investigators and neuroscientists working in the addictions at the time were participating in the conference and/or were in attendance. I was surprised that I should be asked to give one of the main lead papers and that my work (and that of my fellow panelists, Leon Wurmser and Gerald McKenna) was being recognized for an important theoretical perspective and clinical aspect of opiate dependence. Frankly, it was this special honor and invitation that encouraged me to give voice to what would follow in 1985 as the "Self-Medication Hypothesis of Addictive Disorders," a special article that was featured in the *American Journal of Psychiatry* (Khantzian 1985) and appears in this volume as Chapter 11.

As is evident elsewhere in this volume, in chapters that address controversies and polemical arguments on the nature and origins of SUDs, this period of time for me was different and encouraging in that there was considerable respect for and receptivity to a point of view that was grounded in clinical work and guided by a psychoanalytic-psychodynamic perspective. As shown in Chapter 15, the most recent update of the SMH, this perspective has not been so readily accepted in certain quarters. Based on a neurobehavioral perspective and certain empirical studies, arguments are advanced that psychopathology, suffering, and behavioral disturbances are more likely a consequence than a cause of substance use disorders. As I argue, however, in Chapter 10, the in-depth, cross-sectional case study method is as valid and necessary an approach in studying problems such as the addictions as is the approach of the gross anatomist or the pathologist in explaining the structure and function of medical disorders and dysfunctions.

As I already indicated, "The Self-Medication Hypothesis of Addictive Disorders" published in 1985 (Chapter 11) has been widely cited, endorsed, and criticized, and has linked my name to an important if not controversial explanation or theory of addictive disorders. In this chapter I review the clinical observations and theoretical considerations of contemporary investigators of that period, and, combined with the clinical vignettes that I present in the chapter, I believe that there was (and is) a persuasive basis to argue that self-medication motives were compelling reasons for succumbing to a dependency on opiates and cocaine. It would appear that this hypothesis was either sufficiently convincing or repugnant that it was so widely endorsed or discredited over the subsequent decade. In subsequent chapters in this section I address what I believe are the legitimate criticisms and questions raised by the self-medication hypothesis. I also challenge some of the criticisms that I believe are based on misinterpretations of or a failure to understand the essentially important aspects of the hypothesis. As is evident in subsequent chapters, I adopt an overarching perspective of addictions as a "self-regulation" disorder to answer some of the criticisms. Furthermore, in Chapter 15 I apply the SMH to areas I had not previously considered as a basis to further support its utility and applicability for understanding excessive or addictive use of drugs and alcohol.

In Chapter 12, I revisit the problem of human emotional suffering as the basis of addictive illness. I raise the issue that even by the late 1980s few investigators or clinicians attributed drug/alcohol dependency to a need to reduce or control psychological pain and distress. I was invited to write this chapter by the section editor on clinical aspects of alcoholism, Dr. Edward Gottheil, an esteemed psychiatrist working in the addictions, for an annual publication, *Recent Developments in Alcoholism.* He was a great supporter of my work, and this chapter was one of several over a five-year period that he invited me to contribute to this annual publication. In this chapter I was asked, as the title indicates, to compare self-medication factors in alcoholism and other addictions. When I completed it I realized that I had more precisely articulated than previously the notion of addiction as a self-regulation disorder. Thus I placed self-medication factors in that context, and added "self-regulation" to the title, a theme that I further develop in the remaining chapters in this section. In this chapter, I briefly define early drive theory and describe the shift to structural (ego psychology) theory and how this shift meant that a modern perspective of human psychology rested less on the need for reduction (or satisfaction) of sexual (or pleasure) and aggressive drives than on a need for self-containment and self-regulation. This shift necessarily places a premium on comfort, connection, and safety. I delineate the obvious implications that follow in this shift in theory for understanding the addictions. This shift suggests we better understand ourselves and our patients (especially our addicted patients) not so much seeking pleasure as seeking comfort, contact, and a sense of well-being.

As I have already indicated, in Chapter 13, "Self-Regulation Factors in Cocaine Dependence," I further elaborate on addiction as a self-regulation disorder. In this case, I review in more detail the nature of cocaine dependence and how self-regulation and self-medication factors pertain. I also pursue in more detail how characterological style and defenses disguise and at the same time reveal the cocaine addict's underlying vulnerabilities. Again, this chapter was written by invitation in the late 1980s, to be presented at a technical review conference sponsored by the Division of Epidemiology at the National Institute on Drug Abuse. The papers presented at this conference were subsequently published as research monograph 110, *The Epidemiology of Cocaine Use and Abuse* (Schober and Schade 1991). Frankly, I was surprised that I was invited to speak on self-medication factors in cocaine dependence because most of the invitees were epidemiologists or empirically oriented investigators, and I was essentially the sole clinical investigator in attendance. As the title suggests, my main focus here was on cocaine dependence where I elaborate on how self-regulation factors involving difficulties with affects, self-esteem, relationships, and self-care come into play. As I indicate, my perspective, by which I have stubbornly persisted, is a clinical one. This was to forewarn my fellow conferees, I must admit somewhat defensively, about where I was coming from. Early in this chapter I expand on the nature of the data, namely, the clinical-treatment relationship, and how, albeit with an *n* of 1 at a time, it is an invaluable basis for understanding addictive vulnerability. I was further surprised, and pleased, that by the end of the conference my co-participants were more than respectful and receptive to my approach and formulations. Privately, I was satisfied that the inferences I could make about etiological factors in cocaine dependence, based on a clinical approach, were as illuminating as empirical approaches in which the findings were based on samples of hundreds if not thousands of subjects.

In the remaining two chapters in this section I expand on self-regulation vulnerabilities (Chapter 14) and on the self-medication hypothesis (Chapter 15). In this latter chapter I explore in more detail questions raised by and criticism leveled at the self-medication hypothesis. I also suggest that recent areas of application (e.g., nicotine dependence, negative symptoms in schizophrenia, and PTSD) lend further support to the utility and explanatory value of the SMH. Although there is repetition and overlap in these last two chapters with the other chapters in this section, in looking back I am also reassured that there is a progression and refinement in the ideas. The reader can benefit from a selected reading of these chapters on self-medication and self-regulation factors in substance use disorders. However, by reading the chapters in sequence, the reader can form a deeper appreciation, as I know I have, of the development of the clinical perspective and the "practice theory" advanced in this section.

## REFERENCES

Khantzian, E. J. (1985). The self-medication hypothesis of addictive disorders. *American Journal of Psychiatry* 142:1259–1264.

Schober, S., and Schade, C. (1991). *The Epidemiology of Cocaine Use and Abuse*. Research monograph 110. Rockville, MD: National Institute of Drug Abuse.

Vereby, K., ed. (1982). *Opioids in Mental Illness. Theories, Clinical Observations, and Treatment Possibilities*, vol. 398. New York: Annals of the New York Academy of Sciences.

# 8

# Opiate Addiction: Theory and Treatment[1]

With the exception of recent applications of conditioning theory to the problem of drug abuse (Dole 1972, Goldstein 1972, Wikler 1968, 1971), there is little in the psychiatric or psychoanalytic literature that relates theory to treatment approaches. This is most surprising when at least two new treatment approaches have recently obtained wide acceptance, namely the self-help groups or therapeutic communities and methadone maintenance. Although proponents of the methadone maintenance approach have succeeded in better documenting their treatment results, it is probably now safe to say that both treatment approaches are having moderately to fairly successful results in treat-

---

1. This chapter won the Felix and Helen Deutsch Prize, Boston Psychoanalytic Society and Institute, June 1973.

ing and rehabilitating the individuals who remain in these treatment programs (Glasscote et al. 1972). Taking another approach, Vaillant (1966) reported rather dramatic recovery rates in a group of criminal addicts who were imprisoned for at least nine months and were released under supervised parole. These recent developments in treatment approaches have created a new challenge to psychiatry and psychoanalysis to better understand the narcotics addict.

The self-help approaches are admittedly pragmatic; they stress problems with socialization and advance no particular theory to explain addiction or their treatment results (Cherkas 1965, Deissler 1970). The metabolic imbalance theory advanced by Dole and colleagues (1966), and efforts by Dole (1972), Goldstein (1972), Wikler (1968, 1971), and others to apply conditioning theory to explain opiate addiction, though parsimonious and heuristically useful, offer little help in understanding the many other complex psychological factors in addiction. The situation is not much better when one turns to the theoretical discussions in the psychiatric and psychoanalytic literature for an explanation of opiate addiction. Despite the newer treatment approaches and the existent theories of addiction, it is the author's contention that there is little in our theory or practice that offers an adequate understanding of narcotics addicts.

This chapter presents a critical assessment of prevailing theories, and relates some of this theory to our current treatment approaches. Emphasis is placed on psychodynamic factors in trying to understand and treat addicts, with a particular emphasis on problems that addicts have with aggression. On the basis of my clinical experience and observation, I show how a significant number of individuals become addicted to opiates because they learn that the drug helps them to cope by relieving dysphoric states associated with rage and aggression and by counteracting the disorganizing influences of unmitigated aggression on the ego.

Although the review is not a comprehensive one, it is representative. The interested reader is referred to papers by Rosenfeld (1965) and Yorke (1970) for a more detailed review of the psychoanalytic literature on narcotics addiction.

## THEORIES OF ADDICTION

Most of the theoretical discussions on the nature of addiction revolve around the issue of the symbolic and dynamic versus the pharmacogenic action of the drugs. Some investigators minimize the pharmacological action of narcotic drugs and maximize psychodynamic factors, while others underestimate individual psychodynamics and psychopathology and view addiction as a chemical phenomenon caused by physical dependence produced by narcotic drugs. In this section, some representative theoretical views of these various positions are presented.

Freud (1905) and Abraham (1908) stressed the importance of libidinal, particularly oral erotic, factors in addiction. Abraham, in his excellent description of the specific effects of alcohol on the removal of repression, commented on a similar effect of morphine. He linked the use of both drugs to sexuality and advanced the notion that they play a part in overcoming inhibitions, homosexual and heterosexual, especially in men. In these early discussions little distinction was made between the differences among various addicting drugs. Rado (1933) in his early communications minimized the differences between such drugs as alcohol, morphine, and cocaine. He argued that the problem of addiction "begins with the recognition of the fact that not the toxic agent, but the impulse to use it, makes an addict of a given individual" (p. 2). In a later paper (Rado 1957), he shifted in his emphasis and acknowledged that although there are common characteristics among various addicting drugs, there is a need for a special theory for each drug or group.

Although in most of his writings on addiction Rado acknowledged the underlying depression and the pain-removing action of narcotics, it is curious that he tended to stress the pleasurable aspects of taking drugs as the main etiological factor in addiction. He argued that the addict once introduced to narcotics continues to seek a "super-pleasure" due to a "corruption" by narcotics of the individual's normal "enlightened hedonic control." He presented no clinical data to support his conclusion. He likened this state of affairs to the sense of omnipotence of the child. No mention was made by Rado of the part aggression plays in narcotics addiction despite his observations about the relationship between aggression and depression in his classic paper on depression (1928). His undue emphasis on "hedonic control and super-pleasure" to account for the compelling nature of narcotic addiction detracts from his main contribution, which is an appreciation of the underlying depression.

In contrast to the earlier psychoanalytic emphasis on the libidinal and erotic aspects of addiction, Glover (1956) focuses primarily on the aggression and sadism that he believes to be central in the problem of addiction. He also de-emphasizes the difference in action of various addicting drugs, stating "that the pharmacotoxic effects of drugs" (p. 204) are not very specific. According to Glover it is the body part or substance that the drugs symbolize that is important, and by projecting his conflicts onto the drugs he defends against a regression to a more psychotic state.

Diagnostically, Glover believes the addictions represent a fixation to a transitional system between a more primitive "paranoid-schizoid" state and the more advanced obsessional neuroses. The defensive function that is served "is to control sadistic charges, which, though less violent than those associated with paranoia, are more severe than the sadistic charges met with in obsessional formations" (p. 202). Glover views the addict's obsessional involvement with his drugs, and his related unconscious homosexual fantasy systems, as a progressive (as opposed to regressive) and successful defense against paranoid-sadistic tendencies and psychosis. His formulations overall are rich and thought provoking. However, in the author's opinion, he places excessive emphasis on the force and power of the drug's symbolic meaning to the addict, and he makes little distinction between the addicting substances and their pharmacological action.

Wikler (1952) emphasizes the problems addicts have in obtaining satisfactions of their "primary needs." In another paper he and Rasor (1953) contend that neurotics take narcotics to relieve anxiety ("negative euphoria!"), as opposed to the psychopath who seeks the euphoria produced by narcotics. How this distinction is made and what the clinical evidence is to support it is not clear. They fail to emphasize enough their own observations that narcotics have a stabilizing effect on behavior by influencing anxieties related to aggression and sexuality. Rather like Rado and earlier analysts, they focus too narrowly on the pleasure- and satisfaction-producing effects of narcotics.

Formulations by Fenichel (1945), Savit (1954, 1963), and Wieder and Kaplan (1969) emphasize the relief of tension and distress as a motive for taking drugs. Both Savit and Wieder and Kaplan invoke similar mechanisms to explain the relief of psychic pain through the use of drugs, namely by inducing pleasurable regressive states. Wieder and Kaplan refer to a "narcissistic blissful state." Savit goes back one step, giving reductive thinking a new and heroic twist, by speculating that the intravenous use of drugs represents an attempt by the addict to obtain a more primitive state of fusion and regression by achieving a parasitic fetal relationship via the umbilicus (the "vascular channel").

Considering sociocultural variables in relation to addiction, Wikler (1952) and Westermeyer (1971) contrast the effects of opiates and alcohol and of different patterns of use and abuse in Occidental and Oriental cultures. Whereas opium results in reduction and control of drives, alcohol has the opposite effect of implementing and facilitating the expression of internal states. Wikler and Westermeyer both advance the argument that it is not accidental that alcohol is abused more in Western cultures in which the release and expression of aggression is not only more acceptable and valued but is actually encouraged. This is in contrast to Eastern cultures, where placidity and reduced aggression are valued and correspondingly there is a greater consumption and abuse of opium. These assertions and generalizations impressionistically seem correct, but to the author's knowledge there are little or no scientific data to support them.

Chein and colleagues (1964) have ambitiously attempted to account for the sociological, economic, and personality variables involved in the addiction to narcotics. Relevant to this discussion is the material they present on the personality characteristics and psychopathology of the adolescent addicts they studied. Their main thesis is that narcotics addiction is the result of long-lasting severe personality disturbance and maladjustment. They present a rich description of the addict's ego and superego pathology and his many problems with his narcissism and sexual identification. They stress addicts' limited ability to engage their environment in sustained and constructive ways and their general inability to weigh the consequences of obvious destructive or careless behavior. Most interestingly, they state very clearly that addiction is "adaptive and functional"; that is, narcotic drugs are used to help a person get along with himself and the outside world. However, they then go on to give only one example in which narcotics are used in this way, namely, situations in which the drug is taken to dampen anxiety and thereby facilitate sexual performance. Their observations are rich and extensive, but, in the author's opinion, they fall short of substantiating their original thesis that addiction is adaptive. They present an inverse of the usual addictive personality rubric by typifying what an addict is not. They also seem to place undue emphasis on a "nirvana-like" (p. 232) pleasure associated with heroin.

Two papers presented at the Fourth National Methadone Conference in San Francisco (Khantzian 1972, Wurmser 1972) independently of each other came to similar conclusion regarding how narcotics are used adaptively by addicts and how methadone is more effective in controlling addiction because of its greater length of action. Both authors stressed the use of narcotics as a means to counteract the disorganizing influences of rage and aggression, affects with which addicts have particular difficulty. They both view craving as a desire for relief from threatening and dysphoric feelings associated with unmitigated aggression.

On the basis of their work with addicts using controlled amounts of morphine and methadone to try and control patients' addictions, and their subsequent development of the methadone maintenance approach, Dole and colleagues (1966) and Nyswander (1971) concluded that the underlying basis of narcotic addiction is a problem in neurochemical-metabolic imbalance. Accordingly, Dole considers addiction to be a metabolic rather than a psychological disease and thereby justifies the use of methadone maintenance as a means to counteract the neurochemical disorder. In reviewing the physical basis of drug dependence and relapse, Dole (1972) concedes that factors of classical and operant conditioning contribute to problems of narcotic addiction and relapse. However, he still maintains that underlying metabolic disturbances are causal and that the psychological factors play a minimal role.

Wikler (1968, 1971), Schuster (1970), Lindesmith (1965), and others have carefully demonstrated and documented that conditioning factors play a significant role in the development and sustaining of an addiction to opiates. Most of these investigators stress that opiates act as powerful positive reinforcements, in two different ways, to induce and sustain an addiction. First, the self-administration of opiates quickly eliminates the abstinence syndrome once physical dependence is established. Second, the opiate experience is its own reward and causes the addict to repeatedly seek out the pleasurable experience. Along these lines, Goldstein (1972) has proposed that methadone works because it raises the tolerance threshold to the euphorogenic effect of heroin, thereby eliminating the positive reinforcement that results from the "powerfully pleasurable effects" (p. 291) of heroin use. He invokes theories of operant and classical conditioning advanced by Wikler to support his formulations. He boldly asserts that the action of methadone is "purely pharmacologic" (p. 295). He discounts psycho-pathological factors as predisposing to addiction and cites laboratory work with monkeys and rats who self-addict themselves to support his arguments. Undoubtedly conditioning factors are present in nar-cotics addiction, particularly in relation to the problems of physical dependence and the ability of opiates to quickly relieve the symptoms of the abstinence syndrome. However, I believe that it is unwarranted to conclude that laboratory·animals addict themselves because of the euphorogenic actions of ópiates. It is just as reasonable to infer that the animal prefers opiates because of its ability to relieve stress in-duced by laboratory conditions and handling, situations for which the animal is ill equipped instinctively.

Although I differ with some of the inferences drawn from the work of the conditioning theorists cited above, their carefully designed and documented experimental work offers a most useful model to under-stand and influence some of the behavioral aspects of addiction and relapse. I believe, the approaches encompassed by conditioning theory and dynamic psychiatry, along with the physiological aspects of ad-diction, complement one another, and an appreciation of all of these approaches is essential for an adequate understanding of addiction.

## DISCUSSION

The powerful pain-relieving action of opiates is by now well appreci-ated and indisputable. That opiates also relieve other forms of emo-tional suffering is appreciated almost as well. Rado and subsequent investigators, as indicated above, were aware of the relief of tension and distress as reasons for taking drugs. Chein and colleagues (1964) referred to opiates as effective "tranquilizing or ataractic drugs" (p. 228). They, plus Jaffe (1970) in his excellent description of the physi-ological and clinical aspects of narcotic analgesics, seem to have con-sidered some of the specific psychopharmacological and psychotropic properties of opiates. Despite these considerations, it remains impres-sive and puzzling the degree to which the pleasurable aspects of nar-cotics continue to be stressed to explain the compelling feature of opiate addiction. Though the experience of relief of emotional pain and dysphoria obtained through opiate use lends itself equally well to a reinforcement model of drug-seeking behavior, the conditioning theo-rists still stress the pleasurable experience associated with heroin as the main motive for drug taking. Similarly, the focus on the pleasure principle in opiate use is evident in recent and past works by dynamically oriented psychiatrists and psychoanalysts who stress the pleasurable regressive states induced by drugs.

Glover's contributions are important in that he seemed to more adequately understand the defensive and adaptive role that drugs play in the addict's life. Though he failed to appreciate adequately the different action of various addictive drugs, he did seem to appreciate how the sexual and pleasurable aspects of drugs were used defensively against the enormous difficulties that addicted individuals have with aggression. His notion that drugs could be used progressively (as opposed to regressively) to defend against regression to psychotic states is in direct opposition to the still prevalent emphasis on the regressive, pleasurable use of drugs. Consistent with this point of view is the thesis advanced by Wieder and Kaplan, and similarly proposed elsewhere by the author and Wurmser, that drug habituation and addiction represent a process of self-selection in relation to different drugs. Chein and colleagues (1964) have noted how narcotics can help an individual function sexually by dampening anxiety. Khantzian (1972) and Wurmser (1972) have formulated how narcotics specifically attenuate rage and aggression and thereby reverse regressive states.

More specifically, observations of narcotics addicts treated with methadone maintenance have led the author to hypothesize that a significant portion of these individuals becomes addicted to opiates because they discover that the drug acts specifically to reverse regressive states by attenuating, and making more bearable, dysphoric feelings involving aggression, rage, and related depression. The evidence for this is derived from at least four sources: (1) observations of six patients in individual psychotherapy; (2) careful drug and psychiatric histories obtained from 20 patients seeking treatment for opiate addiction; (3) observations of over 200 different addicts coming to the intake group, and other groups, of a drug abuse program over a two-year period; and (4) follow-up evaluations and observations of patients stabilized on methadone maintenance. Repeatedly I observed histories of physical violence, accidents, and physical trauma dating back to childhood among a large percentage of our patients. I was surprised to discover how many patients spontaneously reported physical beatings by cruel, sadistic, and impulsive parents. Similarly, these same patients gave histories of impulsive and delinquent behavior in school, and much antisocial and violent behavior that predated their addictions. In a number of instances, this kind of behavior appeared to be precipitated by major losses and disappointments. In the course of responding to a carefully taken drug history, patients gave ample descriptions of dysphoric states of bodily tensions and restlessness, anger, rage, violent feelings, and depression that were relieved by heroin and other opiates. With an almost monotonous regularity, the patients said they felt "relaxed," "mellow," and "calming," and emphasized a total body response, to describe the effects of opiates when they first began to use such drugs.

Observations of patients in groups, particularly at the time of intake, offered the chance to watch some of these problems played out in the patients' group interactions. Unmitigated angry verbal attacks on each other were not uncommon and in a few instances led to physical attack. The regular use of obscenities, especially with references to genital, fecal, and anal elements, had a definite assaultive quality. Frustrations and attempts to gather information in group meetings led to paranoid outbursts and massive projections with a marked tendency to turn these attacks on the group leader.

In contrast, as patients became stabilized on methadone, I was repeatedly impressed, both in group and one-to-one situations, by significant behavioral and psychological shifts. The patients' aggressive, motoric restlessness disappeared or was more subdued. The patients on methadone maintenance were quieter in their interactions, showing much less lability, angry projections, and paranoia. Many demonstrated and reported a greater capacity for sustained constructive behavior in program activities and outside work. With some exceptions, I generally observed shifts away from regressed states toward less regressed states, from lability toward stability, from egocentricity toward a more concerned interest in others. Conversely, as patients were gradually withdrawn from methadone (for various reasons, but mostly at the patient's request), there was a reemergence of previously observed patterns of aggressive-impulsive outbursts, projections, paranoia, and psychotic patterns of thinking and behavior in a significant percentage of the patients. Wurmser (1972) has described a similar pattern of a reemergence of "rage, hurt, shame, and narcissistic decompensation" (p. 526) as methadone was withdrawn in a group of patients in intensive psychotherapy.

In contrast to the short-acting opiates such as morphine and heroin, where the constant apprehension and anxiety of withdrawal is ever present, methadone maintenance is effective in controlling addiction because it is slowly metabolized and long acting when taken orally. Because of its longer action, it not only relieves emotional pain and distress, but its sustained activity prevents the stress and frustration of frequent withdrawal and thereby lessens the likelihood of regressive reactions. At the same time, like other narcotics, methadone has a specific psychotropic action that attenuates rage and aggression, counteracting the disorganizing influences of these powerful affects on ego functions.

The explanation as to why some patients fail to respond to methadone maintenance is in need of further clarification. It is the subject matter of ongoing clinical investigation and future reports. Briefly, I believe these variations in response to methadone are related to problems of narcissism associated with developmental failures and regressed states. It is my preliminary impression that an important part of how one responds to methadone maintenance is related to the capacity that an individual has to relinquish his narcissistic orientation to life and to discover other satisfactions and healthier modes of adaptation in the real world of people, work, and play.

On the basis of these more recent preliminary observations and formulations there is clearly a need to study much more carefully how narcotic drugs or similar substances are essential and used adaptively by certain individuals in dealing with their instinctual life and their environment. This failure to consider adequately that the psychopharmacological action of narcotics helps with coping and adaptation may explain in part why results with conventional psychotherapeutic approaches have been so uniformly poor. In the author's experience psychotherapists tend to concern themselves prematurely with the maladaptive aspects of drugs when they first engage the patient rather than first trying to understand why the addict so desperately feels he needs his drug.

In attempting to account for the help and relief that some addicts obtain in the self-help approaches, certain features are significant. First, the importance of removing the addict from the street, where relief from distress in the form of heroin is readily available, cannot be underestimated. Second, the early and continuing emphasis on work and the rigorous expectation that all work assignments be carefully executed play an important part in establishing and reinforcing self-regulation and control as well as more healthy attitudes toward work. Also in this regard, forced work and some of the more humiliating tasks and activities to which the addict is subjected are effective because these exercises are in part successful manipulations of the addict's sadomasochistic tendencies. What is probably underestimated by the proponents of such an approach is how they merely play into the addicts' sadomasochism and thereby offer little toward producing permanent change. To the extent that this is not appreciated, there exists the constant danger that the treatment becomes just a symptom of the illness.

How effective the encounter groups have been in these programs in producing permanent change and growth is not clear. Many such groups are run by skilled group therapists, and in these instances such group experiences provide opportunities for significant insight and growth. In other groups, confrontation seems to be the only kind of intervention or interaction and, therefore, they are of questionable therapeutic value. It does appear that the encounter approach often succeeds in breaking down the massive denial and sense of entitlement that is present in many addicts. In these instances some of the temporary dramatic improvements in behavior are more likely based on compliance and thus account for much of the reversion in behavior when the addict leaves this setting. Another nonspecific source of temporary relief in these groups is probably obtained from the sanctioned ventilation of the addict's rage and aggression in a controlled setting.

One of my main criticisms centers around this last-mentioned aspect of the self-help group, namely, the expression and fostering of rage and aggression. Many of these encounter approaches grossly underestimate many addicts limited capacity to deal with intense affect, particularly aggressive feelings. Advocates of these approaches counter by saying that avoidance of such feelings in oneself and others is a copout. Unless patients are carefully selected for such a confrontation, there is the danger that such an approach could lead to further narcissistic injury and sense of failure in people who too often in their lifetime have suffered rejection and failure. Many of these programs also fail to appreciate the dangers of prematurely forcing people to give up their defenses with the result that temporary compliance occurs or, worse, psychotic decompensations are precipitated.

Many programs, including self-help and medical-psychiatric approaches, stress the importance of motivation in treating addicts, and in some programs it is of the highest priority or the most important factor in considering suitability for treatment. This seems remarkable when it is so apparent to even the most untrained observer that much of the addict's life is built on avoidance. Furthermore, most clinicians recognize that motivation is only one consideration in evaluating a patient's suitability for treatment, and often in clinical situations motivation is a luxury hard to come by, whereas treatment may be crucial (that is, for homicidal, suicidal, and psychotic patients). In these instances the responsible clinician is not deterred from trying to gain an alliance and to work with his patient. Vaillant's (1966) findings in instances in which treatment and follow-up were imposed are highly suggestive. Where there are massive gaps in ego and superego functioning, motivation as a prime consideration for treatment seems hardly .relevant. Limit setting is a common practice for borderline patients and those with acting-out character disorders on most psychiatric wards. Often, imposing treatment on an individual is the only way his avoidance can be influenced and thus make possible controls and mastery over ego defects, mood problems, and difficulties in managing affect.

The author is not unaware that little attention has been paid in this discussion to social, economic, and racial problems, factors that are frequently invoked to etiologically account for addiction to opiates. Having touched least upon this aspect of addiction, some final brief comments are included here that I believe are consistent with what has been presented up to this point. The increased use of narcotics in the 1960s paralleled a troubling period of social upheaval, an unpopular war, violence, and a climate of revolution and protest against society and its institutions, and conceivably accounts for some of the increased use of narcotics by young people from middle-class backgrounds. The case of addiction among blacks is well known and perhaps better understood. The lifelong oppression and resultant developmental ego impairments and rage, as well as their limited opportunities to obtain satisfaction in society, must certainly account for part of the black addict's tendency to use narcotics. Antisocial individuals who have a high incidence of narcotic use discover that they become more stable and function better with these drugs (Wikler and Rasor 1953); their difficulties with impulse control, particularly aggression, are probably related to their attraction to narcotics. It is likely that wherever and in whomever there is oppression, developmental impairments, psychic turmoil, rage, and depression, there is correspondingly a ready-made market for narcotic drugs. More specifically, it is postulated that these conditions and situations attract the use of narcotics because they all share in common problems with aggression and the narcotic acts successfully by attenuating and making the aggression more bearable.

## SUMMARY

With the exception of conditioning theory, there is surprisingly little in the psychiatric or psychoanalytic literature that relates theory to current treatment approaches of narcotics addiction. Most theories have appreciated the anxiety- and tension-relieving action of opiates, but there still seems to be a surprising emphasis on the pleasurable aspects of opiate use to explain the compelling nature of narcotic addiction. My own experience has convinced me that problems with aggression predispose persons to becoming addicted to opiates and the problems play a central part. Individuals who become dependent on opiates learn that the drug helps them to cope by relieving dysphoric states associated with rage and aggression. I believe this occurs by the opiate's direct muting action on these powerful affects. In addition to the fact that methadone is more effective in controlling addiction because it is long acting, part of the success of methadone maintenance is related to the specific antiaggression action of methadone. In considering all treatment approaches, I feel it is particularly important to consider the central part aggression plays in opiate addiction, and to appreciate the influences of this emotion and drive on the addict and in our clinical decisions about treatment choice.

## REFERENCES

Abraham, K. (1908). The psychological relation between sexuality and alcoholism. In *Selected Papers of Karl Abraham* pp. 80–89. New York : Basic Books, 1960.

Chein, I., Gerard, D. L., Lee, R. S., and Rosenfeld, E. (1964). *The Road to H.* New York: Basic Books

Cherkas, M. S. (1965). Synanon Foundation—a radical approach to the problem of addiction. *American Journal of Psychiatry* 121:1065–1068.

Deissler, K. J. (1970). Synanon—its concepts and methods. *Drug Dependence, NIMH* Issue 5.

Dole, V. P. (1972). Narcotic addiction, physical dependence and relapse. *New England Journal of Medicine* 286:988–992.

Dole, V. P., Nyswander, M. E., and Kreek, M. J. (1966). Narcotic blockade. *Archives of Internal Medicine* 118:304–309.

Fenichel, O. (1945). *The Psychoanalytic Theory of Neurosis*. New York: Norton.

Freud, S. (1905). Three essays on the theory of sexuality. *Standard Edition* 7:121–145.

Glasscote, R. M., Sussex, J. N., Jaffe, J. H., et al. (1972). *The Treatment of Drug Abuse*. Washington, DC: Joint Information Service.

Glover, E. (1956). On the etiology of drug addiction. In *On the Early Development of Mind*, pp. 187–215. New York: International Universities Press.

Goldstein, A. (1972). Heroin addiction and the role of methadone in its treatment. *Archives of General Psychiatry* 26:291–297.

Jaffe, J. (1970). Drug addiction and drug abuse. In *The Pharmacologic Basis of Therapeutics*, ed. L. S. Goodman and A. Gillman. London: Macmillan.

Khantzian, E. J. (1972). A preliminary dynamic formulation of the psychopharmacologic action of methadone. In *Proceedings of the Fourth National Conference on Methadone Treatment*, pp. 371–374. New York: National Association for Prevention of Addictions to Narcotics.

Lindesmith, A. R. (1965). Problems in social psychology of addiction. In *Narcotics*, ed. D. M. Wilner and G. G. Kassebaum. New York: McGraw-Hill.

Nyswander, M. E. (1971). Methadone therapy for heroin addiction. *Drug Therapy* 1:23–31.

Rado, S. (1928). The problem of melancholia. *International Journal of Psychoanalysis* 9:420–438.

——— (1933). The psychoanalysis of pharmacothymia. *Psychoanalytic Quarterly* 2:1–23.

——— (1957). Narcotic bondage. A general theory of the dependence on narcotic drugs. *American Journal of Psychiatry* 114:165-171.

Rosenfeld, H. A. (1965). The psychopathology of drug addiction and alcoholism: a critical review of the psychoanalytic literature. In *Psychotic States*, pp. 217–252. London: Hogarth.

Savit, R. A. (1954). Extramural psychoanalytic treatment of a case of narcotic addiction. *Journal of the American Psychoanalytic Association* 2:494–502.

—— (1963). Psychoanalytic studies on addiction: ego structure in narcotic addiction. *Psychoanalytic Quarterly* 32:43–57.

Schuster, C. R. (1970). Psychological approaches to opiate dependence and self-administration by laboratory animals. *Federal Proceedings* 29:2.

Vaillant, G. E. (1966). Twelve-year follow-up of New York narcotic addicts: III. Some social and psychiatric characteristics. *Archives of General Psychiatry* 15:599.

Westermeyer, J. (1971). Use of alcohol and opium by the Mao Laos. *American Journal of Psychiatry* 127:1019.

Wieder, H., and Kaplan, E. H. (1969). Drug use in adolescence: psychodynamic meaning and pharmacogenic effect. *Psychoanalytic Study of the Child* 24:399–431. New York: International Universities Press.

Wikler, A. A. (1952). Psychodynamic study of a patient during experimental self-regulated re-addiction to morphine. *Psychiatric Quarterly* 26:270–293.

—— (1968). Interaction of physical dependence and classical and operant conditioning in the genesis of relapse. *Research Publications—Association for Research in Nervous and Mental Disease* 46:280.

—— (1971). Some implications of conditioning theory for problems of drug abuse. *Behavioral Science* 16:92–97.

Wikler, A. A., and Rasor, R. W. (1953). Psychiatric aspects of drug addiction. *American Journal of Medicine* 14:566–570.

Wurmser, L. (1972). Methadone and the craving for narcotics: observations of patients on methadone maintenance in psychotherapy. In *Proceedings of the Fourth National Conference on Methadone Treatment*, San Francisco, pp. 525–528. New York: National Association for the Prevention of Addictions to Narcotics.

Yorke, C. (1970). A critical review of some psychoanalytic literature on drug addiction. *British Journal of Medical Psychology* 43:141–159.

# 9

# Self-Selection and Progression in Drug Dependence

Many explanations have been advanced for why individuals become involved with drugs: they are "pleasure seekers"—their friends do it, so they do it; or "They are medicating themselves"; or it is "Suicide on the installment plan." If one turns to the scientific literature, one can find parallel sophisticated and technical elaborations on these themes. Early psychoanalytic formulations minimized the differences among various drugs (e.g., morphine, alcohol, cocaine, and depressants) and tended to emphasize the erotic, pleasurable aspects of drug-taking (Abraham 1908, Freud 1905, Rado 1933). Many of these and subsequent formulations stressed a regressive form of pleasure, the individual attempting to induce a regressive pleasurable state similar to an earlier phase of his development.

Although later formulations took into account the relief of tension and distress as a motive for taking drugs (Fenichel 1945, Rado 1957, Wikler and Rasor 1953), surprisingly there has continued to be an impressive emphasis placed on the pleasurable aspects of drug use to explain the compelling nature of drug dependence (Goldstein 1972, Savit 1954, Wikler 1968, 1971).

Glover (1932), an exception to these trends, was one of the earlier psychoanalytic investigators who stressed the "progressive [and] protective use of drugs" (p. 189). He believed that the addict's involvement with drugs was akin to an obsessive involvement that protected the individual from more regressive, paranoid-sadistic tendencies and psychoses. Glover minimized the psychopharmacological action of different drugs and emphasized their symbolic meaning to the addict.

Much emphasis has been placed on peer group pressures and the attitudes of the surrounding community as major etiological influences in drug dependence. It is contended here that although peer group influences play a role, it is not a major role. Probably more important are attitudes in the surrounding community that drug use and dependence are deviant. Zinberg (1974, 1975, Zinberg and Robertson 1972) has focused on the important part that the setting, including society's attitudes toward the addict as deviant, plays in determining the users' response to drugs. He maintains that the setting in good part accounts for the withdrawal from society and the regression that become so apparent in drug-dependent individuals. He believes that only a small fraction of people dependent on drugs use them as a function of personality or in response to painful affects.

Our own work (Khantzian et al. 1974) and that of others has picked up on Glover's emphasis on the adaptive use of drugs, while incorporating a better appreciation of the psychopharmacological action of the different drugs. Chein and colleagues (1964) affirmed that narcotic addiction was "adaptive and functional" (p. 227) and referred to opiates as effective "tranquilizing or ataractic drugs" (p. 238). Works by others, emphasizing the use of drugs in the service of drive and affect defense, represent further specific elaborations on a point of view that considers the use of drugs as a way of coping with one's internal and external environment (Khantzian 1974, Krystal and Raskin 1970, and Wurmser 1972).

These more recent formulations have tried to take into account how the specific action of the drug interacts with internal psychological states and reactions. This chapter elaborates and focuses upon how the personality organization and reactive patterns of an individual (hereafter referred to as the psychologic set) interact with various types of drugs upon which individuals become dependent in their attempts to cope. We focus on the drug–set interaction from a psychoanalytic viewpoint in which dynamic (i.e., forces), economic (i.e., energy), structural, and adaptive factors are stressed.

## DRUG–SET INTERACTION AND SELF-SELECTION

People who have become involved with and dependent on drugs have frequently experimented with a wide variety and have become dependent on more than just one type. However, we and others have been impressed with the fact that many of these individuals self-select and seem to have a predilection for a particular drug (Khantzian 1974, Krystal and Raskin 1970, Wieder and Kaplan 1969, Wurmser 1972). This self-selection is related to the fact that the various drugs have distinctive psychoactive actions. In the course of experimenting with different drugs, an individual discovers that the action of one drug over another is preferred. This discussion explores how this preference results and is a function of the individual's discovering that a particular drug relieves internal dysphoric and distressful states and/or leads to improved functioning.

### Energizing Drugs

The main drugs in this category are the amphetamines and cocaine. Although the two drugs are different in their onset of action and metabolism, their energizing properties are well known. From our knowledge of catecholamine metabolism we know that both drugs produce a relative increase in the availability of norepinephrine at key neuroreceptor sites in the central nervous system, which in part accounts for the mood elevation or so-called high with the use of these drugs (Schildkraut 1965). Prior to the widespread use of these substances in the drug subculture of the late 1960s and early 1970s, many individuals had discovered the stimulating properties of amphetamines in the course of studying for exams or using diet pills to lose weight.

It has been our experience that these drugs are effective and take on a compelling quality for many users because they help to overcome the depletion and fatigue states associated with depression. Wieder and Kaplan (1969) observed that the use of amphetamines leads to increased feelings of assertiveness, self-esteem, and frustration tolerance. Wurmser (1972) believes that the use of amphetamines helps to eliminate feelings of boredom and emptiness by producing a sense of mastering aggression, control, invincibility, and omnipotence by overcoming depression.

These reports seem to share in common and take into account the psychic and physical energy problems that are so commonly observed in depression and chronic depressive states. Conversely, but in support of the self-selection hypothesis, we have also been impressed with the fact that certain individuals have an aversion to amphetamines because they discover that in contrast to many depressive individuals, their hyperanxious and/or hyperaggressive tendencies are heightened and made worse by amphetamines. In the case of depression, much more energy is expended in the service of denial, guilt, and shame, with the result that the short-term energizing effects of the amphetamines and cocaine give a sense of relief by overcoming painful feelings of helplessness and passivity.

### Releasing Drugs

Fenichel (1945) has referred to the quotation (source unknown), "The superego is that part of the mind that is soluble in alcohol" (p. 379). This characterization could be applied equally well to the barbiturate and related sedative-hypnotic drugs, and effectively captures the basis for their appeal. Both alcohol and barbiturates in light to moderate doses have the effect of releasing the individual from his inhibitions. This in part is a function of a release of higher, regulatory centers, particularly in the frontal lobes (as demonstrated by the electroencephalogram), and has been referred to by some as a reversible "chemical lobotomy." Smith and Wesson (1974) have used the term *disinhibition euphoria* to describe the action and effect of barbiturates.

Alcohol and sedative drugs seem to exert their influence in individuals by relieving internal distressful states associated with anxiety and conflicts. Although often the anxiety and conflict in drug-dependent individuals seems to be related to a classic neurotic constellation of inhibitions and defense in opposition to unacceptable impulses, it is probably more often the case that the anxiety and conflict are related to rigid (ego) defenses against more primitive and narcissistic longings. Krystal and Raskin (1970) have traced the problems in the object relations of many drug-dependent individuals to early phases of development where parental and environmental failures required the individual to rigidly wall off their self and object representation. They stress the enormous difficulties that the drug-dependent individual has with ambivalence and how he must deny and rigidly repress his aggression and need for love and forgiveness. They stress the aspect of the drug action, particularly with alcohol and short-acting barbiturates, that allows for brief and therefore tolerable fusion in the rigidly split-off self and object representations. That is, the person has an enormous stake in splitting off the "good" and "bad" parts (e.g., feelings, attitudes, ideas) of himself and others. This splitting is in the service of avoiding the ambivalence, which is found by these individuals to be so intolerable. The use of such drugs are therefore less in the service of producing a "high" or euphoria than in the service of relief from dysphoria related to rigid and unstable defenses against painful affects and drives.

## Controlling-Stabilizing Drugs

In our own work with narcotics addicts we have been particularly impressed with the muting and stabilizing action of narcotics. Previous formulations have stressed either the euphorogenic-pleasurable effect of narcotics or their ability to relieve a range of distressful or unpleasant affects as an explanation for the powerful tendency to induce and sustain an addiction. Although these formulations have merit, we have been more impressed with the specific muting action on the individual's rage and aggressive drives.

In previous reports, based on evaluation and treatment of over 200 addicts, we stressed developmental impairments and deficiencies in the egos of the narcotic addicts with whom we had worked (Khantzian 1974). These deficiencies were reflected in outbursts of rage, poor impulse control, and a general sense of dysphoria as a result of the threat they felt to themselves and others because of their violent feelings and impulses. We were repeatedly impressed with the addicts' subjective reports of their initial experience with opiates in which they discovered the immediate calming and stabilizing action of the drug. We describe in more detail the muting and containing action of opiates in

Chapters 4, 8, and 11. On the basis of these findings we hypothesized that individuals were predisposed and became addicted to opiates because they discovered the stabilizing action of these drugs on their egos. The drugs acted specifically (short-term) to reverse regressive states by attenuating and making more bearable painful drives and affects involving aggression, rage, and related depression.

## IMPLICATIONS FOR TREATMENT

Although our main thesis in this chapter has been to stress the predilection and self-selection for certain drugs by different individuals, we have been equally impressed in our work with the tendency for addictions to progress and continue once an individual has heavily used a particular drug.

As we have already indicated, drugs of dependence can exert a powerful influence on various ego states and can induce alterations in functioning and in levels of distress that are more or less adaptive. However, in repeatedly resorting to a drug to obtain a desired state, the individual becomes less and less apt to come upon other human responses and solutions in coping with his internal life and the external world around him. It is in this respect that an addiction takes on a life of its own. Consequently, there is an ever-increasing tendency for regression and withdrawal, which, as Zinberg (1975) has noted, is further compounded by society's inclination to consider such behavior as deviant and unacceptable. The regressed and withdrawn individual discovers that in the absence of other adaptive mechanisms, the distressing aspects of his condition can be relieved only by either increasing the use of his preferred drug or switching to other drugs to overcome the painful and disabling side effects of the original drug of dependence.

In short, the tragedy of drug dependence resides in the fact that heavy drug usage precludes the development of more ordinary human solutions to life problems. This is particularly true of adolescence, when high anxiety levels and tensions are the necessary ingredients for change, growth, and development. The emergence of drug and alcohol problems is notorious during this phase of life and personal development. Life's developmental challenges and crises extend beyond adolescence. The more a person short-circuits and relieves his troubling emotions by resorting to drugs, the less he is apt to discover his own potential and capacities, and the more apt he is to perpetuate and progress in his dependence on chemical solutions in overcoming and muting his difficulties.

## SUMMARY

This chapter has focused on and emphasized the forces at work within individuals that cause them to seize upon the action of various drugs because they have been unable or unwilling to develop alternative ways to cope with dysphoric internal states. We have stressed that different psychological sets predispose different individuals to a particular drug. We believe this emphasis is justified because we feel that the compelling nature of drug dependence cannot be sufficiently explained by simplistic formulations that stress the pleasurable aspects of drug use, peer group pressures, or societal problems and attitudes, to the exclusion of in-depth psychological considerations.

## REFERENCES

Abraham, K. (1908). The psychological relation between sexuality and alcoholism. In *Selected Papers of Karl Abraham*, pp. 80–89. New York: Basic Books, 1960.

Chein, I., Gerard, D. L., Lee, R. S., and Rosenfeld, E. (1964). *The Road to H*. New York: Basic Books.

Fenichel, O. (1945). *The Psychoanalytic Theory of Neurosis*. New York: Norton.

Freud, S. (1905). Three essays on the theory of sexuality. *Standard Edition* 7:125–245.

Glover, E. (1932). On the etiology of drug addiction. In *On the Early Development of Mind*. New York: International Universities Press, 1956.

Goldstein, A. (1972). Heroin addiction and the role of methadone in its treatment. *Archives of General Psychiatry* 26:291.

Khantzian, E. J. (1974). Opiate addiction: a critique of theory and some implications for treatment. *American Journal of Psychotherapy* 28:59–70.

Khantzian, E. J., Mack, J., and Schatzberg, A. F. (1974). Heroin use as an attempt to cope: clinical observations. *American Journal of Psychiatry* 131:160–164.

Krystal, H., and Raskin, H. A. (1970). *Drug Dependence. Aspects of Ego Functions*. Detroit: Wayne State University Press.

Rado, S. (1933). The psychoanalysis of pharmacothymia. *Psychoanalytic Quarterly* 2:1–23.

—— (1957). Narcotic bondage. A general theory of the dependence on narcotic drugs. *American Journal of Psychiatry* 114:165–171.

Savit, R. A. (1954). Extramural psychoanalytic treatment of a case of narcotic addiction. *Journal of the American Psychoanalytic Association* 2:494–502.

Schildkraut, J. J. (1965). The catecholamine hypothesis of addictive disorders. *American Journal of Psychiatry* 122:509–522.

Smith, D. E., and Wesson, D. R. (1974). *Diagnosis and Treatment of Adverse Reactions to Sedative-Hypnotics.* Washington, DC: National Institute on Drug Abuse.

Wieder, H., and Kaplan, E. H. (1969). Drug use in adolescence: psychodynamic meaning and pharmacogenic effect. *Psychoanalytic Study of the Child* 24:399–431. New York: International Universities Press.

Wikler, A. (1968). Interaction of physical dependence and classical and operant conditioning in the genesis of relapse. *Research Publications—Association for Research in Nervous and Mental Disease* 46:280.

—— (1971). Some implications of conditioning theory for problems of drug abuse. *Behavioral Science* 16:92–97.

Wikler, A. A., and Rasor, R. W. (1953). Psychiatric aspects of drug addiction. *American Journal of Medicine* 14:566–570.

Wurmser, L. (1972). Methadone and the craving for narcotics: observations of patients on methadone maintenance in psychotherapy. In *Proceedings of the Fourth National Conference on Methadone Treatment*, San Francisco, pp. 525–528. New York: National Association for the Prevention of Addictions to Narcotics.

Zinberg, N. E. (1974). High states, a beginning study. *Drug Abuse Council*, September.

—— (1975). Addiction and ego function. *Psychoanalytic Study of the Child* 30:567–588. New Haven, CT: Yale University Press.

Zinberg, N. E., and Robertson, J. A. (1972). *Drugs and the Public.* New York: Simon & Schuster.

# 10

# Psychological (Structural) Vulnerabilities and the Specific Appeal of Narcotics

The study of human dependence on opiates offers an opportunity to understand important, if not basic, aspects of mental life, emotional pain, and mental illness. The addictions are a place where the biology and psychology of the mind meet. It is a place that promises to resolve some of the mysterious manners in which the body and the mind affect each other, and to unravel better the "mysterious leap from the mind to the body" (Deutsch 1959) with which psychoanalysts and clinicians have concerned themselves for a long time. The discoveries of the opiate receptors and endogenous opioid peptides have prompted us to consider how the brain and the mind produce their own analgesia for biochemical modulation of physical pain and to consider as well how such processes might also be involved in the modulation and regulation of emotional distress and human psychological suffering.

This chapter is based on my understanding of opiate dependence as a clinician and as a psychoanalyst.[1] However, before embarking on such a task, I experience a certain sense of uneasiness and trepidation in my approach, given that the promising discoveries of opiate receptors and peptides have been based on very sophisticated technical methods of investigation. These discoveries have been the result of a fast-growing, complex technology that has allowed researchers a more concrete, precise means to examine microscopically, molecularly, and quantitatively how the brain and mind function. In contrast, the approach of a clinician and psychoanalyst involves less precise, more abstract techniques and methods of investigation that attempt to understand and explain the problems of opiate dependence in its human, experimental contexts, usually by studying single individuals in great detail and in depth, one at a time. Such an approach utilizes macroscopic constructs concerned with structures, functions, and qualities of the mind and mental life. The two approaches need not compete, and more likely they are complementary, although the focus of their respective interests and observations at times seems far apart.

Having expressed a concern at the outset that sounds apologetic, I set it aside and proceed by assuring myself, and I hope my audience, that my approach is a valid and useful one. It is an approach that needs no apology any more than the pathologist apologizes for the validity and usefulness of autopsies, instead of the electron microscope, in understanding pathology and dysfunction.

From a psychoanalytic perspective, opiate dependence may be approached and considered in terms of human processes involving affects, drives, and behaviors, and the mental apparatus or structures responsible for the regulation of these processes. Addicts become dependent on drugs because they have had general and specific difficulties in regulating their affects, drives, and behaviors. There are different reasons why people use drugs and why a certain individual chooses or prefers a particular drug. Based on a representative clinical example, this chapter discusses the nature of the psychological/

---

1. Psychoanalysis is a method of treatment for emotional problems as well as a method of understanding and explaining mental life and human behavior. Unless otherwise specified, it is applied here in the latter sense as a method of investigation.

structural vulnerabilities that make opiates so appealing to narcotic addicts.

## ARNOLD—A CASE HISTORY [2]

Arnold is a 29-year-old white heroin addict from a wealthy family background. He sought psychotherapy after starting on an outpatient methadone maintenance program. At the time of his evaluation he appeared to be subdued, friendly, and compliant, and he related to the therapist in a strikingly reticent and apologetic manner. In reviewing his history he characterized his parents in idealistic terms and stressed his own culpability in relation to them and the troubles that had emanated from his drug use. His presenting qualities and manner contrasted sharply with a history of violent, sadistic behavior that dated back to his teenage years. As an adolescent he was in many provoked and unprovoked fights. Some of these occurred while under the influence of sedatives and amphetamines. He prided himself on his fearlessness and capacity for brutality.

He indicated that the initial effects of amphetamines appealed to him when he was a teenager because they helped him overcome feelings of vulnerability and weakness in social situations and in contact sports (despite a very hefty muscular physique). With continued use, however, he found himself repeatedly involved in brutally damaging fights, both for himself and his victims. In some instances the fights were provoked and premeditated, but in other instances, they erupted unpredictably and precipitously with little or no provocation. Initially he rationalized and glorified these episodes in a manner consistent with his need to maintain a sense of omnipotence and invulnerability. Later, with more sober reflection, he admitted to enormous terror and dysphoria as a result of his uncontrollable impulses while under the influence of stimulants.

As Arnold approached his early twenties, he found that his often uncontrollable rage and violence was interfering with his friendships

---

2. I elaborate here in more detail on the case of Arnold, first introduced in Chapter 2. His case is particularly apt for stressing the problems of rage in opiate addicts, especially their inability to contain their violent impulses.

and his work. During this period of his life he discovered the calming, subduing influence of heroin, to which he subsequently became heavily addicted.

He stressed how tranquil and relaxed he felt with heroin in contrast to amphetamines and sedatives, and how at first it helped him to feel organized, more energetic, and able to work.

During the initial phases of psychotherapy he continued to present himself in a subdued and deferential way, speaking politely and thoughtfully about his life, his parents, with whom he remained very involved, and his estranged wife. This was during a period of stabilization with methadone maintenance and at a time when he was on good terms with his family and was working regularly in his father's business. After approximately three months of treatment he decided to detoxify from the methadone. As he approached the end of the detoxification, a dramatic shift in his manner, attitudes, speech, and behavior occurred. He was visibly more restless and uneasy during his interviews, he began to falter at work, and he became involved in a barroom fight, sustaining a deep gash in his leg. Repeated fights ensued with his parents during which he was enraged, verbally assaultive, and intimidating. In his therapy he poured out vitriolic hatred and obscenities toward them, revealing for the first time impulses to kill his father; obscenities and paranoid feelings of jealousy were also directed toward his wife. Within two months of discontinuing the methadone, he dropped out of treatment.

## Discussion

Arnold's case reveals remarkable contrasts and shifts over time in his manifest behavior, attitudes, and feeling states. His history reveals he needed drugs both to regulate/overcome feelings of weakness and vulnerability as well as to help in expressing his aggressiveness and to behave more assertively. We also observe that his newly discovered self-assertiveness as a teenager was elusive, short lived, and devastatingly out of control. To combat his feelings of adolescent turmoil and amphetamine-induced rage and aggression, he then began to take advantage of the calming and comforting effects of opiates.

Sedatives and stimulants had initially helped to overcome a sense of inhibition, inertia, and powerlessness in his adolescence. As he approached some of the new challenges in his young adult life, he discovered that the muting and subduing effects of opiates now allowed him to feel more together, integrated, and effective in his personal relationships and work involvements that were otherwise eruptive, chaotic, and overwhelming. However, what was common to both phases of life was his general inability to face some of the specific emotions, affect states, and developmental challenges without relying on a drug to regulate himself and to cope with reality. In the course of therapy, it also became clear how opiate use represented a specific, if not necessary, means to counter the disorganizing effects of his rage and aggression.

Although Arnold is different in a number of respects from some addicts, in many more ways he shares qualities with the narcotic addicts whom I have evaluated and treated in a public narcotic treatment program, as well as with the opiate-dependent patients I have seen in my private practice. The common features are related generally to lifelong problems in regulating one's emotions and behavior, and, specifically, to enormous difficulties in modulating, regulating, and expressing feelings (affects) and drives associated with anger, rage, and aggression.

Some psychoanalysts, particularly those from an earlier generation, might focus and elaborate on Arnold's problems in terms of drive theory, fixations, and disturbances linked to certain phases of psychosexual development. Considered from such a perspective, Arnold's drug use might be interpreted to be the result of unresolved needs to seek regressive, pleasurable states, or caused by explosive impulses and tensions related to early problems around bowel control, or still further, his reliance on drugs might be viewed as a symptomatic expression of anxiety and inhibitions over sexual and aggressive impulses dating back to unresolved oedipal conflicts. This earlier psychoanalytic point of view would place emphasis on the discharge of drives, keeping them at a minimum and how drugs serve such an end.

In more recent years psychoanalysts have concerned themselves less exclusively with the influences of drives and conflicts emanating out of various phases of psychosexual development. Instead they have focused more on structures and mechanisms of the mind that help to regulate human drives, affects, and behaviors. Considered from this more contemporary psychoanalytic perspective, Arnold's problems might be seen more in terms of how unevenly he expressed and managed his feeling. At times he suffered from inertia and states of immobilization; at other times he seemed to be totally out of touch with his feelings, and on many other occasions he was overwhelmed with violent, aggressive, and uncontrollable impulses. In short, this more recent psychoanalytic perspective would focus on developmental impairments and deficiencies in psychological structures that, otherwise not impaired, are responsible for regulating feelings, behavior, inner states of well-being, and satisfactory self-other relationships. This more recent perspective would place greater emphasis on maintaining optimal (as opposed to minimal) levels of feelings (e.g., anxiety and depression) as guides for regulating one's internal life, behavior, and relationships with other people. Viewed in this context, opiate dependence might then be interpreted as a way of shoring up one's impaired capacities to deal with one's feelings and as a means to regulate behavior and interpersonal relations.

## VULNERABILITIES IN AFFECT REGULATION AND DEFENSE

With the benefit of a contemporary psychoanalytic perspective, I would like to review briefly some explanations of why narcotic addicts generally become involved with drugs and find the action of opiates welcome, and to consider in more detail, then, how one of the principal actions of opiates, namely its antiaggression action, provides a specific appeal for narcotic addicts.

Wurmser (1980) has referred to drug use as a "protective system." His term captures the essence of a psychoanalytic perspective of addictions that has better appreciated addicts' structural vulnerabilities and defects in coping with their internal emotions and external reality. In one of our early reports on clinical aspects of heroin use we reviewed some of the causes and consequences of heroin use and how it was used to overcome a range of emotions including pain, stress, and dysphoria (Khantzian et al. 1974). Wieder and Kaplan (1969) refer to the prosthetic function of drugs and their capacity to relieve tension and distress as major motivating influences for dependence on drugs. Milkman and Frosch (1973) present empirical findings suggesting that addicts used drugs either to shore up shaky defenses or to enhance limited ego capacities to engage one's environment. Wurmser (1974) delineates how drugs are used to compensate for defects in affect defense, and, in the case of heroin dependency more specifically, how opiates offer protection against painful affects of rage, hurt, shame, and loneliness. Along similar lines, some of my early work emphasized how the anti-rage and antiaggression action of opiates were used to help addicts cope with defective or nonexistent defenses against these powerful feelings (Khantzian 1972, 1974). The work of Krystal and Raskin (1970) in this context is important in explaining how addicts are developmentally disturbed in recognizing and experiencing their feelings because of the damaging trauma in their backgrounds, and how such individuals use drugs to overcome feeling states that, as a result, were only vaguely perceived, undifferentiated, somatized, and thus overwhelming.

## VULNERABILITIES IN SELF-CARE
## AND NEED SATISFACTION

I have been impressed with two other general influences that predispose individuals to substance dependence. These have to do with addicts' structural vulnerabilities in taking care of themselves, and special problems in accepting and pursuing their dependency needs and wants in more simple and ordinary ways.

Beyond the compulsive and driven aspects of drug dependence, I have been impressed that certain aspects of addicts' dangerous involvements, including the dangers of the drug use and its attendant practices, are results of failures in ego functioning responsible for self-care and self-protection. These functions are related to structures or ego capacities that are acquired in early phases of development and are derived from the caring and protective functions originally provided by the parents. They serve to protect against and anticipate harm and danger. Addicts give repeated evidence in their lives, prior to and while addicted, of being impaired in this capacity. Whereas most people would be fearful, apprehensive, or avoid the many aspects and elements of drug involvement that are dangerous, addicts fail to show worry, caution, or fear, or if present at all, lapse all too readily under the influence of psychological states of disorganization, stress, or other regressive influences (Khantzian 1978, 1980).

In addition to vulnerabilities in self-care, addicts give much evidence of being very uneven, self-defeating, and conflicted in satisfying themselves around the dependency and needful aspects of life. Although they lack a sense of self-worth, comfort, and nurturance from within and thus remain dependent on others and the environment to maintain a sense of well-being, they are just as often counterdependent and disavow their needs. As a result, they alternate between seductive and manipulative attitudes to extract satisfaction from the environment, and disdainful, aloof postures of independence and self-sufficiency that dismiss the need for others. I have described in more detail elsewhere how these counterdependent and self-sufficient attitudes against ordinary forms of dependency leave addicts susceptible to adopting more extraordinary chemical dependencies to meet their needs and wants (Khantzian 1978, 1980).

In brief, then, beyond having troubles (i.e., structural vulnerabilities) in regulating a range of painful feelings, addicts also suffer from an inability to take care of and protect themselves, and to satisfy their needs and wants.

## THE SPECIFIC APPEAL OF NARCOTICS

In the previous sections I have reviewed the general psychological vulnerabilities that predispose an individual to become involved with drugs. In this section I discuss the specific appeal of opiates and how this appeal malignantly combines with addicts' general psychological vulnerabilities to make opiates so devastatingly compelling in their lives.

I believe that one of the major specific appeals of opiates resides in the antiaggression action of these drugs. This action of opiates interacts with general and specific structural vulnerabilities to make opiates very appealing for individuals who suffer such vulnerabilities. In my early work with narcotic addicts I became impressed quickly with addicts' lifelong experiences and problems with rage and aggression, most often dating back to family and environmental influences where they were subject to and victims of physical abuse, brutality, violence, and sadism. I began to suspect that there was a connection between addicts' rageful/aggressive feelings and impulses, their own backgrounds of exposure to violence, and their attraction to opiates. After interviewing many addicts I began to suspect they craved less for euphoria than for relief from dysphoria associated with anger, rage, and related restlessness, which, in the short term, narcotics seem to provide. This was evident in patients' descriptions of how narcotics helped them to feel normal, calm, relaxed, and soothed, and was even more apparent in observing addicts in treatment as they stabilized on methadone and their aggressiveness and restlessness subsided. I subsequently hypothesized that problems with aggression predisposed certain individuals to opiate dependence, and that the appeal of narcotics was related to the antiaggression action of the drug. I proposed that opiates counteracted regressed, disorganized, and dysphoric ego states associated with overwhelming feelings of rage, anger, and related depression. This effect was particularly appealing and welcome, given that the ego capacities in such individuals were shaky or absent, especially against aggressive drives. Opiates reversed regressed ego states by counteracting the disorganizing influences of aggression on the ego, helping addicts to feel and become more organized, and thus better able to cope with life's demands and challenges. It was also this sustained, longer action of methadone that accounted for the "success" and better adaptation of individuals receiving this form of treatment (Khantzian 1972, 1974, 1980).

## COMMENTS AND CONCLUSIONS

I would now like to reconsider briefly this early formulation of the appeal of opiates as an antiaggression agent with the benefit of an added ten-year perspective, and in the context of more recent psychoanalytic formulations and the discovery of naturally occurring endogenous opioid peptides and receptors.

Addicts' survival problems are formidable. They derive from lifelong developmental problems in coping both with their feelings and with external reality. These problems are further compounded by the artificial drives and painful affect states associated with the addictive intoxication-withdrawal cycles, and by the dangerous world of violence and threat in which addicts operate. Internal states of comfort, tranquillity, and satisfaction have all too often been elusive or absent. In addition, although they fail to recognize their self-care problems and the related tendency for hazardous involvements, they nevertheless experience a vague sense of vulnerability in their existence because of their inability to take care of themselves, and as a result they are even more unstable. Whatever equilibrium they attain is usually precarious. Given their unstable ego and self structures for containing feelings and behavior, painful affects of any kind tend to compound further an all-too-ready tendency for psychological fragmentation and disorganization. In my experience, the affects and drives associated with rage and aggression are particularly devastating in this regard. I believe the dysphoria with which addicts suffer is intimately associated with the disorganizing influences of these affects and drives. A vicious cycle is set in motion in which shaky or brittle defenses for coping with internal emotions and external reality are further weakened by the uncontrolled aggression, and, given the subjective and objective threatening nature of these feelings in particular, one's very survival/existence seems more and more at stake. That is, uncontrolled aggression disorganizes from within by eroding ego structures, and threatens from without by jeopardizing needed relationships and by provoking counter-violence from others. The appeal of opiates resides then in the dramatic capacity of these drugs to reverse this state of affairs by muting, containing, and eliminating the rage and aggression that disorganizes and disrupts such individuals.

In closing, I cannot resist speculating how the concept of exogenous opiates as an antiaggression agent might have implications for and be related to the exciting discovery of endogenous opiates, and the role endorphins might play in regulating human aggression. Could it be, under more ordinary circumstances and in the course of development, not only that the brain and mind elaborate endorphins to keep physical discomfort and pain at bay, but also that differential elaboration of these substances plays a crucial role in maintaining *optimal* feeling and comfort states? Endogenous opiates might be especially critical in regulating human aggression, given that it is such a necessary part of human existence in its controlled forms, but can be equally devastating in its uncontrolled forms. As we study further the role and function of endorphins in the workings of the mind, we might better understand how they fuel productivity by maintaining aggression at optimal levels, and how aberration and dysfunction of endorphin activity might be related to the destructive vicissitudes of human aggression. Perhaps it is not too farfetched to suggest that we might some day bridge and better control the "mysterious leap from the mind to the body" (Deutsch 1959) by understanding how ego and self structures function as endorphin regulators.

## REFERENCES

Deutsch, F. (1959). *On the Mysterious Leap from the Mind to the Body.* New York: International Universities Press.

Khantzian, E. J. (1972). A preliminary dynamic formulation of the psychopharmacologic action of methadone. In *Proceedings of the Fourth National Conference on Methadone Treatment,* pp. 371–374. New York: National Association for the Prevention of Addictions to Narcotics.

—— (1974). Opiate addiction: a critique of theory and some implications for treatment. *American Journal Psychotherapy* 28:59–70.

—— (1978). The ego, the self and opiate addiction: theoretical and treatment considerations. *International Review of Psychoanalysis* 5:189–198.

—— (1980). An ego-self theory of substance dependence. In *Theories of Addiction,* ed. D. J. Lettieri, M. Sayers, and H. W. Wallenstein, NIDA monograph 30, pp. 29–33. Rockville, MD: National Institute on Drug Abuse.

Khantzian, E. J., Mack, J., and Schatzberg, A. F. (1974). Heroin use as an attempt to cope: clinical observations. *American Journal of Psychiatry* 131:160–164.

Krystal, H., and Raskin, H. A. (1970). *Drug Dependence: Aspects of Ego Functions.* Detroit: Wayne State University Press.

Milkman, H., and Frosch, W. A. (1973). On the preferential abuse of heroin and amphetamine. *Journal of Nervous and Mental Disease* 156:242–248.

Wieder, H., and Kaplan, E. H. (1969). Drug use in adolescence: psychodynamic meaning and pharmacogenic effect. *Psychoanalytic Study of the Child* 24:399–431. New York: International Universities Press.

Wurmser, L. (1974). Psychoanalytic considerations of the etiology of compulsive drug use. *Journal of the American Psychoanalytic Association* 22:820–843.

—— (1980). Drug use as a protective system. In *Theories of Addiction,* ed. D. J. Lettieri, M. Sayers, and H. W. Wallenstein, NIDA monograph 30, pp. 71–74. Rockville, MD: National Institute on Drug Abuse.

# 11

# The Self-Medication Hypothesis of Addictive Disorders

Developments in psychoanalysis and psychiatry over the past sixty years have provided enabling new insights and approaches in understanding mental life and in treating its aberrations. In psychoanalysis, there has been a shift from a focus on drives and conflict to a greater emphasis on the importance of ego and self structures in regulating emotions, self-esteem, behavior, and adaptation to reality. In psychiatry, we have witnessed the advent of psychotropic medications, a more precise understanding of the neurobiology of the brain, and the development of standardized diagnostic approaches for identifying and classifying psychiatric disorders. Such developments have had implications for understanding and treating addictions, especially given the recent dramatic rise in drug abuse in all sectors of our society and our growing inclination to treat our drug-dependent patients through private practice, in community mental health centers, and in methadone-maintenance or self-help programs, in close proximity to the surroundings in which their addictions evolved.

Popular or simplistic formulations in the early 1970s emphasized peer group pressure, escape, euphoria, or self-destructive themes to explain the compelling nature of drug dependency. In contrast, the work of a number of psychoanalysts in the 1960s and 1970s has led to observations, theoretical formulations, and subsequent studies representing a significant departure from these previous approaches and explanations. On the basis of a modern psychodynamic perspective, these analysts succeeded in better identifying the nature of the psychological vulnerabilities, disturbances, and pain that predispose certain individuals to drug dependence. This perspective, which has spawned a series of diagnostic studies, emphasizes that heavy reliance on and continual use of illicit drugs (i.e., individuals who become and remain addicted) are associated with severe and significant psychopathology. Moreover, the individual's drug of choice is not a random phenomenon.

On the basis of recent psychodynamic and psychiatric perspectives and findings, this chapter elaborates on a self-medication hypothesis of addictive disorders, emphasizing problems with heroin and cocaine dependence. This point of view suggests that the specific psychotropic effects of these drugs interact with psychiatric disturbances and painful affect states to make them compelling in susceptible individuals.

## PSYCHODYNAMIC FINDINGS

An extensive review of the psychoanalytic literature on addiction goes beyond the scope of this chapter. I have reviewed elsewhere the early psychoanalytic literature on addiction, which principally emphasized the pleasurable aspects of drug use (Khantzian 1974, Khantzian and Treece 1977). Psychoanalytic reports that pertain most to this thesis date back to the work of Chein and colleagues (1964) and the earlier related work of Gerard and Kornetsky (1954, 1955), who were among the first groups to study addicts in the community (inner city addicts in New York) and attempt to understand the psychological effects of opiates and how they interacted with addicts' ego, superego, narcissistic, and other psychopathology. They emphasized that individuals use drugs adaptively to cope with overwhelming (adolescent) anxiety in anticipation of adult roles in the absence of adequate preparation, models, and prospects. Because they did not have the benefit of a modern psychopharmacological perspective, they referred to the general "tranquilizing or ataractic" properties of opiates and did not consider that the appeal of narcotics might be based on a specific effect or action of opiates. In addition, their studies were limited to narcotics addicts, thus providing little basis to compare them to addicts dependent on other drugs.

Around 1970, a number of psychoanalysts began to report findings based on their work with addicts, who were coming in increasing numbers to their practices and to a variety of community treatment settings. In contrast to the early emphasis in psychoanalysis on a drive and topographical psychology, their work paralleled developments in contemporary psychoanalysis and placed greater emphasis on structural factors, ego states, and self and object relations in exploring the disturbances of addicts and understanding their suffering. More particularly, this literature highlighted how painful affects associated with disturbances in psychological structures and object relations interacted with the psychopharmacological action of addictive drugs to make them compelling.

Despite a superficial resemblance to earlier formulations that stressed regressive pleasurable use of drugs, work by Wieder and Kaplan (1969) represented an important advance and elaboration of trends set in motion by Gerard and Kornetsky in the 1950s, especially their appreciation of substance abusers' ego impairments and their use of drugs as a "prosthetic."

On the basis of this and other work that considers ego and adaptational problems of addicts, and following lines pursued by Wieder and Kaplan, Milkman and Frosch (1973) empirically tested the hypothesis that self-selection of specific drugs is related to preferred defensive style. Using the Bellak and Hurvich Interview and Rating Scale for Ego Functioning, they compared heroin and amphetamine addicts in drugged and nondrugged conditions. Their preliminary findings supported their hypothesis that heroin addicts preferred the calming and dampening effects of opiates and seemed to use this action of the drug to shore up tenuous defenses and reinforce a tendency toward withdrawal and isolation, while amphetamine addicts used the stimulating action of amphetamines to support an inflated sense of self-worth and a defensive style involving active confrontation with their environment.

The work of Wurmser (1972, 1974) and Khantzian (1972, 1974, 1980, 1982) suggested that the excessive emphasis on the regressive effects of narcotics in previous studies was unwarranted and that, in fact, the specific psychopharmacological action of opiates has an opposite, "progressive" effect whereby regressed states may be reversed. Wurmser believed that narcotics are used adaptively by narcotic addicts to compensate for defects in affect defense, particularly against feelings of "rage, hurt, shame, and loneliness." Khantzian stressed drive defense and believed narcotics act to reverse regressed states by the direct antiaggression action of opiates, counteracting disorganizing influences of rage and aggression on the ego. Both these formulations proposed that the psychopharmacological effects of the drug could substitute for defective or nonexistent ego mechanisms of defense. As with previously mentioned recent investigators, Wurmser and Khantzian also considered developmental impairments, severe predisposing psychopathology, and problems in adaptation to be central issues in understanding addiction. Radford and colleagues (1972) reported detailed case material that supported the findings of Wurmser and Khantzian that opiates could have an antiaggression and antiregression action or effect. They further observed that opiate use cannot be exclusively correlated with any particular patterns of internal conflict or phase-specific developmental impairment.

Krystal and Raskin (1970) were less precise about the specific effects of different drugs but allowed that they may be used either to permit or prevent regression. However, their work focused more precisely on the relationship between pain, depression, and anxiety and drug and placebo effects. They explored and greatly clarified addicts' difficulties in recognizing and tolerating painful affects. They proposed that the tendency for depression and anxiety to remain somatized, unverbalized, and undifferentiated in addicts resulted in a defective stimulus barrier and thus left such individuals ill-equipped to deal with their feelings and predisposed them to drug use. Their work also focused in greater depth on the major problems that addicts have in relation to positive and negative feelings about themselves and in relation to other people. Krystal and Raskin believed that addicts have major difficulties in being good to themselves and in dealing with their positive and negative feelings toward others because of rigid and massive defenses such as splitting and denial. They maintained that drug users take drugs not only to assist in defending against their feelings but also briefly and therefore "safely" to enable the experience of feelings like fusion (oneness) with loved objects, which are normally prevented by the rigid defenses against aggression.

## DIAGNOSTIC AND TREATMENT STUDIES

Partly as an extension and outgrowth of the psychodynamic studies and partly as the result of the development of standardized diagnostic approaches for classifying and describing mental illness, a number of reports over the past decade have documented the coexistence of psychopathology in drug-dependent individuals. Some of these investigators have also reported on the results of conventional psychiatric treatment, including psychotherapy, with drug-dependent individuals. Although the results of such studies to date have been inconsistently successful or inconclusive, they are suggestive enough to further support the concept that drug dependence is related to and associated with coexistent psychopathology.

In a placebo-controlled study, Woody and colleagues (1975) treated a series of narcotics addicts with the antidepressant doxepin and documented significant symptom reduction. Their study suggested that this group of patients suffered with an anxious depression, and as the depression lifted with treatment, there was a corresponding reduction in misuse and abuse of drugs and an improvement in overall adaptation. This group of investigators (McLellan et al. 1979) also reported longitudinal data on individuals dependent on psychostimulants, sedative-hypnotics, or opiates, which suggested that addicts might be medicating themselves for underlying psychopathology. Their study suggested that such individuals might respond to the administration of appropriate psychopharmacological agents for target symptoms of phobia and depression.

Dorus and Senay (1980) and Weissman and Rounsaville and their associates (Rounsaville et al. 1982a, 1982b, Weissman et al. 1976) evaluated large samples of narcotic addicts and, using standardized diagnostic approaches, documented a significant incidence of major depressive disorder, alcoholism, and antisocial personality. The Rounsaville group (1982a, 1982b) concluded that their findings were consistent with the clinical theories of Wurmser and Khantzian, that depressed addicts used opiates as an attempt at self-treatment for unbearable dysphoric feelings.

At a conference sponsored by the New York Academy of Sciences on opioids in mental illness, Khantzian, Wurmser, McKenna, Berken, Millman, Vereby, and others presented clinical findings and theoretical observations that support a self-medication hypothesis of addictions (Vereby 1982). The sponsors of the conference and the participants reviewed the role of exogenous opiates as well as endorphins in regulating emotions. One of the conclusions drawn from these findings was that the long-acting opiate methadone might be an effective psychotropic agent in the treatment of severe psychoses, especially cases refractory to conventional drugs and in instances associated with violence and rage.

Treece and Nicholson (1980), using diagnostic criteria from *DSM-III*, published findings indicating a strong relationship between certain types of personality disorder and methadone dose required for stabilization. They studied this same sample and compared "high drug" and "low drug" users (i.e., in addition to their prescribed methadone dose) and were able to show that the high drug users were significantly more impaired in the quality of their object relations than the low drug users (Nicholson and Treece 1981). Khantzian and Treece (1985) studied 133 narcotics addicts from three subject samples (a methadone program sample, a residential setting sample, and a street sample) and, using *DSM-III*, documented depression in over 60 percent and a range of personality disorders (that included but was not limited to antisocial disorder) in over 65 percent. We also explored the possible relationships between the disturbed/disturbing behavior of addicts as reflected by the personality diagnosis, and the painful affects with which addicts suffer as reflected by the diagnosis of depression.

Blatt and colleagues (1984) used the Loevinger Sentence Completion, the Bellak Ego Function Interview, and the Rorschach to extensively study ninety-nine opiate addicts and compare them to normal subjects. Their findings provide further evidence that opiate addicts suffer significantly in their interpersonal relations and in affect modulation. The authors indicate that addicts use drugs in the service of isolation and withdrawal.

In two carefully executed studies (Rounsaville et al. 1983, Woody et al. 1983) based on the assumption that opiate dependence is associated with psychopathology, the effectiveness of psychotherapy on the psychopathology and presumed related drug dependence of 72 and 110 narcotics addicts, respectively, was tested. Rounsaville and colleagues found no evidence that psychotherapy appreciably influenced treatment outcome. Woody and colleagues demonstrated that the addicts receiving psychotherapy had greater improvement than the addicts who received only drug counseling, and that the psychotherapy subjects required less methadone and used fewer psychotropic drugs.

Finally, carefully executed studies dating back to the early 1970s document that in selected cases and samples of substance-dependent individuals, target symptoms and psychopathology have been identified and successfully treated with psychotropic drugs (Butterworth 1971, Gawin and Kleber 1984, Overall et al. 1973, Quitkin et al. 1972, Woody et al. 1975).

## CLINICAL OBSERVATIONS—NARCOTICS AND COCAINE DEPENDENCE

Clinical work with narcotics and cocaine addicts has provided us with compelling evidence that the drug an individual comes to rely on is not a random choice. Although addicts experiment with multiple substances, most prefer one drug. Wieder and Kaplan (1969) referred to this process as "the drug-of-choice phenomenon," Milkman and Frosch (1973) described it as the "preferential use of drugs," and I (1975) have called it the "self-selection" process. I believe that narcotics and cocaine addicts' accounts of their subjective experiences with and responses to these drugs are particularly instructive. They teach us how addicts suffer with certain overwhelming affects, relationships, and behavioral disturbances and how the short-term use of their drug of choice helps them to combat these disturbances.

### Narcotics Addiction

Although narcotics may be used to overcome and cope with a range of human problems including pain, stress, and dysphoria (Khantzian et al. 1974), I have been impressed that the antiaggression and anti-rage action of opiates is one of the most compelling reasons for its appeal. I base this conclusion on observations of over 200 addicts whose histories reveal lifelong difficulties with rage and violent behavior predating their addiction, often linked to intense and unusual exposure to extreme aggression and violence in their early family life and the environment outside their homes. These experiences included being both the subject and the perpetrator of physical abuse, brutality, violent fights, and sadism. In the course of their evaluation and treatment these patients repeatedly described how opiates helped them to feel normal, calm, mellow, soothed, and relaxed. I have also observed addicts in group treatment whose restlessness and aggressiveness, especially manifested in their abusive and assaultive use of obscenities, subsided as they stabilized on methadone (Khantzian 1972, 1974, 1980, 1982). I was also impressed that many narcotic addicts discovered the anti-rage action of opiates in a context of violent feelings, often of murderous proportion, being released in them by sedatives and alcohol or being manifested as a consequence of amphetamine and cocaine use (Khantzian 1979).

## Clinical Vignette

A 29-year-old ex-felon, admitted to a closed psychiatric ward because of increasing inability to control his alcohol and cocaine use, demonstrated dramatically this special relationship between violence and drug use and why opiates were his drug of choice. I saw this patient in consultation on a day when he had become very agitated and intimidating as he witnessed a very disturbed female patient being placed in four-point restraints. An alert attendant, who was a felon himself on work release, ascertained from the patient that this scene triggered panic and violent reactions similar to those he had experienced when he had been attacked by guards in prison because he had been threatening or assaultive. When I met him I was surprised by his diminutive stature and reticence. I told him I wanted to understand his drug-alcohol use and determine whether our unit was okay (i.e., safe) for him. He immediately apologized for overreacting to the restrained patient and explained how much it reminded him of his prison experience. He quickly launched into his worry that his alcohol and cocaine use was causing increasingly uncontrolled outbursts of verbally assaultive behavior and, as a consequence, an increasing tendency to use opiates to quell his violent reactions. He openly admitted to past overt assaultive behavior, most frequently involving knifings, when he felt threatened, provoked, or intimidated. He kept returning to the confrontation and restraint of the patient, apologizing for his reaction but also explaining how disorganizing and threatening it was for him. He said there had been a time when attack would have been a reflex in such situations, but he wanted to reassure me and the staff that he really understood why we were doing what we were. He seemed to be begging to stay and said he wanted help with his alcohol and drug use.

An inquiry about his drug use and its effect on him revealed that he preferred opiates, so much so that he knew he had to avoid them. (He explained that he knew too many people who had become hopelessly dependent on or had died because of opiates.) Whereas alcohol or stimulants could cause violent eruptions, he explained that opiates—and he named them all correctly—countered or controlled such reactions. He said that the only person he had to rely on was his mother but that she was very ill and in the hospital. He complained that he had suffered as a consequence of his father's alcoholism, the associated violence, and his premature death (alcoholic complications) when the patient was in his early teens. His father's unavailability and early death had left him without supervision or guidance. He bitterly lamented that a brother five years older had been "useless" in providing any guidance on how to control his drug-alcohol use or his impulsive and aggressive behavior ("he didn't help me to smarten up").

The patient's description of his violent side before prison and once in prison, corroborated by the mental health aide who knew him from prison, was chilling and convincing. He was equally graphic in describing the many attacks he suffered at the hands of sadistic correction officers and other inmates. What was clear was that, whether he was the perpetrator or the victim, the violence was a recurrent, regular, and repetitious part of his adult life. I have concluded (Khantzian 1980, 1982) that such individuals welcome the effects of opiates because they mute uncontrolled aggression and counter the threat of both internal psychological disorganization and external counteraggression from others, fears that are not uncommon with people who struggle with rage and violent impulses. The discovery that opiates can relieve and reverse the disorganizing and fragmenting effects of rage and aggression is not limited to individuals who come from deprived, extreme, and overtly violent backgrounds.

*Clinical Vignette*

A successful 35-year-old physician described how defensive and disdainful he had become since his early adulthood as a consequence
of his mother's insensitivity and his father's cruel and depriving
attitude toward the patient and his family, despite their significant
affluence. He said he became dependent on opiates when his defense of self-sufficiency began to fail him in a context of disappointing relationships with women and much distress and frustration
working with severely ill patients. More than anything else, he
became aware of the calming effects of these drugs on his bitter
resentment and mounting rage. He stressed how this effect of the
drugs helped him to feel better about himself and, paradoxically,
helped him to remain energized and active in his work.

I have described (Khantzian 1979, 1982) similar patients from privileged backgrounds in which sadistic or unresponsive parents fueled a
predisposition to angry and violent feelings toward self and others.

## Cocaine Addiction

From a psychodynamic perspective, a number of investigators have
speculated on the appeal of stimulants and, in particular, cocaine. For
some, the energizing properties of these drugs are compelling because
they help to overcome fatigue and depletion states associated with
depression (Khantzian 1975). In other cases the use of stimulants leads
to increased feelings of assertiveness, self-esteem, and frustration
tolerance (Wieder and Kaplan 1969) and the riddance of feelings of
boredom and emptiness (Wurmser 1974). I have proposed that certain
individuals use cocaine to "augment a hyperactive, restless lifestyle
and an exaggerated need for self-sufficiency" (Khantzian 1979, p. 100).
Spotts and Shontz (1977) extensively studied the characteristics of nine
representative cocaine addicts and documented findings that are
largely consistent with the psychodynamic descriptions of people who
are addicted to cocaine.

We have considered from a psychiatric/diagnostic perspective a
number of factors that might predispose an individual to become and
remain dependent on cocaine (Khantzian and Khantzian 1984,
Khantzian et al. 1984): (1) preexistent chronic depression; (2) cocaine
abstinence depression; (3) hyperactive, restless syndrome or attention

deficit disorder; and (4) cyclothymic or bipolar illness. Unfortunately, studies of representative larger, aggregate samples of cocaine addicts do not yet exist to substantiate these possibilities.

*Clinical Vignette*

A 30-year-old man with a ten-year history of multiple drug use described the singularly uplifting effect of cocaine, which he came to use preferentially over all the other drugs. In contrast to a persistent sense of feeling unattractive and socially and physically awkward dating back to adolescence, he discovered "that (snorting) it gave me power and made me happier. It was pleasant, euphoric; I could talk—and feel erotic." Subsequently, injecting it intensified these feelings, but more than anything else, the cocaine helped him to not worry about what people thought of him.

I have been repeatedly impressed how this energizing and activating property of cocaine helps such people, who have been chronically depressed, overcome their anergia, complete tasks, and better relate to others, and, as a consequence, experience a temporary boost in their self-esteem (Khantzian and Khantzian 1984).

*Clinical Vignette*

In contrast, a 40-year-old accountant described an opposite, paradoxical effect from snorting cocaine. Originally, when I evaluated this man, I thought he was using the stimulating properties of the drug as an augmentor for his usual hyperactive, expansive manner of relating. He finally convinced me to the contrary when he carefully acted out how he put down several lines in the morning, snorted it, and breathed a sigh of relaxation and then described how he could sit still, focus on his backlog of paper work, and complete it.

This man's story, a dramatic and extreme case (Khantzian 1983), and two other related reports (Khantzian and Khantzian 1984, Khantzian et al. 1984) suggest that cocaine addicts might be medicating themselves for mood disorders and behavioral disturbances, including a preexisting or resulting attention deficit/hyperactive-type disorder. The extreme case responded dramatically to methylphenidate treatment. I have successfully treated several other patients with methylphenidate, who provide further evidence to support a self-medication hypothesis of drug dependency. At this point it would be premature to conclude precisely what the disorder or disorders are for which cocaine addicts are medicating themselves. However, the pilot cases and my previous clinical experiences suggest several possibilities. The patients share in common lifelong difficulties with impulsive behavior, emotional lability, acute and chronic dysphoria (including acute depressions), and self-esteem disturbances that preceded cocaine use. All of the patients experienced a relief of dysphoria and improved self-esteem on cocaine; they also experienced improved attention leading to improved interpersonal relations, more purposeful, focused activity, and improved capacity for work. The substitution of the more stable, long-acting stimulant drug methylphenidate provided an opportunity for me to observe these patients clinically and to confirm the stabilizing effect of stimulants on them.

## COMMENT

Clearly, there are other determinants of addiction, but I believe a self-medication motive is one of the more compelling reasons for overuse of and dependency on drugs. Clinical findings based on psychoanalytic formulations have been consistent with and complemented by diagnostic and treatment studies that support this perspective, which I believe will enable researchers and clinicians to further understand and treat addictive behavior. Rather than simply seeking escape, euphoria, or self-destruction, addicts are attempting to medicate themselves for a range of psychiatric problems and painful emotional states. Although most such efforts at self-treatment are eventually doomed, given the hazards and complications of long-term, unstable drug use patterns, addicts discover that the short-term effects of their drugs of choice help them to cope with distressful subjective states and an external reality otherwise experienced as unmanageable or overwhelming. I believe that the perspective provided by the self-medication hypothesis has enabled me and others to understand better the nature of compulsive drug use, and that it has provided a useful rationale in considering treatment alternatives. The heuristic value of this hypothesis might also help us to more effectively understand and treat the most recent elusive addiction—cocaine dependence.

# REFERENCES

Blatt S. J., Berman, W., Bloom-Feshback, S., et al. (1984). Psychological assessment of psychopathology in opiate addicts. *Journal of Nervous and Mental Disease* 172:156–165.

Butterworth, A. T. (1971). Depression associated with alcohol with imipramine therapy compared with placebo. *Quarterly Journal of Studies on Alcohol* 32:343–348.

Chein, I., Gerard, D. L., Lee, R. S., and Rosenfeld, E. (1964). *The Road to H: Narcotics, Delinquency, and Social Policy.* New York: Basic Books.

Dorus, W., and Senay, E. C. (1980). Depression, demographic dimension, and drug abuse. *American Journal of Psychiatry* 137:699–704.

Gawin, F. H., and Kleber, H. D. (1984). Cocaine abuse treatment. *Archive of General Psychiatry* 41:903–908.

Gerard, D. L., and Kornetsky, C. (1954). Adolescent opiate addiction: a case study. *Psychiatric Quarterly* 28:367–380.

——— (1955). Adolescent opiate addiction: a study of control and addict subjects. *Psychiatric Quarterly* 29:457–486.

Khantzian, E. J. (1972). A preliminary dynamic formulation of the psychopharmacologic action of methadone. In *Proceedings of the Fourth National Conference on Methadone Treatment*, San Francisco, pp. 371–374. New York: National Association for the Prevention of Addictions to Narcotics.

——— (1974). Opiate addiction: a critique of theory and some implications for treatment. *American Journal of Psychotherapy* 28:59–70.

——— (1975). Self selection and progression in drug dependence. *Psychiatry Digest* 10:19–22.

——— (1979). Impulse problems in addiction: cause and effect relationships. In *Working with the Impulsive Person*, ed. H. Wishnie, pp. 97–112. New York: Plenum.

——— (1980). An ego-self theory of substance dependence. In *Theories of Addiction*, ed. D. J. Lettieri, M. Sayers, and H. W. Wallenstein, NIDA monograph 30, pp. 29–33. Rockville, MD: National Institute on Drug Abuse.

——— (1982). Psychological (structural) vulnerabilities and the specific appeal of narcotics. *Annals of the New York Academy of Science* 398:24–32.

——— (1983). An extreme case of cocaine dependence and marked improvement with methylphenidate treatment. *American Journal of Psychiatry* 140:784–785.

Khantzian, E. J., Gawin, F., Kleber, H. D., et al. (1984). Methylphenidate treatment of cocaine dependence: a preliminary report. *Journal of Substance Abuse Treatment* 1:107–112.

Khantzian, E. J., and Khantzian, N. J. (1984). Cocaine addiction: Is there a psychological predisposition? *Psychiatric Annals* 14(10):753–759.

Khantzian, E. J., Mack, J. E., and Schatzberg, A. F. (1974). Heroin use as an attempt to cope: clinical observations. *American Journal of Psychiatry* 131:160–164.

Khantzian, E. J., and Treece, C. (1977). Psychodynamics of drug dependence: an overview. In *Psychodynamics of Drug Dependence*, ed. J. D. Blaine and D. A. Julius, NIDA research monograph 12, pp. 11–25. Rockville, MD: National Institute on Drug Abuse.

———— (1985). *DSM-III* psychiatric diagnosis of narcotic addicts: recent findings. *Archives of General Psychiatry* 42:1067–1071.

Krystal, H., and Raskin, H. A. (1970). *Drug Dependence. Aspects of Ego Functions.* Detroit: Wayne State University Press.

McLellan, A. T., Woody, G. E., and O'Brien, C. P. (1979). Development of psychiatric illness in drug abusers. *New England Journal of Medicine* 201:1310–1314.

Milkman, H., and Frosch, W. A. (1973). On the preferential abuse of heroin and amphetamine. *Journal of Nervous and Mental Disease* 156:242–248.

Nicholson, B., and Treece, C. (1981). Object relations and differential treatment response to methadone maintenance. *Journal of Nervous and Mental Disease* 169:424–429.

Overall, J. E., Brown, D., Williams, J. D., et al. (1973). Drug treatment of anxiety and depression in detoxified alcoholic patients. Archives of General Psychiatry 29:218–221.

Quitkin, F. M., Rifkin, A., Kaplan, J., and Klein, D. F. (1972). Phobic anxiety syndrome complicated by drug dependence and addiction. *Archives of General Psychiatry* 27:159–162.

Radford, P., Wiseberg, S., and Yorke, C. (1972). A study of "main line" heroin addiction. *Psychoanalytic Study of the Child* 27:156–180. New Haven, CT: Yale University Press.

Rounsaville, B. J., Glazer, W., Wilber, C. H., et al. (1983). Short-term interpersonal psychotherapy in methadone-maintained opiate addicts. *Archives of General Psychiatry* 40:629–636.

Rounsaville, B. J., Weissman, M. M., Crits-Cristoph, K., et al. (1982a). Diagnosis and symptoms of depression in opiate addicts: course and relationship to treatment outcome. *Archives of General Psychiatry* 39:151–156.

Rounsaville, B. J., Weissman, M. M., Kleber, H., et al. (1982b). Heterogeneity of psychiatric diagnosis in treated opiate addicts. *Archives of General Psychiatry* 39:161–166.

Spotts, J. V., and Shontz, F. C. (1977). *The Life Styles of Nine American Cocaine Users.* Washington, DC: National Institute on Drug Abuse.

Treece, C., and Nicholson, B. (1980). *DSM-III* personality type and dose levels in methadone maintenance patients. *Journal of Nervous and Mental Disease* 168:621–628.

Vereby, K., ed. (1982). Opioids in mental illness: theories, clinical observations, and treatment possibilities. *Annals of the New York Academy of Sciences* 98:1–512.

Weissman, M. M., Slobetz, F., Prusoff, B., et al. (1976). Clinical depression among narcotic addicts maintained on methadone in the community. *American Journal of Psychiatry* 133:1434–1438.

Wieder, H., and Kaplan, E. H. (1969). Drug use in adolescence: psychodynamic meaning and pharmacogenic effect. *Psychoanalytic Study of the Child* 24:399–431. New York: International Universities Press.

Woody, G. E., Luborsky, L., McLellan, A. T., et al. (1983). Psychotherapy for opiate addicts. *Archives of General Psychiatry* 40:639–645.

Woody, G. E., O'Brien, C. P., and Rickels, K. (1975). Depression and anxiety in heroin addicts: a placebo-controlled study of doxepin in combination with methadone. *American Journal of Psychiatry* 132:447–450.

Wurmser, L. (1972). Methadone and the craving for narcotics: observations of patients on methadone maintenance in psychotherapy. In *Proceedings of the Fourth National Conference on Methadone Treatment*, San Francisco, pp. 525–528. New York: National Association for the Prevention of Addictions to Narcotics.

———— (1974). Psychoanalytic considerations of the etiology of compulsive drug use. *Journal of the American Psychoanalytic Association* 22:820–843.

# 12

# Self-Regulation and Self-Medication Factors in Alcoholism and the Addictions

It is probably not insignificant that the widespread misuse and abuse of addictive drugs in our society emerged approximately one decade after the introduction of modern psychopharmacological agents. When these drugs were first introduced in the 1950s, they were called "major" (for major mental illness, i.e., psychosis) or "minor" (for minor mental illness, i.e., neurosis) tranquilizers, and as the terms imply, it was believed they worked simply by tranquilizing or attenuating emotional distress. However, with the subsequent advent of the antidepressants in the early 1960s and the identification and clarification of the role of neuroreceptors and neurotransmitters, researchers and clinicians began to appreciate that psychoactive drugs had different sites and modes of action. Consequently, this appreciation modified our designation of these drugs to more precisely describe their action—antipsychotic, antianxiety, antidepressant, and antimanic agents.

As the original and subsequent names of these drugs implied, these agents promised to reduce or counter emotional suffering associated with mental illness. It should not be surprising, then, that some of these drugs (especially antianxiety drugs) and other illicit substances were adopted and used increasingly in the 1960s and 1970s by individuals who were not necessarily patients to relieve and remove emotional distress.

However, for the most part, and until recently, few investigators, clinicians, or theoreticians have considered drugs of abuse to have appeal or addictive potential because of their ability to reduce emotional pain or suffering. Instead, motives of stimulus seeking, pleasure drives, or self-destructiveness are and have been invoked on the psychological side, or biogenetic or addictive mechanisms on the physiological side, to account for why individuals become so dependent on substances of abuse. Notwithstanding the scientific advances that have allowed the measurement of genetic and physiological factors, clinical work with and diagnostic studies of addicts, guided by a modern psychodynamic perspective, offer a basis to conclude that the need to control or reduce emotional suffering is an important motivating factor in addictive disorders. Pleasure- or stimulus-seeking and self-destructive motives are indeed apparent in addictions, but in my opinion they are more often by-products or secondary to problems in self-regulation in which the capacities for managing feelings, self-esteem, relationships, and self-care loom large (Khantzian 1978, 1980, 1991).

This chapter explores how self-medication factors play an important role in individuals' becoming dependent on alcohol and drugs, with an emphasis on alcoholism. The self-medication hypothesis implies that individuals prefer or depend on different drugs because each class of drugs, much like the classes of drugs legitimately used in psychiatry, have a distinctive action and effect that interacts with specific painful feeling states and related psychiatric disorders. I use clinical examples to demonstrate that self-medication factors are as important with alcohol dependence as they are with other addictive drugs. I will compare and contrast the appeal of alcohol with other classes of drugs that are misused and abused (e.g., narcotics and stimulants).

## THE CHALLENGE OF SELF-REGULATION

Because humans are governed less by instincts and more by coping skills and capacities acquired from the caregiving environment, requirements for human survival and adaptation place a lifelong challenge on humans for self-regulation. Regulating emotions is one of the most central of these challenges. I believe self-medication factors in addictive disorders are intimately related to human self-regulation problems, and, in particular, to the regulation of affects. Accordingly, in this chapter I place and discuss self-medication factors and substance abuse in a broader context of the human need for self-regulation.

Clinical investigators working with alcoholics and addicts over the past three decades have accumulated observations and findings suggesting a self-medication hypothesis of addictive disorders (Khantzian 1974, 1985, Krystal and Raskin 1970, Milkman and Frosch 1973, Wieder and Kaplan 1969, Wurmser 1974). Many of these reports stressed major developmental impairments and severe psychopathology and associated painful affect states that made reliance on drugs likely and compelling. Subsequent diagnostic and treatment studies provided supporting and empirical evidence that addicts suffer with coexisting psychiatric disorders and structural psychopathology (Blatt et al. 1984, Dorus and Senay 1980, Khantzian and Treece 1985, McLellan et al. 1979, Nicholson and Treece 1981, Rounsaville et al. 1982a,b, Treece and Nicholson 1980, Weissman et al. 1976, Woody et al. 1975, 1983).

Despite the documented association between substance abuse and psychopathology, I have become convinced that there is a wide range of emotional vulnerability or susceptibility to addictive and alcoholic disorders. Admittedly, the cases of severe psychopathology represent an extreme, but they and the less severely or minimally affected individuals with psychopathology are all more or less subject to human experiences and processes involving distress and suffering. It is distress and suffering that is at the heart of alcoholism and addiction, and cases of more extreme psychopathology are examples of where the emotional pain is greater for such individuals as a consequence of their psychopathology.

The self-medication hypothesis takes into consideration how the effects or actions of the different classes of drugs (i.e., stimulants, opiates, and sedative-hypnotics) interact with states of distress to make them appealing and to cause certain individuals to become dependent on them. The self-medication perspective of drug-alcohol dependence places heavy emphasis on painful affects, but other self-regulating factors involving self-esteem, self-other relationships, and self-care also interact with affect states in substance use and misuse. I will expand on these other factors subsequently.

As I have indicated, my emphasis in exploring self-medication factors in alcoholism and addictions is on suffering and its psychological determinants. There are clearly other determinants, however, in addition to the psychological factors that cause or contribute to the development of dependency on alcohol and drugs. These include genetic, environmental, and cultural factors that may either protect against or heighten a person's vulnerability to substance use disorders. Exploration of these factors goes beyond the scope of this chapter, which is limited to the psychological factors. However, a comprehensive explanation or theory of substance dependence must ultimately attempt to integrate these factors and account for how they interact.

## OLD AND NEW THEORIES OF HUMAN DISTRESS

### Drives and Conflict

Early psychoanalytic theory of the mind advanced by Sigmund Freud emphasized instinctual factors (i.e., pleasure and aggressive drives) and a topographic view of the mind in which much of mental life and psychic process was considered to be unconscious. Freud and his followers later placed greater emphasis on internal processes and states involving wishes and needs and a more detailed appreciation of structural factors and functions involved in regulating psychic life and adjustment to reality. In these earlier psychodynamic formulations, psychic suffering and human distress were viewed for the most part in terms of conflict psychology. Distress was felt to be the result of human drives or wishes pressing for discharge but opposed by inhibitions or repression.

Early psychoanalytic approaches to relieving conflict and distress emphasized making unconscious mental life (i.e., fantasies, wishes, and desires) conscious, and verbalizing and working through pent-up sexual and aggressive drives. Employing free association and cathartic techniques, the objective was to reduce or minimize tensions, conflict, and distress that resulted from excessive control or repression of drives and related impulses.

## Affects and Structure

There has been a decided shift from these early psychodynamic theories, which stressed drives and conflict, and reducing or keeping drives at a minimum as a means to avoid distress and conflict. Contemporary psychodynamic theory has placed affects and feeling life center stage and more systematically considers the ways ego and self structures develop and unfold to optimally regulate affects (i.e., feeling life), self-esteem, relationships, and adaptation to external reality.

Although modern psychodynamic clinicians still employ free association to access the nature and source of emotional distress, greater efforts are placed on actively building empathic connections and contact with patients to help them identify their feelings and needs, to derive a better sense of self and others, and to develop a sense of safety and comfort. Emphasis in contemporary clinical approaches focuses more on fostering improved capacities for containment of feelings and self-regulation. Rather than releasing or reducing drive tensions to minimal levels, modern approaches stress the maintenance of optimal (versus maximum or minimal) affects and helping individuals grow in their capacity to control and transform distress.

## Development and Adaptation

The degree to which individuals can tolerate distress and find relief from human suffering is proportional to the degree they have been able to develop and internalize capacities to regulate feelings, to establish and maintain a healthy regard for self and others, and to take care of themselves. These capacities are incorporated as mental structures and functions in our personality organization and reflect our ego capacities and sense of self.

The development of ego and sense of self begins in infancy and continues over a lifetime. The attitudes and functions that are internalized derive primarily from our parents and, subsequently, from association with other significant individuals and groups. If the growing-up environment is optimally constant, nurturing, and relatively free of major trauma or neglect, ego functions and the sense of self coalesce to give us a mature and adaptable character structure. In contrast, major developmental flaws, defects, and distortions occur in a person's character structure as a function of environmental inconstancy, trauma, and neglect (Khantzian and Mack 1989). Our focus on problems in self-regulation and the use of substances for the purpose of self-medication is based on this appreciation of these developmental processes and disabilities. These developmental flaws and deficits in the character structure of substance abusers are responsible for the difficulties they experience in adapting to their internal emotional life and external world of reality. It is on this basis that addicts and alcoholics attempt to correct these flaws through the use of substances, a "correction" they feel they cannot achieve on their own.

## COMMON FACTORS IN ALCOHOLISM
## AND THE ADDICTIONS

The common factors in alcoholism and the addictions center around the use of substances as a means to achieve and maintain self-regulation. However, considering how disregulated, disorganized, and out of control addicts and alcoholics appear, it is hard to believe that they could be using these substances for purposes of regulating themselves. In fact, it is on the basis of this latter observation that many argue that substances cause distress and disregulation rather than the other way around (Cummings et al. 1985, Vaillant 1980). Such accounts, in my estimation, focus excessively on the admitted regression in psychological function associated with long-term use of drugs, some drugs (e.g., stimulants and sedative-hypnotics) causing more regression than others (McLellan et al. 1979). They fail to take enough into account the more enduring and relatively immutable personality structures of such individuals, which reveal long-standing difficulties in managing their inner psychological life and their external behaviors. Systematic study of such factors reveals that many of the protracted states of dysphoria (or "hypophoria") associated with drug withdrawal are some of the same states that coexisted with other determining personality traits and features predating the substance dependence (Martin et al. 1977, 1978).

I would argue that the regular reliance on any drug causes a "disuse" atrophy in a person's capacity to achieve a subjective or behavioral end in more ordinary ways. That is, the more individuals depend on a drug or alcohol to calm, activate, relate to others, play, and so forth, the less they develop these capacities normally, and more often and tragically they undermine any existing capacities they might have developed. But as we gain an appreciation of substance abusers' life-long difficulties in coping with distress, their initial and subsequent reliance on drugs becomes more understandable. In this section I review how sectors of vulnerability in personality organization common to alcoholics and addicts, involving feeling life (affects), self-esteem, self-other relations, and self-care, can predispose individuals to use and become dependent on substances.

## Affects

The nature of the distress or suffering associated with alcoholism and addiction, I feel, is closely linked with the complex ways in which individuals with these problems experience, tolerate, and express their feelings (i.e., affects). They seem to suffer in the extreme, either feeling too much or feeling too little. Some seem to be more chronically "disaffected" (McDougall 1984) or unable to name their feelings ("alexithymia") (Krystal 1982) and seem more pervasively devoid of feelings; others seem, more often than not, overwhelmed with intense affects, such as rage, shame, loneliness, and depression, and yet others "flip-flop" between the extremes of emotional flooding and emptiness (Khantzian 1978, 1980, 1991, Krystal and Raskin 1970, Milkman and Frosch 1973, Wieder and Kaplan 1969, Wurmser 1974).

Individuals who suffer in these ways use drugs and alcohol to help them cope with emotions. Depending on one's state and the doses of drugs used, drug-alcohol effects may, in some instances, attenuate or allow feelings. When individuals feel a need to repeatedly resort to drugs or alcohol to achieve such effects, it is usually a sign that they suffer with developmental deficits and handicaps and thus need drug-alcohol effects to achieve and maintain states of feeling that they cannot achieve on their own. That is, drugs and alcohol are used as a "prosthetic" (Wieder and Kaplan 1969) to compensate for deficits in regulating affect life.

I will elaborate subsequently on the differences in the effects of the various classes of drugs, including alcohol, and how they interact with specific affect states to make them compelling. However, there is one more general aspect of drug-alcohol use involved in controlling feelings that I believe is important to review. I am referring to a paradoxical aspect of drug-alcohol dependency, namely, that as much as substances may be used to relieve distress and painful affect states, such a reliance also perpetuates and often worsens such states. Although at first this result might seem to be a case of enduring some distress in exchange for even momentary relief, I have realized that substance abusers employ this negative effect in the service of controlling their suffering. In this instance, at least part of the trade-off in accepting the pain of drug use involves converting the passive experience of not knowing or being able to access feelings to an experience where one actively controls feelings, even if the feelings they produce are painful. This seems to apply especially to those patients I described who more often do not seem to feel or are devoid of feelings. Rather than just relieving painful affects when they are overwhelming, drugs and alcohol, and the distress they entail, may also be adopted as a way of being in control, especially when they feel out of control because affects are vague, elusive, and nameless (Khantzian 1987, Khantzian and Wilson 1993).

## Well-Being and Self-Esteem

Basic states of well-being and positive self-regard derive from the earliest stages of development. Addicts and alcoholics suffer with developmental deficits involving a failure to internalize the comforting, soothing, validating, and mobilizing aspects of their parenting or caregiving environment (Khantzian 1978).

I have been repeatedly impressed that drug and alcohol-dependent individuals are vulnerable around problems in soothing and calming themselves, especially when they are stressed and overwrought, and conversely, that they may also suffer with initiative and activation problems when their safety or well-being depends on taking action. Deriving from these basic states, but related to subsequent developmental challenges and need for mastery, substance abusers also suffer because they have not developed a sufficient capacity for self-esteem or self-love to allow them to enjoy confidence in themselves and their potential, and a balanced valuation of their importance in relation to self and others (Khantzian and Mack 1989, Mack 1981). Drug and alcohol effects interact with affect states and characterological or characteristic defenses related to states of disharmony, immobilization, and self-esteem in ways that relieve or alter the suffering entailed with these states. I discuss these interactions more specifically below. When substance abusers speak of the "high" or euphoria that they experience with drugs or alcohol, they are probably referring to the self-soothing, comfort, repair, and sense of well-being and power they cannot obtain or sustain within themselves or from others unless they resort to drugs or alcohol (Khantzian et al. 1974, Krystal 1977, Spotts and Shontz 1987, Woolcott 1980).

## Relationships

The problems addicts and alcoholics have in relation to regulating their feelings and maintaining their self-esteem make relating to and depending on others a precarious, if not erratic, experience. As much as they need others to know how they feel, they often fear and distrust their dependency, disavow their need, and act in counterdependent ways. Their defenses of self-sufficiency and disavowal leave them isolated and cut off, and they disguise from self and others their need for nurturance and validation, which is often excessive, given their developmental deficits. Consequently, there is a tendency to be inconsistent in satisfying their own and others' needs in relationships. They alternate between being selfless and demanding, but more chronically dissatisfied and cut off, and thus more susceptible to using drugs and alcohol to process emotions around their needs and wants (Khantzian 1978, 1980).

## Self-Care

Because of the obvious dangers associated with acute and chronic use of drugs and alcohol, substance abusers are often accused (and they also accuse themselves) of harboring self-destructive motives. Some have suggested that addictive behavior is a form of "suicide on the installment plan." This kind of cynical, negative, destructive motive attributed to addicts derives from early drive psychology (Khantzian and Treece 1977) and detracts from an empathic understanding of addicts' vulnerabilities. Addictive behavior is governed less by self-destructive motives than by the result of developmental failures and deficits that leave certain individuals ill equipped to protect and take care of themselves. Along these lines we have proposed that addicts and alcoholics suffer with deficits or deficiencies in a capacity for self-care (Khantzian 1978, 1989, 1991, Khantzian and Mack 1983). The characteristic patterns of failures to anticipate harm and danger associated with self care deficits are extensively reviewed in Chapters 2, 14, 15, and 19.

As I have indicated, deficits or vulnerabilities in the capacity for self-care cut across all substance abusers. However, the degree of deficiency or disability in self-care may be variable over time in any one individual, but it is more global and pervasive in some types of addictions than others, for example, in certain polydrug addicts and more so in intravenous drug abusers. Self-care functions may be better established in some individuals, but they may lapse or deteriorate under conditions of major stress, depression, or as a consequence of prolonged drug-alcohol use. These functions may also be overridden because for certain individuals survival concerns become subordinate to needs for relief from painful affect states or a drivenness to achieve or perform, which drug effects may enhance (Khantzian 1991). Whether this involves a lapse or is the result of more severe impairment, self-care problems in substance abusers are apparent in addicts and alcoholics in their failure or inability to adequately worry about, fear, or consider the long- and short-term complications and dangers associated with drugs and alcohol.

## DRUGS AND SELF-MEDICATION

Most individuals who become and remain dependent on drugs and alcohol have experimented or tried many drugs and even continue to use more than one drug. However, if asked, most addicts will indicate they prefer a particular drug. Exploring psychological characteristics of such individuals reveals that the drug they select or prefer is a function of characteristic defenses, organization in personality style (or structure), and related affect states that dominate their inner emotional life and their relationships with others. Addicts and alcoholics have a special "discovery" that specific painful feeling states may be relieved or that pleasant, special states of well-being may be achieved through a particular drug.

If an analogy for personality structure and affects can be made to a container and the contents, respectively, one could then say that drugs exercise their effects in the way they alter or modify the container and the contents, the two main factors with which drugs interact. For some individuals, the container is too porous and the contents (e.g., rage and anger) pour out too readily, causing self and others much distress and disharmony. For others, the container is overly restrictive and sealed and thus constricts the experiencing and communication of a range of contained emotions. And for yet others, certain emotions or energy are depleted and diminished. Drugs and alcohol can modify or act on either the container (structure) or the contents (affects). There may be some duplication and overlap in effects from drugs, and, depending on dose and setting, two different drugs might produce similar effects based on different mechanisms of action. For example, both alcohol, in low to moderate doses, and cocaine enhance socialization. Alcohol dissolves the container and lets feelings out, whereas cocaine mobilizes the content and produces increased energy and euphoric feeling. Both effects enhance social interaction. On the other hand, alcohol in heavy doses, like opiates, may have a containing or muting effect on intense, painful emotions. Notwithstanding some of these similarities, the self-medication hypothesis rests on the assumption that the three main classes of drugs of abuse (i.e., stimulants, opiate-analgesics, and sedative-hypnotics) have distinctly different actions and effects.

The process whereby substance abusers discover that the particular action of a drug suits them best has been variously described as the "drug of choice" (Wieder and Kaplan 1969), "the preferential use of drugs" (Milkman and Frosch 1973), "the self-selection process" (Khantzian 1975), and "the drug of commitment" (Spotts and Shontz 1987). In this section I discuss the appeal of stimulants and opiates, and in the next section the appeal of the sedative-hypnotics, in particular, alcohol.

## Stimulants

Within one decade cocaine has gone from being a relatively low-profile, elite, exclusive drug of glamorous, fast-living, and famous people, to a drug that pervades all strata of our society. Because it is the most widespread and prevalent stimulant of abuse, I will consider it the representative drug of the stimulant class of drugs.

The main desired effects of cocaine derive from its activating and energizing properties. It probably has wide appeal because its stimulating effects allure both low-energy and high-energy individuals. For the former, cocaine helps to overcome fatigue and depletion states associated with depression (Khantzian 1975, 1985) or relieves feelings of boredom and emptiness (Wurmser 1974); for the latter, cocaine provides increased feelings of assertiveness, self-esteem, and frustration tolerances or "augments a hyperactive, restless lifestyle and an exaggerated need for self sufficiency" (Khantzian 1979, p. 100).

The affect states that respond to the stimulating action of cocaine are more often than not related to an individual's personality organization and defensive style, which probably predispose to characteristic-associated states of depression, boredom, emptiness, and hyperactivity, and make drug-seeking behavior and involvement more likely. Although an extensive review of these personality factors is not possible, the following are examples of factors that can contribute to cocaine use: (1) states of boredom and emptiness with which certain cocaine addicts suffer could be the basis on which they are described as "sensation" or "stimulus-seeking" personalities; (2) individuals who are overcompensating, ambitious, and driven in their character style use stimulants to augment their drive to achieve, or to compensate for their not infrequent collapse in self-esteem and depression when their ambitions fail; and (3) cocaine may act paradoxically to calm certain restless, emotionally labile individuals with attention deficit disorder (Khantzian 1985, 1991).

*Case Vignette*

Sam, a 39-year-old successful businessman, one year into recovery, poignantly demonstrated many of these features of distress and life-long character flaws that set him up to "love" cocaine. Despite being very personable, handsome, and successful in his businesses, he complained of always being afraid of people, out of touch with his desires and needs, and always pleasing people. Despite many sexual liaisons, he said until recently he never felt close to anyone, and more recently when he did, he "lost" himself in the relationship. He described how minor or major external events could rapidly flip his self-esteem. At these times he would fuel an insatiable need for love and admiration with cocaine. Action and activity, he said, was his main mode of coping, and cocaine provided the means to get started and continue moving. The drug would help him to overcome his overbearing depression and to feel empowered and attractive enough to cruise around and find a woman to satisfy his needs.

## Opiate-Analgesics

In contrast to the stimulants, opiates principally have a muting and containing action. Although opiates mute and relieve physical pain (and on this basis we might surmise that they generally alleviate emotional pain—and they do), I have been impressed that they have a much more specific effect and appeal. Working more exclusively with narcotic addicts in the early 1970s in a methadone treatment program, I became impressed with how many of the narcotic addicts conveyed and demonstrated the muting and containing action of opiates on aggression and violent feelings (Khantzian 1972, 1974). A subsequent series of reports (Khantzian 1980, Vereby 1982, Wurmser 1974) described how individuals who prefer and have become dependent on opiates have had long-standing histories as victims of physical abuse and violence and in many cases often turned into the perpetrators of violence. Such people, whether victims or perpetrators, suffer with acute and chronic states of associated aggressive and rageful feelings. Individuals predisposed to opiates discover that these intense, disorganizing affects are significantly contained or attenuated when they first use opiates, and on this basis they described this action as "calming, feeling mellow, safe, [or] normal for the first time."

In my experience, the problem with aggression in such individuals is a function of an excess of this intense affect—partly constitutional and partly environmental in origin—that interacts with ego and self structures that are underdeveloped or deficient and thus fail to contain this affect. Opiates are compelling because their antiaggression/rage action mutes uncontrolled aggression and reverses internal psychological disorganization and the external threat of counteraggression with which these intense emotions are associated (Khantzian 1982, 1985).

### Case Vignette

A 47-year-old psychologist described graphically how her preference for the containing and soothing effects of opiates compensated for her inability to process emotional distress. Although she was more subdued at the time she offered the following complaints and concerns, early in treatment she had powerfully displayed an intensely angry and intemperate self when frustrated.

Anticipating a stressful, overseas flight that day, she complained, "There's no place in my brain for [dealing with] discomfort." She was expecting to experience a "cranky sleeplessness" on the flight and worried that she would target her husband with her feelings. She was anticipating that her only alternative would be to use drugs. She pointed to a print portraying a mother comfortably and comfortingly holding a child and lamented that she could not calm or soothe herself. Not insignificantly she contrasted her lot to that of two other patients in group therapy who used alcohol to overcome inhibitions and to socialize.

## ALCOHOL AND SELF-MEDICATION

The patient in the above vignette perceptively and intuitively grasped how alcohol affects individuals who prefer it differently from the way it affects those who prefer opiates. Whereas opiate addicts brim with intense and most often angry feeling, alcoholics suffer because they more often are restricted and overcontained in the ways they experience and express emotion. Sedative-hypnotics including alcohol have appeal because these drugs relieve tense, anxious states associated with rigid, overdrawn defenses. The psychoanalyst Fenichel (1945) quotes an unknown source that "the superego is that part of the mind that is soluble in alcohol" (p. 379). This quote corresponds better to the dynamics that are emphasized in early psychoanalytic formulations. These early views stressed that an overdrawn conscience could leave individuals conflicted and tense about sexual and aggressive drives and impulses and that alcohol acted on releasing individuals from their restrictive superego defenses. More recent formulations focus on ego defenses and the subjective aspects of self and self-other experiences.

Alcohol is the main and representative drug for the sedative-hypnotic class of substances. Beyond alcohol, the main types of drugs abused in this class have been the barbiturates (e.g., secobarbital) and the barbiturate-like (e.g., glutethimide) drugs. More recently, these drugs have been replaced by benzodiazepines. The abuse potential of the benzodiazepines is variable and to some degree seems to be a function of pharmacokinetics. On the other hand, Ciraulo and colleagues (1988) suggest that states of distress, "probably discomfort with people and one's surroundings, discontentment and dysphoria" (p. 336), are greater in alcoholics and are probably the main determinants as well in the abuse of benzodiazepines. In this report, Ciraulo and associates provide empirical support for self-medication factors in alcoholism. They show that alcoholics react with a more positive change to the benzodiazepine alprazolam than controls do and therefore are more likely to abuse this drug. Notwithstanding the differences in form (i.e., a pill versus a drink) and meaning, there are enough similarities to use alcohol as the representative drug of this class of drugs to explore their appeal as self-medication agents.

## Affects and Alcohol

Whereas early psychodynamic formulations stressed the dissolving or disinhibiting effect of alcohol on rigid superego mechanisms of defense, more contemporary formulations have placed greater emphasis on alcohol's effect on constricted ego defenses and subjective feelings involving the sense of self and self in relationships with other people. Performing artists and writers understand this distinction well. From ancient times to Shakespeare and up to the present, poets and lyricists through song and words have celebrated the softening and releasing properties of alcohol.

As I have suggested, some substance abusers suffer because they cannot feel their feelings. Our current understanding of why it is that certain individuals cannot feel and need substances to do so is not entirely clear. Some argue that certain patients who are totally out of touch with feelings are "disaffected" and use drugs and activity to ameliorate feelingless, lifeless states related to primitive defenses against anxieties associated with rage and terror (McDougall 1984). This formulation is reminiscent of conflict psychology, but on a more archaic level. Others (Krystal and Raskin 1970) have proposed that feeling life is underdeveloped in alcoholics and that affects, when underdeveloped, tend to remain somatized, not differentiated (i.e., alcoholics cannot distinguish anxiety from depression) and not verbalized ("alexithymia"). Whether deriving from conflict or developmental deficits, sedative-hypnotic abusers' descriptions of their experience may better convey how their preferred drugs alter their feelings, as the following example demonstrates:

*Case Vignette*

> A 30-year-old divorcee, brought up by a restricted and restricting mother and an alcoholic father, withdrew from her family and engaged in much promiscuous activity while a teenager to avoid, in particular, her mother's harsh and critical attitudes. She married in her early twenties and almost totally reversed her behavior and attitudes, adopting strict measures of propriety. By her late twenties, dissatisfaction with her marriage ultimately left her with a chronic sense of dysphoria and disabling migraine headaches. She dramatically discovered that the barbiturates in a commonly prescribed drug for headaches relieved more than her physical distress. Describing the drug effects, she said, "It's wonderful—[it] relieves the boredom and fills the void."

## Well-Being, Self-Esteem, and Alcohol

For some, the principal reason for using alcohol or related drugs is to simply feel. For others, it is to feel better inside oneself or to feel better about oneself. Much of this had to do with splits in personality organization that wall off comforting, soothing, and validating parts of self and do not allow a person to provide these functions for self. Krystal and Raskin (1970) and Krystal (1977) have proposed that this class of drugs has appeal because the drugs dissolve exaggerated defenses of denial and splitting. For some, alcohol allows the brief and therefore safe experience of loving and aggressive feelings that are otherwise "walled off" and leave such individuals feeling cut off and empty. Others discover that the soothing effect of alcohol calms internal clamor and emotional "noise," as the following example shows:

*Case Vignette*

> A 40-year-old psychiatrist described her nightly dependence on a bottle of wine as a means of achieving a sense of "bliss, harmony, and oneness." She emphasized that it was the only time she felt "all right," and that she drank "to maintain a blissful oneness with

the world." Although in her recovery she was discovering that Alcoholics Anonymous, jogging, and music could get her outside of the "inner [emotional] noise," she described how she still had to fight the other alternative that would immediately "quiet the noise," namely, the alcohol.

## Relationships and Alcohol

The notion of alcohol as a superego solvent partly explains why certain tense, neurotically inhibited individuals "enjoy" alcohol as a social lubricant and why this effect is enjoyed by many more in Western cultures for purposes of socializing and partying. Its main attraction, however, is more likely related to more deeply seated defenses related to discomfort and fears about human closeness, dependency, and intimacy. Both superego and ego defenses may, nevertheless, rigidly coalesce in such individuals to leave them feeling chronically distant, cut off, and cold in relationships with significant others. It is often under these conditions that certain predisposed people have a powerful and often dramatic realization as to what alcohol and sedative-hypnotics can do. A popular author-lecturer describes how a child rigidly internalizes harsh parental controls, and subsequently, how the resultant strictures in personality yield to the discovery of drug-alcohol effects: "So you couldn't be mad, you couldn't be sad, you couldn't be glad. You became a walking uptight. Then when you put the chemical in your body—pow! You could relax for the very first time. You were functional! You could feel your feelings, dance, talk to girls. I'm alive! Alive!" (Bradshaw 1988, p. 89).

## CONCLUSION

Self-medication factors play an important role in the development of a reliance on drugs and alcohol. Each class of drugs of abuse interacts with painful affect states and related personality factors to make an individual's preferred drug appealing and compelling. Addicts and alcoholics share in common general problems in self-regulation involving difficulties with affect life, self-esteem, relationships, and self-care. These self-regulation problems combine to make people more desperate, driven, isolated, and impulsive and more likely to assume the risks of drug-alcohol seeking and using behavior. Addiction-prone individuals discover which drug suits them best through the unique qualities of their affect experience, and these choices are what distinguish addicts and alcoholics from each other.

Given that all humans more or less struggle with self-regulation issues, what probably distinguishes substance abusers in general from nonsubstance abusers is the way capacities to experience and regulate feeling interact with the capacity to manage and contain behavior or impulses. We need to study further how, for example, basic states of well-being, a healthy regard for self and others, and mature self-care protect against addictive and alcoholic dependence. Considerable clinical and empirical evidence has accumulated indicating that it is probably the malignant combination of defects in regulating affects and self-care, or problems in managing feelings and impulses, that is necessary and sufficient to produce addiction and alcoholism. Addictive and alcoholic solutions, then, are a way of compensating for self-regulation problems that individuals cannot otherwise correct on their own (Donovan 1986, Khantzian 1986, Spotts and Shontz 1987, Woolcott 1980). Unfortunately, such solutions are short-lived and the attempts at self-correction backfire and fail.

## REFERENCES

Blatt, S. J., Berman, W., Bloom-Feshback, S., et al. (1984). Psychological assessment of psychopathology in opiate addicts. *Journal of Nervous and Mental Disease* 172:156–165.

Bradshaw, J. (1988). Our families, ourselves. *Self Center*, September/October.

Ciraulo, D. A., Barnhill, J. C., and Greenblatt, D. J. (1988). Abuse liability and clinical pharmacokinetics of alprazolam in alcoholic men. *Journal of Clinical Psychiatry* 49:333–337.

Cummings, C. P., Prokop, C. K., and Cosgrove, R. (1985). Dysphoria: the cause or the result of addiction. *Psychiatric Hospitals* 16:131–134.

Donovan, J. M. (1986). An etiologic model of alcoholism. *American Journal of Psychiatry* 143:1–11.

Dorus, W., and Senay, E. C. (1980). Depression, demographic dimension, and drug abuse. *American Journal of Psychiatry* 137:699–704.

Fenichel, O. (1945). *The Psychoanalytic Theory of Neurosis*. New York: Norton.

Khantzian, E. J. (1972). A preliminary dynamic formulation of the psychopharmacologic action of methadone. In *Proceedings of the Fourth*

*National Conference on Methadone Treatment,* pp. 371–374. New York: National Association for the Prevention of Addictions to Narcotics.

——— (1974). Opiate addiction: a critique of theory and some implications for treatment. *American Journal of Psychotherapy* 28:59–70.

——— (1975). Self selection and progression in drug dependence. *Psychiatry Digest* 10:19–22.

——— (1978). The ego, the self and opiate addiction: theoretical and treatment considerations. *International Review of Psychoanalysis* 5:189–198.

——— (1979). Impulse problems in addiction: cause and effect relationships. In *Working with the Impulsive Person,* ed. H. Wishnie, pp. 97–112. New York: Plenum.

——— (1980). An ego-self theory of substance dependence. In *Theories of Addiction,* ed. D. J. Lettieri, M. Sayers, and H. W. Wallenstein, NIDA monograph 30, pp. 29–33. Rockville, MD: National Institute on Drug Abuse.

——— (1982). Psychological (structural) vulnerabilities and the specific appeal of narcotics. *Annals of the New York Academy of Science* 398:24–32.

——— (1985). The self-medication hypothesis of addictive disorders: focus on heroin and cocaine dependence. *American Journal of Psychiatry* 142:1259–1264.

——— (1986). A contemporary psychodynamic approach to drug abuse treatment. *American Journal of Drug and Alcohol Abuse* 12(3):213–222.

——— (1987). A clinical perspective of the cause-consequence controversy in alcoholic and addictive suffering. *Journal of the American Academy of Psychoanalysis* 15:521–537.

——— (1991). Self-regulation factors in cocaine dependence—a clinical perspective. In *The Epidemiology of Cocaine Use and Abuse,* ed. S. Schober and C. Schade. Research monograph 110, pp. 211–216. Rockville, MD: National Institute on Drug Abuse.

Khantzian, E. J., and Mack, J. E. (1983). Self-preservation and the care of the self-ego instincts reconsidered. *Psychoanalytic Study of the Child* 38:209–232. New Haven, CT: Yale University Press.

——— (1989). AA and contemporary psychodynamic theory. In *Recent Development in Alcoholism,* vol. 7, ed. M. Galanter, pp. 67–89. New York: Plenum.

Khantzian, E. J., Mack, J. E., and Schatzberg, A. F. (1974). Heroin use as an attempt to cope: clinical observations. *American Journal of Psychiatry* 131:160–164.

Khantzian, E. J., and Treece, C. (1977). Psychodynamics of drug dependence: an overview. In *Psychodynamics of Drug Dependence*, ed. J. D. Blaine and D. A. Julius, NIDA research monograph 12, pp. 11–25. Rockville, MD: National Institute on Drug Abuse.

————— (1985). *DSM-III* psychiatric diagnosis of narcotic addicts: recent findings. *Archives of General Psychiatry* 42:1067–1071.

Khantzian, E. J., and Wilson, A. (1993). Substance abuse, repetition and the nature of addictive suffering. In *Hierarchical Conceptions in Psychoanalysis*, ed. A. Wilson and J. E. Gedo, pp. 263–283. New York: Guilford.

Krystal, H. (1977). Self-representation and the capacity for self care. *Annual of Psychoanalysis* 6:209–246.

————— (1982). Alexithymia and the effectiveness of psychoanalytic treatment. *International Journal of Psychoanalytic Psychotherapy* 9:353–388.

Krystal, H., and Raskin, H. A. (1970). *Drug Dependence: Aspects of Ego Functions*. Detroit: Wayne State University Press.

Mack, J. E. (1981). Alcoholism, AA and the governance of the self. In *Dynamic Approaches to the Understanding and Treatment of Alcoholism*, ed. M. H. Bean and N. E. Zinberg, pp. 125–162. New York: Free Press.

Martin, W. R., Haertzen, C. A., and Hewett, B. B. (1978). Psychopathology and pathophysiology of narcotic addicts, alcoholics, and drug abusers. In *Psychopharmacology: A Generation of Progress*, ed. V. A. Lipton, A. DiMascio, and K. F. Killam, pp. 1591–1602. New York: Raven.

Martin, W. R., Hewett, B. B., Baker, A. J., and Haertzen, C. A. (1977). Aspects of the psychopathology and pathophysiology of addiction. *Drug Alcohol Dependence* 2:185–202.

McDougall, J. (1984). The "disaffected" patient: reflection on affect pathology. *Psychoanalytic Quarterly* 53:386–409.

McLellan, A. T., Woody, G. E., and O'Brien, C. P. (1979). Development of psychiatric illness in drug abusers. *New England Journal of Medicine* 201:1310–1314.

Milkman, H., and Frosch, W. A. (1973). On the preferential abuse of heroin and amphetamine. *Journal of Nervous and Mental Disease* 156:242–248.

Nicholson, B., and Treece, C. (1981). Object relations and differential treatment response to methadone maintenance. *Journal of Nervous and Mental Disease* 169:424–429.

Rounsaville, B. J., Weissman, M. M., Crits-Cristoph, K., et al. (1982a). Diagnosis and symptoms of depression in opiate addicts: course and relationship to treatment outcome. *Archives of General Psychiatry* 39:151–156.

Rounsaville, B. J., Weissman, M. M., Kleber, H., et al. (1982b). Heterogeneity of psychiatric diagnosis in treated opiate addicts. *Archives of General Psychiatry* 39:161–166.

Spotts, J. V., and Shontz, F. C. (1987). Drug induced ego states: a trajectory theory of drug experience. *Society of Pharmacology* 1:19–51.

Treece, C., and Nicholson, B. (1980). *DSM-III* personality type and dose levels in methadone maintenance patients. *Journal of Nervous and Mental Disease* 168:621–628.

Vaillant, G. E. (1980). Natural history of male psychological health. VIII: antecedents of alcoholism and "orality." *American Journal of Psychiatry* 137:181–186.

Vereby, K., ed. (1982). Opioids in mental illness: theories, clinical observations, and treatment possibilities. *Annals of the New York Academy of Sciences* 98:1–512.

Weissman, M. M., Slobetz, F., Prusoff, B., et al. (1976). Clinical depression among narcotic addicts maintained on methadone in the community. *American Journal of Psychiatry* 133:1434–1438.

Wieder, H., and Kaplan, E. H. (1969). Drug use in adolescence: psychodynamic meaning and pharmacogenic effect. *Psychoanalytic Study of the Child* 24:399–431. New York: International Universities Press.

Woody, G. E., Luborsky, L., McLellan, A. T., et al. (1983). Psychotherapy for opiate addicts. *Archives of General Psychiatry* 40:639–645.

Woody, G. E., O'Brien, C. P., and Rickels, K. (1975). Depression and anxiety in heroin addicts: a placebo-controlled study of doxepin in combination with methadone. *American Journal of Psychiatry* 132:447–450.

Woolcott, P. (1980). Addiction: clinical and theoretical considerations. *Annual of Psychoanalysis* 9:189–204.

Wurmser, L. (1974). Psychoanalytic considerations of the etiology of compulsive drug use. *Journal of the American Psychoanalytic Association* 22:820–843.

# 13

# Self-Regulation Factors in Cocaine Dependence

Unraveling the etiological equation in the addictions has important implications for understanding how biology and psychology intersect in governing human behavior. Technological advances over the past three decades have provided breakthroughs in understanding some of the important biological factors in the equation, the discovery of opiate receptor sites and endorphins being the most recent exciting example. During this same period, extensive clinical work with drug-dependent individuals has also provided a basis for understanding some of the psychological factors that contribute to addictive behavior. A contemporary psychodynamic perspective, complemented by psychiatric diagnostic studies employing standardized diagnostic approaches, has shown that painful feeling states and psychiatric suffering are associated with the addiction and appear to be important etiological determinants (Deykin et al. 1987, Khantzian 1985, Khantzian and Treece 1985, Rounsaville et al. 1982a,b).

This chapter focuses and elaborates on psychodynamic and psychiatric factors observed to be important in the development of dependence on drugs, with particular emphasis on cocaine dependence. The approach is based on the assumption that the clinical context and the in-depth study of individual cases are valuable in explaining what motivates human behavior, in general, and troubling behaviors such as the addictions, in particular. Ultimately, the explanations that will serve best in solving the etiology of addiction will integrate data derived from the biological, social, and psychological perspectives. The aim of this chapter is to delineate more precisely the psychological dimension of cocaine dependence from a psychodynamic perspective with the hope that this approach can shed light on and contribute to an integrated biopsychosocial formulation of cocaine addiction.

As indicated in previous chapters, early psychodynamic formulations emphasized satisfaction of libidinal and aggressive drives and the symbolic meaning of drugs to explain addictions. The reader is reminded that in this volume of my collected works I have been principally guided by a contemporary psychodynamic perspective that focuses on developmental and self-regulation deficits for which addictive substances are an attempt at self-correction.

## NATURE OF THE DATA

The treatment relationship is a valuable source of information for identifying and understanding the psychological vulnerabilities of addicts and how such vulnerabilities might motivate a reliance on drugs. With cocaine addicts, for example, the clinical context offers opportunities to explore how the powerful energizing and activating properties of the drug interact with feeling (or affect) states and personality traits and characteristics to make continued or regular use more likely.

A series of diagnostic studies over the past decade, complementing clinical observations, has documented co-occurring psychopathology predominantly involving depression and personality disorder in cocaine abusers (Gawin and Kleber 1984, Kleber and Gawin 1984, Weiss and Mirin 1984, 1986). These studies, not insignificantly and in contrast to studies among opiate addicts, found a disproportionately higher incidence of bipolar-type affective disorder, and in the case of the Weiss and Mirin studies, a high incidence of narcissistic and borderline personality disorder. Subsequently, Weiss and colleagues (1988) documented a lower but nevertheless substantial incidence of concurrent affective disorder and a higher incidence of antisocial personality disorder.

The main source of data for this report, however, is direct observation and experience with patients in the vis-à-vis context of the patient–therapist relationship, the clinical interview, and group psychotherapy. Such contexts provide unique opportunities to understand the role of state (reactions) and trait (characterological) factors in susceptibility to a reliance on cocaine.

Empathic appreciation of patients' feeling states and analysis and understanding of characteristic patterns of relating and behavior are part of the bedrock of psychoanalysis and psychoanalytic psychotherapy. These clinical traditions instruct us that a great deal can be learned about what motivates mental life and behavior. Following the nuances of reacting and interacting in treatment relationships allows clinicians to appreciate how personality and feeling states interact and play themselves out, both with the therapist (and with other patients in group therapy) and in the patient's life. These observations allow for inferences about a person's strengths, characteristic ways of coping, and dysfunctions and failure to cope in various aspects of life. They can also provide unique and valuable data for understanding how a powerful feeling-altering drug such as cocaine may be adopted functionally and dysfunctionally in an individual's attempt to cope with internal feeling life and adjustment to external reality.

Luborsky (1984) recently summarized the psychoanalytic traditions behind the technique and principles for psychoanalytic psychotherapy. More importantly, for my purposes here, Luborsky and Woody and associates (1986) successfully applied these principles to narcotic addicts, demonstrating that they benefit from psychotherapy, depending on the degree and type of psychopathology present. In their manual for substance abusers, Luborsky and colleagues (1977) described how core relationship conflicts (i.e., characteristic ways of responding to people) emerge in the treatment relationship and provide valuable clues for understanding the meaning of drug dependence, especially factors that precipitate and maintain it. The relationship themes are apparent in many contexts. The "core" issues or the core conflictual relationship theme (CCRT) appear everywhere in the patient's communication: about the past, about the present, and in the treatment relationship. We have found Luborsky and colleagues' approach equally valid and applicable in individual psychotherapy with cocaine addicts in understanding how their feeling states and personality styles contribute to their dependency on cocaine. More recently, we applied these same principles in a National Institute on Drug Abuse (NIDA)-sponsored relapse prevention program for cocaine addicts. Along lines developed by Luborsky, we described how modified dynamic group therapy (MDGT) for cocaine abusers can activate core themes in which we can learn how certain feeling states and relationship, self-esteem, and self-care problems precipitate and maintain cocaine dependency (Khantzian et al. 1992).

My understanding of the appeal of cocaine is an outgrowth of the self-medication hypothesis. The reader is referred to Chapters 11 and 15 for a review of the specific appeal of opiates and depressants. The following description of the psychodynamic factors found to be important in cocaine dependency is based on clinical observations in individual evaluation sessions and treatment relationships, and in the course of group psychotherapy with substance abusers.

## SECTORS OF PSYCHOLOGICAL VULNERABILITY AND THE APPEAL OF COCAINE

Earlier psychodynamic reports had a tendency to associate or equate drug dependency with severe and significant psychopathology (Khantzian 1974, Khantzian and Treece 1977, 1980, Wieder and Kaplan 1969, Wurmser 1974). The emphasis, in my early work, on severe psychopathology as a determinant of drug use was a result of seeing a disproportionate number of heroin addicts in a methadone maintenance program. In more recent years, working with increasing numbers of alcoholics and cocaine addicts seeking treatment, I have found that degrees and sectors of psychological vulnerability are involved rather than global and severe psychiatric disturbance. Degrees of human psychological distress and suffering interacting with other factors seem to be the important determinants in cocaine's subjective appeal. Notwithstanding this shift in emphasis from psychopathology to suffering, my clinical experience continues to suggest that the more extreme cases (i.e., associated with psychopathology where the suffering is invariably greater) serve as valuable guides in understanding the psychological underpinnings of drug dependence.

Sectors of vulnerability in personality organization appear to play a part in predisposing some individuals to cocaine dependence. In my experience, however, no one personality type or "addictive personality" is involved that generally predisposes to dependence on drugs or to dependence on cocaine in particular. Although not exactly personality factors, terms such as *sensation seeking, stimulus seeking,* and *risk taking,* described as risk factors in certain populations (Kandel 1980, McAuliffe 1984, McAuliffe et al. 1987), come closer and describe better how a personality trait or predisposition could be influential in certain behaviors and activities that are forerunners of addictive involvement. Sensation seeking, stimulus seeking, and other traits might be particularly important for certain cocaine addicts.

The remainder of this chapter highlights four sectors of psychologic vulnerability—self-regulation vulnerabilities involving affects, self-esteem, self-other relationships, and self-care—and how such vulnerabilities may be important in the development of a dependence on cocaine.

## Affects

Feeling life, or affects, appear to be distressing for addicts on at least two counts. They either feel their distress as persistent and unbearable or they do not experience their feeling at all (Khantzian 1987). In the latter case, terms such as *alexithymia* (Krystal 1982, Sifneos et al. 1977), *dis-affected* (McDougall 1984), and *non-feeling responses* (Sashin 1986) have been coined or adopted to capture this quality in addicts and special populations. These recent conceptualizations have helped to clarify that dysphoria predisposing to addiction may be unpleasant not only because of painful affects such as anxiety, rage, and depression, but also because feelings may be absent, elusive, or nameless and thus confusing and beyond one's control.

In cocaine addicts, depression or depressive affect has been most frequently identified as a chronic or consistent source of distress that impels individuals to depend on the stimulating and antidepressant action of cocaine (Khantzian 1985, Khantzian and Khantzian 1984, Kleber and Gawin 1984, Kosten et al. 1987, Weiss and Mirin 1986). The ability of cocaine to overcome the fatigue and depletion states associated with acute depression and to activate chronically depressed individuals to overcome their anergia, to complete tasks, and to relate better to others is indeed a powerful short-term antidote to the self-esteem problems associated with these states (Khantzian 1975, 1985, Khantzian and Khantzian 1984). In these cases, self-medication motives seem to play a major part in the initiation and continuation of a dependence on cocaine. Many of these patients predictably and understandably respond to and benefit from the use of tricyclic antidepressant medication (Gawin and Kleber 1984, Rosecan and Nunes 1987). Not all cocaine addicts suffer with clearly identifiable depression. In fact, earlier estimates that as much as 50 percent of cocaine addicts suffered with depression (Gawin and Kleber 1984, Weiss and Mirin 1986) have recently been reduced to as low as 21 percent (Weiss et al. 1988). Weiss and colleagues (1988) attributed this drop in the rate of depression to changing epidemiology and a corresponding change in the characteristics of patients seeking treatment. In support of this change, they also cited the increase in diagnosis of antisocial personality disorder in their more recent study (16 percent), where in the previous (1984) study sample it was nonexistent.

Although the changing epidemiology could be a sufficient explanation for these shifts in diagnosis, the elusiveness of and confusion around affect experience could also explain why it is hard to identify, specify, or elicit the presence of painful affect, including depressive affect, in many patients and in cohort samples. It awaits further study to determine whether vague feelings of dysphoria or atypical depression, not picked up by standardized diagnostic approaches, might also contribute to seeking out the stimulating or activating properties of cocaine. It certainly is not unusual in clinical practice for patients to complain of feeling bored and empty or to seem devoid of affect. Such a state of being could cause sensation seeking or stimulus seeking and/or explain some of the motives of risk takers. Certainly, the qualities of sensation seeking and risk taking are preferred modes for antisocial characters. They are also notorious for being out of touch with or acting out their feeling life. Along lines proposed by Klein (1975) for borderline personality disorder, perhaps it also holds true that individuals with antisocial personality disorder suffer with states of dysregulation of affect and activation, and that many such individuals overcome their often hard-to-identify mood and inertia problems with cocaine.

## Self-Esteem and Relationships with Others

Cocaine is notorious for producing a sense of well-being within one-self and in relationship to other people. Its energizing action produces a sense of empowerment that can enhance a state of self-sufficiency or make contact and involvement with others exhilarating and exciting. Sexually, the user, short term, may also feel increased arousal and potency and a sense of being glamorous and appealing. It should not be surprising, then, that basic aspects of self-esteem and relationships with others are often interwoven in important ways with the fabric of cocaine addiction. Problems with narcissism, or self-love, are often at the root of the self-esteem problems involved with drug dependence. Kohut (1971, 1977) and his followers (Baker and Baker 1987, Goldberg 1978), in their development of self-psychology, proposed that narcissism evolves or unfolds along certain lines and takes mature (normal) and less mature (disturbed) forms and is evident in certain personality characteristics. Healthy narcissism is basic to emotional health and consists of a subjective sense of well-being, confidence in self-worth and potential, and a balanced valuation of one's importance in relation to other people, groups, and places in the world (Khantzian and Mack 1989, Mack 1981). In clinical work with cocaine addicts, I have been repeatedly impressed that vulnerabilities and deficits around these themes have been particularly important influences in explaining the allure of cocaine. Although a majority of these patients have been very successful and/or high achievers and superficially seem psychologically intact, I have been struck by how fragile their basic sense of self-worth has been. This has been most apparent in exaggerated preoccupation with physical or intellectual prowess, major concerns about performance and achievement, exaggerated needs for acceptance and approval, and vaulting ambitions.

Despite the exaggerated striving and needs, however, cocaine addicts are surprisingly uneven and inconsistent in the ways they express their needs and relate to others. They may alternately be charming, seductive, and passively expectant, or they may act aloof and as if they do not need other people. Their supersensitivity may be evident in deferential attitudes and attempts to gain approval and acceptance, but they may rapidly shift and become ruthless and demanding in their dealings with others.

Individual and group psychotherapy provide opportunities to observe the characterological (or characteristic defensive) telltales of these vulnerabilities in self-esteem and in self-other relations. Cocaine addicts have great difficulty in being honest with themselves and others about how driven, ambitious, and needy they are for recognition and acceptance. For many cocaine addicts, high activity levels and an action orientation, augmented by counterdependent attitudes, disguise their dependency needs. For those who are more passive and depressed, postures of helplessness and self-effacement suggest that they are temporarily or more chronically defeated and more obviously struggling with dependency needs. For yet other addicts, disavowal of need and self-sufficiency offer characterological protection from the realization that one is not all-powerful, perfect, and complete. Such patterns are often startlingly apparent in group therapy interactions with cocaine addicts, with their hyperactivity, self-centeredness, and counterdependence often alternating with reactions of passivity, discouragement, and isolation. Cocaine effects interact powerfully with the acute and chronic feeling states engendered by the characteristic needs and personality styles of individuals susceptible to cocaine dependence. Their tendency to be hyperactive, restless, and driving can be augmented and sustained by cocaine's energizing.properties, thus allowing such people a chemical boost or fuel for this preferred style. However, the extreme measures and standards of performance that such individuals maintain are difficult to constantly achieve. Often, such individuals periodically become depressed or chronically suffer with or ward off subclinical or atypical depressive reactions and states. It is not surprising, then, that they find the activating, antidepressant action of cocaine desirable and adaptive on this basis as well.

The diagnostic literature supports these clinical observations; a disproportionately larger percentage of cocaine addicts (compared, for example, to narcotic addicts) suffer with bipolar, cyclothymic, borderline, and narcissistic disorders. All these conditions share a tendency for action, high activity, and rapidly alternating moods, conditions in which the augmenting and/or antidepressant action of cocaine might be desirable.

Finally, consistent with these observations, certain individuals who are driven, hyperactive, emotionally labile, and evidence attentional problems, experience a paradoxical calming response to cocaine much like hyperactive children with attention deficit disorder respond to methylphenidate. In 1983, I reported on such a case involving extreme cocaine dependence that markedly improved with methylphenidate treatment (Khantzian 1983), and Gawin and Kleber (1984), Weiss and Mirin (1984), and Weiss and colleagues (1985) also identified such a subtype. Although this condition has been identified in only 5 percent of cohorts of cocaine addicts, this interesting finding further supports a self-medication hypothesis of addictive disorders. Recent studies have placed the proportion of patients with cocaine dependence and attention deficit hyperactivity disorder (ADHD) at a significantly higher level (Carroll and Rounsaville 1993, Levin and Kleber 1995, Rounsaville et al. 1991).

## Self-Care

Because of the dangerous mishaps and often deadly consequences associated with drug abuse, addicts are often considered to harbor conscious and unconscious self-destructive motives. The highly publicized and untimely deaths of popular athletes and artists suggest that the potential lethal consequence of cocaine use was known by the victims, yet they were not deterred from using it. Are these examples of pleasure instincts overriding survival instincts or, indeed, could this be the "death instinct" (or motive) in action, or are they instinctual at all?

As I have elaborated upon previously (See Chapters 2, 4, and 12) and subsequently, there is little in my experience to suggest that these seemingly apparent self-destructive behaviors are governed primarily by pleasure instincts or self-destructive drives. Rather it is more the results of deficits in self-care which cause addiction-prone individuals to inadequately consider the dangers or harm associated with substances of abuse and related behaviors.

Although we first discovered and described the self-care vulnerabilities in narcotic addicts (Khantzian 1978), I continue to be impressed that in varying degrees this vulnerability cuts across all substance dependency problems, including alcoholism and cocainism. However, rather than being a capacity that is globally or pathologically impaired, self-care functions in cocaine addicts are more or less established but are subject to lapses or regression in function, or on a more persistent basis, are only marginally present, thus causing these patients to not adequately worry, fear, or consider the potential danger or harm involved in using cocaine. Also, considering how needful, driven, or ambitious cocaine addicts can be, it might also be that priorities about achievement and performance override self-care functions and self-preservation concerns that may be less than optimally developed or established. Furthermore, the defensiveness around the self-esteem and relationship difficulties seen in cocaine addicts causes compensatory posturing, counterdependent, and counter-fearful reactions that also interfere with appropriate worry and concerns about self-protection and self-care.

## CONCLUSION

This chapter reviewed the nature of some psychological vulnerabilities that appear to be important in the development of a dependence on cocaine. Clinical observations and psychiatric diagnostic findings associated with cocaine and other addictions suggest that self-regulation problems involving feeling life, self-other relationships, and self-care cause subjective states of distress and behavioral difficulties. The combination of distress and behavior problems leaves people who suffer from such vulnerabilities at greater risk for seeking out and succumbing to the powerful psychotropic effects of cocaine.

This report is not concerned with the issue of the degree or mechanism of interaction with other etiological influences such as biological (e.g., genetic and neurobiological) and sociocultural (e.g., setting, drug availability, environmental stressors) factors. My own experience has led me to conclude that the psychological vulnerabilities delineated in this chapter are important determinants in the development of cocaine dependence in patients seen in a clinical context. It remains unclear whether findings in clinical populations of cocaine addicts are unique to them, or whether there may be implications for understanding cocaine use and abuse in nonclinical populations. For heuristic purposes, I would conclude that psychological factors, as well as social and biological factors, to some degree, play a role in all instances of cocaine abuse. The psychological factors reviewed in this chapter are on a continuum and exercise a greater degree of influence in some cases than in others.

## REFERENCES

Baker, H. S., and Baker, M. N. (1987). Heinz Kohut's self psychology: an overview. *American Journal of Psychiatry* 144:1–9.

Carroll, K. M., and Rounsaville, B. J. (1993). History and significance of childhood attention deficit disorder in treatment-seeking cocaine abusers. *Comprehensive Psychiatry* 34:75–86.

Deykin, E. Y., Levy, J. D., and Wells, V. (1987). Adolescent depression, alcohol and drug abuse. *American Journal of Public Health* 77:178–182.

Gawin, F. H., and Kleber, H. D. (1984). Cocaine abuse treatment. *Archives of General Psychiatry* 41:903–908.

——— (1986). Abstinence symptomatology and psychiatric diagnosis in cocaine abusers. *Archives of General Psychiatry* 43:107–113.

Gerard, D. L., and Kornetsky, C. (1954). Adolescent opiate addiction: a case study. *Psychiatric Quarterly* 28:367–380.

——— (1955). Adolescent opiate addiction: a study of control and addict subjects. *Psychiatric Quarterly* 29:457–486.

Goldberg, A., ed. (1978). *The Psychology of the Self.* New York: International Universities Press.

Kandel, D. B. (1980). Developmental stages in adolescent drug involvement. In *Theories of Addiction*, ed. D. J. Lettieri, M. Sayers, and H. W. Wallenstein, National Institute on Drug Abuse research monograph 30, pp. 120–127. DHHS Pub. No. (ADM) 80-967. Washington, DC: Department of Health and Human Services.

Khantzian, E. J. (1974). Opiate addiction: a critique of theory and some implications for treatment. *American Journal of Psychotherapy* 28:59–70.

——— (1975). Self selection and progression in drug dependence. *Psychiatry Digest* 10:19–22.

——— (1978). The ego, the self and opiate addiction: theoretical and treatment considerations. *International Review of Psychoanalysis* 5:189–198.

——— (1980). An ego-self theory of substance dependence. In *Theories of Addiction*, ed. D. J. Lettieri, M. Sayers, and H. W. Wallenstein, National Institute on Drug Abuse research monograph 30, pp. 29–33. DHHS Pub. No. (ADM) 80967. Washington, DC: Department of Health and Human Services.

——— (1983). An extreme case of cocaine dependence and marked improvement with methylphenidate treatment. *American Journal of Psychiatry* 140(6):484–485.

——— (1985). The self-medication hypothesis of addictive disorders. *American Journal of Psychiatry* 142:1259–1264.

——— (1987). A clinical perspective of the cause-consequence controversy in alcoholic and addictive suffering. *Journal of the American Academy of Psychoanalysis* 15(4):521–537.

Khantzian, E. J., Gawin, F., Kleber, H. D., and Riordan, C. E. (1984). Methylphenidate treatment of cocaine dependence—a preliminary report. *Journal of Substance Abuse Treatment* 1:107–112.

Khantzian, E. J., Halliday, K. S., Golden, S., and McAuliffe, W. E. (1992). Modified group therapy for substance abusers. *American Journal on Addictions* 1:67–76.

Khantzian, E. J., and Khantzian, N. J. (1984). Cocaine addiction: Is there a psychological predisposition? *Psychiatric Annals* 14(10):753–759.

Khantzian, E. J., and Mack, J. E. (1989). AA and contemporary psychodynamic theory. In *Recent Developments in Alcoholism*, vol. 7, ed. M. Galanter, pp. 67–89. New York: Plenum.

Khantzian, E. J., and Treece, C. (1977). Psychodynamics of drug dependence: an overview. In *Psychodynamics of Drug Dependence*, ed. J. D. Blaine and D. A. Julius, NIDA research monograph 12, pp. 11–25. Rockville, MD: National Institute on Drug Abuse.

——— (1985). *DSM-III* psychiatric diagnosis of narcotic addicts: recent findings. *Archives of General Psychiatry* 42:1067–1071.

Kleber, H. D., and Gawin, F. H. (1984). Cocaine abuse. A review of current and experimental treatments. In *Cocaine: Pharmacology Effects and Treatment of Abuse*, ed. J. Grabowski, pp. 11–129. Washington, DC: National Institute on Drug Abuse.

Klein, D. F. (1975). Psychopharmacology and the borderline patient. In *Borderline States in Psychiatry*, ed. J. E. Mack. New York: Grune & Stratton.

Kohut, H. (1971). *The Analysis of the Self*. New York: International Universities Press.

——— (1977). *The Restoration of the Self*. New York: International Universities Press.

Kosten, T. R., Rounsaville, B. J., and Kleber, H. D. (1987). A 2.5 year follow-up of cocaine use among treated opioid addicts. *Archives of General Psychiatry* 44:281–285.

Krystal, H. (1982). Alexithymia and the effectiveness of psychoanalytic treatment. *International Journal of Psychoanalytic Psychotherapy* 9:353–378.

Levin, F. R., and Kleber, H. D. (1995). Attention-deficit hyperactivity disorder and substance abuse: relationship and implications for treatment. *Harvard Review of Psychiatry* 2:246–258.

Luborsky, L. (1984). *Principles of Psychoanalytic Psychotherapy—A Manual for Supportive-Expressive Treatment*. New York: Basic Books.

Luborsky, L., Woody, G. E., Holey, A., and Velleco, A. (1977). *Treatment manual for supportive-expressive psychoanalytically oriented psychotherapy: special adaptation for treatment of drug dependence.* Unpublished.

Mack, J. E. (1981). Alcoholism, AA and the governance of the self. In *Dynamic Approaches to the Understanding and Treatment of Alcoholism,* ed. M. H. Bean and N. E. Zinberg, pp. 128–162. New York: Free Press.

McAuliffe, W. E. (1984). Non-therapeutic opiate addiction in health professionals: a new form of impairment. *American Journal of Drug and Alcohol Abuse* 10(1):1–22.

McAuliffe, W. E., Santangelo, S., Magnunson, E., et al. (1987). Risk factors of drug impairment in random samples of physicians and medical students. *International Journal of the Addictions* 22:825–841.

McDougall, J. (1984). The 'disaffected' patient: reflections on affect pathology. *Psychoanalytic Quarterly* 53:386–409.

Rosecan, J. S., and Nunes, E. V. (1987). Pharmacological management of cocaine abuse. In *Cocaine Abuse: New Directions in Treatment and Research,* ed. H. I. Spitz and J. S. Rosecan, pp. 255–270. New York: Brunner/Mazel.

Rounsaville, B. J., Anton, S. F., Carroll, K., et al. (1991). Psychiatric diagnosis in cocaine abusers: clinical observations. *Archives of General Psychiatry* 48:43–51.

Rounsaville, B. J., Weissman, M. M., Crits-Cristoph, K., et al. (1982a). Diagnosis and symptoms of depression in opiate addicts: course and relationship to treatment outcome. *Archives of General Psychiatry* 39:151–156.

Rounsaville, B. J., Weissman, M. M., Kleber, H., and Wilber, C. (1982b). Heterogeneity of psychiatric diagnosis in treated opiate addicts. *Archives of General Psychiatry* 39:161–166.

Sashin, J. I. (1986). *The relation between fantasy and the ability to feel affect.* Paper presented at grand rounds, Cambridge Hospital, Cambridge, MA, November.

Sifneos, P., Apfel-Savitz, R., and Frank, F. (1977). The phenomenon of "alexithymia." *Psychotherapy Psychosomatics* 28:47–57.

Weiss, R. D., and Mirin, S. M. (1984). Drug, host and environmental factors in the development of chronic cocaine abuse. In *Substance Abuse and Psychotherapy,* ed. S. M. Mirin, pp. 42–55. Washington, DC: American Psychiatric Association Press.

——— (1986). Subtypes of cocaine abusers. *Psychiatric Clinics of North America* 9:491–501.

Weiss, R. D., Mirin, S. M., Griffin, M. L., and Michaels, J. L. (1988). Psychopathology in cocaine abusers: changing trends. *Journal of Nervous and Mental Disease* 176(12):719–725.

Weiss, R. D., Pope, H. G., and Mirin, S. M. (1985). Treatment of chronic cocaine abuse and attention deficit disorder, residual type with magnesium pemoline. *Drug and Alcohol Dependence* 15:69–72.

Wieder, H., and Kaplan, E. (1969). Drug use in adolescents. *Psychoanalytic Study of the Child* 24:399–431. New York: International Universities Press.

Woody, G. E., McLellan, A. T., Luborsky, L., and O'Brien, C. P. (1986). Psychotherapy for substance abuse. *Psychiatric Clinics of North America* 9:547–562.

Wurmser, L. (1974). Psychoanalytic considerations of the etiology of compulsive drug use. *Journal of the American Psychoanalytic Association* 22:820–843.

# 14

# Self-Regulation Vulnerabilities in Substance Abusers

Suffering is at the heart of addictive disorders. It is not primarily the result of marketeering, peer pressure, or the availability of drugs, neither is it the result of pleasure-seeking or self-destructiveness. The suffering that addicts attempt to ameliorate or perpetuate with their use of drugs reflects major difficulties in self-regulation mainly involving four dimensions of psychological life: feelings, self-esteem, relationships, and self-care. This point of view is based on three decades of accumulating evidence derived from clinical work with substance-dependent individuals. Despite this point of view, our collective unempathic if not pejorative view of addicts partly evolves out of outdated psychoanalytic theory, which suggested addicts are pleasure-driven, destructive characters. It is further heightened or aggravated by the judgments we make about addicts based on their behaviors and self-centeredness associated with acute intoxication, or the psychological regression that ensues with chronic addictive illness.

Contemporary psychodynamic approaches to substance abuse problems, guided by structural, self-object, and developmental theory, has allowed for a better understanding of the factors that protect against and those that predispose to addiction. Individuals are not apt to become drug dependent if they are more or less in touch with and able to bear and express their feelings, if they feel good about themselves, if they have reasonably healthy relationships with others, and if they have an adequate capacity for self-care. It is not surprising that traumatizing, abusive, or neglectful parental environments detract from or do injury in all four of these areas. The developmental trauma or damage that addicts experience in this respect is further accentuated when factors of biological or genetic susceptibility, cultural norms, or oppressive social conditions further contribute to or amplify the psychological vulnerabilities. Such interactions make it more likely that affected individuals will experiment with and discover the short-term adaptive and pain-relieving effects of addictive drugs.

This chapter elaborates on the nature of addicts' self-regulation vulnerabilities, which affect their capacities to govern their emotions, self-esteem, relationships, and self-care. My understanding is guided by and based on a developmental and adaptive perspective. I consider addiction to be a solution to life problems for individuals who have varying degrees of vulnerability and resiliency, dating back to the earliest phases of development. I will consider some treatment implications based on my understanding of their vulnerabilities as well as their capacities for recovery and self-repair.

## ACCESSING ADDICTIVE VULNERABILITIES

There are a number of influences that stand in the way of our understanding the addictive process and addicted individuals. Two of the more prominent ones are, first, the pejorative attitudes we harbor toward substance abusers, and second, the problem of competing ideologies. As I have already indicated, the first derives from our tendency to view addicts as pleasure seekers or destructive characters. The second problem of competing ideologies is at least as formidable an impediment when we try to fathom the etiological basis of addictive problems. Although psychological theorists (including psychoanalysts) have always had a penchant for polarizing concepts to explain mental life and human behavior, the debates have been particularly intense and in the extreme in the area of substance abuse. The controversies have more often taken on a quality of religious fervor rather than respectful reasoning and discourse. This has been most evident in debates about whether substance abuse is a disease or symptom, whether biological and genetic factors are more important than environmental and psychological ones, or whether substance abuse is the cause or consequence of the emotional suffering associated with drug-alcohol dependence. An extensive review of these controversies goes beyond the scope of this chapter. In what follows here, I will underscore how clinical work and diagnostic studies with substance-dependent individuals provide an important and legitimate basis to conclude that psychological factors are important etiological determinants in the development of addictive disorders. What is offered here is a perspective based primarily on a psychodynamic appreciation of addicts' self-regulation vulnerabilities. This perspective need not compete with other perspectives that yield different information or conceptualization, such as, for example, a disease concept of addictive illness. This latter formulation provides an appreciation of the progressive, biological nature of addictive illness and a rationale for emergent intervention and control. A psychodynamic perspective provides a basis to intervene and go beyond symptom control and the disease process, and to access and modify the psychological vulnerabilities that predispose to and perpetuate addictive disorders.

## The Clinical Perspective

The treatment relationships that are established and evolve in individual and group work with addicted individuals provide rich and ample clinical data to understand the nature of addictive vulnerability. Patients repeat in their treatment relationships many of the qualities and characteristics of the lifelong dilemmas and problems they have endured, including those that have left them susceptible to becoming dependent on alcohol and drugs.

In what follows, unless otherwise indicated, we draw on the time-proven clinical context of the treatment relationship to understand human problems in addictive suffering. Spanning three decades of clinical experience with addicted individuals, I have found little or no evidence to suggest to me that this context is not as relevant or valid for understanding and treating addicted patients as it is for patients with other symptomatic and characterological problems. Although addicted patients more often have special needs for safety, containment, and control, once provided, clinical work with such patients proceeds and unfolds in surprisingly meaningful and understandable ways and patterns.

The psychotherapeutic treatment relationship, as all therapists come to know, evokes powerful emotions and characteristic patterns of reaction in patients and therapists. When these reactions occur in the patient we refer to them as transference, and countertransference when they occur in the therapist. In the original, more strict definition, transference-countertransference reactions referred to emotions and ways of reacting that derive from early, unresolved conflicts in the child–parent relationship. More generally, transference has taken on a broader meaning to characterize more or less fixed patterns of reacting in a wide variety of relationships and situations, and, along similar lines, countertransference refers to qualities and patterns of reacting that certain patients and treatment situations evoke in the therapist. When Freud first introduced these concepts there was a tendency to consider transference and countertransference reactions as potential barriers to treatment. As these terms are currently viewed, however, we understand that they provide powerful if not essential cues to what patients' psychological dilemmas are about as well as suggesting what it is about the patient's makeup and characteristic responses that is in need of modification and change.

Except for some early noteworthy attempts (Abraham 1908, Freud 1905, Glover 1932, Rado 1933), it is only within the past few decades that we have applied powerful and useful concepts such as transference and countertransference, and psychodynamic theory in general, to our understanding of addicts and the nature of their suffering. This has mainly been the result of the growing and widespread drug use and dependency in our culture, which has afforded psychoanalytically trained practitioners the opportunity to understand and treat large numbers of drug-alcohol–dependent individuals in a variety of settings. Psychodynamic reports growing out of clinical work with addicts during this recent period have stressed major developmental handicaps and structural deficits that have left such individuals impaired in their capacity to manage affect, to maintain reasonable self-other relationships, and to modulate and regulate their behavior (Khantzian 1974, 1978, Krystal and Raskin 1970, Milkman and Frosch 1973, Wieder and Kaplan 1969, Wurmser 1974).

These contemporary psychodynamic findings and understanding have been applied more systematically in individual and group therapy with substance-dependent individuals. Luborsky and colleagues (1981) have demonstrated that an individual psychotherapeutic relationship, and the transferences that develop, can help the therapist and addict-patient to understand the meaning of the patient's drug dependence. They have developed an individual psychodynamic psychotherapeutic approach, utilizing a manual, to treat opiate addicts, which allows a focus on such individuals core conflictual relationship themes (CCRT), and how such themes are intimately involved in precipitating and maintaining drug use. Along similar lines, but with an expanded focus we (Khantzian et al. 1990) have developed a modified dynamic group psychotherapeutic approach for cocaine addicts that allows for an unfolding of their self-regulation vulnerabilities involving problems with affects, self-esteem, relationships, and self-care. The group experience affords opportunities to understand how such vulnerabilities and defenses predispose and cause individuals to relapse to drug use. At the same time that they try to disguise or compensate for their vulnerabilities, addicts betray themselves through their characteristic defenses and behaviors. These responses are played out with the group leader(s) and the other members, and an opportunity is provided for recognition of such patterns in self and other, and thus the opportunity for interruption and modification of the self-defeating patterns, and the development of more mature and less stereotypic responses, especially those involving drugs and related behaviors.

In our approach, as I will elaborate, we have increasingly placed an emphasis on sectors of vulnerability in personality organization related to difficulties with affect defense, self-esteem, relationships, and self-care. I will amplify on primarily two areas, namely those involving affect life and self-care. In my work, starting with opiate addicts and subsequently with other substance abusers, it has constantly impressed me how central these two areas of vulnerability are. My patients have repeatedly revealed that their attempts to medicate or alter their distress, which they experience as intolerable, and their inability to take care of themselves, have combined most powerfully, and more often have been the necessary and sufficient conditions to become addicted. In my opinion it is the deficits in ego-self organization, primarily impacting on affect life and self-care, that is in need of therapeutic understanding and management.

## Diagnostic and Empirical Findings

Notwithstanding my emphasis on a dimensional approach that focuses on sectors of psychological vulnerability, there have recently been a series of diagnostic and empirical studies that should be mentioned because they complement a psychodynamic perspective. Starting in the mid-1970s and over the subsequent decade, a series of diagnostic reports revealed the coexistence of a range of psychopathology among opiate addicts. Reports by Woody and colleagues (1975), Dorus and Senay (1980), Rounsaville and associates (1982a, 1982b), and Khantzian and Treece (1985) documented a high incidence of depression (mostly unipolar), personality disorder, and alcoholism. In the reports by Rounsaville and associates, the authors concluded that their data supported formulations by Wurmser and Khantzian, namely that depressed addicts used opiates to self-medicate feelings that were dysphoric and unbearable. Studying a similar population of ninety-nine opiate addicts, using projective techniques and ego scales, Blatt and colleagues (1984) concluded that these addicts suffer significantly in affect modulation and interpersonal relations, and use drugs to isolate and withdraw. Wilson and collaborators (1989) compared twenty-five opiate-addicted subjects to a normal control group using a scale to measure failures in self-regulation derived from the Thematic Apperception Test. They found that the opiate addicts had greater difficulties than the normal subjects in self-regulatory functions, and further ascertained that their dysfunction derived from early phases of development. And finally, diagnostic studies have shown cocaine addicts to suffer with a disproportionate incidence of bipolar, attentional deficit, and narcissistic disorders (Gawin and Kleber 1984, 1986, Weiss and Mirin 1984, 1986, Weiss et al. 1988), and alcoholics to suffer with significant levels of depression and anxiety (Hesselbrock et al. 1985, Weiss and Rosenberg 1985). These varying patterns of diagnostic findings in relation to the preferred drugs also further support the idea that addicts differentially select a type of drug based on its ability to ameliorate specific painful affects.

# SELF-REGULATION VULNERABILITIES

## Psychopathology Versus Vulnerability

In my own work, I originally emphasized severe and pervasive psychopathology as predeterminants of addiction, involving major deficits in drive-affect defense, narcissistic disturbances, and significant problems in self-care and impulse control (Khantzian 1972, 1974). These observations and formulations, however, were based primarily on clinical work with opiate addicts in a methadone treatment program in which the patients were admittedly more disturbed subjectively and behaviorally. Subsequently, I worked with a broader clientele in private practice and with patients in self-help and outpatient drug-free programs whose choice of drugs predominantly involved marijuana, alcohol, or cocaine. I have been impressed with the high degree of variability in the type and severity of psychopathology and the degrees of resiliency and capacity for recovery in this group of patients. As a consequence, rather than emphasizing severity of pathology and diagnostic categories involved with addictions, I have, as previously noted, increasingly focused on sectors of psychological vulnerability with an emphasis mainly on four dimensions of self-regulation: self-esteem, relationships, affects, and self-care. I will place my main emphasis on the latter two areas of vulnerability.

## Self-Esteem, Need Satisfaction, and Relationships

Addicts suffer because they do not feel good about themselves and as a consequence they are unable to get their needs met or establish satisfying or satisfactory relationships. One of the main complications of their self-esteem dilemma is their extraordinary inconsistency in processing their dependency needs. They alternate between selflessness and self-centeredness; demanding and expectant attitudes are often and quickly replaced by disdainful rejection of help and disavowal of need. Cool and aloof posturing often veils deeper layers of shame and feelings of inadequacy. It is little wonder then that the powerful feeling-altering properties of addictive substances are sought after. They can serve as powerful antidotes to the inner sense of emptiness, disharmony, and dis-ease such people experience. For some it is the boost of an energizing drug such as cocaine or an amphetamine that counters states of inertia and immobilization associated with chronic low self-esteem. On the other hand, these same drugs may act as augmenters for those who compensate with more expansive or hypomanic defenses. Yet for those who react to their inner disharmony with agitation or rage, the calming and muting effects of opiates will be welcomed; and for those who rigidly wall off from themselves and others their needs for comfort, contact, and nurturance, the softening effects of alcohol or other sedatives will be experienced as a warming and magical antidote.

The work of the self psychologists, especially that of Heinz Kohut (1971, 1977), has been most helpful in understanding how the developmental-structural deficits of certain individuals impact on self-esteem maintenance, and how addicts in particular use drugs in this respect in a compensatory way. Kohut observed, "The drug serves not as a substitute for loved or loving objects, or for a relationship with them, but as a *replacement for a defect in the psychological structure*" (1971, p. 46, my italics). His work has helped us to appreciate how self-worth, or self-love, derives from the earliest phases of the child–parent relationship. A basic sense of well-being, inner harmony, and cohesion is established as a function of optimal soothing, nurturance, and protection. Subsequently a capacity for self-other love builds on this foundation through the reactions of admiring and being admired that transpire between the parents and the developing child. When optimal, individuals grow in their sense of self-worth, develop guiding values and ambitions, and establish a healthy capacity for interdependence.

Although Kohut and his followers did not systematically expand on and apply their ideas to addicts, his ideas are germane to their self-other problems. Addicts suffer not only because they experience inner disharmony, discomfort, and fragmentation, or that they are unable to feel good about themselves and thus others. They suffer even more because of the defenses they employ to mask these vulnerabilities. Addictive individuals protect the injured and vulnerable self by employing self-defeating defenses such as disavowal, self-sufficiency, aggression, and bravado. The main costs involve a sense of isolation, emotional constriction, and highly erratic relationships. Subsequently, I will explore a major therapeutic challenge, namely, helping such individuals yield on their distrust, shame, and counterdependence by identifying the shaky sense of self that drives them, and by replacing their bravado and counterdependency with a more balanced interdependent approach to self and others.

## Affects

Addicts constantly convey that they suffer in the extreme with their emotions. At one extreme their feelings are overwhelming and unbearable, and drugs are used to relieve their suffering. At the other extreme feelings seem absent or vague and thus confusing, and drugs are employed to change their suffering. Whether the intent is to relieve or to change suffering, addicts' drug behaviors suggest lifelong difficulties with regulating feelings; drugs represent attempts to control affects that otherwise seem uncontrollable.

Over the past three decades a literature has emerged describing how character-disordered, severely traumatized, psychosomatic, and substance-dependent individuals share certain qualities and dysfunctions in the way they experience their feelings. The works of Krystal and Raskin (1970) and Krystal (1977, 1982, 1988) have been seminal in developing an appreciation of why and how feelings can be so problematic and bewildering for self and others in such conditions. Drawing on extensive clinical work with victims of massive trauma or alcoholism, Krystal has proposed that affects have a normal line of development that is progressive, but subject to developmental arrest or traumatic regression. As a consequence, certain individuals are unable to differentiate their feelings (e.g., they cannot distinguish anxiety from depression), tend to somatize affect, and cannot give words to feelings. In this latter respect, Krystal (1982) has borrowed the term *alexithymia*, coined by Sifneos (1967) and Nemiah (1970) in their work with psychosomatic patients, to convey the special problems substance abusers have in processing and expressing their feelings. As he has witnessed with addicts, and as Nemiah (1975) has also described with psychosomatic patients, individuals so affected cannot identify or tell whether they are tired, angry, sad, hungry, or ill when they are asked about their distress. These deficits may manifest themselves as well in the emotional and cognitive realm. Krystal (1982) cites the work of Marty and de M'Uzan (1963) on operational thinking ("pensee operatoire"), wherein such individuals might display momentary brilliant thinking, but ultimately reveal that their reactions are more bound to events and facts with little connection to emotions. In other instances, the emotional void is interrupted by brief explosions of violence and rage. Related to these observations, McDougall (1984) has referred to such patients as "disaffected," and Wurmser (1974) has used the term *hyposymbolization* to characterize the emotional impoverishment that addicts feel within themselves and interpersonally as a result of such deficits.

In contrast to the developmental problems that cause addicts to have difficulty accessing and expressing feelings, their emotional-developmental impairments just as often cause them to suffer with the opposite problem, namely, that affects are experienced as overwhelming and unbearable. On this basis, early in his writing, Wurmser (1974) placed "defect of affect defense" at the root of addictive disorders, and on this same basis Wieder and Kaplan (1969) referred to drugs of dependence as a "corrective" and "prosthesis." On a similar basis I originally stressed how opiate addicts use opiates to counter the disorganizing influences of rage and aggression on the ego (Khantzian 1974). These formulations shared an appreciation of addicts' limited capacity to bear or sustain painful affects and an understanding of how addicts used the pain-relieving action of the drugs as a way to cope with deficits in affect defense.

One of the main developments that has evolved from these psychodynamic formulations has been the growing appreciation that an addict's main motivation for drug dependence is to use the effects of drugs to relieve or change feelings that are experienced as painful or unbearable. Although addicts experiment with and may use more than one drug, most addicts, if asked, will indicate that they prefer a particular drug. Despite the aforementioned inability to name or express their feelings, when asked what the drugs do for them, it is striking how addicts can differentiate between drug effects and indicate why they prefer one class of drugs over another. Furthermore, they often directly or indirectly indicate the painful states that are ameliorated or altered by their preferred drug. Wieder and Kaplan (1969) were the first to appreciate this phenomenon and coined the term *drug of choice*, and Milkman and Frosch (1973) documented empirical findings to support, as they called it, a "preferential use of drugs." Spotts and Shontz (1987) coined the term *drug of commitment* in coming to similar conclusions. I originally referred to this differential pattern of drug use among various types of addicts as the "self-selection" process (Khantzian 1975), and more recently I reviewed and articulated the basis for a "self-medication hypothesis" of addictive disorders (Khantzian 1985a). In this report, drawing on my own experience and that of others (Krystal and Raskin 1970, Milkman and Frosch 1973, Wieder and Kaplan 1969, Wurmser 1974) I placed emphasis on vulnerabilities and deficits in ego capacities, sense of self, and object relations, which produce psychological suffering and painful affects, and on this basis I proposed that substance abusers discover that the action of addictive drugs counters or relieves the painful states (Khantzian 1990).

The three main classes of addictive drugs—analgesic-opiates, sedative-hypnotics (including alcohol), and stimulants (e.g., cocaine, amphetamines)—have powerful and different psychotropic effects that can relieve or alter psychological suffering. The motives for initial and subsequent use of these drugs can change as a consequence of biological-addictive factors and chronicity, but psychological factors continue to influence the way addicts employ the pain-relieving and pain-perpetuating aspects of addictive drugs. On the side of pain relief, over the past two decades I have reported clinical findings that indicate that individuals use the three classes of drugs to differentially self-medicate painful affect states that result from a range of defects and deficits in defense and personality organization (Khantzian 1975, 1985a, 1990). In particular, I suggested that narcotic addicts are individuals who already have shaky defenses; they take advantage of the anti-rage, antiaggression action of opiates to counter the disorganizing effect of such threatening drives and affects. Sedative-hypnotic or alcohol-dependent individuals are counterdependent; they discover how their drug of choice softens overdrawn and rigid defenses and thus temporarily relieves inner states of isolation, emptiness, and coldness. Stimulant abusers are individuals with deflated (or inflated) ego-ideal structures, and depressive and narcissistic personalities, who use cocaine or amphetamines to treat states of depletion, anergia, and hyperactivity (Khantzian 1990).

Although addicts make it abundantly clear that drugs relieve their suffering, they also make it amply clear that their reliance on such drugs perpetuates and amplifies their distress. That is, an inevitable consequence of drug use and dependency involves the pain and distress of overdose and side effects, painful withdrawal symptoms, and the pain and dysfunction associated with the personal deterioration and regression of chronic, addictive illness. In part this can be explained by addicts' willingness to endure whatever distress is associated with their use of drugs to obtain even momentary relief from their pain. More recently, however, I have come to realize that addicts, in part, actively and even knowingly perpetuate their distress when they compulsively continue their drug use. I have likened this pain-perpetuating aspect of drug use to a compulsion to repeat unresolved pain from early phases of development. Schiffer (1988) has independently come to a similar conclusion, emphasizing self-punitive, sadomasochistic dynamics, deriving from childhood traumatic abuse, to explain the painful, self-damaging aspects of cocaine use and dependence. My own explanation for accepting the pain associated with drug use involves motives to master and convert the passive, confusing experience of being alexithymic or disaffected to an active one of controlling feelings, even if they are painful. Drawing on psychoanalytic and developmental theory that attempts to measure the impact of earliest life vicissitudes on affect and personality development (Gedo 1986, Lichtenberg 1983), I have speculated that the painful, repetitious aspects of drug use and dependence represent attempts to work out painful affect states for which there are no words, memories, or other symbolic representation. This dilemma is especially germane for those patients I described previously who seem not to have or know their feelings (Khantzian 1990, Khantzian and Wilson 1993). Instead of simply relieving painful feelings when they are unbearable or overwhelming, substance abusers may use drugs to control affects, especially when they are vague, elusive, and nameless (Khantzian 1990, Khantzian and Wilson 1993), even if they pay the price of more suffering.

## Self-Care

Addicts constantly give the impression that they are self-destructive. The well-known, well-publicized deadly effects of drugs of abuse and all the related dangerous environments, relationships, and activities associated with the drugs do not seem to deter addicts from their compulsion to use them. They act and often speak as if they do not care about such consequences. On this basis we frequently infer or conclude that they harbor or live out conscious and unconscious suicidal impulses. Such a conclusion is bolstered by evidence that there is in fact a high suicide rate associated with substance abuse (Blumenthal 1988).

In my opinion and experience, the apparent "not caring" and suicidality associated with addictive disorders is a consequence and secondary to, rather than the cause of, the self-destructiveness associated with long-term substance abuse. It reflects more the deterioration, despair, and depression that are the result of an addictive adaptation. The act of using such drugs is less the function of a motivated behavior to actively harm the self, but more an indication of developmental failures and deficits that leave such individuals ill-equipped to take care of themselves. Whether it involves the dangers of drug or alcohol use, or the hazards of daily living (e.g., accidents, health care, finances, etc.), addicts give much evidence that they fail in many contexts to protect themselves. Closer examination reveals that the risks and dangers such individuals constantly encounter are not so much courted or unconsciously harbored, but more often are not anticipated or considered. Based on our experience with these characteristics in addicts, we proposed that substance abusers' self-protective, survival deficiencies are the consequence of deficits in a capacity for self-care (Khantzian 1978, Khantzian and Mack 1983, 1989). Although we first described this deficit in opiate addicts (Khantzian 1978), we subsequently have been impressed that it is present to some degree in all substance abusers.

Self-care is a psychological capacity related to certain ego functions and reactions. This capacity protects against harm and assures survival, and involves reality testing, judgment, control, signal anxiety, and the ability to draw cause-consequence conclusions. The self-care capacity develops out of the nurturance, ministrations, and protective roles provided by the parents from early infancy, and subsequently, out of child–parent interactions. If conditions are optimal the growing child internalizes adequate protective functions and responses to care for him- or herself. The capacity for self-care is evident in adults in appropriate planning, action, and anticipation of harm, danger, or hazardous situations, and involves appropriate degrees of anticipatory affect such as fear, worry, and shame. Such reactions and anticipatory responses are strikingly absent or underdeveloped in addicts. They recurrently fail to consider how their behaviors and reactions fail to take into account situations and conditions that can jeopardize their well-being, especially those involving drug or alcohol use and related activities (Khantzian 1978, 1990, Khantzian and Mack 1983, 1989).

Self-care deficits are more pervasive in some addicts than others. For example, it is more apparent in polydrug or intravenous drug abusers where ego capacities in general are more globally impaired. In other individuals, the capacity for self-care is not as obviously deficient, but under situations of stress, distress, or depression there are lapses or deterioration in self-protective responses. For some individuals, marginally established self-care capacities yield to an overriding need to relieve distress with drugs, or to use them to enhance performance or achieve a goal, which drugs can often provide on a short-term basis. Whether self-care impairments are severe and pervasive, or represent temporary lapses in function, addicts reveal their self-care problems when they do not sufficiently worry about or anticipate the immediate and long-term dangerous consequences of their substance abuse (Khantzian 1990).

We conclude this section by providing a clinical example of how self-regulation vulnerabilities involving affect and self-care deficits combine malignantly to place addicts at risk.

*A Case Vignette*

The following summary of a group therapy meeting for a group of addicts typifies some of their problems with self-care and their confusion and inability to deal with painful or threatening feeling. Although the extra-group event that gave rise to the group interaction was rather dramatic and traumatic for one of its members, it nevertheless demonstrates their not unusual tendency to become involved with the details and logistics of an evocative event or to react with anger and impulsive action.

> The member who related the experience was a recovering physician. He began the group by describing an incident in his clinic in which the boyfriend of a pregnant patient whipped out a knife and slashed her across her shoulder and chest when he misunderstood from the doctor's estimation of gestation that she might have been impregnated by someone else. The doctor first described his shock and his maneuvers to position himself next to the door of the examining room while the boyfriend was angrily screaming and threatening her. The doctor debated leaving until his nurse-assistant (who had called the police) handed him his softball bat and

convinced him that the patient's life was in danger. With the boyfriend's back to him, and without further reflection, the doctor hit the man's arm with the bat releasing his knife, and as he swung around, the doctor then hit him across the abdomen and thereby immobilized him until the police arrived.

Immediately after the doctor completed his story, a lawyer cocaine addict, who was a hyperactive, restless character, launched into an animated monologue on the doctor's potential liability to assault charges by having interceded. As the leader I tried to slow him down, to point out his tendency to be legalistic, and to get more to his feelings. Instead, he and another group member, also a physician, began to argue whether going to the legal aspects of the situation was reasonable. I made several attempts to interrupt by asking them to try and focus on how the story made them feel. Mostly a tone of irritability pervaded the group interaction, with the lawyer and the other physician returning to their argument about the suitability of the lawyer's concerns about the legal implications of the event. The other three members seemed uncharacteristically willing to tolerate this exchange. The doctor who told the story responded to my inquiry about his reactions by telling me and the group how almost immediately after the episode he arranged a "three-day break" in Florida, without his family, to visit a trusted confidant-uncle and ex-marine whom he knew would provide sanctuary, advice, and wise counsel on what had happened. I pointed out to him that he seemed bewildered about and unable to describe his feelings but instead described what he had done. A third physician in the group, in a detached and characteristically analytic manner, commented on the argument between the other two members and then went on to suggest that the doctor had perhaps endangered himself by interceding but also allowed that if he had been involved he might have considered a more devastating blow to the head.

It was only toward the end of the meeting that the fifth member of the group, also a lawyer (the youngest member of the group, who was working as a planner and counselor in a drug treatment program as part of his recovery efforts), forcefully interrupted the proceedings and expressed his shock over the event, his anger and sadness, and his worry for the threat that the doctor had been forced to endure. He also allowed that he might have unnecessarily jeopardized himself had he not been as successful in immobilizing the assailant. The young lawyer also correctly reminded the group that they could usually do better with each other's distress and feelings. I pointed out that it was easier for the group members to pick a fight with each other than to stay with the feelings that had been stirred by the story. By the end of the meeting it had become clear that both the doctor who had experienced the episode and the lawyer who first reacted were the least able to describe their feelings. With some defensiveness the lawyer was able to consider that his preoccupation with the legal aspects of the situation served to avoid his confusion about his feelings, and that the doctor had similarly acted on his own by going to Florida.

## TREATMENT IMPLICATIONS

### General Considerations

Because addicts have so much difficulty in knowing and tolerating their feelings, because their self-esteem, relationships, and self-care are often so precarious, and because drug-alcohol abuse has so many attendant life-threatening dangers associated with it, treatment considerations for substance abusers must place at a premium their needs for comfort, safety, and control. Self-regulation vulnerabilities predispose to, precipitate, and maintain a reliance on drugs, and ultimately it is these vulnerabilities that need therapeutic correction. Nevertheless, we just as strongly believe treatment must rest on a foundation of stability, containment, and control at the outset, and subsequently, of the often emergent and life-threatening nature of addictive disorders. In this respect it does not make sense to pit a disease concept against a symptom approach to substance abuse. Although the former stresses biological and addictive factors, and the latter attempts to understand and modify predisposing psychological factors, ultimately both are in need of attention.

The need to integrate and appropriately sequence these two paradigms, for example, becomes strikingly apparent when we compare the natural history and evolution of a dependence on cocaine to that of alcohol dependence. Whereas the morbid, life-threatening, and fatal consequences of alcoholism usually develop over a period of two to three decades, they often can develop within weeks to months in the case of cocaine dependence, especially when consumed in its free-base form or intravenously. In this respect, the disease concept, as applied in Alcoholics Anonymous (AA) and related self-help and psychoeducational programs, has been enormously successful, especially initially, because it places such fundamental importance on the need to control the addictive process. As I will elaborate subsequently, although the AA disease concept approaches appear to place an absolute emphasis on abstinence as the core and essential requirement of the program, it goes beyond that requirement to help individuals deal with a broader range of psychological issues that have made their lives and their use of substances unmanageable. Clinical-psychotherapeutic and self-help approaches can and need to work in complementary or differential ways to target and modify the self-regulation vulnerabilities of substance-dependent individuals. Effective clinicians can optimally benefit substance abusing patients if they can imaginatively, and oftentimes pragmatically, combine therapeutic elements (clinical and self-help) in meeting such patients' needs.

## The Primary Care Therapist

To be effective in managing and treating substance abusers, clinicians need to play multiple roles and be flexible to assure that patients' needs are met. The treatment relationship can be a powerful vehicle for influencing and modifying behavior, and addicted patients are no exception. Before the leverage of a treatment relationship is employed to access addicts' psychological vulnerabilities, it can and should also be employed to address the needs for safety and stabilization that extra-psychotherapeutic interventions can often better provide. A nonjudgmental, empathic, and authoritative (i.e., confident, hopeful, and instructive) therapist can quickly establish credibility with addicts to help them accept the vitally needed benefits that confinement, pharmacological stabilization, detoxification, or maintenance can offer, as well as involvement in support groups such as AA or Narcotics Anonymous (NA) and assistance with environmental stressors, particularly those involving family.

Considering the multiple clinical management and psychotherapeutic needs of substance abusers, I have proposed that the role of the individual clinician should be that of a primary care therapist, especially in early phases of treatment (Khantzian 1985b, 1986, 1988).

I have suggested that operating in such a role, the involvement of the therapist-clinician in referring addicts to and brokering other treatment elements is not only necessary but, if done carefully, can help in building a treatment alliance. Beyond the initial referral and clinical management aspects, the primary care therapist plays important roles in monitoring and modifying reactions to the treatment components that have been recommended and adopted. This might involve countering avoidant tendencies against attending AA or NA meetings in one instance and, in another, to consider that a particular patient's characterological problem or psychopathology makes such a treatment inappropriate. Simultaneously, the primary therapist remains in a position to gauge how patients make use of and benefit from the individual and group psychotherapeutic relationships that develop. In summary, I have proposed that the primary care therapist can function in direct, coordinating, and monitoring roles to meet patient needs for control, containment, contact, and comfort. Subsequently the treatment relationship can evolve into more traditional psychotherapy. In doing so the clinician is able to maximize treatment retention and assure that what is recommended or provided is effective, and if not, to broker or provide alternative approaches (Khantzian 1988).

### Alcoholics Anonymous—A Vehicle for Control, Support, and Understanding

Alcoholics Anonymous and its derivatives such as NA and Cocaine Anonymous (CA) serve as powerful containers and transformers for addictive behavior. People who are resistant to ceasing a destructive behavior and deny vulnerability can be helped to cease such behavior by admitting to their vulnerability. Self-help groups such as these work not merely by using group pressure to eliminate the offending agent, namely the drug or alcohol, but they also work because they have evolved as extraordinarily sophisticated group psychologies that effectively address the physiological and psychological determinants of addictive compulsions.

Alcoholics Anonymous works as a container, or controlling influence, because it deals effectively with the physiological and psychological factors that drive the addictive compulsivity. It is correctly argued that one of the main reasons people compulsively drink or take drugs is the result of physiological-addictive mechanisms (i.e., tolerance and physical dependence). This has not been the focus of this chapter, albeit it is an important one to appreciate. Helping a person stop the regular use of substances and thus interrupting the physiological basis for desiring drugs or alcohol goes far for many in removing their compulsion. What stands in the way just as often, however, are the predisposing personality characteristics of human beings, including and especially addicts, that make admission of vulnerability so difficult when people most need to do so. Denial is not a defense upon which alcoholics and addicts have sole claim. Nevertheless, it can have more obvious devastating consequences in their case.

The more alcoholics and addicts lose control of their substances and thus their lives, the more they posture to the contrary. Alcoholics Anonymous is most ingenious in confronting this penchant by its traditions, initially on a daily basis, of helping alcoholics and addicts admit to themselves and others that they suffer with a disease or illness and admit that they lost control of alcohol (or drugs) and their lives (i.e., the first step in the twelve steps of Alcoholics Anonymous, "We admitted we were powerless over alcohol . . . that our lives had become unmanageable" [Alcoholics Anonymous 1976]). Stephanie Brown (1985) has stressed how this focus on loss of control and accepting and maintaining an identity as an alcoholic is a key to AA's success. The steps successively build on the admission of vulnerability and the acceptance of humility and altruism as necessary alternatives to the predisposing and progressive self-centeredness and egoism that has been involved in their addictive illness. These defenses are exaggerated and overdeveloped to counter their self-regulation deficits, especially those involving low self-esteem. The many supportive, active, and guiding elements that the addicts immediately encounter in the program provide structure and support that compensate for their self-regulation vulnerabilities. The aphorisms provide a source of soothing and comfort that they desperately need, and the stepwise approach, counsel, and even admonitions (e.g., "Stay in touch, show up, call, don't pick up, go to meetings, ask for help") provide needed consistent guidelines and structure to support and direct individuals to organize their lives, which are often in a shambles. Beyond these practical elements, the use of prayer and spirituality forces the issue of surrendering to a force beyond self, admitting to dependency and the importance of self-other relationships.

As a transformer, AA helps to modify those parts of the self responsible for taking charge and controlling one's life. John Mack (1981) has referred to such a capacity as "self-governance" and described it as a self–other, multiperson psychology. Alcoholics Anonymous compensates for diminished or underdeveloped self-governance capacities that alcoholics and addicts display. Alcoholics Anonymous challenges the assumption of alcoholics and addicts (or, for that matter, of all of us as humans) that we are able to govern our lives and behavior alone. Beyond challenging the "character defects" (i.e., as employed in AA but similar to that used in psychoanalysis) that mask lack of self-esteem and related interpersonal problems, AA also effectively addresses the affect and self-care deficits by inviting its participants to listen to each other's accounts of how they succumbed to and recovered from their addictive illness.

More precisely, we (Khantzian and Mack 1989, 1994, Mack 1981) believe that the storytelling traditions of AA (also referred to as "drunkalogues" or "drugalogues") wittingly or unwittingly are an extraordinarily helpful way for substance-dependent individuals to identify in themselves and others how much their dilemmas with feeling life and self-care have caused their problems. As they tell their stories, often with engaging humor and great eloquence, they perceptively identify and disclose their self-regulation vulnerabilities and reveal the self-defeating characterological defenses that they employ, which are so much a part of their difficulties. The stories reveal they not only did not know, tolerate, or express feelings, but they more often absorb themselves with circumstances, events, and action. Instead of admitting to being lost or confused in matters of self-care, their narratives indicate that they responded to life's hazards and those involving substances with denial of danger, bravado, aggressive postures, and counterphobia. Conversely, their stories of recovery beg the importance of yielding on their self-defeating defenses, admitting to their vulnerabilities, and surrendering to the necessity of accepting distress and interdependence as inevitabilities and requirements of adult life.

## Psychotherapy

Addicts and alcoholics need and respond to psychodynamic psychotherapy. Contrary to the truisms and negative stereotypes of addicts that they do not come for, accept, stay with, or benefit from such treatment, there are now at least two decades of experience by involved clinicians, with preliminary empirical findings, indicating that such pessimism is not warranted. As we indicated at the outset of this chapter, substance abusers can and do respond to psychodynamic treatment relationships, both individually and in groups. Such treatment allows the characterological defenses and underlying vulnerabilities involved in addictive disorders to unfold and be examined and modified in the context of the individual and group relationships that develop. A systematic review of psychotherapy for substance abusers goes beyond the scope of this chapter but I will highlight some themes central to the focus I have placed on addicts' self-regulation vulnerabilities.

In my opinion we now succeed in treating addicts psychotherapeutically when we failed previously because (1) we have better understood their vulnerabilities, and (2) we have modified our psychotherapeutic technique in general and in particular to better respond to addicts' vulnerabilities. The traditions of passivity, uncovering techniques, the blank screen, and strictly interpretive approaches, derived from psychoanalysis of neurotic patients, are not appropriate for either understanding or modifying addictive vulnerability. An appreciation of substance abusers' developmental problems suggests they need greater support, structure, empathy, and contact than that provided by classical psychoanalytic treatments. Accordingly, therapists need to be alerted to the requirements for more actively identifying in individual and group therapy the nature of addicts' self-esteem, relationship, affect, and self-care deficits, as well as the need to constantly point out, clarify, and confront such patients with the self-defeating defenses that they use to disguise or deny their vulnerabilities.

There has been a common thread in our own work and that of Krystal, Wurmser, Dodes, and Luborsky and associates, regarding the advantages of focusing on core areas or sectors of vulnerability to access and modify substance abusers' problems. That is, these approaches stress dimensions of psychological life, or the quality and nature of addicts' distress and suffering, as opposed to more categorical, diagnostic approaches or those that stress the dynamics of a particular type of psychopathology. Krystal's work has stressed the conditions of affect deficit and alexithymia, and how the therapist must be active in explaining to patients how they are different in relation to feelings, and the need to help patients identify and express feelings. Wurmser (1987) has placed growing importance on the need to help addicts understand their problems with shame and with an archaic superego that causes them to repeat humiliating and self-destructive encounters with substances, relationships, and activities. Dodes (1990, Dodes and Khantzian 1991) has drawn attention to states of helplessness and reactive narcissistic rage that precipitate relapse and are in need of therapeutic attention. Woody and colleagues (1986) have explored the importance of the core conflictual relationship themes. In our approaches, we have stressed the four areas of self-regulation vulnerabilities involving affects, self-esteem, relationships, and self-care in understanding how dysfunction in these areas precipitates and maintains drug dependence. All of these approaches share in common an emphasis on activity, support, and empathy and also share the belief that active-supportive methods are not inconsistent or incompatible with expressive approaches that allow for analysis of defenses and the vulnerabilities they mask or disguise.

## CONCLUSION

To be effective, treatment approaches to substance abusers need to constantly appreciate and focus on patients' self-regulation difficulties. At the outset, emphasis needs to be placed on control, safety, and comfort, and early treatment needs to be guided by these considerations. We have proposed that initially a clinician must be prepared to act as a primary care therapist to assure that these initial treatment priorities are adequately managed. Furthermore, because we cannot very well predict who will respond best to what modalities and treatment elements, the role of the primary care therapist is needed to monitor treatment responses and to flexibly combine treatment elements to manage the addictive illness on a short-term basis, and the psychotherapeutic needs on a more long-term basis. It will become evident, for example, that some patients are so disabled and refractory, with their alexithymia or behavioral difficulties, that more long-term confinement or more active self-help and psychoeducative approaches are indicated. In other cases co-occurring psychopathology such as a severe panic disorder or suicidal depression makes the acceptance or suitability of a self-help approach unlikely. The need for an augmented program involving drug therapy to treat co-occurring psychopathology might also necessitate referral or an expanded role for the treating clinician. In either case, the recovery and psychotherapeutic needs of patients are best met by imaginative and pragmatic employment of a combination of treatment elements. In doing so there must be a readiness on the part of the clinician to conclude, based on his or her monitoring efforts and appreciation of the vulnerabilities involved, that a treatment modality is inappropriate or contraindicated and to then consider alternative approaches.

## REFERENCES

Abraham, K. (1908). The psychological relation between sexuality and alcoholism. In *Selected Papers of Karl Abraham*, pp. 80–89. New York: Basic Books, 1960.

Alcoholics Anonymous (1976). *Alcoholics Anonymous*, 3rd ed. New York: World Services.

Blatt, S. J., Berman, W., Bloom-Feshback, S., et al. (1984). Psychological assessment of psychopathology in opiate addiction. *Journal of Nervous and Mental Disease* 172:156–165.

Blumenthal, S. (1988). A guide to risk factors, assessment and treatment of suicidal patients. *Medical Clinics of North America* 72:937–971.

Brown, S. (1985). *Treating the Alcoholic: A Developmental Model of Recovery*. New York: Wiley.

Dodes, L. M. (1990). Addiction, helplessness and narcissistic rage. *Psychoanalytic Quarterly* 59:398–419.

Dodes, L. M., and Khantzian, E. J. (1991). Individual psychodynamic psychotherapy. In *Clinical Textbook of Addictive Disorders*, ed. R. J. Frances and S. I. Miller, pp. 391–405. New York: Guilford.

Dorus, W., and Senay, E. C. (1980). Depression, demographic dimension, and drug abuse. *American Journal of Psychiatry* 137:699–704.

Freud, S. (1905). Three essays on the theory of sexuality. *Standard Edition* 7:125–245.

Gawin, F. H., and Kleber, H. D. (1984). Cocaine abuse treatment. *Archives of General Psychiatry* 41:903–908.

——— (1986). Pharmacological treatment of cocaine abuse. *Psychiatric Clinics of North America* 9:573–583.

Gedo, J. (1986). *Conceptual Issues in Psychoanalysis: Essays in History and Method*. Hillsdale, NJ: Analytic Press.

Glover, E. (1932). On the etiology of drug addiction. In *On the Early Development of Mind*, pp. 187–215. New York: International Universities Press, 1956.

Hesselbrock, M. N., Meyer, R. E., and Keener, J. J. (1985). Psychopathology in hospitalized alcoholics. *Archives of General Psychiatry* 42:1050–1055.

Khantzian, E. J. (1972). A preliminary dynamic formulation of the psychopharmacologic action of methadone. In *Proceedings of the Fourth National Conference on Methadone Treatment*, San Francisco, pp. 371–374. New York: National Association for the Prevention of Addictions to Narcotics.

——— (1974). Opiate addiction: a critique of theory and some implications for treatment. *American Journal of Psychotherapy* 28:59–70.

——— (1975). Self selection and progression in drug dependence. *Psychiatry Digest* 10:19–22.

——— (1978). The ego, the self and opiate addiction: theoretical and treatment considerations. *International Review of Psychoanalysis* 5:189–198.

——— (1985a). The self-medication hypothesis of addictive disorders. *American Journal of Psychiatry* 142:1259–1264.

——— (1985b). Psychotherapeutic intervention with substance abusers—the clinical context. *Journal of Substance Abuse Treatment* 2:83–88.

——— (1986). A contemporary psychodynamic approach to drug abuse treatment. *American Journal of Drug and Alcohol Abuse* 12(3):213–222.

——— (1988). The primary care therapist and patient needs in substance abuse treatment. *American Journal of Drug Alcohol Abuse* 14:159–167.

——— (1990). Self-regulation and self-medication factors in alcoholism and the addictions: similarities and differences. In *Recent Developments in Alcoholism*, vol. 8, ed. M. Galanter, pp. 225–271. New York: Plenum.

Khantzian, E. J., Halliday, K. S., and McAuliffe, W. E. (1990). *Addiction and the Vulnerable Self: Modified Dynamic Group Therapy for Substance Abusers (MDGT)*. New York: Guilford.

Khantzian, E. J., and Mack, J. E. (1983). Self-preservation and the care of the self: ego instincts reconsidered. *Psychoanalytic Study of the Child* 38:209–232. New Haven, CT: Yale University Press.

——— (1989). AA and contemporary psychodynamic theory. In *Recent Developments in Alcoholism*, vol. 7, ed. M. Galanter, pp. 67–89. New York: Plenum.

——— (1994). How AA works and why it is important for clinicians to understand. *Journal of Substance Abuse Treatment* 11:77–92.

Khantzian, E. J., and Treece, C. (1985). *DSM-III* psychiatric diagnosis of narcotic addicts: recent findings. *Archives of General Psychiatry* 42:1067–1071.

Khantzian, E. J., and Wilson, A. (1993). Substance abuse, repetition and the nature of addictive suffering. In *Hierarchical Conceptions in Psychoanalysis*, ed. A. Wilson and J. E. Gedo, pp. 263–283. New York: Guilford.

Kohut, H. (1971). *The Analysis of the Self*. New York: International Universities Press.

——— (1977). *The Restoration of the Self*. New York: International Universities Press.

Krystal, H. (1977). Self-representation and the capacity for self-care. *Annual of Psychoanalysis* 6:209–246.

——— (1982). Alexithymia and the effectiveness of psychoanalytic treatment. *International Journal of Psychoanalytic Psychotherapy* 9:353–378.

——— (1988). *Integration and Self-Healing: Affect, Trauma, Alexithymia*. Hillsdale, NJ: Analytic Press.

Krystal, H., and Raskin, H. A. (1970). *Drug Dependence: Aspects of Ego Functions*. Detroit: Wayne State University Press.

Lichtenberg, J. D. (1983). *Psychoanalysis and Infant Research*. Hillsdale, NJ: Analytic Press.

Luborsky, L., Woody, G. E., Hole, A., and Velleco, A. (1981). *A treatment manual for supportive-expressive psychoanalytically oriented psychotherapy: special adaptation for treatment of drug dependence.* Unpublished manual, 4th ed.

Mack, J. E. (1981). Alcoholism, AA and the governance of the self. In *Dynamic Approaches to the Understanding and Treatment of Alcoholism*, ed. M. H. Bean and N. E. Zinberg, pp. 128–162. New York: Free Press.

Marty, P., and de M'Uzan, M. (1963). Le pensee operatoire. *Review Francais Psycho-Analytique* 27(suppl):345–456.

McDougall, J. (1984). The "disaffected" patient: reflections on affect pathology. *Psychoanalytic Quarterly* 53:386–409.

Milkman, H., and Frosch, W. A. (1973). On the preferential abuse of heroin and amphetamine. *Journal of Nervous and Mental Disease* 156:242–248.

Nemiah, J. C. (1970). The psychological management and treatment of patients with peptic ulcer. *Advances in Psychosomatic Medicine* 6:169–173.

——— (1975). Denial revisited: reflections on psychosomatic theory. *Psychotherapy Psychosomatics* 26:140–147.

Rado, S. (1933). The psychoanalysis of pharmacothymia. *Psychoanalytic Quarterly* 2:1–23.

Rounsaville, B. J., Weissman, M. M., Crits-Cristoph, K., et al. (1982a). Diagnosis and symptoms of depression in opiate addicts: course and relationship to treatment outcome. *Archives of General Psychiatry* 39:151–156.

Rounsaville, B. J., Weissman, M. M., Kleber, H., and Wilber, C. (1982b). Heterogeneity of psychiatric diagnosis in treated opiate addicts. *Archives of General Psychiatry* 39:161–166.

Schiffer, F. (1988). Psychotherapy of nine successfully treated cocaine abusers: techniques and dynamics. *Journal of Substance Abuse Treatment* 5:133–137.

Sifneos, P. E. (1967). Clinical observations on some patients suffering from a variety of psychosomatic diseases. In *Proceedings of the Seventh European Conference on Psychosomatic Research*. Basel: S. Karger.

Spotts, J. V., and Shontz, F. C. (1987). Drug induced ego states: a trajectory theory of drug experience. *Society of Pharmacology* 1:19–51.

Weiss, R. D., and Mirin, S. M. (1984). Drug, host and environmental factors in the development of chronic cocaine abuse. In *Substance Abuse and Psychotherapy*, ed. S. M. Mirin, pp. 42–55. Washington, DC: American Psychiatric Association Press.

——— (1986). Subtypes of cocaine abusers. *Psychiatric Clinics of North America* 9:491–501.

Weiss, R. D., Mirin, S. M., Griffin, M. L., and Michaels, J. L. (1988). Psychopathology in cocaine abusers: changing trends. *Journal of Nervous and Mental Disease* 176(12):719–725.

Weiss, K. J., and Rosenberg, D. J. (1985). Prevalence of anxiety disorder among alcoholics. *Journal of Clinical Psychiatry* 46:3–5.

Wieder, H., and Kaplan, E. (1969). Drug use in adolescents. *Psychoanalytic Study of the Child* 24:399–431. New York: International Universities Press.

Wilson, A., Passik, S. D., Faude, J., et al. (1989). A hierarchical model of opiate addiction: failures of self-regulation as a central aspect of substance abuse. *Journal of Nervous and Mental Disease* 177:390–399.

Woody, G. E., McLellan, A. T., Luborsky, L., and O'Brien, C. P. (1986). Psychotherapy for substance abuse. *Psychiatric Clinics of North America* 9:547–562.

Woody, G. E., O'Brien, C. P., and Rickels, K. (1975). Depression and anxiety in heroin addicts: a placebo-controlled study of doxepin in combination with methadone. *American Journal of Psychiatry* 132:447–450.

Wurmser, L. (1974). Psychoanalytic considerations of the etiology of compulsive drug use. *Journal of the American Psychoanalytic Association* 22:820–843.

——— (1987). Flight from conscience: experiences with the psychoanalytic treatment of compulsive drug users. *Journal of Substance Abuse Treatment* 4:157–168.

# 15

# The Self-Medication Hypothesis of Substance Use Disorders: An Update

> The notion of "self-medication" is one of the most intuitively appealing theories about drug abuse. According to this hypothesis (Khantzian 1985), drug abuse begins as a partially successful attempt to assuage painful feelings. This does not mean seeking "pleasure" from the use of drugs. Rather, individuals predisposed by biological or psychological vulnerabilities find that drug effects corresponding to their particular problems are powerfully reinforcing. [Glass 1990, p. 1583]

Most individuals dependent on alcohol or addictive drugs experience such dependence as unrelenting and persistent. The attendant complications, including loss of control, health, friends and relatives, and self-respect, and even the threat of loss of life, fail to deter those caught in the consuming process of addiction. There is little dispute about the compelling nature and progressively deteriorating course of substance use disorders. There is much debate, however, about the root causes and etiology of these disorders. The above quotation from Glass (1990) suggests that an explanation involving human psychological suffering is important in explaining why people use and become dependent on drugs. In another context, a patient addressed the issue of how drugs help one to cope when he stated, "I take drugs not to escape but to arrive" (H. Kleber, personal communication, 1993). The self-medication hypothesis (SMH) offers an explanation and gives psychological meaning to one of the greatest medical and public health problems to affect our society.

I articulated this hypothesis a decade ago, and I continue to believe that it provides a useful perspective from which to understand some of the powerful emotional factors and pain that govern a person's reliance on alcohol and other addictive drugs. The SMH is not intended to substitute for sociocultural and biogenetic theories in explaining the etiology of substance-related disorders. Rather, it is an explanation that can complement other perspectives. The primary benefit of the SMH is that it addresses important emotional and psychological dimensions of the addictions that have been dismissed (Gold and Miller 1994, Miller 1994), neglected, or inadequately considered in other scientific and clinical investigations.

Although the SMH has received wide recognition and acceptance in general-interest publications (Dranov 1988, Gelman et al. 1989, Goleman 1990) and in the professional literature (Glass 1990, Group for the Advancement of Psychiatry 1991, Ross et al. 1988, Rounsaville et al. 1982a, 1982b), it has also drawn criticism and raised additional questions. This chapter discusses and clarifies aspects of the SMH, considers some of the criticisms and questions raised by this hypothesis, and explores more-recent applications of it in domains that were not originally considered.

## THE SELF-MEDICATION HYPOTHESIS: A RECONSIDERATION AND REARTICULATION

There are two aspects of the SMH that are important and disputed. First and foremost, drugs of abuse relieve psychological suffering. Second, a person's preference for a particular drug involves some degree of psychopharmacological specificity. With regard to the latter, three factors interact to make a particular drug especially appealing

to someone: the main action or effect of the drug, the personality organization or characteristics of the individual, and his or her inner
states of psychological suffering or disharmony. It has been my experience, and that of others (Khantzian 1975, 1978, Krystal 1978, Krystal
and Raskin 1970, Meissner 1986, Milkman and Frosch 1973, Wieder
and Kaplan 1969, Wurmser 1974) that there is a close reciprocal relationship between inner states of suffering and types of personality
or characterological defenses, each heightening the other to make the
appeal of a substance more likely or more compelling.

Patients experiment with various classes of drugs and discover that
a specific one is compelling because it ameliorates, heightens, or relieves affect states that they find particularly problematic or painful.
In my original report on the SMH (Khantzian 1985), I stressed ego
deficits and the inability of individuals with such vulnerabilities to bear
or tolerate a range of affects, and I explained how the main classes of
abused substances could by their specific actions relieve or make more
bearable affect states that otherwise were unbearable. These observations and conclusions were based on careful, in-depth evaluation and
understanding of patients' states of psychological pain and suffering,
characterological traits and defenses related to their suffering, and how
the effects of a particular drug were experienced. With my patients I
empathically explored and discovered how subjective states of distress,
as well as states of confusion and inability to feel their emotions, were
relieved or altered by their "preferred" drug. My clinical findings and
understanding about the suffering and characterological problems that
cause individuals to self-medicate are based on a modified
psychodynamic psychotherapeutic approach. I employ supportive techniques and a semistructured treatment relationship that allow for
more interaction than do classical techniques. This approach provides
better access to a patient's inner life and permits a natural unfolding
of his or her particular ways of experiencing and expressing emotions.
Patients also display characteristic patterns of defense and avoidance
that both reveal and disguise the intensity of their suffering, their
confusion about their feelings, or the ways in which they are cut off
from their feelings. I actively engage with patients and build an alliance that allows them to develop an understanding of how their suffering, defenses, avoidances, and separation from their feelings interact with the specific action of the drugs that they use or prefer. In my
experience these modified psychodynamic techniques yield rich and

ample clinical data that can explain why substances of abuse can become so compelling in a person's life. The findings derived from the use of such psychodynamic methods are empirically testable, as is evidenced by studies (cited below) indicating that subjective states of distress are relieved by substances of abuse.

In the chapters that precede this one on the SMH (see Chapters 8–14), I extensively review the background for this hypothesis and how substances of abuse are adopted as a means to cope with painful affects and external reality. The reader is directed to Chapters 9, 11, 12, and 14, where I more precisely spell out the action of each class of drug and how it predominantly interacts with specific affects states in different individuals to make that particular drug compelling.

I believe that these descriptions capture the compelling nature of the classes of drugs mentioned, but some qualifiers, disclaimers, and special considerations should be offered. It is not unlikely that patients try to make sense out of their addiction by claiming to self-medicate their unhappiness or affect dysregulation when in fact they use such explanations to explain, resist, or rationalize their addiction. In my experience this is frequently the case early in treatment and can be differentiated from a more authentic unfolding of self-medication factors once abstinence is established and mutual trust and a more solid treatment relationship have evolved. Under these latter circumstances, a basis is created for an empathic understanding of why a drug becomes so compelling, which helps to counter patients' previous rationalizations for their drug use.

Although a person may prefer a particular drug, other factors such as cost and availability sometimes preclude its use, causing the individual to substitute other drugs and juggle dosage to approximate the effect of the preferred substance. For example, a person on low to moderate doses of alcohol may appear behaviorally similar to one using moderate amounts of cocaine. In contrast, high doses of alcohol are obliterating (hypnotic) and cause a person to be as obtunded as one who has used large amounts of opiates. The self-selection, drug-of-choice phenomenon also has a corollary. Just as a person may discover the appeal and attraction of a particular drug, he or she may also have the opposite reaction, that is, a marked aversion to a certain class of drugs. For example, an individual prone to aggression might find alcohol to produce a state of marked dysphoria and dyscontrol but experience opiates as soothing and containing. Along similar lines, when a particular drug is used over a prolonged period, its adverse effects can cause "progression" (Khantzian 1975) to another drug to counter those effects. For example, the paranoia- and aggression-producing effects of cocaine not uncommonly make opiates an appealing antidote. Finally, self-medication factors may contribute to relapse. Substance-dependent individuals may refer to "chasing the original high," remembering the marked exhilaration and/or relief when they first began to use a drug. For some, prolonged abstinence can drive relapse because individuals know that they have lost tolerance to their drug of choice and believe that they can come close to experiencing this "original high."

## SUFFERING AND ADDICTIVE VULNERABILITY: CONTRIBUTING AND ESSENTIAL FACTORS

Two of the more obvious criticisms raised by the SMH are that (1) many individuals experience discomfort, pain, and confusion but do not use drugs—or use them and do not become addicted; and (2) becoming dependent on drugs or alcohol causes as much or more distress than it relieves. In this section I review reports and clinical evidence that provide a basis to explain the essential and contributing psychological vulnerabilities that can malignantly coalesce in an individual to increase the likelihood of a substance use disorder. Some of these vulnerabilities help to explain why substance-dependent persons, through their use of alcohol or drugs, wittingly or unwittingly perpetuate the very pain or suffering they are trying to relieve.

### Affect Deficits

As is emphasized by the SMH, a core problem for substance-dependent individuals is the unbearability of affects. But the problem is more complex: the affects are just as likely to be painfully inaccessible, confusing, or inexpressible as they are to be unbearable or intolerable. Adopting a developmental perspective, Krystal and Raskin (1970) and Krystal (1978, 1982, 1988) were pioneers in explaining the way in which affects can be overwhelming and bewildering for persons who abuse substances. They proposed a normal developmental line for affects in which they are undifferentiated, somatic, and not verbalized at the outset; later, they differentiate (e.g., feelings of anxiety and depression can be recognized and distinguished), become desomatized, and are expressible in words. Individuals who abuse substances are either arrested or traumatically regressed in this progression. Adopting the term *alexithymia* coined by Sifneos (1967) and Nemiah (1970), Krystal has repeatedly stressed how the inability to put feelings into words compromises the ability to process emotions and leaves persons more prone to act on their feelings, including substance use. Along similar lines, Wurmser (1974) has referred to "defects in affect defense," describing how at one extreme substance-abusing individuals are overcome by intense hurt, rage, shame, and loneliness, and at the other extreme they seem devoid of inner emotion and fantasy (i.e., the addict's problem of "hyposymbolization"). McDougall (1984) has referred to such patients as "disaffected," and Sashin (unpublished manuscript, 1986) has cataloged a variety of similar "nonfeeling responses" involving failure to experience emotion normally. In our work (Brehm and Khantzian 1992, Khantzian 1993, Khantzian and Wilson 1993), we have emphasized how these patients alternate between intense emotions of rage and suffering and vague feelings of dysphoria and discomfort.

The above observations, based on clinical work with substance-dependent patients and a psychodynamic/developmental perspective, suggest that many individuals, particularly those with a substance use disorder, experience their affects in the extreme. They feel too much, or they feel little or not at all. Some of them learn that drugs and alcohol can ameliorate, relieve, or change these troubling and extreme states of emotions. In the following section I address the contributing and essential factors that make addiction more likely, and the reasons why addicted individuals perpetuate and endure the suffering entailed in substance use disorders. Before doing so, however, I believe that it is important to place the SMH in a broader context of substance abuse as a disorder of self-regulation.

### Substance Abuse as a Self-Regulation Disorder: Contributing and Necessary Conditions

I have hypothesized (Khantzian 1978, 1993, 1995) that substance-dependent persons suffer and self-medicate not only because they do not know, tolerate, or express their feelings but also because they cannot regulate their self-esteem, relationships, or self-care. Blatt and colleagues (1984), Wilson and co-workers (1989), and Shedler and Block (1990) have provided empirical and longitudinal evidence to consider substance abuse as a self-regulation disorder involving affects, self-esteem, relationships, and behavior.

Regulation of painful feelings, in both the unbearable and unrecognizable forms, is a core aspect of addictive vulnerability. Problems with regulating self-esteem and relationships are important contributing factors. Many suffer with such self-regulation problems but do not become addicted. I believe that exposure to drugs combined with the inability to tolerate or to know one's feelings and deficits in self-care is essential for addictive vulnerability. My colleagues and I (Khantzian 1981, Khantzian and Mack 1983, 1989, Khantzian and Wilson 1993) have described impaired survival "instincts" in substance-dependent individuals and the component deficiencies that threaten well-being and survival. They are not so much impaired instincts as compromised capacities to ensure survivability. Such self-care deficits derive from developmental deficiencies that interfere with the ability to anticipate harm or danger. Affected individuals fail to feel apprehension or fear in the face of danger and/or fail to consider, at the cognitive level, cause-consequence relationships involving their behaviors. That is, compared with nonusers they think and feel differently (or ineffectually) in dangerous situations. This is most apparent in relation to the dangers associated with substances of abuse. It is this impaired capacity for self-care that malignantly combines with affect deficits to make experimentation with, dependence on, and relapse to substances more likely and compelling. This is a partial answer to questions of why many people with painful affects do not become addicted. Donovan (1986), considering a multidimensional etiological basis for alcohol dependence, has persuasively argued that the "inability to manage affect and impulse [are the] two psychostructural deficiencies [that] are necessary and sufficient" (p. 4) causes to produce this disorder.

Formulations and hypotheses about substance use disorders implicating self-medication factors and self-regulation vulnerabilities (especially those involving intense affect and self-care deficits) complement empirical and longitudinal investigations implicating emotional dysregulation and behavioral disturbances. Kellam and coworkers (1982, 1991) have longitudinally studied children into young adulthood and documented that childhood aggression and maladaptive social patterns, especially in males, were the main antecedents of later drug use. Similarly, longitudinal data derived from studies by Brook and colleagues (1992) also show childhood aggression and related interpersonal difficulties to correlate strongly with later adolescent drug use. Moss and co-workers (1995) documented a strong relationship between high aggressivity in sons of substance-abusing fathers and the personality trait of "negative affectivity" in the fathers. They suggested that these traits are potential mechanisms for the transmission of substance abuse. It also appears that Cloninger's (1987) differentiation between type 1 and type 2 alcohol dependence is important in this regard; "harm avoidance" and "novelty seeking" are important empirical correlates of the self-care deficits and problems with anticipating harm that I have described (Khantzian 1981, Khantzian and Mack 1983, 1989, Khantzian and Wilson 1993).

Placing self-medication factors in the broader context of self-regulation vulnerabilities also helps to explain some of the psychological aspects, beyond the physiological/addictive ones, of why persons who abuse drugs or alcohol endure or perpetuate the pain and suffering that is associated with substance use disorders. I am referring to the inescapable, painful consequences of acute and chronic drug use, such as the distressful aspects of overdose, the unwanted side effects, the pain of withdrawal, and the personal deterioration, loss of control, and shame. An addiction is often said to take on a life of its own, usually implying physiological/addictive mechanisms to explain the unrelenting negative course of addictive illness. This truism and the underlying assumptions are valid, and I do not mean to minimize them here. But I have also been impressed, both in chronic use and in relapse, that patients are knowingly and unknowingly governed by other motives. Some might argue (and legitimately so) that persons who abuse substances, suffering as they do, are willing to accept such distress in exchange for whatever momentary relief they experience with their drug of choice. However, my patients have convinced me that they actively and often knowingly perpetuate their suffering when they compulsively continue to use drugs or when they relapse after periods of abstinence.

I have likened the pain-perpetuating aspect of drug use to a compulsion to repeat unresolved pain from the earliest phases of development (Brehm and Khantzian 1992, Khantzian 1993). Independently, Schiffer (1988) has come to similar conclusions to explain the self-perpetuating and damaging painful consequences of cocaine use and dependence. My patients' descriptions of how they anticipate and even accept the pain associated with drugs have caused me to conclude that their behavior represents a means to control and work out self-regulation vulnerabilities involving their feeling life. They suggest or demonstrate that they are motivated by a need to "master and convert the passive, confusing experience of being alexithymic or disaffected to an active one of controlling feelings with drug use, even if they are painful" (Khantzian 1995, p. 29). That is, the distressful, repetitive aspects of drug dependence are intimately linked to the effects of early-life trauma on subsequent affect and personality development, representing attempts to work out painful states that cannot always be remembered and are often without words or symbolic representation in the mind (Gedo 1986, Lichtenberg 1983). This aspect of drug use is especially relevant to patients who do not know or recognize their feelings. Rather than simply relieving suffering that is unsustainable, persons who abuse substances often use drugs to control their feelings, especially when they are nameless, confusing, and beyond their control. The motive in these instances shifts from relief of suffering to the control of it (Brehm and Khantzian 1992, Khantzian 1993, 1995, Khantzian and Wilson 1993).

## SUBSTANCE ABUSE, PSYCHOPATHOLOGY, AND THE CAUSE–CONSEQUENCE CONTROVERSY

Presumably, a systematic and empirical examination of the relationship between substance abuse and psychopathology would shed considerable light on the validity of the SMH. Weiss and colleagues (1992a,b) have been among the leaders in exploring this relationship. They noted the paucity of empirical studies testing the SMH and have explored some of the methodological considerations and problems in diagnosing psychiatric disorders in persons who abuse substances. There is, however, a robust literature documenting a strong association between substance abuse and co-occurring psychiatric disorders. From the mid-1970s to the present, numerous reports have documented disproportionately high rates of psychopathology among opiate-, stimulant-, and alcohol-dependent individuals; not insignificantly, these investigations reveal different rates of Axis I diagnoses among specific subgroups of drug-dependent patients (Group for the Advancement of Psychiatry 1991). In most studies depression occurs at a consistently high rate in both its less severe and major forms. One-third to one-half of evaluated patients who are addicted to opiates meet criteria for major depression at the time of evaluation, and as many as two-thirds meet criteria for lifetime depression, mostly of the unipolar type (Khantzian and Treece 1985, Rounsaville et al. 1982a,b, Weissman et al. 1976, Woody et al. 1983). Studies of patients who are addicted to cocaine have consistently revealed disproportionately high rates of affective disorders (especially bipolar types), attention-deficit disorder, and personality disorders, including narcissistic, borderline, and antisocial types (Carroll and Rounsaville 1992, Gawin and Kleber 1984, Halikas 1994, Khantzian et al. 1984, Kleinman et al. 1990, Rounsaville et al. 1991, Weiss et al. 1984, 1985, 1988, Wilens et al. 1994). Although the data have been less consistent in documenting the rates and types of psychopathology co-occurring with alcohol dependence (one review [Keeler et al. 1979] noted that estimates of the co-occurrence of depression and alcohol dependence ranged between 3 percent and 98 percent), epidemiological catchment area (ECA) and clinical studies (Christie et al. 1988, Dorus et al. 1987, Hesselbrock et al. 1985, Penick et al. 1994, Regier et al. 1990, Weiss and Rosenberg 1985) have provided more consistent empirical data and evidence indicating significantly higher rates of anxiety and affective disorders among alcohol-dependent persons than in the general population.

Notwithstanding the numerous studies indicating a strong association between substance use and psychiatric disorders and the possible association between categories of psychiatric disorders and drug preference, these reports vary widely in interpreting whether substance abuse is the cause or consequence of psychopathology. Understanding this relationship may shed light on whether substance abusers are self-medicating preexisting psychopathology.

Although I have cited reports that suggest different rates of Axis I diagnoses among specific subgroups of substance-dependent patients, types of psychiatric comorbidity do not differ that much across the subgroups. This could argue against the SMH by indicating little specificity in one's drug of choice. One argument against drawing such a conclusion is that the actions of abused drugs vary greatly among individuals and may differ according to one's psychological set (i.e., one's unique subjective state of distress) and the situation in which a drug is used. Furthermore, as I repeatedly emphasize in this chapter, it is not so much a psychiatric condition that one self-medicates, but a wide range of subjective symptoms and states of distress that may or may not be associated with a psychiatric disorder. For example, the painful affects and subjective states associated with depression could be predominantly anger, sadness, anergy, or agitation, and it is these specific inner states that one self-medicates.

Several investigators (Dackis et al. 1986, Gold and Miller 1994, Miller and Gold 1991, Schuckit 1986, Schuckit and Hesselbrock 1994, Schuckit et al. 1990, Vaillant 1983) have argued that most of the anxiety and depression associated with substance use disorders is the consequence of chronic use and clears over time with abstinence. The work of Vaillant and Schuckit is particularly important in this respect. These researchers have extensively evaluated and followed populations of alcohol-dependent individuals and have consistently documented low to insignificant incidence of additional psychiatric problems in them. Vaillant has repeatedly emphasized the psychological and psychiatric consequences and the physical morbidity and mortality associated with alcohol abuse and dependence. Vaillant (1996) underscored the long-term physical consequences in his most recent follow-up report of alcohol-dependent males and commented that the incidence of dual diagnosis was minimal in his longitudinal samples. In previous reports Vaillant (1980, 1983, Vaillant and Milofsky 1982) consistently downplayed the role of psychopathology in the "natural history of alcoholism," emphasizing that alcohol dependence plays a greater part in the genesis of psychopathology than does psychopathology in the genesis of alcohol dependence. Furthermore, in contrast to his early publications (Vaillant 1975) in which he underscored narcotics-addicted individuals' problems with sociopathy and depression, he has repeatedly stressed that "genes and culture" play a far greater role than "personality or an unhappy childhood" in the etiology of alcohol dependence (Vaillant 1982, 1983).

In a recent eight-year follow-up study of 453 sons of alcohol-dependent men and control subjects, Schuckit and Smith (1996) reported that family history and level of reactivity to alcohol (i.e., low) best predicted the development of alcohol dependence, and that alcohol dependence was unrelated to prior psychiatric disorders. Similarly, recent and past reports by Schuckit and colleagues (Brown and Schuckit 1988,

Schuckit et al. 1990) have minimized the role of depression and anxiety in the development of alcohol dependence and have stressed that these conditions are more likely induced by alcohol.

The findings and conclusions of Vaillant and Schuckit would appear to argue against an SMH of addictive disorders. However, in their work these investigators have variously failed to consider, not measured for, and/or dismissed the importance of depressive or anxiety symptoms that precede or persist in acute or chronic episodes of alcohol dependence. Actually, with Schuckit's work on the course of anxiety and depression in alcohol-dependent persons, this was further compounded by the fact that his study subjects were a preselected sample of "primary alcoholics" (Brown and Schuckit 1988, Schuckit et al. 1990). By design, anxiety and depression meeting threshold diagnostic criteria would be minimal in such samples. But even if the symptoms do not meet threshold criteria for psychiatric diagnoses, they are still associated with much psychological pain and subjective suffering. The RAND Medical Outcomes Study (Wells et al. 1989) has shown that such distress can lead to significant impairment in physical, social, and role function, and Glass (1990), in discussing the role of depressive symptoms in nicotine dependence, has suggested that such symptoms can produce as much physical impairment as "full-blown depressive disorders." I believe that using Vaillant's and Schuckit's findings to argue against the SMH is not necessarily valid because measures employed in their studies have not addressed or adequately tested the antecedent developmental problems, specific painful affect states, and other subjective states of distress that I have emphasized in this report and previous ones. Furthermore, both Donovan (1986) and Zucker and Gomberg (1986) have critiqued such studies and have argued that these large-scale investigations have difficulty coding and identifying environmental and personality factors that might play an etiological role in substance use disorders. I would add that these studies fail to adequately identify some of the subtle factors relating to self-comfort, personal relationships, and self-esteem. Such factors date back to the earliest phases of development and, as I have suggested, may help to determine whether one is susceptible to becoming substance dependent.

In contrast to the work of Vaillant and Schuckit, numerous other investigations (Carroll and Rounsaville 1992, Christie et al. 1988, Halikas et al. 1994, Hesselbrock et al. 1985, Penick et al. 1994, Regier et al. 1990, Rounsaville et al. 1991, Weiss and Rosenberg 1985) provide evidence of high lifetime prevalence rates of psychopathology in patients with a substance use disorder and a psychiatric disorder preceding the substance abuse. Finally, in cases of comorbidity, one must be aware of Berkson's fallacy (Andersen 1969): disorders that appear to be related in clinical samples may merely be co-occurring because the samples are biased toward severity. A major argument against this possibility is that studies of general population samples (see the ECA studies cited elsewhere in this chapter) have repeatedly shown comorbidity rates that exceed chance.

If one depends on empirical studies employing standardized diagnostic methods, the preceding review of the literature would at best suggest that the "cart/horse" controversy remains unsettled. It does not sufficiently resolve the issue of whether psychopathology is causally linked to substance use disorders.

Interestingly, Rounsaville and colleagues (1991) have argued that even when depressions seem to be the result of substance abuse, the possibility remains that subclinical levels of depression predated and motivated drug use. More recently, McKenna and Ross (1994) have explored the relationship between psychiatric disorders/symptoms and substance abuse and have provided persuasive evidence that substance-dependent individuals use drugs or alcohol to relieve subjective states of distress. In a sample of seventy-nine substance-abusing patients, they found that thirty-six satisfied criteria for co-occurring psychiatric disorders and twenty-three had symptoms considered to be clinically significant. The authors observed that in patients who were dually diagnosed, emotional reasons were involved to a significant (42 percent) or "intermediate" (33 percent) degree in the rationale for their substance abuse. They allowed for methodological problems in making psychiatric diagnoses in this population and for the fact that psychiatric symptoms can often be substance induced, but the findings indicated that the onset of substance abuse was predated by psychiatric disorders and symptoms in a significantly high percentage of the cases. The authors were satisfied that in the majority of cases, substance abuse was related to distress associated with psychiatric disorders and symptoms.

In my experience, Rounsaville and colleagues and McKenna and Ross are correct in allowing for subclinical/subthreshold "variants" of psychiatric disorders and the distress and suffering that these vari-

ants involve. As I have indicated, it is painful affects and related maladaptive defenses and patterns of behavior that cause individuals to
self-medicate states or conditions that might or might not be diagnosable using standardized techniques. In my own work I have used the
generic term *dysphoria* to describe the pervasive, often vague distressful states that substance dependent persons try to self-medicate. Other
terms that describe the same phenomenon have also been introduced—
for example, *affect deficits, alexithymia,* and *disaffected states,* already
described from a psychodynamic perspective, and *hypophoria* (Martin et al. 1977), *atypical depression, subaffective dysthymia, atypical
bipolar,* and *hyperthymics* (Akiskal 1989) on the descriptive/diagnos-
tic side. Such descriptions suggest a wide range of more subtle, but
nevertheless painful, affect states that are involved in the process
whereby patients discover the pain-ameliorating properties of substances of abuse. I believe that further studies of these "borderlands"
of affective distress could help to resolve the debate over the cause-
consequence issues, as well as "diagnostic conundrums" (McKenna and
Ross 1994) as to how psychiatric distress (i.e., disorders or symptoms)
and/or overt or subtle painful affect states may govern drug-seeking/
drug-dependent behavior.

Empirical studies by Weiss, Noordsy, Ciraulo, Milin, and their colleagues (Ciraulo et al. 1989, 1994, Milin et al. 1992, Noordsy et al.
1991, Weiss et al. 1992a) provide data to support my contention that
subjective states of distress (not necessarily psychiatric disorders) are
the important operatives that govern self-medication. Although the
findings in Weiss and co-workers' study (1992a) did not support pharmacological specificity in one's drug of choice for depression, 63 percent of 494 respondents stated that they used drugs for depressive
symptoms (only 10 percent were diagnosed with major depression after
four weeks of abstinence). The authors concluded that patients may
use drugs in response to "depressed mood" without major depression.
Noordsy's group (1991) documented that over half of a sample of
schizophrenic patients ($n = 75$) experienced a lessening of social anxiety, tension, dysphoria, apathy, anhedonia, and sleep difficulties when
they used alcohol. Other nonpsychotic symptoms such as poor interpersonal relationships and shyness were also relieved by alcohol (in
42.4 percent and 39.4 percent of patients, respectively). Ciraulo and
colleagues measured subjective responses to single doses of alprazolam

administered to alcohol-dependent individuals (1994) and non–alcohol-dependent children of alcohol-dependent adults (1989) and demonstrated that mood enhancement was greater in both of the samples than in controls. The authors concluded that these studies provide some support for the SMH. Milin and colleagues (1992), based on responses to an adjective checklist, showed that persons who abuse alcohol, marijuana, or cocaine experience unique subjective reactions to their drug of choice. They concluded that those who abuse alcohol are "stimulus augmenters" and drink to attenuate or reduce their sensitivity, while those who abuse cocaine are "stimulus reducers" and use the drug to increase their level of stimulation.

Although there are diagnostic studies and psychiatric findings that support the SMH, a review of the cause-consequence relationship between substance abuse and psychopathology sheds little light on the role of self-medication factors in the development and maintenance of substance use disorders. I have cited certain empirical studies that give some credence to the role of human psychological distress as a significant influence in the use of addictive substances to self-medicate. What is probably clear from this review is that cross-sectional diagnostic surveys are not very useful in testing the SMH or very well suited to do so. Longitudinal studies (e.g., Brook et al. 1992, Kellam et al. 1982, 1991, Moss et al. 1995, Shedler and Block 1990), which detail family interaction patterns, tolerance/expression of emotions, and behavioral adjustment and track them over time, seem more promising. Such investigations combined with treatment outcome studies would probably be better tests of the hypothesis. Space does not allow for a detailed review here, but future research along these lines might provide more immediate and clearer evidence that suffering and behavioral difficulties are important governing influences that make the use of, dependence on, and relapse to addictive substances compelling.

## RECENT APPLICATIONS OF THE SELF-MEDICATION HYPOTHESIS

In this update of the SMH, I have emphasized the centrality of human suffering, in both its intense and subtle varieties, as a powerful governing influence in the pursuit of, reliance on, and relapse to one's drug of choice. My own experience coupled with recent evidence and clinical studies suggests that these factors are also involved in other areas:

- The use of nicotine to alleviate or remedy subjective states of distress involving dysphoria, dysthymia, and depressive symptoms and/or disorders
- The high incidence of alcohol use, stimulants, and other drugs by persons with schizophrenia or other psychoses, hypothesized to relieve the negative symptoms associated with severe mental illness
- The heavy use of alcohol and other drugs by individuals with posttraumatic stress disorder (PTSD) to self-medicate the affective flooding or numbing involved in this condition

## Nicotine Dependence

A national database (Anda et al. 1990), the ECA studies (Glassman et al. 1990), and other surveys (Breslau et al. 1993a,b) and clinical-investigative studies (Kandel and Davies 1986, Schifano et al. 1994) have all provided evidence of a significant association between heavy smoking (i.e., nicotine dependence) and depression and other measures of subjective distress. Anda and colleagues (1990) using a national database (including self-report scales for depressive symptoms) and nine-year follow-up data, found that smoking rates rose and quit rates fell as depressive symptoms increased. In the follow-up the quit rate was 9.9 percent for depressed smokers and 17.7 percent for nondepressed ones. In a companion article based on an ECA community diagnostic survey, Glassman and colleagues (1990) documented a strong association between cigarette smoking and major depression. They also found that heavy smokers with depression were less successful in quitting and, based on Glassman's clinical observation, noted how in a number of cases serious depression gradually ensued when patients quit smoking, but disappeared within hours after they resumed it. In the same issue of the *Journal of the American Medical Association* in which these two reports appeared, Glass (1990) endorsed the SMH and concluded that it fit the data that they reported.

More recently, Breslau and associates (1993a) studied a randomly chosen sample of 1,007 subjects from a large health maintenance organization. Pertinent to the SMH, they used measures/scales of subjective distress—namely, neuroticism (12-item scale from the Eysenck Personality Questionnaire), negative affect (Positive Affect–Negative Affect Schedule), hopelessness (20-item Beck Hopelessness Scale), and general emotional distress (Brief Symptom Inventory—a 54-item instrument from the Symptom Checklist-90). Nicotine dependence, but not nondependent smoking, was positively associated with all four measures of subjective distress. The authors speculated that neuroticism commonly predisposes individuals to nicotine dependence, major depression, and anxiety disorders.

In a related study Breslau and colleague (1993b) prospectively examined the association between nicotine dependence and major depression in a sample of 995 young adults. They concluded that such an association did exist, but that it might be causal in both directions, noncausal, or reflective of a predisposition to both disorders, raising once again the cart-horse/cause-consequence debate. This investigation relied on the Diagnostic Interview Schedule, a standardized structured interview that, as I previously suggested, is less likely to pick up the subjective signs of distress targeted by the authors' previous study (Breslau et al. 1993a). As that study suggested, subjective signs of distress are probably the important correlates that predispose individuals to nicotine dependence. This perspective is supported by data indicating that depressive symptoms in adolescents predict higher rates of cigarette smoking in adulthood (Kandel and Davies 1986), and that rates of psychological distress (somatization, anxiety, hostility, paranoid ideation) are higher in teenage female smokers than nonsmokers; such symptoms are present when they first begin to smoke (Schifano et al. 1994).

## Comorbid Schizophrenia and Substance Abuse

Most of the observations and conclusions about the SMH that I originally published in 1985 were based on work in my private practice or in a public-sector outpatient substance-abuse program. The patients did not necessarily consider themselves to be suffering from a psychiatric disorder. In 1989 I began working in a state inpatient facility with severely mentally ill patients, many of whom had comorbid substance use disorders. In considering the SMH, I was not sure what symptoms schizophrenic patients might be self-medicating, although

I was aware from my training years that such individuals experienced and had much difficulty in bearing and acknowledging painful affect (Khantzian et al. 1969). After beginning inpatient work, I had the opportunity to interview and/or evaluate many dually diagnosed patients; I immediately became aware of the important distinction between positive and negative symptoms (Andreasen 1982, Andreasen and Olsen 1982, Andreasen et al. 1990, Crow 1980).

I began to suspect that negative symptoms might be an important if not an essential aspect of the appeal of substances for such patients. A case example of a particularly taciturn patient with chronic schizophrenia stands out.

> I was asked to evaluate Barry, a 48-year-old man, regarding suitability for discharge. He insisted that he did not belong in the hospital. With a little prompting on my part, he said that he was an inhibited man who felt uncomfortable with people. He explained that drinking alcohol allowed him to be more talkative and involved. The clinical team members corroborated this by describing his demeanor and interaction just after he returned—still intoxicated—after an escape. He was characterized as being unusually "affable, warm, friendly, and talkative." He agreed when I reflected aloud that alcohol was one of the few ways in which he came alive and felt normal among other human beings. In response, he simply echoed his previous statement: "I am inhibited, I don't say much, and I keep to myself if I am not drinking."

Barry's depiction of himself when not under the influence of alcohol is very much in keeping with Andreasen and colleagues' (1990) description of negative symptoms in schizophrenia: "(1) alogia (e.g., marked poverty of speech, poverty of content of speech); (2) affective flattening; (3) anhedonia-asociality (e.g., inability to experience pleasure or to feel intimacy, few social contacts); (4) avolition-apathy (e.g., anergia, impersistence at work or school); and (5) attentional impairment" (p. 616). The authors indicated that at least two of the above must be present to a marked degree to satisfy criteria for negative symptoms; Barry showed all five.

I believe that tremendous distress, suffering, and dysfunction are associated with negative symptoms, and it should not be surprising that patients with these symptoms find that the specific effects of the various classes of abused drugs can alter, ameliorate, or relieve their pain and discomfort. Evidence and legitimate arguments that use of psychoactive substances precipitates or causes psychosis and/or worsens its course (including heightening negative symptoms) (Breakey et al. 1974, Gold and Miller 1994, Janowsky and Davis 1976, Kleber and Gavin 1985, Miller 1994, Richard et al. 1985) should also not be surprising. The observation that substance abuse more often precedes than follows the development of major mental illness is frequently used to argue against self-medication motives in these disorders. Such arguments ignore the often lengthy prodromal phase of major mental illness, which involves much pain and suffering and social maladaptation. A revealing study by Kelly and colleagues (1992) examined the relationship between premorbid functioning and negative symptoms in schizophrenia. Compared to patients who had no negative symptoms, those with negative symptoms had significantly lower levels of premorbid functioning during late adolescence, and even greater premorbid deterioration between childhood and adolescence. Although the authors did not mention the qualities and elements of premorbid deterioration, it is fair to speculate that significant suffering and maladaptation are key ingredients of poor premorbid functioning, which exists prior to schizophrenia and could predispose individuals to drug and alcohol use at that time.

Based on my clinical experience and recent reports in the literature, there are findings to support the hypothesis that self-medication of negative symptoms (and probably also the prodromes of schizophrenia, which resemble these symptoms) is an important factor in the association between substance abuse and schizophrenia. Based on the assumption that clozapine, an atypical neuroleptic, is more effective in relieving negative symptoms, my colleagues and I (Albanese et al. 1994) followed and reported on two schizophrenic patients whose use of, reliance on, and relapse to alcohol was unrelenting prior to treatment with that drug. Clozapine produced marked improvement in positive and negative symptoms in both patients, and over the subsequent year neither reverted to using alcohol. Complementing our experience and perspective, several reports have appeared in the literature suggesting that psychotic patients self-medicate their distress, and more specifically that they demonstrate a preferential pattern of drug/alcohol use. Reports reviewed by Schneier and Siris (1987) indicate a nonrandom pattern of preferred drug use among schizophrenic patients, with stimulants (i.e., cocaine and amphetamines), hallucinogens, and marijuana being employed at disproportionately high rates. Brady and colleagues (1990) reported on a series of schizophrenic patients who abused cocaine; these authors allowed that the interaction between cocaine and schizophrenia could be causal or a form of self-medication. Most recently, Serper and associates (1995) studied and compared a group of cocaine-abusing schizophrenic patients with a group of abstaining schizophrenic patients. They found that when the patients first presented to the psychiatric service, those who abused cocaine had significantly fewer negative symptoms than did those who abstained. However, after four weeks of hospitalization, there were no group differences in patients' negative signs or mood symptoms. In all of these studies, as well as the report by Noordsy and colleagues (1991) the authors questioned whether the patients might be self-medicating negative symptoms.

From the above, I have concluded that an important factor explaining heavy reliance on drugs and alcohol among patients with schizophrenia is individuals' discovery that substances of abuse offer temporary relief from the distress and suffering associated with their negative symptoms. In the premorbid phases of major mental illness, substance use is an attempt to self-medicate the painful prodromes of these conditions.

## Comorbid Posttraumatic Stress Disorder and Substance Abuse

There is an extensive literature documenting a significant relationship between PTSD and substance abuse. Although the interrelationships are complex and raise many issues, such as (not surprisingly) which comes first (again, the cart/horse debate) and whether both conditions have common antecedents, most of the literature reflects a strong interaction between the two disorders as well as the major suffering and difficulties in coping inherent in them. The seminal and pioneering contributions of Krystal (1988), van der Kolk (1987), and Herman (1992) provide robust and ample documentation of the persistent, pervasive, and significant psychological pain, suffering, and disruption associated with PTSD. These authors have observed and considered the frequent association between PTSD and substance abuse. The trends are strikingly evident in a series of companion reports by Nace (1988), Keane and colleagues (1988), Kosten and Krystal

(1988), and Penk and coworkers (1988) that focused mainly on Vietnam veterans. Nace (1988) noted that 40 to 50 percent of PTSD patients abuse alcohol. More important, he underscored the powerful countertransference reactions that are stirred in clinicians when they work with PTSD patients, which he believes are important indicators of the enormous suffering experienced by trauma victims. Keane and colleagues (1988) reported that PTSD patients seeking treatment in Veterans Affairs medical centers had very high rates (63 to 80 percent) of concurrent substance abuse. In this same series of reports, Kosten and Krystal (1988) considered the importance of self-medication in PTSD. Although they focused primarily on central noradrenergic activity, hypothalamopituitary-adrenal dysfunction, and endogenous opioid disturbances, they linked these factors to suggest that the use of alcohol and heroin could be "an active adaptive style rather than a potentially helpless stance" (p. 60) in the acute stress of war. They described and commented on how alcohol temporarily counters states of anhedonia and numbing in PTSD but also noted the unfortunate disinhibition (i.e., release of aggression) that often ensues, further compounding their PTSD. Penk and colleagues (1988) underscored the role of avoidant coping styles associated with co-occurring substance abuse and PTSD and emphasized the important interactions among substance abuse, trauma, and stress. Their findings support a "traumatogenic" basis for substance abuse in Vietnam combat veterans.

The ECA data and newer reports involving patients in treatment demonstrate important relationships between substance abuse and PTSD in these populations as well. Brady and coworkers (1994) studied female patients in a substance abuse treatment program and found that those with PTSD were more likely to have been physically and sexually abused, especially during childhood, than those who did not have this disorder. The women with PTSD also had elevated scores on the Addiction Severity Index (McLellan et al. 1990) and were more likely to have a comorbid affective disorder. More recently, Grice and colleagues (1995) reported that 66 of the 100 substance-dependent inpatients they studied had been sexually or physically assaulted. Furthermore, half of the assault victims satisfied *DSM-III-R* criteria for PTSD, whereas no one in the nonassault group met them. Swett and Halpert (1994) found that female inpatients who reported histories of physical or sexual abuse scored significantly higher on the

Michigan Alcoholism Screening Test than did patients with a negative trauma history. Windle and colleagues (1995) studied 802 persons admitted to one of five inpatient alcohol-treatment centers and found that 59 percent of the females and 30 percent of the males had been abused during childhood. A history of abuse was also associated with higher levels of antisocial personality disorder and suicide attempts among women and men, with major depression among men, and with generalized anxiety disorder among women. Finally, an ECA study by Cottler and colleagues (1992) identified 430 individuals (out of 2,663 respondents) who reported a traumatic event that could qualify for PTSD. Respondents who used cocaine or heroin were more than three times as likely as those who did not to have experienced trauma, most commonly involving physical attack. According to the *DSM-IV* (American Psychiatric Association 1994) the main features of PTSD are re-experiencing the trauma (including recurrent memories, dreams, and related psychological distress), persistent avoidance or numbing (i.e., avoidance of thoughts and feelings associated with the trauma, amnesia for the traumatic events, decreased interest in important activities, feelings of detachment, restricted affect), and hyperarousal (i.e., sleep disturbance, irritability and anger, poor concentration, hypervigilance, increased startle response).

Recurrent affective flooding and numbing, hyperarousal, and the related states of emotional and behavioral dysregulation interact with drug and alcohol effects and, I believe, are powerful determinants to self-medicate. But it is just as likely that patients self-medicate the negative affects associated with major trauma. In fact, the resemblance between PTSD and the negative symptoms of schizophrenia is striking. In an intriguing review, Stampfer (1990) elaborated on these similarities and concluded that the negative symptoms usually associated with schizophrenia are manifestations of trauma ("of losing one's mind") and that the clinical and pathophysiological phenomena and disturbances are basically similar in PTSD and schizophrenia (i.e., the negative symptoms).

Among the drugs of abuse, drug preference could be determined by whatever symptoms or cluster of symptoms (and associated distress) predominated for any given individual (and/or at any given time). For example, Vietnam veterans with whom I worked gave compelling evidence of how opiates calmed and contained their rage. (Rage and anger are constant companions and concomitants of trauma and violence of any kind.) In the case of alcohol abuse, the alcohol can offset or reverse psychic numbing, feelings of estrangement, and detachment in low to moderate doses, and it can dampen emotional flooding in high, "hypnotic" doses. In these latter cases my patients have referred to the "obliterating" effects of alcohol and other drugs. Finally, it should not be surprising that stimulants such as cocaine are often used by PTSD patients, as Kosten and Krystal (1986) have suggested, to offset the anhedonia and deactivation commonly seen in this disorder. In conclusion, there is evidence that individuals with PTSD are at high risk to become substance-dependent because they discover that the psychotropic effects of drugs and alcohol provide powerful short-term antidotes to the painful positive (e.g., rage, anxiety, panic) and negative (e.g., anergia, anhedonia, affective flattening) affect states associated with trauma histories. That is, they self-medicate the pain associated with symptoms of PTSD.

## CONCLUSIONS

This chapter has highlighted some of the important psychological factors that predispose individuals to substance use disorders. I have placed particular emphasis on clarifying the important role of self-medication factors and how they interact with and are governed by subjective states of psychological pain and suffering that substance-dependent individuals endure; I have also attempted to explain how the SMH applies to nicotine dependence and to schizophrenia and PTSD comorbid with a substance use disorder. What has been left out of this chapter is implications for treatment, and the important neurobiological correlates of addictive suffering. I believe that the SMH has important ramifications and applications in both areas. Empathically appreciating and tuning in to the subjective states of distress that substance abusers self-medicate can help guide clinicians in matching patients to appropriate psychosocial and psychopharmacological treatments. Furthermore, a unified theory or explanation of substance use disorders needs ultimately to address and integrate the neurobiological aspects (including the roles of norepinephrine and the locus ceruleus, as well as of endogenous opioids, dopamine, and γ-aminobutyric acid, the main neurotransmitter systems that correspond to the exogenous substances of abuse) and the psychological correlates (e.g., self-medication factors) of addiction.

In this update of the SMH, I have drawn attention to the nature of the distress that motivates substance abuse, as well as the nature of the person who is unable to control (or self-regulate) the impulse to use and become dependent on drugs. I have focused on three areas of application of the SMH that had not previously been considered. I believe that these applications validate the utility of the SMH and have heuristic value in improving understanding and treatment of the target symptoms and subjective distress that our patients and others self-medicate.

## ACKNOWLEDGMENTS

The author is indebted to Carolyn Bell, Tracy Bucceri, Domenic Ciraulo, Susan Lyden Murphy, Edgar Nace and Steven Nisenbaum for their invaluable assistance, feedback, and support in the preparation of this chapter.

## REFERENCES

Akiskal, H. (1989). Validating affective personality types. In *The Validity of Psychiatric Diagnosis*, ed. L. N. Robbins and J. Barrett, pp. 217–227. New York: Raven.

Albanese, M. J., Khantzian, E. J., Murphy, S. L., and Green, A. I. (1994). Decreased substance use in chronically psychotic patients treated with clozapine. *American Journal of Psychiatry* 151:780–781.

American Psychiatric Association (1994). *Diagnostic and Statistical Manual of Mental Disorders*, 4th ed. Washington, DC: American Psychiatric Association.

Anda, R. F., Williamson, D. F., Escobedo, L. G., et al. (1990). Depression and the dynamics of smoking: a national perspective. *Journal of the American Medical Association* 264:1541–1545.

Andersen, B. (1969). Berkson's fallacy. *Nordic Medicine* 81:729–730.

Andreasen, N. C. (1982). Negative symptoms in schizophrenia: definition and reliability. *Archives of General Psychiatry* 39:784–788.

Andreasen, N. C., Flaum, M., Swayze, V. W. II, et al. (1990). Positive and negative symptoms in schizophrenia: a critical reappraisal. *Archives of General Psychiatry* 47:615–621.

Andreasen, N. C., and Olsen, S. (1982). Negative v. positive schizophrenia: definition and validation. *Archives of General Psychiatry* 39:789–794.

Blatt, S. J., Berman, W., Bloom-Feshback, S., et al. (1984). Psychological assessment of psychopathology in opiate addiction. *Journal of Nervous and Mental Disease* 172:156–165.

Brady, K., Anton, R., Ballenger, J. C., et al. (1990). Cocaine abuse among schizophrenic patients. *American Journal Psychiatry* 147:1164–1167.

Brady, K. T., Killeen, T., Saladin, M. E., et al. (1994). Comorbid substance abuse and posttraumatic stress disorder: characteristics of women in treatment. *American Journal of Addictions* 3:160–164.

Breakey, W. R., Goodell, H., Lorenz, P. C., and McHugh, P. R. (1974). Hallucinogens as precipitants of schizophrenia. *Psychological Medicine* 4:255–261.

Brehm, M., and Khantzian, E. J. (1992). The psychology of substance abuse: a psychodynamic perspective. In *Substance Abuse: A Comprehensive Textbook*, ed. J. H. Lowinson, P. Ruiz, and R. B. Millman, pp. 106–117. Baltimore: Williams & Wilkins.

Breslau, N., Kilbey, M. M., and Andreski, P. (1993a). Vulnerability to psychopathology in nicotine dependent smokers: an epidemiologic study of young adults. *American Journal of Psychiatry* 150:941–946.

——— (1993b). Nicotine dependence and major depression: new evidence from a prospective investigation. *Archives of General Psychiatry* 50:31–35.

Brook, J. S., Whiteman, M., Cohen, P., and Tanaka, J. S. (1992). Childhood precursors of adolescent drug use: a longitudinal analysis. *Genetics, Society and General Psychology Monograph* 118:195–213.

Brown, S. A., and Schuckit, M. A. (1988). Changes in depression among abstinent alcoholics. *Journal of Studies on Alcohol* 49:412–417.

Carroll, K. M., and Rounsaville, B. J. (1992). Contrast of treatment seeking and untreated cocaine abusers. *Archives of General Psychiatry* 49:464–471.

Christie, K. A., Burke, J. D. Jr., Regier, D. A., et al. (1988). Epidemiologic evidence for early onset of mental disorders and higher risk of drug abuse in young adults. *American Journal of Psychiatry* 145:971–975.

Ciraulo, D. A., Barnhill, J. G., Ciraulo, A. M., et al. (1989). Parental alcoholism as a risk factor in benzodiazepine abuse: a pilot study. *American Journal of Psychiatry* 146:1333–1335.

Ciraulo, D. A., Sarrid-Segal, O., Barnhill, J., et al. (1994). Effects of benzodiazepines, buspirone, and placebo on mood and EEG activity in alcoholics and normal subjects [Abstract]. *Scientific Abstracts of the Annual Meeting of the American Psychiatric Association*, Philadelphia, May, p. 159. Washington, DC: American Psychiatric Association.

Cloninger, C. R. (1987). Neurogenetic adaptive mechanisms in alcoholism. *Science* 236:410–416.

Cottler, L. B., Compton, W. M. 3rd, Mager, D., et al. (1992). Posttraumatic stress disorder among substance abusers from the general population. *American Journal of Psychiatry* 149:664–670.

Crow, T. J. (1980). Molecular pathology of schizophrenia: more than one disease process? *British Medical Journal* 280:66–68.

Dackis, C., and Gold, M. (1986). More on self-medication and drug abuse. *American Journal of Psychiatry* 143:1309–1310.

Donovan, J. M. (1986). An etiologic model of alcoholism. *American Journal of Psychiatry* 143:1–11.

Dorus, W., Kennedy, J., Gibbons, R. D., and Ravi, S. D. (1987). Symptoms and diagnosis of depression in alcoholics. *Alcoholism* 11:150–154.

Dranov, P. (1988). The harrowing mystery of addiction. *Cosmopolitan* 205(1):148–151.

Gawin, F. H., and Kleber, H. D. (1984). Cocaine abuse treatment. *Archives of General Psychiatry* 41:903–908.

Gedo, J. (1986). *Conceptual Issues in Psychoanalysis: Essays in History and Method*. Hillsdale, NJ: Analytic Press.

Gelman, D., Drew, L., Hagler, M., et al. (1989). Roots of addiction. *Newsweek*, February 20, pp. 52–57.

Glass, R. (1990). Blue mood, blackened lungs: depression and smoking. *Journal of the American Medical Association* 264:1583–1584.

Glassman, A. H., Helzer, J. E., Covey, L. S., et al. (1990). Smoking, smoking cessation, and major depression. *Journal of the American Medical Association* 264:1546–1549.

Gold, M. S., and Miller, N. S. (1994). The biology of addictive and psychiatric disorders. In *Treating Co-existing Psychiatric and Addictive Disorders: A Practical Guide*, ed. N. S. Miller, pp. 35–49. Center City, MN: Hazelden.

Goleman, D. (1990). Scientists pinpoint brain irregularities in drug addicts. *New York Times*, June 26, pp. C1, C7.

Grice, D. E., Brady, K. T., Dustan, L. R., et al. (1995). Sexual and physical assault history and post traumatic stress disorder in substance dependent individuals. *American Journal on Addictions* 4:297–305.

Group for the Advancement of Psychiatry, Committee on Alcoholism and the Addictions (1991). Substance abuse disorders: a psychiatric priority. *American Journal of Psychiatry* 148:1291–1300.

Halikas, J. A., Crosby, R. D., Pearson, V. L., et al. (1994). Psychiatric comorbidity in treatment-seeking cocaine abusers. *American Journal on Addictions* 3:25–35.

Herman, J. L. (1992). *Trauma and Recovery*. New York: Basic Books.

Hesselbrock, M. N., Meyer, R. E., and Keener, J. J. (1985). Psychopathology in hospitalized alcoholics. *Archives of General Psychiatry* 42:1050–1055.

Janowsky, D. S., and Davis, J. M. (1976). Methylphenidate, dextroamphetamine, and levamfetamine: effects on schizophrenic symptoms. *Archives of General Psychiatry* 33:304–308.

Kandel, D. B., and Davies, M. (1986). Adult sequelae of adolescent depressive symptoms. *Archives of General Psychiatry* 43:255–262.

Keane, T. M., Gerardi, P. J., and Lyons, J. A. (1988). The interrelationship of substance abuse and post traumatic stress disorder: epidemiological and clinical considerations. *Recent Developments in Alcoholism* 6:27–48.

Keeler, M. H., Taylor, C. I., and Miller, W. C. (1979). Are all recently detoxified alcoholics depressed? *American Journal of Psychiatry* 136:586–588.

Kellam, S. G., Brown, C. H., and Fleming, J. P. (1982). Developmental epidemiological studies of substance use in Woodlawn: implications for prevention research strategy. *NIDA Research Monograph* 41:21–33.

Kellam, S. G., Werthamer-Larsson, L., Dolan, L. J., et al. (1991). Developmental epidemiologically based preventive trials: baseline modeling of early target behaviors and depressive symptoms. *American Journal of Community Psychology* 19:563–584.

Kelly, M. E., Gilbertson, M., and Mouton, A. (1992). Deterioration in premorbid functioning in schizophrenia: a developmental model of negative symptoms in drug-free patients. *American Journal of Psychiatry* 149:1543–1548.

Khantzian, E. J. (1975). Self selection and progression in drug dependence. *Psychiatry Digest* 10:19–22.

——— (1978). The ego, the self and opiate addiction: theoretical and treatment considerations. *International Review of Psychoanalysis* 5:189–198.

——— (1981). Some treatment implications of the ego and self disturbances in alcoholism. In *Dynamic Approaches to the Understanding and Treatment of Alcoholism*, ed. M. H. Bean and N. E. Zinberg, pp. 163–188. New York: Free Press.

——— (1983). An extreme case of cocaine dependence and marked improvement with methylphenidate treatment. *American Journal of Psychiatry* 140(6):484–485.

———— (1985). The self-medication hypothesis of addictive disorders. *American Journal of Psychiatry* 142:1259–1264.

———— (1993). Affects and addictive suffering: a clinical perspective. In *Human Feelings: Explorations in Affect Development and Meaning*, ed. S. Ablon, D. Brown, E. J. Khantzian, and J. E. Mack, pp. 259–279. Hillsdale, NJ: Analytic Press.

———— (1995). Self-regulation vulnerabilities in substance abusers: treatment implications. In *The Psychology and Treatment of Addictive Behavior*, ed. S. Dowling, pp. 17–41. Madison, CT: International Universities Press.

Khantzian, E. J., Dalsimer, J. S., and Semrad, E. V. (1969). The use of interpretation in the psychotherapy of schizophrenia. *American Journal of Psychotherapy* 23:182–197.

Khantzian, E. J., Gawin, F., Kleber, H. D., and Riordan, C. E. (1984). Methylphenidate treatment of cocaine dependence—a preliminary report. *Journal of Substance Abuse Treatment* 1:107–112.

Khantzian, E. J., and Mack, J. E. (1983). Self-preservation and the care of the self: ego instincts reconsidered. *Psychoanalytic Study of the Child* 38:209–232. New Haven, CT: Yale University Press.

———— (1989). AA and contemporary psychodynamic theory. In *Recent Developments in Alcoholism*, vol. 7, ed. M. Galanter, pp. 67–89. New York: Plenum.

Khantzian, E. J., and Treece, C. (1985). *DSM-III* psychiatric diagnosis of narcotic addicts: recent findings. *Archives of General Psychiatry* 42:1067–1071.

Khantzian, E. J., and Wilson, A. (1993). Substance dependence, repetition and the nature of addictive suffering. In *Hierarchical Concepts in Psychoanalysis: Theory, Research, and Clinical Practice*, ed. A. Wilson and J. E. Gedo, pp. 263–283. New York: Guilford.

Kleber, H. D., and Gavin, F. H. (1985). Cocaine. *American Psychiatric Association Annual Review* 5:160–185.

Kleinman, P. H., Miller, A. B., Millman, R. B., et al. (1990). Psychopathology among cocaine abusers entering treatment. *Journal of Nervous and Mental Disease* 178:442–447.

Kosten, T. R., and Krystal, J. (1988). Biological mechanisms in post traumatic stress disorder: relevance for substance abuse. *Recent Developments in Alcoholism* 6:49–68.

Krystal, H. (1978). Self representation and the capacity for self care. *Annual of Psychoanalysis* 6:209–246.

———— (1982). Alexithymia and the effectiveness of psychoanalytic treatment. *International Journal of Psychoanalytic Psychotherapy* 9:353–378.

——— (1988). *Integration and Self-Healing: Affect, Trauma, Alexithymia.* Hillsdale, NJ: Analytic Press.

Krystal, H., and Raskin, H. A. (1970). *Drug Dependence: Aspects of Ego Functions.* Detroit: Wayne State University Press.

Lichtenberg, J. D. (1983). *Psychoanalysis and Infant Research.* Hillsdale, NJ: Analytic Press.

Martin, W., Hewett, B. B., Baker, A. J., and Haertzen, C. A. (1977). Aspects of the psychopathology and pathophysiology of addiction. *Drug Alcohol Dependence* 2:185–202.

McDougall, J. (1984). The "disaffected" patient: reflections on affect pathology. *Psychoanalytic Quarterly* 53:386–409.

McKenna, C., and Ross, C. (1994). Diagnostic conundrums in substance abusers with psychiatric symptoms: variables suggestive of dual diagnosis. *American Journal of Drug and Alcohol Abuse* 20:397–412.

McLellan, A. T., Parikh, G., and Bragg, A. (1990). *Addiction Severity Index Manual,* 5th ed. Philadelphia: University of Pennsylvania Center for the Study of Addiction.

Meissner, W. W. (1986). *Psychotherapy and the Paranoid Process.* New York: Jason Aronson.

Milin, R., Loh, E. A., and Wilson, A. (1992). Drug preference, reported drug experience, and stimulus sensitivity. *American Journal on Addictions* 1:248–256.

Milkman, H., and Frosch, W. A. (1973). On the preferential abuse of heroin and amphetamine. *Journal of Nervous and Mental Disease* 156:242–248.

Miller, M., and Gold, M. (1991). Dependence syndrome: a critical analysis of essential features. *Psychiatric Annals* 121:282–288.

Miller, N. S. (1994). The interaction between co-existing disorders. In *Treating Co-existing Psychiatric and Addictive Disorders: A Practical Guide,* ed. N. S. Miller, pp. 7–21. Center City, MN: Hazelden.

Moss, H. B., Mezzich, A., Yao, J. K., et al. (1995). Aggressivity among sons of substance-abusing fathers: association with psychiatric disorder in the father and on, paternal personality, pubertal development and socioeconomic status. *American Journal of Drug and Alcohol Abuse* 21:195–208.

Nace, E. P. (1988). Post traumatic stress disorder and substance abuse: clinical issues. *Recent Developments in Alcoholism* 6:9–26.

Nemiah, J. C. (1970). The psychological management and treatment of patients with peptic ulcer. *Advances in Psychosomatic Medicine* 6:169–173.

Noordsy, D. L., Drake, R. E., Teague, G. B., et al. (1991). Subjective experiences related to alcohol use among schizophrenics. *Journal of Nervous and Mental Disease* 179:410–414.

Penick, E. C., Powell, B. J., Nickel, E. J., et al. (1994). Co-morbidity of lifetime psychiatric disorder among male alcoholic patients. *Alcohol Clinical and Experimental Research* 18:1289–1293.

Penk, W. E., Peck, R. F., Robinowitz, R., (1988). Coping and defending styles among Vietnam combat veterans seeking treatment for posttraumatic stress disorder and substance use disorder. *Recent Developments in Alcoholism* 6:69–88.

Regier, D. A., Farmer, M. E., Rae, D. S., et al. (1990). Comorbidity of mental disorders with alcohol and other drug abuse: results from the Epidemiologic Catchment Area (ECA) study. *Journal of the American Medical Association* 264:2511–2518.

Richard, M. L., Liskow, B., and Perry, P. J. (1985). Recent psychostimulant use in hospitalized schizophrenics. *Journal of Clinical Psychiatry* 46:79–83.

Ross, H. E., Glaser, F. B., and Germanson, T. (1988). The prevalence of psychiatric disorders in patients with alcohol and other drug problems. *Archives of General Psychiatry* 45:1023–1031.

Rounsaville, B. J., Anton, S. F., Carroll, K., et al. (1991). Psychiatric diagnoses of treatment-seeking cocaine abusers. *Archives of General Psychiatry* 48:43–51.

Rounsaville, B. J., Weissman, M. M., Crits-Cristoph, K., et al. (1982a). Diagnosis and symptoms of depression in opiate addicts: course and relationship to treatment outcome. *Archives of General Psychiatry* 39:151–156.

Rounsaville, B. J., Weissman, M. M., Kleber, H., and Wilber, C. (1982b). Heterogeneity of psychiatric diagnosis in treated opiate addicts. *Archives of General Psychiatry* 39:161–166.

Sashin, J. I. (1986). *The relation between fantasy and the ability to feel affect.* Unpublished manuscript.

Schifano, F., Forza., G., Gallimberti, L. (1994). Smoking habits and psychological distress in adolescent female students. *American Journal on Addiction* 3:100–105.

Schiffer, F. (1988). Psychotherapy of nine successfully treated cocaine abusers: techniques and dynamics. *Journal of Substance Abuse Treatment* 5:133–137.

Schneier, F. R., and Siris, S. G. (1987). A review of psychoactive substance use and abuse in schizophrenia: patterns of drug choice. *Journal of Nervous and Mental Disease* 175:641–652.

Schuckit, M. A. (1986). Genetic and clinical implications of alcoholism and affective disorder. *American Journal of Psychiatry* 143:140–147.

Schuckit, M. A., and Hesselbrock, V. (1994). Alcohol dependence and anxiety disorders: What is the relationship? *American Journal of Psychiatry* 151:1723–1724.

Schuckit, M. A., Irwin, M., and Brown, S. A. (1990). The history of anxiety symptoms among 171 primary alcoholics. *Journal of Studies on Alcohol* 51:34–41.

Schuckit, M. A., and Smith, T. L. (1996). An 8-year follow-up of 450 sons of alcoholic and control subjects. *Archives of General Psychiatry* 53:202–210.

Serper, M. R., Albert, M., Richardson, N. A., et al. (1995). Clinical effects of recent cocaine use on patients with acute schizophrenia. *American Journal of Psychiatry* 152:1464–1469.

Shedler, J., and Block, J. (1990). Adolescent drug use and psychological health. *American Psychologist* 45:612–630.

Sifneos, P. E. (1967). Clinical observations on some patients suffering from a variety of psychosomatic diseases. In *Proceedings of the Seventh European Conference on Psychosomatic Research*. Basel: S. Karger.

Stampfer, H. G. (1990). Negative symptoms: a cumulative trauma stress disorder? *Australian New Zealand Journal of Psychiatry* 24:516–528.

Swett, C., and Halpert, M. (1994). High rates of alcohol problems and history of physical and sexual abuse among women inpatients. *American Journal of Drug and Alcohol Abuse* 20:263–272.

Vaillant, G. E. (1975). Sociopathy as a human process. *Archives of General Psychiatry* 32:178–183.

—— (1980). Natural history of male psychological health, VIII: antecedents of alcoholism and "orality." *American Journal of Psychiatry* 137:181–186.

—— (1983). *The Natural History of Alcoholism*. Cambridge, MA: Harvard University Press.

—— (1996). A long-term follow-up of male alcohol abuse. *Archives of General Psychiatry* 53:243–249.

Vaillant, G. E., and Milofsky, E. S. (1982). The etiology of alcoholism: a prospective viewpoint. *American Psychologist* 37:494–503.

van der Kolk, B. A. (1987). *Psychological Trauma*. Washington, DC: American Psychiatric Press.

Weiss, K. J., and Rosenberg, D. J. (1985). Prevalence of anxiety disorder among alcoholics. *Journal of Clinical Psychiatry* 46:3–5.

Weiss, R. D., Griffin, K. L., and Mirin, S. M. (1992a). Drug abuse as self medication for depression: an empirical study. *American Journal of Drug and Alcohol Abuse* 18:121–129.

Weiss, R. D., and Mirin, S. M. (1984). Drug, host and environmental factors in the development of chronic cocaine abuse. In *Substance Abuse and Psychotherapy*, ed. S. M. Mirin, pp. 42–55. Washington, DC: American Psychiatric Association Press.

Weiss, R. D., Mirin, S. M., and Griffin, M. L. (1992b). Methodological considerations in the diagnosis of coexisting psychiatric disorders in substance abusers. *British Journal of Addictions* 87:179–187.

Weiss, R. D., Mirin, S. M., Griffin, M. L., and Michaels, J. L. (1988). Psychopathology in cocaine abusers: changing trends. *Journal of Nervous and Mental Disease* 176(12):719–725.

Weiss, R. D., Pope, H. G. Jr., and Mirin, S. M. (1985). Treatment of chronic cocaine abuse and attention deficit disorder, residual type, with magnesium pemoline. *Drug Alcohol Dependence* 15:69–72.

Weissman, M. M., Slobetz, F., Prusoff, B., et al. (1976). Clinical depression among narcotic addicts maintained on methadone in the community. *American Journal of Psychiatry* 133:1434–1438.

Wells, K. B., Stewart, A. L., Hays, R. D., et al. (1989). The functioning and well-being of depressed patients: results from the medical outcomes study. *Journal of the American Medical Association* 262:914–919.

Wieder, H., and Kaplan, E. (1969). Drug use in adolescents. *Psychoanalytic Study of the Child* 24:399–431. New York: International Universities Press.

Wilens, T. E., Biederman, J., Spencer, T. J., Frances, R. J. (1994). Comorbidity of attention deficit hyperactivity and psychoactive substance use disorders. *Hospital and Community Psychiatry* 45:421–435.

Wilson, A., Passik, S. D., Faude, J., et al. (1989). A hierarchical model of opiate addiction: failures of self-regulation as a central aspect of substance abuse. *Journal of Nervous and Mental Disease* 177:390–399.

Windle, M., Windle, R. C., Scheidt, D. M., and Miller, G. B. (1995). Physical and sexual abuse and associated mental disorders among alcoholic inpatients. *American Journal of Psychiatry* 152:1322–1328.

Woody, G. E., Luborsky, L., McLellan, A. T., et al. (1983). Psychotherapy for opiate addicts: Does it help? *Archives of General Psychiatry* 40:639–645.

Wurmser, L. (1974). Psychoanalytic considerations of the etiology of compulsive drug use. *Journal of the American Psychoanalytic Association* 22:820–843.

Zucker, R. A., and Gomberg, E. S. L. (1986). Etiology of alcoholism reconsidered: the case for a biopsychosocial process. *American Psychologist* 41:783–793.

# PART IV

# Understanding Addictive Vulnerability— Psychodynamics

## INTRODUCTION

In this section the chapters are varied in scope and focus, and cover a wide range of issues on the dynamics of addictive vulnerability. The scope is as narrow as explaining how and why the pharmacological action of methadone for opiate addicts work, as wide as explaining how and why the psychosocial and spiritual influences of twelve-step programs work for alcoholics and others. I also delve into the dynamics of why clinicians and investigators of different persuasions cannot reach consensus on such basic issues as definition, understanding, and conceptualizations of addictive disorders, including issues such as whether the use of addictive substances is the cause or the consequence of psychological and psychiatric suffering.

Throughout this book (and in my career), I have persistently made an appeal to consider the centrality of human psychological vulnerabilities as being very important determinants of addictive behavior. Although I cover more broad areas involving substance use disorders in this section, I also return to and expand on basic clinical aspects of these disorders. In Chapter 17, I review some of the literature on the psychology and psychodynamics of drug addiction; in Chapter 19, in collaboration with John Mack, I elaborate on and explain the nature of self-care vulnerabilities. Applied to addictive vulnerabilities, I believe that beyond self-medication motives, developmental impairments or deficits in self-care function (especially when combined with affect deficits) are one of the most compelling reasons why certain vulnerable individuals are susceptible to becoming involved with and dependent on addictive substances.

Chapter 16 was my first presentation and publication on the addictions. It was written at a time when I was completing my psychoanalytic training, and, as previously indicated, I was under the sway of the ascendant psychoanalytic concepts and argot of that time and, as much, the interests of my training analyst Sidney Levin. A teacher and proponent of instinct theory, he was a man whose zeal for his ideas and concepts was exceeded only by his kindness, and his equal appreciation of the central importance of painful affects, both in practice and in his interactions with others. These two influences (i.e., my psychoanalytic training and my training analyst) are apparent in this chapter on the dynamics of how methadone works. With the hindsight of almost thirty years, my use of psychoanalytic jargon (e.g., "fusion [or, defusion]—of aggressive and sexual instincts," or "instinctual—regression") now seems embarrassingly awkward. Nevertheless, the central point addressed in this chapter, namely, that intense rage and violent feelings were key reasons why opiates could be so compelling, still holds up, as does the idea that the sustained long-acting action of methadone effectively contains such intense affect.

Chapter 17 is interesting and significant in a number or respects. It was a chapter in the proceedings (Pickens and Heston 1979) of a conference on psychiatric factors in drug abuse, convened by the Psychiatric Research Unit at the University of Minnesota in Minneapolis. This chapter, co-authored with Catherine Treece (Khantzian and Treece 1979), was an early attempt to address the cause–consequence controversy issues regarding psychiatric comorbidity associated with substance use disorders (SUDs). Namely, does psychopathology cause SUDs or, is it the other way around (I have elaborated in more detail on this debate in Chapters 15 and 21 on the self-medication hypothesis (SMH). Chapter 17 also included an early articulation of the SMH. Nevertheless, the main objective of this chapter was to explore the diagnostic complexities in assessing and understanding the relationship between psychopathology and heroin addiction. We considered a number of addiction diagnostic models in this respect. Finally, this chapter was the outgrowth of a series of technical review conferences sponsored by the National Institute on Drug Abuse (NIDA) that were first convened in the mid-1970s.

The NIDA technical review conferences supported collaboration with the University of Pennsylvania and Yale–New Haven Medical Centers, and others, and stimulated a series of studies and reports from our Cambridge projects to study and diagnose psychopathology associated with heroin dependence (Khantzian 1978, Khantzian and Treece 1977, 1985, Nicholson and Treece 1981, Treece and Nicholson 1980). Dr. Treece completed her doctorate (Treece 1977) during this period. We were both the beneficiaries of our shared, keen interest in understanding the nature of the human psychological suffering entailed in SUDs, and, in particular, heroin dependence. I felt I was especially fortunate to have a person of Dr. Treece's caliber as a collaborator. Her enthusiasm and clear-mindedness and her ability to articulate her thinking was an especially important source of support and assistance. She was a great impetus in bringing our respective and shared insights to fruition especially in the late 1970s and in the 1980s.

Both Chapters 17 and 2 represent the first definitive articulation of my understanding of drug dependence based on psychoanalytic theory. What is probably most important about our publications and that of our collaborators during this period is that the technical review conferences from which they derive spawned clinical-investigative studies on SUDs and their treatment at major academic and treatment centers at Yale–New Haven Medical Center, University of Pennsylvania–VA Medical Center, and Harvard Medical School at The Cambridge Hospital and McLean Hospital that would continue through the 1980s and 1990s. This includes the pioneering studies of the University of Pennsylvania–VA Medical Center on the efficacy of psychotherapy with methadone patients, diagnostic and outcome studies with psychosocial and psychopharmacological treatments at the Yale–New Haven Medical Center and at McLean Hospital, and our own diagnostic studies and group therapy program for cocaine addicts (the Harvard Cocaine Recovery Project) at the Cambridge Hospital. For those who are cynical about federal efforts to address psychosocial problems, the above initiatives by the National Institute of Drug Addiction, starting in the 1970s and continuing up to the present, were a refreshing and encouraging development. It allowed many of us in the field with a psychosocial bent to pursue clinical-investigative projects in the addictions and to make contributions that had important underpinnings in psychodynamic psychiatry.

Chapter 18 grew out of an invitation to discuss a paper by Dr. David Myerson on dependency and denial problems in aging alcoholics. Dr. Myerson was a singularly dedicated psychiatrist who, uncharacteristically for that time, was devoted to treating alcoholic patients in one of the few outpatient alcoholic clinics at the (then) Peter Bent Brigham Hospital. Discussing his paper was an opportunity for me to apply what I was learning about affect and self-care deficits as a vehicle to counter stereotyped and pejorative attitudes about alcoholics' problems with dependency and denial. In a subsequent publication (Khantzian 1982), not included here, I attempted to link empirical psychiatric studies and psychological profiles to my evolving psychodynamic understanding of alcoholism. I argue elsewhere in this book (especially in Chapter 15) that recent empirical studies both support and fail to support findings derived from a psychodynamic perspective. Nevertheless, in looking back to the 1980s it remains striking to me how much the empirical reports documented behavioral and emotional dysregulation and significant family turmoil in the backgrounds of individuals who later became alcoholic. Although many would now link these findings to temperament, neurobehavioral abnormalities, and cognitive dysfunction as a result of genetic loading, it is at least as striking how these disturbances so closely resemble findings from longitudinal studies (Brook et al. 1992, Kellam et al. 1982, 1991, Moss et al. 1995, Shedler and Block 1990) that document the extraordinary emotional and behavioral disruption in the families of individuals who develop SUD, strongly suggesting environmental factors as important determinants of the emotional pain and behavioral problems that predispose individuals psychodynamically to SUDs. Clearly, hereditary, temperament, and neurocognitive factors play a role in the etiology of alcoholism, and I realize that in the chapters in this section I run the risk of seeming contentious or polemical in arguing for environmental influences and psychological vulnerabilities in alcoholism and the addictions. I run this risk now, as I did then, primarily because we either continually underplay or insufficiently consider psychodynamic factors, a dimension of these problems that speaks to the human, psychological substrate of these disorders. Such a perspective allows patients, families, and clinicians to have a more balanced understanding and dialogue about what it is in the person, or in our human nature, that leaves us susceptible to the ravages of addictive disorders.

As already indicated, Chapter 19 (written with John Mack) explores in more detail what I consider to be one of the core factors involved in the predisposition to substance use disorders, namely, self-care deficiencies. As explained, "self" is used here as it pertains to the whole person and primarily concerns "structures and functions that serve the survival of the self or person as a total organism." This chapter, in an earlier version, applied these concepts to how such structures or functions are deficient or inoperative in substance abusers, but the editor encouraged us to limit its scope. She suggested that we focus more precisely on the theoretical and developmental aspects of self-care functions and how they apply more generally to the human challenge of survival and self-preservation. As we indicate in this chapter, the concept of self-care and its deficiencies stands counterposed to earlier formulations by Freud (1933), Menninger (1938), Tabachnik (1976), and others, who invoked instinctual factors, especially aggressive instincts turned on the self. Through an exploration of the literature on self-preservation (what little there was on the subject at that time, and even up to the present), theoretical explorations, and case examples, we spell out in Chapter 19 what I believe was (and still is) one of the more definitive explanations of what it is in our psychological makeup that ensures (or fails to ensure) our survival and the care for ourselves. As I repeatedly emphasize throughout this book, concerns about self-care (for the patient as well as the clinician) are vitally important in understanding and treating SUDs.

Chapters 20 and 21 were published within one year of each other (1986 and 1987). Although they touch on some common themes, they were presentations for two very different groups; Chapter 20 was prepared for an interdisciplinary/multispecialty group, and Chapter

21 was intended for a more exclusive psychoanalytic audience. In Chapter 20 I examine why we cannot reach consensus on conceptualizations of alcoholism; in Chapter 21 I more narrowly focus on the issue of whether alcoholism causes or is the result of psychological and psychiatric suffering. These two chapters were opportunities to address some of the issues that produced (and to a considerable extent continue to do so, the themes varying only slightly) so much of the conflict and controversy that bedevils our work and collegial relations. These chapters were written at a time when psychiatry was still not well established as having a specialty status in the understanding and treatment of alcoholism; we also had not yet adequately recognized the strong association between major mental illness and substance use disorders. Thus I stated, "Problems with major psychoses and affective disorders rarely involved . . . [alcoholism]," which we now know is incorrect.

In these two chapters I broach the issue of how we all adopt perspectives (and methods of study guided by our perspectives) to the exclusion of considering other perspectives. I even dare to speculate about some of the reasons for this tendency. I consider that each perspective yields data that are of value, but we too often fail to integrate the findings derived from the different perspectives. Instead we separate into opposing camps, bang drums about our viewpoints, and fail to hear above the clamor what we can learn from each other. Thus we are polarized about substance use disorder: Is it a disease or symptom? Is it in our genes or our environment? Or is suffering the cause or consequence of substance dependence?

Chapters 22 and 23 are similar to each other, namely, psychiatric and psychodynamic factors involved in cocaine dependence. They were published within three years of each other during the mid-1980s. This was a period when reports were first appearing in the literature on the so-called cocaine epidemic of the 1980s. The intense interest in cocaine grew out of a pressing concern with the devastating costs and consequences (psychiatrically, medically, and economically) of the emergence and widespread use of cocaine during this period. Much of the material in these two chapters recapitulates material explored in previous chapters, but they also provide a sense of what was being discovered or rediscovered about cocaine dependence that was similar to (or different from) what investigators had learned over the previous three decades about alcohol (and other depressants) and opiate dependence. As I point out in Chapter 22, there was little at that time in the literature or in our clinical experience to guide a practitioner in treating cocaine addicts. Most of what was known stressed the euphorogenic properties of cocaine to explain its appeal. Not surprisingly we (I and my daughter Nancy) raise the likelihood that cocaine for the chronic user has its appeal less because of its euphoria-producing properties than because the stimulating properties of cocaine relieve states of fatigue, depletion, low self-esteem, and boredom associated with depression. We also focus on the use of cocaine as an augmenter for expansive, self-sufficient types, and, paradoxically, its use and preference by individuals with attention deficit hyperactivity disorder (ADHD), who discover its calming and focusing effect. In this latter respect, I make reference in the two chapters to "curing" with Ritalin two extreme cases (Khantzian 1983, Khantzian et al. 1984) of cocaine addiction with co-occurring ADHD, a treatment that at that time was considered very controversial and risky, but less so now. Not without significance, I revisit in Chapters 22 and 23 the cause-consequence controversy with regard to the relationship between cocaine dependence and psychopathology; I also raise and invoke self-care deficits as important determinants in experimenting with, using, and becoming dependent on stimulants.

Alcoholics Anonymous is an extraordinary therapeutic tool and transforming influence in the lives of individuals who suffer with alcoholism and other drug dependencies. In Chapters 24 and 25 I extensively elaborate on these benefits. I wasn't always so persuaded. Early in my career I was put off by the attitudes of territorial and parochial smugness of certain individuals about how alcoholism was a disease and its main, if not only, antidote was reliance on AA to establish and maintain abstinence. Many of these advocates were not in recovery themselves but were working with alcoholics in recovery or studying them. I often had difficulty figuring out how serious or unyielding they were in adopting their views, which bordered on intellectual rigidity if not frank sanctimony. I could not tell if their zeal reflected genuine enthusiasm for a process they were witnessing to be working for others, or whether they were heuristically adopting this paradigm because no others seemed to offer adequate explanations or help for such a deadly, consuming process. Two influences helped me to evolve a more positive appreciation and ultimately an enthusiastic support for its beneficial influences. The first change occurred as a result of a small group of Boston/Cambridge psychiatrists, including myself, forming a group in the early 1970s to discuss some of the dogmas and issues pertaining to alcoholism and other addictions. Fortunately, most of the participants, despite their strong and different persuasions, were not as unyielding as some of their more rigid counterparts whom I first encountered. Most beneficially, the meetings allowed meaningful discussions and exchange of ideas about our points of view. Was alcoholism a disease? Could alcoholics achieve controlled drinking? Was alcoholism a symptom—and if so, a symptom of what? Was there such a thing as controlled heroin use (i.e., "chippers")? This informal group ultimately became established as the Massachusetts Psychiatric Society Committee on Alcoholism and Addictions, which continues up to the present time, a committee that I was privileged to chair for nearly a decade in the 1980s. Although the meetings have evolved to include formal presentations, the core format for interchange of ideas, data, and perspectives has helped us to stay open to appreciating different perspectives for understanding and treating SUDs.

The other main influence to change my mind on the importance and utility of employing AA in my clinical work was the extraordinary strength of character, admirable qualities, and insight (about requirements for abstinence and sobriety) I was witnessing in patients coming into my practice who had benefited from AA. Although I was satisfied with the outcome of my conventional clinical approach with my patients, I began to recommend to most of my patients that they also consider AA as part of their therapy, especially early in their course of recovery. Over time I began to appreciate how my evolving theoretical perspective for understanding addictive vulnerability was entirely consistent with the group approaches of AA. I think this is most evident in Chapter 25. I soon began to appreciate that AA worked not only because it helped individuals acquire tools for establishing and maintaining abstinence, but also because it was an extraordinarily sophisticated group psychology that met the needs of individuals in recovery. Over the past two decades I wrote four papers on AA. I believe the two chapters in this section, one a more in-depth theoretical exploration (in collaboration with John Mack), the other a case study, best expressed my understanding of the importance of AA and how and why it works. Chapter 25 was inspired by an invitation to be the 1994 Distinguished Lecturer in Substance Abuse at North Shore University Hospital, Cornell Medical Center, an honor previously bestowed on Drs. Thomas McLellan (in 1991), Anne Geller (1992), and Mitchell Rosenthal (1993). It was truly an honor to be in such company, and it was a special opportunity to speak somewhat passionately and evocatively about the human bases of addictive vulnerability and about how the group psychology of twelve-step programs accesses, modifies, and transforms such vulnerability. The chapter was published in 1995 in a specialty journal, the *Journal of Substance Abuse Treatment* (Khantzian 1995). In publishing it here in my collected works it is my hope that what I conveyed in this lecture will reach a wider audience because I feel it is one of my best and most humanistic statements about addictive vulnerability and recovery.

Chapter 26 is new, written specifically for this book. As it is abundantly clear in this book, from my perspective, human psychological woundedness and injury to the sense of self and our psychic organization (structures) are at the heart of addictive illness. In these collected works I repeatedly refer to "traumatic abuse—or neglect," going back to my earliest publications. In its more extreme forms we now better appreciate that certain individuals have developed posttraumatic stress disorder (PTSD) as a consequence of these experiences. Over the past three to four decades we have become much more aware of how pervasive PTSD has been in society, and more recently how there is a disproportionate co-occurrence of SUDs associated with it. Although I refer to extreme trauma in many of the chapters in this volume, only in Chapter 15 on the SMH, where I update it and apply it to areas not previously considered, had I in any systematic way tried to explain the relationship between SUDs and PTSD. Chapter 26 expands on Chapter 15. It explores how and why the pervasive and enduring pain, distress, and behavioral disruption associated with PTSD places such individuals at greater risk for developing SUDs. Albeit in the extreme, I describe how PTSD survivors self-medicate their overwhelming pain and chaos with substance to relieve or control their suffering and troubled behaviors. The lot of trauma victims with their all too often involvement with substances provides further poignant if not tragic testimony to the utility and validity of the SMH, a core feature of what this volume is about.

# REFERENCES

Brook, J. S., Whiteman, M., Cohen, P., and Tanaka, J. S. (1992). Childhood precursors of adolescent drug use: a longitudinal analysis. *Genetics, Society and General Psychology Monograph* 118:195–213.

Freud, S. (1933). New introductory lectures on psychoanalysis. *Standard Edition* 22:5–182.

Kellam, S. G., Brown, C. H., and Fleming, J. P. (1982). Developmental epidemiological studies of substance use in Woodlawn: implications for prevention research strategy. *NIDA Research Monograph* 41:21–33.

Kellam, S. G., Werthamer-Larsson, L., Dolan, L. J., et al. (1991). Developmental epidemiologically based preventive trials: baseline modeling of early target behaviors and depressive symptoms. *American Journal of Community Psychology* 19:563–584.

Khantzian, E. J. (1978). The ego, the self and opiate addiction: theoretical and treatment considerations. *International Review of Psychoanalysis* 5:189–198.

—— (1982). Psychopathology, psychodynamics and alcoholism. In *The American Encyclopedic Handbook of Alcoholism*, ed. E. M. Pattison and E. Kaufman, pp. 581–597. New York: Gardner.

—— (1983). An extreme case of cocaine dependence and marked improvement with methylphenidate treatment. *American Journal of Psychiatry* 140:784–785.

—— (1995). Alcoholics Anonymous—cult or corrective: a case study. *Journal of Substance Abuse Treatment* 12:157–165.

Khantzian, E. J., Gawin, F., Kleber, H. D., and Riordan, C. E. (1984). Methylphenidate treatment of cocaine dependence—a preliminary report. *Journal of Substance Abuse Treatment* 1:107–112.

Khantzian, E. J., and Treece, C. (1977). Psychodynamics of drug dependence: an overview. In *Psychodynamics of Drug Dependence*, ed. J. D. Blaine and D. A. Julius, pp. 11–25. NIDA research monograph 12. Rockville, MD: National Institute on Drug Abuse.

—— (1979). Heroin addiction—the diagnostic dilemma for psychiatry. In *Psychiatric Factors in Drug Abuse*, ed. R. W. Pickens and L. L. Heston, pp. 21–45. New York: Grune & Stratton.

—— (1985). DSM-III psychiatric diagnosis of narcotic addicts: recent findings. *Archives of General Psychiatry* 42:1067–1071.

Menninger, K. A. (1938). *Man Against Himself*. New York: Harcourt, Brace.

Moss, H. B., Mezzich, A., Yao, J. K., et al. (1995). Aggressivity among sons of substance-abusing fathers: association with psychiatric disorder in the father and on, paternal personality, pubertal development and socioeconomic status. *American Journal of Drug and Alcohol Abuse* 21:195–208.

Nicholson, B., and Treece, C. (1981). Object relations and differential treatment response to methadone maintenance. *Journal of Nervous and Mental Diseases* 169:424–429.

Pickens, R. W., and Heston, L. L. (1979). *Psychiatric Factors in Drug Abuse.* New York: Grune & Stratton.

Shedler, J., and Block, J. (1990). Adolescent drug use and psychological health. *American Psychologist* 45:612–630.

Tabachnick, N. (1976). Death trend and adaptation. *Journal of the American Academy of Psychoanalysis* 41:49–62.

Treece, C. J. (1977). *Narcotic use in relation to selected ego functions among incarcerated women.* Doctoral dissertation, Boston University. *Dissertation Abstracts International.*

Treece, C. J., and Nicholson, B. (1980). *DSM-III* personality type and dose levels in methadone maintenance patients. *Journal of Nervous and Mental Diseases* 168:621–628.

# 16

# A Preliminary Dynamic Formulation of the Psychopharmacological Action of Methadone

Narcotics addiction is related to states of biological and psychological disequilibrium. An adequate theory of narcotics addition in humans must account for the problems of homeostasis in not only the biological system but also the psychological system as well.

It has been proposed that methadone maintenance works because it restores homeostasis in the biological system by correcting a problem of metabolic imbalance. For the purposes of this discussion it is proposed that methadone maintenance works by also restoring homeostasis in the psychological system. In the latter case the problem is one of imbalance between instinctual and structural factors in the emotional economy of an individual. The clinical improvements witnessed in addicted individuals when they are treated with methadone maintenance can be accounted for better when the influence and interaction of methadone is considered on both the biological and psychological systems.

In this presentation, the problems of imbalance in the emotional and psychological economy of addicted individual will be stressed in accounting for the action and efficacy of methadone maintenance. Our aim is to formulate more specifically how the psychopharmacological action of methadone (maintenance) plays a direct role in restoring improved psychological and behavioral functioning in addicted patients. It should be emphasized that what is advanced in this discussion is by no means considered to be well-developed theory based on systematic collection and analysis of clinical data. Rather, our formulation should be considered more in the nature of an hypothesis based on preliminary clinical observations of patients in our drug treatment program at the Cambridge Hospital.

## REPORT OF CASES

The case material has been selected to highlight some of the particular kinds of emotional difficulties patients have in dealing with their feelings, especially those of aggression and rage. The cases are not necessarily examples to support our thesis for the efficacy of methadone, but for the sake of brevity and because most of us working with methadone maintenance have repeatedly observed its improving the quality of an addicted patient's life, additional case material has not been included. All three individuals are white and from intact middle-class families. In comparison to many patients being treated in large urban communities for opiate addiction, they are perhaps atypical, but they are by no means the exception in our own program.

### Case 1

Jim, a 29-year-old white single unemployed male musician from a lower middle-class background, was one of twelve children (he had seven brothers and four sisters). Father was described as a stringent disciplinarian who regularly beat Jim when he would violate curfew times set down by father. The beatings continued up until the time when the patient was 18 years of age, when he sustained a lacerated lip in one of these beatings and in a rage he viciously turned on and beat his father, resulting in father's incapacitation in bed for three days. Mother was described as a passive compliant woman who catered to the needs of father and the children.

Jim began to use heroin around the age of 25, at first snorting but within a short time shooting the drug. Although there was a previous drug history, he was using heroin almost exclusively at the time of evaluation. Around the same time he started using heroin regularly, he began to participate in activist and revolutionary groups on the East and West Coasts. He claimed that he engaged in the making of bombs and in the planning of violent protests.

He was an attractive, bright, and verbal person who in treatment was observed to alternate between profound feelings of hopelessness and expressions of vitriolic hatred and rage in relation to society and its institutions. He frequently referred to the "shit, oppression, and pain" in society that caused him either to want to shoot people down or to shoot heroin in his veins. This patient was most resistant to the idea of methadone maintenance despite some brief stabilization on methadone during several unsuccessful attempts at detoxification.

## Case 2[1]

Joe, a 23-year-old white married father of one child, was adopted at the age of 5 or 6 months, learning of his adoption only a year prior to evaluation. Both parents were retired, father having worked as an engineer and mother as a teacher. The patient felt he got along much better with his father who was lenient. Mother was described as a very cold and distant person who was inconsistent and indulgent and would occasionally inflict beatings and punishment on him, which he felt were never justified and which he would actively resist.

Although bright, his schoolwork and behavior began to deteriorate in the fourth grade following scarlet fever and pneumonia. In

---

1. The author is indebted to Rick Bickford, Assistant Director, the Cambridge Hospital Drug Treatment Program, for his assistance in evaluating and reporting this case.

the 10th grade he was suspended from school because of a number of "minor incidents." After leaving school in the middle of the eleventh grade, he was arrested for breaking and entering, but charges were dropped when he went into the Navy. Over the next two years he did well, but then a number of incidents, including a car theft while on leave, resulted in an administrative discharge from the military.

The patient began using narcotics on a regular basis intravenously about two years prior to being seen in our clinic after being released from the state hospital following a serious suicide attempt. About a year later he was readmitted to another psychiatric hospital in a confused and apparently psychotic state, reporting that at the time he had cut his coat to shreds with a razor and around that same time strangled two puppies to death that he had purchased in a pet shop. Up to the time of evaluation at our hospital, Joe was averaging four to five bags of heroin a day.

In addition to the already-mentioned sadistic behavior, in his evaluation the patient expressed concern about controlling his impulses. He said he was torturing his father's dog, which he was caring for while his parents were vacationing. He also reported recently burning his wife and then himself with a cigarette after an argument with her and admitted to being genuinely afraid of harming his wife or child.

### Case 3

Tony, a 23-year-old single white Vietnam veteran, was the younger of two children. His sister was 28. He described himself as always being aggressive and difficult growing up. Though his mother was usually the disciplinarian, both parents admitted having difficulty managing him from early childhood. The parents felt that the patient changed dramatically after being in Vietnam, acting more aggressively and moody than he ever had before.

Tony began experimenting heavily with marijuana, amphetamines, and barbiturates in his mid-teens, this being preceded by a history of moderate alcohol consumption in his early teens. Although he experimented with narcotics after first joining the military at age 17, he did not start using heroin regularly until he was wounded in Vietnam. Subsequent to that time and up until the present time, he has used heroin regularly in amounts often exceeding twenty bags per day.

Although Tony indicated great guilt and conflict on a number of occasions regarding his violent and aggressive behavior in the military, he was repeatedly considered to be one of the most aggressive and intimidating patients in our program. Once stabilized on methadone, he was generally more subdued and cooperative, but, nevertheless, in group meetings he gave many verbal indications of his past (and to some extent recent) sadistic and aggressive inclinations. For example, he maintained he began to enjoy killing while in Vietnam, and in another context once described how he enjoyed the grotesque expressions on the faces of people who had been maimed in accidents. He was ultimately suspended from the program for an episode of fighting with a patient in a group meeting and brandishing a 22-caliber rifle in the parking lot of the hospital.

## Discussion

Of the three cases, only Tony was on methadone maintenance. During the brief time that he was stabilized prior to suspension, he was observed to be in better control of his anger. Jim was also noted to be in better control of his angry outbursts when he was briefly stabilized on methadone prior to detoxification at his own insistence. Joe was seen only for evaluation prior to the establishment of our drug treatment program. All three patients were considered to have varying periods of profound depression. What was most striking in all three cases was their intense expressions of rage and aggression. Although in two of the cases violent and aggressive behavior was reported in group activities where the behavior was supported and sanctioned, namely, in Vietnam combat and in militant revolutionary activities, it was felt that in both these cases the aggression expressed was more congruent with preexisting problems of impulsivity, difficulties with control of aggression, and antisocial behavior. Certainly in the case of Joe the problems with aggressive feelings was apparent in his sadistic behavior toward animals and similar feelings toward his wife and child. It is worth noting that in the background of Jim and Joe there was a significant history of receiving physical beatings by their parents. All three patients had definite sadomasochistic elements in their relationships with women. All had erratic work histories and two of the patients (Jim and Tony) showed very poor planning ability and unrealistic attitudes about their future living situation and job prospects.

## FORMULATION OF THE PROBLEM

Before trying to formulate how a drug such as methadone helps in restoring function in an addicted individual, we should first briefly review from an analytic-dynamic point of view what constitutes the normal psychological state of affairs in an individual's adaptation to his environment. To understand this properly, we need to appreciate in particular the relationship between instincts and ego. An analogy to a motor vehicle in which a complicated relationship exists between a structural system and an energy system might be helpful to explain the relationship between ego and instincts. Both the human system and a mechanical system are subject to breakdown in functioning. This can be the result of faulty structure that occurred in the course of development or resulted from stress and damage in the course of normal operation.

Keeping in mind our analogy to the motor vehicle where ideally the combustion and electrical energy systems are interdependent and in synchrony, then in the human system the aggressive and sexual instincts may be viewed similarly as the dual source of energy. In addition to pressing for discharge and satisfaction, this same energy is also harnessed in the process of growth and development for civilized living. The ego is the psychological agency that harnesses, mediates, modifies, and contains the instincts and makes appropriate accommodations for the instincts in relation to the external world and its requirements. When the developmental process is optimal, the aggressive and sexual instincts become fused and interact with the ego in such a way that the individual's activity is constructive and adaptive and his relationships with people are generally satisfactory and satisfying.

A concise way of describing the relationship between the ego and instincts may be stated as follows: The aggressive and sexual instincts are fused and are primarily under the control and influence of the ego. The ego exerts its control and influence through certain ego functions and capacities. This psychological system is subject to breakdown in function either as a result of developmental failure or as the result of trauma and stress after adequate development has taken place. The former situation involves the concepts of impairment and arrest in instinctual and ego development. The latter involves the concept of regression. Whether the situation is one of regression or one of developmental failure, the impairments that result share in common a deterioration in the functions and capacities of the ego on the one hand, and a state of defusion between sexual and aggressive instincts on the other hand.

All psychopathological conditions involve varying degrees of alterations in the ego and defusion of instincts. What is of danger in more serious clinical decompensations is that in the process of defusion the aggression becomes unmodified or uninfluenced by the sexual instincts and further threatens the already compromised ego functions and capacities. It can be seen that a vicious cycle of regression is set in motion. The symptoms of various clinical conditions reflect this regression and are indicators of underlying distress and pain, but the symptoms also represent attempts in the individual to relieve the distress and pain by reversing or arresting the regressive process. It is proposed in this discussion that problems of narcotics addiction are intimately related to processes of defusion of instinct and deterioration in ego function.

Early psychodynamic formulations of addiction (as well as of many other clinical psychiatric problems) unduly stressed the role of anxiety in relation to sexual conflicts as a major determining factor in psychological dysfunction. It is on this basis that the euphoria and pleasure-seeking aspects of addiction continue to be stressed by analytically oriented psychiatrists and others. This kind of thinking explains a recent attempt (and not an uncommon one) by a psychiatrist to account for an individual's vulnerability to addiction by stating that "the drug changes pain into pleasure," and induces "the blissful state of childhood when the mother attempted to keep her infant's frustration minimal by anticipating and gratifying his every wish." Aside from the fact that I have never heard a patient describe this experience, the problem with this view of drug dependency is that it too narrowly focuses on the pleasure-seeking side of an individual's psychology and not enough on problems in development and adaptation, and ego psychological factors and their relationship to instincts, and in particular, to aggressive instincts.

In the three patients described in this chapter, it is difficult to find evidence that their dependence on narcotics is primarily related to attempts to self-induce regressive pleasure as suggested in the "blissful state of childhood" notion. What our preliminary findings suggest is that turning to narcotic drugs actually represents desperate attempts to reverse painful regressed states. That is, addiction tends to occur in states of defusion where aggressive feelings predominate and take the form of severe depression, or the aggression dangerously threatens the individual and others as ego controls fail. These factors of aggression and depression are certainly evident in the patients presented. To date we have been impressed with our patients' accounts of how their short-term behavior often improves when they shoot up heroin. They describe how the drug attenuates internal dysphoric states, particularly states involving anger and depression, and temporarily improves their functioning in situations in which they would not ordinarily be able to cope.

The main problem with prolonged use of most opiates is that the associated continual apprehension and experience of withdrawal acts as a major stress on an ego that is usually already compromised in its function. As ego functions fail because of the stress of physical dependence and withdrawal, a new source of stress develops, namely, a failure in adequate modulation and control of the instincts, particularly aggressive instincts. Unmodified or unchecked aggression does not sit well in any individual because it threatens others and the self. This state is painful, and, like the physical distress of withdrawal, is temporarily relieved by narcotics. Thus a complicated vicious cycle is established where the stress of physical withdrawal is compounded by an associated stress due to psychological disorganization. Both are briefly relieved by the same agents (e.g., heroin) responsible for inducing the stress in the first place.

Methadone (maintenance) is effective in controlling addiction where other narcotics fail because it is a slowly metabolized drug, and taken orally it is long acting. Because of its longer action, it not only relieves pain and distress, it also allows for and directly enhances a reversal of regressive states. Its sustained activity prevents frustration and thereby lessens a regressive reaction. At the same time, like other narcotics, methadone has an action that attenuates rage and aggression. This presumably occurs by the narcotic acting in an inhibitory way on those neurochemical pathways and systems that mediate aggression in the central nervous system.

More specifically, what is proposed in this formulation is that methadone maintenance is effective not only by compensating for what is believed to be a metabolic defect induced by narcotics, but also by its stabilizing, antiaggression action in the central nervous system. By its stabilizing action it counteracts the disorganizing influences of aggression on the ego and thereby reverses regressed states and makes healthier adaptations possible. In the 24- to 48-hour interval free of the apprehension and dread of withdrawal provided by methadone, not only are the usual stresses of frequent withdrawal removed, but in this corresponding time an opportunity is created to provide ego supports and interventions that begin to act as further buffers against stress and regression. From an ego-psychological point of view it cannot be overestimated how critical and immensely supportive it is when caregivers begin to be available on a constant and predictable basis in the form of a nurse giving out methadone, or an interested person helping out with vital issues of self-esteem, namely, work, future career, and family.

## COMMENTS AND CONCLUSIONS

The use of methadone maintenance has provided a new and exciting chance to study the psychological problems involved in addiction. With a better appreciation of adaptational and ego-psychological factors, we are in a position to further our psychodynamic appreciation and understanding of addiction. Methadone is one more instance where a breakthrough in the biological sciences can lead to increasing understanding in the behavioral sciences, which in turn could lead to a richer and more meaningful understanding of a human problem. One example might suffice to support this point. To the author's knowledge there is as yet no adequate explanation for why tolerance to methadone as used in maintenance does not, or is much less likely to, develop. One possible explanation might be that part of the problem of physical tolerance to narcotics in general is related to enzyme induction (and/or some other physiological inactivation system), and that part of the problem is due to instability in the ego. The use of short-acting narcotic drugs introduces a stress of its own on the ego related to the dread of withdrawal, which requires more and more drug to obtain relief. With methadone this need for more drugs becomes less likely, because the addict soon learns that he is free of the symptoms of withdrawal for at least 24 hours, and, with assurances that his next dose is secure, his ego is less stressed and he is able to take advantage of further ego props and supports in the form of involvement with work and family, which leads to a further sense of well-being.

Because so often social factors and problems are invoked whenever the problem of addiction is discussed, one might properly ask what possible relationship might there be between the three addicts from middle-class backgrounds described in this chapter and the addicts who come from a lower socioeconomic background. Furthermore, is there any relevance in the formulation presented here for the person living in a slum or ghetto who seems to be so vulnerable to narcotic addiction? The answer to both questions is in the affirmative. Conditions of oppression and deprivation predispose and lead to developmental impairments, stress, and regressive adaptation. Viewed dynamically, part of the rage and aggression is due to chronic states of defusion. Among a number of constructive and destructive alternatives to the aggression, the victims of slums and ghettos discover that the pain that grows out of their rage subsides when they take heroin. That is, individuals discover that narcotics reverse the process of defusion and regression that grows out of conditions of oppression and deprivation.

As a final observation the author has been impressed with a reluctance among workers in the field of methadone maintenance to consider how the chemical-metabolic problems that underlie opiate addiction interact with the psychological and behavioral manifestations of addiction. It is as though trying to explain this elaboration or interaction would invalidate our theory of addiction as a problem in biological homeostasis, and thus undermine an effective approach that emphasizes a correction in the biological chemical imbalance associated with addiction. Probably the clinician who has seen the efficacy of methadone maintenance with addicted patients is justified in being reluctant to consider in great depth psychological and dynamic factors. He has learned that his approach, combined with brief counseling, has offered more hope than psychotherapeutically oriented approaches. However, it has been my contention that this dichotomy of a biological and a psychological approach to the problem of opiate addiction is not only unnecessary but also unfortunate and counterproductive. Analytic-dynamic psychiatry offers a theoretical basis to account for and support the use of methadone maintenance in the

treatment of the addicted patient. Furthermore, on this same theoretical basis there is evidence to support the disinclination to take an
in-depth psychological approach in many instances and instead to
encourage intervention around practical problems involving family,
work, and concerns about criminal behavior.

# 17

# Heroin Addiction:
# The Diagnostic Dilemma
# for Psychiatry

## *with Catherine J. Treece*

The task we have set for ourselves in this chapter is inspired in large part by our own experience in struggling with the practical and conceptual issues of diagnostic research in a drug-addicted population. This research is part of a group of mandated studies contracted by the National Institute on Drug Abuse (NIDA), Division of Research, to investigate "the implication of psychiatric diagnosis for narcotics dependence treatment." After reviewing other recent work involving similar research efforts, we have concluded that the "dilemma" in our title not only is indicative of our own struggles, but also reflects the struggles of other investigators who have attempted to study the psychopathology of addicts. Specifically the dilemma involves the meaning of diagnosis in the context' of compulsive drug use. Thus, when a psychiatric disorder is manifest in an addict, is it appropriate to consider that we are dealing with addiction as a symptom of a psychiatric disorder, or is the psychiatric disorder a symptom of addiction; or, further still, does a new disorder result for which a special classification and vocabulary is required? Although current research looks promising to resolve such questions, the sum of findings to date reflects long-standing controversies and contradictions. What we hope to do in this report is to clarify some of the issues that perpetuate such controversies.

We begin with a brief overview of findings from earlier studies that reported on diagnosis of addicts. Next we present some preliminary findings from current work in this area, and attempt to organize some of the special difficulties encountered in the diagnosis of addicts. Finally, we propose a set of models around which to conceptualize current research efforts and offer some speculations for synthesizing some of the seemingly divergent results of the overview we have presented.

## ADDICTION AND PSYCHOPATHOLOGY—BACKGROUND

The question of whether all narcotic addicts are necessarily suffering from psychiatric disturbance is an interesting and important one that has been the subject of much controversy. However, this problem is too broad for us to grapple with here. Rather, our present mandate rests on the well-documented fact that among those chronic addicts in our own time and culture who present themselves for treatment, there is a high prevalence of significant psychiatric disorder. Among those investigators who concur in this general observation, there is nevertheless considerable variability as to the nature and frequency of various psychiatric disorders and types of psychopathology that are reported. Much of the variability in the results of diagnostic research can be attributed to factors that affect the epidemiology of drug use in general. Of greater significance to our present task, however, are variations in findings that are an artifact of research design.

A simple example of this is illustrated in Table 17–1, which provides a sampling of several older diagnostic studies of addicts. In these examples, in addition to being different in time frame and in populations sampled, it is evident that the results depended heavily on the type and range of disorders being considered, and implicitly, the specific methods and criteria by which the patients were classified. It would be useful to know, for instance, to what extent "psychopathic," "sociopathic," and "delinquency-dominated character disorder" are describing similar characteristics. Likewise, how much do "overt schizophrenia" and "schizophrenic disorder" or "borderline schizophrenia" and "psychosis" overlap? Given such ambiguity in terms, one can well appreciate the increasing acceptance and use by many researchers of standardized diagnostic criteria and nomenclature for descriptive diagnosis.

**Table 17–1**
**Psychiatric Diagnosis of Various Addict Samples**

| Kolb (1925)—Mixed Sample | |
| --- | --- |
| Pleasure seeking (ill-defined instability of personality) | 38% |
| Psychopathic | 13% |
| Inebriates | 22% |
| Accidental (medical) | 14% |
| Neurotic | 14% |

U.S. Public Health Service Hospital, Lexington,
KY Male Voluntary Inpatient Sample (Valliant 1966)

| | Prescor 1936–37 | Vaillant 1952 | Smith et al. 1965 |
| --- | --- | --- | --- |
| Personality disorder | 76% | 59% | 75% |
| Sociopathic | 12% | 18% | 15% |
| Psychoneurosis | 6% | 5% | 3% |
| Psychosis | 2% | 6% | 2% |
| Addiction only | | 2% | 1% |

Gerard and Kornetsky (1955): Voluntary and Probationary Male
Adolescent Minority Inpatients

| | |
| --- | --- |
| Borderline schizophrenia | 27% |
| Delinquency-dominated character | 40% |
| Disorder inadequate personality | 13% |
| Overt schizophrenia | 20% |
| Serious neurotic | 0% |
| Mild neurotic normal | 0% |

Cohen and Klein (1970):
Mixed Adolescent Inpatients in a Private Hospital

| | |
| --- | --- |
| Character disorder | 85% |
| Schizophrenia | 5% |
| Other (depressed, psychoneurotic, organic) | 10% |

A further point to note in Table 17–1 is a significant omission that points up changing styles in diagnosis, namely the absence of any provision for affective disorders among the classifications offered.

We have observed comparable disarray in the psychoanalytic literature. Although most psychoanalytic writers give ample attention to the prominent depression and anxiety among addicts, their observations, like those of descriptive psychiatry, are subject to disagreement regarding the most relevant constructs to be considered, and subject to styles and fads within their own discipline. Thus, Rado (1926), who has been credited with writing the first psychoanalytic paper devoted specifically to narcotic addiction at about the same time as Kolb's studies appeared, was tied to the limitations of an instinct model. Glover (1932), another early psychoanalyst interested in addiction, observed the extent to which diagnostic conceptualizations about addicts tended to parallel the generalized theoretical interests and controversies in the field at any given time.

Further, the whole area of character disturbance, which has always been strongly implicated in both descriptive psychiatry and psychoanalysis in relation to addiction, has only recently begun to come into its own as more than a vague and general rubric for classifying lifelong disturbances in functioning and adaptation. It is only with the recent elaboration of a comprehensive ego psychology that psychoanalytic observers have begun to develop the theoretical sophistication needed to adequately describe the characterological disturbances so prevalent among addicted patients. Concurrently, descriptive approaches have begun to evolve a more discriminating nosology for the classification of this type of disorder.

Indeed, descriptive psychiatry and psychodynamic/analytic approaches to clinical assessment have grown immensely in precision and subtlety in recent years. In fact, it has been suggested (Freedman 1979) that the trend toward adoption of diagnostic instruments that incorporate operationally explicit criteria for diagnostic classification, such as the *Diagnostic and Statistical Manual* (*DSM-III*) (American Psychiatric Association 1980) and the Research Diagnostic Criteria (RDC) (Spitzer et al. 1978), represents an important step in the direction of incorporating insights from several perspectives, including psychoanalysis, into a more empirical and comparable basis for assessment, classification, and treatment.

## RECENT DIAGNOSTIC FINDINGS

The advances we have noted in modern diagnostic methods give us a basis to be more optimistic about unraveling the diagnostic dilemma with heroin addicts. We now turn to findings from current research efforts that reflect these improvements. At the outset we should stress that much of what we review in this section is based on preliminary data and pilot studies, and thus in no way should be construed as conclusive. However, we believe that the information is sufficiently promising and suggestive to warrant discussion.

### Behavior Disorders and Psychosis

Table 17–2 summarizes the personality-related diagnoses presented in Table 17–1 along with pilot results from two ongoing studies. The latter include our own study (Cambridge Project) and that of Weissman and colleagues (1978), our sister project in New Haven, both of which have used the RDC. Despite previously noted definitional problems, these comparisons are quite interesting.

In Table 17–2, it would appear that Kolb's study is the least consistent with the others. Fifty-one percent (or 72.5 percent if we include "inebriates") of his subjects were diagnosed as having a personality disorder. This sample, however, appears to have included a large number of iatrogenic addicts presumably left over from pre-Prohibition days, and therefore not represented in subsequent studies. The neurotics in this classification may have been the group most comparable to latter-day depressives, although we can only guess about that.

Of the next four studies, all done in Lexington, Kentucky, the Gerard and Kornetsky (1955) study shows a much lower frequency of personality disorders than the other three. Vaillant (1966) provides follow-up data on many of these adolescent addicts who were diagnosed as borderline (or incipient) or acute schizophrenics, but he found that the diagnosis of schizophrenia held up in adulthood in very few cases. He felt that a diagnosis of schizoid or borderline personality would have been more accurate, so that it seems valid to conclude that the Gerard and Kornetsky sample also includes a comparably high proportion of character disorders. Cohen and Klein (1970) likewise report a very high frequency of character disorder, consistent with the Lexington studies. The Cambridge and New Haven projects, on the

Table 17-2
Frequency of Personality Disorder
Among Various Addict Samples

| Authors | Types of Personality Disorder (percent) | | Total Frequency (percent) |
|---|---|---|---|
| Kolb (1925) | "Pleasure seeking" | (38) | 51% (with inebriates: 73) |
| | Psychopathic | (13) | |
| Pescor (cited in Vaillant 1966) | Personality disorder | (76) | 88% |
| | Sociopath | (12) | |
| Vaillant (1966) | Personality disorder | (59) | 77% |
| | Sociopath | (18) | |
| Smith et al. (cited in Vaillant 1966) | Personality disorder | (75) | 90% |
| | Sociopath | (15) | |
| Gerard and Kornetsky (1955) | Delinquency-dominated Character disorder | (40) | 53% (with borderline states: 80) |
| | Inadequate personality | (13) | |
| Cohen and Klein (1970) | Character disorder | (85) | 85% |
| Treece and Khantzian (1978) | RDC personality disorder | | 45% (with schizotypal features: 48) |
| Kleber and Gold* (1978) | RDC personality disorder | | 45% (with schizotypal features: 48) |

*Cited with permission from the authors.

other hand, show lower frequencies of character disorder. However, the estimate of character disorder in these two studies is artifactually lowered by the constraints of the RDC that focuses primarily on affect disorders. It is anticipated that this factor will be corrected in both projects by the addition of *DSM-III* classifications, which, by virtue of its multiaxial system, will permit inclusion of a wider range of personality disorder diagnoses without losing the findings on affective disorders. Although we have only begun to apply *DSM-III* in our diagnostic work, early results are more consistent with our psychodynamic diagnoses in indicating a percentage of character disorder consistent with the others in Table 17–2.

In addition to personality disorder, the other category noted most frequently in the older studies is some form of psychotic disorder. These findings are summarized along with the Cambridge and New Haven pilot findings in Table 17–3. With the exception of the Gerard and Kornetsky (1955) study, which we commented on earlier, the findings are quite consistent over time; that is, there is an existing but quite small percentage of addicted patients who appear to suffer from psychotic disturbances.

Thus we find considerable consistency with regard to the prevalence of both personality disorders and psychotic disorders between the older studies and the two in progress.

## Affective Disorders

We have already noted the absence of comparative data in the earlier studies on affective disorders, despite its persistence as a theme among clinical and theoretical reports. However, there appears to be a major effort under way to make up for the earlier omissions, and to attempt to ascertain the prevalence of affective disorders among addict populations. This kind of diagnostic data has been most readily obtainable among methadone maintenance patients, and several studies have been undertaken recently to look more specifically at this area.

Using several standardized instruments, Weissman and colleagues (1976), Senay (unpublished, cited by Weissman et al. 1976), and Woody and colleagues (1975) have all reported very similar frequencies (about one-third of the patients studied) of manifest depression in samples of methadone maintenance patients. At the same time, two other ongoing studies have indicated both higher and lower percentages of depression. McKenna (1977) reports a pilot finding of 51 percent depression using the Hamilton Scale, but Albech (personal communication) finds that a combination of scales and clinical assessment identifies only about 20 percent of consecutive admissions that would qualify as depressed enough to be appropriate for psychotropic medication. In our own sample, classification as to current depression varies considerably depending on whether it is based on self-report, a clinical rating scale, or assessment by standard criteria.

### Table 17–3
### Frequency of Psychotic Disorder Among Various Addict Samples

| Authors | Type of Psychotic Disorder | (percent) |
|---|---|---|
| Kolb (1925) | No psychotic classifications | (–) |
| Pescor (cited in Vaillant 1966) | Psychosis | (2) |
| Vaillant (1966) | Psychosis | (6) |
| Smith et al. (cited in Vaillant 1966) | Psychosis | (2) |
| Gerard and Kornetsky (1955) | Overt schizophrenia | (20) |
|  | Borderline schizophrenia | (27) |
| Cohen and Klein (1970) | Schizophrenia | (5) |
| Treece and Khantzian (1978) | Schizophrenia | (0) |
|  | Schizo-affective manic | (0) |
|  | Schizo-affective depressed | (11) |
|  | Unspecified psychosis | (0) |
| Kleber and Gold* (1978) | Schizophrenia | (0) |
|  | Schizo-affective manic | (1) |
|  | Schizo-affective depressed | (1) |
|  | Unspecified psychosis | (0) |

* Cited with permission from the authors.

Referring to the RDC lifetime diagnoses, Cambridge and New Haven have both found that about 60 percent of subjects qualify for a depressive diagnosis at some time in their lives. However, the relative frequency of "major," as opposed to "minor" or "intermittent," depressions varies considerably. This may be a reliability problem despite the difficulty of assessing depression in addicts. Both studies, by the way, are also finding an unusually high frequency of hypomania in the subjects' histories, ranging from 10 to 20 percent of the samples studied thus far.

Ambiguities regarding the type, frequency, and severity of depression apparent in these several diagnostic studies are also evident in studies that have tested the utility of psychotropic agents in such cases. Kleber and Gold (1978) have reported on the results of trials of lithium in seven methadone maintenance patients with retarded depression. Lithium treatment was associated with consistent and significant self-reduction in methadone dose, but its effect on the manifest depression was consistent. Another group of patients in their study with a similar depressive picture was treated with tricyclic antidepressants and showed much more consistent clinical improvement, but did not show any significant reduction in methadone dose.

In reviewing the data of a different type of study, that of Woody and colleagues (1975), it is noteworthy that the depression they identified is characterized as "mild" or "neurotic" and that the Hamilton, Zung, and Beck scales showed a significant component of anxiety present in these subjects. Yet the areas of most obvious improvement with antidepressants occurred with just such anxious/depressed subjects. These results are reminiscent of those of Overall and colleagues (1973), who identified a "mild-anxious depression" in a group of alcoholics and chose to test the efficacy of three classes of drugs—antianxiety agents, antipsychotics, and antidepressants—with these patients. Although the clinical symptomatology more closely resembled a mild anxious depression (and therefore was more likely to respond readily to antianxiety agents), the responsiveness to the three classes of drugs revealed the depression to be more like a severe endogenous depression. That is, the antidepressants and antipsychotic drugs were the most effective.

Such apparent incongruities regarding the diagnosis of affective disorder, namely difficulty in assessing the nature of depressive manifestations, and mild depressions that respond to medications like endogenous ones do, is sufficiently inconsistent with our own experience to tempt us to speculate regarding their substantive implications. In short, it may be that a paradoxically mild manifestation of depression among methadone patients, as measured by standard techniques alone, belies a more severe depressive condition that is either missed or muted, or presents in a forme fruste (i.e., an attenuated form).

These speculations are consistent with those of Vaillant (1966), who noted in a series of diagnostic studies he reviewed that addicts rarely displayed symptoms of depression yet appeared depressed on psychological tests. Indeed, in his prospective study of Lexington addicts, Vaillant felt compelled to conclude that by all evidence "the addict patient 'ought' to be depressed but on long-term follow-up is not" (p. 606).

Our speculations regarding such findings, however, must remain guarded since virtually all of the studies just cited represent pilot work, and our comparisons are complicated by differences in research design. We review in the next section some of the reasons this can have a critical bearing on diagnostic findings, and any conclusions drawn from such studies will need to take more detailed note of methodological details than we have the space to do here.

## DIAGNOSTIC PROBLEMS IN WORKING WITH ADDICTS

As already noted, we believe current research shows promise to dispel some of the disagreements and confusion surrounding the clinical understanding of narcotic addiction. However, with regard to affective disorders, we continue to find the diagnosis of an addict to be a difficult task.

In the past, the use of "drug addict" as a diagnostic category all of its own provided a means of sidestepping some of the diagnostic complexity encountered in addicted patients. Indeed, we can appreciate the temptation to classify addicts into a special category, or perhaps, several special categories. This is not only because of the particular complications that addiction itself adds to the clinical picture, but also because of the difficulties in finding a comfortable fit between the clinical presentation and the specifically defined disorders that they so often closely resemble but do not quite represent.

With regard to the complications of addiction per se, assessment of addicted patients requires that in addition to observing the phenomenology of symptoms, behaviors, and emotions, close attention be paid to both the historical context and the environment/setting in which the observations are made. While this is a prerequisite for adequate diagnostic evaluation of any patient group, it presents special challenges when dealing with addicts.

## Current Drug Status

Any clinical observations about drug users must take into account the current condition of the patient with respect to drug state. This can range from acute intoxication by one or more substances, to chronic toxicity, to maintenance on narcotics or other medication, and to withdrawal or drug free states. Systematic experimentation and comparison among groups in different drug states have provided some important clarification of what has been observed anecdotally in clinical settings, though much more remains to be done. A few examples can make the point.

Many diagnostic studies of addicts over the years have used the Minnesota Multiphasic Personality Inventory (MMPI), which provides well-standardized and thus comparable diagnostic data for large and diverse samples. In an attempt to clarify inconsistencies in the various studies, Sutker (1971) and Sutker and Allain (1973) compared incarcerated and outpatient samples of addicts and demonstrated major differences in the profiles reflecting psychopathic deviance and the neurotic triad of anxiety, depression, and hypochondriasis. This was interpreted by the authors as a setting difference. However, subsequent studies provided evidence that this kind of variation can also be shown to be associated with drug status (i.e., using or drug free [Fraccia et al. 1973]), and between voluntary and involuntary treatment status (Gendreau and Gendreau 1973). From still further study it was demonstrated that within diagnostic profiles specific variation was differentially associated with multiple setting factors including inpatient versus outpatient status, and length of hospitalization within inpatient samples. Length of hospitalization as a variable that affects clinical manifestations is further complicated by the fact that the likelihood of staying in treatment is also related to diagnostic differences (e.g., Stewart and Waddell 1972).

One of the research lessons to be derived from these findings is to choose one's variables with care to distinguish between symptoms such as mood or self-esteem, which are highly state dependent, and more enduring traits of personality. However, even broad and seemingly enduring character traits may be highly susceptible to variation due to drug state as was demonstrated by Milkman and Frosch (1973) using a set of clinical ratings of ego functioning under conditions of intoxication and nonintoxication.

Focusing further on the central problem of assessing affective disturbance, Chein and colleagues (1964) noted that narcotics bought on the street at times alleviated psychic distress and at other times led to a general increase in dysphoria. Such complexity of mood and drug interaction has also been demonstrated experimentally in an important series of in vivo studies. Meyer (1976) and Mirin and collaborators (1976) have observed addicts through cycles of self-induced addiction from the drug-free state to withdrawal and readdiction, and have documented major alterations in depressive affect, irritability, and motivation associated with each. Early in the cycle of self-addiction they observed lessening of anxiety and irritability with elevation in mood. With longer term self-administration, irritability, negativism, and depression increased.

In contrast to such apparent regressive responses to self-administration, stand the progressive responses that have been observed in the course of chronic methadone maintenance. Khantzian (1972, 1974, 1978) has stressed the antiaggression action of opiates that appears to counteract the disorganizing influences of rage on the ego. Similarly Wurmser (1974) has stressed the use of opiates in the service of affect defense, suggesting that opiates serve a defensive function with respect to the feelings of "rage, shame, and loneliness" (p. 831) that emerge with overwhelming intensity when subjects are withdrawn from methadone.

McKenna and colleagues (1973) and Kleber and Gold (1978) have been among those who reported the appearance of psychosis among some patients at reduced doses of methadone, with remission at higher doses, implying an antipsychotic function for methadone as well.

## Chronic Drug States

If the acute effects of the drug use complicate the diagnostic picture, so do the chronic effects. There has always been considerable diversity of opinion as to what portion of the psychological functioning of an addict could be attributed to the effects of the addiction, and what portion may reflect a premorbid personality. We are inclined to agree with Kolb (1925) in his report on what must have been the grandfather of our present project. On the basis of a diagnostic study of addicts done under the auspices of the U.S. Public Health Services in 1925, Kolb concluded:

> In evaluating the effect that narcotics may have produced in any given case, it is necessary to have clearly in mind, and to consider collectively, the original character of the person, the physical harm the drugs have done to him, the mental and moral consequences of the physical difficulties, the stabilizing influence, if any, that may have been exerted by the drug, and the demoralizing effect upon the addict of being looked upon as an outcast or a criminal.

Expansion of diagnostic procedures to include in-depth assessment and a lifetime history of disturbances, symptoms, and adaptation can to some extent circumvent the necessity raised in the previous section of asking which is the real diagnostic entity. However, Kolb's prescription remains difficult to follow. A major difficulty in understanding the long-term effects of drugs and addiction on the "original character of the person" is that in so many cases compulsive drug use was initiated in early adolescence, so that determining a premorbid diagnosis becomes a moot point. However, even when it is possible to reconstruct the preaddiction diagnosis, in chronic cases it is very difficult to clearly separate the effect of drug use per se from other life events and from maturation itself.

Results of a line of investigation by Grant and associates (1978) also reminds us that heroin addicts are rarely exclusively using opiates, but that polydrug use is common in such individuals and that neuropsychological deficits are associated with prolonged use of central nervous system (CNS) depressants and possibly opiates. While the possibility of gross impairments in perceptual and other cognitive functions has been fairly well demonstrated for such substances as alcohol and barbiturates, the possibility of subtler deficits involving the capacity to learn from experience and other important adaptive capacities must also be considered. This point has been strongly made by Goldstein (1976) with respect to alcohol and by Gray (1978) with respect to the effects of benzodiazepines. The benzodiazepines are especially important in this respect since they are widely used among methadone patients to boost methadone's effect.

Another aspect of chronic drug status that we must mention briefly is the social milieu in which many addicts become immersed. Zinberg

(1975) has elaborated on the regressive influence of enforced social isolation and deviant status in undermining culturally supported and regulated aspects of social behavior. Khantzian and colleagues (1974) have also discussed the role of the subculture and its attendant rituals on personality organization. From the behaviorally oriented schools we may cite Wikler (1968) and others as to the power of acquired associations to precipitate experiences of intoxication or withdrawal in the absence of drugs.

## Mission Impossible

The long-range intrapsychic effects of narcotic addiction have been the subject of numerous studies. Evidence that suggests long-range deterioration of functioning competes with evidence that suggests ego-supportive, anti-regressive, or prophylactic effects. We have already pointed out that the acute effects of drugs depend on duration and chronicity of drug use, which in turn depend on the psychological makeup, and probably the constitution, of the user. In any event, the evaluation of any chronic effects requires that we provide an adequate description of the current psychological condition of our patients. This brings us to the heart of the diagnostic dilemma, for along with the problem of assessing drug effects, it is the particular qualities of the presenting diagnostic picture itself that make clinically relevant classification so problematic.

For example, at least among the chronic population to which much of the current research is addressed, a major impediment is that subjects tend to be poor self-observers. While this may be pathognomonic in itself, it makes for difficult history taking. Many of our subjects have very poor memories for dates and sequences of events not specifically involving drugs. On the other hand, they often evidence a striking precision and detail in their drug histories, as if their personal histories were measured in these units of pharmacological experience.

There is a pervasive tendency to attribute emotional and psychological phenomena to drug use post hoc, or else to be unable to distinguish drug-related experiences from non–drug-related ones. This seems to us to be more than a problem in reliability. We feel the lack of an appropriate vocabulary with which to document the particular characteristics that are presented to us. The psychoanalytic approach to diagnosis offers a much richer language with which to address some of these issues, but without the methodology of descriptive psychiatry to systematically categorize and classify.

The difficulty in self-observation appears to involve a particular lack of insight or recognition with regard to feelings. This has been described by Krystal (1977) as a developmental problem in differentiation of affect and by Wurmser (1974) as a defect in affect defense that leads to the addict's conviction that he/she needs external substances to manage feeling states. Treece (1977) has emphasized problems in affect tolerance and hypothesized that the drug craving of addicts often represents a defensive transformation or displacement of distressful internal states.

Attempts to explore the validity of such formulations further is frustrated by the very nature of these defensive processes. Many subjects, for instance, are difficult to pin down as to the quality, frequency, or intensity of depressive affect. A subject may seem to acknowledge feeling very depressed one moment, but quickly deny any such feelings when pressed for further details. There is an escapist quality here, as if any introspection might arouse painful memories or emotions that would upset a tenuous equilibrium that permits the warding off of depression. Yet in other cases a depression can be so chronic and pervasive and yet so unrecognized as such that it is taken for normal. Such a subject therefore has no baseline of normal mood against which to measure his dysphoria. Then again, when faced with a patient who describes himself as devoid of interests, accomplishments, or lasting enjoyments, when he maintains that close relationships are not worth the risk of trusting, and he fends off with some success, through a commitment to drug taking, a lurking emptiness, we are tempted to diagnose him as chronically depressed. Yet if he lacks the traditional hallmarks of depression as they have been defined for purposes of classification, if he is not guilt-ridden, does not display vegetative signs, and acknowledges no conviction of personal impairment beyond his compulsion for drugs, does it not violate our nosology to label him a depressive?

Psychodynamic psychiatry provides ample room for considering depression as warded off, masked (Wishnie 1974), or otherwise manifested through characterological adaptations, rather than in the emergence of depressive illness. Still, when the addict interprets and integrates the special transformation of his feelings through drugs, primarily in pharmacological terms, it makes even a character classification inadequate unless we consider these drug defenses as unique and specific to these patients. In short, the drug history and its effects are not simply complications to the psychiatric history; they are, in a very real sense, synonymous with it.

## DIAGNOSTIC MODELS
## OF ADDICTION

The foregoing discussion should make it apparent that diagnosis in regard to chronic addicts cannot be understood without reference to the addiction history. We have found it useful to think in terms of models that by abstraction simplify the different possible kinds of relationships between drug effects and presenting psychopathology.

### The Self-Medication Model

The simplest model for conceptualizing drug use and psychopathology suggests that users are self-medicating an underlying disorder. The observations that we have noted regarding the emergence of manifest psychopathology upon withdrawal from narcotics, and its suppression when narcotics are again administered, form the basis for this model.

A logical application of a self-treatment model has been the trial of alternative or additional psychotropic medications to treat the presumed "underlying" disorder. These kinds of studies are just beginning to be done. Kleber and Gold (1978) have recently reviewed much of the current thinking and experimentation in this area, and integrated it with current knowledge about the biochemistry of endorphins. The sum of these findings clearly indicates interactive effects between methadone and virtually all the major psychiatric mood regulators. This fact makes it easier to understand that methadone, and presumably other narcotics, can have such diverse appeal.

Addiction can best be described as a symptom of underlying psychiatric disorder in those cases where it can be shown that narcotics produce specific desirable medication effects. Such evidence appears to be least ambiguous with respect to the relatively small portion of psychotic disorders. Kleber and Gold (1978) consider the pharmacological evidence to be quite good that methadone has specific antipsychotic action. Case studies being reported likewise support this.

Berken and colleagues (1978) discuss a specific case in which methadone was the treatment of choice for psychotic aggression. McKenna (personal communication) has achieved remission in two cases with a diagnosis of paranoid schizophrenia using higher than normal doses of methadone.

With regard to other kinds of disorders, Khantzian (1974) and Wurmser (1974) have noted repeatedly the efficacy of methadone in suppressing extreme ego-disorganization, especially in the context of rage. Kleber and Gold (1978) believe that methadone also offers antimanic action. And, of course, we have noted the likelihood that narcotics in general have at least short-term antidepression effects.

The effect of narcotics on affect states and disorders, however, seems to require a different conceptualization than that for psychosis. In response to this need we might look at other models of addiction and pathology implicated in some of the recent studies.

## Drug-Induced-Illness Model

A drug-induced-illness model, at its extreme, suggests that addiction produces the psychiatric illness rather than being the consequence of it. Mirin and colleagues (1976), for instance, whom we cited earlier, concluded that depression among addicts was the result, not the cause, of narcotic use. A more subtle explanation requires consideration of the interactive processes leading to psychological regression over time, which may result from chronic self-administration. This was elegantly demonstrated by Wikler (1952) in his observations of individual cases through the cycles of addiction and readdiction. Wieder and Kaplan (1969) illustrate the psychodynamic perspective in suggesting that chronic drug use "always occurs as a consequence of ego pathology," but also "serves in a circular fashion to add to this pathology" (p. 403). Zinberg (1975) has argued that many of the commonalties observed among addicts presenting for treatment, including character features, are better accounted for by the common processes involved in becoming an addict than by common predisposing characteristics.

Combining a self-medication view with findings about long-term consequences of addiction suggests, in the case of depression, that what we are seeing is a disorder that has been altered by the effort to alleviate symptoms. Just as it is now recognized that lengthy pharmacological treatment of insomnia can create a new disorder that perpetuates the malady it was trying to cure, the manifest depression of some methadone patients may represent a similar circular process.

A drug-induced-illness model might also lead to a reassessment of cases in which decompensation during withdrawal is assumed to indicate the unmasking of a psychotic process. An alternative hypothesis in some cases would be that the disruption of the biological and psychological adaptive equilibrium involved in withdrawal produces an acute response to psychic trauma that in a severe character disorder could precipitate a (reversible) psychotic regression.

## The Symptom Model

A third manner of conceptualizing the addiction-psychopathology relationship may prove useful both for integrating the two previous models, as well as for providing a better method for considering longer-term character pathology, in distinction to acute disorder, especially as formulated by the analytic writers. Wurmser (1974) has suggested such a model in describing the compulsion to use narcotics as "co-extensive" with the character pathology. Vaillant (1966) made a similar point in considering that the search (for narcotics) is as important a part of the addiction as the heroin. Khantzian (1974), Wishnie (1974), Milkman and Frosch (1973), and others have indicated as we suggested earlier that drug use can support and enable otherwise defective or inadequate defensive functions. Further, drug use that starts as an attempt to alleviate the psychic distress associated with defective capacities for managing or tolerating affects in the longer run could also act as an impediment to further autoplastic development, and undermine existing internal adaptive options, thus leading to ever greater reliance on exogenous supports. In this manner the drug use, rather than simply masking psychopathology, or in turn producing it, becomes enmeshed in the character adaptation itself and thus essentially becomes the primary symptomatic expression.

Each of the models described thus far can be seen as alternative means of organizing numerous observations. Taken together they can account for the fact that psychic distress motivates initial drug use, may lead to additional symptoms and complications, and is likely to result in a psychiatric presentation that is quite different in different states and stages of drug use. However, it is noteworthy that self-medication and drug-induced-illness models presuppose the presence of depressive illness, and other familiar psychiatric disorders, while the "symptom" perspective tends to emphasize the dissimilarity of addicts to other psychiatric populations including the relative absence of overt depressive disorder. We have observed among our own subjects that some are distinctly conscious of their use of drugs for self-medication, while others are unable to identify any internal or psychological reasons for their drug use beyond a generalized initial sense of well-being or personal integration. While the former subjects are aware of a return of symptoms upon abstinence, the latter can define their need for the drug only in terms of the peremptory craving that arises when they try to wean themselves from it.

It remains open to conjecture whether the different theoretical emphases and the differences we have observed among subjects indicate different types of addicts or different stages in a common process of addiction.

## The Character Disorder
## of Addiction

As a further effort to clarify the diagnostic dilemma, we would like to propose one more model. In this model chronic addiction is viewed as the end point in an evolution from self-medication or symptom expression toward a point in which it becomes functionally autonomous of the original factors that determined compulsive drug use.

This model was to some extent articulated by Chein and associates (1964), who noted that theorists as seemingly disparate as Lindesmith and Wikler both appeared to be describing "the emergence of a personality structure built on narcotics" (p. 26). In making this observation they were able to account not only for their own research findings based on psychiatric and psychoanalytic data, but also for the divergent and seemingly antagonistic findings of social psychology and behavioral research as well.

A model that permits the conceptualization of the chronic addict's personality structure as a specialized disorder indeed seems needed to manage the multiple facets of drug and personality interactions. Simply the fact that not all self-medicators become addicts, and not all addicts become chronic addicts, seems to belie the likelihood that even the three previous models will suffice to account for all of the data.

## SUMMARY AND CONCLUSIONS

If we have overemphasized complexities, we hope that we have also highlighted some useful consistencies in the research on diagnosis of the chronic addicts. In our own work we are trying to integrate a psychodynamic understanding of character disorder with the discipline of a descriptive approach. We have noted a convergence of older and newer research, and of descriptive and psychoanalytic observations, especially around the concepts of personality disorder and affect disturbance, viewed in the long-range context of drug use and pharmacological effect.

Inconsistencies and variation in conclusions are considered more manageable if we understand that different models of addiction are implicit in differing methodologies. The explication of these models should help to generate hypotheses that will clarify whether there are different kinds of addictions, or only many kinds of addicts.

## ACKNOWLEDGMENT

The observations and conclusions in this chapter were based in part on work supported by NIDA Contract # 271-77-3410.

## REFERENCES

American Psychiatric Association (1980). *Diagnostic and Statistical Manual of Mental Disorders*, 3rd ed. Washington, DC: American Psychiatric Association.

Berken, G. H., Stone, M. M., and Stone, S. K. (1978). Methadone in schizophrenic rage. *American Journal of Psychiatry* 135:248–249.

Chein, I., Gerard, D. L., Lee, R. S., and Rosenfeld, E. (1964). *The Road to H: Narcotics, Delinquency, and Social Policy*. New York: Basic Books.

Cohen, M., and Klein, D. F. (1970). Drug abuse in a young psychiatric population. *American Journal of Orthopsychiatry* 40:448–455.

Fraccia, J., Sheppard, C., and Merlis, S. (1973). Some comments about the personality comparison of incarcerated and street heroin addicts. *Psychological Reports* 33:413–414.

Freedman, D. X. (1979). Editor's note. *Archives of General Psychiatry* 36:1.

Gendreau, P., and Gendreau, L. P. (1973). A theoretical note on the personality characteristics of heroin addicts. *Journal of Abnormal Psychology* 82:139–140.

Gerard, D. L., and Kornetsky, C. (1955). Adolescent opiate addiction: a study of control and addict subjects. *Psychiatric Quarterly* 29:457–486.

Glover, E. (1932). On the etiology of drug addiction. In *On the Early Development of Mind*, pp. 187–215. New York: International Universities Press, 1956.

Goldstein, G. (1976). Perceptual and cognitive deficits in alcoholics. In *Empirical Studies of Alcoholism*, ed. G. Goldstein and C. Neuringer. Cambridge, MA: Ballinger.

Grant, I., Adams, K. M., Carlin, A. S., et al. (1978). The collaborative neuropsychological study of polydrug users. *Archives of General Psychiatry* 35:1063–1074.

Gray, J. A. (1978). Anxiety. *Human Nature*, July, pp. 38–45.

Khantzian, E. J. (1972). A preliminary dynamic formulation of the psychopharmacologic action of methadone. In *Proceedings of the Fourth National Conference on Methadone Treatment*, San Francisco, pp. 371–374. New York: National Association for the Prevention of Addictions to Narcotics.

——— (1974). Opiate addiction: a critique of theory and some implications for treatment. *American Journal of Psychotherapy* 28:59–70.

——— (1978). The ego, the self and opiate addiction: theoretical and treatment considerations. *International Review of Psychoanalysis* 5:189–198.

Khantzian, E. J., Mack, J. E., and Schatzberg, A. F. (1974). Heroin use as an attempt to cope: clinical observations. *American Journal of Psychiatry* 131:160–164.

Kleber, H. D., and Gold, M. S. (1978). Use of psychotropic drugs in treatment of methadone maintained narcotic addicts. *Annals of the New York Academy of Sciences* 311:81–98.

Kolb, L. (1925). Types and characteristics of drug addicts. *Mental Hygiene* 9:300–313.

Krystal, H. (1977). Self- and object-representation in alcoholism and other drug dependence: implications for therapy. In *NIDA Research Monograph 12*, pp. 88–100. Rockville, MD: NIDA.

McKenna, G. J. (1979). Psychopathology in drug dependent individuals: a clinical review. *Journal of Drug Issues* 9:197–205.

McKenna, G. J., Fisch, A., Levine, M. E., et al. (1973). The use of methadone as a psychotropic agent. In *Proceedings of the Fifth National Conference on Methadone Treatment*. New York: National Association for the Prevention of Addictions to Narcotics.

Meyer, R. E. (1976). Discussion of preceding five papers. *International Journal of the Addictions* 11:545–549.

Milkman, H., and Frosch, W. A. (1973). On the preferential abuse of heroin and amphetamine. *Journal of Nervous and Mental Diseases* 156:242–248.

Mirin, S. M., Meyer, R. E., McNamee, H. B., and McDougle, M. (1976). Psychopathology, craving and mood during heroin acquisition: an experimental study. *International Journal of the Addictions* 11:525–544.

Overall, J. E., Brown, D., Williams, J. D., et al. (1973). Drug treatment of anxiety and depression in detoxified alcoholic patients. *Archives of General Psychiatry* 29:218–221.

Rado, S. (1926). The psychic effects of intoxicants: an attempt to evolve a psychoanalytic theory of morbid cravings. *International Journal of Psycho-Analysis* 7:396–407.

Spitzer, R. L., Endicott, J., and Robins, E. (1978). *Research Diagnostic Criteria (RDC) for Selected Group of Functional Disorders*, 3rd ed. Washington, DC: American Psychiatric Association.

Stewart, G. I., and Waddell, K. (1972). Attitudes and behavior of heroin addicts and patients on methadone. In *Proceedings of the Fourth National Conference on Methadone Treatment*, San Francisco. New York: National Association for the Prevention of Addictions to Narcotics.

Sutker, P. B. (1971). Personality differences and sociopathy in heroin addicts and nonaddict prisoners. *Journal of Abnormal Psychology* 78:247–251.

Sutker, P. B., and Allain, A. N. (1973). Incarcerated and street heroin addicts: a personality comparison. *Psychological Reports* 32:254–256.

Treece, C. J. (1977). Narcotic use in relation to selected ego functions among incarcerated women. Doctoral dissertation, Boston University. *Dissertation Abstracts International*.

Treece, C. J., and Khantzian, E. J. (1978). Implications of psychiatric diagnosis for narcotics dependence treatment. NIDA contract 271-77-3431. Unpublished quarterly report, December.

Vaillant, G. E. (1966). A 12-year follow-up of New York narcotic addicts. III. Some social and psychiatric characteristics. *Archives of General Psychiatry* 15:599–609.

Weissman, M. M., Kleber, H. D., and Rounsaville, J. (1978). *Significance of psychiatric diagnosis in opiate dependent individuals*. NIDA Contract 271-77-3410. Unpublished annual report.

Weissman, M. M., Slobetz, F., Prusoff, B., et al. (1976). Clinical depression among narcotic addicts maintained on methadone in the community. *American Journal of Psychiatry* 133:1434–1438.

Wieder, H., and Kaplan, E. H. (1969). Drug use in adolescence: psychodynamic meaning and pharmacogenic effect. *Psychoanalytic Study of the Child* 24:399–431. New York: International Universities Press.

Wikler, A. (1952). A psychodynamic study of a patient during experimental self-regulated re-addiction to morphine. *Psychiatric Quarterly* 27:270–295.

—— (1968). Interaction of physical dependence and classical and operant conditioning in the genesis of relapse. *The Addictive States, Association for Research in Nervous and Mental Diseases Research Publication* 46:281–287.

Wishnie, H. (1974). Opioid addiction as a masked depression. In *Masked Depression*, ed. S. Lesse, pp. 350–367. New York: Jason Aronson.

Woody, G. E., Luborsky, L., McLellan, A. T., et al. (1983). Psychotherapy for opiate addicts. *Archives of General Psychiatry* 40:639–645.

Woody, G. E., O'Brien, C. P., and Rickels, K. (1975). Depression and anxiety in heroin addicts: a placebo-controlled study of doxepin in combination with methadone. *American Journal of Psychiatry* 132:447–450.

Wurmser, L. (1974). Psychoanalytic considerations of the etiology of compulsive drug use. *Journal of the American Psychoanalytic Association* 22:820–843.

Zinberg, N. E. (1975). Addiction and ego function. *Psychoanalytic Study of the Child* 30:567–588. New Haven, CT: Yale University Press.

# 18

# Dependency and Denial
# Problems of Alcoholics[1]

David Myerson (1978) has described graphically and specifically four
major areas of loss for the alcoholic as a consequence of drinking, as
he or she grows older, namely, the loss of health, the loss of relationships, the loss of employment, and the loss of freedom through arrest
or court procedures. His thesis is that these losses inevitably lead to
a crisis that challenges the alcoholic's denial of his emotional and
personal bankruptcy in self-esteem and relationships, and that such
a crisis is necessary to effect change. Crisis is a time of both opportu-

---

1. This chapter was a discussion of a paper given by Dr. David Myerson,
   presented at the Symposium on Organic Problems in the Aged: Brain
   Syndromes and Alcoholism, sponsored by the Boston Gerontological
   Society.

nity and danger. (I am told that the Chinese symbol for *crisis* combines the symbols for *opportunity* and *danger*.) It is evident from Myerson's thoughtful paper (and from his well-known and much-respected work with alcohol problems) that he is well aware of both possibilities with alcoholics when the consequences of long-standing or heavy drinking finally erupt into a crisis. His formulation about the nature of the crisis as the alcoholic grows older is most important and useful.

Two aspects of the alcoholic's problems that Myerson repeatedly and necessarily focuses on are the alcoholic's dependency and denial. It is around problems of dependency and denial in relation to loss that the alcoholic's crises evolve. Although Myerson clearly appreciates the dependency and denial problems, it surprises me to see how much he stresses factors of intention, choice, and motivation as being pivotal in determining change in the alcoholic's life. In my own work with drug-dependent and alcoholic patients I have been impressed repeatedly with certain impairments in personality (or ego) functions related to affect tolerance and self-care that are intimately related to the alcoholic's problems with dependency and denial. Perhaps because my work focuses more on impairments in personality structure and function, I have found that factors of intention, choice, and motivation are less useful or helpful in understanding and managing the alcoholic's life problems and crises related to his drinking. What has been more useful to me in dealing with such crises has been to understand better the alcoholic's dependency and denial in relation to developmental problems, problems with managing feelings, and impairments in self-care functions. In this chapter I would like to focus specifically, and with a different emphasis than that given by Dr. Myerson, on the nature of the dependency and denial problem of alcoholics, and the treatment implications for the alcoholic, particularly as such an individual grows older.

Myerson refers to the alcoholic's tendency to resort to suicide or to choose death when faced with the crises of loss associated with alcoholism. His appreciation and concern about this possibility are well borne out by an important study conducted by Murphy and Robins (1967), in which alcoholism ranked second only to affective disorders in accounting for 134 suicides in an urban area. More telling in this study, and consistent with Myerson's thesis, is the finding that frequently (32 percent of the cases) the alcoholic had lost an "affectional" relationship (e.g., through separation, divorce, death, or moving) within six weeks of the suicide. (In 48 percent of the cases this loss occurred within one year of the suicide.) One might cynically conclude from such a study that suicide is the final, dramatic transaction in the life of a person whose course with alcohol has been, in effect, suicide on the installment plan. Others might argue that suicide in such instances results from rage that desperately dependent individuals turn on themselves when they experience loss and/or rejection. Needless to say, such explanations hinge on presupposing the existence of conscious and unconscious destructive motives and impulses. In my experience, however, the self-destructive behavior, including suicide, says less about the intentions and motives of such people, and more about the impairments of their psychological (ego) structure and function. They are particularly ill equipped to deal with their feelings and, because of such ego impairments, depend on others and the effects of alcohol to cope with their emotions and with problems in everyday life.

Much of our thinking about the dependency problem of alcoholics has been influenced by an id psychology that places heavy emphasis on impulses and instincts. I believe this emphasis, unfortunately, leads to reductionistic and speculative formulations that stress the symbolic, oral, regressive aspects of the alcoholic's dependence on ethanol. The personal relationships of alcoholics are similarly characterized as dependent, infantile, and of a clinging kind of attachment or love. Although Myerson stresses qualities of dependency in the alcoholic, he refreshingly avoids such reductionistic speculations. Appropriately, he insists that many of the alcoholic's dependency problems are the result of drinking, rather than unconscious, oral dependency problems causing the drinking.

If one approaches the dependency problem from the structural or ego side, I believe one stands a better chance of observing, understanding, and managing the nature and consequence of the alcoholic's desperate dependency problems. The alcoholic is built in such a way that he has trouble recognizing and experiencing his feelings, whether they are painful, subjective affects such as anxiety and depression, or good and bad feelings about himself or others (love/hate). He discovers, short term, the relief and surcease of painful feelings with alcohol in certain instances, and in other instances how alcohol helps him to experience and express other feelings such as affection and anger (Krystal and Raskin 1970). Similarly, the alcoholic's dependence on people is the result of ego impairments. He seeks out and leans on others not simply for gratification of oral, regressive needs. Rather, and more often, it is to compensate for impairments and defects in the individual's psychological structure, whereby he is ill-prepared to feel good enough about himself (Kohut 1971), unable to comfort himself (Krystal 1978), and unable to care for himself (Khantzian 1978). It is on such a basis that alcoholics turn to and depend on others to provide these missing functions, or as is frequently the case, such individuals become extremely defensive and conflicted over such dependence. In this respect, when we speak of the alcoholic's dependency problems, we say less about the nature of the alcoholic's attachment to his alcohol and/or people as loved or loving objects, and more, as Kohut (1971) has pointed out, about "a replacement for a defect in psychological structure" (p. 46). It is probably for this reason that suicide becomes such an imminent danger with alcoholics—that is, in the absence of his substance, which serves him in relation to his feelings, and in the absence of his dependent attachment to people, who similarly serve his needs and wants, the alcoholic despairs for his existence and his ability to cope, and on this basis perhaps chooses suicide as an alternative.

Our notions about denial, especially in relation to problems such as alcoholism, are also heavily tinged with id psychology influences that assume the existence and presence of conscious and unconscious destructive impulses, intentions, and behavior. In my own work I have again been impressed with ego deficits that fail to protect the individual, in this case, in relation to problems with self-preservation and care. Such problems, for example, are very evident in alcoholics when they deny their inability to control their drinking and maintain that their first drink after months, and even after years, of abstinence will be their only drink, and that they can control their alcohol consumption. In such instances we very often speculate that the individual has potential or real awareness that he is in danger or disaster is imminent, but resorts to an active process of defense or denial in order to justify or maintain his intention, in this case to drink. Needless to say, this much-invoked explanation has considerable explanatory value. However, here too I believe we fail to appreciate sufficiently the more observable ego side of the problem, namely, a lapse and failure in defense against impulses.

All of us as humans are subject to drives, instincts, and impulses. If they were expressed without caution, care, or worry, we would be subject to all kinds of hazardous experiences and involvements. For most of us, cautionary responses, worry, and realistic fear more or less (and automatically) protect us from hazardous involvements. Such self-protective reactions and responses are for most of us integral components of our ego defense mechanisms. However, it is exactly in this realm that so many drug- and alcohol-dependent people are deficient and accordingly complicate and destroy their lives. That is, rather than the alcoholic's destructive behavior being simply motivated or driven, he or she is equally apt to be impaired in self-care ego functions, in the absence of which such an individual fails to appreciate, anticipate, or correct for many hazardous and dangerous involvements, particularly in relation to alcohol use and involvement. I review in more detail in Chapters 2 and 19 the characteristics and developmental origins of self-care deficits.

When we take this type of an approach, in which greater emphasis is placed on ego impairments, then issues of choice, intention, and motivation often seem moot, especially when considering treatment implications. Myerson notes that the crisis the alcoholic eventually experiences causes him to give up his denial and to face the fact that his modus operandi is not viable. He correctly asserts that at this time the alcoholic may give up his alcohol and seek out AA and other forms of help. What is important to stress here is that much of the denial and reluctance to seek or accept help has been intimately related to conflict and impairments around dependency and self-care. Myerson further observes that many alcoholics respond negatively to the crisis precipitated by the alcoholism and persist in and choose a course that continues to be destructive. It is here that he stresses that the alcoholic's course involves a choice, and accordingly the problem may not be a medical or psychiatric one. Such a conclusion (and in an earlier draft he stated this conclusion more strongly) is unwarranted and not as useful as his more optimistic statements about the potential, hopeful possibilities for change, especially at the point of crisis.

I believe that we stand a much better chance of influencing the possibility that the alcoholic will accept or choose help by better appreciating his/her dependency and denial problems more as a structural (ego) impairment problem than as a problem of motivation or choice. Myerson is very tentative about predicting which course will be chosen by the alcoholic at the point of crisis. It also surprises me how much he places the issue of choice on the alcoholic alone, as if the alcoholic could not be influenced. Clearly, others (family, relatives, friends, employers, judges, police, etc.)—as Myerson himself indicates—influence the alcoholic's choice. Certainly physicians, and psychiatrists in particular, have a major opportunity for influencing change. Considering the psychological predisposing and resulting physiological impairments with which alcoholics suffer, it seems to me there is even a greater necessity and responsibility placed on the physician to be active in advocating not only the necessity for treatment, but also the type of treatment. In my own practice, I have been impressed with how such an active approach often overcomes resistance to treatment much more readily than Myerson's paper suggests or my own reading and training initially led me to believe. Assuming then that the problem of choice is not so unpredictable or uninfluenceable, I shall briefly conclude by commenting on some treatment alternatives and implications.

## TREATMENT ALTERNATIVES

### Confinement[2]

Confinement for the treatment of alcoholism is necessary for two reasons: first, for safe and quick detoxification; and second, as Myerson has indicated, for those cases where organic impairment as a result of drinking is advanced and has rendered the alcoholic incapable of caring for himself.

Few alcoholics can stop prolonged or protracted heavy drinking on their own, even with much family support and drug substitution to ease withdrawal. This is even more true for unreliable, deteriorated alcoholics who have lost family supports and contacts, and do not have the means for or access to, outpatient medical and psychiatric care. Confinement for detoxification, then, is often a first and necessary step before any other form of help is possible. Most usually, it is only after detoxification that the alcoholic can realistically consider alternatives, and other treatment interventions can succeed. In the case of confine-

---

2. In our current era of managed care, confinement is often unavailable and the clinician must creatively combine outpatient detoxification and day-treatment rehabilitation in lieu of inpatient confinement and care.

ment for the associated, more severe and chronic organic disability, we have had the salutatory experience of discovering that surprising degrees of function return, and that with adequate availability and variety of supports in the community, including selective use of drugs, a significant number of alcoholics may eventually resume a life relatively free of institutional confinement.

## Alcoholics Anonymous (AA)

AA is one of the best established forms of treatment and rehabilitation. The nurturance, immediate acceptance, understanding, and support of AA serve as an effective response for many to the dependency problems, and as an acceptable replacement for alcohol. The loss and giving up of alcohol is structured by slogans (e.g., "I will stay sober one day at a time"), practical guidelines, the wisdom of experience, and step-by-step approaches. Also, personal disclosures and sharing of experiences help to master the shame of dependency and much of the havoc and loss that have resulted from years of drinking; this is particularly important for alcoholics as they grow older, when they often have little to look back on in their lives that is redeeming. Unfortunately, for just as many alcoholics, if not the majority, AA is never considered or is not acceptable. It is estimated that there are five to ten million individuals in the United States who are alcoholics or have alcohol problems. Despite the widespread nature of the problem and many readily available AA programs, there are only 250,000 to 300,000 members in AA in continental North America.[3]

## Psychotherapy

Although there has been a tendency to eschew individual psychotherapeutic approaches for alcoholism problems, it is a treatment alternative that should be considered because it is a much more acceptable and expected form of help to many alcoholics, especially where

---

3. This estimate has changed drastically since this article was published two decades ago. It is probably the case that more than one million individuals are currently active in Alcoholics Anonymous in North America alone.

AA is the only other widely available form of help. Group psychotherapy should also be considered. In my experience, groups have been extremely useful for some, especially where the group leader feels free to be more active, and even didactic, if necessary. However, this is not universally the case, and, for some, groups are extremely threatening. I suspect in part the abhorrence of some alcoholics for AA is really an abhorrence of groups. AA for the most part is a group approach and as such can be devastatingly threatening when social anxiety and shame are paramount as is so often the case with alcoholics.

In individual psychotherapy, passivity on the part of the therapist in most instances should be avoided, especially initially, because of the danger of stirring up passive longings and concomitant rage. I have reviewed elsewhere (Khantzian 1980) the importance of structure, continuity, empathy, and activity in engaging and retaining alcoholics in treatment. Uncovering techniques and catharsis, especially at an early stage, should also be avoided. Early in treatment (i.e., in the immediate postdetoxification period) the presence of mild organicity should be suspected and allowed for, with lowered expectations for integration of psychotherapeutic work during this early phase.

Myerson cautions about the dangers and possible devastating consequences of couples therapy. In my own work, however, I have found couples group therapy to be a useful, supportive, and corrective intervention once control has been gained over the drinking.

## Psychotropic Drugs

Although controversial, the use of psychotropic drugs has a legitimate place among the treatment alternatives for alcohol problems and alcoholism. Much of the controversy over drug use stems from a distrust of the alcoholic's dependency problems. Again, considered from the motive or intention side, one remains apprehensive about the regressive-oral needs and inclinations of the alcoholic. In considering the problem from the ego side and the nature of the structural impairments, however, the use of psychoactive drugs becomes a logical alternative, if not a necessary one. In many cases it serves as an adjunct to other treatments, in other instances as a definitive treatment for target symptoms and identified psychopathology. This is again particularly true for older alcoholics, especially when dependency on alcohol and people have acted as the main mode of adaptation.

I can only specify briefly here the use of psychoactive drugs, but I have reviewed some of the more recent findings and experiences in more detail in a previous report (Khantzian 1980). Tricyclic antidepressants, and to some extent phenothiazines such as Thorazine and Mellaril, have proven useful, especially in those instances where depression becomes evident after detoxification. Lithium has also recently been shown to be effective in such cases. Quitkin and colleagues (1972) have identified a phobic/anxious state to be causative in a significant number of polydrug- and alcohol-dependent individuals. When treated with imipramine, both the phobia/anxiety and the substance abuse subside and resolve. In some instances, antianxiety agents (e.g., Librium, Serax, and Valium) have proven useful, but these latter drugs remain the most controversial because of their cross-tolerance with alcohol and the similarity to alcohol in their psychopharmacologic effect.[4]

## CONCLUSION

Alcoholic patients do not always accept or comply with treatment that is available or treatment that is recommended and, as Myerson correctly reminds us, continue to persist in destructive behavior. However, part of the problem in helping the alcoholic with his choice is that we as caregivers are victims of our own formulations and stereotypes about the nature of alcoholism and about which solutions are most appropriate. This is particularly true with substance-abuse problems. It is probably safe to say that all of the above-mentioned interventions are suitable and appropriate, but because of parochial attitudes, we have not yet been in a position to answer through clinical trials and investigation the more important question: What is suitable for what type of alcoholic at what point in the course of this most serious and devastating illness?

---

4. I have cited evidence in the introduction to Part II that in carefully selected cases a benzodiazepine might be employed (when all else fails) where severe anxiety or panic disorders co-occurs with substance use disorders. Most clinicians, however, including myself, would agree that a rapidly absorbed, short-acting benzodiazepine such as Valium and Xanax is contraindicated and places the individual at risk to relapse to alcohol.

## REFERENCES

Khantzian, E. J. (1978). The ego, the self and opiate addiction: theoretical and treatment considerations. *International Review of Psychoanalysis* 5:189–198.

—— (1980). The alcoholic patient: an overview and perspective. *American Journal of Psychotherapy* 34:4–19.

Kohut, H. (1971). *The Analysis of the Self*. New York: International Universities Press.

Krystal, H. (1978). Self representation and the capacity for self care. In *The Annual of Psychoanalysis* 6:209–247. New York: International Universities Press.

Krystal, H., and Raskin, H. A. (1970). *Drug Dependence. Aspects of Ego Functions*. Detroit: Wayne State University Press.

Murphy, G. E., and Robins, E. (1967). Social factors in suicide. *Journal of the American Medical Association* 199:503–308.

Myerson, D. (1978). As the alcoholic patients grows older. *Journal of Geriatric Psychiatry* 11:175–189.

Quitkin, F. M., Rifkin, A., Kaplan, J., and Klein, D. F. (1972). Phobic anxiety syndrome complicated by drug dependence and addiction. *Archives of General Psychiatry* 27:159–162.

# 19

# Self-Preservation and the Care of the Self

## *with John E. Mack*

We need not look beyond the past two decades to find ample evidence around us in society and our clinical work of threats to human survival and of self-destructiveness. Despite the fact that ego psychology and object relations theory have become part of the bedrock of psychoanalytic practice and theory, much of our understanding of survival and self-destructiveness continues to be influenced by Freud's early writings. The complex functions relating to self-preservation, self-protection, and survival are relatively neglected in contemporary psychoanalytic literature despite the special urgency of these matters for many of our patients. It is, in fact, surprising, in view of the current interest of mental health workers in disadvantaged individuals and families, for whom survival issues including basic protection from real dangers are conspicuous, that so little attention has been given in psychoanalytic theory to the psychology of self-preservation.

The influence of the early psychoanalytic literature is evident in reductionistic formulations that consider such problems as accident proneness, violent or impulsive behavior, weight disturbances, substance (drug and alcohol) abuse, and other forms of self-neglect in terms of explicit pleasure-seeking and/or unconscious self-destructive motives. Such formulations fail to consider adequately how these problems are just as often a result of deficiencies or failure in ego functions that serve to warn, guide, and protect individuals from hazardous or dangerous involvements and behavior.

This chapter advances a point of view that places greater emphasis on structural and developmental factors to account for certain forms of human self-destructiveness. We describe a complex set of functions that we have designated as "self-care." We believe that failures and impairments in the development of these functions better explain a range of troubled human behaviors. Although denial, conscious and unconscious self-destructiveness, psychological surrender, and other determinants can explain some human self-destructive behavior and impulsivity, we have been equally impressed that the personality structure and character pathology of certain individuals leave them vulnerable and susceptible to various dangers that result in personal injury, ill-health, physical deterioration, and death. We believe such people are often not so much compelled or driven in their behavior as they are impaired or deficient in self-care functions that are otherwise present in the more mature ego. Exploring the components and elements of the functions that constitute self-care not only has heuristic value for a better theoretical understanding of human development and adaptation, but is equally important for understanding and managing destructive behavior in clinical work, particularly in the treatment of impulse and behavior problems.

Self-care as a developed system of functions includes the following elements:

1. A libidinal investment in caring about or valuing oneself—sufficient positive self-esteem to feel oneself to be worth protecting
2. The capacity to anticipate dangerous situations and to respond to the cues that anxiety provides
3. The ability to control impulses and renounce pleasures whose consequences are harmful

4. Pleasure in mastering inevitable situations of risk, or in which dangers are appropriately measured
5. Knowledge about the outside world and oneself sufficient for survival in it
6. The ability to be sufficiently self-assertive or aggressive to protect oneself
7. Certain skills in object relationships, especially the ability to choose others who, ideally, will enhance one's protection, or at least will not jeopardize one's existence.

In this chapter *self*, as used in *self-care* and *self-preservation*, refers to the broader meaning of self pertaining to the entire person. Self-esteem and self-regard also are related to self-care. Unless otherwise specified, however, we are concerned primarily with understanding and explaining the structures and functions that serve the survival of the self or person as a total organism. We also distinguish self-care functions related to protection and survival from self-soothing activities that maintain subjective states of comfort and well-being.

## BACKGROUND

Before he evolved his structural theory of the mind, Freud attempted to encompass what we would now consider fundamental functions of the ego within his theory of instincts (Freud 1933a). Self-preservation, self-care, self-protection, and the like were originally grouped together by Freud as self-preservative or ego instincts. He referred to these as "instincts which serve the preservation of the individual" as opposed to "those which serve the survival of the species" (1913, p. 182). When Freud elaborated his views on narcissism, he regarded the ego instincts as the nonlibidinal aspect of narcissism. Ultimately, Freud rejected this distinction and viewed self-preservation as itself erotic in the narcissistic sense: "The instinct of self-preservation is certainly of an erotic kind, but it must nevertheless have an aggressiveness at its disposal if it is to fulfill its purpose" (1933b, p. 209). Thus we see Freud virtually to the end of his life seeking to conceptualize self-preservation within the framework of his instinct theory, even though in 1938 he finally said, "the ego ... has the task of self-preservation" (p. 145).

Notwithstanding Freud's final admonition that self-preservation was a task for the ego, subsequent psychoanalytic investigators have continued to stress instinctual factors to account for much of human behavior that is dangerous to the self. Works by Menninger (1938) and Tabachnick (1976) are representative examples that illustrate this continuing trend. Menninger believed that Freud's hypothesis of a death instinct could best account for the varied and manifold forms of human self-destructiveness, such as asceticism, martyrdom, invalidism, alcohol addiction, antisocial behavior, and psychosis. He considered such problems as forms of "chronic suicide" and accounted for these tendencies by human aggression turned on the self. Tabachnick came to similar though not identical conclusions in his studies of automobile accidents. He distinguished two types of victims in his study, one group (20 percent) in which the victims were depressed, and another group (80 percent) in which the victims were action oriented but not depressed. Although he identified different features and dynamics in these two groups, he concluded that a "death trend" was common to both groups as a result of tremendous rage and aggression turned on the self. Citing the work of Dunbar (1943) and Alexander (1949), who believe that action-oriented characters are involved in multiple accidents, Tabachnick suggests that a "death or self-punitive trend" might be involved in action orientation. However, Tabachnick concedes that the accident can be an unintended result of conflict in action-oriented characters. In our opinion, such formulations fail to consider sufficiently how the active pursuit of danger, bravado, fatalism, and action substitute for less well-developed, sustaining, stabilizing, and self-preservative functions. These compensatory character traits flourish in lieu of more stable self-care (ego) functions and processes that most often protect human beings from their own self-destructive inclinations.

The functions that are responsible for self-preservation, standing in opposition to self-destruction, have been ascribed to the life or ego instincts, and more generally to the ego. Although an adaptational, ego-psychological view subsumes self-preservation in human existence, there is little in the psychoanalytic literature that specifically identifies or explains the functions and mechanisms that are involved in assuring human survival and self-care.

In concluding remarks in his classic work on the ego and adaptation, Hartmann (1939) observed that although "emphasis on the ego apparatuses may delineate more precisely our conception of the 'self-preservative' drives . . . we have so far treated [them] like a stepchild"

(p. 107). His ideas about the role of the ego apparatus, the part it plays in general adaptation, and its specific role in survival remain central to our understanding of the capacity for self-care and self-protection. In a subsequent paper, Hartmann (1948) allowed that both sexual and aggressive drives contribute to the development of psychic function and ultimately serve purposes of self-preservation. He also stated that the reality, pleasure, and Nirvana principles and the repetition compulsion can under certain circumstances subserve self-protective functions. He concluded, "It is the functions of the ego, developed by learning and by maturation—the ego's aspect of regulating the relations with the environment and its organizing capacity in finding solutions, fitting the environmental situation and the psychic systems at the same time—which become of primary importance for self-preservation in man" (p. 84). It is surprising how little psychoanalysts has expanded upon or advanced Hartmann's thinking in delineating more specifically the component structures and functions that serve survival.

A review of the literature on self-preservation reveals that a number of psychoanalysts are aware of how little we know about its development and the importance of gaining a better understanding of this much neglected area of human adaptation. Glover (1933) appreciated how children early in their development both depended on external objects for self-preservation and also could experience real threat to their survival as a result of external dangers, injury, and aggression. Loewenstein (1949) stated bluntly, "The self-preservative instincts have hitherto been greatly neglected" (p. 388). He felt that the so called self-preservative instincts were not instincts at all (especially not connected with the death instinct), but that they must be seen in relation to the whole development of the ego. In commenting on Loewenstein's work, Zetzel (1949) underscored the importance of the survival instincts and the role of anxiety in relation to real external dangers. Rochlin (1965) states that "instincts of self-preservation" are present earlier than has been supposed and that small children manifest early concerns about death and self-preservation. Mahler (1968) observes, "The function of, and the equipment for, self-preservation is atrophied" in the human species (p. 9). Most modern-day psychoanalysts would agree with this observation, but little systematic attention has been given to how this function and this equipment develop and operate to protect the self from danger and harm. Recent theoretical and clinical work focusing on child development, narcissistic disturbances, affects, impulsivity, and substance abuse has helped, nevertheless, to illuminate how the capacity for self-preservation or self-care develops.

Winnicott (1953, 1960) and Mahler (1968) have stressed the importance of the quality and quantity of nurturance and care in the earliest phases of the mother–infant relationship. The ways in which this maternal care is administered has important implications for the development of self-care. The works of Winnicott and Mahler share an emphasis on optimal nurturance that avoids extremes of deprivation and indulgence and enhances the capacities of the ego to tolerate delay, frustration, and distress. As a result of this process the parent's nurturing and protective functions are incorporated into the child's ego capacities in the service of maintaining adequate self-esteem, ego defense mechanisms, and adaptation to reality. By implication the "good-enough mothering" (Winnicott 1960) and care obtained from the environment during preoedipal development contributes significantly to the individual's eventual capacity to take care of himself or herself.

Through the analysis of narcissistic transferences, Kohut (1971) reconstructed how failures in parental (particularly maternal) care leave certain individuals ill-equipped to maintain and regulate their self-regard and self-esteem because of impairments in ego-ideal formation. He stressed failure in maternal empathy and traumatic disappointments in idealized parental figures as central determinants in narcissistic disturbances. Among the consequences of such disturbances are (1) the external living out of a search for omnipotent, idealized objects that are admired or admiring for achieving a sense of well-being; and (2) the failure to transform through minute internalizations in the preoedipal developmental period various functions of the parents that ultimately contribute to the ego apparatus of the individual. Kohut only touches on the implications for self-preservation of such internalization processes, indicating that the analyst might have to "alert the patient's ego in the interest of self-preservation" (p. 158) to certain impending dangers. His emphasis, however, on the deficits in self-esteem and on failures of internalization in the formation of psychic structure is quite germane to our concept of how the capacity for self-preservation and self-care is acquired from parental figures, particularly from those aspects of parental care that have provided protection and vigilance as the developing and growing child explores his or her environment.

The works of Tolpin (1971) and Sandler and Sandler (1978) are germane to the concept of self-care in that they consider the part early object relations play in the development of psychic structure. They provide a basis for considering what constitute the precursors and components of the capacity for self-care. Tolpin focuses on the part that transmuting internalizations play as a means through which the infant may develop protective, caring, and anxiety-signaling functions. Sandler and Sandler stress how wish-fulfilling relationships with early objects become the basis for incorporating a sense of well-being and safety.

These reports converge to indicate that the various functions required for self-protection and self-care have their origins in the child–caregiver relationship as well as in maturational processes of both drives and ego. For this reason they are best studied from a developmental perspective.

## A DEVELOPMENTAL PERSPECTIVE

Freud (1916–17) clearly appreciated children's initial ignorance of danger and the parents' role in helping them to acquire a capacity to avoid harm:

> It would have been a very good thing if they [children] had inherited more of such life-preserving instincts, for that would have greatly facilitated the task of watching over them to prevent their running into one danger after another. The fact is that children . . . behave fearlessly because they are ignorant of dangers. They will run along the brink of the water, climb on to the window-sill, play with sharp objects and with fire—in short, do everything that is bound to damage them and to worry those in charge of them. When in the end realistic anxiety is awakened in them, that is wholly the result of education; for they cannot be allowed to make the instructive experience themselves. [p. 408]

Anna Freud's (1965) description of the developmental line from irresponsibility to responsibility in body management comes close to some of the processes that concern us in relation to self-care. She reminds us that the satisfaction of essential physical needs, such as feeding and elimination, are only gradually taken on by the child. According to Anna Freud, the slow assumption of responsibility for self-protection occurs in consecutive phases that involve, first, a shift in the expression of aggression away from the body (e.g., biting and scratching) and toward the external world, and second, an increasing orientation in the external world whereby cause and effect and the control of dangerous wishes are understood; these ego functions together with the narcissistic cathexis of the body "protect the child against such external dangers as water, fire, heights." But, she then observed, "There are many instances of children where—owing to a deficiency in any one of these ego functions—this advance is retarded so that they remain unusually vulnerable and exposed if not protected by the adult world" (p. 77). The third phase involves the child's voluntary endorsement of rules of hygiene and physical requirements—normally the latest acquisition (i.e., the latest functions acquired).

Once established, superego functions naturally play a part throughout one's life in protecting the self. In striving to do the right thing, follow the rules, and consistently obey internalized parental admonitions and prohibitions, one is less likely to encounter danger or harm. Too severe or rigid superego representations seem at times paradoxically to inspire dangerous risk-taking, as if the child were trying to escape the hold of a restrictive conscience by seemingly heedless activity. However, self-protection or preservation that relies too heavily on superego strictures is personally costly and likely to limit severely a variety of ego functions and satisfactions. The superego aspect of self-care needs to be distinguished from the complex combination of adaptive and self-caring ego activities, which are the primary focus of this chapter.

The capacity for self-care relates to the broader question of how infants and small children develop the capacity for self-regulation in general. Greenspan (1979) has identified three levels, or stages of learning, in the formation of psychic structures that subserve self-regulation. In the first stage, learning is largely somatic or imitative, dependent on the global fulfillment of body needs by the caregiver. In the second or contingent stage, beginning at 6 to 8 months, affective exchanges with the object become more organized; although imitative modes may still predominate, internalization through identification with elements of the interaction with the parent occurs. In the third phase, beginning at 14 to 18 months, representational learning and more complex affect management and self-regulatory behavior takes place.

Sifneos and colleagues (1977) hypothesize that psychosomatic disorders are related to developmental failures in self-regulation. It is possible that the inability of such patients to recognize and verbalize their feelings grows out of failures of self-regulation in the somatic or preverbal period. Along these lines, Krystal and Raskin (1970) and Krystal (1977) have identified developmental disturbances and traumatic regressed states in substance abusers, concentration camp survivors, and sufferers from psychosomatic illness that we believe are related to self-care disturbances. Such individuals are unable to identify or verbalize their feelings and use them as guiding signals. Similarly, they also suffer because of impairments in self-comfort, self-soothing, and ultimately self-care. Because of difficulties in including these basic life-maintaining and affective functions in their self-representation, they turn outside themselves for care and self-governance.

The complex functions of self-care and self-protection that we are considering take shape largely during the period of representational learning. Precursors of these functions begin to develop during the somatic and contingent stages. It is possible that older children and adults who have a good capacity for self-soothing or self-nurturing but poor ability for self-protection may have identified strongly with nurturant qualities of caregivers during the somatic and contingent periods, while failing later to internalize the more complex representations out of which caregiving and self-protection are structured.

Mahler's (1968) observation of toddlers are consistent with those of Anna Freud and highlight the early appearance of such vulnerability in certain children. Using the case of Jay, Mahler explores how the mother's failures in attending and remaining vigilant as the toddler physically separates from her and explores his environment result in the child's becoming oblivious to dangerous situations. Mahler describes Jay's inability to exercise restraint of his impulses and a recurrent tendency to invite danger as a result of disorientation in space, lags in reality testing, and a tendency to overlook obstacles in his path. Mahler traces some of the origins of Jay's incautious behavior to his mother who maintains a troublesome and bizarre distance and fails to protect Jay's body as he carelessly moves about. Jay obviously was precocious in his locomotor development and was therefore in even greater need of a mother functioning as an auxiliary ego to anticipate and protect him from harm.

We have had the unfortunate occasion to witness a case in which a similar combination of a child's advanced motor skills and aggressive exploratory behavior and the parents' lack of vigilance led to the child's death:

> Bill, an 18-month-old, very active, likable black child, was the son of a patient participating in a methadone maintenance program. He frequently attended his father's group therapy sessions because the baby's mother worked at a full-time position as a secretary. The parents were an attractive couple who cared deeply about each other, but the father.s long-standing addiction to opiates left him discouraged and brooding and his wife depleted.
>
> During the father's group sessions Bill would actively bolt around the large conference room in which the meetings were held. He was noted to pick up anything on the floor that appeared "mouthable," whether edible or otherwise, and put it in his mouth. He frequently stumbled, banging various parts of his body, usually his head. He seemed to sustain his bumps and bruises with impunity, cried rarely, and often appeared to be amused by the looks of shock and startle of the adults in the room. Unfortunately, his father usually was not one of those who was alarmed by and concerned about Bill's behavior and injuries.
>
> Around 10 o'clock one morning Bill was discovered to be cyanotic and apneic in his crib. He was rushed to the hospital and placed on artificial life-support systems. He succumbed ten days later. Subsequent to his admission the staff reconstructed that the child had gone to the refrigerator the previous evening and had drunk a mixture of fruit juice and methadone belonging to his father. Because of the gradual onset of action, Bill had played normally for a while and had then been put to bed by his mother. Unfortunately, neither parent realized that the child had ingested what for him was a lethal dose of narcotics.

In view of the many real dangers in the environment, it is a wonder that children do not more often suffer serious injury and death. That most children escape serious harm suggests how well most parents take care of them, as a result of which they may rather early acquire a capacity to anticipate and avoid danger. The works of Stechler and Kaplan (1980) and Virginia Demos (personal communication to John E. Mack) suggest that, beginning in infancy, a subtle balance exists between the parents' permission for the child to take initiative, to risk and explore, and the parents' protective function, which keeps the risks within reasonable bounds or creates for the child a self-protective representation.

Using videotapes, Demos has documented a range of responses of mothers to the exploratory initiatives of their children. Some mothers allow a rich exploration of the environment up to the point of danger and then set appropriate limits in a finely tuned pattern of interactions. Others show little interest in the child's undertaking and interact only minimally with the child. Gradually, through reciprocal interactions between the small child and his caregivers in the context of explorations of the outside world, the child acquires mental representations of danger, the capacity to anticipate harm, and the ability to renounce unduly risky sorts of gratification.

The acquisition of the capacity for self-care is promoted by intricate, often subtle, reciprocal communications between a child and his parents.

At the age of 22 months, Chris appeared to all who encountered him as a rather reckless, wild boy. He would carom from one piece of furniture to another, from one person to another, sometimes glancing up at his mother with devilish glee before heading off on a new, cyclone-like path. Taking a certain delight in the child's rambunctious, explorative nature, the mother would tolerate a great deal of such activity, but as tensions would mount she would after a while "just blow." When he reached the limits of her tolerance, or was in any danger of hurting himself or destroying property, she would make clear in unequivocal terms that "that was it." He was to stop and to go no further.

When he was older, Chris developed an interest in rock climbing and went on expeditions in which a group would scale precipitous cliffs. His father, a circumspect and thoughtful man, worried about these ventures. He did not stop Chris, but he insisted that there be adequate adult supervision, that Chris learn everything he could about mountain climbing, and that he use proper equipment at all times.

Chris's parents did not simply put a stop to his behavior or demand that he control his impulses. Each parent in her or his way took pleasure in the child's motor skills, his explorations of the world around him, and his mastery of new challenges. They clearly valued him and his efforts at self-development. But, recognizing the danger involved, they set clear limits, thereby conveying the message: we love you and deeply respect that you wish to express yourself and your aliveness and to learn about the world. But we want to protect you, and we do not want you to be hurt or to damage anything else, so we will limit the risks that you will be allowed to take. We wish to get across to you that we love and value you enough to protect you, that you are a being worth protecting.

There is clear evidence that Chris incorporated these messages, which became part of his self representation and ego functioning. He learned to master, first as a 2-year-old, and later in childhood and adolescence, the challenges he undertook. Chris was a boy who from early on liked to "do it my way." The thrust toward mastery, from which he derived satisfaction and considerable self-esteem enhancement, characterized Chris's functioning. Although he clearly was overcoming fears in relation to danger, his activities were not primarily defensive in their function.

We can see in Chris's case, and that of many children like him, that the function of self-care is intimately related to the development of self-esteem. The capacity for self-care grows in the context of a loving parent's communication that he or she values the child and therefore considers the child worth taking care of. The child incorporates this message and comes to value himself enough to protect himself from injury. A complex of functions—expressing pleasure in motor exploration, anticipating danger, setting limits upon oneself when danger is discerned, postponing or modifying the activity to make it safer and more secure—all these depend on valuing oneself enough to invest in self-caring. Small children and adolescents who, in contrast to Chris, take excessive risks and engage in dangerous rebellious behavior show an absence of self-care functioning. Such behavior may be indicative of pseudo-mastery. Exaggerated risk taking is accompanied by denial of fear, which is not mastered. In such instances the self as subject undervalues the self as object and permits undue risks to be taken. True mastery is associated, as in Chris's case, with relatively little self-destructive risk.

A distinction should also be made between self-care, in the sense of taking care of, looking after, or protecting oneself, and self-comforting or nurturing (Dr. Henry Krystal, personal communication). Many individuals are quite capable of soothing themselves, of being good to themselves with food, alcohol, music, or even hypochondriacal behavior. Such individuals may readily stay home from work with minor illnesses or make frequent trips to the doctor. But self-comforting activity of this sort may not be associated with a genuine capacity to look after oneself realistically or to guard against excessive risks and dangers.

Yet, even if a reasonably good capacity for self-care has been acquired, it is, like other ego capacities and functions, subject to erosion and regression, as the following case demonstrates.

Walter, a 12-year-old black boy, was, by his own admission, ordinarily conscientious and always tried to do what his parents wished. He had been admitted to the hospital after accidentally burning his legs while starting a power lawnmower. He described in some detail how he usually would carefully wipe off any residual gasoline and then pull the starter rope to the motor. On this occasion he somehow had neglected to do this. When he started the motor, it suddenly burst into flames. During his hospitalization the psychiatric liaison service was asked to see him because of his excitability and exaggerated sensitivity to pain. The two psychiatrists who saw him learned that there were two small children at home, a sister, aged 2, and a baby brother, a few months old. With a mixture of pride and irritation, Walter described how his parents looked to him as a big brother for assistance in taking care of his younger siblings. He also indicated that he had had his own room until he had been displaced from it by his baby brother. In the course of the evaluation Walter revealed that his usual attentiveness and caution with the mower had not been present because of anger, irritation, and preoccupation with his changed status in the family.

While Walter's immaturity in combination with specific conflicts and stresses led to what one hopes was a temporary lapse in self-protection, there are other cases in which the capacity for self-care develops unevenly.

A 28-year-old single, professional woman in analysis functioned in a highly capable fashion, handling the stressful and at times physically threatening requirements of her job with unusual intelligence and skill. Working in a field close to that of her highly competent father, she could look after herself most effectively. Since age 4 she had suffered from moderately severe attacks of asthma, which continued in her adult life. Her view of her capacity to handle the illness was unrealistic, and as a result she sometimes used poor judgment. On several occasions during the analysis she had permitted asthma attacks, for which there was a clearly effective medical regimen, to reach the point where breathing was severely compromised and her life threatened. The asthma had been heralded in childhood by a severe attack that brought the patient to the point of coma before its nature was discovered in the hospital. The asthma became the arena in which an anxious struggle occurred between the patient and her mother. Constantly fearful for her daughter's safety, the mother held her in an intimate bond, anxiously protecting her and conveying the message that true autonomy was threatening to the mother's survival. The patient failed to develop independent skills in self-care in relation to her health, relying on others to rescue her when asthmatic attacks reached crisis proportions. Sometimes she wistfully communicated longing for a "self-management company." The patient's parents also had failed to protect her as a small child from the violent assaults of her troubled older brother. As a consequence she was drawn to the religiously observing Roman Catholic family next door, who, in their elaborate system of rituals directed by an all-powerful God, seemed to have a way of providing protection from harm for small children.

Specific fantasies, growing out of disturbances in narcissistic development, may interfere with self-protection and self-care. Most important of these are wish-laden, grandiose ideas of protection that interfere with the capacity to guard oneself from danger. There may be the idea, for example, that no harm can befall one, that no matter what risks are taken, a powerful being will look after, protect, or come to the rescue. Often this fantasy is acted out dangerously in trying to rescue others. In these instances the "rescuee" represents the endangered self of the rescuer. The vulnerability and absence of self-care become manifest in the consequences that befall the rescuer, often at the hands of the rescuee, in the course of misguided though well-meaning rescue operations.

The study of children who are accident prone, injure themselves, and become involved in dangerous activities offers an opportunity to understand some of the predispositions and vulnerabilities that result in impairments in self-care. Such vulnerabilities in children also allow for comparisons with other children, such as Chris, who are not accident prone, and enable us to consider what forces compel accidents and self-injury. But even more important, they provide an opportunity to consider the psychological structures and functions that ordinarily stand in opposition to or protect against danger and harm. Several reports (Frankl 1963, 1965, Lewis et al. 1966, Pavenstedt 1967) provide vivid examples and vignettes of children and adolescents who suffer injuries and accidents. Although these reports shed light on important determinants that compel the dangerous activities and behavior of certain individuals, they consider only in passing, if at all, the factors that more usually protect against injury and accidents. As in the adult literature on accident proneness, these reports tend to place undue emphasis on drive theory and aggressive instincts, to the exclusion of other considerations (e.g., structural and maturational deficiencies), in accounting for self-injuries and destructive behavior.

Reviewing problems of self-preservation and accident proneness from a developmental perspective, Frankl (1963) presents many compelling accounts of accidents and injuries sustained by normal and disturbed children and adolescents. She seems to appreciate that among healthy children the caring and protective functions of the parents (or substitutes) are gradually taken over by the child in the course of normal development. The failure to take over these functions leaves the children more susceptible to harm and is the result of deprivation of object love and a lack of cathexis of the child's body. However, in her subsequent discussion and formulations, she repeatedly attributes accidents in childhood and adolescence to conflicts relating to impulsivity, superego representations, and (unfused or defused) aggressive instincts turned on the self. Her observations are graphic and clear, but suggest alternative mechanisms and interpretations. She presents, for example, the case of Eric, who was 14 years old when he put his eye out with a dart by pulling on a string that he had attached to the dart as a means of retrieving it. Frankl interprets this unfortunate accident as the result of the boy's turning aggressive feelings against himself. She supports this interpretation with Eric's own admission that the self-injury was a form of attack on the parents aimed at disappointing and hurting them and making the prospects of success in school less likely. Most striking in Eric's case and Frankl's other cases is the absence of elements of caution, worry, anticipation, or other self-protective measures.

In a study exploring the determining factors involved in accidental ingestion of poisons by children, Lewis and colleagues (1966) evaluated developmental factors and family influences in fourteen children (seven boys and seven girls ranging in age from 14 to 43 months). These children were compared with a control group, for whom it was assumed that the availability of poison and the ability to explore the environment were the same. The most important factors in the accidental ingestion were the child's developmental characteristics (e.g., motor skills, exploratory and imitative behavior, degree of negativism) and the quality of the mother–child relationship at the time of the accident. The latter in particular involved the way the mother organized the family environment, which in this study appeared to have been seriously disrupted within a year before the poisoning event in the majority of the cases. Two factors loomed large as disorganizing influences on the families of the children: (1) a recent birth or death of a sibling, and (2) a loss of adult support for the mother. In this study, spatial or physical elements in the environment invited an accidental ingestion by children who displayed high exploratory activity and superior motor skills, but poor impulse control. These factors combined with a "maternal depletion" that was present in all the cases in which the ingestions occurred. The depletion state consisted of a relative exhaustion of the mother's psychic or emotional resources as a result of inadequate support or a sudden decrease in assistance from other adults upon whom she depended, most usually the husband or the mother's mother.

Lewis and associates' (1966) observations and conclusion underscore the importance of the mother's caring and protective functions in preventing dangerous behavior in children. Their work has implications for understanding how lapses in the early mother–child relationship and maturational lapses contribute to later vulnerabilities in self-care. The authors suggest that most children do not ingest poison because, in the usual closeness of the mother–child relationship, the child senses and anticipates the mother's disapproval of a dangerous act and responds to her guidance to avoid danger. In contrast, when the mother suffers from depletion states as a result of loss or stress, she is less attuned to the child and the positive bond of care and mutual attachment is disrupted. The child is then guided more by the wish to satisfy his own explorative curiosity and/or negativistic pleasure than by the pleasure of pleasing mother. The authors stress that the timing for the establishment of such function as motor skills, impulse delay, anticipation, and reality sense, all of which require some degree of inner guidance, varies from child to child. We would add that the establishment of these and related functions early in life is crucial for assuring ego capacities for self-preservation and self-care later on.

Studies of children from extremely disrupted environments, such as urban slums or poorly run orphanages, provide dramatic evidence of how experiences from such backgrounds can seriously warp, distort, and impair survival skills at an early age. Using a nursery school as a socializing and therapeutic setting, Pavenstedt (1967) and associates observed the disabilities of a group of children who came from disorganized, lower-class families in an urban slum of Boston. In particular, their findings about the children's motor activities and appearance vividly demonstrate what we have referred to as impairments and deficits in self-care. The children "seemed to lack any self-protective measures, being careless with the use of their bodies and seemingly not trying to prevent injuries . . . [and] accidents and injuries were usually not accompanied by expressions of appropriate affect" (p. 57). A general lack of body care, heedlessness, and absence of caution were evident as they "carelessly careened around the room stumbling and bumping into things, tipping over chairs or toys and falling off the climber" (p. 140). The authors stress that such behavior was even more significant in view of these children's otherwise good to advanced motor skills. They poignantly describe how the teachers actively had to intercede and substitute their own protectiveness and caution to avoid injury. But through repeated intervention, instruction, and growing attachment to the teachers, the children seemed to exercise growing caution and to learn to request assistance. Strikingly, the authors also observed reversion and regression to incautious behavior as a consequence of parental separation, harsh punishments, or parental criticism.

Frankl (1963) describes similar findings in children from residential nurseries who had suffered discontinuities in early mothering and subsequent relative deprivation of object love and unsatisfactory care. She indicates that there was a much higher incidence of accidents in children who received unsatisfactory residential care. She contrasts these with children raised in nurseries where they felt greatly valued and appreciated by the staff and where accidents were unheard of or could not be recollected. Frankl invokes the mechanism of aggression turned on the self to explain the injuries sustained by the children who suffered discontinuities in object love and care.

Those who try to explain the behavior of children from extreme environments often fail to distinguish between self-neglect and self-hatred. In fact, Anna Freud (1965) makes this distinction when she differentiates maturational defects from "turning aggression on the self" (p. 76), the latter being a defense mechanism adopted by the ego in conflict situations. Although aggression may play a part in self-destructiveness and accidents in children, we believe that there is more involved than aggression turned on the self or a self-punishment motive. It is likely that aggression in these cases brings about ego disorganization, which in turn causes the individual to become less able to exercise the judgment, control, synthesis, reality testing, and related functions that otherwise assure adequate self-care and protection.

We conclude this section by presenting an example of normal children at play in whom elements of self-care were evident at a relatively early age. The play situation provided a glimpse of one child's appropriate fearfulness and inhibition of impulsive action in the face of what surely constitutes a most common challenge to self-protective aims.

> Three children, aged 6, 9, and 10, were happily running around in a backyard. The two older children decided to climb a tree in which there was a makeshift platform treehouse about 12 feet high. They appeared to do this with skill and ease. A noticeable change in the lighthearted tone of the play could be observed at the point when the older boys began to challenge the younger boy on the ground below to join them. As the boys' challenges escalated to taunts and teasing, the younger boy at first became unhappy and tense, then more obviously fearful, and he then began to cry. Despite the two boys' continued derision, the younger boy refused to join them. Notwithstanding the obvious intense pressure of his playmates and his own shame about his inability to keep up with them, he seemed to respond more to his own fear and apparent awareness that he did not possess his playmates' strength, coordination, and skill to climb the tree.

Our observations of this realistically fearful boy, as well as the cases we cited where such fear was absent, indicate that the functions for self-care and self-protection begin to develop early in life and may operate (or be deficient) in young children. The capacity for self-care is complex and involves multiple affective and cognitive processes; component functions; mechanisms of defense; ego functions such as signal anxiety, reality testing judgment, control, delay, and synthesis; as well as relatively stable superego functions. Cognitively, self-care involves a capacity to perceive, realistically assess, integrate, and attend to relevant cues in the environment. Affects are used as a guide for appropriate action, or as signals to institute defense mechanisms or avoid potentially harmful or dangerous situations. Gradually, in the context of experienced parental protectiveness, the child assumes the process of self-protection and care and incorporates those family and societal rules that help to ensure his safety. When present, these functions operate automatically or deliberately to guide us away from danger or, once in trouble, to guide us out of difficulty. It is the collective action and interaction of these cognitive and affective processes that we refer to as the ego function or capacity for self-care.

Self-care functions become internalized through the ministrations of the caring and protection of parents. In the earliest phases of development self-care begins with incorporative processes in which the nurturing role of the mother contributes to a rudimentary sense of harmony and security (Meissner 1979). In subsequent periods internalization of the caring and protective qualities of the parents occurs as the child, under their watchful eyes, encounters and explores the environment. If the parents' attendance to and care of the child are good, the developing child acquires a capacity to care for himself or herself and to protect against and anticipate harm and danger.

## CONCLUSIONS

We have reviewed a number of reports that document and interpret a range of human problems involving self-injury and harm, including impulsivity and accidents in children. Most of these accounts lay heavy emphasis on drive theory and a motivational psychology that places aggressive drives at the heart of most forms of human self-destructiveness. We have considered the functions that ordinarily stand in opposition to these destructive trends and how normal self-care and self-protection develop.

As with most human functions and reactions, problems of survival and self-destructiveness are multiply determined. Much of human destructiveness, including the self-directed form, may be compelled, defensive, or specifically motivated. In seeking to identify and understand impairments in survival skills and self-care, we have stressed a developmental perspective focused on how early nurturing attitudes and the caring and protective functions of parents, particularly the mother, are internalized and transformed into positive attitudes of self-regard and adequate structures and functions assuring self-care and self-protection.

We have shown that self-care capacities are closely associated with positive self-esteem, for the developing child must internalize the conviction that he is a being of value and that he is worth protecting before he can care for himself. We have noted the disjunction that sometimes occurs between self-soothing or self-nurturing and the full capacity for self-protection or self-care, suggesting that the former function may grow out of earlier, more somatically based experience, while the latter depends on more highly structured representational learning.

This chapter can only be considered preliminary in attempting to explain the complex relationships among self-regard, self-care, and human self-destructiveness. Although self-care functions are fundamental for survival, they build upon an earlier sense of well-being and harmony within the self. It is most likely from such early subjective states that we derive a sense of optimism and aliveness. When this rudimentary sense is lacking or violated, despair and feelings of deadness may later result (Friedman 1980, Kohut and Wolf 1978).

In the developmental model we have presented, self-preservation is contingent upon the establishment of particular structures and ego functions. Furthermore, self-destructiveness results as much from lapses and failures in self-care and protective functions as it is specifically motivated, overdetermined, or driven. Further reports and explorations in this area must ultimately consider self-care functions in dynamic interaction with other operative factors. We have only touched upon how basic attitudes about the self, starting with beginning self-awareness and self-experiences, are crucial for making one feel that the self, and ultimately existence, is worth preserving. We need to understand further how early failures in the development of a cohesive sense of self and the resultant search for self-comfort and self-worth become so overriding that matters of self-care and survival often remain tragically subordinate, secondary, and underdeveloped. We also need to consider how anger, rage, depression, aggression, or other affect states erode or interfere with established self-care functions. We need to explore especially how conditions of depletion, anergia, and inertia associated with intense affective states may cause a lapse or regression in self-care. Further study is needed, for example, of the extent to which self-care functions become relatively immutable and autonomous once established, or, in contrast, may under particular circumstances that burden or threaten the ego become temporarily or permanently lost.

## REFERENCES

Alexander, F. (1949). The accident prone individual. *Public Health Report* 64:357–361.

Dunbar, F. (1943). *Psychosomatic Diagnosis*. New York: Hoeber.

Frankl, L. (1963). Self-preservation and the development of accident proneness in children and adolescents. *Psychoanalytic Study of the Child* 18:464–483. New York: International Universities Press.

——— (1965). Susceptibility to accidents. *British Journal of Medical Psychology* 38:289–297.

Freud, A. (1965). Normality and pathology in childhood. In *The Writings of Anna Freud*, vol. 6. New York: International Universities Press.

Freud, S. (1913). The claims of psychoanalysis to scientific interest. *Standard Edition* 13:165–190.

——— (1916–17). Introductory lectures on psychoanalysis. *Standard Edition* 16:243–476.

——— (1933a). New introductory lectures on psychoanalysis. *Standard Edition* 22:5–182.

——— (1933b). Why war? *Standard Edition* 22:197–215.

——— (1938). An outline of psychoanalysis. *Standard Edition* 23:144–207.

Friedman, L. (1980). Kohut: a book review essay. *Psychoanalytic Quarterly* 49:393–422.

Glover, E. (1933). The relation of perversion-formation to the development of reality sense. *International Journal of Psycho-Analysis* 14:486–504.

Greenspan, S. I. (1979). *Intelligence and Adaptation*. New York: International Universities Press.

Hartmann, H. (1939). *Ego Psychology and the Problem of Adaptation*. New York: International Universities Press, 1958.

——— (1948). Comments on the psychoanalytic theory of instinctual drives. In *Essays on Ego Psychology*, pp. 69–89. New York: International Universities Press, 1964.

Kohut, H. (1971). *The Analysis of the Self.* New York: International Universities Press.

Kohut, H., and Wolf, E. S. (1978). The disorders of the self and their treatment. *International Journal of Psycho-Analysis* 59:413–425.

Krystal, H. (1977). Self representation and the capacity for self care. *Annual of Psychoanalysis* 6:209–246.

Krystal, H., and Raskin, H. A. (1970). *Drug Dependence.* Detroit: Wayne State Universities Press.

Lewis, M., Solnit, A. J., Stark, M. H., et al. (1966). An exploration study of accidental ingestion of poison in young children. *Journal of the American Academy of Child Psychiatry* 5:255–271.

Loewenstein, R. M. (1949). The vital or somatic instincts. *International Journal of Psycho-Analysis* 21:377–400.

Mahler, M. S. (1968). *On Human Symbiosis and the Vicissitudes of Individuation.* New York: International Universities Press.

Meissner, W. W. (1979). Internalization and object relations. *Journal of the American Psychoanalytic Association* 27:345–360.

Menninger, K. A. (1938). *Man Against Himself.* New York: Harcourt, Brace.

Pavenstedt, E., ed. (1967). *The Drifters.* Boston: Little, Brown.

Rochlin, G. (1965). *Griefs and Discontents.* Boston: Little, Brown.

Sandler, J., and Sandler, A. M. (1978). On the development of object relationships and affects. *International Journal of Psycho-Analysis* 59:285–296.

Sifneos, P., Apfel-Savitz, R., and Frankl, F. (1977). The phenomenon of "alexethymia." *Psychotherapy and Psychosomatics* 28:47–57.

Stechler, G., and Kaplan, S. (1980). The development of the self. *Psychoanalytic Study of the Child* 35:85–105. New Haven, CT: Yale University Press.

Tabachnick, N. (1976). Death trend and adaptation. *Journal of the American Academy of Psychoanalysis* 41:49–62.

Tolpin, M. (1971). On the beginnings of a cohesive self. *Psychoanalytic Study of the Child* 26:316–352. New Haven, CT: Yale University Press.

Winnicott, D. W. (1953). Transitional objects and transitional phenomena. *International Journal of Psycho-Analysis* 34:89–97.

——— (1960). Ego distortions in terms of true and false self. In *The Maturation Process and the Facilitating Environment,* pp. 140–152. New York: International Universities Press, 1965.

Zetzel, E. R. (1949). Anxiety and the capacity to bear it. *International Journal of Psycho-Analysis* 30:1–12.

# 20

# Alcoholism: The Challenge of Conceptualization and Consensus[1]

When I started regularly seeing alcoholics in my practice, it was at a time when there were few psychiatrists and fewer psychoanalysts seeing such patients. There was a prevailing attitude then that it was not a good idea for alcoholics to seek help from psychiatrists and psychoanalysts, and, indeed, that it could even be hazardous to their health and recovery. Things have improved since then, but residual if not frank skepticism persists about the relevance of psychiatry and

---

1. Presented at the Joint Meeting of the American Medical Society on Alcoholism and Other Drug Dependencies and the Research Society on Alcoholism Symposium on The Definition of Alcoholism: Why No Consensus? San Francisco, CA, April 20, 1986.

psychoanalysis to alcoholism problems. Some of this skepticism was and still is justified in that the traditions of the symptom approach and the search for psychological etiologies have failed to take into account how the psychophysiological effects of alcohol confound the methods used by psychiatry and psychoanalysis. Worse still, these methods often fail to appreciate and adequately respond to the emergent and life-threatening nature of the alcoholism.

Notwithstanding these previous and lingering pitfalls of psychiatry and psychoanalysis, I propose that the indifference, skepticism, and antipathy toward these disciplines by many workers in the alcoholism field are symptoms themselves of a more pervasive problem in our attempts to define and understand alcoholism. I say "our attempts" because I believe that the most comprehensive and useful understanding of alcoholism will come from a model that integrates the findings of scientists, investigators, and clinicians from our varying disciplines and perspectives.

The assignment for this forum is to consider why we have no consensus on a definition of alcoholism. I do not believe our problem of consensus is in fact a result of problems with definition. Whether we adopt the *DSM-III*, the National Council on Alcoholism (NCA), or the World Health Organization (WHO) definition of alcoholism, most of us are, I think, satisfied with a definition or criteria that address the central issue, namely, that alcoholism is a condition that involves a frequency, amount, and pattern of alcohol consumption sufficient to result in damaging physical, psychological, social, legal, or employment consequences for the individual. I believe our greater problem in achieving consensus has to do with our conceptualizations of alcoholism. All of us depend on concepts to tackle complex problems, and alcoholism is no exception. Our concepts influence the methods, instruments, and techniques we employ, and they yield information unique to that approach. As much as our concepts and related approaches can be facilitating and illuminating, they can also limit and set us apart, and I believe it is in this respect that we have trouble in achieving consensus with each other on our views of alcoholism.

My understanding of alcoholism is necessarily influenced by concepts inherent to psychiatry and psychoanalysis. Unfortunately, attitudes and beliefs about psychiatry and psychoanalysis often conjure up negative images, in part because early and outdated formulations of the mind, derived from psychoanalysis, laid undue emphasis on an instinct psychology, which stressed pleasure seeking and/or self-destruction, and reduced most aspects of life, in health and disease (including alcoholism), to these "base" or basic motives. Psychoanalysis, it appears, has practiced poor public relations. However, we analysts have come a long way since that early time in how we view our patients (including our alcoholic patients) and how we apply our tools on their behalf. Rather than seeing people doomed to hopeless and perverse forms of suffering as a consequence of psychic conflict over pleasure and death instincts, most of us now enjoy the benefit of a more optimistic view of people as individuals seeking a way out from suffering through transformations and growth of the self. I would add that we can also view and understand alcoholic suffering with the benefit of this more hopeful perspective.

This chapter briefly presents a psychodynamic perspective of alcoholism that focuses less on the unflattering and unredeeming views of human mental life and suffering, and more on the nature of the human problems of and potentials for regulating emotions, self-regard, and behavior, and how these capacities and their impairments might relate to alcoholism. I then consider how such a conceptualization might relate to difficulties, opportunities, and challenges for reaching a consensus with others who adopt different conceptualizations of alcoholism.

## THE CLINICAL CONTEXT—A PSYCHODYNAMIC PERSPECTIVE

Until recently, attempts to document coexistent psychiatric findings in alcoholic patients have been muddled by the absence of standardized criteria for the presence of emotional disorders and/or alcoholism, and by the failure to distinguish between primary and secondary illness in relation to each other when these two conditions co-occur. Some of these problems have been worked out better with the other addictions (Khantzian and Treece 1979, 1985, Rounsaville et al. 1982a,b), and only recently have a few studies appeared teasing out these issues for alcoholism. Most of these studies have indicated a coexistence of depression, personality disorder (usually antisocial personality), and, to a lesser extent, anxiety-panic disorders. Recent studies of alcoholics suggest that to a much greater extent than previously believed, depressive and antisocial symptoms are secondary to and a consequence of the alcoholism (Schuckit 1985, 1986). Nevertheless, these findings wait on replication studies, and, performed on special treatment populations, they also defy generalizations at this time. What is still needed are more studies of representative and community samples of alcoholics. It is little wonder then that until recently the incidence of depression among different studies has ranged between 3 and 98 percent (Khantzian 1982). In my opinion, this demonstrates that we cannot yet conclude what psychiatric factors, if any, are involved in the development of alcoholism. However, it is likely that we can learn a lot more about the controversy by defining our populations and better studying representative samples.

In taking a psychodynamic perspective, some of this controversy can be sidestepped in the cause-and-effect debate about psychiatric symptoms in alcoholism. Diagnostic studies provide point-in-time indications of mental suffering. A psychodynamic perspective, on the other hand, provides an understanding of the capacities and vulnerabilities in psychological structure and functions that can explain over time why states of mind and behavior endure or change. Applied to alcoholism, this perspective provides opportunities to examine and understand how psychological structure and function interact with acute and chronic effects of alcohol, and how they are also employed or modified in the process of recovery.

Based on certain concepts and constructs, the psychodynamic paradigm provides a means to organize and explain the complexities of psychological life and behavior. It also provides a way to understand impairments in psychological structure and function that lead to dysfunctional living, including the dysfunctional living associated with alcohol. Considered in this way, alcoholism may be viewed as an expression of an attempt to cure certain disabilities in self-regulation. What it is that has to be regulated, and what the functions and processes are that regulate are the domain of psychoanalytic study. It rests on the assumption that working with individuals in an ongoing treatment (i.e., psychotherapeutic) relationship is a legitimate and special source of data. The approach provides valuable information for understanding the individual and his or her treatment needs. It also yields valuable hypothesis on the nature of human suffering, including that entailed in alcoholic suffering, which may be tested and validated with aggregate samples or populations of patients.

It is within this frame of reference that I have applied psychodynamic concepts to my alcoholic patients as a means to understand, hypothesize about, and treat them. I should clarify that this usually occurs under conditions of control over and stability in their alcohol use, and most usually involves abstinence. In this context my alcoholic patients have taught me how problems with recognizing and tolerating feelings, subjectively evaluating themselves in relation to other people, and in controlling or failing to control their behavior have combined in troublesome ways to make the use of alcohol malignantly compelling. Witnessing my patients' struggles with their emotions and their self-regard and what they do and have done with these struggles suggests to me that they have either been cheated in their development or have lost, as a consequence of trauma, some of the essential psychological equipment necessary for survival and for adjustment to their internal psychological life and external reality.

Interestingly, the diagnostic findings in this respect are reassuring. The types of depression and/or anxiety when present are of the milder types (e.g., dysthymic disorder) and problems with major psychoses and affective disorders are rarely involved. Although alcoholics have problems with psychological pain and suffering and related behavioral difficulties, the evidence suggests that they are relatively free of major disruptive psychiatric disabilities, and thus they are able to employ actual and potential psychological strength in their recovery.[2]

Applying these same concepts to the recovery process, I believe treatments that are successful, whether they are in a psychotherapeutic or self-help context, work because they effectively address, appreciate, and manage fundamental problems with self-regulation. Good psychotherapy as well as Alcoholics Anonymous (AA) recognize that the survival issues and the healing process involved with this illness require structure and needs for safety, comfort, and control, especially early in treatment. Subsequently, both psychotherapy and AA can provide opportunities to understand how alcoholics' "defects in character" (i.e., as borrowed from AA and not neces-

---

2. Based on work over the past decade with dually diagnosed patients, this assertion is no longer valid. There *is* a major association between alcoholism and major mental illness.

sarily from psychoanalysis) and related injuries to the sense of self have evolved out of troublesome and hurtful experiences that have accrued from the past. Viewed in this way, alcoholics' attempts to relieve and perpetuate their suffering through alcoholic and related behaviors may then be understood in the course of treatment as an attempt to repeat old problems in new forms until they get it right.

In adopting this approach, I try to pursue and understand to the fullest extent possible how psychological factors predispose to and perpetuate a reliance on alcohol and how these factors may play a part in relapse. This is not to suppose that these factors are involved to the exclusion of other factors. Rather, my interest and emphasis leads me to explore in each case that I see how and to what extent they are involved and to then consider how they relate to other influences. It is at this juncture that tensions can arise between my point of view and that of others, and why we so often quibble or fight over definitions, concepts, and theories, and fail to reach consensus.

## THE PROBLEM AND CHALLENGE OF CONSENSUS

There are competing ideas in the field of alcoholism and some impediments that stand in the way of consensus, but these problems can be resolved. In my opinion one of the big pitfalls has to do with what happens when we work with ideas applied to life problems. When we come on new and successful concepts that yield new information and useful applications, our success can also have negative consequences. We form groups and meet and share together the advantages of the new way of looking at things, often at the expense of considering alternative explanations and approaches. This happens in all fields of study, and medicine is no exception. For example, the introduction, at the turn of the twentieth century, of psychoanalysis as a theory and a treatment of the mind was revolutionary in more effectively explaining and resolving aspects of psychological life and behavior that were, up until then, bewildering. One of the unfortunate consequences of this success was the development of a sense of exclusivity and elitism and an insistence on reducing all mental life to certain principles that the new paradigm dictated.

I think it can be argued that the same has happened in the field of alcoholism if we smugly insist on what is cause and what is effect. For example, the disease concept has proven that much of the suffering of alcoholism can be relieved by "keeping it simple" and structuring abstinence. This is an important strategy for treatment that is well proven to be effective. However, that definition or concept alone becomes antithetical to understanding and discovering in useful ways the complexities of what else alcoholism is and what can be done about it.

At best we form groups to share and advance ideas, and thus they empower and strengthen us in convictions. However, in so doing, we can also be at risk of developing too strong a sense of being right and others being wrong. Margaret Bean-Bayog (1981) has likened the plight of recovering alcoholics to that of Holocaust survivors and thus suggests that they need to be treated by professionals and each other with much respect for the short- and long-term consequences of their trauma. Holocaust survivors and their offspring often form groups to treat and study their injuries. Interestingly, their suffering often causes them to form either exclusive groups that set them apart or, in contrast, to form more inclusive groups to understand and share their experiences with others who have also suffered. Given that so much of the good work in alcoholism treatment is being done by recovering people, we all need to be careful of a risk that this entails: namely, it can lead to a belief that only those who experienced this disease can understand this suffering, rather than that understanding suffering is an experience that none of us escapes.

Many of us working in the study and treatment of alcoholism are not recovering individuals, but neither this fact nor the concepts we employ should automatically arouse suspicion that we do not understand as professionals or as people the suffering of alcoholics. By the nature of our calling, health care professionals cannot avoid the issue of suffering in their work. Orientation and approach, however, is different for each of us. A lot of this is determined by temperament, which dictates a particular kind of patience with or preference for certain modes of investigation and understanding. Thus, explaining things in terms of hard biological facts is preferred by some of us; for others, reducing things to simple pragmatic concepts is preferable. My own preference and comfort lie with the clinical-narrative modes, and thus I work in the tradition of clinical, psychodynamic psychiatry. (I rarely use slides, graphs, or numbers to make my point. I respect and even envy those who can and do.) These alternative ways can be and often are at odds with each other but they need not be. If Donovan (1986) is correct, and I believe he is, in recently advancing an etiological model of alcoholism that is multidimensional, then we actually need the different temperaments, experiences, and backgrounds that lead us to adopt the different concepts and approaches that yield different kinds of data. The challenge then is not to figure out whose concepts and related data are better or correct, but rather to consider how different concepts and their related findings complement rather than contradict each other. We must respect that our concepts lead us to utilize different instruments that yield different perspectives on the problem of alcoholism. Consensus and enrichment of our understanding of alcoholism, then, will derive from integrating our multiple perspectives and experiences. This is the challenge of the future for all of us.

## REFERENCES

Bean-Bayog, M. H. (1981). Denial and the psychological complications of alcoholism. In *Dynamic Approaches to the Understanding and Treatment of Alcoholism*, ed. M. H. Bean and N. E. Zinberg, pp. 55–96. New York: Free Press.

Donovan, J. M. (1986). An etiological model of alcoholism. *American Journal of Psychiatry* 143:1–11.

Khantzian, E. J. (1982). Psychopathology, psychodynamics and alcoholism. In *The American Encyclopedia Handbook of Alcoholism*, ed. E. M. Pattison and E. Kaufman, pp. 581–597. New York: Gardner.

Khantzian, E. J., and Treece, C. (1979). Heroin addiction-the diagnostic dilemma for psychiatry. In *Psychiatric Factors of Drug Abuse*, ed. R. W. Pickens and L. L. Heston, pp. 21–45. New York: Grune & Stratton.

——— (1985). *DSM-III* psychiatric diagnosis of narcotic addicts: recent findings. *Archives of General Psychiatry* 42:1067–1071.

Rounsaville, B. J., Weissman, M. M., Crits-Cristoph, K., et al. (1982a). Diagnosis and symptoms of depression in opiate addicts: course and relationship to treatment outcome. *Archives of General Psychiatry* 39:151–156.

Rounsaville, B. J., Weissman, M. M., Kleber, H., and Wilber, C. (1982b). Heterogeneity of psychiatric diagnosis in treated opiate addicts. *Archives of General Psychiatry* 39:161–166.

Schuckit, M. A. (1985). The clinical implications of primary diagnostic groups among alcoholics. *Archives of General Psychiatry* 42:1043–1049.

——— (1986). Genetic and clinical implications of alcoholism and affective disorders. *American Journal of Psychiatry* 143:140–147.

# 21

# The Cause–Consequence Controversy in Alcoholic and Addictive Suffering

All of us depend on concepts to understand and respond to complex problems. Alcoholism and addiction certainly are no exception, and, in fact, concepts and theories have abounded to explain this maddeningly elusive and tragic problem in our society. But we have not achieved a consensus on what the various concepts and the approaches that grow out of the concepts teach us. Despite all of our disclaimers that alcoholism/addiction is no one thing and that it has multiple determinants, we almost invariably, if not necessarily, fall prey to considering our own formulations, concepts, and data to the exclusion of other perspectives. Nowhere is this more evident than in the controversy over whether psychological or psychiatric dysfunction is a cause or consequence of substance abuse.

Unfortunately, the cause–consequence debate mirrors and recapitulates old controversies in the philosophy of science in which polemics over nature–nurture, psyche–soma, and environment–heredity dominate. These polemics are counterproductive and reflect linear and reductionistic reasoning. Findings from genetic, neuropsychological, longitudinal, and diagnostic studies are cited to suggest that the effects of chronic and heavy drug/alcohol use produce the psychopathology associated with substance dependence. These arguments are bolstered by observations of alcoholics and addicts who respond favorably to Alcoholics Anonymous/Narcotics Anonymous and experience marked amelioration of their psychological suffering when they abstain from alcohol and drugs.

This chapter explores, from a clinical and psychodynamic perspective, how the complexities of human suffering associated with substance abuse cannot be reduced to simplistic either-or conclusions about whether alcoholism and addiction are a result or cause of that suffering. I focus on how the "normality" of substance abusers is deceptive and how their disabling problems with affect recognition/tolerance and qualities of their self-other relations produce a special relationship with suffering that they seek to relieve at the same time they perpetuate it.

We encounter problems and trade-offs when we adopt approaches that are categorical (e.g., genetic, longitudinal, and diagnostic) rather than those that focus on process and functions (i.e., clinical and psychodynamic approaches). Reviewing the findings of the various perspectives reveals that the cause–consequence debate is not so easily resolved, but that a clinical and psychodynamic perspective provides a basis to understand, integrate, and reconcile some of the findings that at times are contradictions but more often can be seen as complementary and resolvable.

I begin with a case vignette to demonstrate how our patients often instruct us best in understanding the basis and nature of their suffering and disorder(s), and how their responses to what we offer and they offer themselves teach us about their susceptibility and their capacities for recovery.

## A CASE VIGNETTE

"I feel sorry for people who have never been addicts." Thus spoke a Narcotics Anonymous (NA) member, as related by a patient in a psychotherapy group for substance abusers. This occurred in a session that was extraordinary in at least two respects. First, one of the patients reviewed in an extremely compelling manner how intensely painful, out of control, and confusing his feelings were, especially those about his private therapist. Second, the other six members sustained their attention, support, and devotion to this patient's distress, which was noteworthy given the penchant of many of the individuals in this group to be restless and avoidant.

The patient at the time was anticipating the one-week absence of his private therapist. He literally sobbed through a description of how attached he had become to the therapist and what an unreal and bewildering experience it was to have such feelings. He described how out of control he had been after a recent visit to the therapist when he could not leave the therapist's office, had locked himself in the office bathroom for a half hour, punched a hole in the bathroom wall, left abruptly, provoked a near-violent confrontation in traffic, and subsequently had to be physically restrained by his father to prevent further escalation. The patient talked about feeling all alone and how his parents wanted to help but they had never seemed to know how. He told the group of the many fist holes that had accumulated in the walls of his bedroom through his teen years, most of them covered by posters but known to his parents, which they essentially ignored because neither parent seemed to know how to respond. He stressed this quality in his family life, from which he had learned to be self-sufficient and hyperindependent. He referred to a recent family therapy session in which his parents were almost totally unresponsive as he discussed how violent and isolated he felt. He reviewed as well how totally unaware his parents were of his heavy, five-year involvement with cocaine and alcohol until two years before, when his deterioration and a near-fatal drug involvement shared with his disturbed sister finally precipitated a crisis and drew their attention. With the help of a brief exposure to Narcotics Anonymous and beginning individual and group psychotherapy, he had managed to totally abstain from drugs and alcohol, but during this same time he began to, and continued to, experience a persistent gloomy and very angry depression. Despite his negativity and pessimism—he refused to depend on Alcoholics Anonymous (AA) or NA, and he often missed group for weeks at a time—his qualities of extreme intelligence, honesty, intensity, interest in other group members, and flashes of humor (albeit grim) earned him a place in the group as a special person.

In this particular session the efforts of the group leader focused on distinguishing between feelings, acting on feelings, and the need to learn how to bear them and do everything possible to maintain controls, especially for the patient who was suffering so much, to preserve and not injure his relationship with his therapist. It was impressive to observe the sensitive way in which the other patients sustained their appreciation of his emotional turmoil and his loneliness and how they persistently expressed to him their concern about the need for controls and the importance of reaching out to and accepting help from them and other people. One patient predictably suggested he go to NA meetings. He misunderstood this to mean he needed the spirituality and a higher power, and characteristically he resisted this suggestion, protesting his disbelief, and he managed to evoke a sympathetic response from another patient who was similarly skeptical of AA and NA. The patient who suggested attending meetings quietly offered his conviction that meetings had as much to do with understanding feelings and emotions as they did sobriety, and that it occurred through the fellowship with other people. Another patient, a woman who had suffered as much for her sanity and sobriety, offered that what they called sobriety in NA and AA, other people called life. More than anything else in this session, it was impressive to see how unintimidated and undaunted the others had been by his anger or his extreme suffering. By the end of the session he was visibly sad. He thought about the alarm and concern he had aroused, but said, "At least I feel something and I'm less out of contact." As the group neared the end of the session, the leader commented on how well the group had stayed with each others' distress and how well they had conveyed the hope and belief that human connection and contact, such as had occurred in the group and in AA/NA meetings, could substitute for drug connections, especially when feelings seem so unbearable. It was at this juncture that the patient who proposed meetings for the member who was in such distress quietly and movingly concluded with his quotation from NA about feeling sorry for people who have never been addicts.

I think the quotation addresses both the vulnerability and strength in this disorder. I will subsequently try to explain what I think he meant as a patient, and I am discovering as a clinician, about the meaning and function of alcoholic and addictive suffering.

## SUFFERING AND SUBSTANCE DEPENDENCE

### General

Alcoholics and addicts are different from other people. Yet, very knowledgeable people cannot agree on what is different about them. In this chapter I explore from a clinical and psychodynamic perspective my view of what is different and special about them, especially in the way they suffer as a cause and consequence of their substance dependence. I relate my point of view to other points of view and consider why there is so little consensus and so much controversy over the different perspectives, and what can be done about reaching consensus. The controversy and lack of consensus is important because it profoundly influences the way we understand and treat our patients.

The success of the disease concept of alcoholism and recent diagnostic and longitudinal studies have legitimately bolstered arguments that much of the psychopathology associated with alcoholism is the result of chronic alcohol use rather than the cause of it. That is, with the help of AA and NA, many patients and clinicians discover how much emotional suffering abates as one abstains from drugs and alcohol. A number of recent studies show little or no causal association between psychopathology (including childhood, developmental influences) and alcoholism. However, this is not always the case. Many substance abusers who achieve abstinence do not feel better, and some studies do suggest a significant etiological link between psychopathology and alcoholism, and the diagnostic literature on drug addiction indicates an even stronger etiological relationship between the two.

In this section I sample material from the genetic-behavioral and psychodiagnostic perspective and compare them to a clinical perspective with a psychoanalytic orientation. In my opinion, despite some significant, lingering inconsistencies, there is much that can be seen as complementary rather than competing. The issue is not whether substance dependence is a cause or consequence of psychopathology, but how we can begin to integrate the findings of the various perspectives and clarify the complex interrelationships between psychopathology and substance dependence.

## The Genetic Perspective

Proponents of genetics as the main etiological factor in the development of alcoholism make the strongest arguments that the psychopathology associated with alcoholism is a consequence of chronic and heavy alcohol use. There is incontrovertible evidence that heredity exercises a significant influence in the predisposition for alcoholism. What the role of the genetic factor is in the case of drug addiction is less clear. Family, twin, and adoptive studies have established an impressive case for the role of inheritance in the development of alcoholism (Cotton 1979, Goodwin 1979, Schuckit 1981), yet, as Donovan (1986) has suggested, the inherited vulnerability is "significant [but] modest," and in the case of women the role of inheritance is much less clear. What is inherited and how much it influences and interacts with other factors is rightfully still debated and subject to further clarification. For example, studies by Frances and associates (1980), Cloninger and collaborators (1981), and Cadoret and associates (1985) have begun to tease out how other variables such as family drinking patterns, coexistent behavioral problems, and quality of the childhood environment interact with hereditary factors.

The evidence for genetic influences in alcoholism has resulted in a search for biological markers through which the genetic vulnerability might be expressed and predispose to alcoholism. For example, Schuckit (1985b) has recently compared high-risk subjects (HRSs) for alcoholism (i.e., strong family alcoholism history) with low-risk subjects for alcoholism (i.e., negative family alcoholism history) and demonstrated in HRSs a decreased intensity of response to alcohol, including less subjective intoxication after drinking, less induced body sway, less decrement in performance on cognitive and psychomotor tests, and less hormonal changes. He speculates that a major problem for HRSs is that they experience less of an ethanol effect with blood alcohol levels at which most people decide to stop drinking. He has also reviewed the evidence for other markers to support the genetic influence in HRSs, including differences in evoked brain potentials, electroencephalogram (EEG) alpha wave deficiencies, and elevated acetaldehyde levels.

Taking a somewhat different track, Tarter and colleagues (1984, 1985) have extensively reviewed the evidence, much of it based on their own work, that the genetic factors involved in alcoholism primarily exercise their effect through behavior and temperament, and, as a result of differences in these factors, individuals are predisposed to behaviors and reactions that become tied up with excessive alcohol use and alcoholism. They conclude that alcoholics and pre-alcoholics are principally different in temperament in respect to activity level (high), attention span (deficient), soothability (unable), emotionality (labile), reaction to food (extreme), and sociability (disinhibited and nonconforming). The authors link many of these qualities in temperament to the hereditary factors and biological mechanisms invoked by Schuckit. They also correspond to the problems of impulsivity, lack of emotional control, attention deficit, and learning disabilities associated with attention deficit disorder, which Wender and associates (Wender et al. 1981, Wood et al. 1983) have linked genetically and etiologically to alcoholism and substance abuse.

In reviewing the literature on genetic factors in the susceptibility for alcoholism and addiction, it remains impressive how clear and strong a case is made for a genetic model of inheritance when even its strongest proponents concede genetic studies "are still in their infancy" (Schuckit 1985b, p. 2617). It is even more impressive in these studies to see how little consideration is given to how genetic factors may interact with other factors. The genetic studies place emphasis on neurobiological mechanisms that link genetic predisposition to behavior. Although these studies use the language of psychological traits, learning theory, and behavioral psychology, they are totally consistent with contemporary psychoanalytic observations that stress vulnerabilities leading to distortions and disabilities in affect experience, self-esteem, relationships, and behavior. However, where the literature describing temperament and behavior is global and categorical, psychodynamic descriptions place greater emphasis on subjective experiences and a greater degree of specificity on how the vulnerabilities interrelate in a person's life and interact with the effects of substances. For example, when Schuckit suggests that alcoholics feel the effects of alcohol less intensely than low-risk subjects, he could well be describing an aspect of the more global deficits in feeling responses that have been described by Krystal (1982), McDougall (1984), and others (Nemiah 1977, Sifneos et al. 1977), and that have been derived from a psychodynamic perspective. Similarly, when Tarter and associates (1985) speak of "impaired stimulus input modulation" as a prealcoholic vulnerability, it comes very close to what has been referred to as the "deficit in affect defense" (Wurmser 1974) and the "defective stimulus barrier" (Krystal and Raskin 1970) of addicts, vulnerabilities described in psychodynamic terms that implicate early trauma and developmental disturbances.

## The Psychodiagnostic Perspective

Our ability to reliably diagnose psychopathology associated with substance dependence, and our ability to distinguish between primary and secondary illness between these two disorders when they co-occur, has appreciably improved over the past ten years. Actually, more diagnostic studies have appeared on drug dependence than alcoholism, but the situation has also begun to improve with alcoholism as well. These gains have been made mainly as a result of improvements in methodology and diagnostic instruments that have better addressed sampling problems, the requirements for standardized diagnostic criteria, and distinguishing between primary and secondary disorders in relation to each other. Although there are some remarkable consistencies in diagnostic findings between studies and across the specific substance dependencies (i.e., alcoholism, narcotic addiction, and cocainism), some significant disparities and inconsistencies between studies continue to appear and remain unexplained. For example, although we have come a long way since the 1970s when a review of the literature (Keeler et al. 1979) revealed the incidence of depression in various studies of alcoholism ranged between 3 and 98 percent, thus making comparisons or inferences meaningless, it is interesting still to compare and ponder the meaning/significance of two careful studies of alcoholic patients that showed significant differences between them in the co-occurrence of primary (major) depression, namely less than 2 percent in a study reported by Schuckit (1985a) versus 32 percent (and 52 percent among the women) in a study reported by Hesselbrock and colleagues (1985).

Although psychodiagnostic studies with alcoholics and cocaine addicts have only recently begun to appear, and notwithstanding inconsistencies, the findings have in general been remarkably similar to the diagnostic studies with narcotic addicts. There has been a significant co-occurrence of depression, personality disorder, coexistent alcohol dependence among addicts, and coexistent drug dependence in alcoholics, and the incidence of primary disorders and other *DSM-III* axis I diagnoses have otherwise been remarkably low, with the exception of phobic and panic disorders, which have been found to be significant in a few studies (Hesselbrock et al. 1985, Rounsaville et al. 1982b, Weiss and Mirin 1986).

A group of related diagnostic studies of narcotic addicts funded by the National Institute on Drug Abuse revealed a significant and similar incidence of depression, personality disorder, and alcoholism (Khantzian and Treece 1985, Rounsaville et al. 1982b, Woody et al. 1979). As part of that study, our Cambridge group (Khantzian and Treece 1985) documented that 93 percent of the subjects met the criteria for either axis I or axis II diagnoses, that 49 percent had diagnoses on both axes, and only 7 percent of the subjects failed to meet criteria for either axis I or II. Just under half the sample were depressed at interview (two-thirds reported a lifetime history of affective disorder), and two-thirds were diagnosed to have a personality disorder, usually antisocial personality (ASP) disorder but not limited to ASP disorder. These findings were very similar to the Yale–New Haven and the University of Pennsylvania–VA studies (Rounsaville et al. 1982b, Woody et al. 1979). Although these investigators were cautious in making a causal link to the narcotic dependence, a number of the reports suggested that unbearable, dysphoric feelings were related to both the opiate use and the coexistent personality disorder (Rounsaville et al. 1982a,b). It is impressive that the few published studies on cocaine addicts utilizing standardized instruments (Gawin and Kleber 1984, Weiss and Mirin 1986) have also revealed that 50 percent of the studied samples were depressed, and in one of these studies 90 percent of the sample received a diagnosis of borderline or narcissistic personality disorder (Weiss and Mirin 1986). Although comparisons with alcoholism studies are difficult to make because they are still few in number, the findings with narcotic and cocaine addicts are not too dissimilar, to the psychopathology documented, for example, in a study of 321 hospitalized alcoholics by Hesselbrock and colleagues (1985) in which there was a 49 percent incidence of ASP for the men (20 percent for women; 41 percent overall), 43 percent substance abuse, and an overall lifetime prevalence for depression of 38 percent (in 41 percent of the men and 65 percent of the women, alcohol abuse was secondary to major depressive disorder).

As with the case of genetic studies, despite recent advances, the diagnostic findings should be interpreted cautiously given that we still await replication studies and studies of even more representative populations, and, despite qualitative improvements in methodology, these reports include less than a dozen in number documenting an association between psychopathology and substance dependence. Furthermore, my review of the diagnostic reports has skirted other findings that measure dysphoria and dysthymia (which are highly changeable) in association with substance abuse. This literature (Khantzian 1982a) indicated that dysphoria and dysthymia are documented to be consistently present and elevated in association with active phases of alcoholism and addiction, but approach normal levels during abstinence. However, the persistence of more immutable findings such as major affective and personality disorders and characteristic personality traits and profiles (Khantzian 1982a) suggests we need to continue to study and understand the nature of the human suffering that the diagnostic studies reflect and how the suffering might interact with genetic and cultural factors to cause a dependency on drugs and alcohol.

## The Longitudinal Perspective

The prospective, longitudinal studies of alcoholism by Vaillant (1983) shed a unique and important perspective on the issue of cause-and-effect relationships between psychopathology, suffering, and substance use. Vaillant's findings and conclusions are at variance with recent psychodiagnostic and psychodynamic findings in that he concludes that childhood environmental factors and premorbid psychopathology are relatively unimportant as causes of alcoholism. However, Vaillant's documentation of the natural history of alcoholism provides persuasive evidence for the enormous psychological and physical damage, and thus the human suffering, that results from chronic and heavy alcohol use. More central to this thesis, Vaillant's long-term follow-up of the college and core-city sample of subjects (numbering over 600 students over forty years) suggests that alcoholism is correlated more with genes and culture than it is with "orality" and an unhappy childhood. In one of his reports he concludes that once alcohol abuse develops it becomes a disabling disorder affecting all facets of adult development; he states he would not deny the importance of psychopathology in the genesis of alcoholism but would instead emphasize the importance of alcoholism in the genesis of psychopathology (Vaillant 1980).

Vaillant's findings are reassuring because he documents the absence of crippling environmental and developmental damage associated with the development of alcoholism and the hopeful reality that most of the disabling, overt psychological suffering that results from chronic alcohol use is reversible when alcoholics attain sobriety. However, as Donovan (1986) has recently suggested, large-scale studies of alcoholic etiology, even when impeccably designed and executed, as is the case with Vaillant's study, reveal their limitation in their strength, namely that such studies realistically have difficulty coding environmental and personality factors. I would add that such studies are also unable to identify and track subtle variables of early development (especially from infancy), quality of personal relationships, developing sense of self, and the relationship between affect experience and behavior, factors and qualities that a psychoanalytic perspective can better delineate and that could complement and strengthen a longitudinal perspective. Donovan has argued persuasively for an etiological model of alcoholism that would build on a longitudinal and psychodynamic perspective that integrates hereditary, psychostructural, and environmental variables.

## The Psychodynamic Perspective

As previously reviewed in this book, early psychodynamic formulations stressed the unconscious meaning of drugs and aggressive and pleasurable instincts, and on this basis addicts and alcoholics were considered to be self-destructive and oral, concepts that most clinicians find highly speculative and embarrassingly unuseful. Modern psychodynamic formulations have focused on more observable structural impairments that have affected a person's feeling life, the sense of self, the quality of personal relationships, and capacities for self-care.

Central to my thesis in this chapter is how addicts and alcoholics are different in the way they experience their feeling life. However, before elaborating on these feeling problems, I would like to briefly summarize from a psychodynamic perspective how problems with need satisfaction and self-care are part of substance abusers' susceptibility to drug/alcohol dependence and impinge on feelings of self-worth and problems with dependency.

A sense of self-worth derives from the comforting, valuing, and valued aspects of early parenting relationships. When optimal, individuals can comfort or soothe themselves or reach out and depend on others for comfort and validation (Khantzian 1978, 1982b). When developmental deficits and impairments occur in relation to such needs, one sees extreme and contradictory patterns around needs and wants, qualities not uncommon in substance abusers. These problems often attach themselves and painfully play themselves out in the family, personal relationships, and career issues. They also play themselves out powerfully in certain attitudes incorporated into one's personality organization such as excessive self-sufficiency, disavowal of needs, bravado, and counterdependency, all of which make human contact more difficult and drug/alcohol use more likely (Khantzian 1978, Khantzian and Mack 1983).

We have previously reviewed in detail problems with self-care. They develop out of a failure to adequately internalize self-protective survival functions that are established in early phases of development. Self-care problems such as accidents and preventable medical, legal, and financial difficulties in which there is a persistent inability to worry about, anticipate, or consider consequences of action or inaction are evident in histories predating substance abuse. These qualities are flagrantly evident in relation to drug/alcohol use and the associated involvement and activities. Characterologic telltales of this vulnerability are evident in substance abusers' counterphobia, hyperactivity, impulsivity, aggressiveness, and denial of danger (Khantzian 1978, Khantzian and Mack 1983) (see Chapters 2 and 19).

As I suggested, problems with affect defense have been placed at the heart of substance dependence problems (Khantzian 1985). Reports have stressed developmental failures in which substances have been adopted to protect against overwhelming, painful affect as a consequence of structural impairments and a defect in affect defense (Khantzian 1978, Wurmser 1974). Individuals differentially medicate themselves with various classes of drugs to compensate for and to counter intense and threatening affects associated with the defects and distortions in affect defense. However, this is only part of the story. More recently I have tried to address the paradoxical reality that as much as substance abusers attempt to reverse their suffering and distress, and often succeed, they just as much produce suffering as a consequence of their involvement with substances. This is as true for narcotic addicts as it is for alcoholics and cocaine addicts, despite the fact that opiates are a more forgiving drug in this respect (McLellan et al. 1979). I have tried to consider whether there might be a dynamic relationship between the relief of suffering, the production of suffering, the attachment to substances, and other psychodynamic factors. An extensive review of such a dynamic would go beyond the scope of this chapter. Briefly, my clinical experience with patients and what they tell me, and a review of the contemporary psychodynamic literature on affect development, infant research, and repetition suggest that much of addicts' experience of affects is painful, not only because feelings are intense and overwhelming, but also because feelings are just as often absent, confusing, and without words. This quality has been referred to by such terms as *alexithymia, disaffected, affect deficit, hypophoria,* and *non-feeling responses* (Khantzian 1987, Krystal 1982, McDougall 1984). Despite or because of the deficits and distortions around affects, these patients are notorious for superficially seeming normal and free of distress, thus causing McDougall (1984) to term such patients "normopaths" or "pseudonormal."

Based on some of these clinical observations and theoretical developments I have begun to consider a modification of the self-medication hypothesis. Although addicts try to relieve their suffering, more than anything I believe they try to control their suffering. As many alcoholics and addicts have suggested to me, they suffer with their feelings because very often they do not recognize, understand, or control them, but when they take drugs they counter this state of affairs or these feelings because they produce a condition that over time they come to recognize, understand, and control, even if the effects and aftereffects are unpleasant and painful. That is, they often choose to substitute a dysphoria they invent and control in place of a dysphoria that is elusive and that they do not control (Khantzian and Wilson 1993). Perhaps from a psychodynamic perspective this sheds further light on why the issue of psychological suffering cannot simply be reduced to and explained as a cause or a consequence of a substance dependence. But there may be a link psychodynamically between the predisposing and resulting suffering associated with addictive and alcoholic illness.

## DISCUSSION AND CONCLUSION

I began the chapter with a clinical vignette that typifies how substance abusers can suffer because of an inability to regulate feelings and

behavior. It also demonstrates how effectively psychotherapeutic interventions, including AA and NA, can appropriately respond to needs
for regulation of feelings and behavior and ultimately personal survival. I have been impressed with how important it is to address the
human contact issue because the problems with recognizing, managing, and expressing feelings pervade so much of a person's life, cause
so much suffering, and threaten more than anything else to disrupt
and destroy vitally needed relationships. The development of this illness occurs in the context of relationships (albeit often troubled and
troubling), and recovery occurs in a context of caring relationships.
Studying people's responses to treatment is as useful as diagnostic
studies in explaining determinants of addictive illness. Individual and
group treatment and experiences in AA and NA suggest that beyond
establishing abstinence and control, effective treatment, as the case
vignette suggests, provides human contact, which encourages story
telling, recognizing and sharing of feelings, imparting wisdom, containing emotions and behavior, and teaching self-care.

The perspectives of genetics, neuropsychology, psychodiagnostics,
and longitudinal and psychodynamic studies seem at times far removed from the personal and painful realities of drug dependence and
alcoholism. Yet each perspective has an advantage in describing certain features and etiological determinants of substance dependence.
Each also has its limitations. I have tried to sample findings from the
best studies representing the different perspectives. The inconsistencies that my review documents do not necessarily mean contradiction
or negation of competing perspectives. They probably reflect the fact
that some perspectives are better suited for describing and explaining some aspects of substance dependence but are limited in other
respects.

I believe the psychodynamic perspective is valuable because it provides a basis to explain better some of the subjective and experiential
aspects of the meaning and function of substances in a person's life.
It explains some of the more immutable qualities and dysfunctions that
characterize addicts and alcoholics and provides a basis for understanding that individuals are trying to work out and solve human
problems in coping.

Suffering is an inevitable and unavoidable aspect of life, and it
would appear alcoholics and addicts suffer with diagnosable psychiatric conditions that may predispose them to rely on drugs. In other

respects they are not so easily labeled, but their problems with suffering are more discernible in individual and group treatment situations in which their relationship problems become evident in the ways they connect or do not connect to their feelings, in how they do or do not depend on and relate to others, and in the way they succeed or fail in caring for themselves. The quality and intensity of treatment relationships amplify the origins and meanings of their problems, and treatment relationships are a legitimate source of data.

Although our capacity to study addictive and alcoholic illness is enhanced by reducing problems to categories and concepts, these devices are also the basis on which we set ourselves apart from each other and fail to reach consensus. What we need to respect is that the approaches that derive from concepts are enabling and empowering and help us form our convictions. Few of us are dispassionate about our convictions. Our orientation to problems and the concepts we employ are also influenced by temperament. In this respect we prefer to work with different modes of investigation and understanding and thus adopt different perspectives. These differences can enrich our understanding as we need to pursue the different perspectives in order to refine them. However, we need to work better in the margins and borders of our respective disciplines in order to work out what makes alcoholics and addicts different genetically, developmentally, diagnostically, and dynamically, and to understand why they choose solutions that both relieve and perpetuate their suffering.

## REFERENCES

Cadoret, R. J., O'Gorman, T. W., Troughton, E., and Haywood, E. (1985). Alcoholism and antisocial personality: interrelationships, genetic and environmental factors. *Archives of General Psychiatry* 42:161–167.

Cloninger, C. R., Bohman, M., and Sigvardsson, S. (1981). Inheritance of alcohol abuse. *Archives of General Psychiatry* 38:861–868.

Cotton, N. S. (1979). The familial incidence of alcoholism: a review. *Journal of Studies on Alcohol* 40:89–116.

Donovan, J. M. (1986). An etiologic model of alcoholism. *American Journal of Psychiatry* 143:1–11.

Frances, R. J., Timm, S., and Bucky, S. (1980). Studies of familial and nonfamilial alcoholism. *Archives of General Psychiatry* 37:564–566.

Gawin, F. H., and Kleber, H. D. (1984). Cocaine abuse treatment. *Archives of General Psychiatry* 41:903–908.

Goodwin, D. W. (1979). Alcoholism and heredity: a review and hypothesis. *Archives of General Psychiatry* 36:57–61.

Hesselbrock, M. N., Meyer, R. E., and Keener, J. J. (1985). Psychopathology in hospitalized alcoholics. *Archives of General Psychiatry* 42:1050–1055.

Keeler, M. H., Taylor, C. I., and Miller, W. C. (1979). Are all recently detoxified alcoholics depressed? *American Journal of Psychiatry* 136:586–588.

Khantzian, E. J. (1978). The ego, the self and opiate addiction: theoretical and treatment considerations. *International Review of Psychoanalysis* 5:189–198.

——— (1982a). Psychopathology, psychodynamics and alcoholism. In *The American Encyclopedic Handbook of Alcoholism*, ed. E. M. Pattison and E. Kaufman, pp. 581–597. New York: Gardner.

——— (1982b). Psychological (structural) vulnerabilities and the specific appeal of narcotics. *Annals of the New York Academy of Sciences* 398:24–32.

——— (1985). The self-medication hypothesis of addictive disorders: focus on heroin and cocaine dependence. *American Journal of Psychiatry* 142:1259–1264.

Khantzian, E. J., and Mack, J. E. (1983). Self-preservation and the care of the self—ego instincts reconsidered. *Psychoanalytic Study of the Child* 38:209–232. New Haven, CT: Yale University Press.

Khantzian, E. J., and Treece, C. (1985). DSM-III psychiatric diagnosis of narcotic addicts: recent findings. *Archives of General Psychiatry* 42:1067–1071.

Khantzian, E. J., and Wilson, A. (1993). Substance abuse, repetition and the nature of addictive suffering. In *Hierarchical Conceptions in Psychoanalysis*, ed. A. Wilson and J. E. Gedo, pp. 263–283. New York: Guilford.

Krystal, H. (1982). Alexithymia and the effectiveness of psychoanalytic treatment. *International Journal of Psychoanalytic Psychotherapy* 9:353–378.

Krystal, H., and Raskin, H. A. (1970). *Drug Dependence. Aspects of Ego Functions*. Detroit: Wayne State University Press.

McDougall, J. (1984). The "disaffected" patient: reflection on affect pathology. *Psychoanalytic Quarterly* 53:386–409.

McLellan, A. T., Woody, G. E., and O'Brien, C. P. (1979). Development of psychiatric illness in drug abusers. *New England Journal of Medicine* 201:1310–1314.

Nemiah, J. C. (1977). Alexithymia: theoretical considerations. *Psychotherapy Psychosomatics* 28:199–207.

Rounsaville, B. J., Weissman, M. M., Crits-Cristoph, K., et al. (1982a). Diagnosis and symptoms of depression in opiate addicts: course and relationship to treatment outcome. *Archives of General Psychiatry* 39:151–156.

Rounsaville, B. J., Weissman, M. M., Kleber, H., and Wilber, C. (1982b). Heterogeneity of psychiatric diagnosis in treated opiate addicts. *Archives of General Psychiatry* 39:161–166.

Schuckit, M. A. (1981). Twin studies on substance abuse: an overview. In *Twin Research: 3 Epidemiological and Clinical Studies*, ed. L. Gedda, P. Parisi, and W. Nance. New York: Liss.

—— (1985a). The clinical implications of primary diagnostic groups among alcoholics. *Archives of General Psychiatry* 42:1043–1049.

—— (1985b). Genetics and the risk for alcoholism. *Journal of the American Medical Association* 254:2614–2617.

Sifneos, P., Apfel-Savitz, R., and Frankl, F. (1977). The phenomenon of "alexithymia." *Psychotherapy Psychosomatics* 28:47–57.

Tarter, R. E., Alterman, A. I., and Edwards, K. L. (1984). Alcoholic denial: a biopsychological interpretation. *Journal of Studies on Alcohol* 45:214–218.

—— (1985). Vulnerability to alcoholism in men: a behavior-genetic perspective. *Journal of Studies on Alcohol* 46:329–356.

Vaillant, G. E. (1980). Natural history of male psychological health, VIII: Antecedents of alcoholism and "orality." *American Journal of Psychiatry* 137:181–186.

—— (1983). *The Natural History of Alcoholism*. Cambridge; MA: Harvard University Press.

Weiss, R. D., and Mirin, S. M. (1986). Subtypes of cocaine abusers. *Psychiatric Clinics of North America* 9:491–501.

Wender, P. H., Reimherr, F. W., and Wood, D. R. (1981). Attention deficit in adults. *Archives of General Psychiatry* 38:449–456.

Wood, D. R., Wender, P. H., and Reimherr, F. W. (1983). The prevalence of attention deficit disorder, residual type or minimal brain dysfunction in a population of male alcoholic patients. *American Journal of Psychiatry* 140:95–98.

Woody, G. E., O'Brien, C. P., and McLellen, T. A. (1979). Depression in narcotic addicts: possible causes and treatment. In *Psychiatric Factors in Drug Abuse*, ed. R. W. Pickens and L. L. Heston, pp. 105–124. New York: Grune & Stratton.

Wurmser, L. (1974). Psychoanalytic considerations of the etiology of compulsive drug use. *Journal of the American Psychoanalytic Association* 22:820–843.

# 22

# Cocaine Addiction: Is There a Psychological Predisposition?

## *with Nancy Jo Khantzian*

The answer to the question raised in the title of this chapter has important theoretical and clinical implications. To paraphrase Albert Einstein, our theories help us to identify the facts. Our theories also help us in organizing our observations about complex problems. Clearly cocaine addiction is one such complex problem that begs for understanding. Furthermore, if there are psychological factors that predispose a person to cocaine dependence, it would be useful and important to identify such factors and to apply suitable interventions and/or treatment to modify them, and thus eliminate the causative factors that make cocaine use compelling.

Clinical work with addicts, including cocaine addicts, suggests that there are significant psychological factors that predispose individuals to depend heavily on drugs (i.e., we are not referring to recreational or intermittent drug use). Our perspective is based on the experiences of psychoanalysts and psychiatrists and clinical investigators who have worked extensively with drug-dependent individuals over the past twenty years. A psychoanalytic and psychiatric perspective of these patients has provided a means to identify the nature of the psychological vulnerabilities and psychiatric disorders that have been associated with their drug dependency.

One might quickly argue, as I have reviewed in the previous two chapters, that the psychological vulnerabilities and psychiatric disturbances associated with addiction are as much the result of drug use as the cause of it. We have no quarrel with this argument and agree that any addictive involvement entails serious psychopathology as a consequence of the addiction. However, in this chapter we show that there are general and specific predispositions to use and become dependent on cocaine. The psychoanalytic and psychiatric literature and clinical experience support the likelihood that people who become dependent on drugs have a psychological predisposition to do so. Many of the previous chapters have described the general basis for this predisposition. For the purposes of this chapter, we will elaborate on the nature of this predisposition and cite evidence that this holds true for cocaine dependence.

## COCAINE DEPENDENCE—CLINICAL OBSERVATIONS

### General Findings

With some important exceptions, there are few reports of psychiatric evaluations or clinical descriptions of cocaine addicts to guide a practitioner in treating such problems. Most reports of cocaine use emphasize the euphorogenic properties of the drug to explain its appeal (Siegel 1977, Wesson and Smith 1977). In contrast and based on careful clinical evaluation, a number of investigators have identified certain clinical features and characteristics of stimulant abusers that suggest alternative explanations for the specific action and appeal of amphetamines and cocaine. For some, the energizing properties of these drugs are more compelling because they help to overcome fatigue and depletion states associated with depression and dysthymia (Khantzian 1975). In other cases the use of stimulants leads to increased feelings of assertiveness, self-esteem, and frustration tolerances, and the elimination of feelings of boredom and emptiness (Wurmser 1974). Certain individuals use cocaine and other stimulants to "augment a hyperactive, restless lifestyle and an exaggerated need for self-sufficiency" (Khantzian 1979, p. 101). The findings of Spotts and Shontz (1977), who extensively studied the psychosocial characteristics of nine representative cocaine addicts, are largely consistent with these clinical descriptions.

Still lacking are clinical studies of representative samples of cocaine-dependent individuals, using standardized diagnostic criteria, and the application and evaluation of treatment approaches based on careful assessment and understanding of the problem.

As we have repeatedly emphasized in this volume, deficits in self-care functioning create a vulnerability in those who become addicted to drugs. Such individuals lack the self-protective warning system that normally guards against such dangers as those involved with drug use. Addicts' further inadequacies in handling human problems of intense, painful affects lead them to drug use in an attempt to treat themselves for what ails them. Experimentation with different drugs eventually results in addicts' self-selection and preference for the particular drug whose properties best fulfill their unique needs. Cocaine addicts are no exception.

## Recent Findings

In addition to the general problems of affect regulation and self-care problems, our clinical experiences with cocaine-dependent individuals have suggested a number of possibilities more specifically to explain how psychological/psychiatric factors might predispose an individual to become and remain dependent on cocaine. These factors include the following:

1. Preexistent chronic depression (dysthymic disorder)
2. Cocaine abstinence depression
3. Hyperactive/restless/emotional lability syndrome or attention deficit disorder
4. Cyclothymic or bipolar illness

As we have indicated, there is evidence to suggest that the stimulant effects of cocaine counteract depletion and energy problems associated with depression. We have evaluated and treated numerous patients who had long-standing histories of depression, predating their cocaine and other drug use. By current standards, most of them would satisfy the *DSM-III* criteria for the diagnosis of dysthymic disorder. Many of these patients described a mixed, anxious depression in which chronic self-doubt, apprehension, anergia, and initial insomnia were prominent. In taking a careful drug history, these patients stressed how the energizing properties of the cocaine helped them to overcome their anergia, become mobilized, perform tasks, and relate better to others (i.e., short-term), with the result that there was temporary improvement in their self-esteem. A number of these patients also emphasized how this mobilizing action of cocaine paradoxically had a calming effect.

With other patients we have been impressed that the "crash" or depression for which they were treating themselves with cocaine had evolved and was mainly the result of the heavy cocaine use itself, and that it was the principal factor maintaining their reliance on cocaine. These patients described an acute, disabling depression that had all the features of a major affective disorder with endogenous features that developed when they abruptly stopped heavy cocaine use. Repeatedly they emphasized how they felt that the only antidote to this distress was to resume their cocaine and that their craving was mainly fueled by the wish to relieve such dysphoria.

Most recently, we reported on an extreme case of dependence on intravenous cocaine that responded dramatically to methylphenidate treatment (Khantzian 1983). This 33-year-old woman described a history, from adolescence into adulthood, of attentional problems, restlessness, emotional overreactivity, and learning difficulties. In adolescence she discovered that amphetamines, which she continually misused until her late 20s, helped her to be calmer, to concentrate, to overcome her inertia, and to remain more purposeful. As amphetamines became more difficult to obtain, she subsequently discovered the same but more potent effects of cocaine, which quickly resulted in an escalation of the drug and its use intravenously. In another report with Kleber and associates (Khantzian et al. 1984), we have provided follow-up on this patient and two other cocaine addicts who have been successfully treated and stabilized for eighteen months or more with this form of treatment. These patients shared lifelong difficulties with substance dependence (with a preference for stimulants), problems with acute and chronic dysphoria, and a significant history of behavioral disturbances involving impulsivity, hyperactivity, and restlessness. Although some of these symptoms were the result of heavy cocaine use, it was apparent that these patients suffered with long-standing disturbances in affect and behavior regulation, predating their cocaine addiction. We believe that these and other patients like them probably have been treating themselves for a hyperactive/restless/emotional lability syndrome or attention deficit hyperactive disorder (ADHD). All three of these patients described how cocaine, and subsequently the methylphenidate, had a paradoxical action of calming them and improving their concentration and performance.

Finally, in the last-mentioned report, Kleber and his associates suggested that certain cocaine addicts whom they were seeing had features of a cyclothymic or bipolar illness. These patients emphasized how cocaine augmented their hypomanic style or reversed dysthymic cycles in their mood.

## CONCLUSION

There is little in our experience to support pleasure-seeking or self-destructive motives to explain the compelling nature of addictions, including addiction to cocaine. Drug dependency in our experience is better explained by the presence of major problems in adapting to painful internal emotions and adjusting to external, unmanageable realities. A clinical and psychoanalytic perspective has helped us and other clinicians and investigators begin to understand more precisely how certain problems in regulating affects and behavior might predispose certain individuals to cocaine dependence.

From the clinical observations we have presented, it is apparent that many individuals who have come to rely heavily on cocaine have been predisposed to do so as a consequence of preexisting disturbances, most notably disturbances in regulation of behavior and affects. These patients provide impressive, preliminary evidence that a principal motive for their reliance on cocaine was a need to medicate themselves for a range of distressful states. These include depression, self-esteem disturbances, impulsivity, acute and chronic dysphoria, and cyclothymia. Unfortunately, as is so often the case with addictions, cocaine addicts' attempts at self-cure are short lived and, tragically and in most instances, they heighten or worsen the original distress that they set out to treat.

## REFERENCES

Khantzian, E. J. (1975). Self selection and progression in drug dependence. *Psychiatry Digest* 10:19–22.

——— (1979). Impulse problems in addiction: cause and effect relationships. In *Working with the Impulsive Person*, ed. H. Wishnie, pp. 97–112. New York: Plenum.

——— (1983). An extreme case of cocaine dependence and marked improvement with methylphenidate treatment. *American Journal of Psychiatry* 140(6):484–485.

Khantzian, E. J., Gawin, F., Kleber, H. D., and Riordan, C. E. (1984). Methylphenidate treatment of cocaine dependence—a preliminary report. *Journal of Substance Abuse Treatment* 1:107–112.

Siegel, R. K. (1977). Cocaine: recreational use and intoxication. In *Cocaine*, ed. R. C. Peterson and R. C. Stillman, pp. 119–136. National Institute on Drug Abuse Research monograph no. 13. Washington, DC: U.S. Government Printing Office.

Spotts, J. V., and Shontz, F. C. (1977). *The Life Styles of Nine American Cocaine Users*. Washington, DC: U.S. Government Printing Office.

Wesson, D. R., and Smith, D. E. (1977). Cocaine: its use for central nervous system stimulation including recreational and medical uses. In *Cocaine*, ed. R. C. Peterson and R. C. Stillman, pp. 137–152. National Institute on Drug Abuse Research monograph no. 13. Washington, DC: U.S. Government Printing Office.

Wurmser, L. (1974). Psychoanalytic considerations of the etiology of compulsive drug use. *Journal of the American Psychoanalytic Association* 22:820–843.

# 23

# Psychiatric and Psychodynamic Factors in Cocaine Dependence

The powerful effects of cocaine on mood and behavior are by now well known. Early accounts dating back to Freud (1884), and more recently by others (Khantzian and McKenna 1979, Siegel 1977), indicate that, in the short term, cocaine significantly elevates mood, energizes, empowers, and reduces appetite; its negative effects include restlessness, anxiety, excitability, irritability, impulsivity, and paranoia, as well as tactile, visual, and auditory hallucinations. It should not be surprising or unreasonable to expect that some of these effects could interact with preexisting psychopathology to make cocaine compelling, or that these same effects might cause or worsen psychopathology. It is frequently debated, and unfortunately often hotly contested, whether, in general, psychopathology causes a reliance on the effects of addictive drugs, or whether these effects cause psychopathology. There is evidence to support both possibilities, and it is likely that this will prove to be the case for cocaine as well.

This chapter reviews the evidence suggesting that individuals are susceptible to cocaine dependence as a consequence of psychiatric disorders and other psychodynamic factors. The reader is referred to previous chapters where I have extensively reviewed psychodynamic factors related to disturbances in affect regulation, self-esteem maintenance, self-other relations, and self-care.

Considering psychiatric/diagnostic findings together with psychodynamic observations has an advantage over either approach alone. The former allows the objective identification of target symptoms and psychopathology at a point in time; the latter permits, over time, an examination and understanding of those psychological structures and functions responsible for psychological homeostasis. Failures and deficits in these structures and functions account for point-in-time symptomatic and diagnostic findings (Khantzian 1981).

With some important exceptions, until recently there have been surprisingly few clinical descriptions or diagnostic studies of cocaine addicts. Without justification, cocaine has tended to be classified as nonaddictive, a trendy drug for the affluent and the famous (especially performing artists), and a "safe" drug with few or no dangerous side effects. As a consequence, cocaine users and addicts received little clinical or investigative attention until the 1980s, when cocaine use and the devastating consequences of its misuse spread and became evident through all sectors of our society, especially among celebrities and the rich. Notwithstanding these trends, over the past two decades a number of psychoanalytically oriented clinicians and investigators have elaborated on the psychological appeal of and predisposition toward stimulants and, more specifically, on cocaine dependence. Most recently, a few diagnostic and treatment reports have begun to appear documenting the coexistence of psychopathology in cocaine addicts, and the observation that they also may respond favorably to psychopharmacological treatment.

In my own clinical work with cocaine addicts, I have been impressed that they share with other categories of drug/alcohol-dependent individuals some of the same vulnerabilities that generally predispose individuals to become addicted. That is, they are impaired in their capacity to recognize and regulate their emotions, they suffer with significant problems of self-esteem, they experience major difficulties in their relationships, and they can be very erratic and deficient in matters of self-care. They also suffer with coexistent psychiatric disturbances and related painful affect states. It is my impression that some of these painful affects and related behaviors are especially unique to cocaine addicts, and these states interact specifically with the psychotropic effects of cocaine to make them powerfully compelling.

## PSYCHODYNAMIC OBSERVATIONS

A number of psychoanalytic reports and studies have speculated on the appeal of stimulants. Wieder and Kaplan (1969), in their work with adolescent drug users, observed that stimulants, including cocaine, produced increased feelings of assertiveness, self-esteem, and frustration tolerance. They proposed that the associated motoric restlessness contributed to an illusion of activity that subserved denial of passivity. Spotts and Shontz (1977), in their extensive study of nine cocaine addicts, concluded that many of their findings were consistent with the formulations of Wieder and Kaplan.

Wurmser (1974), commenting in general on stimulant abusers, emphasized that they used the effects of these drugs to eliminate feelings of boredom and emptiness by providing a sense of mastery, control, invincibility, and grandeur; he elaborated further that the drug effect served as a defense against depression and/or feelings of unworthiness and weakness. Along similar lines, Milkman and Frosch (1973) concluded that amphetamine addicts used the effects of stimulants to support an inflated sense of self-worth and a defensive style that allowed an active confrontation of their environment.

In my own work with cocaine addicts, I originally emphasized that the energizing properties of stimulants were compelling because they helped addicts to overcome fatigue and depletion states associated with depression (Khantzian 1975). I later expanded on these observations (Khantzian 1985, Khantzian and Khantzian 1984), suggesting that the energizing and activating property of cocaine helped chronically depressed (often subclinical and/or atypical) individuals overcome their anergia, complete tasks, and relate better to others, thus experiencing a temporary lift in their self-esteem. Along somewhat different lines, in another report (Khantzian 1979) I indicated that certain individuals used cocaine as an augmenter.

Although most of these psychodynamic descriptions complement each other, no single effect of cocaine described in these reports adequately explains its appeal. It is probably some combination of cocaine's psychotropic effects on painful affect states (usually depression) and personality traits that interact to make the drug so seductive.

## DIAGNOSTIC AND TREATMENT STUDIES

As already indicated, until recently most of the clinical formulations about and descriptions of cocaine addicts were based on observations of individual cases. Only since about 1983 has there been any indication in the psychiatric literature that cocaine addicts' dependency on their drug might be related to psychopathology. Over this time two diagnostic studies using the *Diagnostic and Statistical Manual of Mental Disorders*, 3rd edition (*DSM-III*) (American Psychiatric Association 1980) and several pilot studies using pharmacological treatments have appeared that suggest that chronic cocaine dependence might be related to or a consequence of coexistent psychopathology.

Weiss and Mirin (1984) reported *DSM-III* diagnostic findings of thirty hospitalized cocaine-dependent individuals. Fifty-three percent of the subjects were diagnosed to be suffering with an affective disorder. Major depression was the most common diagnosis, but they also found a significant subgroup of cocaine abusers with bipolar and cyclothymic disorders who used cocaine to self-medicate their recurrent depressions as well as to enhance their hypomania during manic episodes. Significantly, in their report they also observed that 90 percent of the patients they studied had a *DSM-III* axis II personality diagnosis, with narcissistic and borderline personality disorders being the most frequent, and a very low frequency of antisocial personality disorder (i.e., only one of the thirty subjects). In their report they observed that their subjects perceived cocaine to be useful in regulating both dysphoric and elated moods. Moderate doses relieved symptoms of depression, but increasing doses were necessary to avoid postcocaine depression. The bipolar and cyclothymic patients used the cocaine to enhance their high moods in the manic phase of their illness.

Gawin and Kleber (1984) and Kleber and Gawin (1984) reported a similar rate of approximately 50 percent incidence of affective disorders, *DSM-III* axis I findings, on seventeen outpatient cocaine abusers. In their study, major depression, dysthymic disorder, and atypical disorder accounted for about 30 percent of the cases, and bipolar disorder (including cyclothymic disorder) for the remaining. Both Weiss and Mirin and Kleber and Gawin identified a small but important subgroup of patients with attention deficit disorder–residual type (ADD) in their studies.

Gawin and Kleber (1984) conducted an open-ended clinical trial of desipramine or lithium on sixteen of the seventeen outpatient cocaine addicts described above. Although only three of the six cocaine addicts treated with desipramine were diagnosed as depressed, all six responded to the treatment with decreased craving, and they ultimately stopped cocaine use. The pattern of decreased craving in both groups corresponded to the usual three to four-week response period for tricyclics in general. They also observed that the one feature all six patients shared in common was anhedonia, probably cocaine induced, which also lifted over the several weeks of treatment. Of the six patients treated with lithium, only the three diagnosed as cyclothymic responded to this treatment. They remained cocaine free for more than three months, and their cessation of cocaine use was immediate with commencement of treatment. The remaining subjects treated with lithium and those treated with psychotherapy alone continued to use cocaine. Given the small sample involved, Gawin and Kleber urge caution in overgeneralizing from their study; but their preliminary encouraging findings warrant further study and suggest that, for at least some cocaine addicts, a self-treatment motive might be involved.

Both the Weiss and Mirin (1984) and the Gawin and Kleber (1984) studies indicate that a small but significant subgroup of cocaine addicts suffer with ADD. Although only a small percentage (probably no more than 5 percent)[1] of cocaine addicts suffer with ADD, the existing literature linking ADD to substance abuse and reports of treatment responsiveness to prescribed psychostimulants bears on the general issue of psychopathology in addicts, and specifically on a self-medication motive for cocaine dependence. Tarter and associates (1977) iden-

---

1. More recent reports by Kleinman et al. (1990) and Rounsaville et al. (1991) reveal significantly higher rates of attention deficit hyperactivity disorder (ADHD) in treatment-seeking cocaine abusers.

tified a subgroup of severe alcoholics whose onset of alcoholism occurred at an earlier age and progressed very rapidly, who were diagnosed to be suffering with ADD from childhood. Wender and his associates (Wender 1979, Wender et al. 1981, Wood et al. 1976, 1983), who have written extensively on ADD in adults, have underscored a strong association with alcoholism and drug abuse. In a case study reported by Turnquist and associates (1983), ADD was diagnosed in a severe, chronic 35-year-old man who had failed to respond to previous treatment interventions. Treatment with pemoline resulted in marked reduction of his restlessness, distractibility, and emotional outbursts, and resulted in a significantly improved response to alcoholism treatment and aftercare.

Three recent case reports lend further support to the observation that ADD may be an underlying motive for cocaine dependence. In 1983 I reported on an extreme case of cocaine dependence in a 33-year-old woman who showed marked improvement with methylphenidate treatment (Khantzian 1983). Reconstruction of her childhood and adolescent history with the patient and her mother revealed symptoms consistent with ADD, and it was on this basis that she was treated with the methylphenidate. We subsequently reported further results and follow-up on the first case and two other cases successfully treated with methylphenidate (Khantzian et al. 1984). We concluded from these cases that cocaine addiction might be the cause or consequence of psychopathology and that in all three of the reported cases the cocaine dependence was preceded by major symptoms of ADD in childhood and adolescence. Most recently, Weiss and colleagues (1985) reported on two additional cases of cocaine abusers also suffering with ADD, who showed marked improvement with magnesium pemolate treatment and a significant sustained reduction of cocaine abuse. These reports provide further evidence for a self-medication motive for drug dependence and a basis to suggest that some cocaine addicts treat themselves for ADD.

## COMMENTS AND CONCLUSIONS

I have reviewed evidence indicating that individuals might be predisposed to addiction as a consequence of preexistent psychopathology. I have described the general vulnerabilities and types of psychiatric disorders associated with narcotic addiction and other substance abuse, and I have elaborated on the specific types of distress, dysfunction, and psychiatric disorder in cocaine addicts that seem to cause reliance on stimulants.

There is also a basis for emphasizing that a psychodynamic appreciation of how cocaine addicts experience and regulate their feelings, self-esteem, relationships, and behavior, and an appreciation of overall personality factors provide valuable clues to understanding how or why an individual might be susceptible to cocaine dependence, even in the absence of documentable psychiatric disorder.

I have not addressed in this chapter the question of whether all cocaine addicts suffer with preexisting psychopathology, or whether anyone is susceptible to cocaine addiction. These questions are important, but informed answers will not be forthcoming until we have extensively studied and understood many more cocaine addicts and have better clarified the effects and mechanisms of action of cocaine at the neuronal and biochemical level.

## REFERENCES

American Psychiatric Association (1980). *Diagnostic and Statistical Manual of Mental Disorders*, 3rd ed. Washington, DC: American Psychiatric Association.

Freud, S. (1884). Uber Coca. *Journal of Substance Abuse Treatment* (1984) 1:205–217.

Gawin, F. H., and Kleber, H. D. (1984). Cocaine abuse treatment. *Archives of General Psychiatry* 41:903–908.

Khantzian, E. J. (1975). Self selection and progression in drug dependence. *Psychiatry Digest* 10:19–22.

———— (1979). Impulse problems in addiction: cause and effect relationships. In *Working with the Impulsive Person*, ed. H. Wishnie, pp. 97–112. New York: Plenum.

———— (1981). Some treatment implications of the ego and self disturbances in alcoholism. In *Dynamic Approaches to the Understanding and Treatment of Alcoholism*, ed. M. H. Bean and N. E. Zinberg, pp. 163–188. New York: Free Press.

———— (1983). An extreme case of cocaine dependence and marked improvement with methylphenidate treatment. *American Journal of Psychiatry* 140:784–785.

———— (1985). The self-medication hypothesis of addictive disorders. *American Journal of Psychiatry* 142:1259–1264.

Khantzian, E. J., Gawin, F., Kleber, H. D., and Riordan, C. E. (1984). Methylphenidate treatment of cocaine dependence—a preliminary report. *Journal of Substance Abuse Treatment* 1:107–112.

Khantzian, E. J., and Khantzian, N. J. (1984). Cocaine addiction: Is there a psychological predisposition? *Psychiatric Annals* 14:753–759.

Khantzian, E. J., and McKenna, G. J. (1979). Acute toxic and withdrawal reactions associated with drug use and abuse. *Annals of Internal Medicine* 90:361–372.

Kleber, H. D., and Gawin, F. H. (1984). Cocaine abuse: a review of current and experimental treatments. In *Cocaine: Pharmacology Effects and Treatment of Abuse*, ed. J. Grabowski, pp. 111–129. Rockville, MD: National Institute on Drug Abuse.

Kleinman, P. H., Miller, A. B., Millman, R. B., et al. (1990). Psychopathology among cocaine abusers entering treatment. *Journal of Nervous Mental Diseases* 178:442–447.

Milkman, H., and Frosch, W. A. (1973). On the preferential abuse of heroin and amphetamine. *Journal of Nervous and Mental Disease* 156:242–248.

Rounsaville, B. J., Anton, S. F., Carroll, K., et al. (1991). Psychiatric diagnoses of treatment-seeking cocaine abusers. *Archives of General Psychiatry* 48:43–51.

Siegel, R. K. (1977). Cocaine: recreational use and intoxication. In *Cocaine*, ed. R. C. Peterson and R. C. Stillman, pp. 119–136. Washington, DC: U.S. Government Printing Office.

Spotts, J. V., and Shontz, F. C. (1977). *The Life Styles of Nine American Cocaine Users*. Washington, DC: U.S. Government Printing Office.

Tarter, R. E., McBride, H., Buonpane, N., and Schneider, D. U. (1977). Differentiation of alcoholics. *Archives of General Psychiatry* 34:761–776.

Turnquist, K., Frances, R., Rosenfeld, W., and Mobarak, A. (1983). Pemoline in attention deficit disorder and alcoholism: a case study. *American Journal of Psychiatry* 140:622–624.

Weiss, R. D., and Mirin, S. M. (1984). Drug, host and environmental factors in the development of chronic cocaine abuse. In *Substance Abuse and Psychotherapy*, ed. S. M. Mirin, pp. 42–55. Washington, DC: American Psychiatric Association Press.

Weiss, R. D., Pope, H. G., and Mirin, S. M. (1985). Treatment of chronic cocaine abuse and attention deficit disorder, residual type with magnesium pemoline. *Drug and Alcohol Dependence* 15:69–72.

Wender, P. H. (1979). The concept of minimal brain dysfunction (MBD). In *Psychiatric Aspects of Minimal Brain Dysfunction in Adults*, ed. L. Bellak, pp. 1–13. New York: Grune & Stratton.

Wender, P. H., Reimherr, F. W., and Wood, D. R. (1981). Attention deficit in adults. *Archives of General Psychiatry* 38:449–456.

Wieder, H., and Kaplan, E. (1969). Drug use in adolescents. *Psychoanalytic Study of the Child* 24:399–431. New York: International Universities Press.

Wood, D. R., Reimherr, F. W., Wender, P. H., and Johnson, G. E. (1976). Diagnosis and treatment of minimal brain dysfunction in adults. *Archives of General Psychiatry* 33:1453–1460.

Wood, D. R., Wender, P. H., and Reimherr, F. W. (1983). The prevalence of attention deficit disorder, residual type or minimal brain dysfunction in a population of male alcoholic patients. *American Journal of Psychiatry* 140:95–98.

Wurmser, L. (1974). Psychoanalytic considerations of the etiology of compulsive drug use. *Journal of the American Psychoanalytic Association* 22:820–843.

# 24

# Alcoholics Anonymous and Contemporary Psychodynamic Theory

## *with John E. Mack*

*After a successful psychoanalytic treatment a patient is definitely less neurotic (or psychotic) but perhaps not necessarily more mature. On the other hand after a successful treatment by group methods the patient is not necessarily less neurotic but inevitably more mature.*

Enid Balint (1972, p. 64)

Alcoholism is a devastating illness, eroding every aspect of a person's physical, psychological, and social being. The chronic, unrelenting, yet seemingly self-elected course of alcoholism is so extreme that until recently it caused most people to consider it a hopeless moral or criminal condition. However, over the past fifty years the growing popularity and the success of a natural experiment of extraordinary proportions have proven that alcoholism is a condition that is preeminently responsive to the caring intervention of others. We are referring, of course, to Alcoholics Anonymous (AA), a self-help group that provides in special and effective ways an ongoing source of hope, support, and restoration.

Many of the strongest proponents of AA are recovering alcoholics who have benefited from "keeping it simple and pragmatic." As a consequence, there has been an unfortunate tendency to explain the basis of AA's success merely by its ability to instill and maintain abstinence and in providing a community of others who are understanding because they know the ravages of the illness and know the practical and necessary steps it takes to get better. That is, AA removes the "sufficient and necessary cause" (Vaillant 1983)—the alcohol—from a person's life and replaces it with the support and comfort of AA. As simple and true as they may be, it is our contention that beyond achieving abstinence and providing support, AA is effective because it is a sophisticated psychological treatment whose members have learned to manage effectively and/or transform the psychological and behavioral vulnerabilities associated with alcoholism.

Beyond oversimplifying the basis of its success, one of the by-products of AA has been a corresponding tendency to minimize and eschew the psychological dimensions of alcoholism and to argue that alcoholism causes rather than is caused by psychopathology (Vaillant 1983). Although recent, careful diagnostic studies have produced findings to support both possibilities (Hesselbrock et al. 1985, Schuckit 1985), the emphasis on either-or arguments about etiological links between psychopathology and alcoholism are unfortunate, counterproductive, and defy resolution at this time. In our opinion, a more fruitful line of inquiry is provided if we can explore and try to understand how alcohol, a powerful emotion-altering drug, interacts with a person's emotions and the mental structures and functions that govern and regulate a person's life to make reliance on this substance so compelling. In contrast to earlier psychodynamic formulations that laid heavy emphasis on unconscious pleasurable and destructive instincts and the symbolic meanings of alcohol, modern theorists have placed affects (i.e., feelings) and problems in self-regulation and self-governance at the core of alcoholics' vulnerabilities (Khantzian 1981, Krystal and Raskin 1970, Mack 1981, Wurmser 1974). Approached in this way, reductionistic explanations and either-or arguments about psychopathology and alcoholism can be avoided and, instead, alcoholics' suffering can be better appreciated as a complex interaction between their experience and expression of affect, and the nature and quality of their psychological capacities to govern their affects and their lives. Accordingly, the focus and emphasis in contemporary psychodynamic approaches have been on understanding more empathically how alcoholics experience and express feelings, the quality of their self and object relations, their capacity for self-care, and how these factors interact with the meaning and effects of alcohol.

Alcoholics Anonymous, in common with group therapy, responds to an individual's need for acceptance and sharing to overcome the sense of alienation and shame entailed in a disorder that is so disabling and in which one has lost so much control of his or her life. Like effective group therapies, AA also instills hope, contact, and a climate of mutual concern that provides a basis to regain control of one's life. The encouragement in AA of openness, self-disclosure, an insistence that one cannot get better on one's own, and the repeated emphasis on shared experiences strikes at the core issues of self-regulation and self-care involved in alcoholism as a "multiperson" psychology. In this chapter we examine AA as a special kind of group experience that provides a context for examination, containment, and/or repair of core vulnerabilities involving affects, self-regulation, and self-governance.

## SELF-GOVERNANCE AND AA

Ernst Simmel (1948) was one of the first psychoanalysts to concern himself with AA. In his work he speculated on how the group psychology of AA might therapeutically influence intrapsychic factors that contribute to the impulse to drink. He believed that the therapeutic benefits of AA were consistent with psychoanalytic findings, namely, that AA countered through mass psychology the impulses deriving from the latent, overpowering drives with which alcoholics live. In posthumously published notes he discussed how group dynamics, the community, and religion influence ego structures, and he concluded with the hope that psychoanalysts and AA might collaborate to unravel and resolve the dangers of alcoholism.

The concept of self-governance, introduced by Mack (1981) to underscore the self–other context of self-regulation, represents one attempt to further such a psychoanalytic understanding of alcoholism, particularly the nature of the impulses involved in drinking and how the group dynamics of AA operate to effectively control and transform the impulses:

> *Self-governance* has to do with that aspect of the ego or self which is, in actuality or potentiality, in charge of the personality. Self-governance is a supraordinate function, or group of functions, in the ego system. It is concerned with choosing or deciding, with directing and controlling. The functions of self-governance are similar to what has been called ego executant functions (Hendrick 1943). But "executant functioning" connotes a solitary operation of the ego, while "self-governance" is a psycho-social term, intended to leave room for the participation of others in the governance of the individual. Self-governance as a theoretical concept is intended, unlike ego executant functioning, to allow for the sharing of control or responsibility with other individuals or groups. It acknowledges the essential interdependence of the self and others. . . .
>
> There are many situations in which self-governance is impaired—manic and schizophrenic psychoses and aggressive impulse disorder are obvious examples. The disorders of substance abuse in general and alcoholism in particular offer other striking examples of such impairment. The powerlessness which the alcoholic experiences in relation to alcohol reflects an impairment of self-governance with respect to the management of this substance. It has not been ascertained whether this powerlessness is specific to the drive to drink or is experienced by alcoholics in relation to certain other strong impulses as well. In the AA approach acknowledgment and acceptance of this powerlessness are the first steps in the path to recovery ("We admitted we were powerless over alcohol—that our lives had become unmanageable").
> [pp. 132–133]

The ability to govern oneself is a highly prized capacity. To admit that one is unable to manage one's life, especially the use of alcohol, an accepted and integral part of our culture, represents a major and often inadmissible defeat. Although admittedly there are degrees to which people lose control of their alcohol use, it is clear that those who need to struggle to maintain it are either unable to do so, or are plagued with conflict, self-doubt, and shame. Although debates continue about whether some alcoholics can resume controlled drinking, and whether some alcohol-abusing individuals on the benign end of the spectrum of alcohol excess achieve it, most of the accumulating evidence suggests that a goal of controlled drinking for most, if not all, alcoholics (i.e., those who have lost control of their lives—medically, socially, or legally—as a consequence of heavy, frequent alcohol use) is inadvisable or undoable (Helzer et al. 1985).

The twelve-step tradition (Alcoholics Anonymous 1977) provides an alcoholic with practical tools, suggestions, guiding slogans, and an expanding network of relationships (e.g., participants repeatedly hear the triad slogan, "Don't pick up, go to meetings and ask for help") that help to establish a growing capacity to control his impulse to drink. Alcoholics Anonymous is successful because of its intuitive grasp of the complexities of the biological and psychosocial nature of self-governance, not only in relation to alcohol, but far more pervasively in relation to the conduct of one's life in general. The organization appreciates and underscores that "the self never functions as a solitary entity" (Mack 1981, p. 134). In fantasy or action the self is always participating with others—other people, the family, the neighborhood, and social, religious, ethnic, or national groups—as part of one's existence and development. In this respect the self is a composite structure and an ongoing process, reflecting the interaction with the qualities, values, and norms of the individuals and groups in a person's life. Alcoholics Anonymous capitalizes on this process, recognizing that certain group activities and processes profoundly influence a person's capacity to govern himself, often far more than is possible in an individual psychotherapeutic relationship, and still more so when it occurs in a context of religious experience and values (Mack 1981). Bales (1944) was probably referring to this aspect of AA when he stated, "There is a certain type of control within the individual personality which can have its source only outside of the self—for practical purposes, in the moral principles advocated by a closely knit solidarity group—and can only be internalized and made effective against self-centered, satisfaction-directed impulses by an involuntary feeling of belongingness and allegiance to such a group, i.e., a 'moral community'" (p. 276).

It is little wonder, then, that psychiatric patients outside the AA program often express both envy and a wish to belong, as Bales suggests, when they witness the hope, support, and enthusiasm that its participants derive and reflect. It also partly explains how a patient diagnosed as borderline personality and suffering from the inability to control her emotions, relationships, and behavior exaggerated her alcohol symptoms to justify pursuing the beneficial containing, comforting, and restoring aspects of AA. In this regard, the benefits that alcoholics derive from AA in controlling their alcoholism probably have implications clinically and theoretically for others who suffer from an inability to regulate their emotions and behavior as a consequence of experiencing an injured sense of self (Mack 1981).

## AA, NARCISSISM, AND SELF PSYCHOLOGY

Psychoanalysis is both a method of treatment and a theory of mental life. When Freud first discovered and described his treatment methods, he emphasized instinctual factors (i.e., pleasurable and aggressive drives) and a topographic view of the mind in which many psychic processes were seen as unconscious. Freud and his followers subsequently modified their approach by placing greater emphasis on internal, subjective processes and states (e.g., affects, attitudes, needs, etc.) and structural factors and functions responsible for controlling and regulating one's internal psychic life and adjustment to external reality. Whereas early psychodynamic formulations of mental life and its aberrations (including alcoholism) placed heavy emphasis on drives and the unconscious, more recent approaches stress the importance of affects and ego and self structures in appreciating the unique subjective and observable aspects of how individuals are organized internally and how they adapt to their environment. It is in the context of these developments in psychoanalytic theory that a contemporary psychodynamic view of alcoholism leads us to consider vulnerabilities and deficits in affect management, the sense of self, and the ego in order to understand alcoholics' suffering and decompensations.

### Character Formation, Character Defects, and AA

By the time an individual reaches late adolescence and early adulthood, he or she possesses the capacity to manage emotions, relationships, and behavior with relative success, albeit in ways that are unique to the individual. That is, there are characteristic qualities in a person that set a predictable affective tone and behavioral pattern in that individual. For example, a person may be gloomy versus cheerful, or active and outgoing versus passive and reticent, or expressive versus restrained. Traditionally, in psychodynamic theory we have spoken of this aspect of a person's unique makeup as his or her personality style or personality organization. More precisely, the mental structures and functions determining personality are a reflection of our ego capacities and sense of self. Their development begins in infancy and evolves over a lifetime, incorporating attitudes and functions primarily of our parents and, subsequently, other persons and groups with whom there is significant contact, relationship, and meaning. To the extent that the growing-up environment is optimally nurturing, constant, and relatively free of major trauma and neglect, ego functions and the sense of self coalesce to give us a mature and adaptable character structure. Conversely, major flaws, defects, and distortions develop in a person's character structure as a function of environmental deprivation, inconstancy, trauma, and neglect. These are the flaws to which AA refers when it speaks of character defects in alcoholics.

The salient defects that AA targets so successfully have probably been recognized or identified over its fifty-year history out of the experience and the intuitions of its founders and members, and its insistence on the simple and pragmatic, discarding what is unusable and retaining what has worked. As with psychotherapy in general, AA as a treatment modality for alcoholism has general and specific therapeutic actions. Some elements act to provide symptom reduction and containment; other elements are more curative, seeking to alter the characterologic determinants of the condition. Many in AA, especially some of the older, veteran members, argue that they benefit simply from the removal of alcohol associations, "keeping it simple," and from the provision of a supportive, socializing group committed to abstinence. These supportive elements are often sufficient to explain the benefits of AA. However, we also believe that the curative aspects of AA are probably operative in these cases as well, but in more subtle and less apparent ways.

Obviously the most immediate, general benefit of AA is not at all subtle. AA succeeds in getting people to stop drinking. It is demonstrably effective in setting a limit on the most destructive behavior, the drinking itself. However, what it does even more successfully by addressing the psychological underpinnings of alcoholism (i.e., the defects of character), is to prevent the resumption of drinking. This is the aspect with which we concern ourselves primarily in this discussion.

Bean (1975, 1981), Brown (1985), and others (Alcoholics Anonymous 1978, Bales 1944, Leach 1973, Leach et al. 1969, Stewart 1955, Tiebout

1943–44, Trice 1957, Zinberg 1977) extensively reviewed the history, organization, and procedures of AA and its effectiveness in establishing abstinence and recovery as a process. Bean's focus on how AA successfully challenges alcoholics' denial, and Brown's emphasis on AA's successful management and pursuit of the dynamics of alcoholics' loss of control and the importance of maintaining an identity as an alcoholic, provide important and valuable insights into the group dynamics of AA and the recovery process. We also would stress the importance and centrality of abstinence and the focus on loss of control. We do not dispute the social, biological, and hereditary aspects of alcoholism, and a unified theory must ultimately consider how all these aspects of alcoholism interact with psychodynamic forces. In our view important psychodynamic aspects of alcoholism have been much neglected. Recent advances in psychoanalytic theory and practice provide a better basis for understanding the psychological factors that initiate and end bouts of drinking, maintain sobriety, and predispose individuals to becoming alcoholic (Mack 1981). These are areas that warrant attention, and a psychodynamic perspective can significantly add to our understanding and enable us to help alcoholics overcome their resistance to AA and other treatments that may be helpful.

Beyond the support and containment that AA provides, AA works because it has learned to recognize and respond creatively to the obvious problems alcoholics experience in self-regulation and self-governance (Khantzian 1981, Mack 1981). The problems in self-regulation and self-governance of alcoholics that AA so effectively targets relate to the alcoholic's personality (or character) structure, narcissistic vulnerability, problems in maintaining a cohesive sense of self, affect experience, and certain ego capacities concerned with self-preservation and self-care (Mack 1981). These problems are not unique to alcoholics. They are shared more or less by all human beings but it is the degree of such vulnerabilities, combined with social, biological, and other factors, that needs to be explored to further a comprehensive understanding of alcoholism. We single out these factors for heuristic purposes and because our experience and understanding suggest to us that these are fruitful and helpful avenues to pursue further.

As we have indicated, the strength and vulnerability in a person's character reflects how experiences of nurturing and caregiving have become structuralized (i.e., internalized) over the course of his or her development. The character defects referred to in AA, more than any other aspect of a person's life, include the qualities and flaws in personal organization associated with narcissism and narcissistic development, that is, that aspect of life having to do with self-love.

## Definition of Narcissism

Although AA does not use technical terms, it is clear that it recognizes, as do modern theorists, that alcoholics have problems with self-love and self-regard. Heinz Kohut and his followers (Baker and Baker 1987, Goldberg 1978, Kohut 1971, 1977, Kohut and Wolf 1978, Ornstein 1978), in advancing their concepts about self psychology, have made the important observations that narcissism, or self-love, though linked to object relations, may be considered separately. It has its own developmental line and is manifested in mature (normal) and less mature (pathological) forms, especially in personality organization. Healthy narcissism is basic to our general emotional health and consists of a subjective sense of well-being, confidence in self-worth and potential, and a balanced valuation of our importance in relation to other people, groups, and our place in the world (Mack 1981). Satisfactory relationships and healthy involvement with work and play are fundamental to mature narcissistic development. Pathological narcissism may be expressed as an abnormal or exaggerated preoccupation with the self, its needs, and desires, and in its extreme form expressed as grandiosity. In contrast, it may also be evident in a diminished self-regard and concerns about one's needs and desires. In more extreme forms, narcissistic pathology may produce psychological fragmentation and disorganization of the self as seen in psychosis or in the regressive states associated with acute or chronic intoxication. It is for these latter reasons that alcoholics are often incorrectly diagnosed as schizophrenic or borderline. It is difficult to determine if alcoholic ego disorganization is a consequence of psychophysiological deterioration or narcissistic pathology (Mack 1981).

To this extent, as we explore in this chapter the manifestations of narcissistic vulnerabilities in alcoholics, we wish to emphasize that it would be incorrect and unwarranted to conclude that alcoholics' core problems are a result of narcissistic pathology. It is likely that alcoholics suffer with sectors of narcissistic vulnerability, but that much of the more severe disorganization, regression, and primitive narcissistic pathology and defenses associated with advanced alcoholism is the result of the physical deterioration and the narcissistic hurts and injury that occur with excessive and prolonged drinking.

## Manifestations of Narcissism in Alcoholics

In our experience, one of the most obvious problems associated with narcissism in alcoholics is their inability to acknowledge that they cannot control their drinking. In fact, more often there is an exaggerated belief in the ability to control their impulses, especially the impulse to use alcohol. This aspect of alcoholism has caused Brown (1985) to consider the focus on loss of control as her most central thesis for understanding the psychology of alcoholism and recovery. The alcoholics' problems of control go beyond accepting their inability to limit themselves in relation to alcohol. It is also tied up in the belief, if not insistence, that they are in charge of themselves, that they are autonomous and able to govern themselves. Although alcoholics are not alone in such exaggerated beliefs about self, we suggest that a combination of such a predisposition, interacting with long-term effects of chronic alcohol use, might especially influence alcoholics' drive to drink.

The aphorisms in AA and its literature reflect the appreciation of the healthy and unhealthy ways attitudes about self can affect alcoholics in their attempt to achieve sobriety. For Bill W., the founder of AA, "it meant destruction of self-centeredness" (Alcoholics Anonymous 1978, p. 16). Listening to participants in AA laugh at themselves and at each other in meetings as they tell their stories, and the way they banter lightly and use the aphorisms of AA with each other also show how play, humor, and enthusiasm in the program evoke the healthier aspirations for recovery for themselves and each other. Some of the aphorisms are particularly pointed and witty in puncturing, if not stampeding on, the egoism of alcoholics: they are instructed to "leave their egos at the door" when they attend meetings; the AA KISS motto stands for "keep it simple stupid"; woeful, egocentric laments are met with comments such as, "He suffers from terminal uniqueness" or "Her majesty, the baby"; and should they believe they are too smart or dumb to "get it" in AA, they might hear that "no one is too dumb to get the program; but there are a lot of people too smart."

One of the first psychiatrists to become actively involved with AA, Harry Tiebout (1943–44, 1961), described how AA was an effective treatment for alcoholism because it focused primarily on the egoistic aspect of alcoholics' attitude and behavior. He wrote that the alcoholic realized he always "put himself first" and that getting better required the realization that "he was but a small fraction of a universe peopled by many other individuals" (1943–44, p. 471). The effectiveness of AA hinges on the alcoholic losing "the narcissistic element permanently" (1943–44, p. 472) and trading in the "big ego" (1957, p. 5) of infantile narcissism for a more humble self. As in the following case, continued study of attitudes about self should continue to unravel the issue of how much chronic alcohol use produces the narcissistic element and how much this element might contribute to the development of alcoholism.

> Phil, a very successful businessman and recovering alcoholic, related in psychotherapy how AA helped him deal with alternating attitudes of disdain and shyness in his relationship with people, attitudes rooted in conflicts whereby he constantly over- and undervalued his capacities as a person. He was a man who suffered much neglect as a child because his mother was severely mentally ill and his father was totally absorbed with his career. Despite the neglect and being left to the care of governesses, or because of it, he developed an uncanny ability to observe and imitate others. As an adolescent he overcame his shyness and gained acceptance by entertaining family and friends as a magician. Despite his ability to tune in on what others expected (not uncommon in individuals with narcissistic vulnerabilities) and a deep fear of nonacceptance, he was also aware of his arrogance. Although he had gained eighteen months of abstinence in AA, he knew from the program that he had to deal with and change the attitude of disdain he felt for people in order to maintain his sobriety. He said the "twenty-four-hour book" told him to "pray for [his] enemies." He enthusiastically emphasized that AA really helped him "let go" (i.e., derived from steps 2 and 3 in the twelve steps) of his arrogance and, once again, drawing on an AA aphorism, he said that it really worked after a while, but you had to "fake it till you make it."

From its inception AA has been aware of the pitfalls and potentials rooted in human self-centeredness, especially as it operates in alcoholics, and has been sensitive to the fact that leadership roles can artificially stimulate or inflate self-regard and archaic grandiose self-structures. Thus they have taken measures to circumvent the pitfalls of leadership roles by eliminating permanent offices or leadership positions in AA (Mack 1981). Tradition 2 of AA, for example, emphasizes that "God as He may express Himself" is the ultimate authority and the "leaders are but trusted servants; they do not govern" (Alcoholics Anonymous 1978, p. 136). Yet at the same time that AA challenges the pitfalls of being in a position of authority or leadership in the program, it is clear that the successful elder statesmen of AA are rewarded when personal aspirations and trends are reshaped and transformed by AA. This occurs when AA respects them as inspiring transmitters of the wisdom they acquire in their recovery, one of the cardinal forms of healthy narcissism described by Kohut. In the following section we describe how AA as a special group experience challenges the less healthy forms of narcissism and evokes the healthiest parts of a person's aspirations in satisfying his or her needs.

## Group Psychology, AA, and Self-Governance

Alcoholics Anonymous implicitly adopts principles of group psychology to influence and transform the psychological vulnerabilities inherent in alcoholic suffering. It also shares with group therapy the potential to provide a context for shared experiences, enabling confrontation, support, comfort, and a sense of feeling accepted (Khantzian 1985a). However, beyond a description of these general, beneficial effects (Rosenberg 1984), there is, but for a few notable exceptions (Bean 1981, Brown 1985), little in the group literature that addresses how group dynamics in general or the dynamics of AA in particular influence or modify the intrapsychic dimension of the alcoholic's emotional life. Freud's (1921, 1930) writings about group psychology pertained primarily to mass organizations such as the church, the influence of the leaders, and the effect of large groups on the development of superego and ego ideal structures. The AA reference to "group conscience" is probably significant in this regard. Although other reports on group psychology consider how small and large groups may fulfill needs and be ego sustaining (Calder 1979, Kernberg 1977, Scheidlinger 1964, 1974) and, at the small group therapy level, how they influence and mobilize beneficial interpersonal factors (Brown and Yalom 1977, Vanicelli 1982), there is surprisingly little to explain how groups function to modify and transform personality organization and the vulnerabilities in ego and self-structures that might predispose a person to depend on alcohol. In the following discussion we hope to contribute to such an understanding and to begin to show how AA as a group experience is effective because it accurately targets and modifies those sectors of the self and personality organization that leave alcoholics vulnerable because they are unable to regulate their lives or to take care of themselves.

Alcoholics Anonymous teaches that the human tasks of self-regulation and self-care are not challenges that should be faced or mastered alone. This applies to life in general but it is a particularly crucial realization for alcoholics. When AA places powerlessness center stage as the main source of alcoholics' difficulties, it succeeds almost immediately in providing a powerful counter force (Mack 1981). Through its graduated steps, aphorisms, and structuring the process of abstinence, "keeping it simple," and doing it "one day at a time," AA helps the person to gain a growing sense of confidence in the power to manage his life. In a community that shares the same distresses and losses, accepts its members' vulnerabilities, and applauds and rewards successes, AA provides a stabilizing, sustaining, and, ultimately, transforming group experience.

The focus on helping people to internalize care and controls, and to manage what has seemed so unmanageable, relates to what has been called executive functioning, or what we call self-governance, because this kind of functioning is never altogether a solitary activity. Alcoholics Anonymous is effective because it appreciates that the underpinnings of self are connected with social structures and institutions. Self-governance comprises a set of functions that derive from the individual's participation in a variety of group and institutional activities and affiliations. Alcoholics Anonymous helps alcoholic individuals achieve sobriety by providing a network of stable individual and group relationships that powerfully impact on the governance of drinking behavior (Mack 1981).

Societal norms, social institutions, attitudes, and cultural factors are powerful determinants of drinking practices and behaviors. We either take for granted or, more likely, underestimate how much of our capacity to govern and regulate our drinking patterns and amount consumed are influenced by societal and cultural norms. It is probably safe to say that such influences play a significant ongoing role, along with internalized ego controls, in protecting some individuals who might otherwise become problem drinkers. In fact, it has been proposed that "epidemics" of rampant drinking during periods of U.S. history and in other cultures have occurred when there was a breakdown of family social structures that restricted drinking to special and ceremonial events. With the absence or waning of such sanctions and rituals, men who were socially dislocated because of the industrial revolution and urbanization (Mack 1981, Zinberg and Fraser 1979) began to drink increasingly in taverns and barrooms instead of the home. Perhaps the modern counterpart occurs among high-powered, upwardly mobile, young urban professionals who go to trendy, after-work singles' bars and consume significant amounts of alcohol as a part of their social and work relationships.

Along these lines, we have speculated that the loss of the capacity to govern drinking may go beyond a breakdown of drive and ego structures within an individual and might just as likely be the result of a loss of social and community supports in an individual who is biologically or psychologically vulnerable to alcoholism (Mack 1981). Although the affective component of loss and grief as a consequence of death or separation is often invoked as a precipitant of alcoholic drinking, such explanations more often fail to take into consideration how significant persons in one's life, or related sources of social stability, often represent an important part of the self-governance system. In addition, the person who is lost, because of death or separation, may have served as a stabilizing link to social community resources that aid a person in regulating his or her life.

Most would agree that AA succeeds because it replaces "chemical solutions" with "people solutions." It provides a group of individuals who care and who share similar life experiences. It avoids the confounding and often compounding disappointments of the individual treatment relationship (unfortunately not too uncommon an occurrence) with therapists who are inexperienced in the treatment of alcoholism and/or with patients who prematurely enter therapy before sobriety and stability are well established. It also confronts the defenses of denial and rationalization and the sense of invincibility in alcoholics. The alcohol-controlling capacity of the members of AA becomes part of the self-governing system and helps them to stay humble and to be realistic about their susceptibility to relapse and loss of control (Mack 1981).

Jeff, a man in his mid-30s, aptly described in group therapy how AA served as a protection and antidote against his belief that he was "strong enough" to control his alcohol and drug use alone. He said that his most recent relapse and current hospital admission occurred after he had achieved a total state of abstinence for eight months, but that a few "slips" over several weeks had led to his losing control of his alcohol and cocaine use. He emphasized that his twelve-year history of heavy alcohol and drug use had failed to respond to several detoxifications and attempts at outpatient care until he embraced AA and began to attend daily meetings. He said that although he obtained a great deal of hope and comfort from his meetings, he stopped going regularly after several months but did not drink or take drugs. As a consequence, within a month he felt confident that he could "control things" without attending any meetings at all. He described with insight the progression of rationalizations when he then began to believe that he could take just one drink with some friends, which he did. Shortly thereafter, he said, he allowed himself two drinks and a line of cocaine, whereupon he quickly lost control and within a week was rehospitalized.

The group therapist suggested that perhaps there is some kind of monster inside us, who, it would seem, tell us we could shun or give up such a source of comfort (i.e., the AA meetings) and protection. Perhaps it might help Jeff and the other patients, who all agreed his story sounded too familiar, if we could give a name to the monster. After a short pause, it was Jeff who spoke up and said, "We'll call him King Kong." The groups broke into spontaneous laughter and then animatedly pursued the King Kong in each member. Most members recognized their inflated sense of self in respect to their ability to control drug or alcohol use and how illusory it was. The only reliable antidote, they felt, was the AA/NA program, which kept them more humbly connected to their vulnerability and constantly challenged their self-sufficiency and sense of being invincible by constantly admitting this vulnerability in themselves or witnessing it in others.

## AA and the Religious Dimension

The religious dimension of AA, especially for outsiders, is often considered an off-putting aspect of the program, deterring or discouraging participation. There is a tendency to compare this aspect of AA to formal religions or particular religious sects. This is unfortunate and misleading. Those who understand and appreciate best what is important in the religious dimension of AA place emphasis on spirituality and a flexible approach to defining one's "higher power" or God in the program. In a previous publication we have elaborated on what is essential to the religious dimension of the AA program in addressing alcoholics' vulnerabilities (Mack 1981). We will summarize those observations here.

God as a governing influence or force within an individual may take various forms. For some, religion and religious ideas serve childish and egocentric purposes, where God or religious belief and acts are felt to offer magical protection, or the religious system serves as a rigid and restrictive system of beliefs and practices. For others, the power and awe engendered by the outside universe and our humble place in it instill a sense of a force or power greater than ourselves. The spiritual dimension of AA helps to move a person from a less mature, childish self-centeredness toward a more mature form of object love. The three strands of childhood narcissism described by Spruiell (1975)—self-love, omnipotence, and self-esteem—are helpful and pertinent in this respect, especially omnipotence. The sense of omnipotence begins in the second year of the toddler's life when he begins to sense his power (or the lack of it) and that he can (or cannot) make things happen. It is in this context that the idea of God, or a power greater than oneself, may be a step in the direction of taming and transforming infantile omnipotence and serving in early childhood to establish a capacity for object love (Mack 1981).

The spiritual and religious elements in AA act as an important counterforce to the egoistic aspects of chronic drinking by directly confronting the denial, rationalizations, and allusion of control that support the persistence of alcoholic behavior. Through its appeal to a higher power, AA's insistence on humility acts as an anodyne to the self-serving grandiosity and the wallowing self-pity of the alcoholic. In this context God serves as a self-object in a transition from self-love to object love and provides much needed authority and structure within the self. Step 3 and the remaining steps in the twelve-step tradition of AA help the alcoholic move from a self-centered posture to a more mature one by helping the individual give up the overly prominent, grandiose parts of the self. The self-examination involved in taking "a moral inventory" (step 4), "making amends" (step 9), and "carrying the message to others" (step 12) inspires and instills a real concern for others and an increasing capacity for mature altruism. This effect of AA is genuine and lasting (i.e., for those who embrace it) and suggests that AA may produce permanent structural change, a result that has clinical and conceptual significance for psychoanalytic theory and practice.

## The Self and the Implications of AA

We have emphasized that the core vulnerabilities in the self or the nature of the character defects that AA counters have to do with childish and grandiose attitudes and dispositions contributing to their inability to control their lives or their drive to drink. Our emphasis has been on the total self as a concept involving a multiperson psychology that operates within individuals to govern and regulate their lives.

The growing self-psychology literature, especially the work of Heinz Kohut (1971, 1977), has provided a useful basis for understanding the vulnerabilities in self-organization that AA so effectively contains and transforms. In trying to understand how a cohesive sense of self develops, Kohut focused on early disappointments in the mother–child relationship. He attempted to explain how certain archaic narcissistic structures persist into adulthood and how these infantile structures interfere with the development of more mature adaptations. Attitudes of grandiosity, over- and underestimation of others, and persistent search for comfort from outside the self (i.e., exaggerated self-object needs), as in addictive behaviors, may be adult manifestations of these structures and vulnerabilities, and derive primarily from the disappointments in the early relationship with the mother. Alcoholics Anonymous provides an environment of caring individuals, a supportive group that accepts the alcoholic's frustrated self-object needs. It heals and repairs those parts of the self Kohut found to be especially vulnerable in those suffering traumatic disappointments, especially a capacity for self-soothing and self-comforting and the enjoyment of ordinary exhibitionistic display.

In contrast to heavily and multiply addicted drug abusers, alcoholics, in our experience, do not suffer from global narcissistic personality disturbances. However, the program is sufficiently ingenious (especially in its expanded NA version), in providing sustenance, comfort, and repair that it can be effective in the more extreme cases where there is pervasive character pathology. Our emphasis here has been on poorly developed functions that are precursors of self-governance as opposed to pervasive structural defects in the development of self (Mack 1981).

## AFFECTS AND ALCOHOLISM

Alcoholism is a complex disorder in which problems with self-governance malignantly interact with other vulnerabilities such as disabilities in regulating feelings (i.e., affects) and self-care to cause biologically susceptible individuals and others to become hopelessly dependent on alcohol. In this section we consider how alcoholics and others with related conditions experience their feelings in unusual or atypical ways, so that the feeling-altering effects of alcohol become welcome.

Early psychoanalytic theory placed drives at the root of most emotional and behavioral disturbances. In the case of alcoholism, for example, excessive orality or oral drives were invoked as the main motivation for alcoholic drinking, an explanation most psychodynamic clinicians would now find embarrassingly unuseful (Khantzian 1987). Yet the drive or instincts, as Schur (1966) suggested, are important sources of psychic energy and motivation. They originate in the body and put pressure on ego-executant functions. An adequate account of mental life, including the lives of alcoholics, is needed to take them into account. However, as indicated in an earlier review (Mack 1981), and as Tomkins (1962) suggested, drives are rigid and unmodifiable in nature, whereas affects or feelings, which are more flexible and derive from drives, are the important and prime motivators in human emotions and behavior.

It would appear from our own observations and those of others (Gottheil et al. 1973, Ludwig 1961, Mathew et al. 1979, Pattison et al. 1977) that the powerlessness that alcoholics experience in relation to the impulse to drink is not simply a function of irresistible craving but occurs in a context of psychological distress. We have tried to focus on the nature and quality of affects (or feelings) associated with psychological distress and how a person's feeling life interacts with the effects of alcohol.

A fruitful area for further investigation would be how the unusual and atypical ways alcoholics experience their affects or emotions influence craving and related behavior. We suggest that the flexibility of affects to which Tomkins referred is lacking in alcoholics, because of the atypical ways in which alcoholics experience and express feelings. The expressive aspects of AA may help to increase the flexibility of the feeling life of alcoholics.

Over the past twenty-five years, important clinical and theoretical explorations involving disturbances, deficits, and dysfunction in affect experience have produced findings that are relevant and useful in understanding how the feeling problems of alcoholics may contribute to their reliance on alcohol. Although much of this work has been with addicts and alcoholics, some of the observations have occurred with populations with psychosomatic and characterologic pathology. These observations have made note of and underscored the following:

1. Affects have a normal developmental line and are subject to developmental arrest and traumatic regression (Krystal and Raskin 1970, Lane and Schwartz 1987, Schmale 1964).
2. Addicts, and psychosomatic and acting-out, character-disordered patients display extreme patterns of experiencing affects, some feeling too much and others feeling too little or being devoid of feelings (Khantzian 1979, 1981, Krystal and Raskin 1970, McDougall 1984).
3. Affects may be somatized, undifferentiated (i.e., patients cannot distinguish anxiety from depression), or not verbalized (Krystal 1982, Krystal and Raskin 1970).
4. Affective dysfunction for some is primarily characterized by denial or absence of feelings (e.g., disaffected, nonfeeling responses, or hypophoria) (Martin et al. 1978, McDougall 1984, Sashin 1985).
5. Affective dysfunction may be manifest primarily in an inability to put into words (alexithymia) feelings that are only vaguely experienced or are felt to be diffusely unpleasant (dysphoria, affect deficit) (Khantzian 1987, Krystal 1982, Nemiah 1970, Sifneos 1967).
6. Specific affective states may be overwhelming (e.g., rage, extreme anxiety or dread, mania) as a consequence of early environmental trauma or neglect and/or as a consequence of defects and deficits in ego structure (Khantzian 1985b, Wurmser 1974).

7. The action of the various classes of drugs (i.e., stimulants, analgesic narcotics, hallucinogens, and sedative-hypnotics including alcohol) have specific and different actions that interact with painful or overwhelming affective states and structural deficits to make them appealing (Khantzian 1985b, Wurmser 1974).

It is clear from this partial list that affect deficits may be on a continuum and have differing qualities with regard to the problems of recognition, modulation, tolerance, and articulation of feelings. For some, affect deficits or dysfunction may be within the experiential realm of being unable to identify feelings; for others, it is within the expressive realm where alcoholics and addicts, for example, are unable to display feelings or put them into words, and for yet others the main problem or challenge has been to bear feelings.

Michael, a distinguished, middle-aged scholar with a fifteen-year history of alcoholism, was not as impaired as some in recognizing and expressing feelings. Instead, he aptly described in group therapy how he used alcohol to modulate both pleasant and unpleasant feelings. He described painful conflicts at a family reunion in which he debated taking over the piano playing from his older brother-in-law who was playing insipid and boring tunes. He described how painfully self-conscious he felt about performing and linked it to his puritanical and ambitious mother, who instilled in him at an early age antithetical admonitions: he must achieve great stature when he grew up, yet she often warned him that he must not show off. Finally, overcoming his painful inhibitions, which he realized would have been easily done with alcohol, prior to his having achieved and maintained abstinence, he took over the piano playing and quickly stirred the family into a rousing and enthusiastic sing-along with his spirited, rhythmic, and powerful style of playing. As he told his story in the group, he realized in retrospect that although he had enjoyed himself, he had also worked himself into a "frenzy"; he then also realized that if he had taken a drink it would have calmed his frenzy or, better still, he would not have noticed it at all. He realized further, after this episode, how much he depended on alcohol to dissolve his painful self-consciousness. Michael ruminated for several days after the party that he had "overdone it," until he spoke with a supportive and reassuring older sister who dispelled his anxieties. He also realized that if he had been drinking he might not have experienced, or even been aware of, his anxiety and embarrassment after the party, but he would have also been deprived of his sister's reassurance and the salutary aspect of bearing and working out his worry.

Clinical examples such as this suggest that further exploration of the complexities of alcoholics' experience and expression of feelings, comparing them, for example, with nonalcoholic special populations such as psychosomatic patients, trauma victims, and patients with personality disorders, would add greatly to our understanding of the disorder itself. Such studies should continue to shed further light on the ways alcoholics are different from or similar to these groups in their attempt to use alcohol to relieve the way they experience distress, and the degree to which dependence on alcohol causes regression in ego functions and further perpetuates their distress.

## SELF-CARE AND ALCOHOLISM

It is perhaps not surprising that early psychoanalytic formulations invoking drive psychology, and, more particularly, death instincts or unconscious death wishes or trends, are still often adopted to explain the motivations for heavy alcohol use, given its extreme and devastating consequences (Menninger 1938, Tabachnick 1976). What these explanations often fail to appreciate is that the degree of suffering alcoholics endure, which is often of unusual intensity, and their search for short-term relief through alcohol often override all other considerations. However, beyond this adaptive use of alcohol to relieve suffering, we (Khantzian 1981, Khantzian and Mack 1983, Mack 1981), have been interested in deficiencies and vulnerabilities in a capacity referred to as "self-care." Lack of self-care plays an important part in many impulsive disorders, seems to contribute significantly to the susceptibility of alcoholics and addicts to become involved with substances, and contributes to relapse when abstinence is achieved. There is little evidence that alcoholism is determined by death wishes or even by unconscious destructive motives.

As reviewed in Chapter 19, Freud (1913, 1915, 1916/1917, 1925) almost until the end of his life, considered the self-protective, survival functions in terms of libido theory and the ego instincts, emphasizing the investment of narcissistic libido in the protection and preservation of the individual, as opposed to object libido, which assured the survival of the species. Although toward the end of his life he explicitly indicated that the task of self-preservation was more within the domain of ego functions (Freud 1949), there have been surprisingly few attempts to explain this most important aspect of human existence. As we have emphasized in this volume, such functions are flagrantly or dangerously absent in certain conditions such as alcoholism, obesity, anorexia/bulimia, accident proneness, and other acting out/ impulse problems.

In adult life, healthy self-care concerns are manifested by appropriate levels of anticipatory responses such as embarrassment, shame, fear, worry, and the like when facing potentially compromising, harmful, or dangerous situations where to act or not act could do injury to oneself or others (Khantzian 1981, Khantzian and Mack 1983, Mack 1981). We have been struck by the absence of such anticipatory responses, or the absence of delay with regard to the behaviors and impulses leading up to and associated with the use of substances. Impairments in self-care capacities are even more evident in cases of relapse after prolonged periods of abstinence where one has already had the "benefit" of the disastrous consequences of alcohol use as a guide to knowing about one's vulnerability.

One patient told how an unpleasant encounter with his self-centered father would have precipitated another bout of drinking except for the help of AA. His father visited him and his wife and children. But during the visit the older man constantly seized the conversation from the children at the dinner table, after which the patient found himself becoming increasingly agitated and then unable to sleep. He found himself invoking the AA slogan to "get help," called some friends in AA and spoke about his problems the next day at an AA meeting. In his pre-AA days, despite the availability of his therapist to whom he had easy and frequent access, he said he would have ruminated and remained upset for days, whereas in this instance he found himself remaining safe at first ("I was very anxious—and obsessing—but I didn't drink"). By the next day he felt free of the distress his father's visit engendered. He stressed how the phone calls, the meeting, and "talking myself down" with the aphorisms from AA enabled him to avoid a possible relapse to alcohol and drug use.

Examples such as this suggest that the development and establishment of self-care functions such as self-soothing and delaying pain-avoiding impulsive action are not achieved as a solitary psychological process. Perhaps self-care, more than any other aspect of self-governance, can be seen as a multiperson psychology (see below). Working with alcohol- and drug-dependent patients in psychotherapy has provided constructive observational evidence of the characteristic ways such patients do or do not take care of themselves, how much difficulty they have in availing themselves of other people's help, and how their self-care problems pre- and postdate their alcoholism in the form of preventable accidents, and legal, financial, medical, and related difficulties. Continued psychodynamic and clinical investigation of self-care disabilities will help to clarify the degree to which addictive processes and illness compound and heighten self-care problems.

## EGO DEFENSE AND ADAPTATION

Alcoholics suffer because they have been vulnerable in sectors of their personality organization involving self-governance and the capacity to regulate feelings and self-care. Wherever there are gaps or deficits of functioning in psychological life, individuals develop and display compensatory defenses and characteristic traits and styles of coping, or "defects of character" (step 6 in the twelve-step tradition), such as those that AA asks to be removed.

Many of the defenses that alcoholics use are in the service of compensating for or ameliorating the "defect of affect defense." In some instances these defenses take the form of exaggerated character traits or personality styles that avoid dependency needs and feelings (Khantzian 1981). In other instances, the use of alcohol itself may be seen as a defense. Its effects may relieve unpleasant or overwhelming affects such as intolerable tension and anxiety (Krystal and Raskin 1970), or alcohol may be used to produce feelings of warmth, closeness, and affection by its softening of rigid, counterdependent defenses and character styles that prevent the expression of such needs and emotions (Khantzian 1979, Krystal and Raskin 1970).

Less well-organized patterns of defense against painful affect are evident in impulsive acts, including aggressive and violent behaviors, that ward off feelings of fear, loneliness, and helplessness. The effects of alcohol may augment such defensive behaviors, or may help to alleviate feelings of anxiety or fear that are generated by the behaviors themselves. Thus, self-medication with alcohol becomes a part of the defensive system or adaptation. It may be employed to relieve or eliminate feelings that are experienced as intolerable, or to produce or allow feelings that are otherwise difficult to bear or express (e.g., warmth and affection).

Rationalization and related defenses of denial and justification are prominent defenses associated with alcoholism and the alcoholic's adaptations. In particular, they serve to protect alcoholics from facing their hopeless attachment to alcohol itself and the degree to which their lives have become consumed with alcohol-related associations and activities. Alcoholics employ rationalizations to explain to others and themselves a psychophysiological process of which they are incompletely aware and that they do not understand, a process that constantly erodes and destroys their composure and self-respect (Mack 1981). Furthermore, rationalization may be a characteristic defense in some alcoholic families in which the minimization or denial of heavy alcohol use is transmitted intergenerationally. One recovering 38-year-old alcoholic of a wealthy alcoholic Midwestern family spoke in group therapy about how neither his alcoholic father nor his heavily drinking mother ever mentioned a word about his or their alcoholism or his recovery either prior to his hospitalization for detoxification or in the fifteen months of sobriety after hospitalization. During many subsequent visits with his parents in this time they continued to drink heavily while he was abstinent. The contrast was sharply evident.

Alcoholics demonstrate a range of characterological defenses and traits related to vulnerabilities in self-governance and self-regulation. The twelve steps of AA, especially admitting loss of control and asking a higher power "to remove all the defects of character," challenges such individuals to yield their investment in the primitive defenses they employ. Thus, counterphobic mechanisms, the justification and projection that accompany and compensate for self-care deficiencies (Khantzian 1981), and the attitudes of disdain, counterdependency, and disavowal of needs that are used to shield the alcoholic from old hurts and injury can give way to the beneficial humbling and softening acceptance of support, care, and comfort provided by AA.

The benefit from psychoanalytic treatment hinges less on the removal or reduction of symptoms than on a modification or restructuring of an individual's personality organization. Our own observations and the work of Brown (1985), Bean (1981), and Bateson (1972) suggest that beyond establishing abstinence and providing support, AA's therapeutic effectiveness may also include the production of structural change. Further clinical evidence will be needed to substantiate this possibility.

> For Phil, the patient described earlier, the experience with AA helped him to bring about a significant personality change. In his psychotherapy he described an episode in which he was shocked and hurt after a phone call to one of his sponsors. Without warning this man rejected him brutally with a rage-filled obscene verbal assault. In contrast to a previous pattern in which Phil would have most likely reacted with counterrage and counterattack, he sat and cried, aware of feeling hurt and sad. Guided by his AA program, he called several people for comfort and reassurance. Still feeling rejected and lonely, he then went to his bedroom, literally dropped to his knees (as learned from AA), and prayed intensely. He was surprised and pleased that by the next day his distress had left him. In his therapy hour Phil reflected and contrasted his recent hurt, which he sustained and tolerated, and his subdued response to his sponsor's attack, to his "old self," where, as an example, in his business he had a reputation for being tyrannical, aggressive, and retaliatory. Not insignificantly, during the same hour Phil also recalled that he had suffered from a "mild case of agoraphobia." He recounted examples of social anxiety and shyness, growing up and in college, which he had learned to overcome by medicating himself with alcohol. When he first joined AA and went to meetings without the protection of alcohol's antianxiety effect, he "felt incredibly uncomfortable, and at first stayed in back and didn't talk." But more recently this anxiety was abating and he was confident that he would "get it" even better in the AA program, a striking shift in attitude, given his previous avoidant reactions and behavior.

## COMMENT AND CONCLUSION

Whenever human psychological frailties occur, there is a corresponding tendency to disguise and deny that they exist. A contemporary psychodynamic understanding of alcoholism suggests there are degrees of vulnerability in self-regulation involving self-governance, feeling life (affect), and self-care that are involved in the predisposition to become and remain dependent on alcohol. AA succeeds in reversing this dependency by effectively challenging alcoholics to see that they disguise and deny their self-regulation vulnerabilities. Implicitly, if not explicitly, AA employs group processes to highlight and then modify the vulnerabilities that plague the lives of alcoholics. The focus of AA on the loss of control over alcohol and the insistence on maintaining identity of the suffering individual as an alcoholic (i.e., it is always that one is "recovering," never "recovered") is a useful if not essential treatment device. It permits alcoholics to acknowledge and transform vulnerabilities in self-regulation.

When AA underscores alcoholism as a "disease of denial," it is challenging the alcoholic's attempts to defend against that aspect of the self that is vulnerable, injured, or in a state of disrepair. These defenses are often evident in alcoholics in attitudes of self-centeredness, self-sufficiency, and disavowal of distress, which may alternate with or present as attitudes of abject self-rebuke and pity that defy and reject attempts at comfort and understanding. The organization confronts alcoholics' convictions that they can solve life problems alone or, worse still, that they are not solvable at all. It helps them to see that the challenge of self-governance is not a solitary process, and that yielding to and benefiting from the regulating influence of others in the program, with their care, concern, and even admonishments, is extraordinarily beneficial. By placing the alcoholics' inability to control their alcohol as the central focus, AA creates a basis to address a fundamentally important reality, namely, that as human beings we do not and cannot survive and grow on our own, and that governance of our lives as well as our behaviors is intimately linked and involved with other people.

Once alcoholics surrender to the human reality of interdependence through AA and accept their powerlessness to control their alcohol alone, other beneficial aspects of AA begin to provide a basis to address, repair, and strengthen other vulnerabilities involving deficits and dysfunction around one's feeling life and behaviors.

Alcoholics Anonymous is uniquely suited to provide support, to proscribe detrimental behavior, and to ameliorate guilt. It provides needed, practical coping tools, advice, and admiration—all beneficial elements that are necessary, especially early in recovery, for overcoming the psychological and physical debilitation associated with alcoholism. AA provides human contact in a structured group setting that encourages story telling and the recognition and sharing of feelings, the imparting of wisdom, the containing of emotions and behavior, and the teaching of interdependence and self-care (Khantzian 1987). These elements of the AA treatment approach respond appropriately to alcoholics' narcissistic hurts and defenses and to their incapacity to tolerate intense feelings and to take care of themselves.

The AA program is a special human invention that provides people who have been out of control, uncomfortable, and unable to communicate their distress a forum in which to practice, learn, and internalize growing capacities for containment, self-comfort, and self-expression. Although the treatment strategies are for the most part indirect techniques such as story telling and bearing witness to another's vulnerabilities, AA, as McGarty (1985) suggested, offers universalizing experiences that provide invaluable human association and an opportunity to try out alternative solutions for those who feel too anxious or traumatized to associate or to speak. It is on this basis that Enid Balint (1972) extolled the advantage of group experiences over individual ones for certain problems. She suggests that in individual therapy patients do not tolerate or are not always helped by becoming aware of the analyst's emotions, nor are they helped if the analyst is incapable of them. In contrast, certain emotions and experiences can be best tolerated and enjoyed in a multiperson or group context. When offering these ideas, Balint was not referring to the group experiences of AA but she could have been.

## REFERENCES

Alcoholics Anonymous (1977). *Twelve Steps and Twelve Traditions.* New York: Alcoholics Anonymous World Services.
——— (1978). *Twelve Steps and Twelve Traditions,* 4th ed. New York: Alcoholics Anonymous World Services.
Baker, H. S., and Baker, M. N. (1987). Heinz Kohut's self psychology: An overview. *American Journal of Psychiatry* 144:1–9.
Bales, R. F. (1944). The therapeutic role of Alcoholics Anonymous as seen by a sociologist. *Quarterly Journal of Studies on Alcohol* 5:267–278.
Balint, E. (1972). Fair shares and mutual concerns. *International Journal of Psycho-Analysis* 53:61–65.

Bateson, G. (1972). The cybernetics of "self": a theory of alcoholism. *Psychiatry* 34:1–18.

Bean, M. H. (1975). Alcoholics Anonymous: AA. *Psychiatric Annals* 5:3–64.

——— (1981). Denial and the psychological complications of alcoholism. In *Dynamic Approaches to the Understanding and Treatment of Alcoholism*, ed. M. H. Bean and N. E. Zinberg, pp. 55–96. New York: Free Press.

Brown, S. (1985). *Treating the Alcoholic: A Developmental Model of Recovery.* New York: Wiley.

Brown, S., and Yalom, I. D. (1977). Interactional group therapy with alcoholics. *Journal of Studies on Alcohol* 38:426–456.

Calder, K. (1979). Psychoanalytic knowledge of group processes: panel report. *Journal of the American Psychoanalytic Association* 27:145–156.

Freud, S. (1913). The claims of psychoanalysis to scientific interest. *Standard Edition* 13:165–190.

——— (1915). Instincts and their vicissitudes. *Standard Edition* 14:117–140.

——— (1916–1917). Introductory lectures on psychoanalysis. *Standard Edition* 16:243–463.

——— (1921). Group psychology and the analysis of the ego. *Standard Edition* 18:69–144.

——— (1925). An autobiographical study. *Standard Edition* 20:7–70.

——— (1930). Civilization and its discontents. *Standard Edition* 21:64–145.

——— (1949). Outline of psychoanalysis. *Standard Edition* 23:144–207.

Goldberg, A., ed. (1978). *Psychology of the Self.* New York: International Universities Press.

Gottheil, E., Alterman, A. L., and Skoloda, T. E., and Murphy, B. F. (1973). Alcoholics' patterns of controlled drinking. *American Journal of Psychiatry* 130:418–422.

Helzer, J. E., Robins, L. N., Taylor, J. R., et al. (1985). The extent of long-term moderate drinking among alcoholics discharged from medical and psychiatric treatment facilities. *New England Journal of Medicine* 312:1678–1682.

Hendrick, I. (1943). Work and the pleasure principle. *Psychoanalytic Quarterly* 12:311–329.

Hesselbrock, M. N., Meyer, R. E., and Keener, J. J. (1985). Psychopathology in hospitalized alcoholics. *Archives of General Psychiatry* 42:1050–1055.

Kernberg, O. F. (1977). *Large group processes: psychoanalytic understanding and applications.* Paper presented at the panel on Psychoanalytic Knowledge of Group Processes, American Psychoanalytic Association, New York, December.

Khantzian, E. J. (1979). Impulse problems in addiction: cause and effect relationships. In *Working with the Impulsive Person,* ed. H. Wishnie, pp. 97–112. New York: Plenum.

——— (1981). Some treatment implications of the ego and self disturbances in alcoholism. In *Dynamic Approaches to Understanding and Treatment of Alcoholism,* ed. M. H. Bean and N. E. Zinberg, pp. 163–188. New York: Free Press.

——— (1985a). Psychotherapeutic interventions with substance abusers—the clinical context. *Journal of Substance Abuse Treatment* 2:83–88.

——— (1985b). The self-medication hypothesis of addictive disorders: focus on heroin and cocaine dependence. *American Journal of Psychiatry* 142:1259–1264.

——— (1987). A clinical perspective of the cause-consequence controversy in alcoholic and addictive suffering. *Journal of the American Academy of Psychoanalysis* 15:521–537.

Khantzian, E. J., and Mack, J. E. (1983). Self-preservation and the care of the self-ego instincts reconsidered. *Psychoanalytic Study of the Child* 38:209–232. New Haven, CT: Yale University Press.

Kohut, H. (1971). *The Analysis of the Self.* New York: International Universities Press.

——— (1977). *The Restoration of the Self.* New York: International Universities Press.

Kohut, H., and Wolf, E. S. (1978), The disorders of the self and their treatment. *International Journal of Psycho-Analysis* 59:413–425.

Krystal, H. (1982). Alexithymia and the effectiveness of psychoanalytic treatment. *International Journal of Psychoanalytic Psychotherapy* 9:353–388.

Krystal, H., and Raskin, H. A. (1970). *Drug Dependence. Aspects of Ego Functions.* Detroit: Wayne State University Press.

Lane, R. D., and Schwartz, G. E. (1987). Levels of emotional awareness: a cognitive-developmental theory and its application to psychopathology. *American Journal of Psychiatry* 144:133–143.

Leach, B. (1973). Does Alcoholics Anonymous really work? In *Alcoholism: Progress in Research and Treatment,* ed. P. Bourne and R. Fox. New York: Academic Press.

Leach, B., Norris, J. L., Dancey, T., and Bissell, L. (1969). Dimensions of Alcoholics Anonymous. *International Journal of Addictions* 4:507–541.

Ludwig, A. M. (1961). On and off the wagon: reasons for drinking and abstaining by alcoholics. *Quarterly Journal of Studies on Alcohol* 22:124–134.

Mack, J. E. (1981). Alcoholism, AA and the governance of the self. In *Dynamic Approaches to the Understanding and Treatment of Alcoholism*, ed. M. H. Bean and N. E. Zinberg, pp. 125–162. New York: Free Press.

Martin, W. R., Haertzen, C. A., and Hewett, B. B. (1978). Psychopathology and pathophysiology of narcotic addicts, alcoholics, and drug abusers. In *Psychopharmacology: A Generation of Progress*, ed. V. A. Lipton, A. DiMascio, and K. F. Killam, pp. 1591–1602. New York: Raven.

Mathew, J. R., Claghorn, J. K., and Largen, J. (1979). Craving for alcohol in sober alcoholics. *American Journal of Psychiatry* 136:603–606.

McDougall, J. (1984). The "disaffected" patient: reflection on affect pathology. *Psychoanalytic Quarterly* 53:386–409.

McGarty, R. (1985). Relevance of Ericksonian psychotherapy to the treatment of chemical dependence. *Journal of Substance Treatment* 2:147–151.

Menninger, K. A. (1938). *Man Against Himself*. New York: Harcourt, Brace.

Nemiah, J. C. (1970). Denial revisited: reflections on psychosomatic theory. *Psychotherapy and Psychosomatics* 26:140–147.

Ornstein, P. H., ed. (1978). *The Search for the Self. Selected Writings of Heinz Kohut*, vols. 1 and 2. New York: International Universities Press.

Pattison, E. M., Sobell, M. B., and Sobell, L. C. (1977). *Emergency Concepts of Alcohol Dependence*. New York: Springer.

Rosenberg, P. (1984). Support groups: a special therapeutic entity. *Small Group Behavior* 15:173–186.

Sashin, J. I. (1985). Affect tolerance: a model of affect-response using catastrophe theory. *Journal of Social and Biologic Structures* 8:175–202.

Scheidlinger, S. (1964). Identification: the sense of belong and of identity in small groups. *International Journal of Group Psychotherapy* 14:291–306.

——— (1974). On the concept of the "mother-group." *International Journal of Group Psychotherapy* 24:417–428.

Schmale, A. H. (1964). A genetic view of affects. *Psychoanalytic Study of the Child* 19:287–310. New York: International Universities Press.

Schuckit, M. (1985). The clinical implications of primary diagnostic groups among alcoholics. *Archives of General Psychiatry* 42:1043–1049.

Schur, M. (1966). *The Id and the Regulatory Principles of Mental Functioning*. New York: International Universities Press.

Sifneos, P. E. (1967). Clinical observation on some patients suffering from a variety of psychosomatic diseases. In *Proceedings of the Seventh European Conference on Psychosomatic Research*. Basel: Karger.

Simmel, E. (1948). Alcoholism and addiction. *Psychoanalytic Quarterly* 17:6–31.

Spruiell, V. (1975). Three strands of narcissism. *Psychoanalytic Quarterly* 44:577–595.

Stewart, D. A. (1955). The dynamics of fellowship as illustrated in Alcoholics Anonymous. *Quarterly Journal of Studies on Alcohol* 16:251–262.

Tabachnick, N. (1976). Death trend and adaptation. *Journal of the American Academy of Psychoanalysis* 41:49–62.

Tiebout, H. M. (1943–44). Therapeutic mechanisms of Alcoholics Anonymous. *American Journal of Psychiatry* 100:468–473.

——— (1961). Alcoholics Anonymous: an experiment of nature. *Quarterly Journal of Studies on Alcohol* 22:52–68.

Tomkins, S. (1962). *Affects, Imagery, and Consciousness*, vol. 1. New York: Springer.

Trice, H. M. (1957). A study of the process of affiliation with Alcoholics Anonymous. *Quarterly Journal of Studies on Alcohol* 18:39–54.

Vaillant, G. E. (1983). *The Natural History of Alcoholism*. Cambridge: Harvard University Press.

Vanicelli, M. (1982). Group psychotherapy with alcoholics. *Journal of Studies on Alcohol* 43:17–37.

Wurmser, L. (1974). Psychoanalytic considerations of the etiology of compulsive drug use. *Journal of the American Psychoanalytic Association* 22:820–843.

Zinberg, N. E. (1977). Alcoholics Anonymous and the treatment and prevention of alcoholism. *Alcohol: Clinical and Experimental Research* 1:91–101.

Zinberg, N. E., and Fraser, K. M. (1979). The role of the social setting in the prevention and treatment of alcoholism. In *The Diagnosis and Treatment of Alcoholism*, ed. J. H. Mendelson and N. K. Mello. New York: McGraw-Hill.

# 25

# Alcoholics Anonymous —Cult or Corrective?[1]

I have recently been using an aphorism with patients, most usually in group therapy, about the "two-part secret of making it in life." My aphorism derives in part from what I have heard from patients, usually drawing on their exposure to Alcoholics Anonymous (AA) and its aphorisms, but my two-part secret I patched together on my own. Somewhat lightheartedly but challengingly, I tell my patient(s) that the two-part secret is (1) to keep showing up and (2) to hang in there. In offering it here I realize that removed from the context of a therapeutic relationship, where the timing of such a statement has to be

---

1. This chapter was the 1994 Distinguished Lecture in Substance Abuse, delivered on January 14, 1994 at North Shore University Hospital–Cornell University Medical College, Manhasset, NY.

just right, my two-part secret might sound corny, unoriginal, and possibly not useful; worse still, for the more skeptical or cynical, it could be off-putting. Nevertheless, when I have shared the secret in clinical contexts, it has been met with acceptance, tinged with amusement and curiosity, by most of my patients. It usually draws them in and engages them with me, with themselves, and with the other members in a therapy group. It focuses them on what the problems and benefit are of showing up and hanging in.

It seems to me that one of the most basic problems in life, whether it is in its ordinary dimensions or when it involves impairment and recovery, is the human difficulty in initiating and maintaining human contact. We are told, and presumably it is so, that one of our more unique attributes as a species is that we are social creatures, and by nature we seek and need contact with others. Nevertheless, from infancy through senescence, it has been my experience and observation that human contact and its preservation is one of the aspects of life that at best keeps changing, and at worst is extremely difficult. It often eludes us or we avoid it when we most need it. At other times, we have it and/or discover it, operating unobtrusively and often beyond our awareness, only to realize we miss it and are pained when it slips away from us, sometimes of our own doing and at other times not of our doing.

What I am getting at here is the fundamental fact that most human problems are not best encountered or solved alone. People who have been in small and/or large group experiences for the purpose of obtaining help learn this lesson well. One of the more extraordinary examples of this realization is the benefit that so many participants of AA have derived from their group involvement with each other. The effectiveness of AA in helping people to attend and persist in the program (i.e., to show up and hang in) creates the necessary conditions to recognize, understand, and modify the vulnerabilities in themselves and each other that have devastated them and caused them to lose control of their lives. Twelve-step programs do this not by enslaving or engulfing the self with substituted forms of mind control and subordination of self, as occurs in cults; rather, such programs succeed by creating conditions of interdependence, safety, and comfort, which provide the potential for human maturation and the transformation of self.

In this case study I focus on some of the psychological vulnerabilities involved in alcoholism and drug addiction and examine how AA can succeed in accessing and modifying these vulnerabilities. I compare how twelve-step programs operate to modify the person or self therapeutically with the ways cults access and modify the self, which some have alternatively suggested is the way AA actually works.

I begin with a case example. I then relate my points about the case to my understanding of addictive vulnerability, and discuss how twelve-step programs are an extraordinarily effective antidote and corrective to such vulnerability.

## A CASE STUDY

Gary is a handsome, intense, determined, 30-year-old married anesthesiologist in training, whose decision to pursue medicine initially was postponed, because of certain personality traits, an unrecognized drug dependency, and financial considerations. Although he finally got on track with his medical training, he was crushed when his long-planned-for dream to become a medical practitioner was abruptly interrupted in the middle of his residency training with the program's discovery of his addiction to fentanyl, a short-acting, rapid-onset synthetic opiate used in anesthesia. At first he reacted by vehemently denying wrongdoing or addiction and resisted the intervention that was imposed on him. However, once in treatment, his qualities of determination resurfaced and began to allow him to pursue recovery as earnestly as he had pursued his career.

His boyish, attractive, and casual manner made him appear more youthful, but his youthfulness was strongly juxtaposed with qualities in his speech—articulateness and precision—and a commanding presence, which made him seem older and wiser. Although he was average in height, his compact and rugged physique and imposing style made him an even more formidable character. All in all, he was an attractive and admirable man, notwithstanding that his personal and professional identity and future were in doubt because the discovery of his addiction had left him personally shaken, unemployed, and without a license to practice.

I first met him through his answering machine. He had reached my answering service when he called to arrange aftercare treatment, having been released from an eleven-week inpatient rehabilitation program about one month before. When I returned his call, I was greeted by an upbeat, outspoken voice and quality of speaking on his answering machine that resembled a cross between a southern swaggering cowboy and gunslinger, his greeting ending with the exhortation, "You-all leave a message, you heah?" Frankly, I was put off by the swagger in the recording and anticipated meeting some kind of difficult rogue when I set up an appointment for his evaluation. In fact, once we met, I did not feel put off by him, and my impression was and has continued to be as positive and admiring as I have already described.

From the outset it seemed to me his recovery program was working, in the sense that it had already initiated a healthy process of self-examination and self-reflection. He began the interview by indicating that in admitting to his problems with drugs and alcohol he realized he had always been a "risk taker and stimulus seeker." He said he realized now that he probably was an addict before he ever touched a drink. Gary then abruptly shifted to describing other aspects of himself, saying he was "blessed" with a good mind and athletic ability, which allowed him to excel as a student and athlete. He was first in his high school class of 400 and a four-sport athlete. His rapid-fire characterization of himself was as revealing in his asides about himself as in the impressive accomplishments and activities he enumerated. In describing his gift to read people and relate socially, he casually added he "had a body and mind built for excess." He joined a fraternity in college where drinking and drugging was heavy and pervasive, and he said he "fit right in—yet stayed at the top of my class." When asked, he speculated that the alcohol and marijuana (which he preferred) enhanced his outgoing style. When I asked him if it was easy to be outgoing, he quickly, yet I believe significantly, offered that he was a serious child. He then just as quickly went on to emphasize that once he discovered his success through his personal gifts, he obtained a thrill out of his achievements and liked the attention he derived, especially the thrill and "rush" from winning. Yet, he conceded, it was never enough and he was always anticipating his next conquest.

After fairly heavy experimentation and use of alcohol and other drugs through college and graduate school—and general behavioral excess that earned him the labels of a "maverick" and "diamond in the rough"—he finally began to significantly curtail his drug use (marijuana was always his first choice) once he entered medical school. Looking back, he now realized that his offbeat style and excess probably put people off and had directly and indirectly delayed his acceptance to medical school. Heavy drinking became limited to social functions where it was considered acceptable.

This relative pattern of moderation, especially his curtailment of drugs, continued upon commencing his residency training, but perhaps became even more limited because he had moved, was very busy, and had few friends or contacts in his new city to persist in his previous pattern. As he neared the final phase of his training program, which was short staffed, he had an extra work load and was more often on call. At a time when he was totally inactive physically and suffering many colds and flu-like symptoms, he said he reached for fentanyl. The drug primarily provided a numbing antidote to the progressive sense of feeling tired, sick, and lonely. In retrospect, Gary also realized that his resorting to drugs at that time had occurred in a context of feeling that he was "never happy and had no skills in reaching out or asking for help." He felt his wife was doing the best she could, and he felt he could not reach out to her or anybody else about his anxiety concerning his upcoming boards, his sense of not keeping up, and his feeling mentally and emotionally exhausted.

So much for my initial encounter with Gary as my patient—his strengths, his vulnerabilities, his personality, which served him and defined him, and his fentanyl dependence. I would now like to leap to a session two months later and turn to the strength of his program and his own special capacity to embrace and be embraced by it.

It was clear that the twelve-step program was serving him well in countering his denial and sense of invincibility, and catalyzing an extraordinary process of self-examination, admission of vulnerability, emotional awakening, and reaching out and asking for help. The session followed a five-day reunion with his wife. The discovery of his fentanyl dependence had coincided with her being offered a position back home in the Midwest, which, with his encouragement, she had accepted. They had not been with each other for several months at the time of their reunion. He had anticipated it with considerable apprehension, knowing that one source of his "never being happy" was a sense that he had for a long time felt his marriage had been a mistake. They had been living together when he was accepted into medical school. It was she who suggested marriage at that time, and he had just "gone along." Before the visit with her, he had broached with me his plan to discuss getting a divorce.

But in this session two months after our initial encounter, and five days after the dreaded reunion with his wife, it was not the reunion that he initially spoke of. After some preliminary social amenities, he began by telling me that he was physically sore, explaining that with a friend he had climbed one of the highest mountains in our region two days earlier. He commented, "It's near winter up there," and we both spontaneously acknowledged that he was characteristically and once again "near the edge." As he went on, however, he seemed as if he was near something else as well, and that his ascent to the top of the mountain was also a metaphor for other transformations that were taking place. After clarifying that he and his friend had been painstaking in planning, timing, and safely equipping themselves for this climb (i.e., being more careful and less of a risk taker), he described the beauty and "near spiritual quality" of the climb. It was then that he went on to review the tense, pain-filled, but emotionally satisfying visit with his wife. Gary said, "We talked and talked, took breaks to enjoy ourselves (e.g., go to the movies), talk about things we never talked about—including my intention to seek a divorce—and shared my darkest and worst fear—that our marriage was a mistake." His wife was not surprised, admitting that she too had given thought to a divorce, and sharing as well her apprehension about his addictive illness, recovery, and their future prospects. Although he felt relieved and "off the hook" by her reactions, he went on, nevertheless, to reveal how they openly wept together and continued to open up to secrets they had not previously shared. He confessed to old secrets about money he had used for drugs and two affairs—as he said, "by way of making amends."

As he continued, I was impressed by how reflective he was, his openness, and his vulnerability, thinking he was changing as fast as anyone does, in or out of psychotherapy. I was also remembering that on a recent attempt to call him, even the message on his answering machine was changed, and it was an ordinary one simply asking for the name and telephone number. I chose to comment on all the changes. I observed that there was an absence of the old bravado—that he seemed less shielded and, thus, more open. Gary responded by saying that he had given a lot of thought to, and worry about, shame, regret, and what could have happened. He emphasized his realization that he needed to better know and speak his own feelings. As he did so, he filled up, openly wept, and briefly even sobbed. When I asked where his feelings were coming from he explained that the major problem was his regret that he had never previously been able to do just what he was doing—experiencing and expressing his own feelings. Being unable to do so had not allowed him, he said, to honestly express what he did and did not want to do. In part, he was referring to the deceit in his marriage, but he meant more. He said, "It all has to do with regret about not being open, not being a feeling, human being." He made reference to going around problems rather than through (i.e., facing) them, and that as he was changing he was feeling better and, feeling in a better place, especially realizing how much his secrets (and not feeling) was holding him back. He said that when he had been on the mountaintop two days earlier he had felt as free spiritually and mentally as he ever had, no longer fearing to look back or over his shoulder with regret or shame about secrets, his manipulations, or his conniving. He spoke of his family being there for him (he had opened himself to them as well) and that they were supportive; he expressed the conviction that people thought more of him than ever before, which made him feel "joyful." He underscored the benefit of "dumping" his problems with his family, friends, and myself, and thus no longer being burdened by his guilt.

I have presented Gary's case at some length because he provides illuminating insights into the strengths, vulnerabilities, and pitfalls of addictive illness. But even more important, in what follows, he also reveals the strengths and benefits of twelve-step programs. With very little prompting, during this same visit, he provided, almost point to point, a description of how his recovery program is appropriately attuned to his emotional and relational handicaps, including related self-esteem and self-care deficiencies, and effectively responds to and serves as correctives to his suffering and the characterological style and defensiveness that shielded him from being and becoming a more comfortable, satisfied, and satisfying person(ality).

After reviewing the remainder of this session, in which he gives his own account of this transformation, I will review and elaborate on what it is that is disordered in the person (or personality) of substance-dependent patients, and what I believe are some of the crucial elements in effective recovery programs that provide corrective experience for the disordered person or self that suffers these illnesses.

But for now, let's pick up on Gary's account. As I indicated, it came with only slight prompting.

I said, "It seems your program has had an extraordinary transforming effect on you." He said, in reply, that at the rehabilitation center he had told his counselor he felt he had no further to go (i.e., in his personal and professional descent). The counselor had promptly retorted, "Not quite, you had six feet more to go." The counselor had commented on his bravado and how he had not felt anything in a long time. Gary contrasted that exchange early in his recovery with the present; he said, "I cry on a dime now—and it feels natural." He reflected that the program was the last chance he had, alluding to one of the guides of the program, "Try it for sixty days, and if you don't like it we'll hand back your misery in full." Gary observed that the program had provided some "spark of a sense of self." He elaborated that rehab helped to put things in an "I/we, first person" form, helping him to ask for what he needed and express what he felt. He said, "I found out I wasn't such a bad guy down in there, with all my dire consequences—no job or license, and a likely divorce. I have more meaningful care and relationships than I have ever had." I asked him to elaborate a bit more. He explained that he now had the ability to get his secrets out and to find out, "I am better than I thought." He continued in his description; he said his family, his friends, and his wife embrace him; people in the AA meeting rooms embrace him. He said he now felt he could call people whom he feared—his chief of service, the director of the Physician's Health Program, and colleagues—and could face them and even realize they wanted him to be with them, for example, for the upcoming holiday dinners. He couldn't see this at first, but reminded me that others saw this in the program before he could.

As the end of the hour approached, I reflected out loud some more about his transformations and suggested or requested that I might use his experience to help others in appreciating how AA helps people to change and correct their vulnerabilities. He simply and generously agreed. I reflected a bit more with him about what my patients had taught me from the program that distinguishes between abstinence and sobriety. I told him that beyond the help in establishing abstinence, the program worked because it mainly affects and establishes sobriety by accessing and modifying vulnerabilities involving emotions, relationships, self-esteem, and self-care. I added that his efforts and work over these past weeks and months had gotten him to the top of the mountain, literally and figuratively, in a different way. In response he reflected on the timing of his being out of work and not yet reinstated, and how things work out—in his case, how not working coincided with and helped immensely to deal with his wife's visit and their relationship, one of his most daunting problems. He concluded the hour with this thought: "Coincidences are God's way of maintaining His anonymity."

## SHOULD AA BE CONSIDERED A CULT?

### The Short Answer

All small and large groups run the risk of subordinating the will and identity of an individual to the values, attitudes, and objectives of the group and its leader(s). In fact, in some respects it is an inevitable if not at times a necessary aspect of acculturation and civilized life. A detailed analysis of whether AA is more within the norms of ordinary group formation and participation, which have legitimate expectations and traditions, or whether AA is extreme to the point of subordinating and exploiting members, goes beyond the scope of my presentation. However, I would offer my bias, based on my clinical experience and, for our purposes here, this case study, that AA has much less the characteristics of a cult and more the characteristics of a therapeutic group process that produces personal transformations and maturation. In this section, I briefly present some characterizations and examples of cults, and my thoughts and recent observations of others on how and why some aspects of AA might border on the cultish, but ultimately avoids such a pitfall.

### Cults—Some Definitions and Comments

Louis Jolyon West (1993) offers some characterizations of the type of people who join cultist movements, such as the Branch Davidian cult in Waco, Texas, and presents some definitions based on a consensus derived at the international "Wingspread" Conference held at Racine, Wisconsin, in 1985. The Branch Davidian cult and the People's Temple in Jonestown, Guyana, where 900 followers of Jim Jones committed mass suicide, are extreme examples in which members submit to ideologies and mind control that cause them to follow their leaders to the tragic, violent end of all life (i.e., affirmation of the most deadly, destructive, and dominating motives of the leader).

A totalist type of cult is "a group or movement exhibiting a great or excessive devotion or dedication to some person, idea or thing, and employing unethical, manipulative, or coercive techniques of persuasion and control designed to advance the goals of the group's leaders to the possible or actual detriment of members, their families, or their communities" (West 1993, p. 2). To some extent elements of these risks or consequences are potentially inherent in any human intervention, particularly in those involving group approaches. Cults use the methods of isolation, suggestibility, subservience, manipulation of information, extreme group pressure, total dependence on the group, and fear of leaving it. Leaders in cults are dominant, intense, charismatic, egotistical, and shrewd. Some con men, like David Koresh, are ruthless, clever, dangerous, and unpredictable.

Thus, considering the aims of cults and the modes and qualities of leadership, there is little basis to conclude that AA in its aims or method of leadership is a cult. Mack (1981) has eloquently reviewed and analyzed how the authors of the twelve steps and twelve traditions of AA avoid the risks of "the egocentric pitfalls of leadership that accounts for the *absence* of perpetuating offices or positions of direct authority in AA" (p. 138, my italics), traditions that surely are antithetical to those of cults. More recently, although coming from a more skeptical perspective, where Bufe (1991) emphasizes the irrational, religious, and dogmatic aspects of AA and considers whether AA is a cult, he readily concedes that AA is neither exploitive nor manipulative of its members, nor does it use criticism, mind control, violence, or harassment with its dissident participants.

Notwithstanding the above, there probably is a borderland between cults and self-help groups that should be considered. Marc Galanter (1990) has thoughtfully considered the borderland. It is an excellent review, but his title, "Cults and Zealous Self-Help Movements: A Psychiatric Perspective," detracts from the merits of the paper. "Cults" and "zealous" have pejorative and negative connotations, but only in small part does Galanter focus on the negative or deleterious aspects of cults. As opposed to extreme or totalist-type cults, he considers groups such as the Unification Church ("Moonies"), the Divine Light Mission Hare Krishna, and the Children of God (all of which he studied) as movements that develop when society does not "address fundamental social problems." He draws parallels to zealous healing movements such as AA when professionals are unable to meet the medical problems of its members.

Galanter interchangeably uses the terms *cult, zealous self-help movements*, and *charismatic groups*. He stresses common elements of group cohesiveness, shared beliefs and, to a lesser degree, "altered consciousness" (p. 544). Galanter argues that these elements operate to control behavior and to change and "modulate affect—without overt coercion" (p. 544). Coercion utilizes physical force and confinement. In charismatic groups, psychological forces are employed to instill beliefs and alter behavior. Changes in these respects are socially reinforced, positively or negatively, when members feel (or fail to feel) affiliated with the group. Relief (or distress) results depending on acceptance or rejection of group norms.

Galanter concludes that acute distress is a motivator to joining charismatic groups. He provocatively asks, "How [does] such distress work to motivate engagement and which symptoms are most influential?" (p. 550).

In my opinion and in the opinion of my patient, Gary, distress, linked to core symptoms or vulnerabilities involving affects, self-esteem, relationships, and self-care problems, is at the root of addictive disorders and likely serves to motivate group involvement. Gary also provides evidence that twelve-step groups such as AA get to the bases of members' problems, and they do so therapeutically without subordination or loss of self, and without mind control.

## AA AS A CORRECTIVE

AA serves as a corrective by effectively challenging the part or parts of a person who won't engage or maintain group contact. Once AA overcomes this fundamental resistance inherent in the disease of alcoholism, it works as a corrective by concurrently improving members' awareness and by processing core issues of distress. At the same time characterological flaws and traits of self-deceit, invincibility, and denial are also addressed.

## General

Alcoholics suffer with two fundamental psychological problems—one enmeshed with the other—that require examination and correction. First, they suffer because they are unable to control their alcohol or to control (or regulate) themselves. Their self-regulation problems principally involve their emotions, their self–other relations, and their behavior. Second, they suffer because they cannot admit to their suffering or vulnerabilities, but instead adopt defenses of self-sufficiency and pride, which leaves them isolated and cut off from themselves and others. Their suffering heightens their defensiveness, which, in turn, further perpetuates their suffering. It is in this respect that their pain is enmeshed in their personality, at the same time that their personality heightens that pain.

Alcoholics suffer in the extreme with the human penchant to deceive, disguise, and deny vulnerability when they most desperately need to admit to and accept it. It is a self or person—in disorder around pain and admitting to it—that needs correction. AA succeeds because it first and foremost successfully penetrates the formidable defenses of self-sufficiency and pride that stand in the way of whatever else is in disorder or in need of change. Once this formidable resistance to engage or connect is overcome, all kinds of possibilities open to the individual for self-examination and maturation. AA works as a corrective because it effectively deals with these two challenges that alcoholic patients present. The first involves problems with initiation and engagement, and the second, with the maintenance of contact.

## The Challenge of Initiation, Engagement, and Maintenance of Contact

The steps, traditions, and structure of AA succeed by penetrating the alcoholic individual's defenses of self-sufficiency and pride, especially a pride or arrogance that insists they can control their lives alone and on their own terms, at the same time that they deny their need for or dependency on others. The first two of the twelve-steps are probably the most crucial ones in breaking through the "defects of character," which makes possible the most important admissions that are necessary to get started and to benefit from the rest of the program: (1) the admission of vulnerability ("we were powerless over alcohol"); (2) the admission of loss of control ("our lives had become unmanageable"); and (3) the admission of the need for contact with someone or some power beyond self ("a power greater than ourselves could restore us to sanity").

An extensive literature describes the elements of AA that succeed in helping individuals establish abstinence and address some of their special psychological needs (Alcoholics Anonymous 1939, 1976, 1978, Bales 1944, Bateson 1971, Bean 1975, 1981, Brown 1985, Kurtz 1982, Leach 1973, Leach et al. 1969, Stewart 1955, Tiebout 1943–44, 1961, Trice 1957, Zinberg 1977). The works of several of these authors are especially noteworthy because they go beyond the abstinence issue and address the more fundamental and sophisticated elements of AA that make it a powerful and effective group psychology for instilling personality change and ameliorating alcoholic and addictive suffering. Tiebout, a pioneering psychiatric clinician in alcoholism in the 1940s, was one of the first to comment on the characterological problems alcoholics must face and overcome regarding engagement and contact, namely, an overriding egoism and self-absorption. Bean's (1981) work on breaking through the alcoholic's denial; Zinberg's (1977) review of AA's management of problems with denial, dependency, and fears; and Brown's (1985) focus on the essential and central importance of control problems in alcoholics and their need to maintain an identity as an alcoholic are all more precise advances in appreciating corrective if not curative aspects of AA, especially in providing valuable insights into how AA helps with the challenge to overcome the patient's problems with engagement and contact in and out of the program.

Two names—Gregory Bateson and Ernest Kurtz—stand out in respect to the challenge our patients must face with regard to initiating and maintaining contact. Bateson (1971) published a seminal work adopting systems theory (he refers to cybernetics and the epistemology of the alcoholic), suggesting that alcoholics are locked into a symmetrical (versus complementary) relationship with alcohol and others that is competitive and combative. The need for others is denied and a belief is maintained repeatedly that the alcohol cannot kill and that it can be controlled. Bateson believes that the conversion experienced by AA members reflects a shift from a symmetric habit or epistemology, to a complementary one in which the battle with the bottle is relinquished and there is a shift to and a sense of being part of something larger than self. AA provides a basis to shift from an epistemology based on self-sufficiency and pride to one of complementary and meaningful contact beyond self in the context of supportive, helpful relationships (Brown 1985).

Kurtz (1982) expands on these themes and takes us a step further by underscoring the two main realizations that AA keeps forcing: (1) our essential limitations, and (2) our shared mutuality. Drawing heavily on the parallels with existential philosophy, he observes that for existentialists, acceptance of limitation marks the beginning of sanity, and for alcoholics it is the first step to sobriety. He observes that alcoholics drink to control their feelings and their environment, even though their drinking becomes absolutely out of control; they drink to deny their dependency on others, yet their dependency on alcohol becomes absolute. Beyond seeing AA as therapy for these two problems, he eloquently builds the related case for AA as a therapy for shame. He allows for our human dilemma, one particularly powerful in alcoholic patients, of infinite thirst juxtaposed to essentially limited capacities, and offers that AA helps to transcend this dilemma of shame-filled limitation by being with and accepting the human need for others.

I have highlighted the work of Brown, Bateson, and Kurtz because it directly pertains to the characterological issues that alcoholics knowingly or unknowingly dread, avoid, or struggle against, that is, the challenge I originally spoke of, to show up and hang in, or what I have called here the challenge of engagement and contact. What makes engagement and contact difficult for most individuals, but especially for alcoholics, is their shame. They are limited, but cannot admit it. That is, they fall short of the mark; they suffer one of the worst of human fates—the fate of inadequacy, of being not good (Kurtz 1982). Alcoholic patients endure their guilt—the consequence of being bad or unworthy, which (not insignificantly) is more controllable—better than they endure their shame. This is why Kurtz believes, and I agree, that AA is an effective treatment for shame. It is structured to expose the denial of, and the inability to be honest about, limitation and mutual vulnerability.

Contemporary psychodynamic clinicians and theoreticians, independent of these contemporary perspectives of AA, have come to similar conclusions about core limitations and structural deficits in substance-dependent patients. These limitations and deficits make self-regulation (i.e., emotions, self–other relations, and behavior) and admission of vulnerability difficult (Dodes 1990, Khantzian 1981, Khantzian et al. 1990, Krystal 1989, Mack 1981, Simmel 1948, Wurmser 1974).

AA deals with many "nots" that haunt alcoholic patients and their treators: not showing, not persisting, not contacting, not calling, not asking, not feeling, and not knowing. AA is successful because it is a general and specific corrective for the defects of character or character flaws that make engagement and contact difficult or impossible.

## The Challenge of Self-Regulation

The step-by-step approach, the fellowship, camaraderie, good humor, and story-telling traditions of AA are also ingenious and effective in correcting other aspects of the disordered alcoholic person (i.e., the many "nots" and inadequacies) involving regulation of emotions, self-esteem, relationships, and self-care.

Alcoholics, besides being disordered in their capacity to make and maintain contact, are also disordered or disregulated in their emotions, self–other relations, and behavior. I will only briefly touch on patients' self–other problems, but will stress more their problems in regulating emotions and self-care. I will conclude with some reflections about the program, and about Gary in particular, and about how AA serves as a corrective to these self-regulation vulnerabilities.

Patients with drug-alcohol problems suffer with basic and core deficiencies in their sense of self. It affects their ability to comfort and soothe themselves; it erodes their self-confidence, their self-esteem, and/or their ability to love or think well of themselves. It should not be surprising that their faulty or deficient sense of self makes them shaky, unconfident, and inconsistent in their relationships with others. Matters of dependency, closeness, trust, and intimacy become a major challenge, or they are met with despair, withdrawal, and avoidance. Drugs and alcohol act as buffers, dampers, or augmentors in coping with the painful emotions that one's relationship with self or with others engenders. To this extent, as is the case with disordered emotions, both the use of substances and the characterological defenses employed serve such individuals as an attempt at self-correction that ultimately backfires. But, I conclude, and my patient Gary demonstrates, AA serves as a more enduring corrective to these problems.

Patients with drug/alcohol problems suffer especially because they cannot regulate their emotions or behaviors. These two areas of psychological deficiency are the results of self-regulation vulnerabilities. They cause them great difficulty in knowing, experiencing, or expressing their emotions (affects) at the same time that they demonstrate deficits in their self-care that leave them susceptible to hazards and dangers, not the least of which are those associated with substances.

On the affect side, patients with substance use disorders exhibit extremes in the way they experience affect or feeling life. They feel too much or too little. In the former instance, affects such as rage, dread, or despair are experienced as unbearable, and susceptible individuals discover that the specific action of addictive drugs counter such pain, much the same as legitimate psychotropic medications counter or alleviate psychological suffering and psychiatric distress. In the instances where patients do not know or cannot give words to the more vague states of distress and dysphoria they experience, drugs of dependency are adopted to change or give a sense of control over feelings that otherwise are experienced as confusing and beyond control, even if the drugs make them feel worse.

As my patient Gary reveals, these vulnerabilities are not only painful in and of themselves, but they also impact on character traits and styles that attempt to defend against the pain, but also further perpetuate it. It is not uncommon, and in fact it is more often the case, that these affect deficits are linked to qualities in personality organization in which activity (including hyperactivity), circumstantiality, stimulus seeking, and risk taking are common.

These affect deficits combine malignantly with self-care deficits to give addictive disorders their unyielding, repetitive, compulsive, and destructive characteristic. In the case of the self-care deficits, we have described elsewhere how they result in an inability to ensure or govern one's survivability (Khantzian 1981, 1990, Khantzian and Mack 1983, 1989). This disturbance in regulating self-care involves deficits in signal affects and cognitive responses necessary for guiding action and behavior to ensure safety. Patients with this deficit think and act differently in the face of danger. Fear, worry, apprehension, judgment, and appreciation of cause-consequence relationships are faulty, underdeveloped, or absent in substance-dependent individuals. This explains much of the attendant self-injurious and self-destructive aspects of addictive problems. Characterological signs of self-care vulnerabilities in alcoholic/addicted patients are evident in their qualities of counterphobia, bravado, aggressive posturing, and exaggerated self-reliance.

## GARY—A TRANSFORMATION IN SELF

Before concluding, I will briefly summarize and analyze the corrective influence of Gary's twelve-step program on his character defects and his suffering. As already indicated, his testimony and example are extraordinary because they were forthcoming with so little prompting, yet are so consistent with what AA and contemporary psychodynamic understanding teaches about such patients. From the outset, Gary made it clear that, by temperament, preference, and discovery, he was heavily driven to action and the challenge and thrill of success. His bravado, swagger, and counterdependency, combined (by his own admission) with a penchant for risk taking and stimulus seeking, placed conquest and achievement ahead of comfort and solidity in relationships. His admission that he was at first a serious child suggests that at least in part his counterdependency and self-sufficiency were a compensation or defense for a more vulnerable self. As he engaged with the recovery program and began to "get it," he indicated that AA was succeeding by stimulating an emotional awakening, catalyzing a process of self-examination and admission of vulnerability, and it was countering his considerable denial and sense of invincibility and bravado. The program was fostering a capacity to reach out and ask for help at the same time that he was able to be emotionally open and honest, especially with his wife. His deficiencies in self-care were being influenced by his program and were evident in his more apparent efforts to be careful and take less risks behaviorally. As he was becoming less shielded, a greater capacity to be self-reflective and more subdued was also more apparent. He spontaneously gave more thought to worry, shame, and regret. He saw how important it was to know and speak his feelings, and he was ashamed and regretful that he had been unable to do so, openly weeping about how this inability had been so costly personally. He was regretful and ashamed that he couldn't be honest about what he did and didn't want to do, that he was not open, and that he could not be a feeling human being. He made it abundantly clear that AA was resolving his sense of regret, shame, secrecy, deceit, and manipulativeness. The program had provided "a spark for a sense of self," allowing him to ask for what he needed and to express his feelings. These transformations, finally, were resulting in more meaningful care for himself and in relationships with others. As he said, "I can get things out and be affirmed that I am okay—better than I thought I was."

## CONCLUSION

We have explored elsewhere in more detail the beneficial aspects of the twelve-step/AA programs on the self-regulation vulnerabilities in alcoholic and addicted patients (Khantzian and Mack 1989, 1994). I have only briefly alluded to them here. The narrative traditions of storytelling, sharing, and bearing witness to each other's distress, and the traditions of openness and honesty act as sources of comfort and support for people who otherwise would go on in their lives with their distress unnoticed, unspoken, and unacknowledged. Each story told of succumbing to and recovery from drug or alcohol dependency has aspects in it of vulnerabilities involving troubled and confusing emotions, self–other relations, and behavior. Sometimes told with anguish and remorse, sometimes offered with humor or self-derision, often awkward and stumbling, and at other times spoken with great eloquence and inspiration, the stories not only reveal the core of self that suffers, but they also reveal character strengths and weaknesses that demonstrate the infinite variations and variety of ways in which we succumb or survive, recover, and restore ourselves. This is the profoundly important aspect of groups, which AA exploits as a therapeutic modality. It addresses the problems of the suffering that our patients endure, offering relief, even as it offers extraordinary opportunities for self-examination and personal maturation.

## REFERENCES

*Alcoholics Anonymous* (1939). 1st ed. (1976: 3rd ed., 1978: 4th ed.) New York: Alcoholics Anonymous World Services.

Bales, R. F. (1944). The therapeutic role of Alcoholics Anonymous as seen by a sociologist. *Quarterly Journal of Studies on Alcohol* 5:267–278.

Bateson, G. (1971). The cybernetics of "self": a theory of alcoholism. *Psychiatry* 34:1–18.

Bean, M. H. (1975). Alcoholics Anonymous: AA. *Psychiatric Annals* 5:3–64.

——— (1981). Denial and the psychological complications of alcoholism. In *Dynamic Approaches to the Understanding and Treatment of Alcoholism*, ed. M. H. Bean and N. E. Zinberg, pp. 55–96. New York: Free Press.

Brown, S. (1985). *Treating the Alcoholic: A Developmental Model of Recovery*. New York: Wiley.

Bufe, C. (1991). *Alcoholics Anonymous—Cult or Cure*. San Francisco: See Sharp Press.

Dodes, L. M. (1990). Addiction, helplessness and narcissistic rage. *Psychoanalytic Quarterly* 59:398–419.

Galanter, M. (1990). Cults and zealous self-help movements: a psychiatric perspective. *American Journal of Psychiatry* 147:543–551.

Khantzian, E. J. (1981). Some treatment implications of the ego and self disturbances in alcoholism. In *Dynamic Approaches to Understanding and Treatment of Alcoholism*, ed. M. H. Bean and N. Zinberg, pp. 163–188. New York: Free Press.

——— (1990). Self regulation and self-medication factors in alcoholism and the addictions: similarities and differences. In *Recent Developments in Alcoholism*, vol. 8, ed. M. Galanter, pp. 255–271. New York: Plenum.

Khantzian, E. J., Halliday, K. S., and McAuliffe, W. E. (1990). *Addiction and the Vulnerable Self*. New York: Guilford.

Khantzian, E. J., and Mack, J. E. (1983). Self-preservation and the care of the self—ego instincts reconsidered. *Psychoanalytic Study of the Child* 38:209–232. New Haven, CT: Yale University Press.

——— (1989). Alcoholics Anonymous and contemporary psychodynamic theory. In *Recent Developments in Alcoholism*, vol. 7, ed. M. Galanter, pp. 67–89. New York: Plenum.

——— (1994). How AA works and why it is important for clinicians to understand. *Journal of Substance Abuse Treatment* 11:77–92.

Krystal, H. (1989). *Integration and Self-Healing—Trauma, Affects and Alexithymia*. Hillsdale, NJ: Analytic Press.

Kurtz, E. (1982). Why AA works—the intellectual significance of Alcoholics Anonymous. *Journal of Studies on Alcohol* 43:38–80.

Leach, B. (1973). Does Alcoholics Anonymous really work? In *Alcoholism: Progress in Research and Treatment*, ed. P. Bourne and R. Fox. New York: Academic Press.

Leach, B., Norris, J. L., Dancey, T., and Bissell, L. (1969). Dimensions of Alcoholics Anonymous. *International Journal of the Addictions* 4:507–541.

Mack, J. E. (1981). Alcoholism, AA and the governance of the self. In *Dynamic Approaches to the Understanding and Treatment of Alcoholism*, ed. M. H. Bean and N. E. Zinberg, pp. 125–162. New York: Free Press.

Simmel, E. (1948). Alcoholism and addiction. *Psychoanalytic Quarterly* 17:6–31.

Stewart, D. A. (1955). The dynamics of fellowship as illustrated in Alcoholics Anonymous. *Quarterly Journal of Studies on Alcohol* 16:251–262.

Tiebout, H. M. (1943–44). Therapeutic mechanisms of Alcoholics Anonymous. *American Journal of Psychiatry* 100:468–473.

—— (1961). Alcoholics Anonymous: an experiment of nature. *Quarterly Journal of Studies on Alcohol* 22:52–68.

Trice, H. M. (1957). A study of the process of affiliation with Alcoholics Anonymous. *Quarterly Journal of Studies on Alcohol* 18:39–54.

West, L. J. (1993). Commentary—cult expert explains Waco implications. *Psychiatric Times* 10:1–2.

Wurmser, L. (1974). Psychoanalytic considerations of the etiology of compulsive drug use. *Journal of the American Psychoanalytic Association* 22:820–843.

Zinberg, N. E. (1977). Alcoholics Anonymous and the treatment and prevention of alcoholism. *Alcohol: Clinical and Experimental Research* 1:91–101.

# 26

# Trauma and Addictive Suffering: A Self-Medication Perspective[1]

As many of the chapters and case reports in this book reveal, individuals who suffer with substance use disorders (SUDs) have endured extreme environments in which they have been victims of severe abuse or neglect. In many of the cases, the trauma occurred in early childhood, having a pervasive effect throughout the individual's life and seemingly predisposing them to a dependency on alcohol or other addictive drugs. In other instances, the traumatic influence(s) and the

---

1. This chapter is a version of a paper presented at the New York chapter of the International Society for Traumatic Stress Studies on May 10, 1997. It is in part based on Chapter 15, "The Self-Medication Hypothesis of Substance Use Disorders."

development of a SUD was more contemporary in their life, such as the extreme experience of Vietnam veterans, which for many resulted in a similar chaotic emotional and behavioral disruption, including reliance on drugs, to that of individuals suffering from childhood trauma. Because of the repeated and common association between posttraumatic stress disorder (PTSD) and SUD, this book would be incomplete without a discussion of the relationship between these two conditions.

Individuals with PTSD and SUD share in common suffering and subjective states of distress that do not go away, as many of the case vignettes in this book and in this chapter make so tragically clear. As van der Kolk and colleagues (1996) have evocatively stated, "The posttraumatic syndrome is the result of a failure of time to heal all wounds" (p. 7). Although PTSD and SUD are associated with *DSM-IV* co-occurring psychopathology, the core issues of suffering and distress are not best explained by the axis I and II psychiatric disorders often associated with either or both conditions. Rather, they are subjective states of distress—states that are enduring, distorted, and distorting. That is, more than anything, trauma forever changes our relationship to external reality and our inner subjective world—especially in the domain of affect (or feeling) life.

This chapter reviews how the enduring nature of suffering in PTSD interacts with the pain-relieving and pain-controlling effects of substances, making it more likely that PTSD victims are at risk to use, become dependent on, and relapse to addictive substances. I review core elements of the self-medication hypothesis (SMH) of addictive disorders and how it pertains to traumatic life experiences and PTSD.

## PTSD AND SUDS—A SELECTED REVIEW

There is an extensive literature documenting a significant association between PTSD and SUDs. I will selectively highlight some of this literature to show how early and recent life traumas can cause individuals to suffer and make it more likely that substances of abuse can become compelling.

Clearly the relationship between traumatic life events, an individual's psychological makeup (i.e., personality organization), and the effects of addictive substances involves complex interactions. As I have already suggested elsewhere in this volume, many nonaddicted individuals suffer in the ways that addicted individuals suffer, but they do not develop SUDs; similarly not all individuals who experience trauma go on to develop either PTSD or SUDs. (For a more detailed exploration of these themes, especially on what are the contributing and essential factors that combine to make SUDs likely, see Chapter 15.) Critics of the viewpoint of a causal link between PTSD and SUDs not surprisingly raise the cause-consequence controversy. Namely, does PTSD cause SUDs, or does a reliance on addictive substances cause or precipitate a PTSD syndrome or disorder? Similarly, such critics raise the question of whether both conditions might have common antecedents. These are legitimate questions that must await more studies, especially longitudinal ones, that can track more systematically the impact of trauma, personality development, and the capacity (or incapacity) for resilience and the ability to endure pain and distress.

Notwithstanding these considerations, most of the literature reflects a strong interaction between PTSD and SUDs, underscoring the major suffering and coping problems of individuals with PTSD. As I have noted elsewhere in this volume (see Chapter 15), the seminal works of Krystal (1988), van der Kolk (1987), and Herman (1992) have emphasized the persistent and pervasive suffering and life disruption in the lives of trauma survivors, and all three have noted the frequent association between PTSD and SUDs.

Over the past four decades, our society has witnessed the tragic and persistent consequences suffered by veterans of the Vietnam War. A section of the annual volume of *Recent Developments In Alcoholism* (Galanter 1988) devoted to the Vietnam experience amply documents the pervasive and tragic impact that the war had on many veterans. More importantly, in those cases where PTSD was found, the reports show a disproportionate co-occurrence of SUDs. In a review by Nace (1988), 40 to 50 percent of PTSD veterans abused alcohol. Strikingly, Nace commented on the strong countertransference these patients evoked in the treating clinicians, reactions that he felt were powerful indicators of the enormous suffering these individuals had endured. Keane and associates (1988) studied treatment-seeking patients at a VA medical center and found a very high percentage of them (63–80 percent) suffered with concurrent SUDs. Kosten and Krystal (1988) focused on neurotransmitters and endocrinologic disruptions in Vietnam veterans and linked their findings to the role of the addictive substances to which the veterans had reverted. They suggested that alcohol and heroin probably were a means to actively cope or adapt to an otherwise helpless stance under the acute stress of the war. They further commented that alcohol could temporarily counter states of anhedonia and numbing associated with PTSD. Penk and his associates (1988) similarly concluded that there was a "traumatogenic" basis for substance abuse in Vietnam combat veterans. They documented avoidant coping styles associated with PTSD and SUDs and underscored important interactions between substance abuse, trauma, and stress.

Beyond the Vietnam experience, data gathered from a large epidemiological database and special patient populations also reveal a strong link between PTSD and SUDs. Cottler and colleagues (1992), drawing on Epidemiologic Catchment Area (ECA) data, found 430 out of 2,663 respondents reported a traumatic experience that could qualify for PTSD. In their study, respondents who used cocaine or heroin were more than three times as likely to have experienced trauma as those who did not use; most commonly the trauma was some form of physical attack. Studying a sample of female patients in a substance abuse treatment program, Brady and colleagues (1994) found a high incidence of PTSD, and that these patients with PTSD were more likely to have suffered physical and sexual abuse and to have elevated Addiction Severity Index scores. Along similar lines Grice and colleagues (1995) found that 66 of 100 substance-dependent females had significant abuse histories, and that half of the sample studied satisfied criteria for PTSD. Swett and Halpert (1994) found that female psychiatric inpatients who reported histories of physical and sexual abuse scored significantly higher on the Michigan Alcoholism Screening Test (MAST).

Although this review of the literature is limited, it is representative and shows that empirical studies on PTSD support clinical findings on the nature and degree of psychological pain entailed in addictive suffering. They reveal that trauma in people's lives causes major and persistent suffering and makes it more likely they will use substances in disproportionately heavy patterns and be more severely addicted than those who do not suffer trauma.

## TRAUMA, ADDICTIVE SUFFERING, AND SUBSTANCE DEPENDENCE: A CASE VIGNETTE

"A fate worse than death—endless suffering." Krystal has eloquently and poignantly described the enduring consequences of infantile psychic trauma—that is, when the developing infant is overwhelmed as a result of emotional abandonment or trauma at the hands of an inadequate or damaging caregivers. The above quotation is drawn from his experience observing and describing (personal communication) some of the adult manifestations of such antecedents in individuals who have suffered the burden of such a legacy. Some of these manifestations include the inability to know, endure, or describe their emotions; chronic somatic preoccupations and symptomatology; psychic numbing alternating with affective flooding; and addictive behaviors.

Henrietta was a woman in her late twenties who had suffered such a legacy and who through much of her short adult life persistently displayed all of the painful features associated with infantile trauma. Among her many somatic dysfunctions and complaints were severe and unrelenting headaches that became complicated by the development of a physical and psychological dependence on analgesic opiates. Emotional, anesthetic withdrawal under her bedcovers for days at a time alternated with extended tirades of rage directed at family or anyone else who came within the orbit of her care. The belated realization that as a young child she had been chronically violated sexually by her grandfather had only heightened her volatility and seething anger. I had two occasions to witness these qualities in my capacity as a consultant. The first time was when I was called upon to advise on the suitability of utilizing methadone both for headache relief and as a means to ameliorate her disabling emotional volatility. My brief contact with her helped me to appreciate her endless suffering first hand as I sat with her reviewing her history and symptomatology. Serendipitously, on the second occasion, I had a chance to indirectly observe the unsettling nature, for herself and others, of her intense anger and volatility when I came upon her in the parking area outside of my office screaming at her mother, literally for the community to hear, over some real or imagined outrage she was experiencing.

So I was shocked, yet not surprised, when her mother called me to inform me that she had found Henrietta dead, lying face down in her crumpled bedcovers, having apparently smothered to death. She explained that her daughter had probably oversedated herself, given her penchant to self-medicate her distress, and she assumed her death was accidental. She wanted to emphasize this point because there were no recent suicidal threats, and Henrietta had been more buoyant recently because of a relationship with a new boyfriend. In addition, she was positively anticipating treatment with a new therapist.

As the distressing conversation with Henrietta's mother went on, what became more daunting for me was her preoccupation and insistence that an autopsy not be performed on her daughter. She persisted in asking that I use whatever influence I had to intercede for her and her daughter to prevent what appeared to be a mandatory autopsy by the medical examiner. The mother explained to me that her daughter had anticipated a premature death, dreading that even in death she would be violated. She had expressed the wish that she never be "cut open" under such circumstances.

At first I thought Henrietta's mother's almost sole concern and preoccupation so soon after discovering Henrietta's body represented some misunderstood dynamic between her and her daughter. The next day I concluded that this consideration probably was not the main one for Henrietta's mother. In fact, the real meaning of Henrietta's and her mother's concern became clearer to me the next day, when I was participating in one of many symposia/workshops with Henry Krystal and we had a chance to exchange ideas and experiences on matters involving trauma, addictions, and the human psychological distress these conditions entail. I noticed again in one of his slides the term *endless suffering*. Suddenly it became clearer that Henrietta's mother was the transmitter of what Henrietta knew and felt, at least as well as Krystal knew it as a scholar and as a survivor. I realized how much deeper and more pervasive her fear and terror had been. It was so great, in fact, that she believed her suffering to be endless and that even in death she would be violated. As a footnote to her case, it is also worth mentioning the importance of the opiates in her life. It was one of the few agents that ameliorated the other dominating affect that constantly threatened to overwhelm her, namely her rage. I elaborate below on this appeal of opiates.

## PTSD—*DSM-IV* CRITERIA

I believe that the narrative (i.e., clinical narrative) of a person's life experience can often best evoke and convey the nature of a patient's clinical condition, as the above case vignette poignantly demonstrates. Henrietta's story provides ample testimony to the nature of trauma and the relationship between PTSD and addictive suffering. I would be remiss, however, if I did not include here a formal and accepted criteria/description of the core features of PTSD. The *DSM-IV* (American Psychiatric Association 1994) lists the main features of PTSD as follows:

- Reexperiencing the trauma including recurrent memories, dreams, and related psychological distress.
- Persistent avoidance or numbing.
- Decreased interest in important activities; feelings of detachment; restricted affect.
- Hyperarousal including sleep disturbance, irritability/anger, poor concentration, hypervigilance, and increased startle response.

I believe the recurrent affective flooding, numbing, hyperarousal, and related emotional distress and behavioral dysregulation are the most important criteria. They interact with drug and alcohol effects, and are powerful determinants of the practice of self-medicating.

## PTSD AND SELF-REGULATION

As I have repeatedly indicated in this volume, a major motive for using and becoming dependent on substances of abuse is the discovery of the pain-relieving properties of substances. People learn they can employ these effects to self-medicate their distress. As I have also explained, the self-medication process can best be understood in a broader context of understanding drug/alcohol abuse and dependence as a self-regulation disorder. That is, substance-dependent patients do not suffer simply because they cannot regulate their feelings. They also suffer because they cannot regulate their estimation of themselves (i.e., self-esteem/love), their relationships with others, or their self-care.

These vulnerabilities are profoundly interwoven into the pattern of the lives of individuals who have suffered major traumatic life experiences.

It should not be surprising, then, that PTSD results in a profound psychological rearrangement, and further compounds a person's problems with self-regulation. There are major alterations in affect life, self-image/-esteem, relationships, and self-care. Affect life is experienced in the extreme such that an individual feels too much and is overwhelmed, or he/she feels too little and is rendered emotionally paralyzed. It is on this basis that we speak of PTSD victims as experiencing polar extremes of emotional flooding or emotional numbing. As I will elaborate in the subsequent section, the case vignettes in this book amply document how the various classes of addictive drugs can differentially relieve or alter these extreme emotional states. That one's sense of self, or regulation of self-esteem, can be profoundly effected by trauma should not be surprising.

A 48-year-old, twice divorced mother of five children was evaluated by me in a case conference. She was described as being severely abused through most of her life, first by her stepfather, who tormented her sexually, physically, and verbally from the age of 4 into her early teens; subsequently by an older brother, who sexually violated her when she was 8 to 13 years old; and then, as an adult, by two husbands, who severely physically abused her. Anticipating the case conference, she was extremely apprehensive and focused in particular on how I and those in attendance would judge her. As the following essay, written for the conference by the patient exemplifies, her concern about others' view of her touchingly reveals a deeper and persistent problem with her view of herself.

### My Care Cup

Way down, deep inside me, I have a "care cup" where I care so much about what people think of me. But even a little deeper I feel compassion for how uncomfortable others are who know the truth about the things I have been through. I imagine I feel the same way as a burn survivor or a person that's all twisted up in a wheelchair from a crippling disease. So, in response to their response I try to act OK and not let others see the damage and my traumas from the abuse that I have experienced in my past. I'll call it "Hiding the Monster" that others seem to see in me, the thing that makes them so uncomfortable around me. Actually, the "monster" is how their reactions make me feel. Way back when I told my mother what my stepfather had been doing to me, her reaction made me feel like a monster because that's how she treated me. She seemed to get very angry at me and she acted like she was scared to death. I'm not saying that all people respond this way. I'm only saying that's why I try to hide, so they won't run away, leaving me alone like my mother did when I was only 4 years old. When she turned her back on me, I turned and ran to find a corner of another room where I could bury my face and cry. I felt like my heart had broken and I was so ashamed of my mother for that response. That shame has made me very sad and lonely for many years.

This case exemplifies many of the features of PTSD. The pain she endures is self-evident; it affects her view of herself as well as her view of others and how they see her. I need not argue too strongly that her perceptions are both distorted and distorting, and her capacity for self-regulation has been profoundly rearranged, especially in the domain of self-esteem. Initially, starting in her teens, heavy doses of alcohol ameliorated the resultant emotional turmoil. Later, as an adult, she found crack cocaine to be an effective and preferred antidote for her persistent anhédonia and psychic numbing.

An accomplished 38-year-old alcoholic attorney who came from a privileged but nevertheless abusive background (she was repeatedly sexually violated by her older brother and his friends from the age of 12), revealed in group therapy how profoundly her experience and regulation of her relationship with others were affected by her sexual trauma. She repeatedly commented in a cynical manner about her circle of "friends." She especially delighted in making a caricature out of a psychiatrist friend. In group she made a split between her male buddies in the group and myself as the group leader, who she considered a "phony." As she elaborated in several exchanges, she vocalized how, despite her high ethical standards and other admirable professional qualities, she considered herself and just about everyone else (again not hesitating to single me out) as being insincere in their expressions of care for one another. She was most visibly uncomfortable in group when I or other members offered positive feedback or expressions of concern for her distress or well-being. She had discovered alcohol was a more reliable way to warm up and regulate her relationship with others.

Finally, if it is true that as human beings none of us escapes the tendency for vulnerabilities in our psychological apparatuses (structures), then the capacity for regulating our self-care is no exception. Developmentally, the capacity for self-care is more or less established in early childhood, and the degree to which it is intact ensures our survival; when it is damaged or underdeveloped, our survival is jeopardized. Trauma often causes people to seem to not care about self-harm or behaviors that are obviously self-destructive. This apparent indifference for one's safety has the appearance of an active self-injurious or even suicidal element. Upon closer examination, however, these behaviors and other more subtle aspects of self-protection more often result from deterioration in an individual's psychological functions and defenses as a consequence of trauma, where otherwise a person would more ordinarily be anxious, aware, and vigilant in the face of harm or dangerous involvements. Paradoxically, in one respect PTSD leaves individuals hypervigilant as if threat was ever-present; in other respects trauma causes failures in basic self-care. Further, individuals so affected just as frequently lapse in self-protective measures and reactions to a variety of hazards and threats, and all too often these involve the dangers of addictive drugs and related behaviors. As I have reviewed elsewhere in this collection, it is the self-regulation disturbances in affects and self-care that malignantly combine to make dependence on substances of abuse more likely and compelling.

Given the major impact that psychic trauma has on a person's life, the impact on a person's capacity for self-regulation is tragically amplified with all its attendant complications including those involved with drug-alcohol use and dependence. Thus, substances of abuse serve as a prosthetic for vulnerabilities in self-regulation, and especially so for those who suffer with PTSD.

## PTSD AND SELF-MEDICATION

The two fundamental aspects of the SMH—(1) that addictive drugs relieve human psychological suffering, and (2) that there is pharmacologic specificity that causes preference for one class of drugs over another—preeminently apply to self-medication factors being involved in PTSD. I have extensively reviewed these two aspects of the SMH in Chapters 11, 12, and .15. To briefly summarize here, opiates (e.g., heroin, Percodan, Demerol) have their appeal because they are powerful antiaggression and anti-rage agents. They quiet and counter these powerful affects and produce a sense of calm from within, and make self–other relations feel more safe and manageable. Depressants, such as alcohol and short/rapidly acting benzodiazepines (e.g., Valium, Xanax, Halcion) have their appeal because they have a softening or relaxing action on tense, rigid defenses that guard against needs for trust, emotional, warmth, and closeness. Stimulants such as cocaine and amphetamines have appeal because of their energizing and activating properties. They counter states of inactivation and low energy present in overt clinical depression or in its more subtle or atypical forms, thus explaining the surge of well-being and enhanced self-esteem produced by stimulants. Drugs such as cocaine also appeal to high-energy, hypomanic (i.e., not quite manic), "fast-lane" types because they augment such modes, making it easier for such people to be that way. Stimulants also have an opposite effect (thus widening the net of their appeal), in that they paradoxically calm and focus individuals who suffer with attention deficit hyperactivity disorder (ADHD); this is as true in the case of illicit cocaine use as it is when it is legitimately prescribed in the form of Ritalin for individuals who suffer with ADHD.

Considering these specific effects or actions of these various classes of drugs, it should not be surprising that they powerfully interact with the intense, painful affect (feeling) states and behavioral dysregulation associated with PTSD.

Violent and aggressive feelings are an (almost) invariable feature of PTSD. Henrietta's case makes this amply clear. Early in my career, working with opiate-dependent Vietnam veterans in a methadone program, I was repeatedly impressed with how such patients described the calming, normalizing, and muting action on persistent feelings of anger and violent affect. This was evident in their interactions with staff and each other in the methadone program, and especially apparent in our intake rap groups before they had been stabilized on methadone (a long-acting synthetic opiate used to substitute for their drugs and to prevent relapse to street narcotics, especially heroin). These rap groups were used as a vehicle for transitioning people to methadone while the program and the federal requirements for methadone treatment were being processed. The use of obscenities and vitriolic attacks on each other or the group leader was not uncommon. As the individuals stabilized on the long-acting opiate methadone, there was a striking diminution in the aggressive use of the obscene language and the violent and aggressive group interactions. As already noted, a majority of these patients were trauma victims and/or Vietnam veterans.

More recently, evaluating borderline patients (a condition strongly associated with histories of severe abuse and trauma) in a long-term residential facility for addicted females, I have been impressed with how the use of opiates had forestalled or precluded more regressed manifestations of this condition, such as self-mutilation and rage turned on self or others. In this case, the calming and containing action of the drug had seemed to protect against the trauma-induced rage. This contrasted sharply to the ravaging effects that had occurred in their counterparts who had not discovered or used opiates in our long-term psychiatric facility, where I also evaluated many borderline patients. In these latter cases the uncontained rage and violent feelings/impulses were apparent in the form of self-mutilation, swallowing of objects, assaults on self and others, and repeated violent emotional outbursts. Although many of these patients were dually diagnosed and had experimented with other drugs, fortunately (or unfortunately) opiates were not one of them.

In contrast to the uncontrolled feelings of aggression and rage in certain traumatized patients who find opiates compelling, some of these same patients and others self-medicate the sense of emotional volatility, constriction, and numbness with depressants such as alcohol and related drugs. Alcohol, depending on the dose, can release or contain emotions. In low to moderate doses, it causes people to experience both positive and negative emotions that they otherwise cannot feel or express, including feelings of affection, warmth, and dependency, or irritability, anger, and dislike. Not uncharacteristically, under such conditions individuals describe how they can relax, warm up, and enjoy the company of others. One patient described how a drink could help her "achieve a sense of bliss, harmony, and openness." These liberating or loosening-up reactions, in the absence of the alcohol effect, are hardly like the ones of anhedonia and psychic numbing experienced by severely traumatized individuals. However, used in high doses, alcohol can obliterate or numb affects that become over-whelming or unbearable, as is so often the case when trauma victims periodically experience affective flooding.

As I indicated in the previous section, the energizing properties of stimulants can counter states of anergia and inactivation associated with overt and subclinical forms of depression. Severely traumatized patients not only experience subtle and more severe forms of depres-sion, but also are crippled by a pervasive anhedonia and psychologi-cal paralysis (numbing). When such individuals experiment with or use cocaine and other stimulants, they discover, short term, how pow-erfully these agents can reverse their depression as well as the emo-tional paralysis associated with their traumatic experiences. Used long term or in high doses, stimulants can be extraordinarily disruptive and produce unwanted effects such as agitation, intense aggression, para-noia, and/or overt psychosis. Despite experiencing these intense un-pleasant effects, substance use disordered individuals, nevertheless, continue to use stimulants. Of interest and more troubling, PTSD individuals are not only not an exception to this tendency, but they often seem even more compulsively captivated by these harsh, pain-producing effects. I and others (Schiffer 1988) have commented on how these severely traumatized individuals who are cocaine dependent are drawn to repeat and reexperience these harsh effects as a way of ac-tively controlling and mastering their pain and the disruption that were much like the distress and suffering they passively experienced and did not control when they were originally traumatized. This seems to be the case independent of whether the trauma was long ago or recent in a person's life. I have elaborated in more detail on this dual aspect of substance use in this volume (see Chapters 7, 14, and 15) and elsewhere (Khantzian 1995, Khantzian and Wilson 1993).

## COMMENT AND CONCLUSION

The clinical examples and formal diagnostic criteria make it amply clear that PTSD survivors suffer endlessly and in the extreme. They continue to remember and reexperience the trauma in their waking hours, and they are unable to escape them in sleep, which for them is disrupted and repetitiously nightmarish. They remain avoidant and emotionally blunted, they lose interest in their surrounds, and they are detached and emotionally restricted. As much as trauma has shut them down, traumatized individuals are just as apt to be overaroused; sleep is disrupted by trauma replays, irritability, anger, and rage are constant companions, and the ability to focus and concentrate is offset by their hypervigilance or startle response. It should not surprise us then that the powerful feeling-altering action of addictive drugs can be so gripping and irresistible.

Patients self-medicate both the positive (e.g., agitation, rage, hyperactivity, and violence) and the negative (e.g., depression, numbing, anhedonia, inactivation) symptoms of PTSD. Their drug preference might be more exclusive because a particular affect might predominate, such as the continually enraged Vietnam veteran relying on heroin to contain his violent feelings. In other instances one's drug preference (or dose) might vacillate and be dictated by whatever symptoms predominate at any given time. A period of shutdown or numbing might be lifted by a low to moderate dose of alcohol or cocaine; emotional arousal and painful trauma recall might most readily be obliterated by consuming large amounts of alcohol or opiates. In general, and on the specific bases I have elaborated, PTSD victims are at high risk to discover that substances of abuse relieve states of anger, anxiety/fear, and panic, or in the other extreme, states of anergia, anhedonia, and affective flattening. Once this hook is set, the foundation for a substance use disorder is established.

Thus, PTSD causes major changes in ones capacity for self-regulation. These changes tend to endure and be long-lasting. Substances of abuse have powerful pain-relieving and pain-controlling properties. PTSD victims discover this, and as a consequence, such individuals are at high risk to become and remain dependent on addictive drugs.

## REFERENCES

American Psychiatric Association (1994). *Diagnostic and Statistical Manual of Mental Disorders*, 4th ed. Washington, DC: American Psychiatric Association.

Brady, K. T., Killeen, T., Saladin, M. E., et al. (1994). Comorbid substance abuse and post traumatic stress disorder: characteristics of women in treatment. *American Journal of Addictions* 3:160–164.

Cottler, L. B., Compton, W. M. III, Mager, D., et al. (1992). Posttraumatic stress disorder among substance abusers from the general population. *American Journal of Psychiatry* 149:664–670.

Galanter, M., ed. (1988). *Recent Developments in Alcoholism, Vol. 6.* New York: Plenum.

Grice, D. E., Brady, K. T., Dustan, L. R., et al. (1995). Sexual and physical assault history and post traumatic stress disorder in substance dependent individuals. *American Journal on Addictions* 4:297–305.

Herman, J. L. (1992). *Trauma and Recovery.* New York: Basic Books.

Keane, T. M., Gerardi, P. J., and Lyons, J. A. (1988). The interrelationship of substance abuse and post traumatic stress disorder: epidemiological and clinical considerations. *Recent Developments in Alcoholism* 6:27–48.

Khantzian, E. J. (1995). Self-regulation vulnerabilities in substance abusers: treatment implications. In *The Psychology and Treatment of Addictive Behavior,* ed. S. Dowling, pp. 17–41. Madison, CT: International Universities Press.

Khantzian, E. J., and Wilson, A. (1993). Substance dependence, repetition and the nature of addictive suffering. In *Hierarchical Concepts in Psychoanalysis: Theory, Research, and Clinical Practice,* ed. A. Wilson and J. E. Gedo, pp. 263–283. New York: Guilford.

Kosten, T. R., and Krystal, J. (1988). Biological mechanisms in post traumatic stress disorder: relevance for substance abuse. *Recent Developments in Alcoholism* 6:49–68.

Krystal, H. (1988). *Integration and Self-Healing: Affect, Trauma, Alexithymia.* Hillsdale, NJ: Analytic Press.

Nace, E. P. (1988). Post traumatic stress disorder and substance abuse: clinical issues. *Recent Developments in Alcoholism* 6:9–26.

Penk, W. E., Peck, R. F., Robinowitz, R., et al. (1988). Coping and defending styles among Vietnam combat veterans seeking treatment for posttraumatic stress disorder and substance use disorder. *Recent Developments in Alcoholism* 6:69–88.

Schiffer, F. (1988). Psychotherapy of nine successfully treated cocaine abusers: techniques and dynamics. *Journal of Substance Abuse Treatment* 5:131–137.

Swett, C., and Halpert, M. (1994). High rates of alcohol problems and history of physical and sexual abuse among women inpatients. *American Journal of Drug and Alcohol Abuse* 20:263–272.

van der Kolk, B. A. (1987). *Psychological Trauma.* Washington, DC: American Psychiatric Press.

van der Kolk, B. A., McFarlane, A. C., and Weisaeth, L. (1996). *Traumatic Stress.* New York: Guilford.

# PART V

# Treatment of the Addictions

## INTRODUCTION

This final section of the book focuses on the treatment of individuals who suffer with substance use disorders (SUDs). Treatments that succeed effectively respond to patients' needs and to the vulnerabilities that are at the root of SUDs. As the previous sections have shown, I have evolved a perspective that suggests addictive vulnerability is a result of individuals' being unable to regulate or control their feelings (affects), self-esteem, relationships, and self-care. The most effective treatment interventions rest on an empathic appreciation of these vulnerabilities. This is the case whether they entail self-help, individual or group psychotherapy, or pharmacotherapy. Clearly there is much pain and suffering involved, there is an inability to control one's life, and there are flaws (or defects) in character that govern or determine these vulnerabilities. With any approach, all these vulnerabilities or deficits must be addressed. In the chapters that follow I spell out from my perspective and experience how and why I think effective treatments work, how and why a range of treatment approaches need to be coordinated, and how to prioritize (and stage) treatment interventions in order to best target and alleviate the suffering and behavioral dysregulation involved in addictive disorders.

Chapter 27 was published in *Psychiatric Annals*, a popular trade journal that has been read by psychiatrists since 1970. This paper was published in 1976, when I, the addiction field, and the *Annals* were in an early phase of development. The *Annals* edition in which this article appeared was devoted to the emerging interests in self-help programs and how or if psychiatry could help addicted individuals deal with their dependence on drugs. At the time self-help groups seemed to have a stronger foothold in arguing for what was in the best interest of addicted individuals, and I and the few psychiatrists who were treating addictive disorders were struggling, often (as is apparent in this chapter) defensively, to establish that psychiatrists had a legitimate and necessary role to play in understanding and treating these disorders. In Chapters 20 and 21 in the previous section, I described what I thought were some of the unnecessary and counterproductive controversies between the AA/self-help approaches and traditional psychodynamic and psychiatric approaches to understanding and treatment. That was contentious enough, but the contention and conflict between self-help groups of the encounter or confrontational type, popular in the early 1970s, and the professional community were even more daunting and bitter. Consistent with my attitudes and temperament about this kind of divisive clamor, one of my objectives in writing this chapter was to make peace rather than war, and to tactfully address potential and actual pitfalls as well as strengths in the competing models. Of special interest, and as a sidelight, was the public and private debate I was carrying on (as I do in this chapter) with Dr. Mathew Dumont, a lovable but contentious ideologue and the then commissioner for drug rehabilitation in Massachusetts, who was an arch spokesperson for the self-help movement.

Chapter 28 on group treatment of unwilling addicted patients was my first paper (in collaboration with William Kates) on group psychotherapy for SUDs. At the time I was still learning about treating substance-dependent patients, in this case narcotic-dependent individuals in a methadone maintenance treatment program that we started in 1970 at the Cambridge Hospital and that continues to this day on a much larger scale as the North Charles Institute for the Addictions. The chapter also captures some of the very difficult aspects of narcotics addiction as well as the special challenges such patients present for the treating clinician and the treatment staff. Although I did not write again about group therapy until fifteen years later, it has been a therapeutic mainstay in my practice dating back to when this chapter was first written. As is evident in a number of the concluding chapters in this section, I am convinced that group therapy is a vital if not essential treatment for addictive disorders. Groups allow for a natural unfolding of patients' core issues of pain and suffering as well as the characteristic ways' such individuals deceive, defend against, and deny (to themselves and others) their suffering. Chapter 28 is an early representation of these factors, the power of groups, and some of their hazards, pitfalls, and strengths. Clinicians need to be alerted to these factors for effective leadership and therapeutic benefit. This chapter also graphically depicts some of the major difficulties opiate addicts experience with rage, violent behaviors, and compensatory disdainful and aggressive defenses and attitudes, especially evident in those patients who have experienced major trauma developmentally and experientially, such as Vietnam veterans.

Chapters 29 and 30 address the issue of understanding and treating substance-dependent physicians. Although they were published within three years of each other, I think it is fairly evident in Chapter 29 that it was less clear to me and others (even in the early 1980s) what clinical, programmatic, and regulatory elements were important or necessary to help substance-dependent physicians face their disabilities, engage in recovery, and reestablish themselves as valued and contributing health care professionals. In one case I found myself in the unenviable position of serving a substance-dependent physician simultaneously as treater, advocate, and monitor; in another case I was witness to the tragic consequences of poor communication, mutual distrust among the parties involved, and lack of coordination between clinician, the hospital, and the board of registration. I plead for better coordination of clinical care, advocacy, and regulatory sanctions because the stakes are high and the consequences often tragic when these elements are not well coordinated.

In Chapter 30 I speak with a clearer voice and with more understanding about how to appreciate and to work with the similarities and differences between nonphysician and physician addicted individuals. The psychodynamic understanding of addictive vulnerability will sound familiar here. It is not too different from much that precedes these two chapters in my reviews on the internal world of the addicted person, the self-medication hypothesis, and understanding the psychodynamics of addictive vulnerability. Although I make the case for there being more similarities than differences in physicians and nonphysicians who are dependent on drugs, I explore how addictive vulnerability might interact with an individual's "call to medicine" and the special ways that medicine as a profession can tug at susceptible individuals. In later chapters I spell out in much greater detail what best serves the needs of patients with SUDs, and what constitutes effective treatment, but in this chapter I discuss five principles of treatment and recovery to achieve these ends with substance-dependent physicians.

Chapters 31 and 32 were two of my first publications in which I more extensively describe from a psychodynamic perspective the treatment implications of addictive vulnerability. Chapter 32 was prepared at the invitation of the 1984 Bond Symposium of the Psychiatric Institute of the University of Pennsylvania Medical Center Hospital. The invitees where asked to consider the why, when, and how of psychotherapy with substance abusers. I chose to frame the issue around the broader question of what is psychotherapeutic for substance abusers and to consider how psychotherapy fits into the various treatment modalities for patients with SUDs. I review the benefits and limitations of the approaches we use and how we need to consider from a clinical perspective when and why one approach might be preferred over another (e.g., AA and confinement vs. psychotherapy). I addressed these broader issues because I was continually impressed with practitioners' prejudices and insularity about treatment; for example, addictionologists might recommend AA, and other clinicians psychotherapy, to the exclusion of alternative or combined treatment approaches. To this end I argue that a clinician must play multiple roles, and I introduce the concept of the primary care therapist. I expand on this concept in Chapter 33, but in introducing it here I emphasize that the alliance that develops in the individual psychotherapy relationship (which I argue should be considered for all patients) can be leveraged to help patients pursue other needed treatment options such as AA and other modalities. I elaborate on these themes in the next two chapters.

In Chapter 32 I stress the importance of keeping a central focus on affect and self-care disturbances when we consider treatment modalities for patients with SUDs. I unequivocally advocate that individual psychotherapy be considered for all substance abusing patients. Psychotherapy is beneficial and often necessary in its own right, and such a treatment relationship can be crucial in keeping patients in other effective treatments and maximizing their benefit. I anticipate here as in the previous chapter the role of the clinician as a primary care therapist, which I expand upon in Chapter 33. I also critique and analyze some of the pitfalls of passivity and uncovering techniques deriving from traditional psychodynamic approaches, and suggest specific modifications to more actively engage patients around their affect and self-care deficits. Active, supportive, and empathic appreciation of these vulnerabilities plays an important role in retaining patients in treatment and improving treatment outcome. I apply these same basic principles in the remainder of this chapter in considering the benefits, limits, and contraindications of twelve-step/AA meetings, individual and group psychotherapy, and pharmacotherapy, depending on patients' needs or their tolerance for these approaches.

Because we are poor predictors of which substance abusing patients will respond to what treatment modality, and because their needs are multiple and often emergent, in Chapter 33 I advocate that clinicians play the role of a primary care therapist (PCT) to ensure that appropriate interventions are provided to meet patient needs. Part of my motivation to write this chapter was a pet peeve of mine, going back to the beginning of my training, that psychodynamic psychiatrists too often become involved with esoteric or convoluted concepts to guide their understanding and treatment, and fail to appreciate enough their patients' basic needs regarding their suffering and self-management. It has been my experience that this is equally true with clinicians who treat patients with SUDs. In this chapter I discuss patients' needs for the four C's of control, containment, contact, and comfort, and I use these four needs to orient and guide a PCT in the care of patients. In particular, I elaborate on the PCT functioning in directing, coordinating, and monitoring roles to optimally combine psychotherapeutic, psychopharmacologic, and self-help elements in meeting patients' needs.

Although this chapter is brief, I think it is one of my more helpful statements in concisely guiding a clinician to what is essential in meeting the immediate and long-term treatment needs of patients with SUDs.

Chapter 34 was presented in 1989 and published in 1992 as a preliminary report on modified dynamic group therapy for substance abusers, a group treatment approach that codified my years of experience using psychodynamic group psychotherapy with substance abusing patients. Although group therapy had been a mainstay for me as a therapeutic tool with my patients over the previous fifteen years, I had not, up until the publication of this chapter, written or lectured in any systematic way on how I conceptualized and practiced group therapy with substance abusing patients. The impetus to do so developed when in 1986 I joined with Dr. William McAuliffe, a premier researcher/investigator/methodologist, in the Harvard Cocaine Recovery Project, a National Institute on Drug Abuse (NIDA)-sponsored project for which McAuliffe was the principal investigator. We agreed, as I explain in the chapter, that we would compare two group approaches—a cognitive behavioral one, Recovery Training/Self Help (RTSH), and a psychodynamic one, Modified Dynamic Group Therapy (MDGT). In addition to my role as the clinical co-investigator for the project, one of my main responsibilities was to supervise the group leaders for MDGT. This gave me the opportunity to work with two colleagues, Drs. Sarah Golden and Kurt Halliday, who are especially creative and imaginative clinicians who understand how groups can benefit patients with SUDs. They used what I knew from experience and practice and what they were learning through their participation in the project, namely that group psychotherapy could be a preeminently useful instrument to target and modify addictive vulnerability. We had the luxury of reviewing together many hours of group psychotherapy, and the opportunity to conceptualize and put into words the essential elements, assumptions, norms, and focus that make group therapy a very useful and powerful corrective. The work was mutually validating for all of us, and I have remained grateful that McAuliffe stimulated me to develop my ideas (he was a daunting but effective taskmaster) and that Halliday and Golden were so enthusiastic and receptive to my ideas, and even more, so effective in articulating what we were doing, which eventually culminated in a book, *Addiction and the Vulnerable Self: Modified Dynamic Group*

*Therapy for Substance Abusers* (Khantzian et al. 1990). Chapter 34 was our first articulation on group psychotherapy, and in part the foundation for the first chapter and overview of our book. More particularly, in Chapter 34 we highlight how vulnerabilities around regulating affects, self-other relations, and self-care emerge in the context of the group experience. We describe how such a group allows for a natural unfolding of these vulnerabilities and at the same time how characterological styles and defenses surface that are attempts to cope with these vulnerabilities, but instead interfere with satisfactory or satisfying connection or contact with others. After reviewing the assumptions and focus of MDGT, we discuss how we foster a sense of safety, control, comfort, and contact, in contrast to traditional approaches that place a greater emphasis on uncovering and interpretive techniques.

In Chapter 35 John Mack and I state our conviction that AA works because it is a powerful group psychology that not only arrests uncontrolled drinking, but more importantly corrects core problems in self-regulation. Although much in this chapter recapitulates the ground covered in Chapters 24 and 25, it is much more geared to patients' experiences in AA, providing clinical examples to support our theoretical perspective. We wrote this chapter, as the title indicates, as a guide to help clinicians understand how and why AA works. Mack and I were invited by one of the editors of the *Journal of Substance Abuse Treatment*, Dr. John Imhoff, to be guest editors for the edition in which this chapter was the lead paper. A number of distinguished investigators/clinicians, including Mark Gold, John Chappell, and David Smith, were asked to write rebuttals and to offer their perspectives on addictive vulnerability and their understanding of the utility of AA. Not surprisingly, much of the debate boiled down, once again, to the nature-nurture and cause-consequence dichotomies in which there was a characteristic polarization and, with some exceptions, a failure to reach any consensus on how and why AA worked. In fact the rebuttals for at least two of the authors, Gold and Chappell, were used by them, to my dismay, as a springboard to again critique the self-medication hypothesis of SUDs. As we indicate in the chapter, our approach was primarily that of an "outside-in" view of the clinician, mainly using case vignettes of individuals and patients' accounts of their experiences and the benefits they derived from their involvement with AA. As the case vignettes in Chapter 35 reveal, the storytelling traditions of AA help alcoholics face their shared experiences of human woundedness, especially their inability to regulate their emotions, self-esteem, and behaviors. These traditions also help individuals face and acknowledge their characterological defenses of self-absorption, disavowal of need, and denial of their vulnerabilities.

In Chapters 36 and 37, with my colleagues Sarah Golden, William McAuliffe, and Kurt Halliday, I return to group psychotherapy as a key therapeutic modality for accessing and modifying the self-regulation vulnerabilities that significantly contribute to the development of SUDs. Chapter 36 reviews theoretical and clinical aspects of the range of group treatments for addictive disorders. We then focus on dynamic group therapy, and on how effective groups must respect patients' needs for control, safety, and comfort, especially at the outset, and to then target patients' characterological problems and self-regulation vulnerabilities involving feelings, self-esteem, relationships, and self-care.

In Chapter 37 the emphasis shifts to a consideration of technical issues and techniques that help clinicians appreciate the importance of the leader's attitudes and ways of conducting groups to best address the needs and vulnerabilities of substance abusing individuals. We consider the importance of the leader's combining individual therapy with the group treatment. We also discuss how to structure safety, comfort, and stability, and we guide the clinician in adopting an empathic approach to deal with the patients' need for abstinence and the prospect of relapse when (or before) it occurs. Issues of self-disclosure by the leader and the need to be real are explored as well as modes of activity and passivity (in the leaders and members) that can be crucial in helping patients better express themselves and listen. We also guide the clinician in addressing the vicissitudes of departures from group and the integration of new members, how the group leader's empathy is informed by appreciating the nature of the addicted person's vulnerabilities, and what the essential elements are that make a group supportive.

The last two chapters of this book, both of which are previously unpublished, are devoted to psychotherapy. Chapter 38 centers around a case vignette primarily involving group psychotherapy, and Chapter 39 describes how I conduct individual psychotherapy based on my understanding of the patient's needs and the nature of addictive vulnerabilities. In both chapters I highlight some of the contemporary literature on psychotherapy, which reports how and why our more recent use of psychotherapy has been more successful than in the past. In part this has been the result of our better appreciating the special needs of substance abusing patients (e.g., safety, control, comfort, and contact) and our modifying our techniques to better bring into focus such patients' vulnerabilities. The case vignette in Chapter 38 demonstrates how the sources of an individual's suffering involved in reverting and relapsing to alcohol may be rooted in experiences that go beyond memory. Nevertheless, in the context of a therapeutic group these early, preverbal origins of distress can be activated, examined, and modified.

Chapter 39 demonstrates how I conduct individual psychotherapy with patients who suffer with substance use disorders. It is proper that I should conclude this volume of my collected works with a chapter that shows how the theoretical framework that I adopt (i.e., a psychodynamic perspective) can effectively guide the treating clinician and how the clinical process can validate and enrich the theory. Elsewhere in this volume I paraphrase Einstein on how our theories help us to identify the facts. It is my hope that this last chapter succeeds in making it clear how patients' histories, stories, and psychotherapeutic interactions reveal recurrent themes that are meaningfully explained by the theoretical frame I have employed in this book. Understandably, then, I return in this chapter to self-regulation vulnerabilities, but I amplify on how these vulnerabilities shape and influence the ways in which the personalities of individuals suffering with drug-alcohol dependency become disordered. Using two brief vignettes and one that is more in-depth, I show how affect, self-esteem, relationship, and self-care deficits shape patients' character styles and structures. These structures are attempts to cope with the deficits and related pain; at the same time they perpetuate and just as often heighten them. As the cases reveal, both the deficits and the attempts to defend against them predispose susceptible individuals to become dependent on and relapse to addictive substances. I stress two core issues—problems with control, and problems with suffering—and basic manifestations of self-regulation problems, and how empathically engaging patients around these core issues becomes crucial in treating individuals with SUDs.

## REFERENCE

Khantzian, E. J., Halliday, K. S., and McAuliffe, W. E. (1990). *Addiction and the Vulnerable Self: Modified Dynamic Group Therapy for Substance Abusers.* New York: Guilford.

# 27

# The Self-Help–Psychiatry Controversy in Addiction Treatment[1]

Until recently, the contributions of medicine and psychiatry have been unable to offer adequate understanding and treatment of drug dependence. In response to the void that has existed, self-help philosophies, such as those of Synanon, Daytop, and Phoenix, have developed as alternative approaches to help people with drug dependence problems.

---

1. This chapter is in part based on two unpublished reports (Khantzian 1974a, 1975). The first was prepared by the author for the Drug Rehabilitation Advisory Board, Commonwealth of Massachusetts, of which he was a member and chairman. The second was a report to the American Psychiatric Association (APA) on the North American Congress on Alcohol and Drug Problems, San Francisco, 1974, which the author attended as the official representative of the APA.

Many of these programs were surprisingly effective for a significant number of people where other approaches had failed (Glasscote et al. 1972). In the mid-1960s, shortly after self-help programs' emergence, methadone maintenance was introduced as another effective intervention model for people dependent on narcotics. A growing controversy has since developed over the merits and shortcomings of these different approaches.

The self-help programs have stressed residential treatment, abstinence, and aggressive "encounter" or confrontation. The methadone programs have used a medical-psychiatric model that emphasizes the physiological and psychological impairments associated with addiction. The methadone programs have necessarily been staffed in large part by physicians and nurses, and the self-help programs by nonprofessionals and ex-addicts. Based on their respective features, a polarization has tended to develop, in which adherents of one approach have argued the superiority of their program over the other in such matters as client attraction and retention, effectiveness, and appropriate response to the assumed causes of addiction.

In my opinion, much of this controversy has been fed by unnecessary contentions and divisive arguments put forth by the more militant and extreme self-help advocates, and has been unwarranted and counterproductive. In this chapter I address this controversy, highlighting some recent clinical-psychiatric work with drug-dependent persons and reviewing some sources and examples of both dissonance and complementariness between these two approaches. My emphasis is on the need to develop and maintain sound clinical approaches to the problems of substance dependence.

## THE SELF-HELP APPROACH

Dumont (1974) has traced the origins of the self-help movement and has particularly stressed the relevance and importance of this approach for drug problems. Despite his professional training as a psychiatrist, he has been one of the most aggressive and eloquent spokesmen for the self-help point of view, and has rigorously rejected professional approaches or a psychopathological model for understanding drug dependence. Under his leadership, the Division of Drug Rehabilitation in Massachusetts has produced the "Comprehensive Plan for Drug Abuse Prevention" (Commonwealth of Massachusetts

1974), which reflects Dumont's commitment to this orientation and is supported by a funding policy favoring self-help programs. Although Dumont probably represents an extreme position in his statements and programmatic policies, his example is not atypical of national trends, and his work and achievements are a useful reference point.

Dumont stresses societal influences and peer-group pressures as the root cause of and impetus for drug use in contemporary society (Dumont 1971). He also emphasizes problems of young people's alienation and deep distrust of the values and leadership of our society. He is explicit in condemning the professional sector, along with many others, for being caught up in "plastic values" and for being abusive of status and power. He argues that the power invested in the psychiatrist as a professional plays into the excessive dependence of those who are served and into the rescue fantasies of those who serve them. Comparing the power-authority structures of psychiatric wards with those of self-help settings, he maintains that the former are closed and the latter open and that, despite the authoritarian and often demeaning structures that are imposed in self-help groups, the main obstacle to achieving that purpose (i.e., reaching the top of the system) is self-imposed (Dumont 1971, 1974).

The typecasting and characterizations by Dumont and other self-help advocates frequently portray psychiatrists as at best a pathetic extension of the vested values and interests of a sick society and at worst as cynically subjecting their patients to their own power needs. Psychiatrists and allied professionals are further portrayed as persons who see the client as passive and helpless, rather than an active colleague.

The eloquence here begs an issue and misleads the reader into believing that psychiatrists and professionals do not share in such concerns and values. This point of view maintains that only peer relationships have potential for growth, understanding, and change—an assumption used to support other assumptions often made without adequate documentation. For example, though they acknowledge that addiction has no single cause, self-help advocates affirm that continuation and discontinuation of drug use for the great majority are a conscious and deliberate choice and that peer-group factors are of paramount importance. This thinking ignores a whole range of human activity based on compulsive and driven behavior that has both puzzled and challenged students of the mind and behavior for centuries. It also fails to acknowledge unconscious needs and longings, such as the need to imitate and master, the need for approval, and so on. Although professionals have perhaps erred in viewing addiction simply as a function of psychopathology or disordered physiological processes, the imbalance in their approach is not corrected by totally discounting such factors and creating new etiologies that are equally reductionistic.

Many besides myself would seriously question whether peer-group pressure is central for those who become and remain addicted. The large and carefully reported evidence documenting addiction as entailing serious psychological impairments cannot be ignored. The assumed strategy in many self-help approaches is appropriately aimed at prevention with young people in order to preclude the development of serious, chronic addiction. However, strategies must also include the recognition that such addiction problems exist and will continue to exist. Medicine and psychiatry have not had a glorious track record for cure in this area, but this fact does not justify rejecting such efforts any more than we would suggest ceasing the treatment and study of other chronic problems for which the solutions are still insufficient.

Furthermore, the indictment of psychiatric approaches overlooks the many problems that self-help groups encounter in retaining clients, for example, 75 to 90 percent of their clients drop out within a months (Dumont 1974, National Clearinghouse for Drug Abuse Information 1975), and the psychological casualties that often result from exposure to such programs. We agree that peer-group influences are important and can be a powerful means of intervention, influence, and change. However, a cautionary note is warranted in that peer-group influences can just as powerfully mobilize destructive forces that can undermine confidence, growth, and development.

## PSYCHIATRIC EXPERIENCES WITH ADDICTION

We have heard often enough that psychiatric approaches to drug-dependent persons are irrelevant and fail, but in my experience such conclusions are not warranted. Despite all efforts to combat drug problems, the attempts so far to gain a thorough psychological understanding of the origins and consequences of drug dependence have been minimal. Until ten years ago, most of our efforts to address the problem were through the criminal justice system, particularly at the federal level—the prime example being the federal prison at Lexington, Kentucky. More recently, the self-help groups and methadone maintenance programs have gained wide acceptance. The involvement of psychiatry and the behavioral sciences in these diverse programs has been spotty and uneven. However, when serious students of addiction have become clinically active in all these approaches, including the federal prisons, they have produced encouraging evidence that the problem of drug dependence does indeed fall within our domain as psychiatrists, and that we have much to offer as well as much to learn.

In clinical work with addicts, we have become more aware of the intrapsychic and character problems of drug-dependent persons. Early psychiatric literature stressed the regressive, pleasurable (libidinal) use of drugs and the psychopathic character problems (Khantzian 1974b). In my experience, this emphasis has been misleading and has failed to appreciate the defensive nature of addicts' character structures, including the defensive use of sexuality. The clinics and other programs established during the past ten years to treat heroin addicts have provided definite evidence that these people suffer from acute and chronic depression, anxiety, and underlying psychosis (Johnson et al. 1973, Khantzian 1974b, McKenna et al. 1973, Vaillant 1966, Wishnie 1974) and that they use such substances as amphetamines and barbiturates, in addition to opiates, to treat themselves for psychiatric syndromes. This evidence also indicates that there is a specificity in relation to the substance that is used: many persons select drugs in accordance with their underlying psychiatric problems. For years, people from middle-class backgrounds have used barbiturates and amphetamines in this way; with the burgeoning drug problems among our youths, these two types of drugs have found their way into the hands of young people suffering similar problems.

Until the early 1970s, federal efforts (through the Special Action Office for Drug Abuse Prevention and the National Institutes) were limited primarily to the heroin problem. Over the past two to three years, however, a number of programs developed through the National Institute on Drug Abuse (NIDA) have tried to identify and evaluate many of the so-called young polydrug users. NIDA has financed twelve demonstration projects in which over 2,000 patients have been seen for detoxification and evaluation of polydrug problems. The most commonly abused substances have been the barbiturates and other sedative hypnotics, with amphetamines and other central nervous system (CNS) stimulants also in wide use.

In December 1974, the preliminary findings of these demonstration projects were reported at the North American Congress for Alcohol and Drug Abuse. Dr. John Benvenuto of NIDA presented an overview on national patterns of nonopiate polydrug use based on these demonstration projects. Psychological profiles of the patients treated revealed abundant and significant psychopathology; 50 percent had had psychiatric treatment, and depression was a common finding in many. Benvenuto concluded that such persons might be treated more appropriately within the mental health system by health professionals and health workers with mental health skills, and that the aggressive approaches often used in therapeutic communities were ineffective and contraindicated.

In a clinical paper on the treatment of polydrug abusers presented to the same congress, Dr. David Smith reported findings that upheld Benvenuto's conclusions. He questioned the effectiveness of therapeutic approaches previously devised to treat heroin addicts, stating that the polydrug users treated in his clinic showed more psychological impairment than the overall patient population or groups of heroin users of the same age. Although it had been anticipated that therapeutic communities would be effective in handling these patients, Smith concluded that young polydrug users found it difficult to gain admission to such communities or, if admitted, to complete treatment. More flexible, nurturing treatment settings with a supportive and activity-oriented environment seemed more promising. Smith discovered that many patients required specific psychoactive agents—such as antidepressants, lithium, and antipsychotics—for treatment of underlying mood disorders and psychoses. He advocated the use of antianxiety agents, combined with psychotherapy and other support services, to bring about greater stability in the patient's life.

In my own work, which is primarily with heroin addicts, I have been impressed with the part that drugs in general and heroin in particular have played in people's attempts to cope with their environment. In previous reports, we have studied the use of heroin to ward off a range of underlying problems associated with depression, anxiety, and other forms of human suffering (Khantzian et al. 1974). More specifically, we formulate the role of heroin use as an attempt to mitigate problems of depression and aggressions. In my general practice of psychiatry, I have treated a number of polydrug-dependent patients, and my experiences concur with those of Benvenuto and Smith: addiction occurs when there are significant psychopathological problems, particularly depression, anxiety, and psychotic processes, and when the patient has used available drugs to ward off the unbearable feelings related to those states.

## TOWARD A BALANCED VIEW

Caplan (1974) has recently traced how groups develop their own responses to crises when institutions and professionals fail to respond adequately. He calls such self-help groups "support systems." He stresses the importance of appreciating the significant role played by nonprofessionals and the necessity of learning to support such efforts. "We must develop sufficient respect for our own contributions and sufficient personal and group security not to attack or defensively belittle the nonprofessionals as though they were competing with professionals. They complement the professionals; they cannot replace them." Alcoholics Anonymous and self-help drug treatment programs represent an enormous resource in this country in response to the pervasive problems of alcohol and drugs. Despite psychiatry's limited successes in these areas, we possess expertise in the processes and problems surrounding substance dependence; we clearly have contributions to make and need not apologize or compete. We must learn, however, to appreciate the contributions of others, particularly the paraprofessionals, and must foster opportunities to maximize support, interaction, and collaboration.

We must also better realize the enormous clinical and investigative challenges that drug and alcohol problems present for psychiatrists as clinicians and scientific investigators. Although the self-help approaches are effective for many, others find them either unacceptable or ineffective. Many patients and their families continue to seek mental health professionals for guidance, assistance, and care.

## CONCLUSIONS

We believe there is compelling evidence that drug dependence is a major clinical problem that begs the involvement of clinical psychiatry. Less conventional, nonprofessional approaches certainly have contributions to make; however, the problems of polemics and attitudes remain as major obstacles to establishing more reasoned solutions. Drug dependence is one of many problems to be solved. There is much work to be done, and we agree with Caplan that we should not compete.

The issue of client failures in any treatment approach is one that ought not to be politicized or used as the basis for attack on other approaches. Rather, it should remind us all of the serious and humbling nature of any work concerning human troubles and human change, and compel us to take a more dispassionate view of what approaches work best for what people at what times in their lives.

# REFERENCES

Caplan, G. (1974). *Support systems and community mental health*. New York: Behavioral Publications. Unpublished report.

Commonwealth of Massachusetts (1974). *Comprehensive plan for drug abuse prevention*. Unpublished report.

Dumont, M. P. (1971). Why the young use drugs. *Social Policy*.

——— (1974). Self-help treatment programs. *American Journal of Psychiatry* 131:636–640.

Glasscote, R. M., Sussex, J. N., Jaffe, J. H., et al. (1972). *The Treatment of Drug Abuse*. Washington, DC: Joint Information Service.

Johnson, B., Corman, A. G., Khantzian, E. J., and Long, J. (1973). Rehabilitation of narcotic addicts with methadone: the public health approach versus the individual perspective. *Contemporary Drug Problems*, pp. 565–578.

Khantzian, E. J. (1974a). *Critique of the Comprehensive Plan for Drug Abuse Prevention (Commonwealth of Massachusetts) with a special emphasis and comment on self-help and professional approaches*. Unpublished report.

——— (1974b). Opiate addiction: a critique of theory and some implications for treatment. *American Journal of Psychotherapy* 28:59–70.

——— (1975). *North American Congress on alcohol and drug problems—A Report to the A.P.A.* Unpublished report.

Khantzian, E. J., Mack, J. E., and Schatzberg, A. F. (1974). Heroin use as an attempt to cope: clinical observation. *American Journal of Psychiatry* 131:160–164.

McKenna, G. J., Fisch, A., Levine, M., et al. (1973). The use of methadone as a psychotropic agent. In *Proceedings of the Fifth National*

*Methadone Conference,* Washington, DC. New York: National Association for the Prevention of Addictions to Narcotics.

National Clearinghouse for Drug Abuse Information (1975). Report series 34, no. 1, April. Rockville, MD: NIDA.

Vaillant, G. E. (1966). 12-year follow-up of New York narcotic addicts. Some social and psychiatric characteristics. *Archives of General Psychiatry* 15:599–609.

Wishnie, H. (1974). Opioid addiction: a masked depression. In *Masked Depression,* ed. S. Lesse, pp. 350–367. New York: Jason Aronson.

# 28

# Group Treatment of Unwilling Addicted Patients

## *with William W. Kates*

The treatment and management of unwilling drug-dependent patients raise challenging questions about human rights and coercion. Such questions have been raised with the two most prevalent types of programs for addiction treatment, namely, methadone maintenance and self-help. Both approaches have been accused of using coercion in a way that infringes on the civil liberties and rights of the individuals in these programs. Some of the self-help approaches and their extensive use of group pressure to exact conformity have been cited as violations of human rights and dignity. Similarly, concerns are often expressed that methadone can be used as a means of controlling and limiting a patient's freedom and rights by using the required daily maintenance dose as a "club" to influence various aspects of the patient's life.

Clearly, addicted patients ought to have the right to choose whether they want treatment or not, even if the unpleasant alternative is jail, which often is the case. They should also have the right to be informed about how a program operates and what treatment will consist of, and then to decide whether such a program is suitable for them. They should also have the option to leave the program after commencing treatment if they wish to do so. However, once a person joins a program with informed consent, and assuming programmatic content is not capricious and that there exist sufficient means to monitor activities such as community boards and other regulatory agencies, then a program must maintain considerable freedom and responsibility to decide what the content and conditions for treatment shall be. As an example, and for the purposes of this discussion, we shall review how a particular program decided to impose mandatory group treatment as one of the major conditions for participation in a narcotics addiction treatment program.

To impose treatment or change a person (even if it is dignified by such labels as "therapy") runs certain risks, such as fostering a regressive and/or hostile dependency in the person being treated and an arbitrary and patronizing attitude in those doing the treatment. But the disadvantages of compulsory treatment are outweighed by the benefits.

This chapter focuses on group psychotherapeutic work with narcotics addicts in an outpatient program using methadone maintenance and other support services, and demonstrates some of the problems and challenges of working with such a group of patients. We shall delineate how our program structure and therapeutic strategies evolved in response to observed clinical characteristics and features of our patients (personality and drug-related) such as regression, impaired judgment, narcissistic conflicts, cognitive deficiencies, self-care problems, intolerance of painful affects (particularly depression), and other ego impairments.

After a brief description of our program, we shall present clinical vignettes from two distinctly different periods in the program's history. The first group vignette is taken from an early period in the program's development when group therapy was voluntary and the program was rather unstructured, and staff expectations were relatively low. The second vignette is taken from a more recent period, subsequent to programmatic changes that made group treatment mandatory, and more limits and structure were instituted, resulting in higher staff expectations. We shall attempt to establish through our clinical material that imposition of treatment, including mandatory group therapy, is a suitable and appropriate response to the characteristic defenses and clinical features of our patient population.

## PROGRAM HISTORY AND CLINICAL OBSERVATIONS

The clinical observations in this report are based on experiences with narcotics addicts in an outpatient treatment program. The program currently consists of methadone detoxification and maintenance, individual and group treatment, and social and vocational rehabilitative services. The drug treatment program is a component unit in a community-based mental health center and is also affiliated with the Department of Psychiatry of a municipal hospital. At the present time methadone is dispensed daily to all patients (i.e., no take-home methadone) from the hospital, and the treatment and vocational services are provided at a decentralized location in another part of the community. The program is run entirely on an outpatient basis and the majority of the patients are voluntary. A small percentage of the patients are probated from the courts and pressured to come from other parts of the criminal justice system. Other informal pressures related to the family, friends, finances, and anticipated or pending legal action are often factors that motivate an individual to seek treatment. However, the major source of compulsory program participation derives from the fact that once a person is initiated to and maintained on methadone, he becomes relatively dependent on the program for his/her need for narcotics to stem the pain and discomfort from narcotics withdrawal.

Over the past four years the program census has ranged between 50 and 100 patients, and has recently leveled and been maintained at 100. The mean age is 24 years; 20 to 25 percent of the patient population are women and 20 percent of the patients are black.

Practically without exception, all patients applying for treatment have been physically dependent on opiates, and, by definition, those on methadone maintenance (60 to 75 percent) have been addicted for two years or longer. More significantly, the majority of individuals seeking treatment evidence many of the characteristic physical and psychological features and complications associated with serious narcotics addiction. A significant number of the patients manifest nutritional deficiencies and/or various stages of self-neglect in grooming, dress, and hygiene. At the time of admission many of the patients show physical complications of prolonged intravenous drug use, such as recent and old thrombosed veins (tracks), hepatitis, abscesses, and other nonspecific pulmonary and systemic problems. Regressed behavioral and psychological features are also prominent. A desperate and chaotic life existence is often thinly veiled by a cool and at times contemptuous request for methadone alone, with the patient insisting his/her problems are the result of drug addiction. Some clamor more loudly and belligerently and show very low frustration tolerance. Hypochondriacal preoccupations are very common. Others are grossly hostile and mistrustful, reacting with outbursts of rage, projections, and distortions that are conveyed through obscenities and street language. Still others present themselves as very passive and/or depressed and often come for many clinic visits and meetings before they speak up about themselves, and then often only after being actively engaged by staff and other patients.

At its inception, the main features of the program consisted of an intake group, methadone, small groups, and vocational counseling when indicated; otherwise, the program at this early phase was relatively unstructured. Group meetings were entirely voluntary, and placing individuals on methadone and further assignment to small groups was decided by staff on the basis of observations in groups and elsewhere about the individual's willingness to cooperate with the program and motivation to stop using narcotics. The observations in the first vignette are taken from this early period in the program's development when group therapy attendance was voluntary and not a condition for participation in other phases of the program.

### Vignette 1

During the first meeting of this group (nine members), the group leader asked the members what they hoped to gain for themselves in treatment. After a number of patients talked about vocational plans and ambitions, a 24-year-old black patient spontaneously introduced the problem of how his wife did not give of herself emotionally. He acknowledged how attentive she was regarding his material wants, but he complained vaguely about her not being open emotionally. He was quickly joined in this by the other addicts, who for the most part agreed that this was true of women. Toward the end of this discussion, the patient who had introduced the subject began to qualify his earlier statements and then offered that he "might be greedy." At the end of the meeting some basic ground rules were reviewed by the co-leaders, and it was emphasized that "we all have a responsibility to see that nobody gets hurt, emotionally or physically, and that we call each other on this when we see it developing."

In the next meeting, a 22-year-old, white, Vietnam veteran who had just been started on methadone maintenance stridently walked in ten minutes late and announced that the large bag of pink popcorn that he was carrying was his new "dope." When he was gently questioned by one of the group leaders about his provocative attitude, he quickly launched into a discussion about how he had always had "a chip on the shoulder." This then led to a discussion between himself and another patient about violent behavior. Some of the other patients commented about their mutual tendency to laugh inappropriately when someone was hurt. The veteran, with no apparent reluctance, spoke of how he enjoyed hurting people. He spoke of being amused by the grotesque faces of people who had been dismembered in an accident. A female patient prodded him on one of his comments. He became more angry and countered her queries with a loud invective. Later, this woman left, giving the excuse that she did not feel well. Despite some long, loud, and angry protests by the veteran, the leaders repeatedly pointed out that it was difficult for people to bear so much exposure to troubling matters and feelings so soon, and that it was destructive and would drive members away if the patients were not considerate of what other members of the group could handle.

The next meeting was much quieter; in particular, the veteran was much more subdued and the other members were attentive to and supportive of each other. The content of the meeting was striking. The patients shifted back and forth from talking about the hopelessness and helplessness of their present life situations and their future outlook, to angry assaults on society and its institutions. A white, 29-year-old ex-musician seemed intent on convincing the leaders that life on the street was more grim and ugly than could possibly be imagined. He described how in earlier years he had "worked over" people in obtaining and selling narcotics, referring to both physically violent and sadistically manipulative behavior. He proclaimed that as soon as he got "cleaned up" (i.e., withdrawn from narcotics) he was going to leave for the countryside and mountains with his woman; otherwise, the alternative to this would be to either shoot somebody or else continue "shooting (heroin) into my veins." After one of the leaders asked about his family background, this same patient went on to describe the many brutal beatings meted out by his father as punishment for family cur- few violations. He then described with exhilaration the last beating he received at age 18 when he turned on his father and severely beat him.

## Comment

This vignette, taken from one of the first groups in the program, oc- curred at a time when group treatment was not mandatory. Atten- dance in this group was sporadic, tardiness by most of the members was very common, attrition was high, and within seven months of its formation the group disbanded. It was a group that was formed at a time when the program was very small and there had been much informal contact between the staff and patients elsewhere in the pro- gram. There had been a great deal of discussion about forming small groups, and because of this fact and probably as a result of the extra- group contact with the group leaders, we believe that many unrealis- tic expectations were set up among both staff and patients. Group leaders encouraged patients to discuss directly their wants early in the group meetings. This approach, compounded by lack of a formal program structure and by staff ambivalence about setting limits on patient behavior, allowed certain group members to reveal their "greediness" and related depression.

We believe that some of the dramatic interactions, particularly the outburst of rage with references to violent and sadistic attitudes and assertions of aggressiveness, were expressions of and defenses against personal issues related to dependency wishes and longings for com- fort and care. It has been our experience with individuals such as those we are describing that groups tend to mobilize such longings as well as defenses against them. There is much pain and conflict associated with such longings. In the absence of other holding influences, there is a tendency (in addition to the manifest dramatic reactions cited) for many group members to avoid such groups, to become restless and walk out, and ultimately to drop out of such groups. In retrospect, we also believe that it is generally contraindicated for group leaders to encourage, implicitly or explicitly, the direct expression of passive needs and longings, especially early in the history of a group. As indicated in the example above, this kind of premature exposure is often precipitated by a seemingly reasonable question asked by the therapists about what the members expect to gain from treatment. In a subsequent example, we show that the group leader does better to avoid such leading questions in favor of allowing a more natural unfolding of the group process based on directions and material introduced by the group members.

## Program Changes

The consequences of lack of structure and unrealistic expectations in the early phases of the program were high dropout rates after initial contact, highly variable attendance and much tardiness in group and individual counseling sessions, escalating demands from the patients, and much demoralization among both staff and patients. One of the first responses to these problems was early assignment of individual counselors; attendance for individual counseling was made mandatory. Patients were assigned to small groups more selectively after careful staff observation of individuals in intake group and individual counseling. Limits and sanctions on unacceptable behavior, such as drug dealing, threatened or actual violence, repeated absences from counseling sessions, and repeated lateness for methadone doses, were carefully spelled out in the form of written rules that were given to and verbally reviewed with the patients early in their contact with the program. Isolated and/or repeated infractions became grounds for definite, time-specified suspensions from the program. Attendance at group continued to be voluntary, and missed group meetings or dropping out of group continued to be dealt with as a therapeutic issue. These gradually instituted measures resulted in improvement in patient cooperation and related program morale.

However, there continued to be problems in the small groups, with high turnover, irregular attendance, tardiness, eating and drinking during meetings, and easy distractibility. Although the staff was experiencing a growing conviction that group therapy was very useful in influencing and effecting change with those who were attending, there was continuing expression of concern among staff and patients that the inconstancies and inconsistencies in group participation continued to have a major demoralizing effect.

In the initial one and a half years of the program's operation the issue of mandatory group treatment was repeatedly considered by the staff. A lengthy staff meeting was then held to force closure on the issue. Ethical and philosophical concerns were expressed and reviewed. However, the main concerns focused on the clinical and programmatic impact of such a policy. Some of the staff favored mandatory groups, stressing the patients' ego gaps and weaknesses in making and following through on treatment plans, as well as a defensive need to fend off help and care from others in the group. Others felt that mandatory group attendance would result in a higher dropout rate, thus confining treatment to only a few exceptionally motivated individuals. Those arguing for imposition of mandatory group treatment felt that it would maximize chances of holding people in groups and the program, and that assuming responsibility for this decision would allow for initial treatment contact in the group until such time as the individuals could overcome their fears and resistances. A consensus was finally reached to institute mandatory group treatment. More specifically, a policy was established that once the staff had evaluated and determined that group was indicated and the patient had agreed to participate as part of his overall program contract, then the patient would be expected to come to group on time and would be allowed only three missed meetings, after which, short-term and subsequently indefinite suspension from the program would result.

For the past three and a half years this program policy has been in effect and there have been none of the serious consequences or complications originally anticipated. With the exception of patients with marked paranoid tendencies, inability to concentrate, diffuse ego boundaries, and marked lability, most patients are routinely assigned to small groups. The institution of this policy has corresponded to a period of marked expansion in program census. Despite this expansion, overall retention of patients in the program has increased, with significant improvement in morale for both patients and staff. The effect on the efficacy of treatment has been less clear. However, it is our impression that the potential problems produced with mandatory groups are understandable, manageable, and resolvable as one more reality problem to be faced by the leader and members in the therapeutic work of the group. By way of illustration, the following vignette is taken from a different group, run by a different group leader, well after the above changes, including mandatory groups, had become well established.

### Vignette 2

A most reluctant male patient came to group only because he was required to do so in order to obtain methadone. He would arrive late, sit at the periphery of the group, and look out the window while the group was in process. He often read a book or magazine. When invited to make comments, he would protest how worthless the group was, how angry he was about being there, and he would insist that he didn't care about anybody in the group. The group co-leaders responded to this posture initially by allowing the patient his peripheral place in the group and avoiding challenges to his protests that he did not need to be in the group. He was asked to listen, and attempts were made, verbally and nonverbally, to encourage him to maintain at least peripheral participation. During this phase, he often appeared paranoid and seemed threatened by any direct confrontation. Gradually there was a shift over a period of months, and when invited to participate or give an opinion, he would do so in an arrogant and hostile manner. Several years later, in the same group, he accounted for some of his previous behavior as having been a "test." He revealed that in his individual counseling sessions he would often read a magazine upside down and his therapist was "too dumb to notice." Similarly, he described his position in the group as being outside the group, "ignoring other group members as a test to see if people were sharp and sensitive to my feelings."

The strategy adopted by the group leaders was not to try to force this patient to think of himself as in need of the group but instead to ask him to back off and let other people continue doing the work of the group. During the course of this man's participation in the group, an incident occurred that suggested the extent of his pathology. In the middle of a meeting, one of the co-leaders asked him to remove his sunglasses because she could not see his eyes. He reacted with anger and became paranoid, with obvious looseness and disorganization in his thinking and associations. It was as if her invitation for greater intimacy made him briefly psychotic. Much later, this impression of fragility was confirmed when he experienced a more protracted psychotic break in the context of marital discord.

After several years of participation in the group, during which time he gradually became more integrated and involved, he developed an intense, positive relationship with the male co-therapist in the group. He was explicit in indicating his feelings of trust and his wish for help with his marital problems, which included his wife's depression and suicidal attempt. That is, the same patient who had protested so violently about his unwillingness to be in group and who was most explicit about how worthless group was for him in his life was also the patient who eventually formed a most intense, trusting, and gratifying relationship with the group leader. This same patient also formed an intense relationship with an older female member of the group that has lasted for a number of years and has involved trust, advice-giving, some mutual sharing, and some semblance of understanding each other.

## Comment

Since group attendance was mandatory in order to participate in the other phases of the program, this man's participation in the group at the outset was largely determined by his wish to receive methadone. The basic therapeutic approach consisted of accepting the patient's unwillingness to be in the group as a frequent but not insoluble problem. We try to avoid direct confrontation of this resistance, try to understand its dynamic significance, and allow, even encourage, the patient to be a silent and peripheral participant until such time as problems related to trust, protest, and paranoia are overcome. One of the leaders' tasks is to enlist others in the group to aid in asking such a patient to wait and to allow other people to continue doing their own work. At times the group leaders must become more active and confrontive in setting limits on such patients, particularly when such a patient is articulate, loud, and apt to overwhelm more reticent and less aggressive group members. Although a few such patients have had to leave the group and the program when these limits and constraints were imposed, such instances have been surprisingly few in number. This approach requires a certain time perspective in which it is accepted that there is no rush for the patient's recovery nor for the therapist to know the patient better. More precisely, little attempt is made to force an individual to relinquish his defensive posture in order to join the group. Becoming a group member is one of the goals, not a prerequisite, of the therapeutic process.

## DISCUSSION

Although the unwilling patients' various expressions of resistance to group appear similar on the surface, we view these expressions as primarily defensive and as serving different purposes. We have formulated three sources and levels of resistance: (1) unwillingness as a "ritual protest," (2) unwillingness as a defense against acknowledging problems as internal, and (3) unwillingness as a defense against wishes for and fears of closeness.

We refer to the first category as ritual protest because it is brief, requires little intervention, and is easily recognized by the other members because most have experienced it. It dissolves as the new member gets to know the group and begins to talk about himself. Characteristically, upon joining the group individuals announce that drugs, not their feelings or relationships, are the source of their difficulties. This reaction, which is more common in men than women, seems to serve the purpose of maintaining an image of strength and independence in a situation that elicits longings to be taken care of and to be close to other people.

In the second category, in which the individual is defended against acknowledging problems as internal, when such people join the group they stress that their problems stem from family, society, and, in particular, from drugs. They view their original drug involvement not as a result of internal problems but as a wish to have fun and get "high." Subsequently, they view the drug as taking over their lives and eventually becoming the source of all their difficulties, such as problems with the law, family, sexuality, and impulses. This is a position not readily relinquished because projecting difficulties onto the outside world is less painful than to acknowledge a need for treatment. Within the group, this posture results in denying that other members and the leader can be a source of help. Blame is placed on the leader for failures, regression, and other problems in the group, and outside life difficulties are blamed on methadone and the program. In contrast to the members expressing ritual protest, these patients are initially willing to be in the group as long as it is a forum for discussing the evils of the outside world, injustices of the program, or the power of drugs. However, when group membership is proposed as important for intrapsychic or interpersonal needs, the importance or use of the group is denied.

The third source of unwillingness to be a member of the group appears to be defensive against needs and fears associated with closeness. The group is devalued and declared worthless: "I don't need any help." "I'm my own person." "I solve problems on my own and don't discuss them." "There is nothing here anybody can offer." "I don't like or trust anybody in group." More often than not, such reactions represent a paranoid position and these patients are extremely frightened of the prospect of being in a group with other people. Frequently, such individuals are unable to sit close to other people and may be unable to attend meetings.

### Self-Care Problems and Treatment Strategies

Narcotics addiction may be viewed as an extreme attempt at solving problems of self-care and self-regulation. In a previous report (Khantzian et al. 1974), we indicated that both deprivation and indulgence can result in early impairments in ego function related to self-care and self-regulation that later may lead to addiction problems. We proposed that adequate establishment of these functions were the result of optimal nurturing in the early mother–child relationship. It is our impression, along lines developed by Kohut (1971), that some of the extreme patterns of demand, neediness, and passivity, alternating with disavowal of needs, contemptuous rejection of assistance, and exaggerated postures of self-sufficiency observed with our patients, are expressions of deeply experienced but often highly defended against conflicts around unresolved and inadequately satisfied needs for love, nurturance, and care. These failures and lapses in nurturance predispose these individuals in later adult life to narcissistic conflict and problems with aggression and depression for which they seek relief through the use of narcotics.

In our clinical experience with addiction problems, we have repeatedly observed how desperately needy, disorganized, and out of control narcotic addicts are when they first contact the program. Despite their desperate need for help and stabilization, these same individuals are expert in actively resisting and failing to follow through when help is offered, and they have an uncanny ability to undermine and sabotage their treatment once they have been accepted into the program. Although much of this behavior is dynamically motivated and defensive in nature, as well as being symptomatic of regression, in other respects these individuals' apparent self-disregard, failure to comply with assigned treatment plans, missed appointments, and tardiness reflect a particular kind of impairment in ego function that predisposes people to mishaps and mistakes. These are functions that, when better established, either automatically guide most of us away from trouble, or once in trouble, are mobilized, again fairly automatically, to direct us out of trouble. This is not the case with most addicts, and the treatment strategies we have adopted attempt to take this into account.

We have attempted to structure into the program, particularly in the group therapy, provisions and responses that actively and directly respond to both the overdetermined need to fend off help as well as the tendency of these individuals to be insufficiently anxious, concerned, and responsive about many aspects of their life, in particular, about self-care measures. As we have instituted more structure and limits in the program, including mandatory group treatment, we believe we have created a treatment environment that places pressure on individuals gradually to assume increased responsibility and control over their lives. In our opinion this is not a process that can be hurried or forced through confrontation and exhortation. It is a process in which the treatment staff and therapists must be willing to play a very active part in the growth, healing, and change process.

As we have indicated, our basic strategy with these unwilling patients is an approach that is nonpressured and nonconfrontive, that allows the patient to participate in silence and at the periphery of the group. However, we try to remain sensitive, flexible, and responsive to his movement toward and into the group process. Like other strategies that deal with defenses of denial, projection, and avoidance, our goal is to maintain self-esteem and to try to focus, gently and slowly, on the underlying painful affects and the defenses against them, rather than insisting that the defenses must be surrendered.

## ACKNOWLEDGMENTS

The authors are indebted to Ms. J. Long and Drs. H. Grunebaum, N. Zinberg, and M. Burglass for their helpful criticisms and comments in the preparation of this manuscript.

## REFERENCES

Khantzian, E. J., Mack, J., and Schatzberg, A. F. (1974). Heroin use as an attempt to cope: clinical observations. *American Journal of Psychiatry* 131:160–164.

Kohut, H. (1971). *The Analysis of the Self.* New York: International Universities Press.

# 29

# The Substance-Dependent Physician

Over the past decade, the impaired physician has become the focus of increasing attention and concern among the general public, as well as within the medical profession. As a result, in recent years, medical professionals, societies, and boards of registration have responded with increasing sensitivity to the need for recognizing and dealing with such problems (Green et al. 1976, Talbott and Benson 1980, Talbott et al. 1981). Prevailing attitudes toward the impaired physician once ranged from indifference and apathy to contempt and rejection. However, in more recent years, awareness has been growing that the problems of the impaired physician are manageable and remediable and that impaired physicians can be restored to assume full professional responsibility.

More than forty states now have medical society programs to assist impaired physicians. Although one can safely say that these programs lack uniformity, since few guidelines have been established to deal with this sensitive problem on a national level, effective programs do exist and are increasing in number (Cloutier 1982).

The majority of cases of physician impairment involve drugs and/ or alcohol abuse. My interest in such cases derives mainly from my clinical investigations of substance dependency in general. My research (Khantzian 1978, 1980) has been directed toward understanding some of the causes and consequences of substance use and dependence, particularly the psychological and/or structural impairments that cause individuals to find the specific effects of various classes of drugs appealing (Khantzian 1975). I have attempted to study more precisely what particular adaptation is sought from or achieved with a drug that so compels an individual to constantly pursue and revert to drug use despite its frequently devastating consequences.

This chapter explores some of the clinical, monitoring, and disciplinary problems encountered when dealing with substance-dependent physicians. Some of the special requirements and considerations of the parties who share the responsibility for such cases are also discussed. My perspective is that of a clinician who has treated substance-dependent physicians and who has been an active member of a state medical society committee for impaired physicians.

## PROFILE OF THE SUBSTANCE ABUSER

In my experience, an individual's dependence on substances stems from an impairment in those psychological functions that regulate behavior, emotions, and self-esteem, that is, ego and self capacities.

Most substance-dependent physicians I have treated are extremely competent and devoted to their patients and to their work. However, they are almost equally remiss in matters involving their own self-care and emotional needs. Interestingly, this feature persists even when these physicians gain control over their substance dependency. This special type of passivity is less a motivated behavior than a result of underdevelopment in certain ego and self capacities. Such persons are insufficiently worried about the consequences of their actions or their lack of initiative. In the absence of such responses, behavior may be ill-considered or thoughtless, and, in some instances, have harmful consequences.

## REACTIONS TO THE PROBLEM

As the physician's dependence on chemical substances progresses, the well-being of his or her patients is increasingly jeopardized. Unfortunately, whether we respond as professionals or as citizens, our reactions to drug or alcohol dependency are too often ill-considered. That is, we tend either to overreact to the problem or to play it down. On the one hand, we can be judgmental and punitive. On the other hand, the abusers' denial of the problem may be exceeded by that of their colleagues and family members.

An intoxicated physician's expansive behavior may be passed off as an attempt to "let one's hair down." Competing pressures of professional responsibilities and family obligations may be said to justify an extra dose of a tranquilizer or pain killer taken to relieve a "backache." A physician's reliance on sedatives for fitful sleep may be similarly condoned. Even worse, indiscreet or explosive behavior, which often surfaces with reliance on addicting substances, may be dismissed as a personal quirk.

A balanced approach to the problem combines three priorities: (1) understanding and dealing with why and how the individual developed a need for drugs; (2) planning ways in which medical professional and regulatory agencies can intervene to protect the public from harm; and (3) ultimately restoring the substance-dependent physician to a productive life, as a contributing member of the medical profession and of society at large.

## MANAGEMENT

Effective treatment depends on a thorough appreciation of the substance abuser's impairments. Out of this fundamental appreciation arose my conviction that substance-dependent individuals, including physicians, need careful psychiatric evaluation and treatment, that they respond favorably to such approaches, and that sanctions (disciplinary actions) and limits, which are often invoked in such cases, are not necessarily incompatible with effective treatment. Although clinical work with substance dependency is often extremely difficult and may yield disappointing results, many patients recover with effective management.

## Psychotherapy

Clearly, the patient's deficiencies must become the focus of a therapist's attention. Patients must be helped to appreciate the relevance of their impairments, not only to substance abuse but also to the wide range of activities in which anticipation of danger is essential. Thus, the role of the therapist, at least initially, is to identify the patient's impairments and actively point out their consequences.

## Advocacy and Limits

Since self-care disturbances beg the issue of control, substance-dependent physicians are unwittingly their own worst advocates. This places the burden of regulating the patient's behavior, particularly during the recovery period, on all parties involved in the case. Thus, the Committee for Impaired Physicians must assume the role of advocate and troubleshooter for the substance-dependent physician. At the same time, the therapist and disciplinary boards must set firm limits and guidelines as key parts of the rehabilitative process.

## PRINCIPLES OF SUCCESSFUL REHABILITATION

Growing experience with substance abuse problems suggests that successful rehabilitation rests on the following principles: a commitment to advocacy and restoration of professional activities; careful administration of a recovery program that includes regular, documented psychiatric treatment; separation of the treatment and advocacy roles; frequent, random urine surveillance; and active coordination between the activities of the treating, advocating, and sanctioning parties. These principles and the problems encountered in their evolution are highlighted in the following case studies.

## Case Study 1: Conflicting Roles

A 55-year-old physician began to use barbiturates and, subsequently, opiates when his oldest child developed a serious illness. The physician's reliance on drugs ultimately affected his work, but despite alarm over his patients' safety, both he and the medical executive committee of his hospital let a period of two months elapse before seeking medical advice. The patient was suffering from a masked depression, which was chiefly manifested as intractable insomnia. His inability to articulate his feelings was extreme, and his superficial banter masked his sense of deep despair and helplessness.

As the treating physician, my efforts were directed toward helping the patient understand his depression and its relationship to his drug dependence. However, over the next two years, my energies in this case were also divided between my other roles as patient advocate and consultant to the executive committee of the medical staff and board of trustees of the hospital in which the patient worked.

Understandably, the trustees remained extremely concerned over continuing the physician's staff privileges, given the hospital's liability for his professional conduct. It was therefore clear that the patient needed an advocate, and his extreme passivity made this issue critical.

My initial reluctance to undertake this role stemmed from my lack of experience in this capacity and of any guidelines or models to follow. However, there were several reasons that I ultimately decided to meet with the board of trustees, as well as the medical executive committee. First, there were no formal mechanisms for peer review by the medical society, at either the local or state level. (The medical society committee for impaired physicians had not yet been established, and the board of registration's disciplinary powers in such cases were ill-defined.) Second, the hospital board seemed perched for disciplinary action alone. Third, the patient had stopped using drugs and was recovering and able to work. Fourth, it was my belief that the patient's continued clinical improvement depended on his continued employment. Fifth, it was my responsibility to deal with the alarm surrounding this case, given the absence of any other mechanism to deal with the problem.

Although this patient seemed to greatly appreciate my involvement in his case, in retrospect my multiple roles had at least two undesirable consequences. First, my efforts to forestall precipitous disciplinary measures by the hospital board played all too readily into the patient's characteristic passivity in assuming responsibility for himself. This was compounded by the actions taken by everyone else, whether against him or on his behalf. Second, my efforts placed me in the unenviable position of being viewed by the hospital board as a "do-gooder." My credibility was compromised because the trustees considered my efforts to be at cross purposes with their concerns, that is, patient safety and hospital liability.

Today, the situation has improved significantly. Our state medical society has established a committee for impaired physicians (now called the Physicians Health Services), and the board of registration has assumed greater responsibility for constructive intervention and sanctions. The current problem, which is explored in the case below, seems to be one of self-definition, territoriality, communication, and responsibilities.

## Case Study 2: Poor Communication

A young physician was referred for mandatory psychiatric evaluation and treatment after the hospital pharmacist had discovered that he had been writing narcotic prescriptions for his own illicit use. The pharmacist, circumventing the hospital administration and chief of staff, reported the physician to the Drug Enforcement Agency (DEA). In turn, the DEA informed the hospital administration about the situation, and the physician was subsequently placed on probation.

Over the next 18 months, the patient became increasingly involved with the hospital board, the committee for impaired physicians, and the board of registration. Ultimately, he fell under the ongoing scrutiny of state narcotics agents. Unlike the physician in case 1, this patient could not readily control his dependency on opiates.

The most disconcerting elements in this case were secrecy, miscommunication, and failure to coordinate the efforts on behalf of this physician. This situation resulted, in part, from the insidious distrust by the patient of all parties involved in the case, including the therapist, and, in part, from the failure of the involved parties to adequately coordinate their activities and effectively communicate information relevant to the patient's care. For example, at one point, the patient seriously considered voluntary hospital confinement; at the same time, however, law enforcement agents and family members had again discovered that he was writing illicit prescriptions, but they did not inform the patient's therapist or the committee for impaired physicians and the hospital board, which might have pursued the patient's hospitalization.

In the midst of this communications breakdown, the chief of service decided to suspend this physician permanently. This complication occurred at a time when there were no formal policies or procedures on how the disabled physician or treating therapist should relate to the involved hospital board and medical society committee or on what responsibilities each of the parties had vis-à-vis the other. It subsequently became clear in other, less complicated cases that once policies and procedures were in place things went more smoothly. However, this was not to be the case for this physician. Ultimately, treatment and disciplinary measures failed to restore him to his professional status. Given that he had otherwise been considered a superb technician who showed great promise, this was sad indeed.

## CONCLUSION

The physician who abuses a controlled substance is involved in an extreme attempt at self-cure that is doomed to fail. Such physicians require good clinical care and demand control. Clinical efforts need not conflict with disciplinary measures, which are invariably invoked in such cases. Rather, successful rehabilitation rests on sound clinical evaluation and care, advocacy, and, when necessary, discipline and sanction. Furthermore, responsibility for intervention must constantly be clarified by the treating, advocating, and disciplinary parties involved.

## REFERENCES

Cloutier, C. (1982). An analysis of formal controls on impaired physicians. *Psychiatric Annals* 12:225–237.

Green, R. C., Carroll, G. J., and Buxton, W. D. (1976). Drug addiction among physicians: the Virginia experience. *Journal of the American Medical Association* 236:1372–1375.

Khantzian, E. J. (1975). Self selection and progression in drug dependence. *Psychiatry Digest* 10:19–22.

——— (1978). The ego, the self and opiate addiction: theoretical and treatment considerations. *International Review of Psychoanalysis* 5:189–198.

——— (1980). An ego-self theory of substance dependence. In *Theories of Addiction*, ed. D. J. Lettieri, M. Sayers, and H. W. Wallenstein, pp. 29–33. NIDA monograph 30. Rockville, MD: National Institute on Drug Abuse.

Talbott, G. D., and Benson, E. B. (1980). Impaired physician: the dilemma of identification. *Postgraduate Medicine* 68:57–64.

Talbott, G. D., Richardson, A. C., Mashburn, J. S., et al. (1981). The Medical Association of Georgia's disabled doctors program. *Journal of the Medical Association of Georgia* 70:545–549.

# 30

# Understanding and Managing Addicted Physicians

Our call as physicians to the profession of medicine involves complex motives. It is probably safe to say, however, that for most of us, making people healthier, taking care of patients, or repairing them plays some part. As we attend to the injuries and dysfunctions of our patients, we also attend to our own. The healing traditions constantly challenge us and our patients to address the need for restoration and well-being.

I believe that most physicians are motivated by idealism and commitment in choosing medicine, and that our choice is rooted in a desire to offer comfort and care to others. In fact, much of our stress and burdens as well as our satisfactions derive from this deeper personal and professional meaning in our lives.

The substance-dependent physician is a casualty of life's human challenges and the special challenges of the profession of medicine. Addiction can best be understood, I believe, in terms of problems with self-regulation. Most substance-dependent physicians' problems represent a condition in which the complex motives involved in choosing medicine as a career have interacted with self-regulation deficits not unique to physicians. The stereotype of addicts, including physician addicts, as untreatable, hopeless individuals is unwarranted. Substance-dependent physicians consistently respond favorably to supervised treatment and advocacy, and they are most often able to resume their work after successful intervention (Shore 1982).

This chapter reviews three areas of self-regulation deficits in substance-dependent physicians that I believe are the main bases of their difficulties, namely, vulnerabilities in regulation of feelings, self-esteem, and self-care. From a clinical perspective and my work with an impaired physicians' committee, I discuss how such vulnerabilities interact with the powerful challenges and human struggles that confront physicians and then consider what some of the treatment implications of these problems might be.

## CLINICAL OBSERVATIONS

### Recognition and Regulation of Feelings

The frequently referred to altered state of consciousness that addicts seek with their drugs is a misnomer. More correctly, what addicts seek is an altered state of feeling. The state of feeling that they are seeking is not one of pleasure or euphoria, however, as is commonly thought. In fact, what such people actually seek through their continual use of drugs is a relief from displeasure and dysphoria. The nature of this dysphoria is complicated. It is not that their feelings are simply overwhelming; it is more accurate to say that their feelings are more often elusive, vague, confusing, and even absent. The term *alexithymia*, derived from the Greek, meaning "no words for feelings," which was originally coined by Sifneos and associates (1977) and Nemiah (1977) to describe certain psychosomatic patients, has also been adopted by Krystal (1982) to underscore this problem in addicts. Most recently McDougall (1984) has referred to such individuals who lack feelings as "disaffected." Conversely, when such persons do feel, it can also be extreme. They feel not at all or they feel too much, and thus their feeling life can be overwhelming. As such patients begin to feel, their anxieties border on panic or terror; depressive feelings may suddenly become violently suicidal ones, and anger and aggression often assume murderous proportions.

The drug that individuals prefer or on which they come to rely is intimately related to the presence or absence of feelings or impulses with which they struggle. In some instances, drugs are used to enable the experiencing and expression of feelings. Sedative-hypnotics and alcohol are notoriously effective in this respect. Most of us take for granted that our feelings serve as signals or activators for necessary action. This is not the case for most addicts, and in this respect their feelings fail them. For some, this is chronically the case and is a cause and/or a consequence of a restricted personality style. For others, their inability to activate and mobilize themselves is related to the energy and inertia problems associated with depression. This is why stimulants appeal to chronically and acutely immobilized persons. More recently, I have been impressed that some individuals use stimulants for the drugs' paradoxical calming effect on hyperactivity and restlessness. This has been particularly apparent in a number of cocaine addicts I have treated (Khantzian 1983, Khantzian and Khantzian 1984). For many of these individuals, hyperactivity is a compensation for depressive feelings. Opiates are notoriously effective for modulating and relieving a range of intense, painful feelings; this is particularly true when anger or aggression is involved. One of the most specific appeals of opiates resides in their ability to quell or mute rageful feelings. Such feelings are particularly dysphoric and threatening because they disorganize from within by producing a subjective experience of disruption and fragmentation, and they disorganize from without in that such emotions invite counteraggression and retaliation from others (Khantzian 1982).

Physician addicts are just as subject to the predispositions to self-select their drugs as are any other individuals, and their all too easy access to drugs leaves them especially vulnerable to addiction.

Many physicians who are drug dependent are nevertheless remarkable for their skillful and sensitive devotion to their patients' distress, especially severely and terminally ill patients. For some, their sensitivity to their patients' suffering is related to their own personal suffering and dysphoria, and their care for their patients represents a

partially successful transformation and resolution of their own conflicts. To the extent that they fail to recognize, regulate, or transform
their emotional pain, they are prone to rely on drugs for relief. I have
been especially impressed that certain predisposed physicians have
found mounting anger and rage in the context of frustrating personal
and professional experiences to be dramatically reversed with opiates.
The calming and paradoxically energizing effects of opiates in such
cases often are the basis for vulnerable physicians to become increasingly dependent on narcotics.

Although these patients instruct us that a major motive of drug
use is to obtain relief from suffering, they also suggest there is a more
subtle motive linked to the suffering of the addiction-withdrawal cycle.
A physician addict explained that he was as much involved with the
misery drugs cause as with the relief they offer. He added that at least
he produced and controlled this misery, whereas he did not understand
and could not control the misery that had caused his drug use. Such
patients learn (and if we listen, they instruct) that their self-imposed
suffering is a way to master and control painful feelings that are otherwise confusing and beyond their control.

## Self-Esteem Regulation

Addicts frequently invite pejorative characterizations of themselves as
dependent personalities. They are referred to as "oral" characters,
infantile, clinging, and weak. I believe that the nature of addicts' (including physician addicts) dependency problems is poorly understood
and that these unflattering labels detract from understanding and
managing their dependency disturbances. Recent clarifications advanced by the self psychologists offer better clues as to the nature of
addicts' dependency problems. Balint (1968), a forerunner of the self
psychologists, suggested that the dependency of addicts and alcoholics was the result of a "basic fault" and a "yearning for this feeling of
harmony" (p. 56) that alcohol and drugs could supply. Kohut (1971),
the pioneer of modern self psychology, proposed that substances acted
as a substitute for a "defect in psychological structure" (p. 46). This
fault or defect produced in a rudimentary way a pervasive lack of well-
being, which could extend through a lifetime. It was probably this
chronic state of affairs to which Silkworth (Alcoholics Anonymous
1978) was referring in the Alcoholic Anonymous (AA) "Big Book," for

which alcoholics well knew the antidote, namely, a "sense of (elusive) ease and comfort which comes at once by taking a few drinks" (Alcoholics Anonymous 1978, p. xxvii).

One of the major consequences of this defect or deficiency is the failure to value oneself. For many physicians, their successes as students, clinicians, teachers, and researchers become a vehicle to compensate for self-esteem problems. They also often discover, however, that these "success cures" carry them only so far. Subsequent challenges in life and the insults and disappointments in their work, family life, friendships, and health precipitate crises and make any sense of well-being that their careers provided elusive. At such times of crisis and distress, individuals discover the short-term uplifting and pain-relieving effects of drugs and alcohol.

## Self-Care Disturbances

Too much has been written about the self-destructive drives and motives of addicts. Clinical, theoretical, and popular accounts take for granted or actively advance a stereotype of addicts as people who both consciously and unconsciously court self-destruction and death. In my opinion, the "suicide by installment" view of addicts is a gross violation and distracts from our understanding their inability to care for themselves. It is an aspect of addictions that needs to be better understood. My own clinical experience suggests that dependency on drugs is less related to a motive to self-destroy and more indicative of major problems of self-care and self-preservation, resulting from a deficiency or absence of a capacity for self-protection.

Addicts simply do not anticipate or fear the consequences of their action (or inaction) in the face of danger; they fail to be attentive to cues that ordinarily cause most of us to be aroused and alerted to potential mishap or harm. This vulnerability, evident in its more benign forms in a tendency to forget and to sustain minor accidents, is often evident in carelessness with daily living habits, poor money management, accidents, and preventable legal, surgical, medical, and dental problems. The same failure is also involved in the unthinkingness and flagrant lack of concern that lead to involvement with substances (Khantzian 1981, Khantzian and Mack 1983).

Working with recovering drug-free physician addicts through an impaired-physicians committee and in my clinical work, I have been impressed that although they have been woefully neglectful, imprecise, and careless in managing their personal lives, ironically they often enjoy the opposite reputation with colleagues as being very precise and careful in their treatment of patients. Not insignificantly, a number of them have also been accomplished airplane pilots, race-car drivers, and mountain climbers. I suspect they have transformed and attempted to work out problems with self-care through their painstaking, deliberate efforts to take care of others and to master dangerous pursuits.

## TREATMENT IMPLICATIONS AND PRINCIPLES

Addicted and alcoholic physicians are particularly subject to receiving poor treatment because of their special status. We consider it indelicate to question physicians about their excesses. We shy away from expecting them to adhere to a strict monitoring of their behavior and to put self-care ahead of patient care while recovering. We also often fail to take a careful drug-alcohol history lest we seem disrespectful and distrusting. And too often the treating and treated physicians exempt themselves from the following basic management principles that are applicable to all substance-dependent individuals:

1. *Good basic care begins with a careful drug and alcohol history.* It is extremely important to ascertain the amounts, patterns, and effects of drug or alcohol use and attempts to curtail or control them. Most patients, and especially physicians, appreciate such a careful inquiry and are cooperative and honest. Persistent inquiry about what users seek or experience from the action of their preferred drug(s) provides a means to emphatically tune into their distress and identify the nature of the dominant, painful feelings with which they struggle. This empathic, understanding attitude and approach helps to overcome a major treatment block—a sense of shame—and becomes the basis for building an alliance rather than an adversarial relationship.
2. *Early confinement and achievement of abstinence are essential.* The compulsion to use drugs for painful feelings coupled with self-care problems can malignantly combine to make abstinence difficult and reversions common. Hospitalization early in treatment and other interventions can significantly contribute to es-

tablishing and ensuring control. The utility of the adjunctive alternatives we can employ can materially assist in maintaining abstinence when a patient is or becomes ambulatory. Urine surveillance, naltrexone (Trexan),[1] and disulfiram (Antabuse) provide valuable safety nets and important delay factors. Disulfiram, in particular, provides a prosthetic, anticipatory alarm system for patients who all too often are lacking in the normal capacity to anticipate danger and protect themselves.

3. *Impaired physician committees are important in the treatment and recovery process.* My experience as a member of the Massachusetts Medical Society's Committee on the Impaired Physician (now the Physician Health Services) has convinced me that the advocacy they provide physicians who cannot provide it for themselves, the confrontation needed to make impaired physicians accept their illness and its treatment, the monitoring, the peer assistance, and the support are all vital parts of treatment for colleagues who often take poor care of themselves and thus are their own worst advocates. When combined with active treatment, impaired physician committees can ensure recovery and full resumption of work for a majority of those who participate in such programs.

4. *Alcoholics Anonymous and its offspring Narcotics Anonymous (NA) are invaluable in helping substance-dependent individuals with their vulnerabilities.* They are as effective for physicians as they are for those from other walks of life. Our profession, however, sometimes leaves us short on lessons in humility. It is, therefore, often difficult for physicians to submit to what AA insists on, namely, that they are powerless over alcohol, that they cannot recover on their own, and that they accept a "higher power." When it does work, AA is one of the most ingenious, dynamic psychological approaches for helping people with life's problems. For many, it goes beyond providing support and becomes the basis for significant and permanent psychological growth and change (Mack 1981). There are those, however, who

---

1. Interestingly, naltrexone, used originally to block the effects of opiates, has recently been employed and marketed under a new name (REVIA) to help alcoholics curtail their desire for alcohol (Volpicelli et al. 1992).

will not accept this kind of help but will respond to other interventions.

Initially, for many physicians, the idea of entering into discussion and stepping forth as an alcoholic or addict in a large AA or NA meeting is particularly abhorrent, given concerns about their reputations in the community and among colleagues. International Doctors in AA (IDAA) provides a transition experience, and similarly, physician support groups, which have become increasingly common, help physician alcoholics and addicts overcome their shame and fear of exposure and accept the benefits of AA, NA, and other treatment alternatives.

5. *Psychotherapeutic and psychopharmacologic approaches to substance-dependency problems should be considered and utilized.* Most important, parochial views should be avoided. Psychotherapeutic and psychopharmacologic treatments rest on a tradition of identifying underlying causes of presenting symptoms. But the problem with treating life-threatening symptoms is that they often cannot wait while one finds root causes. Whether one is dealing with malignant hyperthermia, hypertensive crises, or a consuming addiction, issues of control and safety must be placed ahead of understanding etiologies. Once control and safety have been established for the patient, then conditions exist to address, through a psychotherapeutic relationship, the underlying problems that led to the loss of control. Sensible clinicians understand this, and sensible people working with alcoholics and addicts quickly come to realize it as well.

Psychotherapy provides an opportunity for people to find a better self through a relationship with another human being. They learn in this psychotherapeutic relationship that their feelings can be identified and contained, and that they can grow to value themselves more and to regulate their behavior better, particularly in regard to self-care.

In selected cases a human (treatment) relationship alone is not enough. Feelings are truly overwhelming for some patients, especially when they first give up their alcohol and rely on others. In extreme and unresponsive cases involving major affective disturbances, anxiety-phobic disorder, dyscontrol syndromes, attention deficit disorder, and others, appropriate pharmacological agents are available and ought to be considered. The pharmacological agents that we use in these cases may become means to enable other human interventions and solutions, whereas the drugs addicts and alcoholics use or revert to become tragic ends in themselves.

## CONCLUSION

Substance-dependent physicians, like most drug- or alcohol-dependent individuals, need to understand how they have adopted extraordinary drug solutions for a range of human problems. They need to learn how to better regulate their feelings, how to value themselves more, and how to take better care of themselves. They also need to learn that their drug-alcohol "solutions" preclude more ordinary human solutions to the problems in their lives.

I believe that human relationships can best provide opportunities to understand these problems through either a professional psychotherapeutic relationship or peer group experiences, such as group therapy and self-help groups such as NA or AA. To gain understanding and forestall progression of the addictive process, however, it is imperative to establish control over the use of drugs or alcohol at the outset. In less severe cases, initial control and abstinence may be obtained without confinement, but for more severe cases, confinement and the use of drug substitution for stabilization and detoxification may be required to establish this control.

One of the great tragedies in modern medicine is that decisions about treatment approaches to addictions and alcoholism are too often influenced by controversies and polemics about beliefs and ideologies. We need to be more concerned with what works for and is acceptable to each individual. We need to apply these principles not only when we care for the addicts and alcoholics who treat themselves on the street with their substances, but also when we care for our colleagues who medicate themselves in their own consultation rooms and in our hospitals.

## REFERENCES

*Alcoholics Anonymous, 4th Edition.* (1978). New York: Alcoholics Anonymous World Services.

Balint, M. (1968). *The Basic Fault.* London: Tavistock.

Khantzian, E. J. (1981). Some treatment implications of the ego and self disturbances in alcoholism. In *Dynamic Approaches to the Understanding and Treatment of Alcoholism*, ed. M. H. Bean and N. E. Zinberg, pp. 163–188. New York: Free Press.

——— (1982). Psychological (structural) vulnerabilities and the specific appeal of narcotics. *Annals of the New York Academy of Sciences* 398:24–32.

——— (1983). An extreme case of cocaine dependence and marked improvement with methylphenidate treatment. *American Journal of Psychiatry* 140:784–785.

Khantzian, E. J., and Khantzian, N. J. (1984). Cocaine addiction: Is there a psychological predisposition? *Psychiatric Annals* 14:753–759.

Khantzian, E. J., and Mack, J. E. (1983). Self-preservation and the care of the self—ego instincts reconsidered. *Psychoanalytic Study of the Child* 38:209–232. New Haven, CT: Yale University Press.

Kohut, H. (1971). *The Analysis of the Self*. New York: International Universities Press.

Krystal, H. (1982). Alexithymia and the effectiveness of psychoanalytic treatment. *International Journal of Psychoanalytic Psychotherapy* 9:353–378.

Mack, J. E. (1981). Alcoholism, AA and the governance of the self. In *Dynamic Approaches to the Understanding and Treatment of Alcoholism*, ed. M. H. Bean and N. E. Zinberg, pp. 125–162. New York: Free Press.

McDougall, J. (1984). The "disaffected" patient: reflections on affect pathology. *Psychoanalytic Quarterly* 53:386–409.

Nemiah, J. C. (1977). Alexithymia: theoretical considerations. *Psychotherapy Psychosomatics* 28:199–207.

Shore, J. H. (1982). The impaired physician: four years after probation. *Journal of the American Medical Association* 248:3127–3130.

Sifneos, P., Apfel-Savitz, R., and Frankl, F. (1977). The phenomenon of "alexethymia." *Psychotherapy Psychosomatics* 28:47–57.

Volpicelli, F. J. R., Alterman, A. I., Hayashida, M., and O'Brien, C. P. (1992). Naltrexone in the treatment of alcohol dependence. *Archives of General Psychiatry* 49:876–880.

# 31

# Psychotherapeutic Interventions with Substance Abusers

With the alarming rise of substance abuse in all aspects of our society over the past quarter century, there has been a growing awareness that addiction and alcoholism represent major public health problems. The health care professions have been ill prepared for this "epidemic" and slow in responding with effective interventions for understanding and care. In the absence of suitable professional responses, self-help programs of all types, of which AA and NA are the most effective and beneficial, have sprung up as an accepted intervention for the tragic consequences and suffering associated with substance dependency. The great community psychiatrist Dr. Gerald Caplan has observed that self-help groups (he calls them "support groups") emerge and develop when existing professional approaches to a problem are slow in responding or are not effective. He assures us that this is a natural evolutionary process in which at best the self-help community draws attention to and legitimatizes a problem and creates a context for professionals to take up the challenge for understanding and dealing with it. Furthermore, they need not and should not compete with each other (Caplan 1974).

Unfortunately, Caplan's reassurances have not always held up in the field of substance abuse treatment, and the politics and economics of it and our individual and collective vanity have not always allowed self-help programs and professionals to learn from each other about the advantages, limitations, and complementarity of the two approaches. Since nonprofessional, self-help approaches have been tremendously influential and effective, we need to consider how these programs fit in therapeutically, technically, and practically with what we do as clinicians and practitioners. I remain convinced that, as clinicians and mental health professionals, we have a great deal to offer in understanding and treating substance abuse disorders, but we also need to work out better the politics and dynamics of how our approaches relate to alternative ones, particularly AA, NA, and other modalities (e.g., educational and instructional interventions) that are safe and effective.

This chapter considers "the why, the when, and the how" of psychotherapy with substance abusers. Given the growing involvement of clinicians and psychotherapists in substance abuse treatment over the past fifteen years, the topic is timely and apt. However, I would like to add "the what" to the list of considerations, namely, what is psychotherapy for substance abusers, and what is psychotherapeutic for substance abusers, and why, when, and how does psychotherapy fit in. From my perspective as a practitioner and psychotherapist, I will discuss some of the advantages and challenges of a clinical approach to substance abusers, as well as consider some of the tensions and limitations associated with the approaches we employ, whether they be professional, psychotherapeutic ones or nonprofessional, self-help ones.

## THE CLINICAL CONTEXT

A concept (e.g., Synanon) or self-help approach has advantages because it simplifies and reduces problems to basic assumptions about causes and adopts interventions that are pragmatic and workable. Notwithstanding the advantage of such an approach, I adopt and maintain a clinical approach and tradition in considering the utility of the therapeutic modalities that we employ including concept or self-help approaches. This tradition requires us to link treatment modalities to history, diagnosis, and identifiable etiologies. Although all the answers are not yet in, wherever possible I try to link treatment approaches to an understanding of substance abusers, and, where it is less clear what is going on, I use the clinical measure of safety and efficacy as a guide to what we do.

Substance abusers suffer because they are unable to manage their feelings, self-esteem, relationships, and behavior (Khantzian 1978). It is for these reasons that they need treatment in general, and psychotherapy in particular. They have substituted extraordinary chemical solutions for more ordinary human ones and as a consequence they need to discover in the context of a human relationship with another individual or a group of individuals that their problems can be identified, understood, and treated in more ordinary ways. They need to understand their special relationship with suffering both as a cause and as a result of their involvement with substances. They need much assistance in overcoming their belief, if not insistence, that they cannot cope with their distress in any other way, and they need special help and intervention to appreciate how much they complicate their suffering and add to it by adopting a chemical response.

Although much remains to be identified and understood concerning addicts' suffering, psychodynamic and psychiatric diagnostic studies of the addictions over the past twenty-five years have yielded significant findings that have important implications for treatment. An extensive review of these findings goes beyond the scope of this chapter, but I will briefly highlight the prominent clinical and psychopathological features of substance abusers that have the greatest implications for psychotherapeutic interventions.

The most prominent findings in substance abusers center on major problems with painful affects and impulsivity. It is thus not surprising that diagnostic studies have documented a high incidence of depression and personality disorders, including but not limited to antisocial personality disorder (Khantzian and Treece 1985, Rounsaville et al. 1982a,b). Beyond the descriptive findings, the problems with painful affects seem principally related to deficits in recognizing, regulating, and tolerating their feelings; narcissistic disturbances reflected

in troubled self–other relations and self-esteem problems are intimately related to the affect disturbances and interact with them to
make reliance on the psychotropic effects of substances malignantly
compelling (Khantzian 1978, 1980a, Krystal and Raskin 1970,
Wurmser 1974). The often referred to impulsivity of addicts is one of
the most maddening and maladaptive aspects of addiction. It seems
to be a reflection of failures to value the self enough, combined with
self-care deficits wherein addicts and alcoholics do not worry, anticipate, or think enough about dangerous or hazardous involvements,
particularly those associated with substance abuse (Khantzian 1981,
Khantzian and Mack 1983). Certain characteristics in the personality
organization of substance abusers derive from these disturbances.
Some of the most prominent characteristics of substance abusers with
which our treatment interventions ultimately must wrestle include
alexithymia, counterdependence, and counterphobia.

The impairments and disturbances of substance abusers have clear
implications for addressing needs for safety, comfort, and control, especially initially, but also throughout treatment, when we assume responsibility for their care. Establishing and maintaining these provisions are necessary and essential conditions for treatment and they
are an integral part of therapy. Some of this occurs or is mediated in
the individual treatment relationship. More particularly, I believe that
a therapist functioning in a primary care role can build an effective
alliance with his/her patients and significantly increase the patients'
chances of better appreciating and integrating the provisions they
must make to better regulate and care for themselves. In other instances the mechanics and requirements of institutional responses,
when applied in an enlightened way (e.g., the confinement and control provided by prisons, parole, probation, and hospitals), are equally
important therapeutic factors. In yet other cases the advantage of peer
group experiences seem most enabling in containing and regulating
addicts' tendencies to avoid their pain and escape into action.

I believe the issue of when and how to provide psychotherapy for
substance abusers, and more precisely what kind of psychotherapy,
should be kept in this context of the need to establish and maintain
safety, comfort, and control. Some of our confusion and inconsistency
about our psychotherapeutic role with addicts and alcoholics derives
from traditions and expectations in clinical practice that often unwittingly and unnecessarily compete. I am referring to the curative and

healing traditions in medicine, and the investigative and understanding ones in science, psychoanalysis, and psychology. The physician acts and does; the psychotherapist empathizes and investigates. In training psychiatrists, some of my colleagues insist that we have to train the physician "doer" out of psychiatric residents. Of course there is much to this in that much of our work as psychotherapists in the psychodynamic tradition requires us to set aside the modes of active intervention—procedures, operations and the like—and instead cultivate modes of listening, investigation, and understanding. I maintain that these modes are not mutually exclusive, and, more than we care to admit, good psychotherapy in general requires us to work in both modes, and when working with substance abusers it is imperative. If we can be honest with ourselves about these tensions and seeming contradictions, then we can more flexibly and effectively manage and negotiate our patients' needs. This might require us to combine strange psychotherapeutic bedfellows such as drug substitution, limits, analysis of transference distortions, confinement, and so on.

## PSYCHOTHERAPEUTIC INTERVENTIONS

In this section I review the main psychotherapeutic interventions that we employ and consider their indications and benefits. In the final section I consider differentially some of the special problems, limitations, complications, and contraindications of these therapeutic modalities.

### Individual Psychotherapy

I believe individual psychotherapy should be routinely considered for substance abusers. Its usefulness and advantages have been recently documented in two studies (Woody et al. 1983, 1984). These studies and a number of clinical reports (Khantzian 1978, 1981, Wurmser 1984) suggest that the type and degree of psychopathology associated with substance abuse can be identified, that suitable subjects may be effectively dealt with in a psychotherapeutic relationship, and that the addition of this modality is more efficacious than drug counseling alone. However, in my opinion, individual psychotherapy for substance abusers should be broadly defined to include all those interventions and roles a therapist must play in ensuring that a substance abuser's physical and psychological needs are understood and managed.

The initial multiple roles that the therapist must play with substance abusers may be likened to the functions a primary care physician assumes. Accordingly, in this aspect of our work I conceive of the intervening clinician as a primary care therapist whose aggregate roles and responsibility for care accrues to what is psychotherapeutic. In this respect it is essential in early phases of treatment that a therapist concern and involve himself with the vitally important matters of safety, stabilization, and control. Carefully obtaining a drug history including the amounts and patterns of drug(s) used, and the empathic exploration of the drug effects sought and experienced, can contribute significantly to a strong treatment alliance with the patient. Identifying and modifying external/environmental precipitants and aggravants, especially within the family, which predispose and worsen the substance abuse can also help to instill added stability and further strengthen the treatment relationship. Also, it is important for the therapist to involve himself/herself early and to follow through with decisions about and support for confinement, detoxification, involvement with Alcoholics Anonymous (AA) or Narcotic Anonymous (NA), and pharmacological treatment modalities.

In addition to brokering and facilitating other interventions, a major area of attention in early phases of treatment should be monitoring the patient's capacity to benefit from individual psychotherapy and to tolerate and endure exposure to groups. The therapist can play an important role in helping to overcome some patients' fears and resistance to AA and NA, thereby providing the crucial added safety and support that is essential for them. As I discuss in the next section, in other instances the therapist may ascertain that coexistent psychopathology and other symptomatic or characterological difficulties make referral to self-help and/or traditional group treatment unlikely or undesirable (i.e., contraindicated), but that other treatment alternatives are acceptable and indicated.

As stabilization is achieved, one can begin to ascertain the capacity to develop a more traditional psychotherapeutic relationship. However, this may involve a protracted period of months to years as a person makes the internal psychological and external adjustments involved in establishing a drug-free life. Furthermore, substance abusers' difficulties with affect recognition and modulation often require increased therapist activity, initially and subsequently, in helping them to label and tolerate their feelings. Similarly, problems with self-care predispose such patients to impulsive and injurious action, and these tendencies call for the therapist to act as an auxiliary protection system by actively helping them to anticipate problems and to contain their behavior.

Although it is frequently maintained that addicts and alcoholics are poorly motivated, lack insight, and develop destructive and unworkable psychotherapeutic relationships (e.g., negative transference/countertransference reactions), I believe that these characterizations are more the result of excessive passivity and neutrality on the part of therapists, and an outmoded model of therapy that rests on uncovering techniques alone. More contemporary psychotherapeutic approaches appreciate the importance of structure, activity, warmth, flexibility, and empathy in helping these patients to identify and better manage their disabilities in the context of a caring relationship. Finally, I think it is safe to say that once stability has been well established and allowances made for the vulnerabilities and disturbances unique to substance abusers, then the vicissitudes and complications of psychotherapy are not too different from those encountered when treating patients with character pathology and other severe neurotic and affective disturbances (Khantzian 1980b, 1981). In the last section of this chapter I refer to certain cases in which, for reasons special to substance abusers, transfer to another therapist might be considered.

## Self-Help Groups

Until recently and as a consequence of ineffective or nonexistent professional treatment approaches, addicts and alcoholics have learned that they can help themselves and each other through group interactions, sharing experiences, self-disclosure, and support to abstain from drug and alcohol use, and, to confront their biological, psychological, and moral "defects" that have predisposed them to their illness. Alcoholics Anonymous (AA) and Narcotics Anonymous (NA) are examples of our human capacity to be at least as ingenious and creative in restoring ourselves as we are inventive in destroying ourselves. In my own work, I have been interested in how effective group approaches (i.e., self-help and psychotherapeutic) are in helping substance abusers acquire from each other coping devices, tools, and practical guides to repair their self-care impairments. My colleague at the Cambridge

Hospital, Dr. John Mack, has focused on how AA effectively and in the best psychodynamic traditions addresses "self-governance" problems of alcoholics (Mack 1981). His formulations are applicable as well for NA and addicts. He uses the term *self-governance* to refer to those psychological functions concerned with choosing, deciding, directing, and controlling the person, that is, those sets of ego functions responsible for taking charge of the personality. He allows that such functions have been referred to as "executant function" but he prefers the term *self-governance* to allow for a broader connotation of other individuals and groups being involved in the governance of a person. He attributes, in part, the success of AA, and similar group experiences, to its recognition that alcoholism represents a failure in self-governance, that the self never functions as a solitary unit, and that recovery requires a caring community of others. He suggests that their caring for and attending to each other, especially examining their defects of character, goes beyond abstinence and sobriety and in fact produces permanent change, growth, and maturity in personality organization.

There are many types of self-help approaches for substance abuse that have emerged over the last twenty years, and many have incorporated the best of AA, NA, and traditional group psychotherapy. Unfortunately, it is not always the case that self-help modalities adopt or develop the best in these traditions. In the last section of this chapter I comment briefly on some of the more aggressive and confrontational self-help approaches and their disadvantages and contraindications.

## Group Therapy

In many respects the support, change, and growth opportunities derived from more traditional group psychotherapy are based on similar dynamics of AA and NA—universal shared experiences, enabling confrontation, support, and the comfort of feeling accepted and understood by others. Beyond these elements, group therapy, utilizing the skillful leadership of a trained therapist, allows a more focused examination of characteristic, self-defeating behavior patterns, helps people recognize and better sustain their feelings, and more precisely identifies self-care and self-esteem problems and some of the compensatory attitudes of bravado and counterdependency. More specifically, group members can be effectively guided to spot and respond to their exaggerated efforts to ward off help and the tendency to be incautious and insufficiently anxious about dangerous situations and behavior, particularly those associated with drug use. In the case of self-care impairments, cognitive disabilities interact with problems of experiencing and recognizing affects to leave substance abusers vulnerable to hazards; in this respect, specialized, tasks-oriented/didactic group experiences and those utilizing behavioral-cognitive techniques can be extraordinarily helpful in repairing self-care, self-regulating deficiencies (Marlatt and Donovan 1982, McAuliffe and Gordon 1980).

## DIFFERENTIAL TREATMENT CONSIDERATIONS

As clinicians consider treatment approaches to complex clinical problems, I recommend an approach that links treatment with the patient's history, the identification and organization of symptoms and signs, and the search for etiologies. When we do this in considering treatment modalities for substance abusers, we can then think critically and differentially about the efficacy of different treatment modalities, as well as their unwanted, deleterious effects. This time-proven tradition learned from basic pharmacology, namely to consider effects, side effects, and toxic effects for whatever we offer our patients, holds up for our human interventions as well as those involving drugs. I will explore briefly in this final section some differential considerations, pitfalls, and hazards of the treatment interventions we employ.

There is a tendency for treatment personnel and programs to prescribe group treatment experiences and to broadly extol their advantages for all substance-dependent individuals. Indeed, group experiences, whether of the self-help variety or the traditional psychotherapeutic type, are powerful and effective in challenging defenses and producing change. However, for this very reason it is just as important to consider the potential threat, harm, and contraindications for assigning certain individuals to group treatment modalities in general, and to be aware of the discomfort and threat that group experiences can produce for certain individuals. The aggressive, heavily confrontative group approaches employed by some of the original concept programs such as Synanon offer little advantage, are risky, and for the most part are contraindicated. This is especially so given the lifelong difficulties addicts have had managing intense, angry affects, because such approaches greatly stir these emotions.

Although AA and NA generally do not produce such problems, in other respects they can cause or underestimate other problems. Most notably, substance-dependent patients often suffer with shame and anxiety, often of immense and phobic proportions, which make large group experiences very difficult or unthinkable. For others, a rigid personality organization makes the "surrender," "belief in a higher power," and "keep it simple" messages of AA and NA unacceptable. In still other cases professionals and paraprofessionals rigidly insist that patients accept and/or attend AA and NA to the exclusion of other alternatives, and thus compound further the substance abusers' sense of hopelessness, and probably contribute to lost opportunities for intervention.

Because many patients will not or cannot accept AA or NA, we need to consider alternative treatments, and we should not label their intolerance to these programs as a resistance. Both the success and the limitations of AA and NA challenge us to learn what is the beneficial nature of their effect as well as to consider the implications for alternative approaches when they are not accepted or they don't work. That is, it places consideration of this treatment in a more familiar clinical context in which we consider alternative approaches when there are contraindications or when a patient does not tolerate a particular treatment.

Group psychotherapy has its own hazards and pitfalls, and therapists need to appreciate the special vulnerabilities and propensity of addicts in groups. Substance-dependent patients tend to function in the extremes when in groups and as a consequence may either overexpose themselves or remain isolated and withdrawn. This has implications for other group members and/or the leader, namely, to adopt containing/modulating or activating/supportive roles. Problems with paranoia, shame, severe depression, and aggression often call for increased activity and attention on the part of the group leader, and in extreme cases might mean participation in groups is contraindicated for the sake of both the individual and the group.

In the case of individual psychotherapy some substance-abusing patients continue to have major difficulties in recognizing and dealing with their feelings, and self-esteem problems or behavioral difficulties persist with little evidence of benefiting from the treatment relationship. In such cases the primary therapist has the responsibility to broker other combinations or interventions and perhaps to de-emphasize the individual work. In other cases a transfer to another therapist is sometimes required given the many real-life crises and threats therapists and patients endure together, especially early in treatment. For example, the common problems with ambivalence, which occur in individual psychotherapy, especially feelings of anger and distrust, often are especially difficult for a patient to experience and/or to express if the patient feels the therapist saved his/her life; as one patient put it, "How can you be angry at or hate someone who saved your life?" Similarly, in other instances there is a need for a change in therapists because the therapist has become too real in meeting the patient's needs. In such instances a new therapeutic relationship is often needed to foster more traditional transference and countertransference reactions in order to work out unconscious conflicts and related character pathology.

## SUMMARY AND CONCLUSION

Drug/alcohol-dependent individuals need to discover and understand how they have adopted extraordinary drug solutions for a range of problems. I believe human relationships can best provide this opportunity through either a professional psychotherapeutic relationship or peer group experiences such as group therapy and self-help groups such as AA or NA. Addicts need to learn that drug solutions preclude more ordinary solutions to life problems, and that therapeutic and peer group experiences can provide the creative challenges, tools, and impetus to find alternative solutions.

Clinical work with severe and disabling human problems teaches us the humbling nature of our work as health care professionals. Clearly, work with substance abusers is no exception. As we gain in our scientific, technical, and clinical understanding of these problems, we are able to help our patients make enlightened choices about what is useful and effective in their treatment and recovery. However, there is much we do not understand about substance abuse, and there are many affected by the problem who cannot accept what we have to offer. Effective practice must still be guided by practical and empirical measures of what is safe and what works. Health care professionals do not have a corner on this market of what is safe and what works.

Practitioners need to honor their traditions where treatment is guided by careful collection of data and continual pursuit of root causes, mechanisms, and etiologies. But, above all, rigid attitudes about the advantages of our own approach and the limitations of other approaches need to be avoided. In this respect we honor "above all" the primary tradition in clinical practice—"to do no harm."

## REFERENCES

Caplan, G. (1974). *Support Systems and Community Mental Health.* New York: Behavioral Publications.

Khantzian, E. J. (1978). The ego, the self and opiate addiction: theoretical and treatment considerations. *International Review of Psychoanalysis* 5:189–198.

———— (1980a). An ego-self theory of substance dependence. In *Theories of Addiction*, ed. D. J. Lettieri, M. Sayers, and H. W. Wallenstein, pp. 29–33. NIDA monograph 30. Rockville, MD: National Institute on Drug Abuse.

———— (1980b). The alcoholic patient: an overview and perspective. *American Journal of Psychotherapy* 34:4–19.

———— (1981). Some treatment implications of the ego and self disturbances in alcoholism. In *Dynamic Approaches to the Understanding and Treatment of Alcoholism*, ed. M. H. Bean and N. E. Zinberg, pp. 163–188. New York: Free Press.

Khantzian, E. J., and Mack, J. E. (1983). Self-preservation and the care of the self-ego instincts reconsidered. *Psychoanalytic Study of the Child* 38:209–232. New Haven, CT: Yale University Press.

Khantzian, E. J., and Treece, C. (1985). *DSM-III* psychiatric diagnosis of narcotic addicts: recent findings. *Archives of General Psychiatry* 42:1067–1071.

Krystal, H., and Raskin, H. A. (1970). *Drug Dependence: Aspects of Ego Functions.* Detroit: Wayne State University Press.

Mack, J. E. (1981). Alcoholism, AA and the governance of the self. In *Dynamic Approaches to the Understanding and Treatment of Alcoholism*, ed. M. H. Bean and N. E. Zinberg, pp. 128–162. New York: Free Press.

Marlatt, G. A., and Donovan, D. M. (1982). Behavioral psychology approaches to alcoholism. In *Encyclopedic Handbook of Alcoholism*, ed. E. M. Pattison and E. Kaufman, pp. 560–577. New York: Gardner.

McAuliffe, W. E., and Gordon, R. A. (1980). Reinforcement and the combination of effects: summary of a theory of opiate addiction. In

*Theories of Addiction*, ed. D. J. Lettieri, M. Sayers, and H. W. Wallenstein, pp. 137–141. Rockville, MD: National Institute of Drug Abuse.

Rounsaville, B. J., Weissman, M. M., Crits-Cristoph, K., et al. (1982a). Diagnosis and symptoms of depression in opiate addicts: course and relationship to treatment outcome. *Archives of General Psychiatry* 39:151–156.

Rounsaville, B. J., Weissman, M. M., Kleber, H., et al. (1982b). Heterogeneity of psychiatric diagnosis in treated opiate addicts. *Archives of General Psychiatry* 39:161–166.

Woody, G. E., Luborsky, L., McLellan, A. T., et al. (1983). Psychotherapy for opiate addicts. *Archives of General Psychiatry* 40:639–645.

Woody, G. E., McLellan, A. T., Luborsky, L., et al. (1984). Severity of psychiatric symptoms as a predictor of benefits from psychotherapy: the Veterans Administration-Penn Study. *American Journal of Psychiatry* 141:1172–1177.

Wurmser, L. (1974). Psychoanalytic considerations of the etiology of compulsive drug use. *Journal of the American Psychoanalytic Association* 22:820–843.

———— (1984). More respect for the neurotic process: comments on the problem of narcissism in severe psychopathology, especially the addictions. *Journal of Substance Abuse Treatment* 1:37–45.

# 32

# A Contemporary Psychodynamic Approach to Drug Abuse Treatment

A modern psychodynamic perspective of the addictions suggests that addicts do not turn to drugs, as often stated, to seek pleasure or self-destruction. This is a pejorative view heavily influenced by an earlier psychoanalytic perspective of addiction that laid heavy emphasis on instincts and drives and a topographical model of the mind that attached unconscious meaning to the effects and practices associated with drug use. A more contemporary psychodynamic approach places greater emphasis on disturbances in psychological structures and capacities responsible for (1) regulating internal emotional life, and (2) the adjustment to external reality. The former perspective involves the inability to recognize, modulate, and tolerate feelings (affects), and to maintain internal states of well-being and safety; the latter involves deficits in the capacity to control impulses and activity and to exercise adequate judgment in assuring self-care and self-preservation (Khantzian 1980, Khantzian and Treece 1977).

This more recent psychodynamic understanding of addicts' impairments complements recent discoveries and findings documenting the existence of opiate receptors and transmitters in the brain, the co-occurrence of a range of psychiatric disorders, and the presence of psychopathology in the families of addicts. It is significant that among a number of functions that the endorphins serve, a main one appears to be that of regulating emotions (Martin 1980). Dysregulation of these neurotransmitters is probably related to addicts' difficulties with regulating their feelings and other subjective states. The psychiatric diagnostic findings documenting depression, personality disorder, and alcoholism in addicts also indicate a relationship between addicts' distress and behavior and their reliance on addictive drugs (Khantzian and Treece 1985, Rounsaville et al. 1982a,b). The study of the interactions and dynamics of addicts' families provides further evidence to support clinical observations that addicts have often suffered unfortunate exposure to troublesome and disturbed emotional patterns and behavior. These include extreme styles of expressing and processing affects, bizarre communications that undermine autonomy and self-esteem, and the overt and covert fostering of unusual behaviors that become linked to drug-dependent individuals' impulsivity and self-care problems (Khantzian 1979).

This chapter considers how a modern psychodynamic appreciation of addicts' vulnerabilities and disturbances relate to the treatment modalities we employ. I focus on individual psychotherapy, group treatment approaches (i.e., self-help and professionally led), and psychopharmacological modalities.

## SELF-REGULATION DISTURBANCES

Effective treatment of addicts must respond creatively and imaginatively to the two central disturbances that malignantly combine to make dependence on drugs compelling, namely defects in regulating affects and behavior.

The nature of addicts' difficulties in managing their feelings is complex. They experience their feelings in the extreme (i.e., they feel too much or too little), but just as often their feelings are vague, ill-defined, and confusing. In addition, when they do experience their feelings, they are poorly regulated, hardly tolerated, and more frequently expressed through action (Khantzian 1979). The reader is referred to previous chapters on self-regulation and self-medication factors (Chapters 2, 11, 14, and 15) where I have extensively reviewed the basis for addicted individuals' problems in regulating their feelings and behavior, especially self-care.

## TREATMENT MODALITIES

The treatment modalities that we employ for addicts must keep their affect and self-care disturbances as a central focus. Whether we choose confinement, individual psychotherapy, group treatment, or drug substitution, addicts' difficulties in regulating feelings and taking care of themselves make it especially important that needs for comfort, control, and safety be considered and/or integrated into the treatment or combination of treatments that we adopt or prescribe (Khantzian 1985).

A detailed exploration of the content and techniques involved in the various treatment modalities is beyond the scope of this chapter. Instead, I will highlight from a psychodynamic perspective and my experience as a clinician what I believe to be some important factors about patient needs and treatment dynamics that should be kept in mind when we consider our therapeutic interventions.

### Individual Psychotherapy

Individual psychotherapy should be considered for drug-dependent individuals. Evidence from three recent studies from the Pennsylvania VA group indicates that individual psychotherapy for addicts has advantages over drug counseling alone (McLellan et al. 1985, Woody et al. 1983, 1984). These findings plus reports by a number of psychoanalytic investigators (Khantzian 1985, McDougall 1984, Wurmser 1984) begin to suggest that the type and degree of psychopathology may be indicators about how our patients should be approached psychotherapeutically, and whether our efforts will be efficacious.

I discuss individual psychotherapy first, not because it is necessarily the most effective modality, but because an individual/one-on-one treatment relationship can be primary and central in encouraging an addicted patient to participate in the other treatments that are recommended, thus maximizing their benefit. I have been impressed with the utility of conceptualizing the role of the individual clinician as that of a primary care therapist (Khantzian 1985). Especially early in treatment, an individual therapist cannot and should not avoid involvement and decisions about treatment matters that address the requirements for comfort, control, and safety, namely the need for confinement, the need for drug substitution (i.e., for detoxification or stabilization/maintenance), the need for Alcoholics Anonymous (AA) or Narcotics Anonymous (NA) and other support groups, and the need for identification and modification of environmental stressors and aggravants, especially within the family. Beyond these initial concerns, the primary therapist also plays an important role in monitoring and modifying reactions and capacities to tolerate the treatments that have been adopted. In some instances this might involve helping a patient to overcome prejudices against and resistances to AA and NA. In other instances it might mean that the therapist needs to intercede because the patients' needs, personality characteristics, or psychopathology suggest that certain treatments are contraindicated.

Beyond the initial supportive, management, and monitoring roles a psychotherapist must play with addicted patients, the special disabilities and characteristics of addicts require other modifications and provisions in our therapeutic approach to them. Traditions of passivity, the blank screen, and uncovering techniques derived from psychoanalysis of the neurosis are ill-suited for responding to the treatment needs of most drug-dependent patients (Khantzian 1985). Instead, they need active approaches to appreciate how their difficulties with affect management and self-care deficits so seriously compromise their lives and predispose them to depend on substances.

Krystal (1982), probably better than anyone else, has cogently described how essential it is for addicts to understand their difficulties with recognizing and tolerating their feelings. His work once again helps us to appreciate the importance of being active, open, and supportive in helping patients to identify, label, and express their feelings with words versus action. He has also stated that these problems with recognizing their feelings are probably related to coexistent anhedonia and that we need to explore with our patients how disturbances in the realm of affects impact on and interact with the experiences of pain and pleasure. He has proposed a pretherapy phase of treatment to help patients see and understand that they are different in the way they experience their inner life, and an emphasis is placed on modes involving instruction, encouragement of restraint, and labeling. His work is consistent with my own observations of narcotics addicts whose intense and overwhelming experiences with rageful and violent emotions suggest they need much help in learning about the importance of tolerating and containing such affect, and that affects need not and should not be expressed through action and destructive impulses (Khantzian 1985, McDougall 1984).

It is much more alliance building to help addicted patients understand their problems with taking care of themselves than to suggest that they are trying to kill themselves. In my own work with addicts in psychotherapy, I place great emphasis on empathically identifying the self-defeating and self-destructive consequences of their self-care deficits and how this vulnerability has left them susceptible to addictive involvement. I try to clarify that they have not necessarily intended to be destructive, but rather that they have had lifelong difficulties in reacting appropriately to potential harm and danger, particularly involving substances (Khantzian 1985, McDougall 1984).

This failure in self-protective functions is linked to their difficulties and confusion around their feeling life. Detailed and repeated psychotherapeutic examination of feelings in response to life situations are necessary to help such patients see that their feelings can serve as guides to appropriate reactions and self-protective behavior rather than signals for impulsive action and the obliteration of feelings with drugs.

Beyond the heavy emphasis and focus in psychotherapy on affect and self-care impairments, several additional points should be made here on individual psychotherapy with addicts. First, except for their special difficulties, much of long-term, individual psychotherapy with addicts is not too different from long-term therapy in general in that characteristic conflicts, traits, and related distress unique to the individual become the principal foci. Second, the therapist needs to consider the special characteristic reactions and compensations that addicts display that are related to their vulnerabilities, namely those involving alexithymia, anhedonia, counterdependency, and counterphobia.

Finally, among the various brokering and monitoring roles that a therapist must play, some of the most important ones involve monitoring the patient's progress and responses in the individual psychotherapeutic relationship, and considering whether and/or when a shift to another modality or another therapist might be indicated. In some cases the disabilities in recognizing and modulating feelings and behavioral difficulties persist or worsen and suggest the need for another treatment or combination of treatments and a de-emphasis of the individual psychotherapy. In the previous chapter we also indicated that transfer to another therapist might be indicated because the many interventions around real-life issues, crises, and threats during treatment make transference and countertransference issues too difficult to work out, especially those issues involving ambivalence where the patient does not feel free to experience or express anger and disappointment because of the feeling that the therapist saved his or her life (Khantzian 1985).

## Group Approaches

Whether of the self-help variety or a psychotherapeutic one, group approaches for addictive disorders generally serve as antidotes to the sense of alienation that is pervasive among addicts, and they provide important related experiences of universality, sharing, mastery, overcoming shame, and acquiring practical, human tools for self-care.

### Self-Help Groups

The development of AA over the past 50 years, and more recently NA, represents an extraordinarily successful and natural experiment demonstrating that people can help themselves overcome major life problems by providing for each other a context of sharing experiences, self-disclosure, and support, in this case to abstain from drugs and alcohol. By keeping it simple and practical AA and NA have been masterful in providing step-by-step approaches and coping devices to achieve abstinence and avoid relapse. Their spirit and ethos challenge their participants to examine their mistaken assumptions that life's vicissitudes, stresses, and crises can justify or make acceptable reliance on drugs or alcohol (Khantzian 1985).

Self-help groups such as AA or NA go beyond providing support and sustenance. I have been impressed lately to hear my patients emphasize how there has been a shift in AA and NA meetings away from drunkalogs and drugalogs to a greater emphasis on members' understanding their feeling life and coping behaviors. In my own work I have not only been impressed that AA/NA helps individuals to cope with their feelings as a cause and consequence of their alcoholism, but I have been most impressed with how important the practical, step-by-step approaches are in repairing addicts' and alcoholics' self-care impairments. In chapter 31 we also noted how Mack (1981) has focused on the self-governance problems of alcoholics and how AA in the best psychodynamic tradition helps individuals modify those parts of themselves responsible for taking charge and controlling them.

*Group Psychotherapy*

Group psychotherapy shares elements of enabling confrontation, feeling understood, acceptance, and support in common with self-help groups. Appreciating the clinical nature of addicts' disturbances, a trained group therapist can effectively help members face their characteristic difficulties with managing feelings, self-esteem, relationships, and self-care, particularly keying on self-defeating, compensatory attitudes of self-sufficiency, disavowal of need, bravado, and counterdependency.

## Some Caveats

There is a tendency to overprescribe self-help and psychotherapeutic group approaches as an anodyne for severe psychopathology. This is especially so for addicts and alcoholics. Clearly, groups are powerful means for producing change. On this basis they can be beneficial, but they can also be disruptive and harmful. It is important to consider individual patient needs in groups, and in certain instances why groups might be contraindicated for some patients or impossible for others to consider. In general, problems with shame, severe social anxiety, paranoia, or depression can make group experiences very difficult. Given addicts' special problems with managing and regulating affects, most heavily confrontive, aggressive group approaches are probably contraindicated. Although AA and NA do not produce such problems, their participants and advocates often underestimate how the problems with shame and anxiety, often of phobic proportions, make AA and NA inappropriate treatments. For others a rigid personality structure makes the "surrender," "higher power," and "keep it simple" messages of AA and NA unacceptable. In traditional group therapy, group therapists need to keep in mind addicts' tendencies to react in the extremes with regard to their feelings, needs, and behavior, and thus there is a need for the leader to adopt and to foster in the group appropriate activating/supportive or containing/modulating roles.

## PSYCHOPHARMACOLOGICAL TREATMENT

This section briefly considers drug treatment approaches as they pertain to psychotherapeutic approaches.

Addicts and alcoholics suffer with treatable psychiatric disorders related to their disturbances in affect and behavior regulation. It should not surprise us, then, that they suffer with affective disorders, phobic anxious syndromes, psychosis, dysphoric states, and hyperactive/restless conditions (Khantzian 1979, 1981). Although in a majority of instances patients recover without drug therapy, there still remain many who are truly overwhelmed as a consequence of painful affect states and coexistent psychopathology. Treating these patients with psychotropic medications often makes possible other human, psychotherapeutic interventions, and their use should be considered accordingly, especially in extreme cases. In these cases our medication may become a means to other therapeutic ends, otherwise our patients' self-medication may become a tragic end in itself.

## CONCLUSION

Our growing psychodynamic, clinical, and scientific understanding of addicts suggests that there is growing rationale to apply our therapeutic modalities selectively and differentially based on patients' characteristics and degrees and types of psychopathology. Special attention to the way disturbances in affect recognition/tolerance and self-care disturbances combine to make drug dependence malignantly compelling has important implications for considering the treatment or combination of treatments we employ. We also need to consider when, why, and how the treatments we employ could be harmful and thus contraindicated. Addicts need more than anything else a variety of therapeutic contexts to discover that they can adopt more ordinary human solutions in place of their extraordinary chemical ones. A clinician's understanding of addicts' problems can be vitally important in assuring such an outcome.

## REFERENCES

Khantzian, E. J. (1979). Impulse problems in addiction: cause and effect relationships. In *Working with the Impulsive Person*, ed. H. Wishnie, pp. 97–112. New York: Plenum.

—— (1980). An ego-self theory of substance dependence. In *Theories of Addiction*, ed. D. J. Lettieri, M. Sayers, and H. W. Wallenstein, pp. 29–33. NIDA monograph 30. Rockville, MD: National Institute on Drug Abuse.

—— (1981). Some treatment implications of the ego and self disturbances in alcoholism. In *Dynamic Approaches to the Understanding and Treatment of Alcoholism*, ed. M. H. Bean and N. E. Zinberg, pp. 163–188. New York: Free Press.

—— (1985). Psychotherapeutic interventions with substance abusers—the clinical context. *Journal of Substance Abuse Treatment* 2:83–88.

Khantzian, E. J., and Treece, C. (1977). Psychodynamics of drug dependence: an overview. In *Psychodynamics of Drug Dependence*, ed. J. D. Blaine and D. A. Julius, pp. 11–25. NIDA research monograph 12. Rockville, MD: National Institute on Drug Abuse.

—— (1985). DSM-III psychiatric diagnosis of narcotic addicts: recent findings. *Archives of General Psychiatry* 42:1067–1071.

Krystal, H. (1982). Alexithymia and the effectiveness of psychoanalytic treatment. *International Journal of Psychoanalytic Psychotherapy* 9:353–388.

Mack, J. E. (1981). Alcoholism, AA and the governance of the self. In *Dynamic Approaches to the Understanding and Treatment of Alcoholism*, ed. M. H. Bean and N. E. Zinberg, pp. 128–162. New York: Free Press.

Martin, W. R. (1980). Emerging concepts concerning drug abuse. In *Theories of Addiction*, ed. D. J. Lettieri, M. Sayers, and H. W. Wallenstein, pp. 278–285. Research monograph 30. Rockville, MD: National Institute on Drug Abuse.

McDougall, J. (1984). The "disaffected" patient: reflection on affect pathology. *Psychoanalytic Quarterly* 53:386–409.

McLellan, A. T., Luborsky, L., and O'Brien, C. P. (1985). Sociopathy and psychotherapy outcome. *Archives of General Psychiatry* 42:1081–1086.

Rounsaville, B. J., Weissman, M. M., Crits-Cristoph, K., et al. (1982a). Diagnosis and symptoms of depression in opiate addicts: course and relationship to treatment outcome. *Archives of General Psychiatry* 39:151–156.

Rounsaville, B. J., Weissman, M. M., Kleber, H., et al. (1982b). Heterogeneity of psychiatric diagnosis in treated opiate addicts. *Archives of General Psychiatry* 39:161–166.

Woody, G. E., Luborsky, L., McLellan, A. T., et al. (1983). Psychotherapy for opiate addicts. *Archives of General Psychiatry* 40:639–645.

Woody, G. E., McLellan, A. T., Luborsky, L., et al. (1984). Severity of psychiatric symptoms as a predictor of benefits from psychotherapy: the Veterans Administration-Penn Study. *American Journal of Psychiatry* 141:1172–1177.

Wurmser, L. (1984). More respect for the neurotic process: comments on the problem of narcissism in severe psychopathology, especially the addictions. *Journal of Substance Abuse Treatment* 1:37–45.

# 33

# The Primary Care Therapist and Patient Needs in Substance Abuse Treatment[1]

Clinical experience and research evidence instructs us that alcoholics and addicts respond beneficially to an array of interventions (Emrick et al. 1977, Woody et al. 1986). Self-help groups have been preeminently successful in helping individuals to discover that they are not alone, that talking and listening to each other helps, and that focusing on the achievement and maintenance of abstinence is essential for most people to get better. Others discover that traditional clinical interventions such as individual and group psychotherapy and/or pharmacological interventions are central in treating coexistent psychiatric disorders and psychological suffering, thus making reliance on drugs unnecessary.

The main problem, however, is that individuals are often at the mercy of chance, what is available, or the particular leanings or prejudices of professionals and nonprofessionals in deciding the kind of help they will receive. The traditions of medicine, social work, and clinical practice in general are well suited for responding to the diagnostic and treatment needs of substance-dependent individuals. However, failure by many clinicians to consider the confounding and life-threatening nature of excessive drug and alcohol use has often caused clinicians' responses to be ineffectual. Beyond successfully countering legal and moralistic attitudes about alcoholism, the disease concept of substance dependence has helped recovering individuals and caregivers to appreciate that the essential first step in treatment is the necessity for control of drug and alcohol use, most usually and best achieved through abstinence. Nevertheless, because we cannot yet predict who responds to what kinds of interventions, and because all approaches produce treatment failures, there is a need for clinical approaches that will effectively serve, broker, and coordinate patients' needs, and it is cruel if not poor practice to insist on any one approach or conceptualization in deciding on a suitable intervention.

It is important that a clinician play the role of a primary care therapist (PCT) in meeting the needs of substance-dependent patients for safety, stabilization, control, and comfort (Khantzian 1985, 1986). The treatment needs of substance abusers are often complex. The medical and psychiatric complications associated with substance dependence often initially require simultaneous responses to needs for evaluation, confinement, detoxification, involvement with AA/NA, and pharmacological treatment. Subsequently, there is a need to observe and monitor the patients' responses to individual treatment relationships as well as their ability to utilize and tolerate group experiences, whether they be of the self-help or traditional group therapy variety (Khantzian 1985). A primary care therapist, if flexible and responsive, can ensure safety and stabilization at the outset, and then provide a multiplicity of treatment elements that meet intermediate and long-term clinical needs for support and understanding. The PCT also can appropriately respond to the vulnerabilities associated with the patients' drug/alcohol dependence.

This chapter considers the four C's of patient needs—control, containment, contact, and comfort—and how the PCT can function in directing, coordinating, and monitoring roles to maximize retention in treatment and to make sure that what is recommended or provided is effective, and if not, to intervene with alternative approaches. The considerations outlined here are guided by a psychodynamic understanding of substance-dependent individuals' problems and vulnerabilities around affect deficits, self-esteem maintenance, relationships, and self-care (Khantzian 1978, 1980).

## CONTROL

Substance abusers' need for control must necessarily include but also go beyond concerns about abstinence. Difficulties with affect tolerance and impairments in self-care have combined in addicts' lives to make reliance on drugs malignantly likely and compelling (Khantzian 1978). The term *loss of control* so often applied to the alcoholics' and addicts' use of substances might also be used as a metaphor for alcoholics'/addicts' feelings and behavior. The inability to recognize and regulate their feelings and problems with considering the consequences of their actions are intimately associated, both as cause and effect, with their substance abuse. Out of this association, addicts and alcoholics develop a conviction that they cannot get along without drugs or alcohol. We need to keep this reality in mind when we adopt treatment strategies to help substance abusers regain, and, for some, obtain for the first time, control over their substance use, feelings, and behavior.

Strategies for establishing control begin with the drug history. The PCT is in a good position to form an alliance with the patient and to constructively link him with treatment by empathically inquiring about when the patient first began to use substances; the context or associations involved; the pattern, progression, and amounts used; and the subjective effects that were sought and achieved. If asked, patients will also reflect on and describe the deleterious consequences of their involvement with drugs and alcohol. This process of interacting with a clinician/therapist is surprisingly useful and enlightening to both patient and clinician in thinking about and collaborating on decisions about the severity of the individual's substance dependence and what needs to be done about it (Khantzian 1981).

Not all substance abusers first seeking help are so out of control that they need confinement. Loss of control around substances, feelings, and behavior is on a continuum on which, at one extreme, the patients' physical and psychological deterioration, loss of family and social contacts, and/or active processes of resistance and denial make emergent, unilateral intervention by the PCT imperative. In less severe circumstances, the patient and PCT may work in a psychotherapeutic mode on the importance of controlling drug and alcohol use. For example, PCTs may stress abstinence as the most reliable means of control and create pressure to identify feelings and behaviors that govern substance abusers' drug/alcohol use, but operationally they may agree to allow the patients to establish with them that they can or cannot significantly curtail or control the substance abuse.

Self-help approaches are most effective in helping substance abusers retest and reverse their hypotheses that life is unbearable or unmanageable without substances. Although the success of AA/NA is said to hinge on primarily structuring and maintaining the central importance of abstinence, it succeeds because it is also extremely effective in using group psychology in addressing substance abusers' problems with managing and understanding their feelings and behavior through the alcohol and drug stories, aphorisms, and formal and informal confrontations of each others' psychological vulnerabilities (i.e., defects in character) (Khantzian 1985, 1986). Unfortunately, not all alcoholics and addicts will accept AA or NA. Here, too, the PCT can play a vital role in overcoming prejudice and resistances, and, if not, can substitute or offer a combination of other approaches, including individual and group psychotherapy, in grappling with the importance of controlling/abstaining from substances and examining and understanding how problems with regulating emotions, self-esteem, relationships, and self-care have caused patients to opt for drug-alcohol solutions.

The PCT is ideally suited to evaluate the usefulness of adjunctive pharmacological agents and diagnostic aids that can help establish and maintain control over the use and abuse of substances. As I have already indicated, substance abusers need much help to circumvent and compensate for vulnerabilities around affect intolerance and self-care. Methadone maintenance, for example, is effective not only because it corrects states of biological disequilibrium produced by chronic use of exogenous opiates, but also because it is a powerful psychotropic agent that counters a range of painful affects, especially those of aggression and violence, affects that have often predated the addiction (Khantzian 1982). Along somewhat different lines, pharmacological deterrents such as disulfiram and naltrexone and the use of urine monitoring/ surveillance are often extremely valuable in maintaining control by building in delay factors and thus compensating for deficits in self-care wherein addicts and alcoholics often do not delay and do not worry enough about their impulsivity (Khantzian 1986).

## CONTAINMENT

Substance abusers' penchant for action and drug/alcohol use is often an indication of major problems with controlling emotions, relationships, and behavior, and the relationship with the PCT may be an important first step in providing the containment necessary for other aspects of recovery. An important aspect of the PCT's role is to test out and build possibilities for psychotherapeutic relationships. Once control/abstinence is achieved and the person's life is reasonably stabilized, the PCT may begin to ease into a more traditional psychotherapeutic relationship. A number of recent reports have established the efficacy of individual psychotherapy based on an appreciation of the types and degrees of psychopathology present (Khantzian 1985, Woody et al. 1986). Psychodynamically oriented psychotherapeutic approaches have stressed the need for activity, support, empathy, and the employment of special techniques such as labeling, instruction, and explanation to help substance abusers appreciate their special problems with affect recognition and affect tolerance. As these basic disabilities around affects are explored and resolved in the safety of a relationship with the PCT, the patient benefits from an often new sense of feeling understood. This becomes a basis to work out how deficits and distortions around feelings have deleteriously influenced the patient's self-esteem and relationships with others. Even if the individual PCT's efforts are not entirely successful, the substance abuser may use the stabilizing and supportive aspects of this relationship to accept additional interventions such as traditional and self-help groups to help the patient contain and understand damaging and self-defeating behavior.

The ongoing nature of the PCT's role may also be invaluable in evaluating and making judgments about the necessity of psychotropic drugs, acceptability or nonacceptability of group treatments and emerging issues, and reactions that might suggest a need for confinement.

Substance abusers, as already indicated, need as much help with their self-care problems as they do with understanding their feelings (Khantzian 1986). There is a tendency to confront substance abusers with statements indicating that they are governed by self-destructive motives. This is not useful and usually counterproductive. The PCT is again in an advantageous position to explore and identify with substance abusers their developmental and situation-dependent disabilities that cause them to not worry about or anticipate danger, and that these are correctable disabilities. This is an approach that builds alliances and is better than the accusations of destructiveness that are often implied or explicitly stated as motives for drug/alcohol use. The empathic appreciation of affect and self-care disabilities, best provided initially in the relationship with the PCT, begins to have ramifications for accepting other treatment elements. It often serves as an especially helpful preparation for group experiences where members are better alerted to identify and contain these affect and self-care vulnerabilities in themselves and each other when they observe them in their group interactions and elsewhere.

## CONTACT AND COMFORT

When addicts and alcoholics adopt drug/alcohol solutions to self-medicate their painful affect states, they wittingly and unwittingly produce functional and psychological isolation. Recovery most often hinges on reversing this isolation by replacing drug solutions with human (relationship) solutions. Thus, restoration of comfort, without relying on drugs, becomes vitally linked to the establishment and maintenance of human contact. Individual and group psychotherapy, self-help groups such as AA and NA, and other types of support are effective because they creatively combine elements of support, clarification, confrontation, and understanding—factors that foster the contact necessary for trust and reliance on others. This contact and reliance over time provide substance abusers with new ways of coping with the feelings, relationships, and behavior problems previously associated with drug/alcohol dependence.

For many, the contact that self-help groups supply is accepted surprisingly well and begins almost immediately to help patients feel more comfortable and thus relatively free of the impulses and cravings that lead back to drugs and alcohol. Others find that their distrust, problems, counterdependence, and/or shame anxiety make reliance on and involvement in groups inconceivable. For yet others with a rigid personality organization, the "surrender," reliance on a "higher power," and "keep it simple" statements of AA and NA are rarely experienced as sources of comfort. Here, too, a PCT is well situated to act as a suitable alternative resource, who, over time, can work on such attitudes psychotherapeutically with patients and examine with them how their attitudes contribute to reliance on drugs.

The PCT provides a traditional treatment relationship in which disturbances around human contact and involvement can be played out, examined, and resolved. Subsequent to this more intensive process, some individuals can then work out residual problems with contact and comfort in self-help or traditional psychotherapeutic group experiences that the PCT can broker when the time is right. In my own experience of playing a PCT role, I have found that direct and continued involvement is especially important in working out and providing combined individual and group treatment, a blend that I have found to be especially beneficial. I have found that I can help patients initially overcome symptomatic and characterological problems that interfere with needed relationships and predispose to drugs, and then I place them in a dynamic group, also run by myself, with varying amounts of overlap between the individual and group treatment. Based on need and the degree to which they tolerate one or the other, I work out a flexible combination that provides the contexts to work on their discomfort with a range of feeling states and characterological traits that predispose to addictive suffering. Detailed description goes beyond this review, but the focus is on helping addicts and alcoholics face both the absence of and confusion around feelings as well as intolerance of feelings that are experienced as unbearable and overwhelming. Characterological traits including paranoia, counterdependence, counterphobia, and disavowal also become therapeutic targets of concern. Depending on the timing and patient, group, and therapist characteristics, some of the symptomatic and characterological problems are better dealt with in the individual therapy and others in the group therapy, and the PCT is well positioned to make judgments about patient needs and receptivity in both contexts.

Treatment relationships provide human contexts for individuals and therapists to appreciate how much emotional suffering has contributed to their substance dependence. Patients and therapists not only discover the possibilities for comfort that psychotherapeutic relationships provide, but also discover their limitations. At these times they can begin to consider alternative and ancillary ways to provide and obtain relief. A PCT observing these unfoldings can play an active role in encouraging, recommending, and integrating additional interventions such as pharmacotherapy, meditation, biofeedback, and hypnosis into the treatment that, combined with more traditional psychotherapy and self-help treatments, can significantly alleviate addictive suffering.

## CONCLUSION

Addicts and alcoholics suffer not only because they lose control of their substance use. They suffer as much because of long-standing problems with regulating their emotions, self-esteem, relationships, and behavior. The treatments that succeed do so because they respond appropriately to patient needs for control, containment, contact, and comfort. Unfortunately, the degree to which these needs are met is often the result of chance and of what is available. This chapter described how a clinician can function as a primary care therapist to ensure and maximize the possibilities that such needs are met and provided for. In many instances the PCT plays a secondary or brokering role; in other instances he/she becomes involved directly and actively as an individual and group therapist because patients cannot accept other approaches.

Treatment should be guided primarily by patients' needs, conditions, and treatment responses rather than by a particular concept or approach alone. A primary care therapist is invaluable for assessing patient needs, monitoring treatment response, and then combining and modifying treatment elements that will best ensure control, containment, contact, and comfort.

## REFERENCES

Emrick, C. D., Lassen, C. L., and Edwards, M. T. (1977). Nonprofessional peers as therapeutic agents. In *Effective Psychotherapy: A*

*Handbook of Research*, ed. A. S. Gurman and A. M. Razin, pp. 120–161. New York: Pergamon.

Khantzian, E. J. (1978). The ego, the self and opiate addiction: theoretical and treatment considerations. *International Review of Psychoanalysis* 5:189–198.

—— (1980). An ego-self theory of substance dependence. In *Theories of Addiction*, ed. D. J. Lettieri, M. Sayers, and H. W. Wallenstein, pp. 29–33. NIDA monograph 30. Rockville, MD: National Institute on Drug Abuse.

—— (1981). Some treatment implications of the ego and self disturbances in alcoholism. In *Dynamic Approaches to the Understanding and Treatment of Alcoholism*, ed. M. H. Bean and N. E. Zinberg, pp. 163–188. New York: Free Press.

—— (1982). Psychological (structural) vulnerabilities and the specific appeal of narcotics. *Annals of the New York Academy of Science* 398:24–32.

—— (1985). Therapeutic interventions with substance abusers—the clinical context. *Journal of Substance Abuse Treatment* 2:83–88.

—— (1986). A contemporary psychodynamic approach to drug abuse treatment. *American Journal of Drug and Alcohol Abuse* 12(3):213–222.

Woody, G. E., McLellan, A. T., Luborsky, L., et al. (1986). Psychotherapy for substance abuse. In *The Psychiatric Clinics of North America*, ed. S. M. Mirin, pp. 547–562. Philadelphia: W. B. Saunders.

# 34

# Modified Group Therapy for Substance Abusers: A Psychodynamic Approach to Relapse Prevention[1]

*with Kurt S. Halliday, Sarah J. Golden, and William E. McAuliffe*

It is easier to stop using substances than it is to not resume using them. Relapse prevention has legitimately gained much attention because it deals with this essential aspect of managing substance abuse disorders (Marlatt and Gordon 1980, Washton 1988, Zackon et al. 1985). Clinical reports and psychiatric studies from the past two decades indicate that substance abusers have psychological vulnerabilities and psychiatric disturbances that can lead to dependence on sub-

---

1. This chapter was presented at the National Institute on Drug Abuse Symposiums at the Annual Medical Scientific Conference of the American Medical Society on Alcoholism and Other Drug Dependencies (AMSAODD), Atlanta, April 30, 1989.

stances to relieve their states of distress and suffering (Khantzian 1985a, McLellan et al. 1979, Rounsaville et al. 1982a,b). These vulnerabilities and disturbances can also lead to both psychological difficulties and drug relapse.

In contrast to relapse prevention approaches that stress cognitive and behavioral factors, the modified psychodynamic model described here attempts to focus on the emotional aspects of relapse and on the psychological vulnerabilities in the personality organization of individuals that leave them susceptible to emotional reactive patterns that make relapse more likely. Moreover, we believe that the psychological factors involved in relapse are much the same as those that originally predisposed individuals to a reliance on substances. In these respects, we consider our approach a definitive treatment that goes beyond concerns about abstinence and relapse and addresses interpersonal and characterological insight and change. We believe that effective treatments must target and modify substance abusers' psychological vulnerabilities and disturbances to make reliance on or reversion to substances less likely. We have reviewed elsewhere how self-help, psychotherapeutic, and psychopharmacological treatments may be employed to modify the psychological vulnerabilities and emotional distress associated with a patient's substance abuse (Khantzian 1985b, Khantzian and Mack 1989).

More recently, we have been interested in applying group psychotherapeutic approaches to our clinical understanding of addictive vulnerabilities. As part of a National Institute on Drug Abuse (NIDA)-sponsored project comparing behavioral and psychodynamic models in group treatments of cocaine addicts, we have devised a manual for the group treatment of cocaine addicts titled *Addiction and the Vulnerable Self: Modified Dynamic Group Therapy (MDGT) for Substance Abusers* (Khantzian et al. 1990). This chapter is a preliminary report on MDGT for substance abusers. We define the essential elements of MDGT, the assumptions on which the approach is based, and the focus of the group treatment, namely, areas of vulnerability involving affects (i.e., feelings), self-esteem, relationships, and self-care, which make dependence on and reversion to drugs likely. We discuss the modified dynamic group therapy approach in a context of what the therapy has in common with other effective group approaches and what distinguishes it from these other approaches.

## THE HARVARD COCAINE RECOVERY PROJECT

The MDGT group treatment is a component of the Harvard Cocaine Recovery Project (HCRP). The HCRP is a NIDA-sponsored project designed to compare two group treatments. The main comparison group in this project, recovery training and self-help (RTSH), is a group method devised for heroin addicts by Zackon and colleagues (1985) and modified for cocaine addicts in this project. RTSH is a relapse-prevention model focusing on behavioral factors. A standard treatment group consisting of Cocaine Anonymous (CA), Alcoholics Anonymous (AA), and Narcotics Anonymous (NA) members was used as a control group. Although all patients in the project were encouraged to attend CA, AA, and NA, in the two experimental conditions (i.e., MDGT and RTSH), the participants attended two group treatment sessions per week for twenty-six weeks. All participants, including those in the control group, were assigned an individual counselor with whom they met weekly. After intake evaluation and counselor assignment, participants were randomly assigned to the experimental or control groups. Participants in the project were required to be abstinent for a minimum of two weeks but not more than one year.

## GROUP APPROACHES TO SUBSTANCE ABUSE

### General

Groups have powerful effects on their members' states of well-being, comfort levels, and feelings about themselves and other human beings. Depending on their construction and aims, groups may heighten individuals' self-esteem and the sense of belonging or they can have just the opposite effect, producing self-contempt and a sense of deviance. For example, substance abusers may be admired as recovering individuals if they belong to an NA group in which they feel cared about and care for others, or they may be seen and see themselves as hopeless "junkies" who are untrustworthy and care only about themselves. Although we all have tendencies for isolation, shame, and affect intolerance, substance abusers suffer more of these problems. Groups may be powerful vehicles for reversing these tendencies in addicts and alcoholics because they create conditions and opportunities to examine and correct them. Groups that effectively deal with addicts' difficulties, whether the groups are self-help, didactic, or dynamic, succeed because the individuals in these groups share and combine elements of support, understanding, information, and behavior change necessary to reverse the isolation, shame, and affect intolerance entailed in substance abuse.

## Self-Help Groups

At first glance, self-help groups appear to be effective simply because they succeed in using peer pressure to achieve and maintain abstinence. As Vaillant (1983) has suggested, AA succeeds in removing the "sufficient and necessary cause," the alcohol, from the person's life and thus arrests the disease. Our experience, however, suggests another reason for the success of self-help groups. They are extremely sophisticated psychological approaches that force the issue of involvement with others and thus counter the human tendency for self-centeredness, especially when members feel inadequate and powerless about their lives. We have recently summarized how self-help groups such as CA, AA, and NA examine and modify character defects related to attitudes about self and others that make interdependence, experiencing, and expressing feelings and self-care difficult (Khantzian and Mack 1989). AA challenges these defects by advocating surrender, acceptance of a higher power, and the denouncement of self-absorption. AA's emphasis on openness, support, and sharing of experiences allows the treatment to address problems in self-regulation involving self-governance, feelings, and self-care.

## Didactic Rehabilitation Groups

With the burgeoning of inpatient and outpatient facilities to address widespread use of drugs and alcohol in our society, group-oriented experiences have evolved to educate individuals about the biological and psychological aspects of the addictive process, especially early in recovery. Much of this psychoeducational approach is based on the disease concept of addictive disorders in which people are instructed about the progressive nature of the biological process of addiction, and how the physical and psychological dependence on drugs and the inability to control use are consequences of that process. Again, the emphasis in these approaches is on the importance of removing the offending substance and on the importance of abstinence. Most of these approaches have evolved from the AA tradition, but the emphasis in these didactic approaches is to impart information about the disease process with less emphasis on the personal experiences.

Nevertheless, these approaches work because the information and explanations are usually presented in a context of effective communication. Our observations indicate that the lecturers are wittingly or unwittingly chosen to do this work because they do it with feeling, if not passion, and often this strong feeling is based on personal experiences. Individuals learn and internalize the information offered because the lecturer effectively combines knowledge, personal experience, and feelings about the subject. Such an approach inspires individuals to reconsider attitudes and behaviors that have governed their addictive disorders.

### Relapse-Prevention Groups

The realization that educative approaches can significantly influence the course of addictive disorders has in part contributed to the development of a number of relapse-prevention approaches focusing on cognitive and behavioral factors that cause individuals to revert to drugs (Marlatt and Gordon 1980, Washton 1988, Zackon et al. 1985). Zackon and associates (1985) have applied a relapse-prevention model to a group method for substance abusers. These approaches all recognize that drug craving is often precipitated by external cues; that high-risk situations and experiences can be cataloged and avoided; and that alternative coping skills, attitudes, and behaviors can be acquired to avoid situations, relationships, and activities that result in relapse. Although relapse prevention emphasizes cognitive and behavioral factors, these groups are also successful because they reverse the sense of confusion and helplessness addicts and alcoholics experience in response to internal emotional and external environmental cues. These approaches empower individuals to believe in their ability to control their emotions and behavior.

### Psychodynamic Groups

Psychodynamic group psychotherapy rests on the assumption that the relatively unstructured nature of the group experience allows for a natural unfolding of individuals' characteristic way of relating to people and external reality and the subjective emotions and attitudes about self and others that their experiences evoke. In the case of substance abuse, psychodynamic group therapy is designed to evoke salient themes of psychological vulnerability and characteristic defensive styles (what AA calls character defects) that make dependence on drugs and relapse likely. The remainder of this chapter defines MDGT and describes the assumptions and focus of a modified dynamic group approach and how it targets and modifies the vulnerabilities and defenses involved in addictive disorders and relapse (Khantzian et al. 1990).

## DEFINITION OF MDGT: THEORY AND PRACTICE OF PSYCHOANALYTIC PSYCHOTHERAPY

Early psychoanalytic theory placed heavy emphasis on pleasurable and aggressive drives and the unconscious meaning of drugs and alcohol to explain the substances' compelling nature. Treatment based on these early concepts emphasized the relief of conflict by making the unconscious determinants conscious, thus releasing pent-up drives that were otherwise expressed or released through drug or alcohol use. More recent psychoanalytic approaches stress the centrality of affect (or feelings), problems with human contact and safety, and the psychological functions that regulate them. Psychoanalytic psychotherapy assumes that the treatment relationship activates the affects and drives operating beyond an individual's awareness and that the process of treatment creates opportunities to examine and modify these forces and regulating factors. A psychodynamic approach applied to group therapy for substance abusers provides a means to examine and change particular psychological vulnerabilities and character traits that emerge in the group interactions that are intimately involved in the predisposition for drug-alcohol dependency and relapse.

MDGT's conceptualization of dynamic psychotherapy differs in its basic assumptions from the earlier theoretical approaches to the understanding and treatment of substance abusers. In contrast to concepts of psychotherapy that emphasize instinctual strivings and conflicts, we place greater emphasis on developmental and structural deficits that have affected our patients' capacities for self-regulation.

Rather than encouraging the expression of painful affects and the exploration of unconscious material, we see modified dynamic psycho-therapy as an approach in which an active and friendly therapist, with the help of a supportive group, encourages and facilitates patients to look at the four primary dimensions of MDGT, namely, self-care, relationship conflicts, self-esteem, and affect regulation. These four dimensions are examined as they play themselves out in the group and in the patients' lives. Through this experience, group members discover alternative ways of seeing, experiencing, and exonerating themselves, thus allowing for greater flexibility and awareness of choice in their lives.

## ASSUMPTIONS OF MDGT

MDGT is based on the assumption that leaders are most effective if they adopt certain basic concepts about their roles, the substance abuser in a group, how modified psychodynamic groups differ from other group therapies, and the nature of addictive vulnerability and suffering.

### The Group Leader and Members

The group leader in MDGT facilitates interactions that foster sharing and comparing of experiences, empathy, and expanding awareness. In MDGT, group leaders are trained to actively provide structure, ensure safety and comfort, and specifically key on the patients' issues and reactions related to feelings, relationships, self-esteem, and self-care problems. Although clarification and interpretation are provided, equal emphasis is placed on empathy, involvement, and support.

A group creates a special interpersonal context of relationships and experiences among the members and leader that constitutes a forum for examining and modifying members' problems. In group therapy, therapists are not the only curative agent, and they constantly foster the realization that members, as well as therapists, are aware, insightful, supportive, understanding, and corrective.

Notwithstanding the emphasis on an egalitarian model, group leaders must also be aware of their special position in the group and of the fact that they will be targeted recurrently with certain powerful needs that are central to addicts' disabilities and dysfunction. Given substance abusers' special problems with self-regulation, they are more likely than those in other groups to turn to the leader for comfort, protection, clarification, admiration, and guidance. The leader's skillful management and response to these requirements will balance the legitimate need for assistance and support from the leader with the need for further exploration of these themes by the group members. This in turn will lead members to the discovery that they can also provide what is needed for themselves and each other. As is so often the case in psychotherapy, the timing of when to provide and when to explore is important, especially when the disabilities of addicts are considered. When a group temporarily becomes fragmented, overwhelmed, stuck, or inhibited, the leader may need to provide what the group and its members cannot provide for themselves.

## The Interpersonal Context

Although MDGT is designed specifically to examine, modify, and compensate for the vulnerabilities in ego and self structures in addicts, the group experience provides a powerful interpersonal context that influences these structures. The essentially important elements of interpersonal factors in groups for substance abusers have been well described in the contemporary literature on alcoholics by Brown and Yalom (1977, Yalom 1974, Yalom et al. 1978) and by Vannicelli (1982). Brown and Yalom (1977) stress basic assumptions for understanding self and others in interpersonal situations. They argue that groups are powerful vehicles for imparting information, instilling hope, providing human contact, and facilitating personality change and symptom reduction. Emphasis is on here-and-now issues. Vannicelli emphasizes the interpersonal pathology in the group interactions as a means for members to understand their maladaptive and self-defeating ways of relating to others. MDGT builds on the interpersonal context to provide a more specific focus on addicts' self-regulation vulnerabilities and the associated characterological patterns that predispose addicts to their general symptoms and to the specific symptoms involving the drugs they choose or prefer.

## The "Modified" and "Dynamic" in MDGT

To help addicts understand their vulnerabilities, MDGT requires modification of both interpersonal and classic psychoanalytic techniques of group psychotherapy. These modifications in turn influence both individual and group dynamics. In contrast to groups that focus primarily on interpersonal factors, MDGT emphasizes understanding one's structural or characterological disturbances and deficits as they emerge in the course of the group experiences (Khantzian 1978, 1980, Treece and Khantzian 1986). MDGT is also geared to actively address the feelings of isolation and the sense of aberration and shame that addicts share. This active mode and focus on commonalties are at variance with classic psychoanalytic group treatment. Furthermore, because the symptom of substance abuse is a life-threatening one, group requirements for safety become paramount. Thus, the modification of fostering a shared goal of control or abstinence (and safety) as a requirement for treatment imposes a greater degree of homogeneity than is usually encountered in psychoanalytic group psychotherapy.

Finally, although our MDGT approach aims to elucidate and modify individual psychodynamics, we employ a rather generic concept of "dynamic" in MDGT. This concept assumes that in addition to individual psychodynamics, the structure, norms, context, and aims of any group also generate their own dynamics that cannot be explained or understood by the summing of the individual psychodynamics alone.

## FOCUS OF MDGT

Similar to Luborsky and his collaborators (1981), we believe that we can be more effective in psychotherapy if we can narrow our focus to issues or themes that repeatedly seem central to substance abusers' reliance on drugs and their associated relationships and activities. The focus for Luborsky and associates in supportive-expressive treatment is on two main aspects of substance abusers' problems: (1) the meaning of drug dependence, especially factors that precipitate and maintain drug use; and (2) substance abusers' core relationship conflicts. Luborsky and colleagues (1981) state, "The way the therapist gains understanding of the intrapersonal and interpersonal context for the patient's symptoms is mainly by figuring out the core relationship themes . . . [that] contain within it the patient's relationship problem" (pp. 14–15). Luborsky's group point out that the relationship theme is apparent in many different relationships, and the core theme appears everywhere in the patient's communication about the past and the present, and in the treatment relationship (i.e., transference). In our experience, it is even more apparent how the core relationship theme plays itself out in group treatment with other members and the leader/therapist. This theme is often expressed more intensely with some members than others. The group leader often becomes a likely target of these relationship themes. This provides the group leader, the members, and eventually the individual patient a chance to see and understand how the theme plays itself out in the person's life, in the group, and especially in the symptomatic patterns of drug use and related involvements.

The focus on core relationship problems and patterns as embodied by the Luborsky group in supportive-expressive treatment is very applicable to MDGT. However, we specify and stress a focus on certain key vulnerabilities to guide the therapist, and ultimately the patients, in appreciating particular aspects of their life and behavior involved with their disabilities. As we will describe further, there is a need to focus on how particular involvement with drugs and their effects is related to subjective affect states, relationship and self-esteem problems, and self-care disturbances. MDGT provides a context to elaborate and identify vulnerabilities and compensatory mechanisms (i.e., psychological defenses) that perpetuate maladaptive responses, including those involving drugs. Leaders and group members are encouraged repeatedly to observe and describe in each other how difficulties in recognizing and regulating feelings, self-esteem, and relationship and self-care problems have been and are intimately related to their susceptibility to drug involvement, relapse, and drug effects. Constant attention is directed in MDGT to monitoring self and others about drug use, exposure, and related activities.

## Affect Recognition, Tolerance, and Regulation

The nature of affect disturbances that cause substance abusers to seek substances to alter their distress is complex. Group leaders and members need to appreciate these disturbances to avoid premature conclusions about or impatience with a patient's feelings and the related reliance on drug effects. A number of investigators have underscored the defects and deficits in substance abusers' experience of their feelings. Emphasis in these observations is on defects in the psychological apparatus that cause substance abusers to experience their emotions in the extreme—feeling too much or too little. In this sense drugs are used as a prosthesis or as a remedy against defects in affect tolerance involving distress, tension, rage, shame, and loneliness. There is also a corresponding tendency to respond with activity or passivity to the individual's environment (Milkman and Frosch 1973, Wieder and Kaplan 1969, Wurmser 1974). In other cases, the vagueness and confusion around feelings are such that patients are either unable to give words to them (alexithymia) or hardly seem to have feelings at all (disaffected) and defensively fight rather than feel (Krystal 1982, McDougall 1984). Furthermore, the drug of choice or self-selection phenomenon suggests that for many substance abusers certain kinds of feelings predominate. Thus, patients with feelings of rage and anger often find opiates to be most appealing (Khantzian 1980, 1985a), and individuals with energy problems associated with depression respond to stimulants, and restricted, anxious, closed-off, counterdependent people find the softening effects of alcohol and sedatives soothing and releasing (Khantzian 1975, 1985a).

An appreciation of some of these complexities can help substance abusers adopt a new repertoire of responses to their problems after they experience and process their feelings with each other. In some meetings, emphasis on empathy and on individual or group distress might be of paramount importance; there might be a need to use such an occasion to acknowledge how such states lead to avoidances, or drug craving and use. On other occasions group members and the leader might have to spend more time helping a person label and describe the feelings that a certain life event might stir. At these times groups help individuals to see that they sometimes even use the distressing, confusing, and disruptive effects of drugs as a controllable substitute for their feelings, which they otherwise experience as uncontrollable and even more confusing (Treece and Khantzian 1986). At other times, it is extremely useful and illuminating to point out to a patient how a specific affect state evoked in group treatment leads to a craving for a very specific effect offered by a particular drug.

## Self-Esteem, Need Satisfaction, and Relationships

Much of substance abusers' distress revolves around their inability to feel good about themselves and their relationships with others. These themes play themselves out powerfully in groups and in this respect make Luborsky and colleagues' (1981) conceptualization about core relationship problems very useful. Substance abusers display how they have failed to adequately internalize that part of development that allows one to sustain the comforting, admiring, and being admired experiences of childhood. These early relationship experiences provide a sense that one can feel good or validated from within, or that one can reach out easily, when necessary, for nurturance and validation. The resulting deficits and disabilities that are so often present in substance abusers produce extreme and uneven patterns in satisfying needs around dependency, self-worth, and comfort. As a consequence, "They alternate between seductive and manipulative attitudes to extract satisfaction from the environment, and disdainful, aloof postures of independence and self-sufficiency that dismiss the need for others . . . [and thus they are left] susceptible to adopting more extraordinary chemical dependencies to meet their needs and wants" (Khantzian 1982, p. 28).

As we have already indicated, many of the interpersonal aspects of groups provide curative responses for self-esteem and relationship problems in an ongoing way through the shared, universal aspects of group, the ongoing support and acceptance, and the instillation of caring, respectful modes of listening and interacting. Beyond these general elements, the group leader who is sensitized to these issues can be instrumental in pointing them out and fostering responses that allow more precise examination of the self-esteem and need-satisfaction issues that cause substance abusers to posture in extreme and characteristic ways. Key areas to focus on include self-defeating behaviors, compensating attitudes of self-sufficiency, disavowal of need, bravado, and counterdependency (Khantzian 1986).

## Self-Care

Addicts are often accused or accuse themselves of harboring and living out suicidal motives because of the life-threatening nature of drug dependency. Our own work has shown that the self-defeating and destructive aspects of drug abuse are a reflection of a more pervasive disability and impairment around self-care and self-preservation. Our view has been influenced by a developmental perspective in that we have been able to ascertain and identify with our patients how they have suffered with lifelong vulnerabilities around self-care. This has been evident in patient histories (predating and postdating their substance abuse) of accidents and preventable medical, dental, legal, and financial difficulties in which there has been a persistent inability to worry about, anticipate, or consider consequences of their action or inaction. With regard to involvement with drug-related environments and ultimately the drug use itself, it has been striking to see how little fear or worry substance abusers showed about the meaning or consequences of their use of drugs. These relapses in self-care are the symptomatic reflection of deficits in psychological structures and functions that normally protect us from danger. That is, whereas most people fear the many dangerous aspects of drug use, addicts fail to show such concern. When they are fearful, their fear fails to guide them and they are more apt to lapse or relapse under states of stress, disorganization, and regression (Khantzian 1978, 1982, Khantzian and Mack 1983).

Alliance building is much more likely with addicts if we help them learn about their vulnerabilities and deficits in self-care than if we suggest or point out that they are self-destructive. Group leaders and members can get to this vulnerability in self-care if they can cultivate an empathic understanding of the substance abusers' inability to exercise caution; mishaps and disasters occur as a result of this problem. Just as often, the patients can be encouraged to observe the characterological symptoms associated with this vulnerability such as counterphobia, hyperactivity, aggressive posturing, denial of danger, and bravado. In sum, we place great emphasis on actively and empathically identifying the self-defeating and self-destructive consequences of patients' self-care deficits and how their problem has left them susceptible to addictive involvement. We clarify that substance abusers have not necessarily intended to be destructive, but rather that their self-care susceptibilities have caused them lifelong difficulties in reacting appropriately to dangerous situations, in particular those involving drugs (Khantzian 1978).

## SUMMARY AND CONCLUSIONS

In response to the widespread use of drugs in our society and with all the disabilities that substance abuse disorders entail, a variety of treatment approaches, differing in conceptualizations and methods, have evolved. One of these, relapse prevention, has gained a high degree of popularity and acceptance because it deals with one of the most bedeviling aspects of substance abuse, namely, the tendency to resume using drugs after weeks, months, and even years of abstinence. Models for relapse prevention target cognitive and behavioral factors that precipitate reversion to drug use. These approaches, along with psychoeducative and self-help groups, acknowledge that individuals with substance abuse disorders benefit from acquiring information and modifying their behavior in relation to here-and-now internal and external cues that govern dependence on and relapse to substances. In these approaches information and behavior modification are considered central for the prevention of relapse.

Our MDGT approach to substance abusers works on the assumption that the emotional distress and suffering associated with certain psychological vulnerabilities are equally important and need to be modified if treatment and relapse prevention are to succeed. Although the best approaches operationally combine elements of support, information, behavior modification, and psychological understanding, MDGT is designed to focus primarily on substance abusers' psychological vulnerabilities as a means to avoid substance dependence and relapse.

In our work on the psychological vulnerabilities of addicts, we have emphasized affect recognition/regulation, self-esteem, relationship, and self-care problems. MDGT provides a context for these vulnerabilities and related compensatory characterological styles to emerge in the group interaction. The group leader and group members examine and modify the characteristic responses that reveal the repetitious, self-defeating personality characteristics and defensive styles that both betray and attempt to compensate for substance abusers' vulnerabilities. In this approach emphasis is on affects, sense of self, relations with others, and self-care.

## REFERENCES

Brown, S., and Yalom, I. D. (1977). Interactional group therapy with alcoholics. *Journal of Studies on Alcohol* 38:426–456.

Khantzian, E. J. (1975). Self selection and progression in drug dependence. *Psychiatry Digest* 10:19–22.

——— (1978). The ego, the self and opiate addiction: theoretical and treatment considerations. *International Review of Psychoanalysis* 5:189–198.

———— (1980). An ego-self theory of substance dependence. In *Theories of Addiction*, ed. D. J. Lettieri, M. Sayers, and H. W. Wallenstein, pp. 29–33. NIDA monograph 30. Rockville, MD: National Institute on Drug Abuse.

———— (1982). Psychological (structural) vulnerabilities and the specific appeal of narcotics. *Annals of the New York Academy of Science* 398:24–32.

———— (1985a). The self-medication hypothesis of addictive disorders: focus on heroin and cocaine dependence. *American Journal of Psychiatry* 142:1259–1264.

———— (1985b). Therapeutic interventions with substance abusers—the clinical context. *Journal of Substance Abuse Treatment* 2:83–88.

———— (1986). A contemporary psychodynamic approach to drug abuse treatment. *American Journal of Drug and Alcohol Abuse* 12:213–222.

Khantzian, E. J., Halliday, K. S., and McAuliffe, W. E. (1990). *Addiction and the Vulnerable Self: Modified Dynamic Group Therapy for Substance Abusers*. New York: Guilford.

Khantzian, E. J., and Mack, J. E. (1983). Self-preservation and the care of the self-ego instincts reconsidered. *Psychoanalytic Study of the Child* 38:209–232. New Haven, CT: Yale University Press.

———— (1989). AA and contemporary psychodynamic theory. In *Recent Development in Alcoholism*, vol. 7, ed. M. Galanter, pp. 67–89. New York: Plenum.

Krystal, H. (1982). Alexithymia and the effectiveness of psychoanalytic treatment. *International Journal of Psychoanalytic Psychotherapy* 9:353–388.

Luborsky, L., Woody, G. E., Holey, A., et al. (1981). *Treatment manual for supportive-expressive psychoanalytically oriented psychotherapy: special adaptation for treatment of drug dependence*, 4th ed. Unpublished.

Marlatt, G. A., and Gordon, J. R. (1980). Determinants of relapse: implications for the maintenance of behavior change. In *Behavioral Medicine: Changing Health Lifestyles*, ed. P. O. Davidson and S. M. Davidson, pp. 410–452. New York: Brunner/Mazel.

McDougall, J. (1984). The "disaffected" patient: reflection on affect pathology. *Psychoanalytic Quarterly* 53:386–409.

McLellan, A. T., Woody, G. E., and O'Brien, C. P. (1979). Development of psychiatric illness in drug abusers. *New England Journal of Medicine* 201:1310–1314.

Milkman, H., and Frosch, W. A. (1973). On the preferential abuse of heroin and amphetamine. *Journal of Nervous and Mental Diseases* 156:242–248.

Rounsaville, B. J., Weissman, M. M., Crits-Cristoph, K., et al. (1982a). Diagnosis and symptoms of depression in opiate addicts: course and relationship to treatment outcome. *Archives of General Psychiatry* 39:151–156.

Rounsaville, B. J., Weissman, M. M., Kleber, H., et al. (1982b). Heterogeneity of psychiatric diagnosis in treated opiate addicts. *Archives of General Psychiatry* 39:161–166.

Treece, C., and Khantzian, E. J. (1986). Psychodynamic factors in the development of drug dependence. *Psychiatric Clinics of North America* 9:399–412.

Vaillant, G. E. (1980). Natural history of male psychological health. VIII: antecedents of alcoholism and "orality." *American Journal of Psychiatry* 137:181–186.

—— (1983). *The Natural History of Alcoholism.* Cambridge, MA: Harvard University Press.

Vannicelli, M. (1982). Group psychotherapy with alcoholics. *Journal of Studies on Alcohol* 43:17–37.

Washton, A. M. (1988). Preventing relapse to cocaine. *Journal of Clinical Psychiatry* 49:34–38.

Wieder, H., and Kaplan, E. H. (1969). Drug use in adolescence: psychodynamic meaning and pharmacogenic effect. *Psychoanalytic Study of the Child* 24:399–431. New York: International Universities Press.

Wurmser, L. (1974). Psychoanalytic considerations of the etiology of compulsive drug use. *Journal of the American Psychoanalytic Association* 22:820–843.

Yalom, I. D. (1974). Group psychotherapy and alcoholism. *Annals of the New York Academy of Science* 233:85–103.

—— (1975). *The Theory and Practice of Group Psychotherapy,* 2nd ed. New York: Basic Books.

Yalom, I. D., Block, S., Bond, G., et al. (1978). Alcoholics in interactional group therapy. *Archives of General Psychiatry* 35:419–425.

Zackon, F., McAuliffe, E. W., and Ch'ien, J. M. N. (1985). *Addict Aftercare: Recovery Training and Self Help.* DHHS publication no. ADM-85-1341. Washington, DC: U.S. Government Printing Office.

# 35

# How AA Works and Why It Is Important for Clinicians to Understand

*with John E. Mack*

The success of self-help programs such as Alcoholics Anonymous (AA) and Narcotics Anonymous (NA) has tremendous implications for the medical profession in general and for psychiatric practice in particular. The physical and mental ravages caused by alcohol and drugs are inescapably evident to most practitioners; yet we are often ineffective in our clinical attempts to treat alcoholic and drug-addicted patients. Until recently, many of us considered alcoholism and addiction to be hopeless, debilitating, and progressive conditions. However, there is increasing evidence that AA helps patients succeed not only in arresting their uncontrolled drinking and drugging but also in transforming their lives physically, emotionally, and spiritually. For many, the transformation is dramatic. Individuals who at one time appeared totally unraveled and self-absorbed and preoccupied with obtaining and using alcohol and/or drugs, suddenly, with abstinence and recovery, appear more whole, and they begin to show concern for the care of others as much as for themselves.

Can the medical and psychiatric professions afford to ignore the utility of such transformations and "cures" in a condition that so adversely affects so many patients? Might medical and psychiatric practitioners also have something to learn about how other patients, with conditions in which self-care also suffers, benefit from self-help groups that use the model of AA and NA?

AA is based on a powerful group psychology that addresses and modifies core problems in self-regulation. Early psychodynamic theorists stressed destructive and pleasure motives for addictions. Modern theorists have focused more on certain developmental and structural deficits that adversely affect a patient's feelings and behaviors that predispose biologically susceptible individuals to become reliant on drugs and alcohol (Donovan 1986, Khantzian 1981, Krystal and Raskin 1970, Mack 1981, Wurmser 1974). This chapter examines how sectors of psychological vulnerability involving self-governance, affects, and self-care contribute to this predisposition. We highlight and describe some of the essential features and dynamics of AA that help to correct the psychological vulnerabilities of alcoholics and addicts.

Alcoholism and drug dependence are the result of complex interactions of biological, psychological, and cultural factors, yet the most promising and successful interventions in these disorders are psychosocial in nature. It is our contention that an understanding of the individual and group psychology involved in a patient's succumbing to and subsequently recovering from alcoholic and addictive disorders will help professionals to accept and recommend self-help modalities as an important or essential part of their patients' treatment. The more clinicians understand about the AA model, the more skillfully they will be able to intervene therapeutically with patients who are substance dependent as well as with other patients with related conditions who are in the process of recovery and self-repair.

## THE WORKINGS OF AA: A CLINICAL PERSPECTIVE

A thorough review of the literature on the efficacy of AA is beyond the scope of this chapter. In fact, the empirical evidence documenting the effectiveness of AA is scanty because of the program's voluntary nature and its tradition of anonymity. When studies have been done, they have failed to distinguish which members benefit (Emrick 1989). However, there is evidence that those who stay and embrace the program derive benefit from it (Emrick 1989). In this chapter we stress a clinical perspective and understanding of AA, and delineate how the structure and content of AA effectively target and modify particular vulnerabilities that have perpetuated alcoholic and substance abuse disorders in biologically susceptible individuals.

This section focuses on the workings of AA, based on our clinical view of patients who are struggling both in individual treatment and in AA to gain, or to regain, control of their psychological health, their drug/alcohol use, and their lives in general. Our observations also stem from opportunities we have had to observe a range of group approaches in inpatient and ambulatory settings. These approaches ranged from a strict AA/NA format to therapeutic and experiential groups that, to varying degrees, incorporate elements and aspects of the AA and NA model. Our understanding of AA is guided primarily by a perspective that is an "outside-in" view of the clinician as opposed to that of an "inside-out" view of AA by the recovering person. In the latter case, there are numerous compelling and well-known accounts in the literature of AA that provide helpful, inspiring reports of recovering alcoholics' and drug-addicted individuals' testimony to the program's benefits (Robertson 1988, Wholley 1984, Wilson 1957). These accounts help other recovering individuals and their loved ones and families understand more about the disorder and find hope.

Our aim in this chapter is to provide similar help to clinicians by describing essential elements of AA and by using case vignettes to illustrate the usefulness of AA as a resource and treatment modality. Although the vignettes have been obtained from patients in treatment, it is probably safe to argue that AA works for many even without the help of clinicians, especially early in recovery, because it is an intervention that avoids the many complications engendered by the transferential and countertransferential reactions that develop in therapy. For instance, powerful and common reactions of shame by the patient and antipathy by the therapist are avoided and diluted, or they are worked out indirectly through the storytelling, acceptance, and approbation that are so fundamental to AA.

Clinicians and theoreticians debate, often divisively and counterproductively, whether psychological disabilities are the cause or the consequence of alcoholism and drug dependence, and the relative importance of psychological and biological factors (Khantzian 1987, Schuckit 1985, Vaillant 1983). Operationally, AA and NA do not make these distinctions. The groups clearly recognize both aspects of the addictive process and provide opportunities for members to discuss and bear witness to one another's vulnerabilities whatever the origin. For example, it is not uncommon to hear alcoholics or drug-dependent individuals describe in meetings how inept, isolated, and unattractive they felt as adolescents and young adults. Some describe how they compensated by posturing to the contrary; others tell how they dealt with painful self-esteem problems. It is in the context of these remembered painful subjective states that people reveal the exhilarating and liberating effects of alcohol and drugs, which suddenly made them feel "normal" (a term often used by substance abusers when they discover their drug of choice) for the first time. This sense of feeling normal can mean anything from feeling calm, soothed, or subdued to suddenly feeling more integrated, socially engaging, powerful, effective, or attractive. These accounts provide compelling testimony to the human psychological suffering that is often at the heart of the psychological predisposition to these disorders.

The self-help programs also provide ample opportunity for members to describe the psychological debilitation and deterioration that resulted from chronic use of alcohol and drugs. The program effectively reminds its participants how cruelly progressive addictions are if individuals continually attempt to self-medicate their emotional suffering. The meetings help individuals to discover that they are not alone in their suffering, that the shame associated with their problems is not unique, and that they need the help of others to obtain and maintain their sobriety and to understand their own and others' "defects of character" (Alcoholics Anonymous 1977) that led them to the point where they could not control their addictions or their lives.

Self-help groups such as AA provide a special forum to examine the human tendencies toward arrogance, self-centeredness, psychological denial, and self-destructiveness. They offer powerful antidotes to these tendencies through a group psychology that insists on the members' admitting their inability to control substances and their vulnerability as an alcoholic and/or drug-addicted individual. Active alcoholics, for example, maintain they can control their drinking without the help of others, despite devastating evidence and repeated experiences to the contrary; "to the last drop" they will insist that they will not let the bottle beat them; rather, they will "beat the bottle." At meetings they are patiently and firmly instructed otherwise. The members' self-absorption and psychological deterioration associated with alcoholism and addiction are addressed; they are told that they suffer with a disease they are "powerless" to control and that they can get better by going to meetings, asking for help, and not using drugs or alcohol "today."

Alcoholics are advised to go to meetings to be reminded on a regular basis of "who and what they are." Sometimes they are told it is not enough to say "alcoholic" or "addict" but more provocatively to admit to being a "drunk" or "junkie." The simplicity and pejorative aspects of these directives are an essential first step toward recovery and the realization and acceptance of one's human vulnerability. It is especially useful for people who have postured with attitudes of entitlement, complacency, or pseudo–self-sufficiency as a means of coping with the helplessness, loss, and despair often underlying their disorder. They are encouraged or directed to participate, in a new and beneficially humbling way, in a group involvement that forces them to examine the issues of helping self and others. The importance of meetings is constantly stressed and is reflected in the aphorism "More meetings, more sobriety; fewer meetings, less sobriety; no meetings, no sobriety." Yet if people "slip," they are neither scolded nor banished but are exhorted to use their slips as reminders of their susceptibility, that they are "always recovering/never recovered" and that they can learn from their mistakes. The timid and constrained learn by listening. Some overcome and eventually master their timidity; but even as they do, following the AA credo of openness and honesty, they speak with shaky voices of their timidity and shame, thus helping others to dare speak up to tell their story. Others who never dreamed of public disclosure become eloquent, inspirational lecturers who pull in and convert others who are reticent or skeptical. It is striking to witness many of these people, who were previously restless, disdainful, action oriented, or inattentive to human emotion, as they sit riveted to the speaker, watching, studying, and listening to one another's stories as they attempt to describe and redefine themselves.

Although personal experiences of immensely painful proportions that involve humiliation, loss, and death are repeatedly reviewed, the reparative value of commitment to a group and the use of humor, surrender, and prayer are also always apparent at AA/NA meetings. The members constantly speak of near-death experiences, personal losses, and the death of many drug abusers and alcoholics they have known. Despite, or because of, these tragedies, they instruct themselves and one another that the losses are not in vain but that they serve as grim reminders of human self-destructiveness; at the same time, they serve as guides for commencing and sustaining self-repair and recovery. A story told at an AA meeting humorously captures and counters the tendency among alcoholics and drug abusers to resign themselves passively to the progressive and destructive forces involved in alcoholism and addiction. The story was told at a point in a meeting when one of the speakers had made reference to the many alcoholics he had known who had died because of their disease. The speaker was an "old timer" in the program, who spoke reticently but reflectively as he told the story:

> A traveling salesman is in search of a special gift for his very wealthy mother who had all the possessions one could desire. He is persuaded to pay $5,000 for an exotic, expensive tropical bird who speaks four languages. He ships the bird to her. Arriving at his next destination, he excitedly calls her to inquire if she liked the gift. He said, "Mother, did you receive the bird?" She replies, "Oh, you mean the one we ate for supper last night?" In dismay the son responds, "But Mother, that was a very expensive, exotic, and intelligent bird who spoke four languages. How could you?" To which Mother replied, "If it was such an intelligent bird, why didn't it speak up?"

## THE INJURED SELF AND SELF-GOVERNANCE

The story of each of our lives repeats the story of the fall from paradise. Once, the inner narrative that expresses the memory of our intrauterine and early infantile experience tells us, all our needs were blissfully met and we were bathed in love and pleasure. But this joy did not and could not last, and although we sought gratification through new relationships and other sources outside the family to perpetuate or restore this state, our lives were beset with a host of disappointments, such as competitors for our parents' affections, discrepancies between our wishes and our inability to fulfill them, failures, separations, losses, and even abuse and attacks by others. Each of us has a story to tell, in our own way, a tale of universal woundedness. Indeed, one of the most brilliant devices in AA is the use of the shared narrative or story, dubbed the "drunkalogue."

The psychobiological residue or indicators of our hurts or wounds are the painful affects we must endure, which may, if we can endure them and use the pain constructively, direct us to new possibilities, solutions, and satisfactions. But if the pain is too great and our psychological and material resources disproportionately meager, we will turn to maladaptive or pathological forms of affect management or regulation. These include the compartmentalizations of the self or the driven activity we observe in the neuroses; the unrealistic distortions of consensus reality in the psychoses; the excessive dependence or pseudo-independence patterns of the personality disorders; and, especially germane for this discussion, the heavy reliance on chemical substances to relieve pain, provide pleasure, regulate emotions, and create personality cohesion—a process we have called "self-governance" (Khantzian and Mack 1989, Mack 1981).

The relationship between personal historical wounds and affective experience is not simple or linear. In the course of childhood, adolescence, and young adult life, we experimented consciously and unconsciously with a variety of behavioral and emotional responses to the challenges and disappointments that confronted us and to the universal or existential threats that are an inescapable part of the human condition. Some of these adaptations seemed to work better than others in getting our needs met or managing our affects. So we became, more or less, specialists in the use of anger, overactivity, joviality, manipulation, intellectuality, sentimentality, seduction, generosity, helplessness, and self-sufficiency, in a complex mix or layering that gave us our style and provided the tone or character for our adult personalities. We all, to a degree, rely on "outside" (we use quotation marks because "outside" so immediately becomes "inside" and the distinction is often difficult) stimuli or substances to reduce pain, give satisfaction, regulate affects, or complete the sense of self. We might, therefore, think of the substance-addicted population as being composed of individuals who cannot achieve a style of affect regulation or self-governance that relies enough on internal resources or strength, or upon human relationships that are sufficiently mutually enhancing or integrating, to avoid excessive substance dependence. We use so many qualifying words because such great numbers of people, who only get into limited amounts of difficulty, rely heavily on alcohol, sweet foods, prescribed tranquilizers, sleeping pills, cigarettes, marijuana, coffee, and other substances for the regulation of their affective lives and general well-being that distinctions between addicted or drug abusing and normal or healthy individuals are not easy to make. We cannot, therefore, emphasize strongly enough that, when we focus on the difficulties in affect regulation of a pathologically addicted population, such as alcoholics, we are talking about degrees of wound. We are speaking of special intensities of troubling feelings, such as fear and emptiness (or the inability to tolerate intense affects of any kind, even positive ones—"Easy does it," says AA), and relative oversensitivity or vulnerability to emotional pain.

Alcoholic beverages are so ubiquitous in this culture, and drinking is so heavily sanctioned and promoted through advertising that appeals to vanity and self-esteem, that we wonder sometimes how most of us avoid becoming addicted. Martin, in the following case vignette, observed about alcohol drinking, "It just seemed like what everybody else did." Nevertheless, studies show that only 5 to 10 percent of the adolescent and adult population in the United States rely heavily on alcohol for feeling management or well-being and are adversely affected in physiological, psychological, vocational, and social functioning (Kamerow et al. 1988). AA is particularly effective with alcoholics in this category (for whom alcohol is an essential, if not the essential, mode of self-governance), once they make a commitment to becoming and staying sober. The vignette illustrates the way AA works to bring about and support sobriety and to enhance personal growth.

### Case Vignette

Martin was in his late 30s, and his life was profoundly changed by his experience with AA. He was a highly intelligent and gifted internist, writer, and performing artist. He was seen by one of us [J.E.M.] to assess the progress of his recovery after he was arrested and his medical license suspended for issuing Demerol prescriptions in patients' names and taking the drugs himself. After seeing Martin twice, Dr. Mack wrote the following note to Dr. Khantzian, who was the referring physician from the Committee on the Disabled Physician:

> I have seen Martin now in two interviews. On the basis of the interviews and other conversations, I am firmly convinced that he has done

a remarkable job of personal rehabilitation. He has, as far as I am able to ascertain, been drug and alcohol free for a period approaching fifteen months. He has been able to achieve this largely through attending Alcoholics Anonymous, which has provided him not only with support, but with valuable personality structures that have helped him to take charge of his problem.

Dr. Mack met with Martin seven times as part of a project aimed at adding to our understanding of his alcohol and drug dependency and the role of AA in his recovery. Martin comes across as a gentle, thoughtful, intelligent, and charming person. He has now been sober and drug free for eleven years. Martin has continued to distinguish himself professionally and to mature. He has become an extraordinarily kind, altruistic person who has helped many others as a leader in the alcoholic community and beyond.

Martin had used alcohol heavily for about fifteen years and Demerol for three years when his license to practice medicine was finally suspended. He had lost his marriage, his work, and most of his friends and had diminished contact with his two sons when he began his recovery process. He is the eldest of three children, the only son of middle-class Jewish parents, and felt he was raised "like an only child." When he was 4 or 5, his mother was hospitalized for some weeks with an illness, the nature of which he did not know or could not recall. He is virtually amnesic for what happened from that time until age 12. At 12, he began a pattern of minor delinquency, stealing small things, charging calls illegally on other people's phones, and lying. According to Martin his parents would say, "We're really disappointed in you," but they were largely permissive, indulgent, and inconsistent in their discipline. "I was a charming kid with a lot of ability and I could always work around these things," he said.

Martin thrived in high school. His many talents enabled him to excel in sports, music, theater, and cards. He was popular with other teenagers and active in a fraternity. But he started to become aware in adolescence that he was beset with sexual fears, which he tried to cover up with bravado (he later thought of himself as "this rugged hard drinking person") and promiscuous behavior. He suffered from impotence and premature ejaculation, and his early relationships ended in failure. Looking back, he observed that it was when he was an adolescent that he first realized, "There's a big hole inside of me and I can't fill it up." Martin had always felt a kind of emotional stunting, a distancing from others and situations, an inability to feel. He did not remember being able to cry, except at the happy endings of movies. "But in my real life situation, it was like I was seeing through some kind of a filter. And the emotional impact of what I was encountering never hit home. It still doesn't a lot. It makes me an incredible doctor in certain instances. I am so cool in horrible situations because something in me doesn't see them as being as horrible as someone else might."

Martin always felt that his self-worth was affirmed almost entirely from the outside, and he constantly looked for approval from others, feeling desperate that he might lose it. "I used to cheat in college to get from a 90 to a 94, that kind of thing. It was like being on an unending treadmill because there's no rules. The only rules are that it's like a bottomless well and you just keep sucking in the fuel that keeps you going, which is people telling you that you're OK. It's like the death sentence for a lot of people."

During the summer, between college and medical school, Martin got a job driving a beer truck, which allowed him to drink heavily. He continued to drink upon his return to medical school and reported loving alcohol. He particularly loved tequila during those years. Alcohol helped Martin to feel "more content" and "it made it easier to live with myself." Drinking sharply reduced his feelings of "self-loathing" and gave him an "instant" sense of self-worth. Alcohol was also useful to Martin in quickly muting, blunting, or handling all strong feelings, including good ones, as, for example, his excitement when he sold his first book.

After drinking beer, tequila, and other spirits for four or five months, Martin realized that he had lost control. He could not drink at all without getting drunk, which, in fact, had become the intention. He was particularly dependent on using alcohol before examinations and for dealing with his social fears.

> I watched an actress in a play one night and I thought she was wonderful. She was just a marvelous actress and I went out of my way to find her. I called her and invited her to come over and spend a day at my house down on the Cape. And about an hour before she came I decided I couldn't face her. I don't know why, but I just couldn't. I didn't feel right. So I drank some wine, about three glasses of wine, and by the time she came over I couldn't carry on a conversation and I was

just drinking more wine and drinking more wine and finally I got sick about an hour and a half or two hours after she arrived and she left.

Most of Martin's insights about the years of his dependence on alcohol and drugs were retrospective. For a long time, he denied that there was anything the matter with him or that he cared one way or another about his life. There was a "big element" of "just not giving a good shit." In sum, he said, the alcohol took care of the "only needs I ever had." It also relieved him of the need to even recognize that he had emotional needs, especially for relationships, although a Minnesota Multiphasic Personality Inventory test he had taken three years before his license was suspended indicated strong dependency needs and depression. Interestingly, in this regard, Martin did not distinguish his opiate habit from his alcoholism. The psychological predisposition, he said, was the same, at least for him, but alcohol was generally more available. The fear that alcohol is also more socially acceptable fit Martin's need to maintain his place in society. Opiates, on the other hand, were faster-acting substances, and Martin apparently became more willing to participate in a socially less acceptable or deviant, more isolating, activity.

Martin managed because of, or in spite of, his alcoholism and drug dependency to complete medical school and residency and developed a highly successful free-care clinic in the Midwest. He even did research for the Public Health Service after residency. He was married after medical school and had two sons, who were 10 and 13 at the time of Martin's arrest. But he became increasingly unable to function with or without alcohol, suffered from blackouts on drunken binges, lost his marriage, and for about two years before his arrest he began to supplement his drinking with Demerol injections.

A year before his license was suspended, Martin was caught illegally prescribing drugs for himself. He voluntarily entered a psychiatric hospital for four weeks, was diagnosed as depressed, saw a psychiatrist afterward several times a week, and returned to work. But in a few months he resumed his drinking and drug habits until his arrest. About six weeks after that, he took a room in a motel with the intention, and enough drugs, to kill himself. He did not do it that night but "knew" he would the next. During the next day, he saw in the back seat of his car a notice from a professional association for a meeting of "International Doctors in AA." He went to the meeting where three "most verbal, most interesting" physicians told their stories. "I was cry-ing after the first five minutes of the first person. And then by the middle of the second one I started to feel strange, like I'm going to make it. I could see there was an answer for me here."

This was the turning point and the end of Martin's drinking and drug use. He began attending AA meetings seven or eight times a week, tapering to four when he was especially busy. His own sharing in the group was an especially valuable experience for Martin. "To get up and tell a lot of the same things I have just told you, a lot of things that I would never have told my best friend that were my deepest, darkest, most horrible secrets and tell them in front of a huge group of strangers and to walk away from that encounter and count fingers, count toes, and like I am 'Okay, I said these horrible things.' "

Martin emphasized the transformative power of being able to share truthfully in front of many other people. He said he had lied even to therapists but not to the AA group, and after that experience, he said, "I don't lie anyplace. I say whatever comes to my mind in front of groups of 200 people. It is just getting the words out in front of another person . . . to suddenly discover that all of these things I have been frightened about are okay and to reaffirm that by saying it to a lot of people." "Do they reaffirm it back to you?" he was asked. "Yes, by just looking at you, and the point is to do it not once, but for me to do it over and over and over."

In reviewing his vulnerability or predisposition to alcoholic addiction, Martin placed the greatest emphasis on "the lack of spiritual sense" and his tendency to externalize the management or regulation of his affective life, looking to the affirmation of others, and especially to alcohol and opiates, to enable him to tolerate his inner self-experience and the demands and stresses of his life. He attributed these deficiencies to what he called "a spiritual bankruptcy," which he defined as the failure to identify or own his inner values, purpose, direction, and responsibility. AA addressed specifically the vulnerable personality elements that Martin and others have identified as being at the root of their alcoholism or drug addiction. Martin credited AA with the largest part in his recovery, but he also had important support from clinicians, including a psychiatrist, who were knowledgeable and experienced in the addiction field.

Martin emphasized the significance of AA's specific attention to the regulation or management of affects. "At the very core of what everybody in AA recognizes is that something is really screwed up in the way they've dealt with feelings." The first job is to identify feelings, even the fact that we have them. "They do encourage you to try to get in touch with your feelings all the time. In the beginning it's not a question of what feeling it is, but rather that you're feeling. For a long, long time it's, 'Oh, my God, what is this? Am I hungry? Am I angry? Am I tired? Am I lonely? Whatever, I just know that I'm feeling something.' And that's really what it amounts to for a long time, and then gradually you're encouraged to try to sort those feelings out."

Of particular value, Martin said, was AA's focus on avoiding intense affect/feelings. "I know what's getting me better; what's getting me better is directed at those little banners that are up at every AA meeting and that are on the bumpers on all the AA cars and everything: 'Easy does it,' 'First things first,' 'Keep it simple,' 'One day at a time,' 'Live and let live'—those kinds of things that sound so absurdly simple to somebody who's got them. It's like a revelation to somebody who hasn't."

Small stresses of life become tests of progress in managing feelings. "You test it out on these very, very concrete things in life: When you get a busy signal. Somebody dents your fender. The grocery bag breaks on the bottom and all your groceries fall out and, you know, the minute the bag breaks, that's it. You can either get upset about it or you can pick up your groceries."

Successful management of emotions means giving up the immediate highs that the drugs provided in favor of the deeper but delayed satisfactions that come with sobriety.

> In AA, they're worried that any excessive emotion in either direction is something that, for whatever reason, I'm not ready to handle. Or maybe none of us is ever ready to handle it, because certainly AA teaches emotional moderation. I see my life in AA as being one of these things far below the euphoric highs that I used to get, but with my work I'm gradually pushing that whole thing higher and higher, and that sooner or later I'm going to constantly surpass my greatest joys. And I can feel it happening. I can feel my whole level of being get higher every day.

The group sharing and the rituals that are an important part of AA meetings are an important source of structure and support. Martin calls it a support "system" or "a reprogramming process." He feels that the group's acceptance and affirmation have been essential to the internalization of positive self-esteem. The AA group provides a feeling of self-worth "by just looking at you," Martin said. As I (J.E.M.) got to know him better and became clearer about what he was telling me, I would offer my own observations regarding what seemed effective about AA, especially about its structure. In our fifth session I said, "Let's not fuss about whether it's genetic, development, biological, emotional, parent–child—the hell with that. It exists. A person is helpless in the face of alcohol, etc. Let's devise a strategy that will provide what people cannot provide for themselves, but giving them as much responsibility as they're able to take along the way, ideally reaching the point where their most effective way to meet their needs is by giving to others."

Martin responded, "What you just said is the absolute essence of AA. It's my understanding of it, and I think my understanding is a good one. That's exactly what it does. They have all these catch phrases in AA for that. They say, 'Utilize, don't analyze.' And then somebody else will say, 'Wait, it's a simple program for complicated people.'"

AA defines alcoholism as a spiritual, physical, and mental disease. Mental health clinicians are generally more knowledgeable and comfortable with the physical and mental dimensions, regarding the spiritual aspect as perhaps too vague and unreal, or belonging to the province of others, especially to the clergy. But AA's contribution to the spiritual understanding and treatment of alcoholism may be its greatest and most unique achievement and deserves more of our attention as clinicians.

Spirituality is, of course, difficult to define. It usually refers to a deep sense that there exists in the universe a deeper structure of being, a purpose or possibility, or even a divine design. This divine design may be experienced as mysterious, or not readily manifest, but it can be approached or experienced through surrendering one's egoistic sense of separateness and self-focused strivings. For some people, especially those who have remained active in established religions, the divinity of creation is embodied in God or a godlike presence. For a particular individual, participation in the divine design means discovering one's purpose or destiny.

Martin, whose religious background was that of a nonpracticing Jew, emphasized the relationship of his sobriety and personal growth to his spiritual development. He was not reluctant to speak of God.

Basically AA for me has been a reprogramming process to learn, first of all, that it is okay to be imperfect. That it is okay to screw up. That it is okay to believe in God. ["I use the word *God* because it's easy," he said later.] That it is okay to believe that you were born with intelligence for a purpose, and that the purpose wasn't to be miserable, that it wasn't to be unhappy, and that you don't even have to know the purpose beyond that. You just have to go about your daily business and try and handle situations as they come up with an understanding that you weren't put here to be miserable. And I don't have this great idea of a cosmic God or anything. I have a feeling now and understanding that there is a power in me to become the best possible Martin that I'm capable of being.

I asked him to say more about what God was for him. He replied, "I was so superficial in my whole life that I never really gave it much thought. God or no God. I never had one." The idea of believing that a "power greater than yourself can restore you to sanity and keep you from taking drugs or drinking—well that's a problem for somebody that doesn't have any belief in a power greater than himself." He continued,

What I have been able to work with—and it has been expanding a little bit now—is that the power is a power inside me to be a better person, to be greater than I am right now, the power instinctively to know what the right thing is to do with a given situation or with my life, that I have to tap into that power and find it and it is that power that will tell me that it's wrong, that I don't have to take drugs, or that I don't have to drink. It's a power that will say, "Look at what you have done to your life."

Martin noticed the changes in himself on a day-by-day basis.

I don't look up to the sky or anything. It's more of the "Stay cool please, God. Help me stay cool. Help me do what I have to do today. Help me not want to drink, or take a drug. Help me not to hurt anybody. Help me to not lie." And then at night when I realize another day has gone by and I haven't done any of the things that I asked not to do today, I do the same thing. I get down on my knees and I thank God.

I can feel myself changing in terms of a bigger concept of God. It's starting to flow into me. I don't know where it is coming from, but I sense it now. I sense I am starting to connect with just natural things. I am starting to feel more comfortable. I am starting to sense an or-

der to my life that I have never felt before. A purpose that has something to do with just being.

Toward the end of my last meeting with him, Martin said, "There
is this feeling-sense that I have that there is a destiny built inside of
me to be Martin, whatever that is, and that I am never really going
to find out, but that the whole thing of life is that process, each day
trying to learn a little more about yourself, each day trying to become
a better person."

For Martin and for many people in AA, the unfolding of a sense of
purpose leads to a shift from the experience of the universe as a place
of coldness, emptiness, and rejection to a viewing it as a more positive, even embracing, surrounding. Ultimately, this may lead to deep
self-acceptance.

> Sometimes I play mental games and put myself in situations. I put
> myself in mental situations of blindness. How would I do, what would
> I feel? Would I be all right if I became blind? The answer is yes. Would
> I be all right if I was told today that I was going to die next week? I
> swear I would be. I just have the sense that I will be okay. I would
> understand that I couldn't do anything about it. And I don't know what
> that is except that I really have started to get an identity that I never
> had before. I don't have to put on as many airs. I don't have to lie to
> people, I don't have to do anything like I used to try to create a per-
> son. This is where the God sense comes, that it's not a negative world,
> it is not a negative universe, and we are not negative people. Basi-
> cally, I mean people get hurt, people die, but there has to be some
> kind of method to it all. It has to do with acceptance.

## AFFECT DEFICITS AND AA

The character defenses of self-centeredness and invincibility often
mask substance abusers' sense of low self-esteem and impairments in
their feelings. Recent elaborations on these affective vulnerabilities
have placed early developmental deficits at the root of the difficulties.
Powerful feelings naturally arise in the areas of self-esteem and relationships. It should not be surprising that affective dysfunctions would
then interact with the feeling-altering, and ultimately compelling, effects of drugs and alcohol. In our opinion, AA succeeds in penetrating
the characterological defenses among alcoholics and drug abusers, as
Martin's case illustrates. It also benefits individuals who have been

restricted in their feeling life by helping them to access, experience, and express their emotions.

## Developmental Line for Affects

Psychodynamic descriptions of alcoholics as oral or impulsive characters are based on early drive theory and have led to the common clinical view that substance abusers are pleasure-seeking and/or self-destructive individuals. This pejorative perspective has prevented practitioners from understanding better the drug abusers' and alcoholics' internal suffering. Clinicians are beginning to appreciate better the adaptive functions that substances serve in personality organization and to see why drugs and alcohol seem to be so necessary for certain individuals. Studies of other special populations, such as victims of massive trauma and psychosomatic or character-disordered patients, have also revealed that developmental vicissitudes such as unresponsive or insensitive parents or psychic trauma can significantly alter or distort the ways individuals experience and express their feelings and adapt to life's challenges.

## Manifestations of Affect Deficits

As we stated earlier, the emphasis on drives and instincts in the psychiatric literature has been misleading in understanding substance-dependent individuals; nevertheless, drives serve an important function in mental life. They are the wellspring of human vitality and the fuel for our emotions. Drives and instincts have their origins in biological processes and are important sources of psychic energy and motivation (Schur 1966). They also help to organize psychic life and functions. However, as we suggested in a previous report (Khantzian and Mack 1989), and as Tomkins (1962) indicated, drives tend to be rigid and unmodifiable, whereas affects, which, in a metapsychologic sense, may be considered drive derivatives, are more flexible. Affects are the principal motivators of human relationships and behavior (Khantzian and Mack 1989, Mack 1981).

Our clinical experience, and that of others (Gotteil et al. 1973, Ludwig 1961, Matthew et al. 1979, Pattison et al. 1977), suggests that craving alcohol and the impulse to drink are as much governed by psychological distress as they are by biological or addictive factors. Alcoholics and substance abusers lack the flexibility of affects to which Tomkins refers. This inflexibility, which can derive from developmental (or traumatic) deficits, may explain some of the peculiar qualities and manifestations of affects and suffering that patients experience and why they may depend on substances to artificially alter or manipulate their feelings.

Observations from clinical work with special populations and infant and child development studies suggest a developmental line for affects and conclude that traumatic neglect, abuse, or victimization can cause significant deficits and dysfunction in affective experience. Clinical work with substance-dependent patients and with psychosomatic, traumatized, and character-disordered individuals has yielded useful information on how aberrations in feeling life may influence drug- or alcohol-seeking behavior. We have reviewed previously in this volume the psychodynamics of these aberrations. Evidence of affect dysfunction may be seen in patterns of denial, emotional flooding, paralysis or numbing, or impulsive action.

In the case of substance abusers, specific affect states such as rage, dread, or depression, or a more diffuse unpleasant dysphoria (as a consequence of alexithymia or disaffection), may lead to the compulsion to use opiates, sedatives, or stimulants (Khantzian 1985, 1990, Wurmser 1974).

### Case Vignette

Tom, a 32-year-old real-estate salesman, had a history of heavy drug and alcohol use. He demonstrated a number of extreme characteristics, including diffuse musculoskeletal distress, denial of feelings in the face of intense emotional exchanges (observed in group therapy), morbid preoccupations about cancer, periodic storms of rage or anxiety, and stretches of near-paralyzing depression. Despite his enormous private, chronic suffering, on the surface he appeared to be a young, polished professional who projected an aloof, disdainful attitude that alternated with a cynical and biting humorous banter.

In an interview about one year into treatment, and shortly after a brief impasse in his therapy, Tom reflected out loud on some of the recent distress he had been experiencing. He displayed how the treatment relationship could activate his distress; he also demonstrated how therapy provided an opportunity to examine and work out his underlying vulnerabilities and the characterological defenses and traits that mask them and, at the same time, how such characteristics had perpetuated his suffering. As we demonstrate in a subsequent example, this same patient was benefiting significantly from AA in identifying and understanding his self-centeredness and isolation and how it contributed to his distress.

Tom began the interview by saying he felt as if he had been through a "physical illness." He said, "I feel tired from the inside out, like when I had mononucleosis years ago . . . exhaustion!" He spoke of sleeplessness from the night before and how he had taken a benzodiazepine. Otherwise, he said, he would have felt out of control and might have cried profusely as he had several nights before. He expressed concern that he would "never have a good day again." Although he complained of still feeling anxious and depressed, he said he felt more in control. Previously, his distress "had taken on a life of its own." He added that he experienced periods of distress and feeling overwhelmed much less frequently, whereas several years ago he would regularly (and deliberately) get drunk at these times. I [E.J.K.] reminded him that this recent period of distress had developed in the context of frustration with his individual and group therapy. I recalled a metaphor he had recently used of how a "just-right" breeze can cause a threatening sway in a bridge. Spontaneously, Tom began to review the ongoing sense of inconstancy he had felt growing up in relation to his mother, who was "catatonic with anxiety," and his father, who was unstable, violent, and unavailable because of his alcoholism. What Tom learned from this, as he put it, was to become "tough and uncaring." He compared himself to nine other young men with whom he grew up in the same "transient environment," and all of whom had gone to reform school.

After comparing his situation to that of another man in group therapy who came from a similar "tough" environment, but where the man's father was present, Tom concluded with the following reflection: "That's the background I have come from—a world full of tragedy . . . one that didn't work. Now I'm seeing a psychiatrist." [The therapist said, "Maybe it worked better than you think; at least you're not seeing a parole officer."] Tom continued,

> I went to college with that background. It's when the anxiety began to occur and I had poor relations with girls. My drive got me through graduate business school but my nerves were shot. That's too bad [a

rare moment of empathy for himself]. As to where you [the therapist] fit in with my dependency, possibly you were stepping in as a parent, someone who could provide emotional support and respond to life's glitches. Then your glitches became untenable flaws. As for turning to my parents, it was a totally futile exercise. *I have a very hard time being dependent on people, it can be extremely hard. It's entirely against my mind set* [italics added].

He shifted to talking about a somatic concern as the end of the session neared. Then he described how he could employ his toughness to handle "notoriously tough underworld hoodlums" and to make them act deferentially toward and be dependent on him. He reflected on the need to change his image of himself, adding, "Now I feel I don't have any answers." But then he said, "What do you make of this feeling I have these days in the pit of my stomach?"

## AA, Feelings, and Storytelling

AA is a special interpersonal experience that takes advantage of those aspects of group process that foster human contact, self-examination, and self-expression. Storytelling is its main vehicle. By telling and listening to stories about one another's deterioration and recovery, lonely and despairing people discover and appreciate that they are not alone or unique in their suffering and that there is hope. Although the stories are about serious, if not life-threatening, matters, they are most often conveyed with healthy measures of humor, forbearance, and wisdom. In our opinion, one of the main benefits of AA is that it helps and, more often, inspires people who have been out of touch with or inattentive to their feelings to attend to and take charge of them.

The support, contact, concern, and understanding that the stories evoke are also powerful corrective experiences that address the affect deficits of drug-dependent people. A prominent journalist told her story: "You switch from pills and booze to people and feelings. It's like going to church or to see a psychiatrist; you do it because it makes you feel better. The thing that always strikes you is there's a lot of laughter. It's like being with combat veterans—the common bond is suffering" (Robertson 1989). It is not uncommon to hear participants speak of how their families "didn't do feelings" when they were growing up and about how AA was the place where they were introduced to feelings. AA members learn to appreciate how much, throughout their lives, they have resorted to "action" or using substances instead of feeling the feelings. The aphorisms, truisms, and even the admonitions that are repeated in the stories (e.g., "Don't pick up" [don't use substances]; "Go to meetings"; "Ask for help") also help people to compensate for another aspect of their affect deficits, the inability to comfort or soothe themselves (Krystal 1989).

Taking action and using substances are often conscious attempts in the lives of drug-addicted people and alcoholics to avoid feelings and/or distress. At other times, the avoidant, addictive behavior is automatic, beyond awareness. In the former instance, the desire to self-medicate seems to be the main motivation for resorting to substances (Khantzian 1985). In those instances, however, where alcoholics or drug-addicted people are less aware of their feelings, or they experience none, the motive to "use" or "act" seems more to involve the need to control or alter feeling states that are inaccessible or cannot be put into words (Khantzian 1989).

The AA method subtly, and almost uncannily, works to address and repair the affect deficits from which substance abusers suffer and helps them to develop more mature and flexible management of affects. In recovery, alcoholics often speak of discovering "what life's about," and especially of how important feelings are. As one recovering person concluded, "Alcoholism is a disease of disordered emotions." For some substance abusers, hearing the stories helps them experience and identify feelings for the first time; others grow in their capacity to express emotion; yet others learn to better endure or bear psychological pain.

AA works because it provides ongoing support. The self-help group model conceived by AA also succeeds because it creates a human context of listening and attending to the others' stories and provides a place to help people to understand and feelingfully express their own history.

## Case Vignette

Tom, the previously mentioned real-estate broker, who suffered so much in his feeling life, described how his self-absorption often keeps him out of touch with his own feelings and those of others and how AA and the stories he now hears at meetings counter his tendency for self-centeredness, providing alternatives for dealing with his anxieties.

Tom began one session expressing how "crummy" he had felt over the past several weeks and how the worse it became, the less inclined he was to attend AA. He said he finally forced himself to attend a meeting, realizing he would otherwise eventually drop out. He then spoke enthusiastically of a very special AA discussion group in which "I had an incredible experience around the issue of self-centeredness, a sense of looking at myself totally differently as if I were outside myself, very contented as if my focus was outside-in as opposed to inside-out." Tom referred to hearing a number of members explain how much their recovery had hinged on understanding and helping other members in their recovery program. He speculated on the possible implications the program might have for anxiety management and how he needed "to look forward, not backward." Later, he talked about the religious aspects of AA and mentioned that he had been reading William James, who saw religious experiences as a way of getting outside of the self. Then he emphatically stated that one has to get out of his or her own body and get a focus on others and see that "the welfare of others and their well-being was of greater concern than one's own." He said he used that insight to focus on how he might better comfort his wife and baby son instead of "rolling over" or worrying that his smoking would cause lung cancer. Tom was relieved to discover that he could be more concerned for his family and speculated that religion is important because it gets people outside themselves. He said, "You can only get so anxious [about oneself] if you are concerned about others." Referring to how he felt after that special AA meeting, Tom said, "I actually had a day where I felt content." He compared this to his former feelings while on drugs: "It's not the same as on a drug—it's contented versus sedated."

## Discussion

The case of Tom illustrates how attempts at self-medication ultimately fail and how being with others at AA can better help individuals sustain and tolerate their feelings. As noted earlier, storytelling is an important, if not central, part of the group process of AA. The stories highlight and help to modify substance-dependent individuals' tendency to avoid distress through substance use. The repetition of stories serves to reinforce the participants' need to accept their identities as alcoholics or addicts. This method assists them to acknowledge their vulnerabilities and to face their inability to control the substance abuse. Ultimately, the stories lead people to realize that the "way they are" (whether it is the physiological compulsion or the character defects that govern their addiction) makes it extremely difficult to control their feelings or their behavior through their previous adaptive strategies involving substances. In the following section, we review how feeling problems (or affect deficits) and self-care problems can malignantly interact with substances and their effects to set the stage for substance dependence.

## SELF-CARE AND AA

Individuals who abuse drugs and alcohol are often considered to harbor, consciously or unconsciously, self-destructive motives, given the obvious physical and social dangers associated with drugs and alcohol abuse. Such individuals themselves often reinforce this conclusion or impression when they actively deny or claim not to care about these dangers. Much of the more obvious destructive and suicidal behavior may be the consequence of chronic involvement with substances. There is little in our experience to suggest that self-destruction is a primary motive or intent when one becomes dependent on substances. Rather, addictions may stem from a developmental deficit in self-protective or survival functions, which we have referred to as a capacity for self-care. We originally described the problems in self-care among opiate-addicted individuals, for whom the problem was more severe or pervasive than for nonintravenous drug abusers (Khantzian 1978). Subsequent work with alcoholics, cocaine-addicted individuals, and other patients with impulse disorders suggests that, although less apparent than with opiate-addicted individuals, vulnerability or impairment in self-care functions is present more often than not, to some degree, in all people with addictive behaviors (Khantzian and Mack 1983, 1989).

In addition to acting as a corrective for self-governance problems and affect deficits as described earlier, we believe AA works to address and repair self-care vulnerabilities, which are a major source of difficulty for drug abusers and alcoholics.

## Manifestations of Self-Care Deficits

We first described and developed our ideas about self-care impairments based on clinical work with opiate abusers. In taking careful drug histories on over 200 patients, we were impressed by how deficient or oblivious these narcotic-dependent patients seemed to so many of the dangers involved in all aspects of their drug use. The risks these patients faced included menacing relationships, dangerous environments, and life-threatening practices such as sharing needles. We have subsequently been impressed by the etiological role that self-care deficits also seem to play with cocaine abusers and alcoholics (Khantzian 1981, Khantzian and Khantzian 1984). In the case of the latter two groups, however, it has been our impression and experience that their capacity for self-care is not nearly as impaired or deficient as it is in the case of opiate abusers. Alcoholics' and cocaine users' self-care functions seem to be better established or developed, but this population is still vulnerable to lapses and regression in self-care or to functioning marginally or ineffectively (Khantzian 1990). Often, in these cases, in the context of emotional distress or deflation, painful affects have interacted with failures or lapses in self-care, causing these individuals not to consider or worry enough or anticipate the harm involved with the regular and heavy use of drugs.

Although self-care deficits and dysfunction are most apparent among people who are in the process of becoming addicted, or who are relapsing once abstinent, they are also evident in preaddiction and postsobriety histories. Some examples include their failure to seek treatment for preventable medical and dental problems, their tendency for physical mishaps and accidents, their chronic financial instability, and the generally chaotic management of their lives (Khantzian 1978, Khantzian and Mack 1983).

## Case Vignette

Nancy is a 34-year-old vascular surgeon, four years into recovery from dependence on opiates and benzodiazepines. She is a good example of someone who, despite abstinence from drugs and significant time in recovery, still has structural deficits and uses the defenses of expansiveness, invincibility, and counterphobia to mask an underlying sense of being lost and an inability to use that distress to guide her toward better self-care.

During one of her treatment sessions, Nancy commented on how she felt literally "pinched" with the schedule of activities she was maintaining. She also reported a recurrence of migraine headaches. She complained about how unaware she could be of her feelings and needs and remarked that a friend told her that her migraines were her "ego." I [E.J.K.] reminded her that she had recently described feeling "high" when she solves problems with a person whom she sponsors in AA or when she deals with a medical crisis. She said she understood now what her friend meant about the ego and that it's related to the high she gets. For example, she would choose to eat chocolate, although it causes her headaches; she confessed, "I really believe I can get away with it. I do have a problem with acceptance, as they say we addicts do." She was reflecting on the day ahead and thought that if her borderline headache, which she was experiencing, blossomed into a full-blown one, she would go home and go to bed. Otherwise, consistent with her inability to admit to vulnerability and to use ordinary distress as a guide, she said, "I won't take on or attend to the tension to make it better for me before it does get worse. I need to be one of the guys." She added, "It's like when I used to try to please my father and I always felt that I was too frail." And then she thought, "And now as a doctor I *can* be [one of the guys]." Nancy was determined to make her practice successful, no matter what it took; yet she also expressed that she would like ideally to make her own well-being a top priority and hope and trust that her surgical practice would work out. I commented that it was as if she needed the wham of a headache to remind her of the fact that she was an ordinary human being. She quickly rebutted jokingly by saying, "Call me anything, but don't call me ordinary." (See Kurtz's observation in Chapter 25 on accepting "essential limitation" as a necessary condition for sobriety.) Near the end of the hour, Nancy referred again to feeling "pinched" in her schedule and joked about how she thought it was probably ironic that she thought of relieving the "pinch" by adjusting her backbelt, the supportive belt she used for chronic back pain, instead of adjusting her schedule.

## Discussion

Nancy refers to "we addicts" as having a problem with "acceptance." Although the statement is simple enough, it is another example of how deceptively sophisticated the AA approach is in identifying personality characteristics common to substance abusers that predispose them to their difficulties. Nancy's case unveils the typical counterphobic and hyperactive modes that compensate for and mask self-care vulnerabilities. Her case also helps us to appreciate how useful the program is for so many similarly addicted individuals in regulating and containing the characterological flaws and in compensating for the self-care deficits that often lead to self-neglect and hazardous behaviors.

## AA, Storytelling, and Self-Care

Earlier, we wrote of how intensely riveted AA participants are to the stories told in the meetings. This phenomenon is especially impressive given the addicts' previous tendencies to be counterdependent, restless, and inattentive to their own and others' emotions and behaviors. Patients in therapy repeatedly convey the compelling influence that AA exerts in forcing them to examine the many forms of self-disregard and carelessness that have contributed to their self-care deficits. It is probably the power of AA's group psychology and the evocative stories that draw people in, inspire, and positively affect self-care. At one level, this occurs by participants simply admitting to and telling stories about how inadequately they took care of themselves as addicts and alcoholics and how lost they were. At other times, through the use of reflection or self-deprecating humor, banter, and aphorisms (e.g., "No one is too dumb to get the program, but some might be too smart," or, "KISS—keep it simple stupid"), the storytelling might serve to address the character flaws or defects that disguise personal vulnerability.

Tom, whom we discussed earlier, revealed his growing awareness of both sides of the problem—his vulnerability and the self-deception— as the following example reveals.

## Case Vignette

During one session, Tom spoke of his "discomfort and rebellion around dependence" and how the fellowship of AA served as a constructive antidote to his self-defeating counterdependence. The story he told indicates that he was learning to view other people's perceptions of substance abuse, and life's problems in general, in helpful ways in order to better regulate and take care of himself.

I [E.J.K.] reminded him that his frustration with dependency had been a recurrent relationship theme in and out of therapy. He recalled how his heaviest periods of drug and alcohol use had occurred when he had been most isolated and had renounced people's dependency on him and his on other people. He stressed how he was disdainful of people's support and encouragement and more apt to take in negative feedback, but admitted that therapy and AA were helping and that he felt he was "coming out of some kind of dense fog" that he was at a loss to explain.

As Tom continued, it became clear that he knew better than he thought he knew about how people can help each other to regulate their behaviors. AA and his therapy were important, if not essential, human connections, he realized. Tom's case helps us to appreciate how new forms of relationships help us to gain perspective on our limits and capabilities and how even having good feelings, or an excess of feelings, can sometimes fail to guide us as well.

Tom described in another session how he had come close to drinking the previous weekend. The near relapse had occurred in the context of having had a good day on a Friday that then led to "feeling grandiose, or, as they say in the [AA] program, not right-sized." This was Tom's pattern, and at those times, he would turn up his radio very loud and begin to feel "expansive" and unable to control the "good feelings." It was at that point that he most wanted to drink, but he knew that if he did he "would go all night." He told of an AA friend who referred to a "blowfish" state, in which the friend felt intensively uncomfortable, that the feeling was not a result of drinking but was "very inconsistent with reality." The friend noted that "five or six beers would be insufficient to manage the uncomfortable feeling." Tom linked this comment to his own father who, he said, had a "blowfish sense of reality." He then said he had felt "right-sized" on the following day, when he had attended a wedding with his wife. Using the lessons of the AA program, he decided not to drink even though he felt he could control his drinking. He referred to being in the "second stage of sobriety," namely, coming to believe that he was an alcoholic and knowing he would get into trouble if he drank at all. He expressed a sense of humility at this realization.

Tom was able to articulate in a personal way some of the universal insights about and modifications in self that can be derived from AA. People in and out of the program refer to alcoholism as a "deadly and progressive disease" that can only be arrested, not cured. For this reason, alcoholics and addicts are said to be always recovering and never recovered. We believe that this hyperbole is wise and necessary and serves to constantly help protect against the common susceptibility in alcoholics and addicts to lapse in self-care and to reveal and address positively the personal vulnerabilities that defend against that susceptibility.

## CONCLUSION

AA effectively uses general group psychological principles, as well as newer ideas in group dynamics unique to the self-help movement, to help alcoholics and drug-addicted individuals break through their isolation and denial and to contain and modify the vulnerabilities and resistances that precipitate and perpetuate addictive illness. (See Chapters 24 and 25 for a more detailed review of how group psychology in general, and AA in particular, modify the psychological vulnerabilities and behaviors of alcoholics and addicts.)

AA stresses the importance of human interdependence. It replaces a chemical solution for disordered impulses, distress, and suffering with a human one. The journalist mentioned earlier described some of the helpful elements of AA (Robertson 1989) and justified the value and guiding influences of the aphorisms of AA by saying, "They are true!" She referred to the acronym HALT (hungry, angry, lonely, and tired) as an example. HALT is often used in AA to warn alcoholics and addicts of psychological states and feelings that can lead to reverting to drugs and alcohol. Robertson simply but eloquently indicated why alcoholics and addicts need such guides for their emotions and behaviors: "Alcoholics can't think straight; they need [these truisms or guides]; they are not obvious to alcoholics—you learn to protect yourself in those meetings."

AA works because it employs group psychology (1) to compensate for and/or to modify alcoholics' vulnerabilities and (2) to penetrate and dislodge the characterological defenses that they use to counter or overcome their vulnerabilities. The program demonstrates that the barriers of self-centeredness and related defensiveness can be surmounted when the need to belong or believe is met or satisfied. In the context of the newly discovered acceptance, comfort, and understanding that AA provides, drug/alcohol-dependent people can begin and continue to identify, examine, modify, and repair the distress and behavioral difficulties that have resulted from their self-governance, affect, and self-care deficits.

Finally, the model of treatment that AA represents has important implications for psychiatry and the mental health field in general. The self-help groups model represents a paradigmatic shift from the traditional, mechanistic view of a person as a discrete and separate entity, bound by his or her integument, and governed by defenses, feelings, and impulses to a relational view that perceives the individual, paradoxically, as both unique and simultaneously connected in a system or flow of relationships. We are already seeing evidence of theoretical and clinical shifts in the field of psychiatry:

1. A greater emphasis on the individual as a self system (rather than a solitary ego) embedded in a network of relationships and cultural influences.
2. More attention to the therapeutic impact of values and to value differences or commonalties between and among clients and therapists.
3. A focus on the spiritual life of the individual, defined as the longing for or experience of meaning, purpose, or connection with an unknown reality behind the manifest one and a higher self both within and outside the person.
4. Greater emphasis on relationships of all kinds—intrafamilial, collegial or professional, friendship, erotic, and spiritual—and their centrality for self-governance or for maintaining or disturbing well-being and health.
5. The importance of group relationships (including group treatments), organizations, and the community as natural extensions of the emerging paradigm of the self system.
6. An increasing recognition that each of us has a social or political self; a self-in-connection in the larger society; and, whether we are politically active or passive, our social and political identifications strongly affect our experience of power or powerlessness in the world.
7. Our changing view of the earth as an entity to be exploited or consumed for human purposes to a new perception of the planet as our home or "mother" with which we have a profound, mutual, and eternally dependent relationship.

The value of AA in the treatment of alcoholism and addiction derives from its attention, deliberate or fortuitous, to all of these emerging transformational trends in the mental health field.

# REFERENCES

Alcoholics Anonymous (1977). *Twelve Steps and Twelve Traditions.* New York: Author.

Donovan, J. M. (1986). An etiologic model of alcoholism. *American Journal of Psychiatry* 143:1–11.

Emrick, C. D. (1989). Alcoholics Anonymous: membership characteristics and effectiveness in treatment. *Recent Developments in Alcoholism* 7:37–53.

Gottheil, E., Alterman, A. L., Skoloda, T. E., and Murphy, B. F. (1973). Alcoholics' patterns of controlled drinking. *American Journal of Psychiatry* 130:418–422.

Kamerow, D. B., Pincus, H. A., and McDonald, D. I. (1988). Alcohol abuse, other drug abuse and mental disorders in medical practice: prevalence, costs, recognition and treatment. *Journal of the American Medical Association* 225:2054–2057.

Khantzian, E. J. (1978). The ego, the self and opiate addiction: theoretical and treatment considerations. *International Review of Psychoanalysis* 5:189–198.

——— (1981). Some treatment implications of the ego and self disturbances in alcoholism. In *Dynamic Approaches to the Understanding and Treatment of Alcoholism*, ed. M. Bean and N. E. Zinberg, pp. 163–188. New York: Free Press.

——— (1985). The self-medication hypothesis of addictive disorders: focus on heroin and cocaine dependence. *American Journal of Psychiatry* 142:1259–1264.

——— (1987). A clinical perspective of the cause-consequence controversy in alcoholic and addictive suffering. *Journal of the American Academy of Psychoanalysis* 15:521–537.

——— (1989). Addiction: Self-destruction or self-repair? *Journal of Substance Abuse Treatment* 6:75.

——— (1990). Self regulation and self-medication factors in alcoholism and the addictions: similarities and differences. In *Recent Developments in Alcoholism*, vol. 8, ed. M. Galanter, pp. 255–271. New York: Plenum.

Khantzian, E. J., and Khantzian, N. J. (1984). Cocaine addiction: Is there a psychological predisposition? *Psychiatric Annals* 14:753–759.

Khantzian, E. J., and Mack, J. E. (1983). Self-preservation and the care of the self—ego instincts reconsidered. *Psychoanalytic Study of the Child* 38:209–232. New Haven, CT: Yale University Press.

——— (1989). Alcoholics Anonymous and contemporary psychodynamic theory. In *Recent Developments in Alcoholism*, vol. 7, ed. M. Galanter, pp. 67–89. New York: Plenum.

Krystal, H. (1989). *Integration and Self-Healing—Trauma, Affects and Alexithymia*. Hillsdale, NJ: Analytic Press.

Krystal, H., and Raskin, H. A. (1970). *Drug Dependence—Aspects of Ego Functions*. Detroit: Wayne State University.

Ludwig, A. M. (1961). On and off the wagon: reasons for drinking and abstaining by alcoholics. *Quarterly Journal of Studies on Alcohol* 22:124–134.

Mack, J. E. (1981). Alcoholism, AA and the governance of the self. In *Dynamic Approaches to the Understanding and Treatment of Alcoholism*, ed. M. H. Bean and N. E. Zinberg, pp. 125–162. New York: Free Press.

Mathew, J. R., Claghorn, J. K., and Largen, J. (1979). Craving for alcohol in sober alcoholics. *American Journal of Psychiatry* 136:603–606.

Pattison, E. M., Sobell, M. B., and Sobell, L. C. (1977). *Emergency Concepts of Alcohol Dependence*. New York: Springer.

Robertson, N. (1988). *Getting Better—Inside Alcoholics Anonymous*. New York: Morrow.

——— (1989). *Recovery: a personal experience*. Presented at the Cambridge Hospital Annual Addiction Conference, Cambridge, MA, March.

Schuckit, M. (1985). The clinical implications of primary diagnostic groups among alcoholics. *Archives of General Psychiatry* 42:1043–1049.

Schur, M. (1966). *The Id and the Regulatory Principles of Mental Functioning*. New York: International Universities Press.

Tomkins, S. (1962). *Affects, Imagery, and Consciousness*, vol. 1. New York: Springer.

Vaillant, G. E. (1983). *The Natural History of Alcoholism*. Cambridge: Harvard University Press.·

Wholley, D. (1984). *The Courage to Change—Personal Conversations with Alcoholics with Dennis Wholley*. Boston: Houghton Mifflin.

Wilson, W. G. (1957). *Alcoholics Anonymous Comes of Age—A Brief History of AA*. New York: AA.

Wurmser, L. (1974). Psychoanalytic considerations of the etiology of compulsive drug use. *Journal of the American Psychoanalytic Association* 22:820–843.

# 36

# Group Therapy for Psychoactive Substance Use Disorders[1]

*with Sarah J. Golden and*
*William E. McAuliffe*

Group treatment modalities are almost universally adopted as the preferred or predominant therapeutic modality for patients with psychoactive substance use disorders, despite the presumption that our ideologies or conceptualization about problems often dictates different approaches. In the field of substance abuse treatment there are strong and often polarized etiological views of substance dependency in which biological, psychological, and/or social factors are often invoked and pitted against one another. Nevertheless, regardless of

1. Portions of this chapter are a version of a chapter published in *The American Psychiatric Press Textbook of Substance Abuse Treatment*, edited by M. Galanter and H. D. Kleber. Washington, DC: American Psychiatric Press, 1994.

orientation or conceptualization, treatment approaches predominantly place patients together in groups to consider the nature of their addictive vulnerability and what course of action can be taken in response to it.

A systematic review of outcomes of efficacy studies is beyond the scope of this chapter. In fact, there has been little systematic study comparing or evaluating the efficacy of group treatment with that of other treatments. However, a number of more recent studies indicate that treatment efficacy and outcome are improved by better matching patient characteristics, needs, and vulnerabilities to the different individual and group methods that we employ (Cooney et al. 1991, Khantzian et al. 1990, McAuliffe and Albert 1992, Poldrugo and Forti 1988).

This chapter reviews theoretical and clinical aspects of the variety of group treatments commonly employed and examines the commonalities as well as the differences in these group approaches. We stress the special needs of substance-dependent persons, their special vulnerabilities, and the characteristic and characterological problems they present that are associated with their addiction. We also demonstrate how group therapy can effectively help patients with psychoactive substance use disorders effectively access, target, and modify the factors that govern their dependency on alcohol and drugs.

## GROUPS AND ADDICTION

Groups are effective treatment because they embody an appreciation of the healing power of the connection with others. Groups address the universal need to belong and at the same time counter the tendency to believe one is unique in one's plight and distress. Elements of information, support, understanding, and confrontation act as important, if not powerful, antidotes to and respite from the shame, isolation, and loneliness that is so central a determinant of addictive illness. Whether the aim of the group is education or therapy, patients can be extraordinarily helpful to each other in the group context (Herman 1992, Khantzian 1986, Tuttman 1990, Yalom 1985).

### Overview and a Review

As we have indicated, each group approach reflects a particular view of addiction. The self-help groups, epitomized by Alcoholics Anonymous

(AA), constitute one of the most widely recognized and successful group approaches. These groups are so widely used not only because they were some of the first to be established but because they were also clearer and more effective in providing practical explanations and solutions. AA was and still is successful because it offers a corrective psychological, spiritual, and moral approach to the problem of addiction. Founded in 1935 by Bill Wilson and Dr. Bob in an attempt to help each other, AA derived from a model of Christian fellowship that fostered self-examination, acknowledgment of character defects, restitution, and "working with others" (Orford 1985). AA targets both deficits and the attitudes about self and others embodied in character traits and styles that make interdependence, experience, and expression of feelings and self-care difficult. Participation in AA counters and transforms these difficulties by effectively advocating surrender and acceptance of a higher power and by challenging human self-centeredness (Khantzian and Mack 1989).

The concept of an individual's submitting to a group's treatment ideology has perhaps found its fullest expression in therapeutic communities for the treatment of addiction. Synanon, established in the 1960s to address heroin addiction, aggressively used the group modality to change attitudes through confinement, structure, daily work assignments, and oftentimes demanding interpersonal confrontation (Cherkas 1965). This total group approach, in which every aspect of daily life is regimented, continues to thrive in such programs as Daytop and Phoenix House.

Other major group approaches in the treatment of addiction have developed and evolved from the cognitive-behavioral and psychoanalytic/psychodynamic clinical traditions. From these schools of thought have emerged both individual and group therapies for addiction. In what follows, we focus on the group models. One form of cognitive-behavioral group therapy, the psychoeducational group, uses the group format to inform addicted persons about the behavioral, medical, and psychological consequences of their addiction. Such groups are a staple of most rehabilitation programs (Nace 1987) and are often seen as the first step of a more comprehensive treatment program. By raising awareness of the consequences of addictive behavior through informational materials, didactic presentations, and group discussions, this method is intended both as education and as persuasion, an attempt to show the group members how addiction "complicate(s) their lives"

(Drake et al. 1991). As agencies of persuasion, these groups foster members' commitment to further treatment.

Cognitive-behavioral theory holds that addiction is learned behavior that is reinforced by such contingencies as the pleasurable effects of drugs (McAuliffe and Ch'ien 1986). The addictive behavior is conditioned and then generalized to a range of stimuli in the environment that continue to perpetuate the addiction. The treatment for addiction thus involves learning to recognize and avoid these stimuli and, ultimately, to extinguish conditioned responses to them. Cognitive-behavioral therapy aims to develop alternative thoughts and behaviors to the conditions that have triggered addictive responses. Based on such an understanding, McAuliffe and Ch'ien (1986) developed a cognitive-behavioral group treatment for substance abuse—recovery training/self-help (RTSH)—to prevent relapse. RTSH uses a curriculum, a didactic group format, and discussion groups to recognize social and environmental cues that lead to relapse. Based on these assumptions and a similar format, McAuliffe and Albert (1992) developed an outpatient cessation model for early recovery from cocaine dependence.

A number of group models have emerged from the psychoanalytic/psychodynamic tradition. Most relevant for the treatment of addiction have been those groups that have a psychodynamic, interpersonal focus and that address the addicted person's particular needs for safety and structure in the group setting (Brown and Yalom 1977, Khantzian et al. 1990, Matano and Yalom 1991, Vannicelli 1982, Yalom 1974).

In the psychoanalytic/psychodynamic tradition, addiction is understood as the person's "solution" to the problem of psychological vulnerability. Contemporary psychoanalytic theory has elaborated on these vulnerabilities as defects of self, both intrapsychic and characterological, that can lead to addiction in an attempt by the person to regulate and medicate the distress caused by the defect (Kohut 1977, Meissner 1986, Wurmser 1978). Khantzian (1974, 1978, 1985) has addressed the particular psychological and narcissistic vulnerabilities of the potential "addict"; Khantzian's self-medication hypothesis holds that addiction results when a person seeks to relieve the suffering and distress resulting from deficits in ego capacities involving affects, self-esteem, self-care, and relationships with others as these deficits play themselves out in everyday life. Heightening awareness of self and changing characteristic patterns of handling these vulnerabilities in everyday situations are addressed in the psychodynamic group treatment of addiction.

Perhaps the most important aspect of Khantzian's model is that it is "modified" dynamic group therapy (Khantzian et al. 1990). The therapy is modified in that the vulnerabilities and difficulties of the addicted person are recognized in the format of the treatment; the group model is one that establishes maximum safety for addicted persons in requiring and helping to maintain abstinence, in providing outreach and support, in using an active style of leadership, and in always addressing the potential for drug and psychological relapse. Structure and containment are emphasized rather than confrontation. This group model has been studied experimentally as part of the Harvard Cocaine Recovery Project (Khantzian et al. 1990).

## Group Therapy as Treatment of Choice

Group psychotherapy has been described by Alonso (1989) as "the definitive treatment for producing character change" (p. 1), because in a group setting, as Alonso explains, the "cost of character defenses is illuminated and presents a conflict which can render the same traits dystonic and thus available to interpretation and change" (p. 8). Similarly, group therapy has been described by Matano and Yalom (1991) as "the treatment of choice for chemical dependency" (p. 269). Matano and Yalom attribute this choice to the "power of groups—the power to counter prevailing cultural pressures to drink, to provide effective support to those suffering from the alienation of addiction, to offer role modeling, and to harness the power of peer pressure, an important force against denial and resistance" (pp. 269–270).

Our own work with modified dynamic group therapy and the work of R. H. Klein and associates (1991) place a premium on helping group members recognize their characterological and personality problems. The group provides a "supportive, holding environment" that fosters conditions for examining the character flaws that perpetuate the group members' suffering and addictive behavior.

## Special Needs of the Addicted Person in Group Therapy

Whether persons are seen as vulnerable to addiction because they are narcissistically compromised through early experiences of deprivation and damage, with the persistent feelings of shame, loneliness, depression, defectiveness, and emptiness described by Kohut (1977) and Meissner (1986); whether they are understood to be narcissistically vulnerable and impaired secondary to the addiction (Vaillant 1983); or whether they are thought to have some "common shared factor" responsible for both the addiction and their character problems (Flores 1988)—the addicted person faces particular difficulties in the therapeutic process. A narcissistically vulnerable person may crave empathy and contact with others and yet fear and reject such contact (Liebenberg 1990). The characteristically "uneven and inconsistent" way in which cocaine-addicted persons relate suggests their dilemma upon entering therapy: "They may be alternately charming, seductive, and passively expectant, or they may act aloof, as if they do not need other people. Their supersensitivity may be evident in deferential attitudes and attempts to gain approval and acceptance, but they may rapidly shift and become ruthless and demanding in their dealings with others" (Khantzian et al. 1990, p. 40).

Klein and colleagues (1991) have outlined the relevant issues in providing outpatient group psychotherapy for persons with character disorders, with comorbid addiction: (1) these persons must be viewed as having a dual diagnosis; (2) the "recurrent dangers these individuals pose to themselves and/or to others" must be recognized; and (3) "their intense demands, during repeated crises, . . . their propensity for acting out anxiety and aggression, and [their] tendency to split clinicians and systems" (p. 99), and the difficult countertransference these patients can evoke must all be addressed. Taking action, rather than bearing affect or anxiety or talking about things, is the preferred expressive mode in these patients, and the acting out may well involve relapsing to the addictive behavior (e.g., drinking, using drugs, gambling). Other characteristic acting-out behaviors may involve splitting and violations of boundaries and of the group contract (e.g., attempting to conduct group business outside the group either with therapists or with other group members).

Matano and Yalom (1991) identified the tendency of alcohol-abusing persons to externalize, to "see themselves as being influenced or controlled primarily by external events," and, by way of compensation, to employ the defenses of "defiance, grandiosity, and counterdependency" (pp. 288–289). Because they do not experience themselves as being effective or in control, they rebel against control experienced as coming from outside. These defenses, or characteristic ways of coping, are taken into account in tailoring the group therapy to the needs of the addicted person.

Khantzian (1986) has identified four areas of psychological vulnerability in the addicted person that may be viewed as disturbances or deficits in ego functioning and that potentiate characterological problems: (1) regulation of affects, (2) self-care (i.e., the capacity to protect oneself from undue risk or danger), (3) relationships with others, and (4) self-esteem. The difficulty in regulating affects manifests itself in an intensity of unmodulated feeling, often dysphoric, or in being unable to identify one's own emotions. Self-care deficits find their expression in poor attention to health, engagement in high-risk behaviors such as unsafe sex, and a general lack of concern for emotional and physical self-preservation. Relationships with others can be problematic in many ways—tumultuous, dependent, or lacking because of the individual's isolation and withdrawal. Finally, self-esteem is compromised or shaky, and this problem may manifest itself as idealization or devaluing of others, feelings of shame and inadequacy, or bravado and grandiosity.

In group treatment modified for the special needs of the addicted person, these four dimensions of everyday intrapsychic and social life become the organizing foci for understanding the addicted person's distress, behavioral difficulties, characteristic ways of handling problems, and possibilities for change. These foci provide a clarity and structure for handling complex issues with action-oriented, crisis-prone, and affectively constricted or volatile group members.

## FEATURES OF GROUP PSYCHOTHERAPY
## WITH ADDICTED PERSONS

Specific features of group therapy for the addicted person derive from the consideration of the person's special needs and have been discussed by several authors in the literature of addiction and group psychotherapy (Brown and Yalom 1977, Flores 1988, Golden et al. 1993, Khantzian et al. 1990, 1992, Matano and Yalom 1991, McAuliffe and Albert 1992, Vannicelli 1982, 1988, Yalom 1974). In addition, the emerging literature of group psychotherapy of the "difficult" patient —one whose character defenses and acting-out behavior challenge the traditional group therapy format—contributes to our understanding of what is needed in the group psychotherapy of addicted persons (Fenchel and Flapan 1985, Klein et al. 1991, Leszcz 1989, Liebenberg 1990, Rice and Rutan 1987, Roth et al. 1990, Stone and Gustafson 1982) Finally, the literature of dual diagnosis of major mental illness and substance use disorder offers guidance in modifying group therapy for this population (Levy and Mann 1987, Minkoff and Drake 1991).

## Pregroup Preparation

Preparation for group increases motivation, reduces premature dropouts, and eases fears and resistances. Khantzian and colleagues (1990) point out that the therapist can play a critical role at this point in establishing optimistic and realistic member expectations regarding the efficacy of the group. The therapist (in this case for a psychodynamic group treating cocaine addiction) not only "acquaints the new members with the established ground rules, which include strict confidentiality, attendance and promptness, and abstinence from drugs and alcohol," but also discusses the benefits of group therapy, defines the focus of the group, acknowledges the difficulty of joining groups, "explains the work of therapy" (Khantzian et al. 1990, pp. 46–48), and helps new members to identify their goals. Reaching out to the prospective group members, anticipating what will follow, and concretely outlining the expectations provide necessary structure to allay overwhelming anxiety in group members.

## Structure and Safety

Structure and safety in the group for addicted persons are provided in a number of ways. The group contract initially serves as an organizing feature, and as the group progresses, it will be tested and perhaps hotly debated, which is part of the work of the group. Shared norms, explicitly stated and reiterated, also provide structure. Abstinence from the problematic addictive behavior, a commitment to talking about feelings and problems rather than acting on them in the group, and agreement about the goals of the treatment are important. Maintaining enhanced structure in a psychodynamically oriented group means explicitly endorsing certain group norms, adopting an active leadership style for the therapist, and, as in Khantzian's modified dynamic group therapy model, keeping the group's focus on specific character and interpersonal problems.

Treaters of addiction must place at a premium, and remain eternally vigilant about issues and themes of sobriety, self-preservation, and self-care (Khantzian et al. 1992, Matano and Yalom 1991). Emphasis is placed on support and on alertness for early signs of psychological relapse such as the company patients keep and potentially risky environments. At the same time, group leaders act as facilitators, catalysts, and modulators to ensure optimal interaction and to discourage member overactivity or premature self-disclosure. In doing so, the group leader creates conditions for listening, empathy, participation, and patience for the invariable resistances that occur, as well as toleration of the anxiety and discomfort that group participation can repeatedly evoke.

## Confrontation Versus Support

Matano and Yalom (1991) point to the dangers of an overly confrontational approach in the group. Although the necessity of increasing the addicted person's honesty with himself or herself and others is real, the group leader's attempt to break down denial can backfire, causing the patient to "leave the treatment program or to dissemble compliance while inwardly retreating" (p. 291). The key is to treat addicted patients like "other patients—that is, by relating to them in an empathic, supportive, and understanding manner" (p. 291). A central task of the group leader is thus to manage the anxiety that the group process, particularly confrontation, inevitably stimulates in the group members and to keep it at a tolerable level.

Leszcz (1989), discussing the group treatment of the characterologically difficult patient, views the group as first of all providing a holding environment, a place that is reliable, constant, and accepting, where group members can "relate in a nonrelated way, until they are able to ascertain that it is safe" (p. 326). The confrontation itself is spelled out as "a forceful, but supportive pressure on the patient to acknowledge something that is conscious or preconscious, but avoided because of the distress that it involves" (p. 327).

The group model of Khantzian and associates (1990) encourages an understanding of addictive behavior as an attempt to deal with feelings and experiences and as an adaptation that has outlived its usefulness. In their resistance to change, group members are guided "to appreciate how their ways of coping and the crises they precipitate are linked to the past; they need to acknowledge their painful feelings from the past and in the present, and to support each other in finding alternative ways to cope with their painful feeling states and problems in living" (p. 76). In other words, the group members, although they are held responsible for their choices and actions and are asked to look squarely at themselves, are not blamed and judged.

The group modality offers a particular advantage when it comes to confrontation: group members are more likely to respond to confrontation by their peers—that is, as Leszcz (1989) notes, "Group members are less restricted in their range of responses and may be better able to use humor, cajole, or shock one another to force attention to a disavowed issue" (p. 327).

## The Group Therapist

The therapist in the group therapy of addiction has an active, demanding role to play. Concerns for safety and structure require an alert presence and a readiness to manage and help to modulate anxiety, to address acting-out behavior, and to intervene if necessary to set limits and uphold the group contract, even as building cohesion and developing the work of the group proceed. This active mode of leadership is important because addicted persons with histories of neglect and trauma "do not respond well to the traditions of therapeutic passivity . . . [but] instead they need therapists who can actively and emphatically help to engage them and each other around their vulnerabilities and the self-defeating defenses and behaviors they adopt to avoid their distress and suffering" (Khantzian et al. 1990, p. 162).

The therapist may become the focus of anger and dependency, the mediator of struggles, and the unintentional voice of the superego. Co-therapists are split into good and evil. Countertransference feelings may be difficult, especially when helplessness and fear are evoked, as they often are in these groups (Klein et al. 1991). Undergoing supervision, taking opportunities to share the work, using concurrent therapies or supports (when indicated) for the group members, working as part of a team or a program—all help to make group therapy for addiction possible and effective.

## CONCLUSIONS

Current group approaches to the treatment of addictions have emerged from several traditions: self-help fellowships; the psychoeducational cognitive-behavioral modality; and the psychodynamic, interpersonal tradition. Although group approaches have evolved from these diverse theoretical and ideological viewpoints, there is a dearth of controlled studies of efficacy and outcome that could support a particular school of thought. Conceptually and pragmatically, practitioners working with addicted persons have come to similar conclusions regarding these patients' special needs in a group setting. If addicted persons are to receive the full benefit of treatment, their characterological and psychological vulnerabilities must be recognized and addressed. Traditional treatments are then modified, particularly if they do not already provide the high degree of structure and safety necessary for engaging and holding the addicted person. The group approach—in its powerful capacity to support and confront, to comfort and challenge, and to involve its members in encounters that vividly heighten awareness of interpersonal and characterological problems and provide a safe place for change—is now viewed as the treatment of choice for the addicted person. Special features of group therapy for the treatment of addiction are an emphasis on outreach and preparation for involvement in the group, a high degree of structure and active leadership, a concern for safety (particularly an awareness of the risk of relapse to the addictive behavior), a balance between confrontation and support, and a goal of moving beyond the initial cohesiveness of the group members' identification as addicts to helping them discover common bonds in living ordinary life.

## REFERENCES

Alonso, A. (1989). *Character change in group therapy.* Paper presented at Psychiatric Grand Rounds, Cambridge Hospital, Cambridge, MA, September.

Brown, S., and Yalom, I. D. (1977). Interactional group therapy with alcoholics. *Journal of Studies on Alcohol* 38:426–456.

Cherkas, M. S. (1965). Synanon foundation—a radical approach to the problem of addiction. *American Journal of Psychiatry* 121:1065.

Cooney, N. L., Kadden, R. M., Litt, M. D., and Getter, H. (1991). Matching alcoholics to coping skills or interactional therapies: two year follow-up results. *Journal of Consulting Clinical Psychology* 57:598–601.

Drake, R. E., Antosca, L. M., Noordsy, D. L., et al. (1991). New Hampshire's specialized services for the dually diagnosed. In *Dual Diagnosis of Major Mental Illness and Substance Disorder*, ed. K. Minkoff and R. E. Drake, pp. 57–67. San Francisco: Jossey-Bass.

Fenchel, G. H., and Flapan, D. (1985). Resistance in group psychotherapy. *Group* 9:35–47.

Flores, P. J. (1988). *Group Psychotherapy with Addicted Populations*. New York: Haworth.

Golden, S., Halliday, K., Khantzian, E. J., and McAuliffe, W. E. (1993). Dynamic group therapy for substance abusers: a reconceptualization. In *Group Psychotherapy in Clinical Practice*, ed. A. Alonso and H. Swiller, pp. 271–287. Washington, DC: American Psychiatric Press.

Herman, J. L. (1992). *Trauma and Recovery*. New York: Basic Books.

Khantzian, E. J. (1974). Opiate addiction: a critique of theory and some implications for treatment. *American Journal of Psychotherapy* 28:59–70.

——— (1978). The ego, the self and opiate addiction: theoretical and treatment considerations. *International Review of Psychoanalysis* 5:189–198.

——— (1985). The self-medication hypothesis of addictive disorders. *American Journal of Psychiatry* 142:1259–1264.

——— (1986). A contemporary psychodynamic approach to drug abuse treatment. *American Journal of Drug Alcohol Abuse* 12:213–222.

Khantzian, E. J., Halliday, K. S., Golden, S., and McAuliffe, W. E. (1992). Modified group therapy for substance abusers: a psychodynamic approach to relapse prevention. *American Journal on Addictions* 1:67–76.

Khantzian, E. J., Halliday, K. S., and McAuliffe, W. E. (1990). *Addiction and the Vulnerable Self: Modified Dynamic Group Therapy for Substance Abusers*. New York: Guilford.

Khantzian, E. J., and Mack, J. E. (1989). AA and contemporary psychodynamic theory. In *Recent Developments in Alcoholism*, vol. 7, ed. M. Galanter, pp. 67–89. New York: Plenum.

Klein, R. H., Orleans, J. F., and Soule, C. R. (1991). The axis II group: treating severely characterologically disturbed patients. *International Journal of Group Psychotherapy* 41:97–115.

Kohut, H. (1977). Preface. In *Psychodynamics of Drug Dependence*: NIDA Research monograph no. 12, ed. J. D. Blaine and D. A. Julius, pp. vii–ix. Washington, DC: Superintendent of Documents, U.S. Government Printing Office.

Leszcz, M. (1989). Group psychotherapy of the characterologically difficult patient. *International Journal of Group Psychotherapy* 39:311–335.

Levy, M. S., and Mann, D. W. (1987). A change in orientation: therapeutic strategies for the treatment of alcoholism. *Psychotherapy: Research and Practice* 24:786–793.

Liebenberg, B. (1990). The unwanted and unwanting patient: problems in group, psychotherapy of the narcissistic patient. In *The Difficult Patient in Group*, ed. B. Roth, W. Stone, and H. Kibel, pp. 311–322. Madison, CT: International Universities Press.

Matano, R. A., and Yalom, I. D. (1991). Approaches to chemical dependency: chemical dependency and interactive group therapy—a synthesis. *International Journal of Group Psychotherapy* 41:269–293.

McAuliffe, W. E., and Albert, J. (1992). *Clean Start*. New York: Guilford.

McAuliffe, W. E., and Ch'ien, J. M. N. (1986). Recovery training and self help: relapse prevention program for treated opiate addicts. *Journal of Substance Abuse Treatment* 3:9–20.

Meissner, W. W. (1986). *Psychotherapy and the Paranoid Process*. Northvale, NJ: Jason Aronson.

Minkoff, K., and Drake, R. E., eds. (1991). *Dual Diagnosis of Major Mental Illness and Substance Disorders*. San Francisco: Jossey-Bass.

Nace, E. P. (1987). *The Treatment of Alcoholism*. New York: Brunner/Mazel.

Orford, J. (1985). *Excessive Appetites: A Psychological View of Addictions*. New York: Wiley.

Poldrugo, F., and Forti, B. (1988). Personality disorders and alcoholism treatment outcome. *Drug Alcohol Dependence* 21:171–176.

Rice, C. A., and Rutan, J. S. (1987). *Inpatient Group Psychotherapy*. New York: Macmillan.

Roth, B., Stone, W., and Kibel, H., eds. (1990). *The Difficult Patient in Group*. Madison, CT: International Universities Press.

Stone, W., and Gustafson, J. P. (1982). Technique in group psychotherapy of narcissistic and borderline patients. *International Journal of Group Psychotherapy* 32:29–47.

Tuttman, S. (1990). Principles of psychoanalytic group therapy applied to the treatment of borderline and narcissistic disorders. In *The Difficult Patient in Group*, ed. B. Roth, W. Stone, and H. Kibel, pp. 7–29. Madison, CT: International Universities Press.

Vaillant, G. E. (1983). *The Natural History of Alcoholism*. Cambridge: Harvard University Press.

Vannicelli, M. (1982). Group psychotherapy with alcoholics. *Journal of Studies on Alcohol* 43:17–37.

——— (1988). Group psychotherapy aftercare for alcoholic patients. *International Journal of Group Psychotherapy* 38:337–353.

Wurmser, L. (1978). *The Hidden Dimension: Psychodynamics of Compulsive Drug Use.* New York: Jason Aronson.

Yalom, I. D. (1974). Group psychotherapy and alcoholism. *Annals of the New York Academy of Science* 233:85–103.

——— (1985). *The Theory and Practice of Group Psychotherapy.* New York: Basic Books.

# 37

# Modified Dynamic Group Therapy: Technique and Technical Issues

## *with Kurt S. Halliday and William E. McAuliffe*

In this chapter on modified dynamic group therapy (MDGT) we offer some guidelines on technique and technical issues. In our book, *Addiction and the Vulnerable Self: Modified Dynamic Group Therapy for Substance Abusers* (Khantzian et al. 1990), from which this chapter is taken, we show how groups work by highlighting certain foci and overriding themes, and in particular by presenting process material to demonstrate group interaction, development, and progression. In more narrowly focusing on certain issues in this chapter, the guidelines offered are intended to be neither exhaustive nor definitive. They are offered as suggestions and examples to assist the therapist in anticipating recurrent themes, concerns, and problems that arise in group psychotherapy with substance abusers. Our hope is that the experience and views reflected in these guidelines will help the practitioner to maintain a healthy balance between the inevitable uncertainties and the exciting possibilities that group members present to us as therapists as they attempt to work out their substance abuse and life problems with each other in group therapy.

## THE REQUIREMENT OF INDIVIDUAL COUNSELING OR THERAPY

The reasons that people, especially substance abusers, need groups, are often the same reasons that keep them out of groups. Substance abusers are avoidant, counterdependent, and self-absorbed. Groups are powerful antidotes to these characteristics, but substance abusers need special individual psychotherapeutic help to overcome their resistances and avail themselves of the corrective experiences groups can provide.

Working with addict's problems of distress, self-contempt, loneliness, and dependency, the empathic clinician is often able to understand why they have chosen a drug-alcohol "solution." Yet, even as they recover from their drug solution and abstain, it becomes evident that the substances and the vulnerabilities they mask are only part of their problem. What is more formidable and in greater need of modification is the range of characteristic defenses and traits that addicts adopt to disguise or deny their suffering or their being lost. Instead of revealing or admitting to difficulty, they more often posture with attitudes of self-sufficiency and disavowal of need and act as if they can solve their problems on their own, if they can even admit to having problems at all.

To place individuals in groups without lending individual therapeutic guidance, especially at first, can be extraordinarily threatening and bewildering to them, and for addicts even more so. Given their intolerance of distress and contact and the isolation and distrust that their concerns engender, we should not be surprised that asking such individuals to join a group and rely on and expose themselves to others may seem heroic if not futile. Their often profound counterdependence and deeper layers of shame make it unlikely that they will accept the care and help of others or will reveal their more engageable human qualities.

In our experience we have been impressed with how important an individual counseling or therapeutic relationship can be in helping substance abusers join a psychotherapeutic group. As we have discussed elsewhere (Khantzian 1985, 1986), the active, supportive, and empathic roles that an individual therapeutic relationship provides can be powerfully alliance building and assist addicts in facing many aspects of life that have otherwise seemed impossible without drugs. This relationship can also be employed in the service of enlisting addicts to accept the beneficial experiences of group psychotherapy. Fears, prejudices, shame, and resistances about groups can be identified, voiced, and explored. When the individual treatment relationship overlaps with and/or parallels the group experience, the therapist and patient are afforded a unique opportunity to monitor and focus on the sources of difficulties of being in group, which might not soon enough or effectively enough be addressed to avoid premature dropouts.

Our experience suggests that for the most part a flexible arrangement is possible when deciding whether the group and individual therapists should be the same or different, the duration of simultaneous individual and group therapy, the possibility of involvement with self-help groups, and the ongoing focus of the individual versus the group therapy. There are advantages and disadvantages when the group therapist is the same as the individual therapist. One advantage is that the therapist is better positioned to evaluate patient needs and receptivity in both contexts and judge which symptomatic and characterological problems are better dealt with in individual therapy and which are better dealt with in group (Khantzian 1988).

## ABSTINENCE AND RELAPSE

Achieving and maintaining abstinence from substances is an ongoing process. Although some group members surprise us and themselves by achieving it almost immediately, for others, especially at first, the craving or desire to use substances remains a major challenge and source of difficulty. In fact, much of the success of self-help groups such as Alcoholics Anonymous (AA) and Narcotics Anonymous (NA) rests on their ability, literally in a stepwise fashion, to help individuals establish abstinence by focusing on their inability to control the use of substances and to acknowledge that they are addicts or alcoholics (Brown 1985). By espousing a disease concept of alcoholism and addiction, self-help groups place emphasis on the substance as the necessary and sufficient causative agent, and thus insist on absolute control, namely abstinence, as the only way to arrest the disease process or illness. Although at first glance a self-medication hypothesis of addictive disorders might seem at odds with a disease concept, we do not believe operationally or clinically that these formulations or approaches are incompatible or need compete. Dodes (1988), for one, has eloquently articulated how and why a psychodynamic approach can be effectively combined with self-help groups.

Self-regulation problems involving affects, self-esteem, relationships, and self-care are at the root of addictive disorders, and the use of substances is a symptom of these vulnerabilities. At the same time they are an attempt to "cure" the vulnerabilities. Such a perspective necessarily requires the clinician to understand that for many the use of substances and/or the felt need for them is a symptom that does not go away easily. The substances have become an important part of the addict's or alcoholic's psychological organization, often as an important coping mechanism. On this basis, addicts' dread of abstinence is understandable. Nevertheless, it must also be acknowledged that it is a symptom that can kill. In this respect alcoholism and addiction must often be treated as a condition that cannot wait for an understanding of root causes. This has become dramatically evident with cocaine dependence in which the progression of the addictive process with all its attendant risks of morbidity and mortality is often measured over weeks or months (e.g., compared to the more often indolent, but just as devastating, course of alcoholism, which more often spans two to three decades).

The challenge in group psychotherapy is to harness and integrate the uncompromising insistence of self-help groups on control (i.e., abstinence) with the best of clinical traditions that place a premium on empathy and understanding as the pathway toward a more permanent and long-lasting recovery. The group leader in this respect, as in so many other respects, has a major responsibility for demonstrating, modeling, and evoking responses among the members that address the emergent and symptomatic aspects of relapse. There is a need for the leader as well as the members to balance the requirement for abstinence with a measure of forbearance and understanding when the inevitable lapses and relapses occur. In some instances this might require that the leader and members focus on and explore the subtleties of an affect state or a blow to one's self-esteem that caused a relatively benign isolated use of drugs for one of the members. Or the challenge might be to harness the passion and power of group concern and influence when another member requires major confrontation, such as when a relapse is unrelenting and life threatening. In the latter instance, the best outcome might be for the group leader and members to have the member in jeopardy accept more intensive help such as hospitalization. Moreover, in our approach, just as abstinence involves a process, relapse involves a process as well. The resumption of drug/alcohol use is usually predictable psychologically far in advance of the act of using. In this respect we view relapse as a process that involves psychological factors and vulnerabilities. Accordingly, we cultivate among the members the need to alert themselves and each other to pre-drug use symptomatic behaviors and characterological signs that might herald relapse.

## THE STRUCTURE OF THE GROUP: SAFETY, COMFORT, AND STABILITY

For any therapeutic group to function effectively, constant consideration must be given to factors of safety, comfort, and stability. This is especially so for substance abuse groups, given the major difficulties addicts have experienced with the dangers, diseases, and instability involved in drug and alcohol adaptations. To structure and maintain these conditions for safety, comfort, and stability, the leader must pay special attention to the composition of the group and how people listen to and talk with each other, deal with disruptive destructive behaviors (in and out of group) and foster the specific and general factors that assure group cohesiveness. Beyond the factors of confidentiality, consistency, and support, which are the mainstays for safety, comfort, and stability, we expand further here on several other important considerations.

Most group therapists would agree that the composition of a group—the number and characteristics of its members—is an important determinant of a group's viability and effectiveness. Groups for substance abusers are no exception. In our experience we have found that eight to ten members is the optimal number to permit a more natural unfolding, interaction, and progression, without placing an unnecessary burden on the leader or on any one member (as is often the case when only three or four members are present) to speak or provide the needed responses. It also makes it more manageable and comfortable for those who need or prefer to listen and to be more passive until they are ready to speak, and yet for those who speak and actively interact more readily and are able to focus on their own needs, this group size forces them to be more conscious and responsive to the needs of others. Furthermore, when a reaction of understanding, empathy, or validation occurs from members in response to a particular member in crisis or distress, it is strikingly more effective and meaningful when it is spontaneous and forthcoming from a group of eight to ten members, compared to how a similar response can feel forced or begged in a smaller group. This becomes even more apparent and important at times of group attrition when old members are leaving and have not yet been replaced by new members. Furthermore, as we have indicated, because MDGT assumes that what is therapeutic or corrective does not rest with the leader alone, the number of members is particularly important in determining the possibilities for the imaginative, unforced, and insightful responses necessary for understanding self and others in group.

In addition to the number of members in the group, the characteristics of the members, including issues of severity of dysfunction, balance, and matching, are important. Generally (but there are exceptions), severely immobilized and/or suicidally depressed members do not do well in group because they heighten the group's and their own sense of inefficacy. Similarly, severely disorganized or threatening individuals can demoralize or retard group morale and effectiveness. Yet invariably, to some degree these problems emerge in the history of a group and the members, and especially the leader, are forced to play more active, intervening, limit setting, and modulating roles to contain or offset the effects of disturbed or disturbing members. For example, the group leader might need to actively draw out or speak for a very depressed, withdrawn member, even at the risk of the patient's striking out. In doing so, the leader gives voice to his or her and the member's sense of helplessness, in order to demonstrate that the other members are neither alone with nor responsible for the despair such members engender. In other instances, for example with a verbally aggressive or abusive member, the leader might need to intervene to draw the anger to him/herself in order to counter the disorganizing and destructive effect on the member(s) and the group as a whole if it goes unchecked.

People are remarkably sensible and sensitive when they gather in groups to help each other. To this extent, it is reasonable to assume there are at least as many forces at work in a group to ensure cohesion and growth as there are forces that threaten fragmentation and regression. The group therapist in assuming the mantle of leadership can operate to co-opt and harness these positive elements and forestall the negative ones. In his or her manner of listening and speaking he can demonstrate, evoke, facilitate, and produce responses that contain or discourage fragmentation and reinforce those that result in group cohesion. Especially early in a group's history, the leader must be evocative, active, and if necessary forceful, to create the proper climate for safety, comfort, and stability. Woodward and McGrath (1988), in this respect, have legitimately argued that the leader might even function charismatically (e.g., by being authoritative, helpful, and giving) to meet patient needs, especially early in treatment. Subsequently, the leader and the members can trust that, properly led and maintained, the group will progress and grow in providing the responses that are needed to maintain abstinence, recovery, and individual maturation.

## SELF-DISCLOSURE AND BEING REAL

It is difficult to pretend or practice pretense in groups. This is as true for the leader as it is for the members. In this section we deal with the ways group leaders respond when their feelings and behavior are questioned, how leaders should respond to questions directed to them about their personal lives, and whether they should generally be reserved or open in their style. Freud's dictum to be oneself is still a useful guide. Nevertheless, the need (and we believe the necessity) to be genuine must also be balanced against the need to not excessively burden the work of the group by disclosures and responses that cause excessive focus on the leader and his/her issues. In this respect it is our opinion that the leader should practice what we have preached elsewhere (Khantzian et al. 1990), namely to strive for a middle ground.

Part of the balance the leader strikes between disclosure and reserve should be guided by the balance MDGT attempts to achieve between the supportive and expressive aspects of the work. On the supportive side we encourage authentic concern and responsiveness for the real achievements, distress, and problems the members experience or endure; on the expressive side we allow enough ambiguity and detachment to help the members identify and play out with each other the character flaws that govern or perpetuate their dilemmas. To this extent questions or issues directed to or focused on the leader might be part of a genuine need to know or to identify with the leader or part of the often warm and friendly interplay characteristic of MDGT. At other times they might represent a resistance and the playing out of a member's character defects by making the leader an external target of the member's internal and interpersonal difficulties. Some questions and issues directed to leaders are so loaded in their nature or timing (for example, has the leader used cocaine or is he/she recovering?) that an answer would stimulate too much diversion or dissatisfaction. In such instances our experience indicates that it is best not to answer, but to explain the reasons behind the decision, including the leader's discomfort and concerns about how his/her responses might deleteriously affect the work and participation of the group as a whole or some of its members. In other instances during light banter, especially as sessions are starting or ending, members often inquire about family ("Do you have children?"), or talk about sports or movies ("Did you see the ball game? The Dustin Hoffman movie?") or vacations. Most of the time these questions are benign and friendly in nature. In these instances it is our belief that a friendly and honest exchange is advisable; moreover, to do otherwise would artificially engender and unnecessarily amplify the interaction.

## ACTIVITY/PASSIVITY IN THE LEADER
## AND THE MEMBERS

People are either burdened or blessed by their psychological nature and the way that this nature is expressed in their basic modes of responding to the world. This is temperament and it is not easily modified. We believe the modes of activity and passivity are particularly important ones to focus on and be aware of in group psychotherapy. Whether exercised or expressed without awareness, or unbridled and in the extreme, by either the leader or members, excessive activity or passivity can produce some of the most bedeviling and demoralizing aspects of group work.

The group leader has a particular responsibility to be aware of his/her penchant for activity or passivity and its effect on the group and on the members. Similarly, the leader needs to be aware of how the activity-passivity modes are expressed by the group as a whole (each group develops its own dynamics), and how the extreme activity or passivity of any one member affects that member, other members, and the group. The leader needs to be aware in extreme cases of the need for him/her to play containing, initiating, activating, or modulating roles, to model for the group members and to encourage them to do the same for each other. Often for the leaders it is useful to reflect on or speak openly of their own tendency for activity (or passivity) and to speculate on how it interferes or helps with the work of the group. At other times the leader might contrast opposite modes in several members to help them appreciate how their modes affect their relationships in and out of group. In our opinion it is less important whether one is cryptic and passive or expansive and active. Rather, the leader and members must develop a growing awareness as to how they are and how this affects others, and the possibilities, and at times necessity, for change.

## COMINGS AND GOINGS

Someone has referred to the departures, absences, disappointments, and changes that occur in relationships as the "little deaths." How we deal with them often forebodes how we deal with life's more threatening losses and eventualities. Because substance abusers and addicts so frequently court "near-death" experiences with their substances and attendant behaviors, we believe there is a basis to speculate that they test or court in the extreme feelings about life that they are otherwise unable or unwilling to endure in more ordinary ways. Groups can be extraordinarily beneficial in countering these extreme tendencies and helping substance abusers test out a middle ground for experiencing and bearing emotions. The comings and goings in the life of the group are particularly important in this respect.

Although absences, tardiness, growth, and attrition in groups can be the stuff of group dysfunction and crisis, these developments can also be the basis for the leader and members to explore and work out the range of feelings and reactions they evoke that might otherwise, and characteristically, go unrecognized and/or expressed maladaptively. In our approach, although we place expectations on members' behaviors involving absence and tardiness, for example, our emphasis is on converting troubling behaviors into opportunities for self-examination, change, and growth. The group leader can be invaluable in helping the members create a practicing ground for accessing, identifying, and expressing emotions that the group life engenders, especially those involving the inevitable departures, absences, changes, and special relationships that occur. In our experience, however, there is a considerable degree of variability in how these developments are experienced and manifested. The group leader needs to be vigilant in creating a climate that allows a natural unfolding of reactions suited to the unique qualities of the group and the persons involved, while at the same time avoiding the pitfalls of the extreme, namely, to ignore or overplay how, for example, a member's absence, tardiness, or planned termination affects the members, the leader, and the group as a whole. Once again, we strive for the middle ground and work to circumvent the extremes of paralysis and no reaction at all on the one hand, and inauthenticity and pseudo-emotion on the other.

These principles of responding apply not only to the tardiness, absences, and the departures of group members, but to other developments in the life of the group such as growth, attrition, and extragroup relationships. The reactions of the leader, individual members, and the group as a whole can vary considerably depending on the situation or the members involved.

At times, anticipated or not, groups lose or gain members. Sadness or a sense of loss (i.e., for the former members or for the group as it was) might be the dominant affect or theme for some or all of the members. In another group the attention might shift to a theme of enjoying the emergence of untapped leadership qualities in one of the members engendered by group growth or attrition. A word is also in order about extra-group relationships and activities. Although a risk always remains about unfair and divisive pairings or groupings outside the group, in general we believe it is both unnatural and impossible to prohibit them. This is especially so given the contemporary trends for so much formal and informal contact (often very needed) that occurs among members participating in self-help groups. The leader should neither encourage nor discourage these relationships, but he/she can share concerns and experiences about potential problems and risks, and single out obvious hazards as they develop. The main concern of the group leader and members should be an expressed awareness of the possibility of unfair or divisive groupings, and that the members must remain open and honest about their extra-group relationships and activities. Whatever the changes or developments, their significance should not be condemned or exaggerated. Rather, they should be seen as opportunities to enjoy gains and successes and to bear disappointment and distress in the group, while at the same time linking the group experiences to life events outside the group. In this way the group developments impart to the members a growing and deeper appreciation of how similar life events outside the group, unrecognized and unprocessed, have precipitated drug use.

## STYLES OF THE LEADERS

Therapeutic technique and style is best guided by our understanding of the origins and nature of the members' vulnerabilities. Our work with substance abusers indicates that most of them have been exposed to extreme environments developmentally, involving traumatic abuse, deprivation, or neglect. As a consequence they suffer from special disabilities and character structures that affect their capacities for self-regulation and relationships. Group therapists as much as, if not more than, individual therapists must keep these considerations in mind in the way they conduct themselves and their treatment of substance abusers. For the most part, then, and understandably, substance abusers do not respond well to the traditions of therapeutic passivity, the blank screen, or the uncovering techniques derived from psychoanalysis of the neuroses (Khantzian 1986). Instead they need therapists who can actively and empathically help to engage them and each other around their vulnerabilities and the self-defeating defenses and behaviors they adopt to avoid their distress and suffering.

In general, MDGT allows for a range of qualities and styles in the leader. However, extremes in modes of behavior or style on the part of the therapist as well as members, especially ones of extreme passivity and unresponsiveness, are counterproductive if not antitherapeutic. A friendly, unpretentious, and reasonably open manner, within the constraints of one's temperament, will serve the therapist and group best. As circumstances and group and individual needs dictate, the therapist should be flexible enough to fill and model a range of roles, one moment prepared to be firm and directive if the group founders or a member behaves offensively, at another time prepared to yield when, for example, the group members need feedback and modification if they excessively focus on a particular issue or person.

The main allies for therapeutic practice, nevertheless, remain the listening and observing modes. The involved group therapist is constantly challenged to empathically fine tune to whatever is said at the same time he/she scans for how what transpires affects the other members. Furthermore, as much as there are central concerns in our roles as therapists for carefully taking in, absorbing, and integrating what our group members say and reveal (or disguise) in the group transactions, clearly there are ways and ranges of responding to group members that should also concern us. A strict and narrow focus on resistances and transference, for example, in our opinion, will not work. More often the responsive therapist facilitates or evokes group discussion when sensitive problems or painful affect are skirted or avoided. The therapist might label an emotion when a member or the group cannot identify it. At other times a simple statement of clarification might be sufficient. It is not unusual in our approach for the group leader to seize a moment of crisis or breakthrough to reflect out loud about a person or an issue. The leader in these instances may guide members in cultivating a capacity to integrate thoughts and feelings about life situations in the service of forestalling impulses and cultivating in their place more self-reflection, restraint, and circumspection. More rarely, but nevertheless effective and necessary to reach more refractory members, active measures such as coaching, guided focusing, or confrontation on an issue might assist members to understand a situation that otherwise escapes them.

## THE SUPPORTIVE METHOD

MDGT occurs within a supportive, friendly context. This develops through the members' and leader's active responses of respect, admiration, empathy, and real concern for distress. The leaders in MDGT take special measures to enlist the members as collaborators with them in self-exploration and understanding. There is a shared responsibility in the group for establishing and maintaining the conditions of safety, comfort, and stability, which are the essential underpinnings of the work. The leader constantly models and demonstrates how respect, curiosity empathy, undivided/attentive listening, and tactful/careful speaking foster these ends. The members and leaders repeatedly reinforce and encourage these responses. The group discourages pretend and pretense, and in their place fosters honest self-examination and authentic self-expression. The guidelines and reflections we have presented in this chapter are offered not as rigid precepts or practices. They are offered more to convey a philosophy and attitude about group work with addicts and how the leaders and members can function to best accomplish the task of being helpful to each other.

## REFERENCES

Brown, S. (1985). *Treating the Alcoholic: A Developmental Model of Recovery.* New York: Wiley.

Dodes, L. M. (1988). The psychology of combining dynamic psychotherapy and Alcoholics Anonymous. *Bulletin of the Menninger Clinic* 52:283–293.

Khantzian, E. J. (1985). Therapeutic interventions with substance abusers—the clinical context. *Journal of Substance Abuse Treatment* 2:83–88.

——— (1986). A contemporary psychodynamic approach to drug abuse treatment. *American Journal of Drug and Alcohol Abuse* 12(3):213–222.

——— (1988). The primary care therapist and patient needs in substance abuse treatment. *American Journal of Drug and Alcohol Abuse* 14:159–167.

Khantzian, E. J., Halliday, K. S., and McAuliffe, W. E. (1990). *Addiction and the Vulnerable Self: Modified Dynamic Group Psychotherapy for Substance Abusers.* New York: Guilford.

Woodward, B., and McGrath, M. (1988). Charisma in group therapy with recovering substance abusers. *International Journal of Group Psychotherapy* 38:223–236.

# 38

# Preverbal Origins of Distress: Substance Use Disorders and Psychotherapy

This chapter reviews some of the preconditions for psychotherapy with substance abusing patients, and some of the ways contemporary psychotherapists have learned to better focus on their vulnerabilities to make psychotherapy more effective. With this as backdrop I review what I believe is a special vignette demonstrating some of the subtleties and developmental origins of addictive suffering and how psychotherapy can evoke and ameliorate such suffering.

Psychotherapeutic work with patients suffering with substance use disorders (SUDs) occurs in the context of considering the special needs of such patients. Once these special needs are considered and allowed for, the psychotherapeutic task of unraveling the meaning of our patients' symptoms and helping them to change becomes not too dissimilar to the more ordinary tasks and challenges of psychotherapy in general.

One of the first problems that must be assessed in treating substance abusing individuals is the degree to which the patient's use of substances is out of control. In the more obvious extreme cases where physical dependence exists and alcohol or other addictive drugs have become an invariable, daily, and consuming aspect of a person's life, traditional psychotherapeutic approaches are wasted on a mind and "a brain that is very hard to treat" (H. Rosette, unpublished manuscript). The quotation refers to the obvious severe physiological and psychological disruption caused by the chronic and heavy use of addictive substances. In such cases, the first priority must be to help the patient gain control over drinking and/or drug use, which more often than not means achieving abstinence. In less severe cases, where the use of substances is periodic and less consuming (e.g., binge drinking or drugging), a more flexible approach might be adopted and psychotherapy can be considered, focusing on how the patients' use of substances fits into their perceived treatment needs and goals as well as their overall adaptation. An extensive review of these considerations is beyond the scope of this chapter, but they are considerations that have been controversial and extensively debated. Particularly controversial are the questions of when, in the process of recovery from substance abuse, psychotherapy should commence, and what type, and for some who are more skeptical (Vaillant 1981), whether it should be considered at all. Some of the most cogent and useful contributions in this area have been by Brown (1985), who stresses the importance of helping the patient to develop an identity as an alcoholic; Bean-Bayog (1985), who focuses on ways to stay sober and to face and mourn the losses resulting from their drinking; Dodes (1984), who emphasizes the need for abstinence as part of internalizing more healthy self-care functions; and Kaufman (1994), who advocates stages of psychotherapy in which phases of therapy must successively address abstinence, early recovery, which involves stabilization and relapse prevention, and advanced recovery, which involves addressing issues of intimacy and autonomy.

While one fundamental task of the psychotherapist is to consider the effects of active, heavy use of substances on the process of psychotherapy, the therapist must also consider the patient's core areas of psychological vulnerability. These vulnerabilities predispose susceptible individuals to substance abuse, relapse, and renewed dependency. I have reviewed elsewhere (Khantzian 1995) how we have become more successful in the psychotherapy of patients with SUDs as we better consider their needs for safety, control, comfort, and contact, especially at the outset of treatment (Khantzian 1988), better understand their vulnerabilities, and modify our techniques to better manage such patients' special needs.

A number of contemporary investigators and clinicians share this shift in focus. Rather than considering categories of psychopathology which predispose to SUDs (e.g., borderline or narcissistic pathology), they have more precisely identified core sectors of vulnerability, deficits, and conflicts that govern addictive behavior. Krystal (1988) has focused on deficits in affect development and alexithymia. He emphasizes the need for therapists to explain to patients that they are different in the ways they experience feelings; specifically, their feeling are somatized, undifferentiated, and nameless, and the therapist's task is to help such patients identify and express their feelings. Wurmser (1987) has emphasized the importance of helping addicts understand their problems with shame; they feel a pervasive sense of weakness and helplessness, which juxtaposed to an archaic superego, causes them to repeat humiliating and self-destructive behaviors, including those involving the use of substances. Dodes (1990) advocates that therapist and patient be aware that the patient's states of narcissistic rage and feelings of helplessness precipitate relapse and require special therapeutic attention. Woody and associates (1986) have targeted in psychotherapy how core conflictual relationship themes are operative in dictating reliance on and relapse to alcohol and drugs; specifically, characteristic relationship patterns, and related distress, are evident in and outside of therapy, as well as in their present and past histories. In my own work (1995) I have stressed that SUDs are best understood as disorders in self-regulation of affects, self-esteem, relationships, and self-care. Walant (1995) has underscored the infantile origins of the contact and interdependence problems in substance abusers' relationships with others that promote addictive adaptations.

The following case vignette involves a patient who demonstrates a number of these vulnerabilities (e.g., affect dysregulation and related characterological defenses), and the surprising and interesting turns that psychotherapy can take in understanding the sources of our patients' distress and suffering. Although the unfolding of this patient's dilemmas occurred in the context of group psychotherapy, previous individual psychotherapy with her referring therapist and myself laid the groundwork for what emerged in the course of her group therapy. Psychotherapeutic work with substance abusers provides a special opportunity to understand the recurrent association between psychological distress/suffering, the personality organization of an individual, and the penchant of such individuals to resort to the use of and dependence on substances to deal with their suffering. Sometimes the suffering is intense and overwhelming; at other times it is vague, elusive, and confusing. The following case example illustrates the way in which preverbal traumatic experiences may be linked to a patient's tendency to relapse to alcohol use and dependence.

## ADDICTIVE SUFFERING AND SUBSTANCE ABUSE: A CASE VIGNETTE

When I met Nancy, an attractive, lively 52-year-old mother of two daughters, she struck me as being an atypical alcoholic in that she seemed more genuinely expressive, articulate, and in touch with her feelings. She had been referred by her individual therapist because of a history of periods of heavy drinking (almost exclusively involving wine), interspersed with periods of abstinence of varying duration. Her most recent relapse (after a five-year abstinence) to daily, heavy use of wine (up to a bottle or more per day) had been precipitated by seeing the movie *Babette's Feast*, which prominently features a gourmet dinner served with wine. The movie centers around the hard and barren lives of the inhabitants of a remote island in the North Atlantic. A former famous chef from France, who has taken up residence on the island, orchestrates a sumptuous gourmet feast with very fine wines to break through the literally and symbolically barren lives of the members of the community she has joined. It was on the occasion of seeing this film that Nancy ended her five-year period of abstinence, quickly escalating to her previous daily consumption of large amounts of alcohol.

When I first started seeing her, I explored how she might be self-medicating painful affect that was either of an intense or elusive and confusing nature. I identified a part of her that could be passionate and even sensual, which was somewhat walled off, but could be released by alcohol. However, I was not impressed with this as a prime motivator for her use of alcohol. She was aware of this aspect of herself and was at ease enough to joke about her passionate side and her inhibitions.

As she became engaged in her individual and group therapies, we became aware of a more harsh, judgmental, and controlled/controlling part of her that she would turn on herself and others in the group. She made harsh judgments about many things, including addictive behavior, which she continued to view as a moral shortcoming in herself and others. Yet in other respects, she was a warm, caring, and supportive group member who could be as empathic and insightful as she was judgmental.

It was not until two years into her group therapy that I was able to fathom a core of unspoken or unspeakable anguish that might fuel her desire for alcohol. The group therapy meeting in which her suffering emerged began with her joking about the group taking a summer "sabbatical." She further hinted that she might take a more permanent sabbatical given that she was feeling so well and had learned much about her own and others' alcoholism. She joked about her tendency to take aim at one of the members whose behavior she frequently questioned or criticized. As she went on there was an almost hypomanic quality to the way she described how much better she was feeling, emphasizing how active and productive she was with her time, and how little wasting there was of it. She said that more often than not she was doing two things at a time, giving examples of listening to a book on tape while crocheting (she was an avid reader and unpretentiously very literary) or painting an outside deck or potting flowers. In this context, Nancy alluded to moments of elation and feelings of being at one with nature.

It was hard for me and other group members to tune in to her seemingly upbeat, buoyant mode of speaking. One of the older male members hesitantly reminded her that they had both been speaking in group recently of life's "finiteness." This caused her to pause, and she began to speak lovingly and with sadness and about her mother. (She had always spoken of her parents in very endearing terms. She was an only child who was adored by both parents. Her mother was from a strict European background, and propriety was very important to her.) Nancy shifted the topic again and rather mischievously revealed to me and the group for the first time that her mother was a flirt, leading a glamorous life as a beautiful and fashionable lady prior to marriage, and she hinted of some possible brief liaisons after her mother was married. As Nancy went on speaking she became very moved, choking back her tears, referring to a well of sadness, and holding her hand over her chest as if she was having trouble breathing as she spoke. She said she did not understand her strong emotional reaction. Feeling her deep level of sadness myself, and feeling a bit awkward, I tried to intervene supportively. I commented on how deep her sadness ran, noting that it was not surprising that her emotions were confusing as well as painful. I also commented that these fluctuating feelings during our session paralleled some of her reactions of sadness and anxiety (including unexplained shortness of breath) outside the group. I also said I suspected that there was more to make clear about her mother's life that might clarify the welling-up of sadness when Nancy spoke of her. Nancy quickly reacted by explaining that her birth had "ripped Mother's previous life away"—that is, her mother settled down to give Nancy her devoted, undivided love and attention in a marriage that was one of convenience. Nancy's father's love for her mother was considerable, but her mother's feelings for him were more of affection and respect.

At this point the group's attention shifted to a younger and newer member, Jane, who was a victim of sexual trauma, for whom Nancy usually mustered maternal concern and support. During this exchange Nancy was quiet. As the group meeting was nearing the end, I noticed that Nancy looked even more sad and remote. I asked her about her appearance. Bitterly and sadly she blurted that when the group had shifted its focus to Jane, Nancy had felt "dismissed" and that she wanted to quit the group. This response was much out of character for her in or out of group. Although she was expressing bitterness and anger, the sadness was still more gripping and evident. Her associations led back to her mother, and I questioned whether there was any more to tell about her relationship with mother. I wondered whether it was always the case that mother was so available and adoring. Again I was surprised at the matter-of-fact way she recalled that when she was born, mother did not want to nurse her and in fact pushed her away. Nancy was quick to assure us that this soon changed to the way she remembered things—idyllic and loving.

The group ended with my reflecting out loud that much of the pain we bear in life stems from a time when we were too young to formulate our experience in words and for which we have no verbal memories. Later in life these vague and confusing feeling states can emerge in a variety of ways. I noted that Nancy might be experiencing this kind of feeling state both in the group session that day and during episodes of panic and difficulty breathing that occurred recently outside the group. I shared with her my confidence that the preverbal emotional memories, pain, and anguish could be better understood and made more bearable.

## Comment

Nancy is a gifted, buoyant, and feelingful person. She has a character structure that is solid (if not too solid), confident, and self-sufficient. Unlike many substance abusers who might be outwardly outgoing but inwardly more shy or restricted, she seemed more authentically gregarious, able to make good contact (albeit most easily on an intellectual plane), and was emotionally expressive. Yet she and I were both aware that alcohol interacted with some core part of herself that was confusing, inaccessible, and painful. For a while I was not sure my ideas of self-medication pertained to her; but as all of us in the psychotherapy group better appreciated that day, there was a core of anguish that was rooted in a nameless and not rememberable ancient sense of feeling dismissed that had played itself out in group. It is not too great a leap, then, to conclude that some individuals can and do resort to substance abuse to alter preverbal emotional memories that remain largely out of awareness and beyond understanding. It is not insignificant that the movie *Babette's Feast*, in juxtaposing austerity and sensuality, could trigger Nancy's long-standing sense of austerity and being cut off ("dismissed"). This deeply rooted and nameless pain probably occurred after viewing the film and again in the group therapy session described above. In the first instance relapse to alcohol was the result; in the second, there was the opportunity for openly experiencing, bearing, and understanding a vital aspect of Nancy's emotional life.

## Addendum

The vignette involving Nancy occurred after two years in treatment and ten months before she terminated her group therapy with me. By the time she stopped group she had been abstinent for about three years. One year after her termination I contacted her to evaluate her overall status and her ability to abstain from alcohol. She was buoyant and pleased to hear from me, and said that she was feeling and doing well, having remained totally abstinent since she ended treatment. She stressed that her individual therapy (with me and her other therapist) "would not have done it alone," and that the combination of the individual and group therapy were necessary to the success of her treatment. She stressed that the big breakthrough was "to get angry with you and to test the preverbal thing you were getting at." She said that although she did not totally agree with my ideas about the preverbal distress, she knew it was important to experience and express her feelings, especially anger. She repeated, "Although I do not necessarily agree, you made me think about it [the preverbal interpretation] and I still percolate with it. I keep rejecting it, but on the other hand I don't forget it."

Nancy and I did not entirely agree at the cognitive level what had benefited her. However, it was apparent to me and her that reexperiencing feeling dismissed in the group, and the resulting anger, and continuing to think about it (i.e., working it through) had helped her to feel better and to not drink.

## REFERENCES

Bean-Bayog, M. (1985). Alcoholism treatment as an alternative to psychiatric hospitalization. *Psychiatric Clinics of North America* 8:501–512.

Brown, S. (1985). *Treating the Alcoholic: A Developmental Model of Recovery*. New York: Wiley.

Dodes, L. M. (1984). Abstinence from alcohol in long-term individual psychotherapy with alcoholics. *American Journal of Psychotherapy* 38:248–256.

——— (1990). Addiction, helplessness, and narcissistic rage. *Psychoanalytic Quarterly* 59:398–419.

Kaufman, E. (1994). *Psychotherapy of Addicted Persons*. New York: Guilford.

Khantzian, E. J. (1988). The primary care therapist and patient needs in substance abuse treatment. *American Journal of Drug and Alcohol Abuse* 14:159–167.

——— (1995). Self-regulation vulnerabilities in substance dependence: treatment implications. In *The Psychology and Treatment of Addictive Behavior*, ed. S. Dowling, pp. 17–41. New York: International Universities Press.

Krystal, H. (1988). *Integration and Self-Healing: Affect, Trauma, Alexithymia*. Hillsdale, NJ: Analytic Press.

Vaillant, G. E. (1981). Dangers of psychotherapy in the treatment of alcoholism. In *Dynamic Approaches to the Understanding and Treatment of Alcoholism*, ed. M. H. Bean and N. E. Zinberg, pp. 36–54. New York: Free Press.

Walant, K. B. (1995). *Creating the Capacity for Attachment: Treating Addictions and the Alienated Self*. Northvale, NJ: Jason Aronson.

Woody, G. E., McLellan, A. T., Luborsky, L., and O'Brien, C. P. (1986). Psychotherapy for substance abuse. *Psychiatric Clinics of North America* 9:547–562.

Wurmser, L. (1987). Flight from conscience: experiences with the psychoanalytic treatment of compulsive drug abusers. *Journal of Substance Abuse Treatment* 4:157–179.

# 39

# Psychotherapy of Substance Abusing Patients: Engaging and Treating the Disordered Person

Although the field is young, over the past two decades there has been a growing and significant literature on a multiplicity of types and modalities of psychotherapy for substance-dependent individuals. A systematic review of this literature is beyond the scope of this chapter. The interested reader is referred to Krystal (1982) and Wurmser (1987) (both of whom are pioneers), Woody and colleagues (1986), Frances and colleagues (1989), Dodes and Khantzian (1991), Khantzian (1988), Galanter (1993), McAuliffe and Albert (1992), Levy (1990), and most recently Kaufman (1994) and Walant (1995). These investigators have in common a rich and extensive clinical experience in working with substance abusing patients. They discuss the special needs of substance abusing patients and how individual psychotherapeutic approaches can be creatively combined with other therapeutic approaches to ensure sobriety and recovery.

This chapter presents my approach to psychotherapy, which is based on a psychodynamic perspective, focusing on some of the special vulnerabilities and related characterological problems that predispose to an individual to reliance on substances. I pay special attention to how psychotherapists should operate to initiate contact, understand how patients are disordered and how they suffer, and focus on the ways they are vulnerable and dysregulated.

## INITIATING CONTACT AND ENGAGEMENT

Two issues are invariably at the core of addictive disorders: problems with control, and psychological suffering. As much as alcoholics and addicts demonstrate their repeated loss of control of their substances with all the attendant complications and harm, they also reveal how much they try to maintain control through their repeated attempts to not use or to limit their use, and much psychological suffering is associated with substance abuse. They use drugs because they suffer, but they also suffer because they use drugs. Empathically engaging patients around the control problems and suffering entailed in their disorder becomes crucial for initially establishing and then maintaining an effective treatment alliance that addresses the core issues of addictive vulnerability.

### Case Vignette 1

At the outset, when Don called and subsequently arrived for his first appointment, he seemed lost, confused, and rather naive about his alcoholism, even after a twenty-year history of drinking. He knew he drank heavier than most of his high school peers, he spent a night in jail during college after a driving while intoxicated (DWI) arrest, and he periodically worried through most of his adult life that his drinking was out of control.

This 38-year-old single man worked as an analyst-manager in telecommunications, and just recently relocated from another state. He showed up for his first visit (an early morning appointment) twenty minutes late. He said he had missed the highway exit. He gave the appearance of a successful executive, dressed in suit and tie, except that he was somewhat disheveled, carried a small canvas workout bag, and wore sneakers, thus causing him to look somewhat unpolished and uncoordinated. He spoke reticently through pursed lips, but otherwise gradually opened up and described his problems and concerns about his alcohol use. His initial complaint was that he was "tired of my basic routine." Don emphasized his recent relocation, an absence of a network of friends, and his daily routines of work, an occasional physical workout, and going home and drinking five quarts of beer each evening. With little prompting by me, he let me know that his pattern was leaving him fatigued and "not clear minded." When I asked him if he were getting so unclear as to have blackouts, he replied in the affirmative and added that he "avoided situations where it would matter." I gently prodded to clarify the amount and pattern, to which he replied by saying it was steady, daily, and that he probably needed the alcohol by the end of the day to feel normal.

Although he was reticent and soft spoken, I was impressed that he was engaging, and ready to discuss his alcoholism. He wanted my help as he tried to understand his situation and change things. As I always do, but sooner with Don than others, I sought a drug/alcohol history, directly but gently asking when he first used, what he used and preferred, and what his drug of choice did for him. Over the years I have discovered that such a direct approach not only elicits needed facts and patterns of use, but that it is alliance building. An empathic and interested approach most often conveys that there is much to be understood and appreciated about how and why patients have depended on drugs and alcohol. This approach stands in contrast to and counters the shaming and judgmental attitudes about their substance use they have repeatedly experienced from others, and from themselves, through most of their life. Don told me that the first time he drank, he drank heavily (it was wine, consumed in a park with friends from his junior high school class), and it was an elixir for "fun, to loosen up, and laugh a lot." In high school he would periodically drink heavily and smoke marijuana with friends. In college the pattern and frequency escalated such that it became more persistent and heavy, but as he said "not yet day in and day out" as it was now. However, at the end of college the DWI arrest caused him to worry that he was "getting out of control." As the initial session was nearing the end I asked him what he thought he needed to do and what he expected I would offer. He reflectively and quietly replied, "Enough is enough.

As for what I expect, I expect to have reasonable and private conversations with someone who is experienced in these problems, and to get this resolved." He then added that he was not happy with his pattern of going home every night, drinking, and going to bed intoxicated.

In contrast with many other patients, and especially given the reserve he showed, Don did not require much probing or prodding to relate his drug alcohol history, indications of a lifelong inhibition, a tendency toward isolation (both causing and heightening his drinking), and his openly conceding an awareness of the deleterious effects of drinking in his life. I concluded the hour by offering him an opinion that I said might surprise him, namely, that he suffered with a condition from which "you might have to get better before you got better." I pointed out that we might have to do whatever we could figure would help to stop drinking first, before we could adequately work on the causes and the consequences of his drinking. I explained to him what I meant by relating how my patients' experiences had taught me that one of the reasons we drink a lot is because we drink a lot, and that it is a process that fuels itself and is self-perpetuating. I also asked him to consider his own awareness of how much distress and dysfunction he was experiencing given his current pattern of use. I added that we could put to good use his worries about his long-standing and continued inability to control his drinking.

He began his second session by saying he had thought about my comment that "you might have to get better before you got better." I asked for his reaction. He said that if it was true, it meant he was in a place he'd not like to be—"pretty far down—and it probably was a true statement—but in a way it was encouraging." He then reflected on the amount he was using, that he was going out less and less and not pursuing his other interests such as working out and photography, and that he had been entrenched in this pattern for the past eight to ten years. I asked him who the person was that was shielding or immersing himself in alcohol this way. After again describing his tendency to be very active physically (e.g., skiing, cycling, aerobics), he then explained that because of his heavy pattern of drinking, he was progressively losing interest in activity, engaging with people, and the world in general. Pursuing my sense of him, I asked if he was a loner and what was his status with men or women friends. With little hesitation, he said, "I tend to be a loner." I then asked, "What about relationships?" He, replied, "In some respects, I have just given up." He referred to a painful entanglement and breakup with a woman six years earlier, how it had "exhausted" him financially and emotionally, and left him weary and worried about getting involved again. Although he said he had women and men friends whom he had left behind when he relocated, he had not made many friends since moving. I tried to pin him down further: "How do you feel in relationships—are you a shy guy?" He said he was shy and had a tendency to not speak unless spoken to. He gave an example of this being so even with his mother. When his mother calls on a weekend morning, he often finds himself automatically reaching for a beer. We spent the remainder of the hour discussing some of the practicalities of getting outside help from Alcoholics Anonymous (AA) or a partial care or ambulatory program to establish some abstinence. He said the religious element in AA tended to put him off, but he was looking into some meetings and was considering Rational Recovery (RR), an alternative self-help group that eschews the spiritual and "powerlessness" elements of AA, and instead fosters attitudes that individuals can rationally explore their reasons for drinking and drugging, and thus be empowered to not use substances. It is also referred to as Smart Recovery.

I saw Don for his third appointment about three weeks later. He promptly informed me that over the past twenty-five days, he had drank on only five days. Not insignificantly, he volunteered that when he drank, he drank heavily, "but nothing bad happened," although he had then felt "unusually bad" (i.e., hung over) the next day. On the other hand, he had also had the experience of generally feeling and sleeping better during the time he had not been drinking. Again to his credit, he spontaneously reflected on how alcohol was causing a decrement in his work performance. He then added that he had begun to attend AA meetings more regularly, especially on those days that he did not drink, adding that he had found one meeting that was particularly comfortable and compatible for him. He said it was useful to see and hear people who had recovered from situations worse than his. We later agreed he was making progress, but a pattern had been established, as he put it, "of drinking to oblivion." He said you hear about it in the program (i.e., twelve-step/AA) but that he didn't believe it yet, adding, "I have known that for a long time." He conceded that going to meetings was helping, but concluded that his visits with me were forcing him to think about his alcoholism.

Although Don is not entirely atypical, he makes it evident how much addictive disorders entail struggles with controlling (or not controlling) one's use of substances, and how much painful emotions (in Don's case, around connecting and relating to others) are involved in a person's drug/alcohol history. Don allows, with only the slightest prompting, that he worries about controlling his use and he also allows that alcohol simultaneously makes relationships both easier and less likely, especially as he escalates and loses control of his drinking. As his therapist, I remain attuned to the signs of control problems and his pain, both in and out of our visits, as he gives his history. In this initial phase of contact and engagement, I try to remain empathically attuned to the critical issues of control and distress. At the same time I begin a dialogue and discuss with him how a program of abstinence will help, short and long term, to regain control not only of his alcohol use, but of his life in general, including better knowing, understanding, and regulating his emotions without the "benefit" of alcohol.

## ACCESSING THE DISORDERED PERSON

There is a significant literature linking substance abuse with personality disorders. Although most of the personality disorders are represented in these findings, the most prevalent ones are antisocial personality disorder and borderline personality disorders. In actual practice, the personality disorder of an alcoholic or addict more often has mixed elements with borderline and narcissistic features predominating (Kohut 1971, Mirin and Weiss 1991, Nace et al. 1983). The problem for therapists with findings from this literature is that what is diagnosed is based on standardized categorical findings that are descriptive and empirical, whereas a therapeutic approach is facilitated by clinical findings that are dynamic and explanatory. For this reason I prefer to consider the disordered person(ality) and its relationship to addictive suffering and substance use.

A person's way of being may cause characteristic suffering, and the more the person suffers the more the characteristic way of being is heightened. The avoidant and isolated person feels alone, depressed, and not understood, which perpetuates further distrust and isolation. Others start with bravado and aggressive posturing when they are frightened, but strut even more ardently in order to hide their vulnerability. The disdainful and counterdependent types mask their dependency and loneliness, but the inadmissibility of their need for others fuels and amplifies their posturing of self-sufficiency. Isolated people compulsively use drugs or alcohol. Related depression, fear, and loneliness interact powerfully with the ameliorating action of abused substances to make them so appealing.

The psychotherapeutic challenge for clinicians is to be attuned to and to remain aware of the reciprocal interactions between the way(s) a person is disordered in their personality makeup and their suffering, and how these two factors predispose to and cause reliance on drugs or alcohol, and threaten relapse if and when abstinence is achieved. Luborsky and colleagues (1981), employing psychodynamic techniques in supportive-expressive therapy, place emphasis on "core conflictual relationship themes" to access how recurrent relational problems have persisted in a patient's life and how such relational factors precipitate and maintain a reliance on substances. The relational themes are apparent in patients' character style and are revealed in their past and present behaviors outside of treatment; at the same time they become apparent or surface in the treatment relationship. They become the basis for the therapist to supportively explore with patients how core relational difficulties influence their reactions in and out of treatment and influence a range of behaviors including those involving substance use and dependence.

In our own work, in the supportive-expressive, psychodynamic traditions, we have broadened the focus to four areas of vulnerability: affects, self-esteem, relationships, and self-care. The suffering entailed with these vulnerabilities becomes linked to characteristic styles that compensate for them. People become more defensive as they wittingly or unwittingly react to their suffering. The psychotherapeutic relationship needs to be empathic and supportive, at the same time that it is reasonably open and structured. The therapist addresses these four areas by gently and persistently exploring problems with how career and relationship issues have produced pain, and how characteristic ways of coping amplify the patient's pain and defensiveness.

## Case Vignette 2

Bob, a 49-year-old Catholic, divorced, successful entrepreneur had many of the qualities of a Marine Corps officer. Besides his crisp, matter-of-fact way of describing elements of his business life, personal relationships, and concerns about his family (especially how his alcoholism had affected his children), he made it abundantly clear that he had a ramrod attitude about judging himself and others.

With reticence and a hint of shame, Bob described how he had reverted to using alcohol after a ten-year period of abstinence mostly achieved and maintained by dedicating himself to his AA recovery program where he was as much "committed" to the recovery of others as he was to his own recovery. He clarified that he "loved the macho cops and firemen" aspects of going on missions (in the program they are called "commitments") to drying out/drunk tanks to work with skid-row alcoholics. His matter-of-fact description of his active, dedicated involvement with confronting other people's alcoholism contrasted sharply with his own vagueness and lack of clarity about what he thought or felt when he picked up his first drink after ten years in a program that drums into members the absolutely disastrous consequences of such behavior. He was equally unclear about what effects he felt from the alcohol when he relapsed, which was consistent with his previous or initial reactions to alcohol and his past history of alcohol use. With regard to his most recent relapses (there were three over the two years prior to seeing me), he explained that he "was being nice" to himself and focused on how special the gourmet olives were that went with the vodka martini. As for his past history of alcoholism before he became sober, the best he could offer was he "always felt alcohol was fun."

Although I knew his recovery program stressed that an alcoholic can always find a reason, positive or negative, to drink, I suspected there were distressing precipitants to his drinking after ten years of abstinence, and I also felt his relapse was also interwoven with his intense, tightly wrapped manner of being. In my initial intake, I noted the year of Bob's relapse coincided with a bottoming out of the commercial real estate market, in which he was heavily invested. I shared with him that another patient in the same business had said to me that he did not know anyone presently in the business that wasn't effectively bankrupt. In response, he initially minimized his business reversals and gave me sophisticated technical reasons why he would eventually emerge whole and solvent, but even more significantly he stressed that during his previous decade of prosperity he had arranged for the financial security of his ex-wife (with whom he remained on good terms) and children.

Given his defensiveness and the magnitude of his losses, I first explored other aspects of his life, such as his explanation that he saw his relapse to alcohol as "being nice" to himself. I gently asked if there was anything that was not feeling "nice" at the time. In passing, he again acknowledged how his real estate holdings were in the pits at the time, but went on to contrast how easy it was to be sober over the previous ten years; he said he was a rich bachelor, living in an attractive metropolitan area, business was great, and he was well thought of by his peers. He referred to a girlfriend whom he liked and with whom he had great fun, but was quick to point out she was a "mature woman" (i.e., a contemporary) and that they "did not do decadent things." He explained that shortly before his financial reverses, his girlfriend's work began to require more travel and resulted in her protracted absences and unavailability. He sheepishly said that he became involved with another woman and explained that at first he felt it unimportant to disclose his other involvement, as he chose not to tell his old girlfriend. However, as his new relationship became more serious, he admitted things were "more stressful"; he guessed he was "guilty" of protecting himself and avoiding confrontation, which he said he didn't like. He hoped that his previous girlfriend would get a message when he stopped being sexually intimate with her, yet he wanted to "be available" to her. He said, "I felt guilty, and still do, and the long and short of it was there were two relationships going on, one winding down and one coming on, and what was stressful was the secretiveness." I asked him how Catholic he was. He said, "Very strict— I was an altar boy—and I still sneak a trip to the cathedral if I feel no one is looking."

I wondered out loud with whom he shared his distress. I knew he was in group therapy during that time and queried if he had shared any of his conflicts about his guilt and being torn between two women, or whether the group knew about the seriousness of his financial reversals. As an aside, he first clarified what a "big leap" it was for an "Irish Catholic to be in therapy"; he then added that he talked a little about his finances, but lamented it was embarrassing, stressing that laying off a chauffeur, for example (i.e., a big deal for him because it clearly mirrored how dire finances were) paled in comparison to the problems of others in the group. Furthermore, he was emphatic that dealing with male/female issues were difficult if not impossible to discuss in the group. Further gentle probing revealed that in fact he was bordering on personal insolvency and that he was unable to share with anybody either the facts of his finances and relationship problems, or to say anything about the feelings involved.

As the hour's end neared, I shared with him my sense of how much he was his own man and drew on himself alone for counsel about his pain if he felt his pain at all. I reminded him that he was in a recovery program that taught people the importance of asking for help and how to do it. I stressed he couldn't, partly because he was so out of touch with his feelings, but also because his best sense of himself and his pride did not allow for it. The issue of alcohol came up again, and he repeated alcohol was a fun drug. I told him that for him it was a "feeling" drug. He said he was not a mean drunk but in fact was more garrulous, expressive, and sentimental when he drank.

This man, in contrast to many other substance abusing patients, is not devoid of feelings. More than anything, he was cut off from them. I sensed that his worries and concerns for his two women friends as well as those for his family were genuine and authentic. I felt his sadness, shame, and guilt, but as is often the case, the feelings were palpable and experienced more by me than by him. What was most evident was Bob's self-sufficiency and pride, his need to be respected and honorable, and most of all his need to be his own man who took care of others and their needs, but could not acknowledge or express his own. The therapeutic task in Bob's case is to engage him in a dialogue about the presence and legitimacy of his feelings and needs, the pain and tension he endures, and how his tight and constrained way of being is an impediment to feeling more comfortable and at ease. Over time, in addition to using his recovery program tools to maintain sobriety, this man is significantly helped in his therapy by seeing that alcohol is not so much for "fun," but in fact is an agent to feel and soften up a significant part of himself that he cannot otherwise allow or express. Whatever else alcohol does to them, patients like Bob also gradually discover what alcohol does "for them"; they learn that it has been an attempt at correcting their disordered emotions and sense of self, a correction that ultimately fails them and further heightens their dilemmas.

## UNDERSTANDING ADDICTIVE SUFFERING

Addicts and alcoholics repeatedly discover that a particular drug helps in the short term to control or regulate what feels so uncomfortable and uncontrollable in their lives. They learn that their drug of choice (which they invariably can specify but not always obtain—thus they substitute) can relieve states of distress or suffering that are often unbearable or overwhelming. It also quickly becomes apparent that the control or relief that is obtained is usually fleeting, and their problems with control and suffering are often amplified and are further perpetuated. Self-medication motives (Khantzian 1975, 1990) for using and becoming dependent on drugs suggest that the various classes of addictive drugs have a specific action or effect on particular affects states (e.g., rage, fear, tension, dysphoria, and depression).

As the following case illustrates, there is pharmacological specificity in the individual's drug(s) of choice. Exploring this factor is alliance building and provides entrée into understanding the ways individuals have both endured and perpetuated distress and suffering in their lives. Identifying the suffering involved in substance use is a valuable vehicle for getting to know people who suffer and the characteristic ways they have coped with their pain and distress. The following case demonstrates how a patient can effectively respond to a combination of group and individual therapy, and how pain and confusion about identity, self-esteem, and affect deficits can be at the core of psychoactive substance use disorders.

## Case Vignette 3

In her initial description of her alcohol use, Ann, a 43-year-old, poised, animated, and seemingly articulate woman, said she used it "almost daily" to achieve "varying degrees of anesthesia." Although she could not describe what she was trying to numb, she just as quickly added that she invariably felt bad the next day, indicating it was "such a waste, and I felt hung over." Yet almost in the same breath she also volunteered, with some confusion, "I miss it if I don't have it." She repeated several times how much her drinking was a "waste and stupidity." With further prodding by me, we clarified that she looked forward to the *New York Times* and her martini at the end of the day and was able to say, "It settles me down—I get numbed, buzzed. It doesn't give me energy, but it takes the hassles of the day away." She denied lessening any particular tension but instead offered, "Whatever I am, alcohol lessens." She further clarified that her pattern of use literally and figuratively allowed her to withdraw (she used the word *jump*) into a corner of the room that was her own private and special place.

In describing this pattern of alcohol use, Ann was struggling to explain that she used alcohol to withdraw, mute, and contain feelings that were both troublesome and elusive. She also made it abundantly clear that her hangover and the sense of wasting time the next day were more clearly palpable than the pain she was trying to mute, and that she felt ashamed and stupid for this pattern that she repeated and could not resist. As I got to know her, I became even more aware of how much her smooth and buoyant veneer was a cover-up, and that she had adopted it (consciously developing and cultivating it as a young adolescent), to compensate for a tragic, lonely, and painful childhood and adolescence, as a result of her mother's lifelong alcoholism and her father's lingering lymphoma of fifteen years to which he succumbed when Ann was 14. Later, when she was a young adult trainee in medicine, she jokingly allowed that easy access to drugs (she tried most of them) resulted in the realization that she "loved them all" and made for "better living through chemistry."

It was difficult at first to pin down any overriding specificity in her drug preference. As she said, she loved them all. But as I soon learned, the effects of each class of drugs served her differently during successive phases of her life. During her medical training her polysubstance abuse seemed to produce effects that could artificially alter or ameliorate emotions that she otherwise did not experience, tolerate, or know. She was discovering that the customary effervescent style she had adopted in adolescence could be augmented and make her "the belle of the ball" in one situation (stimulants and low-dose depressants, e.g., Seconal, succeeded here), whereas Percodan (a synthetic opiate) could smooth out and make her mellow in other situations.

During one of our early sessions, I asked who was the person that she was medicating these days with alcohol, which had evolved as her drug of choice. She indicated it appealed in two ways: it could still bring out the "fun-loving" part of her, but is also helped to "numb" her in ways and for reasons she was less clear about. As the work progressed, it became more clear that she didn't like herself, and felt fraudulent, unloving, and unsuccessful.

As I customarily do, in our second session I inquired how she felt we had done during our first session. She referred to a "positive chemistry," indicating she needed a "coach," and compared me to another alcoholism specialist/therapist she was also considering. She said the other therapist was too open-ended and "toned down," whereas I was "very clear about the diagnosis of alcoholism and why you thought I was alcoholic." (She was referring to my exploring the appeal of the alcohol effects, focusing on the pattern and amounts of use, and the adverse consequences she was experiencing.) She amplified on needing a coach, saying she needed "someone who when it was necessary would beat me over the head" to make it clear what was happening and what was required to get better. I felt she was indicating that she needed someone to be direct and instructive if necessary, modes by which substance abusers benefit, I believe, because there is so much confusion about regulating their emotions, which can be so painful and/or bewildering.

After six weeks of sessions, Ann agreed to join a therapy group that I was running, and to work concurrently with me as well in individual therapy. To my surprise, she abruptly stopped drinking entirely just prior to joining the group. I believe this was partly influenced by her knowledge that all group members were abstaining, and her need to be abstinent was leading her to be a good (i.e., compliant) member; her resolve was also probably made easier in that she had cut back in the amounts she was drinking and had switched from gin to wine. As I often do when someone stops drinking, I asked about the status of her desire to drink. She said she experienced a desire only when she "felt harried and frustrated and didn't feel good" about herself. Not insignificantly, she was describing feelings and attitudes about herself that were constants, and feelings that likely sustained her alcohol use and could precipitate relapse. When she joined the group and introduced herself, I was impressed with how she awkwardly revealed to the group members that she "didn't know what my story was."

Group therapy for substance abusers has some aspects of twelve-step/AA traditions with respect to storytelling, which is especially useful in uncovering or clarifying their problems with regulating their emotions, self–other relationships, and self-care. I thought it curious and significant that she could not even begin to tell her story, especially given her poise and articulateness. As her therapy progressed, Ann gave evidence that her inability to know and talk about herself was not isolated to her group experience. For example, in her relationship with her fiancé, it was rare to discuss or share her feelings and when asked about family life in this respect, she was explicit that her parents "did not do feelings" especially around her father's illness and mother's alcoholism.

As her therapy progressed (she made sure we both worked hard to ensure progress) and she remained abstinent, she marveled at the growing clarity in her mind, the pride in her not drinking (i.e., regaining control over it), and finding a more comfortable and peaceful space within herself. In one session she contrasted the public persona of poise and attractiveness of one of the group members, Helen, with the pain Ann observed and experienced in Helen in the group. I reminded her that Helen's pain was more evident outside of the group than Ann realized. Commenting on how hard Ann wanted to get sober ("sober" meaning mature, versus "abstinent" meaning simply not drinking), I replied that getting sober might mean knowing and developing a new or clearer narrative about herself. In saying this, I had in mind how hard she had worked to successfully develop an upbeat, personable, and "most popular" image (albeit false) in high school to overcome her woes, the same image she further molded and cultivated into adulthood. We repeatedly explored how real comfort was elusive because she could not access or express her inner pain. Instead she was more governed by her need to achieve and maintain her upbeat style. She could hardly think about her mother, especially her death, without panic, but as she did she revealed how her mother had died in her arms. She concluded that session by sorrowfully elaborating on the theme of trying to fix Mother all of her life right up to her death and how guilty and ineffective she felt about her inability to do so. I concluded by saying it was a hallmark for much of her life, namely, to attend to and fix the needs and feelings of others rather than to know or be in touch with her own.

In contrast to her struggles about her poor sense of self and her teetering self-esteem, I continued to be struck by and to admire her earnestness to change and grow. She seemed to resonate positively to my actively taking exception to her dismissive and/or self-deprecating remarks and would often insightfully and reflectively consider my contrary observations. For example, she responded to my active focus on her shame and self-deprecation by giving careful thought to what I said. She then said, "I have never recognized shame or my inability to get a grip" (i.e., referring to the legitimacy of her needs and distress).

To her credit, six months into therapy (with minimal prodding by me) she could speak pensively and more directly about the frustrations concerning her fiancé's unresponsiveness, and when for example I was late for a session, she could speak of her tension about time and money lost. Her evolving qualities of pensiveness and directness gave evidence that she was yielding on the "popular/buoyant" and unreflective (about self) front she customarily adopted, and was learning to better monitor her feelings and needs and to be more aware and forthcoming in her reactions.

As she was yielding on her defensive style, she became more open to the pain of the other group members with whom she was getting more involved. In one group session that had much distress and sadness, with several members speaking of a "dark cloud" they carried, she was especially taken aback when another attractive and upbeat (like herself) professional, Bill, spoke poignantly about his feeling ineffectual and unworthy.

In her subsequent individual session(s) it was evident she was profoundly affected by Bill's story and his feelings of guilt and inefficacy—the latter feeling being one that had so powerfully pervaded her life. She said she was "drawn in and confused by Bill's pain." In response, I underscored the undeniability of pain and its inescapability; I offered that it was especially hard and it frightened and confused her more because she was so unaccustomed, past and present, to sustaining her emotions, and it was made all the more difficult because she was underdeveloped in her capacity—given her background—to reassure and comfort herself, capacities that otherwise might help to offset and make her emotional pain more endurable. Ann reemphasized how taken aback she was by Bill and wondered out loud where she was with her "dark cloud and bad feelings." She appreciated one group member's noticing the hard time she was having in group when Bill told his story. She reflected with me that "living on the edge" and her self-esteem and relationship problems (e.g., with her fiancé) re-created her unrest that was always present about her mother. She came back to her inability to let her mother into her memories, and a wish to do it over with her, but this time wondering what it would be like now, as an adult. I encouraged her to go on, and picking up on her term, I asked her to wonder out loud. After wondering about what or who her mother's parents had been to her, Ann said her mother became sad, confused, and childlike after her brain hemorrhage and repeatedly spoke to her deceased father. She then shifted and feelingly said, "I'd like to tell her to stop drinking and that she'd feel better." I asked what she was feeling. She said, "I feel good about myself." I said, "But it must be sad that she's not here to share that feeling." Ann replied that perhaps she might transmit her feeling spiritually, and then touchingly amplified on what she was feeling, saying, "I tried to fix her all my life, and I couldn't. I'd like to hold her and weep in her arms—and she in mine." I simply said, "That was touchingly put."

Not without significance, subsequent to the above group and individual sessions, she was able to begin telling and retelling her story in her group and individual sessions, and she, the other members, and I were better able to understand the reasons for her special brand of earnestness and social veneer. She was able to elaborate on her sense of feeling unworthy and how striving for the "best" had worked (e.g., voted most popular senior and president of her class), but it had been at the expense of never allowing for her true self and painful existence. She said, "It brings tears to my eyes to admit my low esteem of myself [and avoiding it] caused me to run in the wrong direction."

Even as she allowed her weeping and sadness to enter our work, she did not, nor did I, lose a sense of humor about our task and each other. For example in one session, we both laughed when she asked if I had studied at Harvard; I replied, "No, I couldn't go to Harvard, but I teach there."

Her early comment in group, that she "didn't know what my story was," lingered with me. I believe when she made that statement, she was at odds (i.e., low self-esteem, superficially connected, and cut off from her emotions) and out of touch with herself. I believe the repetitious processing of her self-doubt, pain, and disconnectedness in her therapy over time helped to make her more comfortable in facing a false self she had adopted, and in understanding and accepting the reality and legitimacy of her pain and how much of herself she had given up at the expense of impressing, serving, and fixing others. We often refer to the disorganizing effect of intense affect, but in Ann's case, her being opened gradually (and then more intensely by Bill's sad story) to her lifelong sadness and pain gave her more self-coherency and an increasing sense of well-being over time. Around this time she responded to an inquiry about how treatment was helping her: "It works by helping me stay with my feelings."

She told me a story near the end of her therapy that compellingly symbolized her life dilemmas. While exercising, about six years before, involving a monotonous routine in which she meditated, she had a vision of uncovering a "huge room," in one corner of which was her father and brother, in another, all her toys, and most starkly in the remaining corner was her mother, but more startlingly her mother was in pieces, "dismembered—but not decomposed." Ann joked what a psychiatrist would make of it. She quickly inserted that the image made her feel "undone—the way (she) was always undone—that the pieces of her life were undone, no closure." I commented on how her history had left her feeling undone, and I then suggested she associate to the rest of the vision. She said, "The only other piece were all the toys, untouched; the toys represented a childhood that was never lived or experienced." I commented that finding her mother in pieces gave new meaning to the "fix it/fix mother" theme in her life; I also suggested how fragile her mother must have been. She repeated, "It is true, she was fragile." She had more childhood recollections—a dream of her mother being caught in a toaster and Ann being unable to extricate her, reflectively adding, "Back then how much of Mother's discomfort and pain I had taken on," concluding, "I was such a schmuck!" I observed it was sad that she was not left with any dignity or self-credit for trying. She made reference to the fact that we were finding some dignity working together. After checking whether she was okay with all the remembering, I offered an interpretation having to do with her life: "Maybe it was your history and feelings, forgotten, not remembered, and not told, that was the history that drove you to drink."

## THE VULNERABLE AND DYSREGULATED
## SELF—A FOCUS

As the case vignettes demonstrate, when individuals "choose" a symptom of substance abuse, the complexities and problems of this symptom become interwoven with, reflect, and further amplify problems involving dysregulated emotions, self-esteem relationships, and self-care. In my work with such patients in psychotherapy, now spanning three decades and probably 250 patients (i.e., conservatively averaging ten patients a year who were in treatment on average 1.5 years), I have found that addressing the complex interactions of substances with the ways such individuals are organized in their personality, their behavior, and their suffering is made easier by focusing on essential features of their disorder.

When I first began working in psychotherapy with individuals with psychoactive substance use disorders, I was in the middle of my psychoanalytic training. My training, then and now, persuaded me to adopt a perspective that a reliance on drugs and/or alcohol served an adaptive purpose in the lives of such individuals. This perspective further led me to appreciate how internal states of distress caused such individuals to discover that substances could ameliorate, make more bearable, or alter a wide range of affects that otherwise were confusing and unbearable. As I soon discovered, the various classes of drugs that are abused had a pharmacological specificity that could interact with particular affects (e.g., rage, depression, anergia, anxiety—often subclinical and not readily apparent) and personality factors to make a drug powerfully compelling. As previously reviewed, this process or aspect of becoming substance dependent has been variously characterized, and has been referred to, for example, as "the drug-of-choice" phenomenon (Wieder and Kaplan 1969), "the self-selection process (Khantzian 1975), preferential use of drugs (Milkman and Frosch 1973), and "the drug of commitment" (Spotts and Shontz 1987). In 1985 I published a summary of these reports and presented and amplified on my own findings indicating that self-medication factors were important in the development of a dependency on and relapse to the use of substances (Khantzian 1985).

Subsequently, because the self-medication hypothesis did not sufficiently explain such factors as the perpetuation of suffering entailed in substance abuse, and that many individuals suffer the way addicts and alcoholics do but do not invariably become drug dependent, I found it necessary to adopt a more overarching view of substance-dependence problems as a self-regulation disorder (Khantzian 1990). This perspective expanded my focus, beyond the painful and confusing affect states that individuals self-medicated, to consider additionally self-regulation problems involving self-esteem, relationships, and self-care. Whereas I and my predecessors had originally considered global and pervasive psychopathology in association with substance dependence, I was witnessing significant resiliency, recovery, and psychological strength in patients undergoing treatment and care through professional treatment and self-help (i.e., twelve-step, AA-type programs). As a result of my evolving experience, I have more recently tried to understand substance abusers' self-regulation problems with a view that there are degrees of vulnerability involving problems, with feelings (affects), self-esteem, relationships, and self-care. As is the case in general with human psychological life and suffering, wherever there is pain, hurt, or vulnerability, we more often find compensations, denial, or the inadmissibility of such suffering. Substance abusers are no exception in this respect, and I have found it especially useful to work in psychotherapy with them, keeping in mind the constant interplay between their vulnerabilities and the ways they defend against, compensate for, or adopt characterological traits to protect themselves from their vulnerabilities. The three cases in this chapter illustrate that the initiation, maintenance, and relapse of substance abuse disorders are traceable to self-regulation disorders involving disordered affects, self-esteem, relationships, and self-care.

## Disordered Affects

Painful, inaccessible, and confusing affects are at the core of addictive suffering. Alcoholics and addicts experience their emotions in the extreme—they seem overwhelmed with distress or they seem to not feel their feelings at all. As a consequence, substances are or become compelling because they can ameliorate suffering that addicted individuals experience, or they can produce feelings, often painful, when individuals are devoid of or are unable to feel their feelings. Psychotherapy with substance-dependent patients, to be successful, must constantly keep in mind these aspects of their problem. I have explored elsewhere this dual feature of how alcohol or drugs remove at the same time they perpetuate pain (Khantzian and Wilson 1993). This duality has to do with relieving unbearable, painful affects, but to the extent that one's feelings are not known, confusing, or uncontrollable, substance-dependent individuals also knowingly or unknowingly opt for the painful consequences when they use drugs and alcohol. Then substances produce a suffering that they do understand and is less confusing, and thus they "choose" a symptom they do control. In one instance (i.e., pain) the operative is *relief* of suffering and in the other (i.e., confusion) the operative is *control* of suffering.

The cases of Bob and Ann gave considerable evidence that alcohol served both purposes. Ann began therapy quite unknowing and unable to articulate what her distress and suffering was about, but that it was tied up with her alcoholism. At first she described alcohol as providing surcease from the psychological "noise," which she did not understand; it also was a vehicle for withdrawing and isolating herself. She also made reference to the fact that as much as alcohol could ameliorate her distress, it just as much caused and perpetuated her pain—the pain and cloudiness of the hangovers, and the more protracted and chronic dysfunction it caused (i.e., psychophysiologically), as well as the pain of guilt, shame, and humiliation about how "stupid" she felt about her inability to control or stop her use of alcohol. Ann's and Bob's cases also reveal that they were cut off from, unaware of, or bewildered by their emotions. It was striking how Bob was unable to describe any feelings about his financial reversals or his relapse, both of which on closer examination had catastrophic meaning, at least on a cognitive level. It became clear that Ann's inability to tell her story was in part due to her inability to access any of the pain and suffering she endured. Only as she began to feel her pain and express her suffering could she bring any sense of coherence or understanding to her poor self-esteem and feelings of unworthiness.

The therapist functions to alert patients such as Ann and Bob to their affect deficits and to fine-tune how they experience or fail to experience their pain and distress. In Ann's case, allowing her to gradually find out how out of touch she was with her pain was important. My main challenge was to tactfully and persistently point out and remind her that there was more to her then her superbuoyant and upbeat manner. I followed her words and pointed them out to her (e.g., "noise," "numb," "suppress," as well as her frustrated ambitions), and used the clarifications we made together about the alcohol effects to further help her understand there were painful feelings in general, and, more precisely, pain about her self-regard (see below) that drove both her manner of being as well as her use of alcohol. In Bob's case the challenge was to be more direct in labeling and/or drawing out his feelings, to which he otherwise seemed oblivious. I respectfully acknowledged his need to draw his own counsel, to be strong, courageous, and even macho, but I stressed that for him the challenge was to yield on his tough veneer and to begin to take more chances in facing and sharing his feelings about the financial reversals and problematic relationships. In both of these cases, it is apparent that there is a vulnerable, pained, and hurting person, but there is a person who is also unaware, who deceives, and who cannot admit to vulnerability.

Working with substance abusers in psychotherapy, fine-tuning to the pain and confusion involving affect life and how it gets linked to substance abuse is especially important and alliance building. At the same time this kind of therapy also requires the tactful and gradual challenging of defenses and the cover-up that protects against their pain. This was the case with Bob and Ann and is a standard and necessary part of the work. It is not too different from the work of psychotherapy with patients in general who are not substance dependent.

## Disordered Self-Esteem and Relationships

Difficulties in establishing and maintaining adequate self-esteem and satisfactory relationships are not problems unique to alcoholics, but as the three case vignettes suggest these factors are often woven into the fabric of addictive problems and often are important contributing determinants in substance use disorders. A sense of inner well-being is a bedrock for an evolving sense of self, and ultimately the capacity for self-respect and self-love. To the extent that people do not feel good about themselves, it permeates their relationships with others and makes satisfying or satisfactory relationships unlikely or more difficult. It is not surprising, then, that individuals who suffer in their self–other relations discover that the various classes of drugs can interact with their pain and suffering, and related characterological traits, to act in the short term as a corrective for these difficulties. Alcohol softens overdrawn, self-sufficient, and rigid defenses that are often adopted to cover a shaky self-esteem, or a sense of feeling cut off and empty. This short-term softening effect of alcohol often makes inner comfort with self and others more possible. Stimulants will energize those suffering with depressive anergia and self-doubt, and help to overcome related characterological attitudes of apathetic indifference, which are defensive. Stimulants also augment and make it easier for expansive, hypomanic types to be the way they like to be, especially when their style does not allow them to accept their limitations. Opiates soothe and quiet those individuals who are racked by rage and related agitation, and in doing so opiates make it less necessary to defend against these inner states with postures of self-sufficiency and bravado. I again mention these recurrent, interrelated patterns of distress, defense, and substance abuse to alert psychotherapists to the vulnerabilities substance abusers endure and the ways they become disordered in trying to manage their self-esteem and relationships, and ultimately cause them to become dependent on substances. The challenge in therapy is to identify the vulnerability, the defenses, and the characterological signs, and to help patients appreciate that the more extraordinary drug and characterological solutions can be replaced over time by more ordinary human solutions of self-acceptance, self-respect, and connectedness to others.

Although Ann's problems with her feelings were important, it was also clear how unconfident, self-judgmental, and unworthy she felt. Besides the upbeat, buoyant veneer she had adopted and cultivated, she, like Bob, had also striven for what I call the "success cure." I suspected, and over time tried to clarify with her, that the "noise" or clamor that she tried to numb with alcohol derived from never feeling free of her demanding aspirations and ambitions, which alternately paralyzed and agitated her. Similarly, her need to be more "loving and caring" was secondary to an overdemanding ego-ideal system that straitjacketed more than guided her. Similarly, in Bob's case it was striking how his best sense of himself rested strictly in relying on his "own counsel," his counterdependency, and maintaining the trappings of propriety. Although alcohol dissolves our superego, a modern ego-psychology perspective would suggest that alcohol is at least as good an ego solvent; as the case vignettes suggest, alcohol softens or acts on overdrawn ego defenses that leave one feeling isolated, cut off, or empty.

### Disordered Self-Care

In addition to the obvious self-damaging aspects of the use of substances and the related attendant practices, addicts and alcoholics often give the appearance of generally being reckless, self-destructive, and even suicidal. In my experience, some of this is defensive and much of it is a consequence of chronic addictive illness. The apparent not caring and suicidality is a consequence and not the cause of substance abuse problems. What is primary is self-care deficits and related compensatory defenses.

From the outset of treatment, Don gave evidence of self-care problems. There was a general uncoordinated appearance about him: he was twenty minutes late for his first appointment, missing a clearly marked highway exit ramp on his way to my office. In reviewing his history, although he was clearly shaken fifteen years before when incarcerated for DWI, he admitted that subsequently, as his alcoholic illness progressed, he had never given much thought to the DWI and its aftermath. Although he would worry about things, he was ineffectual in acting on and following through on his worries. Ann glorified and rationalized her risk taking, especially the dangers of stealing and stockpiling drugs as a health-care professional, as well as her freespirited, partying style. What seemed more apparent to me was her not knowing what she felt, and she was thus unable to more carefully guide her behaviors professionally and socially. Bob's explanation for the reversion to drinking (after not drinking for ten years)—namely, that he was "being nice" to himself and that he was intrigued with some gourmet olives that would go with that first fatal martini—exemplifies the denial and rationalizations associated with alcoholism. In fact what is often explained under the rubric of denial and rationalization in alcoholic behavior more precisely involves deficits in self-care. As Bob's case reveals, I was able to elicit little evidence of anticipatory alarm or worry about the significance of that initial drink, as was the case with the dire circumstances involving his financial holdings. Ultimately, the combination of deficits in affect life and self-care are the two most compelling factors in substance abuse, and are the necessary and sufficient causes for addictive vulnerability.

In facing self-care problems with patients such as I have described, it is important and at times necessary that the therapist intervene, and be active and instructive. Self-care deficits are on a continuum, and in the more extreme cases it is necessary to actively intervene in order to help patients see how blind they are to danger and mishap. As Havens (1984) has pointed out along other lines (i.e., the need for admiration in certain patients), the therapist employs a "performative" role in which he/she can speak and act authoritatively, literally in the service of survival. It has been surprising and gratifying for me to discover that patients accept such active approaches when they are applied with tact and proper timing. Such approaches probably work because they represent the antitheses of what addicts and others have been saying to them for a long time, namely, they are killing themselves; it seems obvious to me that it is more alliance building and corrective to say, "You are not able (and probably have been unable) to take care of yourself," and exploring with patients what this underdeveloped capacity is about.

## THE SYMPTOM/DISEASE DEBATE—A CONCLUSION

Clinicians and patients debate, often contentiously, whether dependence on substances is a disease or a symptom. The material I have presented in this chapter might suggest my bias is with the latter. However, common sense, clinical observations, and the apparent cruel and progressive nature of addictive disorders would dictate that the debate is silly and counterproductive. Addictive disorders have the characteristics of both symptom and disease. A partial explanation of this dual aspect of these disorders is that the original reasons for becoming addicted (or relapsing once under control) are different from the reasons that individuals drink or drug compulsively once they become addicted.

Psychotherapeutically, it is useful to help patients see that there is a progressive and unrelenting deteriorating aspect of substance dependency that is rooted in addictive processes that are physiological in nature, and that makes the use of substances so unrelenting, cruel, and devastating in its consequences. It is on this basis that in advanced phases of the disorder addicts and alcoholics look and act alike. Referring to this aspect of addictive disorders as a disease has objective validity that is appreciated by both clinicians and recovering patients; it helps with understanding the loss of control, debasement, and stigma of their illness. However, as I hope this chapter has adequately illuminated, there is also an aspect of addictive disorders that is rooted in human psychological suffering and difficulties in controlling and regulating one's life.

Psychotherapy with alcoholics and addicts is an effective tool for engaging such patients in a meaningful dialogue that goes beyond disease or symptom, to help them understand that in some very important respects their "symptom" has represented solutions and attempts at self correction and self-cure that have backfired. But it also is a statement about human vulnerabilities and denial of vulnerabilities that beg for alternative solutions. Psychotherapy with alcoholics and addicts is and should continue to be a legitimate and effective method to help our patients find alternative solutions to endure and transform their pain and to have a more satisfactory life.

## REFERENCES

Dodes, L. M., and Khantzian, E. J. (1991). Individual psychodynamic psychotherapy. In *Clinical Textbook of Addictive Disorders*, ed. R. J. Frances and S. I. Miller, pp. 391–405. New York: Guilford.

Frances, R. J., Khantzian, E. J., and Tamerin, J. S. (1989). Psychodynamic psychotherapy. In *Treatment of Psychiatric Disorders*, a task force report of the American Psychiatric Association, T. B. Karasu, task force chair. Washington, DC: American Psychiatric Association Press.

Galanter, M. (1993). *Network Therapy for Alcohol and Drug Abuse—A New Approach in Practice*. New York: Basic Books.

Havens, L. L. (1984). Explorations in the uses of language: counterintrojective statements (performatives). *Contemporary Psychoanalysis* 20:385–399.

Kaufman, E. (1994). *Psychotherapy of Addicted Persons*. New York: Guilford.

Khantzian, E. J. (1975). Self selection and progression in drug dependence. *Psychiatry Digest* 10:19–22.

——— (1985). The self-medication hypothesis of addictive disorders. *American Journal of Psychiatry* 142:1259–1264.

——— (1988). The primary care therapist and patient needs in substance abuse treatment. *American Journal of Drug and Alcohol Abuse* 14(2):159–167.

——— (1990). Self-regulation and self-medication factors in alcoholism and the addictions. In *Recent Developments in Alcoholism*, vol. 8, ed. M. Galanter, pp. 225–271. New York: Plenum.

Khantzian, E. J., and Wilson, A. (1993). Substance dependence, repetition and the nature of addictive suffering. In *Hierarchical Concepts in Psychoanalysis: Theory, Research, and Clinical Practice*, ed. A. Wilson and J. E. Gedo, pp. 263–283. New York: Guilford.

Kohut, H. (1971). *The Analysis of the Self*. New York: International Universities Press.

Krystal, H. (1982). Alexithymia and the effectiveness of psychoanalytic treatment. *International Journal of Psychoanalytic Psychotherapy* 9:353–388.

Levy, M. S. (1990). Individualized care for the treatment of alcoholism. *Journal of Substance Abuse Treatment* 7:245–254.

Luborsky, L., Woody, G. E., Hole, A., and Vellelco, A. (1981). *A treatment manual for supportive-expressive psychoanalytically oriented psychotherapy: special adaptation for treatment of drug dependence, 4th ed.* Unpublished.

McAuliffe, W. E., and Albert, J. (1992). *Clean Start*. New York: Guilford.

Milkman, H., and Frosch, W. A. (1973). On the preferential abuse of heroin and amphetamine. *Journal of Nervous and Mental Diseases* 156:242–248.

Mirin, S. M., and Weiss, R. D. (1991). Substance abuse and mental illness. In *Clinical Textbook of Addictive Disorders*, ed. R. F. Frances and S. L. Miller, pp. 271–298. New York: Guilford.

Nace, E. P., Saxon, J. J., and Shore, N. (1983). A comparison of borderline and non-borderline alcoholic patients. *Archives of General Psychiatry* 40:54–56.

Spotts, J. V., and Shontz, F. C. (1987). Drug induced ego states: a trajectory theory of drug experience. *Society of Pharmacology* 1:19–51.

Walant, K. B. (1995). *Creating the Capacity for Attachment: Treating Addictions and the Alienated Self*. Northvale, NJ: Jason Aronson.

Wieder, H., and Kaplan, E. H. (1969). Drug use in adolescence: psychodynamic meaning and pharmacogenic effect. *Psychoanalytic Study of the Child* 24:399–431. New York: International Universities Press.

Woody, G. E., McLellan, A. T., Luborsky, L., and O'Brien, C. P. (1986). Psychotherapy for substance abuse. *Psychiatric Clinics of North America* 9:547–562.

Wurmser, L. (1987). Flight from conscience: experiences with the psychoanalytic treatment of compulsive drug users. *Journal of Substance Abuse Treatment* 4:157–168.

# PART VI

# Epilogue: Future Prospects for Understanding and Treating the Addicted Person

The biological, social, and psychological substrate for understanding substance use disorders is complex. Understanding how these three basic aspects of addictive disorders interact to make such problems likely is even more complex. In this respect, I anticipate or hope, health and time permitting, that I have one more book to write. It will not per se be about addictive disorders, but about many of the controversies involved in trying to gain a consensus about the nature of human psychological vulnerabilities and how to best understand and treat them. The book will also discuss "marginality," not in its modern usage, of being peripheralized, but in the sense popularized more than a half-a-century ago in a book by a Harvard sociologist, Everett Stonequist, entitled *The Marginal Man* (1937).

For Stonequist, marginality meant residing between different worlds, or more precisely, being in the margins between different cultures, different ethnic/religious groups, and different ways of thinking and/or viewing the world. He described how it was the lot of certain individuals to never feel entirely comfortable in one world or another but rather to reside between them, never totally free to join one or the other, and ultimately positioned to see both the folly and wisdom in different domains. In this respect, I consider myself a "marginal" man. My parents came from a different country and thus I am a first-generation ethnic, which by Stonequist's description makes me a marginal person.

Nevertheless, it would appear that in this book I have joined one camp—the psychodynamic one. I confess, however, that the marginal man in me is not entirely comfortable with this choice. When I am with clinicians or practitioners of the same persuasion as myself, I am often put off or even embarrassed when I hear or see how doctrinaire my colleagues can be, such as in not seeing the utility of adopting a biological treatment or considering the relevance of the disease concept of alcoholism. I am also aware of my marginal disposition when our refined technologies more and more precisely map out brain morphology and function. These technologies reveal findings that have far-reaching implications for understanding human nature and the biological underpinnings of the mind, including implications for explaining addictive vulnerability. Accordingly, when challenged by people who are skeptical about such concepts as the self-medication hypothesis, I sometimes offer, with amusement, that I believe in it more on some days than others. This is my way of conceding that my perspective and the explanation it yields cannot be the only valid one.

In concluding this volume, I plead with those who raise such questions, and this book raises many such questions, to try residing in between the biological, social, and psychological domains, because no one domain explains best the nature of our human vulnerabilities. Each powerfully offers advantages and there is legitimacy if not the necessity to assume a perspective and "milk it for all it is worth." It is the way advances are made in the social and biological sciences. Ideally, we all wait on a unified theory that can explain it all, but in reality these are rare occurrences in the evolution of ideas and theory. Most of the time we must reside in the margins of different ways of thinking. The marginal person in each of us can consider the potentials and limitations in one another's perspectives and then we must wait on the rare Renaissance person who can ultimately bridge the different domains and explain how they all come together. This is how we advance our sciences and our civilization, and it is how we address what ails us as individuals and as a society. The perspective I offer in this book, I am convinced, is a powerful and useful one. I do not intend it to be a perspective to the exclusion of other ones. At the same time there is explanatory power here, even if it is only a partial explanation. I challenge my colleagues and readers of different persuasions to consider the power and limits of their persuasions from a similar vantage point. Ultimately we should all try to clamor less about our convictions and to more readily concede that we simply prefer and profit from different approaches. Our differences need not invalidate one another's perspective, and over time, if we can allow for the differences, we can achieve more consensus, and ultimately we can better integrate our theory and practice.

## REFERENCE

Stonequist, E. V. (1937). *The Marginal Man: A Study in Personality and Culture Conflict*. New York: Scribner's.

# Credits

The author gratefully acknowledges permission to reprint the following:

Chapter 1: Heroin use as an attempt to cope: clinical observations. (With J. E. Mack and A. F. Schatzberg.) *American Journal of Psychiatry* 1974; 131:160–164. Copyright 1974, the American Psychiatric Association. Reprinted by permission.

Chapter 2: The ego, the self and opiate addiction: theoretical and treatment considerations. *International Review of Psychoanalysis* 1978; 5:189–198. Copyright, Institute of Psycho-Analysis.

Chapter 3: Impulse problems in addiction: cause and effect relationships. In *Working with the Impulsive Person*, ed. H. Wishnie, pp. 97–112. New York: Plenum, 1979.

Chapter 4: An ego/self theory of substance dependence. In *Theories of Addiction*, ed. D. J. Lettieri, M. Sayers, and H. W. Wallenstein, pp. 29–33. NIDA monograph no. 30. Rockville, MD: National Institute on Drug Abuse, 1980.

Chapter 5: Ego functions and psychopathology in narcotics and polydrug users. (With G. J. McKenna, first author.) *International Journal of the Addictions* 1980; 15(2):259–268. Reprinted by permission of Marcel Dekker.

Chapter 6: Some treatment implications of the ego and self disturbances in alcoholism. In *Dynamic Approaches to the Understanding and Treatment of Alcoholism*, ed. M. H. Bean-Bayog and N. E. Zinberg, pp. 163–188. New York: The Free Press, 1981. Reprinted by permission of the publisher.

Chapter 7: Addiction: Self-destruction or self-repair? *Journal of Substance Abuse Treatment* 1989; 6:75. Copyright 1989. Reprinted by permission of Elsevier Science–NL, Sara Burgerhartstraart 25, 1055 KV Amsterdam, The Netherlands.

Chapter 8: Opiate addiction: a critique of theory and some implications for treatment. *American Journal of Psychotherapy* 1974; 28:59–70. Reprinted by permission of the Association for the Advancement of Psychotherapy.

Chapter 9: Self selection and progression in drug dependence. *Psychiatry Digest* 1975; 10:19–22.

Chapter 10: Psychological (structural) vulnerabilities and the specific appeal of narcotics. *Annals of the New York Academy of Sciences* 1982; 398:24–32. Reprinted by permission of the New York Academy of Sciences.

Chapter 11: The self-medication hypothesis of addictive disorders. *American Journal of Psychiatry* 1985; 142(11):1259–1264. Copyright 1985, the American Psychiatric Association. Reprinted by permission.

Chapter 12: Self-regulation and self-medication factors in alcoholism and the addictions: similarities and differences. In *Recent Developments in Alcoholism*, vol. 8, ed. M. Galanter, pp. 255–271. New York: Plenum, 1990. Reprinted by permission of the publisher.

Chapter 13: Self-regulation factors in cocaine dependence—a clinical perspective. In *The Epidemiology of Cocaine Use and Abuse*, ed. S. Schober and C. Schade, pp. 211–216. Research monograph no. 110. Rockville, MD: National Institute on Drug Abuse, 1991.

Chapter 14: Self-regulation vulnerabilities in substance abusers: treatment implications. In *The Psychology and Treatment of Addictive Behavior*, ed. S. Dowling, pp. 17–41. New York: International Universities Press, 1995. Reprinted by permission of International Universities Press.

Chapter 15: The self-medication hypothesis of substance use disorders: a reconsideration and recent applications. *Harvard Review of Psychiatry* 1997; 4:231–244. Reprinted by permission of Mosby-Year Book.

Chapter 16: A preliminary dynamic formulation of the psychopharmacologic action of methadone. *Proceedings of the Fourth National Conference on Methadone Treament*, San Francisco, 1972. Reprinted by permission of the National Association on Drug Abuse Problems.

Chapter 17: Heroin addiction—the diagnostic dilemma for psychiatry. (With C. J. Treece.) In *Psychiatric Factors in Drug Abuse*, ed. R. W. Pickens and L. L. Heston, pp. 21–45. New York: Grune & Stratton, 1979.

Chapter 18: On the nature of the dependency and denial problems of alcoholics. *Journal of Geriatric Psychiatry* 1978; 2(2):191–202. Reprinted by permission of International Universities Press.

Chapter 19: Self-preservation and the care of the self—ego instincts reconsidered. (With John E. Mack.) *Psychoanalytic Study of the Child* 1983; 38:209–232. New Haven, CT: Yale University Press. Reprinted by permission of Yale University Press.

Chapter 20: Alcoholism: the challenge of conceptualization and consensus. *Journal of Substance Abuse Treatment* 1986; 3:251–254. Reprinted by permission of Elsevier Science–NL, Sara Burgerhartstraart 25, 1055 KV Amsterdam, The Netherlands.

Chapter 21: A clinical perspective of the cause–consequence controversy in alcoholic and addictive suffering. *Journal of the American Academy of Psychoanalysis* 1987; 15(4):521–537. Reprinted by permission of the American Academy of Psychoanalysis.

Chapter 22: Cocaine addiction: Is there a psychological predisposition? (With N. J. Khantzian.) *Psychiatric Annals* 1984; 14(10):753–759. Reprinted by permission.

Chapter 23: Psychiatric and psychodynamic factors in cocaine dependence. In *Cocaine*, ed. A. M. Washton and M. S. Gold, pp. 229–240. New York: Guilford, 1987. Reprinted by permission of Guilford Publications.

Chapter 24: Alcoholics Anonymous and contemporary psychodynamic theory. (With John E. Mack.) In *Recent Developments in Alcoholism*, vol. 7, ed. M. Galanter, pp. 67–89. New York: Plenum, 1989. Reprinted by permission of Guilford Publications.

Chapter 25: Alcoholics Anonymous—cult or corrective: a case study. *Journal of Substance Abuse Treatment* 1995; 12:157–165. Reprinted by permission of Elsevier Science–NL, Sara Burgerhartstraart 25, 1055 KV Amsterdam, The Netherlands.

Chapter 27: Perspectives on the self help–psychiatric controversy in addiction treatment. *Psychiatric Annals* 1976; 6:8–15. Reprinted by permission.

Chapter 28: Group treatment of unwilling addicted patients: programmatic and clinical aspects. (With W. W. Kates.) *International Journal of Group Psychotherapy* 1978; 1(1):81–94. Reprinted by permission of Guilford Publications.

Chapter 29: The substance-dependent physician: where care and discipline meet. *Drug Therapy* 1982; 12:190–196.

Chapter 30: The injured self, addiction and our call to medicine (understanding and managing addicted physicians). *Journal of the*

# Index